The Slender Thread

This work is a partial representation of *The Slender Thread* by Willeen Keough, a multimedia work of scholarship published in the Gutenberg-e online history series. As such, this print edition does not include the images, maps or the index contained in the online edition. The Gutenberg-e series is part of our commitment to create new kinds of scholarly and educational publications through new media technologies. Our mission is to make these works as innovative, efficient, and cost-effective as possible. We encourage reviewers and readers to also consult the complete work online at the free access site: http://www.gutenberg-e.org/ or through ACLS Humanities E-Book (HEB) at: http://www.humanitiesebook.org/series_GUTE.html

The online version of this work contains all the printed text here, in addition to digital images, artwork, audio, video, and hyperlinks that allow the reader to experience the full meaning of this scholarly work. The organizing structure, content, and design of the online work was created by the author in collaboration with a team of editors, web developers, and designers in order to give the richest meaning to the historical narrative and argument. The intellectual content of this work is designed to be read and evaluated in its electronic form. This text is not a substitute for or facsimile of the online version of this work.

The Slender Thread

Irish Women on the Southern Avalon, 1750–1860

Willeen Keough

www.gutenberg-e.org

COLUMBIA UNIVERSITY PRESS
NEW YORK

Columbia University Press
Publishers Since 1893
New York Chichester, West Sussex

Library of Congress Cataloging-in-Publication Data

Keough, Willeen G., 1955–
The slender thread : Irish women on the southern Avalon, 1750–1860 / Willeen Keough
p. cm.
Includes bibliographical references.
ISBN 978-0-231-13202-2 (cloth : alk. paper)—ISBN 978-0-231-50693-9 (e-book)
1. Irish—Newfoundland and Labrador—Avalon Peninsula—History—18th century.
2. Irish—Newfoundland and Labrador—Avalon Peninsula—History—19th century.
3. Women immigrants—Newfoundland and Labrador—Avalon Peninsula—History.
4. Working class women—Newfoundland and Labrador—Avalon Peninsula—History.
5. Sex role—Newfoundland and Labrador—Avalon Peninsula—History.
6. Fishing villages—Newfoundland and Labrador—Avalon Peninsula—History.
7. Avalon Peninsula (N.L.)—Social life and customs—18th century.
8. Avalon Peninsula (N.L.)—Social life and customs—19th century.
9. Avalon Peninsula (N.L.)—Emigration and immigration—History.
10. Ireland—Emigration and immigration—History. I. Title.
F1124.A85K46 2008
305.48'89162071809033—dc22
2008037640
www.gutenberg-e.org

Columbia University Press books are printed on permanent
and durable acid-free paper. This book is printed on paper
with recycled content. Printed in the United States of America.

c 10 9 8 7 6 5 4 3 2 1

CONTENTS

ACKNOWLEDGMENTS

Throughout the research and writing of this book, I have benefited tremendously from the collegial atmosphere of the academic community. In particular, I would like to extend my very deep appreciation to Linda Kealey, Shannon Ryan, and Peter Hart for their wise counsel and friendship throughout my doctoral and postdoctoral work. I owe a tremendous debt of gratitude to John Mannion for sharing his insights on Irish migrations to Newfoundland and to both him and his wife, Maura, for providing me access to their extensive name file collection on Irish immigrants to the island. I also want to thank Greg Kealey, Terry Murphy, Hans Rollmann, Tom Nemec, Christopher English, Robert Sweeny, Valerie Burton, Christopher Youé, Terry Bishop-Stirling, Maudie Whelan, Carla Wheaton, Tracy English, and John Fitzgerald for their interest and encouragement through the years. And to Cyril Byrne, a special thank-you for friendship, support, and sharing "stories."

I wish to acknowledge that earlier versions of portions of this book have appeared in two articles: "The 'Old Hag' Meets St. Brigid: Irish Women and the Intersection of Belief Systems on the Southern Avalon," *An Nasc* 15 (spring 2001); and "The Riddle of Peggy Mountain: The Regulation of Irish Women's Sexuality on the Southern Avalon, 1750–1860," *Acadiensis* 31:2 (spring 2002).

I gratefully acknowledge the financial support of the Social Sciences and Humanities Research Council of Canada and the Institute of Social and Economic

Research, Memorial University of Newfoundland, through doctoral and postdoctoral fellowships and research grants. I also wish to thank the American Historical Association and the Andrew W. Mellon Foundation for their financial support in developing this monograph through the Gutenberg-e project.

For their expert and unstinting guidance throughout the production of the book, I am extremely grateful to the members of the Electronic Publication Initiative at Columbia University and the staff of Columbia University Press. I especially wish to thank Paul Erickson and Nick Frankovich for their attentive and sensitive reading of my manuscript and their patience throughout the copyediting process. And I am very grateful to Kate Wittenberg, Sean Costigan, and Gordon Dahlquist for their good humor and calm in the face of many storms. To Sharene Azimi, who steered my project home after transitions at EPIC, a special thank you. Many thanks as well to the production team of EPIC, especially Clif Jackson, who worked so diligently on the final version of this e-monograph.

I am also heavily indebted to a number of people who volunteered their time and expertise to come to the assistance of this technologically challenged author. In particular, I wish to thank Tracy English for transforming my hand-scrawled graphs into digitized charts and figures, Alice Nolan at the Open Learning and Information Network, Memorial University, for helping me work through numerous technical crises, and the many kind people at TETRA, Memorial University, for their guidance as I worked my way through the brave new world of scanners, digital cameras, and digital voice recorders.

For their patience and expertise, I am also very grateful to the staff members of the various archives and museums I visited in the course of my research. In particular, I wish to thank the staff of the Provincial Archives of Newfoundland and Labrador, especially Cal Best and Melanie Tucker, for their good-natured support throughout my endless visits to their facility. I am also very grateful to the staffs of the Centre for Newfoundland Studies, the CNS Archives, the Maritime History Archives, the Memorial University of Newfoundland Folklore and Language Archive, and the Provincial Reference Library for their invaluable assistance. I extend special thanks to Dorothy Agriesti and Maxine Dunne of the Ferryland Museum for generously sharing their time and historical materials with me.

I owe a very deep debt of gratitude to all the people from the southern Avalon who agreed to be interviewed during my oral history project. They were extremely generous with their time, their knowledge, and their hospitality as they opened their homes and their collective memories to me. They have enriched my understanding of the area immeasurably. In addition, I want to thank Margaret Wakeham for her spirited rendition of "Betsy Brennan's Blue Hen" and Eddie O'Brien for his readings from Jim Joe's community history.

On a personal note, I wish to thank all my friends for their humor, interest, and uncritical acceptance of my academic reclusion over the past several years. To my family, for their infinite patience, encouragement, and support, I am grateful beyond measure. And to Michael, a special thank-you for riding out another very long "two years."

This monograph is dedicated to Julianne, whose life story inspired it, and to Gertrude, who encouraged me to write it.

LIST OF ABBREVIATIONS

CNS	Centre for Newfoundland Studies, Memorial University of Newfoundland
Cy.	Newfoundland Currency
FMDB	Ferryland Museum Database, Ferryland
ISER	Institute of Social and Economic Research, Memorial University of Newfoundland
MHA	Maritime History Archives, Memorial University of Newfoundland
MUNFLA	Memorial University of Newfoundland Folklore and Language Archive
NLGS	Newfoundland and Labrador Genealogical Society, St. John's
PANL	Provincial Archives of Newfoundland and Labrador, St. John's
PCA	Presentation Convent Archives, Mother House, Cathedral Square, St. John's
PRL	Provincial Reference Library, St. John's
RCAASJ	Roman Catholic Archdiocese Archives, St. John's
SPG	Society for the Propagation of the Gospel in Foreign Parts
Stg.	British Sterling (all amounts refer to British currency during the study period)

PREFACE

> Three slender things that best support the world: the slender stream of milk from the cow's dug into the pail; the slender blade of green corn upon the ground; the slender thread over the hand of a skilled woman.
>
> —Irish triad (trans. Kung Meyer), ca. 9th century

This study of the lives of Irish women on the southern Avalon emanates from more than academic interest. My maternal roots are in the area, and I have encountered there a tradition of strong, resourceful Irish Newfoundland foremothers: my great-great-great-great-grandmother Catherine, who raised a large family in Ireland, often alone while her husband worked at the Newfoundland fishery, until she finally joined him on the southern Avalon in the 1790's; my great-great-great-aunt Margaret, who came out from Ireland, became mistress of a planter household, and inherited from her first husband land and fishing premises—property which she gave to her brothers upon her remarriage and which is still in the family today; my great-great-aunt Sally, who provided board and medical services to fishermen to earn extra income for her family; my great-grandmother Bridget, who nursed her family alone during a diphtheria epidemic, carrying the black waste of infection down to the sea in the early morning under the watchful eyes of the quarantine officer; my great aunt

Sarah, who kept a gracious three-story home in Shore's Cove on the proceeds of a shebeen she ran on the side; my grandmother Julianne, her hands as large as oven mitts and work-roughened from making fish and hay and clothing and endless loaves of bread to feed her brood of twelve; and my own mother, Gertrude, whom a priest warned my father not to marry because Southern Shore women had "far too much to say for themselves."

Yet Irish Newfoundland women appear to be curiously passive, when they are mentioned at all, in the historiography of early settlement in Newfoundland. In my examination of their lives on the southern Avalon, I hope to bring these women more clearly into focus in the discussion of migration and settlement experiences, to stretch the slender thread across the ocean, to understand the source of its suppleness and strength.

1. PICKING UP THE THREAD

Locating Irish Newfoundland Women in the Narrative of Migration and Settlement

The southern Avalon Peninsula of Newfoundland[1] is one of the oldest sites of European endeavor in North America. English, Portuguese, Spanish, and French vessels fished along the coast from Bay Bulls to St. Mary's Bay throughout the sixteenth century, and a migratory fishery from the West of England, or West Country,[2] continued in the area in the seventeenth and eighteenth centuries. Four English attempts at colonization also took place on this portion of the island in the early seventeenth century, although the patentees' ambitions did not come to fruition except, to a limited extent, at Ferryland.[3] Early census reports, however, indicate that individual English *planter* (resident fisher) families were established in a number of harbors in the study area by the late 1600s. The southern Avalon was also one of the earliest destinations of Irish migration to North America. The Irish began arriving there in the late seventeenth century as cheap labor for West Country fishing ships and planter families, and their numbers increased with the development of a flourishing Ireland–Newfoundland trade in provisions and *passengers* in the eighteenth century. Overwhelmingly, they were Catholic migrants from the southeastern ports of Ireland and their hinterlands. In the early decades of the nineteenth century, there were further large waves of Irish migration to Newfoundland, particularly during the periods 1811–16 and 1825–33;[4] by mid-century, a substantial population of Irish settlers, and particularly a vibrant Irish plebeian community (see Appendix A), had established itself along the southern Avalon. The following pages will explore Irish women's[5] lives within this context, focusing on the period from the 1750s, with the first major influx of Irish migrants into the area, to 1860, when the transition to a family production unit in Irish fishing households was demonstrably complete.

Using gender as an category of analysis, refracted through the lenses of ethnicity and class, the discussion will concentrate on the female dynamics of immigration and community formation, attempting to discern the meanings that women ascribed to their experiences and the understandings of Irish Newfoundland womanhood that were constructed within this New World environment. It is not my intention, however, to examine women's lives in terms of a separate women's culture, but rather to root them firmly within the family and community contexts in which they evolved. Nor will some essentialist "woman's experience" unfold in the following chapters—for women's lives on the southern Avalon were marked by difference as well as similarity. Finally, I do not mean to equate *gender* with *women*, or to suggest that understandings of masculinity within this historical setting are unproblematic and unchanging. Rather, the female-centered perspective of this study is meant to contribute to an ongoing and necessary corrective in two broad areas of historiography: the literature on early European settlement in Newfoundland and Canada, and the history of the Irish diaspora (the following is an abridgement of a fuller historiographical discussion, with citations, in Appendix B).

EARLY EUROPEAN SETTLEMENT IN NEWFOUNDLAND AND CANADA

> Almost every family history here begins with "Two brothers came out from Ireland or England . . ."
>
> —HE, resident of Ferryland, 20 July 1999[6]

This insight came from one of my oral informants as she tried to warn of the difficulties in mining the oral tradition for information about women's contribution to early community formation on the southern Avalon. She had certainly arrived at the crux of a methodological problem, for she was not only articulating the conventional opening for, but also identifying the main protagonists in most family histories in the Irish Newfoundland or English Newfoundland tradition. There are, of course, some departures from the formula: in one variation, an older brother remains in the home country while the younger leaves for Newfoundland; in another, a father and his sons cross the Atlantic to seek their fortune in the fishery. But in plot and focus, the stories are similar. The family narratives tell how those men carved a living out of relentless sea and barren soil, and how they bred large families in a mysterious process that, with its seeming absence of women, must surely have equaled the miracle of the Virgin Birth.[7] The sagas continue to follow the male line: sons and grandsons are named, their lives chronicled, while daughters remain peripheral—sometimes numbered, rarely named, often ignored altogether.

While my informant was discussing the oral tradition, her comments could also have applied well to the traditional historiography on Newfoundland settlement, in which this male-centered focus resounds. Granted, this preoccupation was rooted in the nature of the main industry of Newfoundland—the cod fishery—which, until the second half of the eighteenth century, was largely migratory in aspect and carried out primarily by men, with a smattering of planters' wives and female *servants*. Logically linking the course of settlement with the pursuit of the fishery and the vicissitudes of its migratory and sedentary branches, earlier writings either overlooked or vastly underplayed the one ingredient essential for the stabilization of the local population: the presence of women.

Traditional historiographical offerings explained settlement as a process that occurred within the context of conflict between inhabitant fishermen and avaricious merchants from the West of England, who controlled the migratory trade and effectively pressured successive governments to prohibit settlement, or at least to discourage it actively, in order to block the development of a competitive resident fishery. Hence, these historians argued, settlement in Newfoundland followed an erratic course, with resident fishermen relegated to marginal areas, their premises hidden in tiny coves or hanging precipitously off cliff faces—out of the way of the privileged migratory fishermen and out of the sight of visiting *fishing admirals* and naval authorities.

This theory of "retarded settlement" was roundly challenged by later writers, who argued that, although the Western Adventurers had briefly opposed settlement, many of them soon came to realize that the migratory and sedentary branches of the fishery could be complementary, and evolved into suppliers and marketers for the inhabitant fishery while maintaining their migratory interests into the eighteenth century. The home government, spurred by its desire to preserve a "nursery for seamen" through the traditional migratory ship fishery, did attempt to restrict settlement by delaying the development of governance and property ownership in Newfoundland. Ironically, they were forced to establish increasingly sophisticated agencies to enforce the restrictive laws they were passing and to maintain law and order between residents and visiting fishermen (Web Link). The scattered nature of fishing communities therefore reflected not a fear of discovery by officials or harassment by migratory fishermen, but rather the suitability of the sites for exploiting the inshore cod resource.

Yet as the historiographical debates on settlement in Newfoundland evolved, the movements of men were carefully traced and analyzed while the activities of women remained out of focus. Even though the Newfoundland fishery had been primarily (although not exclusively) a male enterprise up to the middle of the eighteenth century, in Newfoundland, as elsewhere, populations and communities did not stabilize until women were present in increasing numbers. But while the historical literature spoke of the rising supremacy of the resident fishery and the increasing stability of the population in the latter eighteenth century, women's experiences were absent, their voices muted. Occasional references appeared to fishermen's marrying "local women" (a term that generally referred to women of English or Irish, not aboriginal, descent)—as if their presence needed no further explanation, as if these women had somehow sprung from the ground. Like Topsy, a character of nineteenth-century American fiction, they had apparently just "grow'd."[8] Treating them as merely a factor in a demographic equation, the literature said little or nothing of their motives for emigrating, their lived experiences, or their role in early community formation.

By the late 1970s and early 1980s, feminist scholars outside the disciplines of history and historical geography were offering insights on women's roles in fishing families of the late nineteenth and early twentieth centuries and questioning women's absence from historians' accounts of early Newfoundland communities. Whether coincidentally or in response to this critique, some necessary (if somewhat conservative) adjustments were made to the historiography in the late 1980s and early 1990s. Scholars began to include a section or a chapter about women in their writings about the settlement process; they also made the link between the presence of women and population growth, although they underplayed women's importance in terms of settlement continuity. But there was an assumption in these writings of an inexorable "evolution" towards a patrilineal, patrilocal, patriarchal society in which women's status and experiences were seen as secondary, diversionary, or anomalous.

In recent years, important contributions in the field of legal history have delved into the impact of both formal and customary legal practices on women in Newfoundland. Still, there are significant gaps in our understanding of how women's lives, especially in early fishing communities, played out on the ground. And there is still reluctance in the literature on early settlement to perceive gender in terms of a dynamic, ongoing process that did not follow a straight and uncontested "evolutionary" course towards patriarchy.[9] But was the "march of patriarchy" as unproblematic in the Newfoundland context as much of the historiography has presupposed?

The paucity of scholarship on women in early Newfoundland communities corresponds with a traditional obscuring of the female experience in the Anglophone literature[10] on early European immigration to the rest of the territory that today forms Canada.[11] Since the late 1980s, women's historians have been working towards a more balanced interpretation of immigration history that incorporates more gender-inclusive categories of analysis. But there is a late-nineteenth- and/or twentieth-century concentration in this literature and a focus on ethnic minorities and urban experiences. The history of women in earlier migrations from the British Isles to Canada has, until recently, remained largely unexplored terrain; in much of the literature, these women have remained part of an amorphous entity, *white settler society,* with little recognition of the gendered dynamics of their experiences or the ways in which dimensions of race, ethnicity, and class also affected their lives.

The Anglophone literature on colonial women in Canada has lagged behind its American counterpart, although some significant contributions have been made in the past two decades to our understanding of women's lives in the pre-confederation period. Yet many of these writings demonstrate a difficulty that is still pervasive in women's history—the problem of uncovering the experiences of women from marginalized groups. Evidence from the white colonial elite—statutes, newspapers, diaries, correspondence, prescriptive writings—dominates the historical record for the period of early settlement. We can see how hegemonic feminine ideals were constructed and have some insight into their impact on elite women, but we have much more limited access to the meanings they created for women of aboriginal societies, ethnic minorities, and working-class or plebeian cultures. We can read interpretations of the lives of women on the periphery, but they have been mediated by middle-class editors, clergymen, and officials and, occasionally, gentry women. But although the presence of plebeian women in *white settler society* is quite muted in the written records, historians are increasingly finding traces of their lives. This study will be a further contribution to that body of literature, although it is merely one small drop in a slowly filling well.

THE IRISH DIASPORA IN NORTH AMERICA

The literature on Irish migrations to North America has traditionally been preoccupied with famine and post-famine migrations, resonating with motifs of disruption and alienation.[12] This concentration has had a profound impact on popular understandings of the diaspora on both sides of the Atlantic. There is a timeless sorrow, a lingering sense of mourning and loss, that clings to our perceptions of Irish movements to the New World. The very phrase *Irish emigration* evokes images of poverty and desperation—of suffering masses huddled in the dank holds of coffin ships, fleeing hunger, disease, and economic devastation in the home country. Such impressions emanate from one relatively brief but intensely poignant moment in the history of Irish emigration: the Great Famine and its immediate aftermath. But because of the magnitude of this mid-nineteenth-century trauma, such images linger in the popular consciousness as the essence of the Irish diaspora through time.

These shades and specters haunted the traditional historiography on Irish emigration. Up to the mid-1980s, the *Great Hunger* often cast its pall over discussions of other movements of Irish people: vestiges lingered in explanations of later relocations; its shadow also stretched back in time as historians used earlier migrations to set the stage for the famine exodus without considering that previous movements may have had dynamics of their own. When movements in the late eighteenth and early nineteenth centuries were mentioned at all, they were usually presented as a prologue to the great Irish emigration drama of the mid-nineteenth century, and images of exile and exclusion pervaded the texts.

This is particularly true of the works of historians of the American Irish, from William Forbes Adams to Kerby Miller, whose writings, until the past decade or so, have tended to dominate the literature on Irish immigration to North America.[13] The perspectives they provide of the ghettoization of impoverished and unskilled Irish immigrants in urban landscapes do not supply useful models for understanding the experiences of Irish immigrants on the southern Avalon or in rural areas in general. Indeed, this portrayal of the Irish as predominantly disadvantaged urban dwellers has been roundly challenged by writers such as Donald Akenson, David Doyle, and Cecil Houston and William Smyth, who have effectively demonstrated that most of the Irish in North America ultimately fanned out into rural areas and were employed in primary industries, with a smaller but still significant number entering skilled trades and professions. This was especially true of pre-famine immigrants: the processes of urbanization, ghettoization, and proletarianization were a later phenomenon in the United States, and that model does not apply at all to Canadian experiences.[14]

In addition to his urban bias, Miller has also come under fire for his representation of Irish Catholics as a group handicapped by religious and cultural traditions in adapting to their new environments—casualties of modernization who clung to traditional goals and lifestyles. This examination of the southern Avalon Irish will challenge his findings, portraying a largely Catholic migrant group as responsive to opportunity and often upwardly mobile in their new communities.

Here, it will follow a major paradigm shift in the historiography since the late 1980s—a movement away from discourses of exile and alienation toward a view of Irish migration as a rational, adaptive strategy employed in response to changing social and economic conditions in Ireland and the demands of an increasingly international economy. A warning bell must be sounded, however, about the economic reductionism that often underscores this type of interpretation, with its tendency to portray emigration purely as a "transfer mechanism" while muting the negative aspects of the experience—the fragmentation of families and home communities, the re-mapping of social and political terrains. As Jim Mac Laughlin argues, this type of interpretation is an over-correction of the traditional literature and overly sanitizes the phenomenon of emigration.[15]

Furthermore, there has been a continuing reluctance among historians of Irish emigration—particularly quantitative historians, who rose to prominence in the latter part of the twentieth century—to delve too deeply into pre-famine experiences because of the lack of "hard" evidence on population sizes and emigration figures for the period. Even writings that draw more heavily from qualitative sources, or use a combined methodology, rarely reach back further than the 1840s, particularly works dealing with movements beyond the British Isles. Discussions of earlier emigrant groups are usually preliminary and tentative. There is thus still a need for Irish migration studies that emphasize earlier movements and emigrant agency without underplaying the human costs or reducing the phenomenon to a purely economic response mechanism.

John Mannion's work on the Irish in Newfoundland follows more recent trends in the literature, emphasizing the influx of Irish servants into the Newfoundland fishery as an adaptive response to declining opportunities in the homeland.[16] His writings, however, illustrate a further limitation of the historiography until recent years: a tendency to homogenize Irish emigration in terms of male experiences. As late as 1993, Akenson aptly noted that women in the Irish diaspora were still "the Great Unknown."[17]

The low visibility of Irish women in emigration studies reflected a deficiency in the broader corpus of Irish historical writings. Irish women's history in general had lagged behind its British and North American counterparts, although it has certainly come out of its pioneering stages with a growing body of research of increasing analytical rigor from the 1990s to present day. Still, the search for Irish women emigrants is doubly confounded by gender imbalance and a lack of attention to the pre-famine period. While the literature about Irish women emigrants has grown, most offerings have examined movements from the mid-nineteenth century and beyond, when the Great Famine had established a new set of parameters for Irish emigration. This concentration is understandable, for the demographic and economic changes of the famine years and their aftermath had particular impact on women and wrought a profound change in their status in Ireland. But few of these writings provide insight into the motivations and experiences of earlier women emigrants.

In looking for the Irish woman emigrant of the late eighteenth and early nineteenth century, we find ourselves staring down a historiographical funnel. As we shift our perspective from overseas Irish emigration in general to focus on Irish female emigration experiences in particular, and finally hone in on earlier movements, our viewing screen becomes increasingly constricted. The story of the Irish women who emigrated to North America before the 1840s can only be patched together from pieces and fragments of evidence of an emigration phenomenon that is, in itself, fragmentary in the literature.

Much of the information provided by historians about early women emigrants is statistical: a relentless array of sex ratios, average ages, marital categories, fertility rates, and occupational profiles, drawn from aggregate data for a broad range of destination areas and extended time periods. After parading out this statistical data, many of these writers then allow the female emigrant of the pre-famine period to be once again eclipsed by male experiences.

Perhaps one of the most well-known proponents of quantitative over qualitative approaches in studying Irish migration is Donald Akenson, who has used aggregate data to provide a "yardstick"—based on average sex ratios and age, religious, and occupational profiles—against which Irish migrations to various parts of the English-speaking world can be measured. For the late nineteenth and early twentieth centuries, he also provides a breakdown of women emigrant "types" based on marital status and number of children. Again, however, his indices are based on data from the post-famine period to Partition. The pre-famine period remains veiled in mystery, he claims, although he does venture some aggregate findings and a periodization of women's migration from 1815 onwards.[18]

Akenson is trying to provide a tool to gauge the typicality of specific movements against a broad geographical and temporal canvas. Yet the problem in presenting the average as typical is that it overlooks the possibility that this statistical measurement may not reflect the actual experience of many, or even most, of the emigrants involved. In his effort to provide a template for the Irish diaspora worldwide, Akenson tends to blur the nuanced edges of specific migrations, seeming to imply that those experiences that do not fit the mold are irrelevant, or so anomalous as to be unworthy of historical examination other than as a curiosity. More troubling, his analysis leaves us with a series of unrelated, unexplained, and non-contextualized statements that provide little insight into migration experiences as they were actually lived by the people involved.[19]

Akenson's writings are representative of an increasing focus in the Irish historiography on quantitative analysis in the latter decades of the twentieth century, a shift which has led some critics to bemoan the predominance of cliometricians in the field. Nonetheless, these approaches have been quite useful in banishing stereotypes and blanket assumptions, and other historians have often been pleased to cite their findings (as I have done), secretly relieved that someone else has performed the task of crunching the numbers. But without context and anecdotal vitality, such analyses remain clinical and bleak; without interpretation, they are unsatisfying. They demonstrate little understanding of emigration as a movement of people, not just economic or demographic variables. And they provide little insight into the multi-layered dynamics of emigration: how gender, ethnicity, and class affected emigration experiences, or how emigration, in turn, affected the negotiation of gender, ethnicity, and class in the New World.

HOOKING INTO THE PAST

My approach to uncovering the lives of Irish Newfoundland women combines elements of poststructuralism and empiricism—strange bedfellows indeed, given the tension that has existed between these two methods of accessing the past. Poststructuralists have struck at the very core of empiricists' methodology by positing that there can be no such thing as documentary objectivism, because the very language that supposedly reflects reality in documentary evidence is itself involved in the process of constructing experience and meaning. Furthermore, these meanings themselves are unstable—shifting and changing over time as they are contested and either legitimated or reconstructed.

Poststructuralists' critique of conventional readings of language has instilled in many empiricists a fear that they are bent on paralyzing all efforts at communication and debate. However, poststructuralism has opened up whole new avenues of exploration in history by challenging the traditional white, male, middle-class bias of the discipline. It has provoked a re-examination of the content, methods and epistemology of the discipline to determine how "knowledge" is constituted, how some people are assigned to the center of the historical narrative while others are relegated to the margins, how evidence is selected, verified, and transmitted to portray a particular vision of social reality, and how the silences in history speak as much about biases as the written text. Poststructuralists have deconstructed language to understand how gender, as a system of meaning, is used to legitimize power relations in society, and how gender intersects with other constructions of difference, such as race, class, ethnicity, and sexual orientation, in creating and maintaining strategies of domination and subordination.

Discourse analysis has proved to be an effective method of shaking the tree of conventional wisdom, and poststructuralist theory has strongly informed my thinking about the lives of Irish Newfoundland women. However, I do not concentrate exclusively on discourse analysis in retrieving understandings of the past, for therein lies the danger of abandoning experience altogether, to the extent that discourse itself becomes the sole focus of historical study. While it is useful and necessary to deconstruct language in order to understand the processes by which meaning was (and is) created, discourse must still be situated in the context of specific lived experiences—in terms of both the subjects and the objects of the discourse—in order to understand how these systems of meaning actually functioned. In short, it is essential to monitor the interplay between rhetoric and reality.

Thus, I have not abandoned the research methods of empiricism, for to do so would distract me from the agency of the women I had hoped to incorporate into the historical narrative. Irish Newfoundland women of the late eighteenth and early nineteenth century left few texts in the historical record (even given the broader interpretation of that word to include many forms of cultural symbols), and I do not wish to treat them as mere objects of the hegemonic discourses that attempted to shape their lives. In order to find the Irish Newfoundland woman as subject of the historical narrative, then, I have regarded her lived experiences as text. And in order to uncover this text, I have relied heavily on empirical research techniques, with all the problems and limitations they entail.

My examination of the construction of Irish Newfoundland womanhood is thus grounded in historical context and lived experiences as they can best be determined from available sources. I analyze the hegemonic discourses that attempted to set parameters for women on the southern Avalon, but I also present evidence that these discourses were slow to intrude into the day-to-day life of plebeian culture. This is not to dismiss the effects of the persistent legal, social, and political discrimination that permeated the environment in which women moved; indeed, much insightful literature has already been written in these areas. But, as Bridget Hill warns, it is important in women's history not to focus only on patriarchal mechanisms by which women have been oppressed, for such an approach distorts our understanding and misses "the subtlety of the complex interaction of the many other factors" that have shaped women's lives.[20] Irish Newfoundland women on the southern Avalon did exercise a significant degree of authority at the local level and reached beyond the boundaries of the prescribed gender roles of hegemonic culture in myriad ways. It is these phenomena I am most interested in exploring: how and why they deployed this informal power, despite increasing pressures from certain quarters to resign their authority, and how they manifested agency within the contours of family and community power relations.

This blending of methodologies may not find favor in all quarters. When Akenson speaks of women in the Irish diaspora as "the Great Unknown," for example, he urges historians to resist the temptation to reconstruct the past from bits and pieces of anecdotal evidence, calling for a systematic gathering of "hard" evidence on women emigrants. But this demonstrates a lack of sensitivity to the dilemma that confronts historians of women and other groups who have been marginalized by the keepers of the written record in earlier periods. If historians remain fixated on "hard" evidence, the absence of these groups from the historical narrative may never be corrected. If we limit ourselves to studying only those who are more easily traced in order to ensure the certainty of our conclusions, we are in danger of losing large segments of our past.

Decades of poring over statistical information have not lifted the veil of mystery from the history of early Irish women emigrants, and it is highly unlikely that a hidden stash of data lies waiting for discovery. Nor would such a cache, if it did exist, necessarily provide us with a perfect picture of the past. Qualitative material is necessary in order to contextualize and explain the phenomena that the quantitative data reveal; anecdotal evidence is needed to help us understand the dynamics that shaped specific movements and the meanings that migrants derived from particular migration and settlement experiences.

This study provides a blend of quantitative and qualitative evidence, using a range of traditional historical sources, from census reports, parish records, business accounts, and estate records, to government correspondence, court records, missionaries' reports, newspapers, and diaries (see Appendix B). But most of this evidence was generated by middle-class administrators, clergymen, newspaper editors, and mercantile families. What are missing are the voices of the Irish women themselves. Most of these women would not have had the luxury of time, or likely the necessary literacy skills, to correspond or maintain journals; those pernicious silencers, time and illiteracy, have muffled the cadences of their daily lives.

Because I am attempting to reconstruct the past of a group so muted in the written record, I have used the oral tradition of the area to help flesh out information I found in documentary sources. Although this approach has gained considerable legitimacy as a means of retrieving the history of marginalized groups, it still requires justification to some. Indeed, with its increasing use by scholars in the social sciences and humanities in the 1960s and 1970s, the method quickly came under attack from traditional documentary historians, who warned of the indiscriminate acceptance of oral evidence at face value. Memory was unreliable, they argued, subject to the distortions of time and age, personal bias, and the impact of retrospective interpretations of the past. Oral historians countered with arguments that traditional documentary sources were also selective and biased; furthermore, they channeled thinking towards traditional methodologies and categories of understanding, thus reinforcing the continuing exclusion of certain groups from the historical narrative.[21]

Still, in response to concerns about the "accuracy" of oral history, an effort was made to lend "scientific rigor" to the gathering and evaluation of oral evidence: methodologies were devised to measure bias in oral evidence, to quantify oral responses and codify the results, and to corroborate oral testimony with written sources. By the 1980s, however, theorists were realizing that the subjective elements of oral history were not necessarily methodological flaws. Distortions and lapses in memory could actually provide insight into, not distraction from, the process of historical understanding and help scholars arrive at a more nuanced "truth" than the unidimensional accuracy of "facts." Practitioners were urged to deconstruct memory—to understand the process of remembering itself, the link between memory and identity, and the significance of memories to individuals and cultures. But as memory has become an object of study in its own right, the original intention of using oral history to retrieve information about the past of minority groups has somewhat faded from view.[22] And, as Michael Frisch has noted, rather than using theory to help interpret experiences, the experiences are being used to help make sense of theory.[23]

This is not to dismiss the importance of the complex workings of memory, and, indeed, a study of the retrospective nature of collective memory and the ways in which Irish migration experiences to the southern Avalon have been imagined and remembered would reveal much about how such processes contribute to the negotiation of ethnic identity over time. But that is not the focus of this work. My use of oral history harks back to the original aim of recovering the history of a marginalized group—in this case, a group sidelined by gender, ethnicity, region, and class.

Oral history has been used effectively in other migration studies, although it should be noted that most practitioners have actually been able to interview the emigrant generation as well as succeeding generations about migration and settlement experiences. Interviewing informants about the more distant past, which they did not actually live through, but about which they have received (and adapted) collective cultural memories, is another matter. Nonetheless, others have tapped oral traditions successfully to recreate historical contexts and flesh out details that do not exist in the written record—for example, information about kinship ties, informal belief systems, or the rhythms of daily and seasonal work and leisure routines.[24] I too have found the oral tradition invaluable in recreating historical cultural landscapes and provoking insights about Irish Newfoundland womanhood that would never have emanated from a study of the documentary evidence alone.

In collecting and interpreting oral testimony,[25] I have treated it like all my other sources—trying to ascertain bias or hyperbole, and looking for corroboration (either oral or documentary) when available. Occasionally, the oral evidence roughly corresponds with the written record, which will placate traditional documentary historians (although missives begrudgingly penned by frustrated colonial civil servants and irate priests require careful scrutiny as well, and I could just as easily argue that the oral tradition corroborates the documentary evidence in these cases). If the material presented comes from oral sources alone, I identify it as such. Information introduced with phrases such as "according to the oral tradition" meet the following criteria: a large majority of my informants have provided me with the same information, and it passes the *common sense* test—that is, the crux of the material (minor hyperbole need not discredit the essence of the anecdote) makes sense within the context of other information I have gathered. I also use material provided by only one or two informants if it passes the common sense test, but I specify the more individual nature of the memory in the text or by endnote to differentiate it from broader collective historical memories.

This lack of corroboration, however, does not diminish the significance of individual renderings in my eyes. Like Samuel Schrager, I acknowledge my oral informants to be "bearers of truth" in their telling of oral history in the sense that they are providing an interpretation (not necessarily a literal transcription) of processes or events based on their best understanding and knowledge of the matter, tempered by what they feel is significant and worth repeating to the interviewer. This does not mean that their renderings should not be problematized or contextualized like other types of sources, but simply that in the oral tradition, there is a Audio Sample marked difference in informants' attitudes towards the retelling of oral history and the retelling of a legend or tall tale.[26] With the retelling of their communal past, there is a deep-seated feeling that the information they are imparting is important: they want to *get it right*, and they want the historian to get it right as well.[27] And if there has been some refashioning of material in the process, so has there been in all historical accounts—written or oral, past or present. As Selma Leydesdorff, et al., point out, "no history reaches us unmediated."[28]

TRANSITION

In the current historiography on early Irish immigration and settlement in North America, Irish women are shadowy figures. They speak to us in sighs and whispers only from footnotes and after-thought chapters, mere helpmates to male migrants who are presented as the active shapers of New World experiences. This study will attempt to retrieve at least one group of these Irish women—the multi-generational group who settled in the southern Avalon up to the mid-nineteenth century—from the periphery of the record. Hopefully, it will encourage the custodians of the historical narrative—oral and written—to find a more gender-inclusive way of recounting early European settlement in the Americas than the conventional "Two brothers came out from Ireland or England . . ."

NOTES

1. The term *southern Avalon* in this study incorporates the area from Bay Bulls to Dog Point in St. Mary's Bay, the latter being the cut-off point in early census material dealing with St. Mary's Bay.

2. The West of England, or West Country, was comprised of six counties on the southwestern corner of England: Devon, Dorset, Cornwall, Hampshire, Somerset, and Wiltshire. Devon, Dorset, Cornwall, and Hampshire were all involved in the Newfoundland fishery, with Devon and Dorset having the longest and most significant involvement in the trade. The Channel Islands of Guernsey and Jersey also participated.

3. Several proprietary grants in the early 1600s incorporated the study area, including patents to Sir William Vaughan (primary site established at Renews, ca. 1617), Henry Carey, Lord Falkland (Renews, ca. 1623), George Calvert, Lord Baltimore (Ferryland, 1621), and Sir David Kirke (Ferryland, 1638). See: Gillian Cell, *English Enterprise in Newfoundland, 1577–1699* (Toronto: University of Toronto Press, 1969); and Peter Pope, "The South Avalon Planters, 1630–1700" (Ph.D. diss., Memorial University of Newfoundland, 1992).

4. John J. Mannion, "Introduction," in *The Peopling of Newfoundland: Essays in Historical Geography*, ed. John J. Mannion, Social and Economic Papers, no. 8 (St. John's: Institute of Social and Economic Research [ISER], Memorial University of Newfoundland, 1977), 1–13.

5. The terms *Irish woman/women* and *Irish Newfoundland woman/women* apply to both Irish immigrant women and women within the multi-generational Irish ethnic group in Newfoundland (including those with mixed English-Irish ties) in the study area. Occasionally, Irish women in Ireland are discussed, but the context will make the distinction clear.

6. HE, interview by author, Ferryland, 20 July 1999.

7. The Christian belief that Jesus Christ was miraculously conceived in the womb of his mother, Mary, through the power of the Holy Spirit, without sexual intercourse with a man.

8. Topsy is a young female slave in Harriet Beecher Stowe's novel *Uncle Tom's Cabin*. When quizzed about her parentage and where she has come from, Topsy has

no knowledge of her background, but ventures an opinion nonetheless: "I spect I grow'd. Don't think nobody never made me." See Joan D. Hedrick, *The Oxford Harriet Beecher Stowe Reader* (New York: Oxford University Press, 1999), 256.

9. This lack is discussed in "Editors' Note: Women, the Migratory Fishery and Settlement," in *Their Lives and Times: Women in Newfoundland and Labrador: A Collage*, ed. Carmelita McGrath, Barbara Neis, and Marilyn Porter (St. John's: Killick Press, 1995), 22–26.

10. I confess my unfamiliarity with the Francophone literature on this period.

11. The confederation of Canada took place in 1867, when Canada West (Ontario), Canada East (Quebec), Nova Scotia, and New Brunswick tentatively joined forces (with little in common, some have argued, but debt and the fear of American expansionism). By 1905, all remaining provinces and territories had been brought into the union with the exception of Newfoundland, which entered the confederation in 1949.

12. Although Ireland experienced a number of local crop failures and some widespread famines in the eighteenth and nineteenth centuries, the famine that is the focus of much of the historical literature on Irish emigration in that period is the Great Famine, which occurred in the late 1840s through the early 1850s. The term *famine* in this discussion refers to that mid-century disaster, unless the context specifically indicates otherwise.

13. See, for example, William Forbes Adams, *Ireland and Irish Emigration to the New World from 1815 to the Famine* (1932; reprint, New York: Russell and Russell, 1967); Oscar Handlin, *Boston's Immigrants* (Cambridge, MA: Harvard University Press, 1941); William V. Shannon, *The American Irish* (New York: Macmillan, 1963); Lawrence J. McCaffrey, *The Irish Diaspora in America* (Bloomington: Indiana University Press, 1976); Kerby A. Miller, "Emigrants and Exiles: Irish Cultures and Irish Emigration to North America, 1790–1922," *Irish Historical Studies* 22, no. 86 (September 1980): 97–125; Miller, *Emigrants and Exiles: Ireland and the Irish Exodus to North America* (New York: Oxford University Press, 1985); and Miller, "Emigration, Capitalism, and Ideology in Post-famine Ireland," in *Migrations: The Irish at Home and Abroad*, ed. Richard Kearney (Dublin: Wolfhound Press, 1990), 91–108.

14. See Donald H. Akenson: *Being Had: Historians, Evidence, and the Irish in North America* (Don Mills, ON: P. D. Meany, 1985), 40–42, 69–72, and 84–85; and *Small Differences: Irish Catholics and Irish Protestants, 1815–1922: An International Perspective* (Kingston: McGill-Queen's University Press, 1988), 102–3. See also Cecil J. Houston and William J. Smyth: *Irish Emigration and Canadian Settlement: Patterns, Links, and Settlers* (Toronto: University of Toronto Press, 1990), 21; and "The Irish Diaspora: Emigration to the New World, 1720–1920," in *An Historical Geography of Ireland*, ed. B. J. Graham and L. J. Proudfoot (London: Academic Press, 1993), 338–65, particularly 353. See also David Doyle, "The Irish in North America, 1776–1845," in A New History of Ireland, ed. W. E. Vaughan, vol. 5 (Oxford: Clarendon Press, 1989), 706.

15. Jim Mac Laughlin: *Historical and Recent Irish Emigration: A Critique of Core-Periphery and Behavioural Models* (London: University of North London Press,

1994), 9–11 and 45–46; and "Emigration and the Construction of Nationalist Hegemony in Ireland: The Historical Background to 'New Wave' Irish Emigration," in *Location and Dislocation in Contemporary Irish Society: Emigration and Irish Identities*, ed. Jim Mac Laughlin (Cork: Cork University Press, 1997), 5–35.

16. See, for example: John Mannion, Mannion, *Irish Settlements in Eastern Canada: A Study of Cultural Transfer and Adaptation* (Toronto: University of Toronto Press, 1974); Mannion, "The Impact of Newfoundland on Waterford and Its Hinterland in the Eighteenth Century" (paper presented at the Annual Conference of Irish Geographers, University College, Galway, 22 April 1977); Mannion, "Tracing the Irish: A Geographical Guide," *The Newfoundland Ancestor* 9, no. 1 (spring 1993): 4–18; and John Mannion and Fidelma Maddock, "Old World Antecedents, New World Applications: Inistioge Immigrants in Newfoundland," in *Kilkenny: History and Society-Interdisciplinary Essays on the History of an Irish County*, ed. William Nolan and Kevin Whelan (Dublin: Geography Publications, 1990), 345–404. For a more extensive list of Mannion's writings, see Appendix B and the Bibliography.

17. Donald Akenson, *The Irish Diaspora: A Primer* (Toronto: P. D. Meaney, 1993). The quotation comes from the title of chap. 7: "Women and the Irish Diaspora: The Great Unknown."

18. Akenson, *Primer*, particularly chap. 7.

19. Akenson's study of the Irish in Ontario is an exception, although it focuses primarily on men's experiences. See Akenson, *The Irish in Ontario: A Study in Rural History*, 2nd ed. (Montreal: McGill-Queen's University Press, 1999).

20. Bridget Hill, "Women's History: A Study in Change, Continuity, or Standing Still?" in *Women's Work: The English Experience, 1650–1914*, ed. Pamela Sharpe (London: Arnold, 1998), 42–58, particularly 55.

21. Katherine Jensen, "Oral Histories of Rural Western American Women: Can They Contribute to Quantitative Studies?" *International Journal of Oral History* 5, no. 3 (November 1984): 159–67; quotation from 160.

22. Alistair Thomson, "Tales of the Century: Biennial National Conference of the Oral History Association of Australia, 2–5 September 1999, State Library of Victoria, Melbourne," *Oral History* 28, no. 1 (spring 2000): 25–27.

23. For a discussion of some of the debates in the field, see: Alistair Thomson, Michael Frisch, and Paula Hamilton, "The Memory and History Debates: Some International Perspectives," *Oral History* 22, no. 2 (autumn 1994): 33–43; Jensen, "Oral Histories"; Rebecca Sharpless, "The Numbers Game: Oral History Compared with Quantitative Methodology," *International Journal of Oral History* 7, no. 2 (June 1886): 93–108; Joan Sangster, "Telling Our Stories: Feminist Debates and the Use of Oral History," *Women's History Review* 3, no. 1 (1994): 5–28; Selma Leydesdorff, Luisa Passerini, and Paul Tompson, eds., *Gender and Memory*, International Yearbook of Oral History and Life Stories, vol. 4 (Oxford: Oxford University Press, 1996); and Anna Green and Kathleen Troup, eds., *The Houses of History: A Critical Reader in Twentieth-Century History and Theory* (New York: New York University Press, 1999), 230–38.

24. See, for example: Gerald L. Pocius, *A Place to Belong: Community Order and Everyday Space in Calvert, Newfoundland* (Athens: University of Georgia Press, 1991);

Thomas Nemec, "Trepassey, 1505–1840 A.D.: The Emergence of an Anglo-Irish Newfoundland Outport," *Newfoundland Quarterly* 69, no. 4 (1973): 17–28; Nemec, "Trepassey, 1840–1900: An Ethnohistorical Reconstruction of an Anglo-Irish Outport Society," in *Through a Mirror Dimly: Essays on Newfoundland Society and Culture*, ed. Maura Hanrahan (St. John's: Breakwater, 1993), 145–62; Nemec, "An Ethnohistorical and Ethnographic Study of the Cod Fishery at St. Shott's, Newfoundland" (Ph.D. diss., University of Michigan, 1980); Margaret MacKay, "Nineteenth Century Tiree Emigrant Communities in Ontario," *Oral History* 9, no. 2 (autumn 1981): 49–60; and Alistair Thomson, "Moving Stories: Oral History and Migration Studies," *Oral History* 27, no. 1 (spring 1999): 24–37.

25. The oral testimony presented here is drawn primarily from interviews conducted from 1999–2001 with twenty-one male and female informants from seven communities in the study area: Brigus South, Cape Broyle, Calvert, Ferryland, Renews, Trepassey, and St. Mary's. Several of the interviewees had moved from their home communities in adulthood, but all had spent their childhood and early adulthood on the southern Avalon and all have roots in the plebeian fishing community of the area. Because a number of them did not wish to be identified, I refer to all informants throughout this study by initials that I have assigned to preserve their anonymity.

The informants were advised of the general subject areas to be covered in the interview either in an advance meeting or by correspondence. A questionnaire with broad, open-ended questions was used in the actual interviews, but only to give the interviews shape and flow, not for statistical purposes. The interviewing process itself was as interactive and open as possible. My original intent was to audio-record as many interviews as possible; however, most informants were quite dismayed by the sight of the recorder, and in order to maintain a more relaxed and productive atmosphere, I often resorted to careful note-taking only. (All interview notes remain in my possession.) Because I was seeking historical context rather than personal narratives, this method was not problematic. As a result, however, the only direct quotations that appear in the text are short and those of which I am certain of the accuracy of the wording. This recent interview material has been supplemented by oral material that I gathered as an undergraduate in the early 1970s (see Bibliography), as well as by a small amount of material collected in the study area by other interviewers that is housed at the Memorial University of Newfoundland Folklore and Language Archive (MUNFLA) and several undergraduate student papers using oral history (including one of my own) that were prepared for anthropology, geography, or history courses in the 1970s and are available at the Maritime History Archives, Memorial University of Newfoundland (MHA).

Of the audio clips presented in this work, two are actually my retelling of anecdotes that I had collected from several informants who were reluctant to be recorded. I have done this because the oral retelling is so much more effective than a written version. I feel that this decision is further justified by the fact that I have maternal roots on the southern Avalon and have spent much of my life there, so I am a legitimate bearer of the oral tradition of the area. One of the two anecdotes relates to Mrs. Clancy (at the end of this section), and the other, to a widow's curse (Chapter 5).

26. Samuel Schrager, "What is Social in Oral History?" *International Journal of Oral History* 4, no. 2 (June 1983): 76–98, particularly 78. In only one interview did I feel that the informant was not making this distinction, and I have used his information minimally and with due caution.

27. I am aware, here, of my own participation in shaping the interview—that, despite the flexible nature of the interview, my research interests have taken priority in the selection of subject matter for discussion. I also realize that this selection process, in itself, may have affected the processes of collective historical memory and the way the material may be remembered and retold in the future.

28. Introduction to *Gender and Memory*, ed. Leydesdorff, Passerini, and Tompson,12.

2. THE SLENDER THREAD CAST OFF

Migration and Reception in Newfoundland

> When Michael and Mary Ryan were coming from County Wexford Ireland to Nfld. their first child was Born at sea. It was the year 1826. The boy was named Thomas Ryan . . . Michael Ryan . . . was drowned near Petty Harbour Motion, in the year 1830 on a sealing voyage. His wife Mary Ryan was left with 3 young children, Thomas who was born at sea, Michael and Thimothy Ryan. After some years Mary Ryan Married again. Edward Coady also a native of County Wexford. They had a family of 2 sons and 1 daughter . . . They have many decendents at Cape Broyle, many places in Canada and also in the United States. Audio Sample

These homespun words, transcribed from the oral tradition by an elderly community historian in 1971, provide a skeletal story of an Irish woman who came to Cape Broyle on the southern Avalon in the early nineteenth century.[1] It is a sparse and plainspoken chronicle of her life, but Mary Ryan's story could be the stuff of movie directors' dreams. A young Irish woman leaves her home in Wexford to accompany her husband on a perilous journey that will bring her to a landscape quite different from the green farmlands of her home country. There has been some urgency in their leaving, for Mary is well into her pregnancy upon departure, and the transatlantic crossing, difficult at best, will be a dangerous venture for a woman about to give birth. Perhaps they are responding to economic recession or land shortage. Almost certainly, they have heard of the potential for earning a livelihood in the Newfoundland fishery. And so they leave, despite Mary's condition, and somewhere on the heaving mass of the North Atlantic, she gives birth to a boy named Thomas. Despite the primitive conditions on board the passenger vessel, she and her newborn son both survive the journey. The Ryans begin to carve out a living in Newfoundland, supplementing their fishing livelihood with subsistence farming—all that is possible in the short growing season and the rock-strewn soil of the southern Avalon. Michael also finds winter employment in Newfoundland's second industry, the seal fishery. Then, tragically, he dies on a sealing voyage, leaving Mary with three young boys to raise on her own. Still, she remains in her new home and eventually remarries. Mary and her new husband, Edward Coady, another native of Wexford, go forth and populate the new world . . . *Fade to black.*

The narrative of Mary Ryan's journey to the southern Avalon can easily be burnished with dramatic gilt. But how much of the story is representative of the experiences of other Irish immigrants to that shore? Certainly, when Michael and Mary Ryan left County Wexford in 1826 to come to the southern Avalon, they were not venturing into the great unknown. Ireland–Newfoundland trade connections had been forged long before, and news of living conditions and employment opportunities in Newfoundland would surely have permeated all but the most hidden villages of southeast Ireland. Indeed, it is not only possible but likely that Michael had already been out to the southern Avalon; the Pole Papers list a Michael Ryan as a *dieter* with Richard Down in Cape Broyle in the winter of 1799–1800 and a fishing *servant* of John Mackey in Brigus South the following summer.[2] Perhaps Michael had participated in the Newfoundland fishery from his teenage years and was now a man in his forties, emigrating to Newfoundland with his younger bride (a common marriage pattern along the southern Avalon in the period). Or perhaps he was a son or other relative of an earlier Michael Ryan who had been involved in the fishery. More assuredly, the Ryans were part of a larger swell of Irish immigrants who came to Newfoundland in the period 1825–33. And this movement was, in turn, part of an extended period of Irish migration to Newfoundland dating back to at least the late seventeenth century.

EARLY MIGRATION

Early nominal census material, haphazardly recorded in the crabbed hands of British naval officers stationed at Newfoundland, indicates a strong presence of English planter families on the southern Avalon by the late seventeenth century, the demographic outgrowth of a West of England-Newfoundland fishery that was almost two centuries old.[3] But the naval officers also enumerated servants working for the planters, and although ethnicity was not revealed in the records, there is no question that an Irish element had crept into this migration stream—an element that included Irish women, for as early as 1681, Capt. James Story made the following marginal note in his accounting of the fisheries and inhabitants in Newfoundland:

> The trade of Irish to Newfoundland is all sorts of frises, linen cloath, candles, cloath Hatts, shooes, stockens, beefe, porke, bread, butter, cheeze & all sorts of small merch'dise, there returnes for it are fish, they like wise bring over a great many women passeng[ers] wch they sell for Serv^s & a little after theire coming they marry among the fisherman[men] that live with the Planters . . .[4]

But while there were some Irish vessels trading at Newfoundland,[5] initially the primary carriers of Irish *passengers* to the island were vessels from the West of England (Web Link). Certainly by the late seventeenth and early eighteenth centuries, fishing ships from north Devon ports (Bideford and Barnstaple especially, but also Appledore and Northam) were regularly stopping at southeast Irish ports for cheap salted provisions and labor for the Newfoundland fishery. In 1720, British naval authorities on the island noted the "great numbers of Irish roman Catholick servants, who all settle to the southward [of St. John's]."[6] At this time, however, the migration to Newfoundland was largely temporary, for, while the fishery at Newfoundland had both a migratory and a resident component, the majority of fishing servants, regardless of which branch they served, returned home after the period of time contracted by their *shipping papers*—usually a summer, or two summers and a winter (*a Newfoundland summer*).[7] Even many planters (still a predominantly English group in the early eighteenth century) would eventually return to their home country to pursue other work or retire.

But wartime conditions wreaked havoc on the West of England–Newfoundland trade, particularly the migratory sector, and wartime conditions were almost continuous for Britain in the latter half of the eighteenth century. North Devon's traffic collapsed during the Seven Years' War, but its role in the Irish passenger and provisions trade was assumed by ports in south Devon and Poole, in Dorset. At the same time, the Irish migration stream swelled as increasing numbers of Irish fishing servants filled the void left by English servants who had either been pressed into naval service or had moved inland to avoid roving press gangs. After the war, some merchants in southeast Irish ports—especially Waterford, but also New Ross and Youghal—developed an independent trade with the southern Avalon and Burin, and these ports and their hinterlands would become a major source area for Irish emigrants to the study area (and to Newfoundland in general). Other southern Avalon Irish initially entered through the port of St. John's, attracted by its increasing commercial activity and potential for employment, ultimately wending their way southwards from the town (mirroring a similar diaspora northwards into Conception Bay).

A "NOTORIOUSLY DISAFFECTED" AND "WICKED & IDLE" PEOPLE: EARLY RECEPTION

Meanwhile, as the eighteenth century unfolded, British authorities in Newfoundland watched the growing numbers of Irish migrants with levels of concern ranging from wariness to near-hysteria. In March of 1702, in the midst of Anglo-French hostilities which had manifested themselves in local confrontations between the French at Placentia and the English along the *English Shore,* local English authorities charged that several French and Irish Catholics at St. John's were "spyes, corupting & debauching his Maj^ties^ Servants, and other his subjects to desert their Service and bring in a French power."[8] That autumn, the principal inhabitants of the town requested that the naval commodore ban the hiring or entertaining of "any foreigner or Roman Chatholick" without the permission of the commanding officer at Fort William.[9] In 1705, the naval officer at St. John's articulated a theme that would echo throughout the eighteenth century and into the next:

> That Care may be taken of the Irish residing in the Country, for they by our daily Experience have proved very detrimental to the Governm^t^. hereof, for when the Enemy makes any Incursion upon us they doe take up armes and informe our Enemy and prove very treacherous and our greatest Enemy.[10]

In 1738, naval governor Capt. Philip Van Brugh (Web Link) fired a similar volley, suggesting that Irish migration to Newfoundland be stemmed:

> The most material and universal complaints are against the great numbers of Irish Roman Catholics yearly brought into Newfoundland, and remain the winter season, to the very great prejudice of His Majesty's Protestant subjects, who dred the consequense that may attend them in case of war; and humbly beg their case may be laid before your lordship that a method may be found to prevent such imbarkation in Ireland.[11]

But there was a tension in official attitudes towards Irish servants, for although they were seen as undesirables, they were becoming increasingly essential to the operation of the fishery on the island. So the numbers of Irish arriving in

Newfoundland grew, but so too did concerns about their loyalty to the Crown. In 1749, Governor George Rodney warned the Colonial Office that the Irish Roman Catholics in Newfoundland were not to be trusted.[12] The following year, Governor Francis Drake (Web Link) wrote in a similar vein that the Irish "are notoriously disaffected to the government, all of them refusing to take the oath of allegiance when tendered to them."[13] The southern Avalon, with its growing numbers of Irish wintering over, was seen as one of several potential breeding grounds of Irish treachery.[14] Drake, for example, specifically drew the Colonial Secretary's attention to the fact that "the majority of inhabitants to the Southward of St. John's are Papists."[15]

During the American Revolutionary War, a petition to Governor John Montagu (Web Link) from the merchants and principal inhabitants of Renews, all of English ethnicity, stated that, despite depredations committed by American vessels along that shore, "we are more in danger from some of them [Irish inhabitants], than from the Americans, as they are determined to plunder the Stores & turn Rebels."[16] That same year, Montagu issued a general admonition to the people of Ferryland district for their refusal to assist in defending the interests of the Crown from enemy vessels along that coast.[17] In 1800, when the failed United Irish rebellion of 1798 sparked a mutiny among Irish troops in the Newfoundland Regiment at St. John's (Web Link), concerns were again expressed about the disaffection of the Irish population, hundreds of whom were thought to be involved in a larger plot to murder British authorities, merchants, and their supporters on the island. Particular concern was expressed about the southern Avalon. Debriefing Governor William Waldegrave on the episode, Surrogate and Deputy Naval Officer (later, Chief Justice) John Ogden reported:

> . . . we knew not who we could depend upon for support in case of resistance, having every reason to believe the defection was very extensive not only through the Regiment, but through the Inhabitants of this and all the *Out Harbours*, particularly to the Southward almost to a Man have taken the United Oaths . . . it would be absurd to suppose it might not take place again . . . the security of Trade and Fishery, nay the security and salvation of this Island itself will entirely depend upon a proper Military Force [of 800–1,000 men] at this place, with sufficient strength to afford small detachments to some of the Out Harbours to the Southward to watch their motions, and assist the Magistrates when necessary.[18]

Traditional fears that England's difficulty would prove Ireland's opportunity had clearly been carried over from the Old World to the New. 10

Official discourse also equated the Irish with vagrancy, drunkenness, and disorder. Concern was frequently expressed, for example, about the idle and unruly conduct of Irish men and women left to winter over in Newfoundland without employment. Lord Vere Beauclerk, a naval commodore stationed at Newfoundland, articulated such fears in 1728, as did naval governors George Clinton (in 1731), Thomas Cadre Smith (in 1742), and John Byng (in 1743).[19] On 22 September 1755, Governor Richard Dorrill (Web Link) ordered that all masters of ships bringing passengers to Newfoundland must return them home after the fishing season unless special permission was granted otherwise. The measure dealt with fishing servants in general, but it was particularly aimed at reducing the Irish element of the population, as revealed by the wording of the preamble:

> Whereas a great Number of Irish Roman Catholicks are Annually brought over here, a great part of which have but small wages, so that after paying their Passages to this Place, and the charges of Clothing & during the fishing season, their whole wages are spent & they have not wherewith either to Pay their Passages home, or to Purchase Provisions for the Winter, by which means they not only become chargable to this Place but many Robberys and Felonys &c are committed, by them to the great Loss and Terror of His Majesty's Liege Subjects in this Island . . . [20]

Two years later, Governor Richard Edwards complained to the Board of Trade in a similar vein that too many Irish servants were being abandoned by fishing masters during the winter, often without their summer wages, and left at large "to the great terror and distress of the Inhabitants."[21]

Three important contextual elements must be noted in relation to the attitude of British authorities towards the Irish Catholic population of Newfoundland. First, their opinions reflected contemporary English perceptions of difference between the Anglo-Saxon and Gaelic-Irish "races."[22] Second, their actions were justified by law, for Newfoundland Catholics (a predominantly Irish group) were subject to a punitive legal regime up to the early nineteenth century that drew from the Penal Laws that existed in Great Britain and Ireland at the time.[23] For example, Catholics in Newfoundland could not hold office within the rudimentary system of governance on the island because of the requirement to swear an oath repudiating transubstantiation. They were not permitted to bear firearms, hold property, or run public houses. A special tax was imposed on Catholics involved in trade on the island.[24] Catholics were not permitted to exercise their faith openly until Governor Jonathon Campbell (Web Link) issued a Declaration of Liberty of Conscience in 1784. Before this edict, a handful of priests operated underground (and often without official church sanction), traveling incognito to various harbors to serve the growing Catholic population. The oral tradition of the southern Avalon, for example, tells of a priest who escaped authorities at Witless Bay disguised as a fisherman, and of another priest who had to hide in a cellar in Toad's Cove (now Tors Cove) to avoid detection. It also tells of midnight meetings at the *Mass Rock* in Renews to say the Mass, the rosary, and other prayers.[25] The potential consequences for those who harbored priests or permitted the Mass to be said in their homes were heavy fines, house burnings, and deportation.[26] Granted, this regime was enforced with varying degrees of rigor, depending on the individual attitudes of governors and surrogates of the day; but certainly, the intensity of enforcement increased in proportion to the numbers of Irish arriving in Newfoundland from the mid-eighteenth century onwards.

Finally, it is also important to view many of these regulations within the context of a struggle on the part of British authorities to promote the migratory fishery at the expense of a resident fishery in order to preserve the hub of the industry in the West of England and to maintain Britain's nursery for seamen. Throughout the latter seventeenth century, the English government had tried to discourage settlement altogether; but by the turn of the next century, after several successful incursions by the French into the English Shore (inroads later reversed by treaty), Britain was beginning to see the wisdom of maintaining a year-round presence in Newfoundland. Still, the migratory fishery retained its priority in official policy as the British endeavored to limit settlement, especially by limiting the degree of government instituted in Newfoundland. While some elements of rudimentary governance had to be established throughout the eighteenth century in order to maintain a semblance of order on the island,[27] various governors in Newfoundland upheld the privileges of the ship fishery that had been introduced by Western Charters in the previous century and legislated by the *Act 10 and 11 Wm. III, Cap. 25* (the *Newfoundland Act* of 1699).[28]

One of the strongest advocates of the ship fishery in the eighteenth century was Hugh Palliser (Web Link). While governor of Newfoundland during the summers of 1764 through 1768,[29] he unleashed a battery of orders and proclamations to prohibit the enclosure of lands suitable for the ship fishery and to remove any buildings, gardens, or other encroachments thereon.[30] He also enforced strict adherence to the law that fishing servants who had not been contracted for winter work were to be returned to their native countries at the end of each fishing season, and he ordered that sufficient money be held back from their wages to pay their passages home. Like Dorrill and Edwards before him, he noted that thousands of servants were left behind each winter in "misery, distress and hardships," with no money and no employment to provide for themselves, and thus became a burden on the community.[31]

But while Palliser expressed concern about fishing servants in general, his regulations, like those of Dorrill and Edwards, targeted Irish servants in particular. Palliser wildly overestimated the proportion of Roman Catholics (and hence Irish) in the population at three-quarters of the total, reflecting a commonly held attitude that the Irish were profligate in their family sizes.[32] He spoke generally of the inhabitants of Newfoundland in disparaging terms, arguing that for a full six months, "they are perfectly Idle, abandon'd to every sort of Debauchery and Wickedness, become perfect Savages, are Strangers to all good Order, Government and Religion by habitual Idleness and Debauchery's." They would never become industrious fishermen or seamen, he continued, and would always pose a security risk, "for they always did and always will join an Invading Enemy and full 3/4 of them are Roman Catholics."[33]

On 31 October 1764, Palliser issued the following regulations for the upcoming winter:

> For better preserving the Peace preventing Roberies, Tumultuous Assembly's, and other disorders of Wicked & Idle People remaining in the Country during the Winter
>
> Order'd -
>
> That no Papist Servant man or Woman shall remain at any Place where they did not Fish or serve during the Sumer Preceeding.-
>
> That not more than two Papist men shall dwell in one House during the Winter, except such as have Protestant Masters.-
>
> That no Papist shall keep a Publick House or Vend Liquor by Retail.-
>
> That no Person keep Dyeters during the Winter.-
>
> That all Idle disorderly, useless men & Women be Punish'd according to Law and sent out of the Country.[34]

The order clearly conflated "Wicked & Idle People" with "Papists," and the Papists in Newfoundland at the time were virtually all Irish. The majority of dieters in Newfoundland were also Irish by this period, so the order was specifically aimed at reducing the numbers of "disorderly, useless" Irish on the island after the fishing season. Even Palliser's efforts to remove encroachments from fishing rooms targeted Irish inhabitants. A large number of Irish Catholics were erecting huts, he observed, in which they entertained "Rogues and Vagabonds" and encouraged them to remain on the island "to the great disturbance of the Peace, and danger of His Majesty's Subjects Lives, and to the exceeding great prejudice of the Fishing Trade." The magistrates were to tear down the offending buildings immediately and not permit any similar encroachments in the future.[35] The Irish were a "problem" that must be controlled.

While Palliser was one of the most virulent of Newfoundland's governors in his mistrust and even dislike of the Irish, the spirit and intent of his regulations were carried out by succeeding governors up to the turn of the nineteenth century. Regulations concerning the removal of fishing servants over the winter were re-issued by governors Jonathon Byron, Molynoux Shuldham, Robert Duff, John Montagu, Mark Milbanke, Richard King, William Waldegrave, and John Gambier.[36] (Web Link) Until the late 1770s, they appeared overtly in conjunction with the anti-Papist regulations initiated by Palliser. Indeed, Byron's 1770 order respecting over-wintering Catholics included the additional provision that "the Children of Roman Catholic's born in this Country be Baptized according to Law [that is, according to the precepts of the Church of England]."[37]

In the last two decades of the eighteenth century, the explicitly punitive tone of the regulations disappeared, but its spirit could still be felt in the enforcement of the regulations respecting the largely Irish Catholic dieter population. When Catholic Prefect-Apostolic James O Donel requested permission from Governor Milbanke (Web Link) to build a chapel at Ferryland, for example, Milbanke dictated the following response on board the vessel that was returning him to Britain for the winter:

> The Governor acquaints M^r^. O'Donell that so far from feeling disposed to allow of an increase of places of Religious Worship to the Roman Catholics of this Island, he very seriously intends next year to lay those already established under particular restrictions. M^r^. O Donnell must be sensible that it is not the Interest of Great Britain to encourage people to winter in Newfoundland, and he cannot be ignorant that many of the lower Order of those who now stay, would if it were not for the Convenience with which they obtain absolution here, go home for it at least once in two or three years; And the Governor has been misinformed if M^r^. O'Donell instead of advising their return to Ireland does not rather encourage them to winter in this Country.[38]

Orders prohibiting the enclosure of lands also continued to be anti-Irish-Catholic in tenor after Palliser's term. In 1771, for example, Governor Byron ordered the justice of the peace at Bonavista to remove some marking posts which an "Irish Papist" had put up on a vacant fishing room "with an Intent to Build a *stage & Flakes* thereof, & Possess the same as his Right & Property," contrary to the *Newfoundland Act* of 1699, and to warn him and all other Papists from marking vacant fishing rooms as property.[39] Gubernatorial ire was not limited to cases of Irish encroachments on shore space that should have been reserved for the fishery. Irish servants who were squatting inland in Ferryland district, particularly Renews, provoked the following directive by Governor Montagu in July 1777:

> Whereas information has been made to me that there are a great number of Irish Servants belonging to *Boatkeepers* in the District of Ferryland and particularly in the Harbour of Renewse who have inclosed Lands and built Hutts, at half a mile Distance at the Back of their Fishing rooms, without any permission for so doing which is not only a great Violation of the Law, but will be the means, if not timely prevented, of contention and strife.
>
> These are therefore to require & direct all people who may have fenced in any Lands and built Houses thereon, without my Permission immediately to cause all such Fences to be pulled down, and that they do not presume to build any Hutts, Stages, or *Cookrooms*, or to inclose any Lands at the back thereof, otherwise than for the service of the Fishery without my Permission for so doing, upon paid of Forfeiture of Five Pounds for every such offence, to be stopped out of their Wages if Servants and have no other Effects. And I do hereby require and direct all His Majesty's Justices of the Peace within the said District to see this My Order is strictly obeyed.[40]

The proclamation was accompanied by a letter to local justice of the peace Robert Carter advising that if the fences were not taken down voluntarily and expeditiously, Carter was to make arrangements to have them removed by force.[41]

British authorities stationed at Newfoundland were not bending the rules to harass the growing Irish population on the island. All these orders and regulations were in keeping with the laws that governed Newfoundland in the eighteenth century. Furthermore, it was not unusual for local officials in colonial contexts to be concerned about large numbers of unemployed, unsettled people within their jurisdiction, even if they were often unreflective about the underlying causes of the undesirable behavior they were trying to curtail. The focus of these official efforts in Newfoundland, however, was decidedly anti-Irish-Catholic in nature, aimed at reducing the numbers of Irish remaining on the island; there were no corresponding proclamations respecting English Protestant inhabitants, for example, who were also enclosing land and building houses without formal permission.[42] And throughout this official discourse ran a construction of "Irishness" as inherently feckless, intemperate, and treacherous; the Irish were a problem group that required constant regulation and surveillance.

Part of this discourse focused particularly on an image of the Irish woman immigrant as vagrant and whore. Again, this must be seen within the broader context, in which British authorities had discouraged the presence of all women in Newfoundland. Amidst the debates leading up to the revision of the Western Charter of 1671 (the most oppressive revision in terms of settlement[43]), the specter arose of the inherently immoral woman, a threat to the orderly operation of the fishery. West Country merchants involved in the Newfoundland trade, not yet convinced that settlement was to their advantage, claimed that planters used their womenfolk to "debauch ignorant mariners."[44] The "respectable" inhabitants of St. John's at the turn of the eighteenth century requested special monitoring of single servants (male and female), but especially those "scandalous & prostitute Women" who remained after the fishing season, to the "great prejudice & ill Example to y^{e}. sev^{ll}. Harbours."[45] This was a construction of womanhood that British authorities did nothing to discourage in relation to Newfoundland, for, ironically, the very characteristics touted by British colonial policy in encouraging women to participate in colonizing ventures on the North American mainland—their stabilizing effect on community formation, their essential role in permanent settlement—were perceived as threats to British enterprise in Newfoundland, where a resident fishery would weaken the migratory sector (and, hence, Britain's training ground for seamen).[46] As Capt. Francis Wheler, a naval officer stationed at Newfoundland, reported to the home government in 1684: "Soe longe as there comes noe women they are not fixed."[47]

The policy of discouraging women migrants to Newfoundland persisted well into the eighteenth century, and local authorities found occasion to remark particularly about the undesirability and unsuitability of Irish women in the population. When Captain Story had commented in 1681 on the Irish women servants who came out as servants and married fishermen, he had added:

> . . . & a little after theire coming they marry among the fisherman[men] that live with the Planters, & being Extreamly poor, contract such Debts as they are not able to pay so yt if course be not speedily taken for the preservation of such passengers coming over the Countrey they will be ruined.[48]

In particular, the construction of the undesirable woman took on ethnic undertones as the numbers of Irish increased after the mid-eighteenth century.[49] In 1764, for example, Governor Palliser linked Irish women servants with poverty, improvidence, and disorder when he issued the following notice:

> Whereas great Numbers of Poor Women are frequently brought into this Country, and Particularly into this Port by Vessels arriving from Ireland who become ditress'd and a Charge to the Inhabitants, and likewise Occasion much disorder and Disturbance against the Peace of our Sovereign Lord the King.-
>
> Notice is hereby given to all masters of Vessels arriving in this Country that from the First day of April next no Women are to be Landed without Security being first given for their good behavior and that they shall not become Chargable to the Inhabitants.[50]

Although Palliser was generally wary of the increasing numbers of Irish arriving in Newfoundland (often through the administrative center of St. John's, and hence right under the governor's nose), it was significant that with this—the very first of his anti-Irish-Catholic proclamations—the governor homed in on the perceived threat of the unattached Irish woman. Two years later, the alleged sexual immorality of just such a woman provoked another strong reaction from Palliser and the magistrates in St. John's. In the case of *Pendergrass v. Blakener*, fishing servant Thomas Pendergrass sued for wages denied him by his master, John Blakener, because Pendergrass had been having sexual relations with Blakener's Irish female servant. Pendergrass recovered his wages "without any Deduction on acc^{t}. of his Intercourse with [the] Woman Servant to the said Blakener," but the magistrates were instructed "to Order the Woman who occasion'd this disturbance, to leave the Country, & oblige the master of the Ship who brought her, to carry her away."[51] Both the 1764 proclamation and the 1766 deportation order reflected a fear of the single Irish woman, whose sexual autonomy and social and economic independence from father or husband cast her, in the eyes of colonial authorities, as deviant—a danger to the social and moral order of the island.

The discursive construction of Irish women servants as immoral, unproductive, and menacing was reiterated in Governor Montagu's proclamation of 1777, which expressed particular concern about their arriving in Newfoundland pregnant and becoming a drain on the populace:

> Whereas it has been represented to me that the Ships and Vessels that come from Ireland frequently bring unmarried Women, and Young [Girls], who are destitute of Friends and come over with no other View but to be hired as Indentured Servants, that on their arrival and having hired themselves to Masters, have proved to be with Child, which is attended with Difficulties to the Masters, and is the cause of bringing many Incumbrances upon the Inhabitants of this Island and of this Place in particular.
>
> These are therefore to forbid all Masters of Vessels from bringing any Women as Servants from Ireland, on pain of Forfeiting Ten Pounds for every Person so found on board, or that can be proved by Information to have been brought over by them.
>
> And I do further Declare if any such Women be hired to a Master on Shore and she proves to be with Child at the time she was so hired, the Master [of the vessel] shall not be paid for her passage.
>
> But in the Case he shall be paid for such passage before the Person so brought over is Discovered to be with Child, He [the master of the vessel] shall be obliged to refund whatever Sum he received.[52]

This order fashioned an image of the Irish woman servant as promiscuous and conniving. It implied that large numbers of such dissolute women (or at least sufficient numbers to warrant an official proclamation) became pregnant outside of wedlock, either in the home country or on board vessels bringing them to Newfoundland, where they entrapped unwary employers by contracting their services without revealing their condition. Ultimately (and here was the oft-repeated theme on the "feckless" Irish), they would become a charge on the more "respectable" inhabitants of the island.

In 1805, Governor Erasmus Gower observed that "a considerable number of unmarried women" were arriving on the island "without having any relatives or Friends residing here." Having "reason to fear" that many of them were "persons of bad character," he resurrected Palliser's regulations of 2 July 1764, and ordered that the masters of vessels bringing passengers to the island be advised that they would be held accountable for the financial security and moral behavior of female passengers.[53] Although Gower did not specify ethnicity in his order, there can be little doubt that the target group was Irish, given their predominance in the passenger traffic at that period. The same regulations were re-invoked by Governor John Holloway three years later.[54]

The Irish woman immigrant, then, was a particular "problem" for local authorities, requiring special regulation of her own. In particular, the single Irish female servant required monitoring, for her independence from a patriarchal family context and her potential sexual agency contravened hegemonic feminine ideals that embodied domesticity, dependence, fragility, and sexual passivity. Yet all Irish women immigrants were pariahs, for implied (though not directly stated) in this discourse was the fear that once these women were permitted to remain, the equation for reproducing this undesirable ethnic group on the island would be complete.

The linkage of degeneracy and Irish womanhood was further reinforced when an Irish convict ship put ashore 114 Irish convicts—including twelve women—at Bay Bulls and Petty Harbour in late August of 1789.[55] After using up the provisions that had been left them, the convicts dispersed to communities in the area and, according to reports, "committed various depredations upon the Fishermen and Inhabitants."[56] A large group moved on to St. John's, where sixty-three of the male convicts were rounded up and confined in a former hospital located on the barrens about a mile inland from the town. While inhabitants of the area feverishly made plans to have this menace removed from the island, steps were taken to protect the town from those convicts who were still at large. Even so, particular concern was expressed about the twelve women convicts who remained at liberty:

> . . . the most effectual step that has been taken is the appointment of a Patrol of six to Eight men, a Constable and a reputable Housekeeper at their head properly Armed who Walk the paths from ten in the Evening till Gun Firing in the Morning . . . *this even may be insufficient to keep Good order while twelve women Convicts (more abandon'd than you can conceive of) are suffer'd to remain at Large* . . . [57]

As women convicts would not likely have posed more of a threat to life and property than male convicts, the perceived danger of leaving these women at large must have been the threat they represented to the moral order and masculine self-control. The extra attention and concern they attracted arose from the perception of these women as social pollutants.[58]

Yet despite official discourses that equated Irishness with rebellion and disorder, and Irish womanhood in particular with vagrancy and immorality, Irish servants—men and women—continued to be hired for service in the fishery and domestic work, particularly in Conception Bay, St. John's, and along the southern Avalon. Poole merchants defended their use of Irish servants to the Commissioners for Trade in 1752, arguing, in response to concerns that Irish Catholics bred in prodigious numbers, that they increased "in no greater proportion than protestants" and that "their behavior has given no cause to apprehend any dangers to the well being affected to His Majesty's person."[59] Indeed, regardless of the unavailability of English servants in wartime, some employers preferred Irish servants to English. For example, Saunders and Sweetman—a mercantile firm operating at Placentia, St. Mary's Bay, and Trepassey—sent at least one vessel, and in some years two, to Waterford to pick up Irish passengers for the fishery. As Pierce Sweetman noted in 1788:

> We have been very lucky in having no runaways, this Spring we have lost but 2 men & an Engh. Boy, I would advise you never to send out more Engh. youngrs. [*youngsters*] than will just clear the Vessels, the most of all that ran away from this [firm's service] the Winter before this were Engh. Boys & youngrs. they never any of them stick to the place or have any attachment to it, & for hard labour one Irish youngr. is worth a Dozn. of them . . .[60]

Sweetman's attitude may have been shared by other employers along the shore; certainly, the Pole Papers (1799–1800) indicate an overwhelming majority of Irish among the fishing servants in Ferryland district at the turn of the nineteenth century. In addition, court records for the study area are peppered with cases involving Irish Newfoundland women who were contracted servants or were providing other services (washing, sewing, nursing, hospitality trade) particularly for the single male fishing population and a small number of middle-class customers.

Furthermore, regardless of official regulations aimed at preventing Irish settlement, the predominantly temporary nature of the Irish migration stream was assuming more permanence, as the migratory fishery, plagued by almost continuous years of warfare, declined and the resident fishery grew in both absolute and proportionate terms, especially from the American Revolutionary War period onwards. And while large numbers of migrant servants were still hired for the fishery—whether in the migratory or the resident sector—there was an increasing tendency for these servants to stay in Newfoundland beyond their contracted period of service. The letterbook of Saunders and Sweetman for 1788–1804 indicates a general reluctance of servants to return to Ireland, especially from 1789 onwards,[61] and the Pole Papers indicate that, while large numbers of servants were still being hired in the fishery in Ferryland district in 1800, many had "dieted" during the winter of 1799–1800. Furthermore, a number of these male servants had wives and children living with them in the summer of 1800. And a number of Irish masters were hiring servants of their own for the fishery. Along the southern Avalon, removed from the watchful eyes of visiting governors, an Irish planter society was taking root in most harbors and would be reinforced through increasing Irish migration, both temporary and permanent, through the close of the eighteenth century and into the middle of the nineteenth century. Irish women like Mary Ryan were an integral part of that migration in terms of community formation, economic production, and community power dynamics; they would also play an essential role in establishing an essentially Irish society on what had once been part of an English planter shore.

But before examining the role of Irish women in early settlement on the southern Avalon, let us first board them on passenger vessels of the day and try to understand their experiences of leaving home and crossing the North Atlantic to a new world.

". . . THERE IS NOT A SAINT IN THE CALENDAR THAT WAS NOT INVOKED . . .": PASSAGES

Mary Ryan did not keep a journal of her 1826 passage from Wexford to Cape Broyle. Indeed, there are no surviving written accounts by women passengers from Ireland to the southern Avalon from the period of this study. Most of these women would have had neither the luxuries of time, paper, and ink, nor the level of literacy required to maintain records of their journeys. But several accounts of the Atlantic crossing by Irish women who arrived in St. John's have survived from the period; these were letters written by Presentation nuns to their home convent in Galway shortly after they came out to Newfoundland in 1833 (Web Link). Although the sisters did not initially settle on the southern Avalon, one of them, Mother Mary Bernard Kirwan, would later establish the first convent school in the area in 1853 at Admiral's Cove, Fermeuse (now named Port Kirwan in her honor[62]). But even without this connection to the southern Avalon, as Irish women travelers of the day, their writings can help us gain some insight into the experience of leaving home and starting a new life in an unfamiliar land.

> My ever dear Revd. Mother,
>
> I am sure you will be delighted to hear we are at last arrived at St. John's after a most unpleasant voyage of 25 days . . . We were only a few hours on board when we all got sick and were obliged to go to our berths. We were almost insensible. Any expressions I can make use of could give you but a faint idea of Dr. Fleming's kindness and attention. Nothing was left undone which could in any way contribute to our comfort. He was like tender parent, physician and priest . . . We had one consolation . . . that was he would allow no passenger on board so that we had the vessel to ourselves and when we were a little recovered we went occasionally on deck. These arrangements must have been very expensive . . . , but it was a great comfort to us.
>
> On the third day after we left Ireland we had a storm. One of the masts was broken and some others damaged. It lasted for three days but we were not much frightened because we were almost regardless of what was going on we were so deadly sick, but we soon had another storm to encounter which was most awful. It was on the 10th. It lasted 36 hours. The sails were torn in pieces, it came on so suddenly, the waves were monstrous high and used to wash over the deck in so terrific a manner that you would suppose every moment was your last. We were obliged to stay in bed because the vessel heaved so much that we could not stand for a minute. You may be sure there is not a saint in the calendar that was not invoked during this violent storm . . . [As we came in view of land, we] were in great spirits thinking we could go on shore in a short time, but we met another disappointment: heavy fogs and contrary winds prevented us from landing and we were for three days tossed about within a few miles of St. John's . . .
>
> At length the joyful day arrived. We entered the harbour on the 21st, St. Matthew's day . . . [Sister Magdalene O'Shaughnessey][63]
>
> We crossed the harbour in a small boat and when we came near the shore there were crowds of small boats full of people, the banks and hills were crowded and as soon as the boat that the Bishop and we were in arrived there was nothing to be heard but shouts of joy and acclamations . . . Protestants, Orangemen and all kinds of people came to welcome us and you may guess how we felt when we found ourselves in the midst of such a concourse of people and received in the most flattering manner . . . As soon as we arrived, they had a carriage ready to receive us . . .
>
> We are as happy as can be, separated from our dear Sisters. Tell each and every one of them that I can never forget them and that no distance or

length of time shall ever alter my love, affection or gratitude for my dearest Community . . . [Sister Mary Xavier Lynch][64]

I almost despaired of ever writing to you again. I was so ill for ten days I was almost insensible to everything. The Sisters thought I would never reach St. John's . . . I would be happy if I could forget all those I parted with that were so dear to me. I can never think of them without regret. This day six weeks we left Galway. I can scarcely think it possible, dear Rev. Mother, that I am never again to see you and all my dear Sisters for whom I every day feel a greater affection but we will I hope yet be united . . . [Mother Mary Bernard Kirwan][65]

We are just beginning to feel the severity of the weather . . . You may imagine what the cold is when in our bedrooms we cannot leave a drop of water in the basins or jugs. We must wait ever so long before we can get it to melt. As for our towels you might as well have a sheet of paste board for after using them and putting them to dry they are frozen quite hard and stiff. I washed my stockings and put them to dry. What was my amazement when going to mend them to see them stiff as a board and icicles hanging from them. Water freezes in a room even with a fire and the water which is left on the altar for the priest is in ice before he uses it, though only left a little before he comes. As for the milk for breakfast it is like lump sugar and we are obliged to cut it with a knife . . . When we are out walking our breath freezes on our cloaks . . . As for the clothes, when they are put in to steep they become a complete mass of ice; and the meat is obliged to be sawn. I suppose, dear Ann, you think all this incredible for we thought so ourselves until we began to experience it . . .

Once more give my love a thousand times to all my dear Sisters . . . It is often I think of you all. I must do violence now and stop for if I were to indulge myself much longer my tears would flow . . . [Sister Mary Xavier Lynch][66]

We had ice-cream for weather to-day . . . [Sister Magdalene O'Shaughnessey][67]

Of course, the nuns' experience in many ways provides a study in contrast with that of most Irish women who immigrated to Newfoundland during the study period. The sisters' passage was not typical in terms of either accommodations or reception. They were well-educated, middle-class women, traveling as the invited guests of Newfoundland's Roman Catholic bishop Michael Anthony Fleming on a ship purposely hired to bring them to the island as safely and comfortably as possible. Indeed, Bishop Fleming had rejected the first ship that had been provided for their passage, judging it "rather small to make comfortable accommodation for the ladies," and had gone in search of a better vessel at Liverpool, where he had considered several ships before finally settling on the *Ariel*.[68] Certainly, then, the sisters' accommodations were as comfortable and commodious as the bishop could provide; their diet, although uninspired, was adequate; they were not crowded into the bowels of a passenger vessel with hundreds of other emigrants, fighting for scarce provisions and sleeping space; and their privacy was assured. They did not have families to tend to, nor did they have the additional stress of being pregnant on the journey—a condition that was not uncommon for Irish women passengers, judging from Mary Ryan's experience and the rationale for Governor Montagu's 1777 edict. Neither did they have to ward off the unwanted advances of the ship's crew or male passengers, as was likely the case of other single women traveling without family.[69] Furthermore, they crossed the ocean in the gentler weather of September, while most Irish passengers came out to the island before the fishing season, in the spring, when cold weather, frost, snow, sleet, and coastal ice added to the discomfort and anxiety of the journey.

Consider, by contrast, the experience of John and Nellie (Lyons) Welsh, who left Wexford for the southern Avalon in 1784; their ship was driven into Petty Harbour by heavy ice, and John had to tow Nellie and their belongings over the icepack to safety (they arrived in Cape Broyle the following year with an infant son named Michael).[70] Or consider the ordeal of emigrants on board an 1817 Irish passenger ship that could not enter Renews harbor because of coastal ice the passengers had to leave the ship and crawl ashore on their hands and knees.[71] Furthermore, while the nuns were destined to hard work in difficult conditions, they did not have the immediate concerns of finding work, shelter, and food upon arrival. And the welcoming "shouts of joy" they received from people of all classes and religious persuasions were far different from the condemnations of the Irish immigrant woman "problem" by local authorities. Still, there were elements of their experience that would have been shared with other travelers of the day, both male and female: sorrow and misgivings about leaving home, fear of the Atlantic crossing, a sense of adventure and new beginnings, and the process of adjusting to a new environment until one could finally shrug aside the task of sawing frozen milk and meat to observe, "We had ice-cream for weather to-day."

Other written accounts of passages from Ireland to Newfoundland, while less personal in tone and content, do exist. They survive in governors' correspondence, business records, and newspapers of the period, and several are outlined below. Most deal with vessels that arrived in St. John's. However, they still provide insight into the experiences of migrants to the southern Avalon, for sometimes vessels that cleared customs at St. John's moved on to the study area; and, as noted earlier, St. John's was also a stop-off and dispersal point for many passengers who ultimately made their way to the southern Avalon, particularly that section from Bay Bulls to Trepassey. It is important to note in relation to these accounts that much of Newfoundland's passenger traffic from Ireland was excluded from British passenger legislation of the early decades of the nineteenth century. The British government passed a series of passenger acts, beginning in 1803, which sought to increase the safety and comfort of emigrants by restricting the ratio of passengers to vessel tonnage and requiring certain minimal amenities on board. In 1804, however, the legislation was rescinded in relation to fishing vessels carrying *shipped* servants for the Newfoundland fishery. Furthermore, because of insufficient supervision, owners and masters of passenger vessels that were covered by the legislation could easily circumvent the regulations, transporting people (whether shipped or not) under the fiction that all had employment and thus avoiding the niceties of sufficient space and provisions for their complements.

By 1815, the governor and the local Board of Trade were calling for a more stringent regulation of passenger traffic, and their suggestions were incorporated into the British *Passenger Act, 56 Geo. 3 Cap.* 83, passed in 1816.[72] Local authorities carefully monitored the arrival of passenger vessels thereafter; even the slightest infraction was reported to the governor and attracted a fine for the master and/or the owner.[73] However, large numbers of Irish migrants continued to arrive in St. John's (the major port of disembarkation) without employment prospects. They came, one magistrate observed, "in consequence of the most flattering and fallacious prospects of advantage" offered by unprincipled vessel owners "merely from the mercenary motive of procuring additional freights for their Vessels bound from [Ireland] for Newfoundland." As soon as they arrived in St. John's, the magistrate continued, "these unfortunate poor wretches were all turned on shore to shift for themselves without any possible means of Subsistence, or of getting employment."[74] Despite local protestations, in 1825, restrictions on the Newfoundland passenger trade were lifted altogether, possibly triggering, or certainly facilitating, another major wave of Irish migration to the island and provoking concern among local authorities and merchants.[75] Not surprisingly, then, most of the following accounts deal with voyages ending in tragedy, and feature prominently in materials dealing with the peak periods of Irish immigration (1811–16 and 1825–33).

In 1811, for example, Governor John Duckworth reported to the Colonial Office on the trial of James Lannon, master of the schooner *Fanny* out of Waterford, who was charged and convicted of a "misdemeanor" under the *Passenger Act.* The vessel had carried a passenger complement of 184 men, women, and children: a full seventy passengers over the number permitted by the ship's tonnage. Depositions of various survivors of the voyage—testimony that was remarkably consistent in its details—revealed a serious lack of water and provisions on board the vessel. For the first three days, the passengers had received no water or food. For the remainder of the first week, adults had received one quart of water per day, an allowance that had dwindled to one-half pint by the third week (children's allowances had been one-half the adult amounts). The only provisions that had been made available were sporadic rations of bread.[76] One passenger stated that he had been in such distress from lack of water that he had preserved his own urine and drunk it. In all, thirty-two passengers died on the voyage, and several others expired after landing in St. John's.[77] Roughly twenty women and ten children survived the trip; how many women and children had originally left Ireland is not known.[78]

Negligence and tragedy in the passenger trade from Ireland continued as ever increasing numbers of Irish sought passage to Newfoundland over the following years. In 1815 alone, eleven overcrowded and under-provisioned passenger vessels from Ireland (seven from Waterford, three from New Ross, and one from Youghal) arrived at St. John's, carrying 2,232 passengers, including 172 female immigrants.[79] One of the vessels was the brig *Grace*, which had cleared Waterford for Newfoundland with 150 male and twenty female passengers. The water allowance on board was only one quart per person per day, and provisions were vastly inadequate: seventy bags of bread, and twenty-eight barrels of spoiled pork, a portion of which was so inedible that the passengers threw it overboard. Ultimately, the passengers were forced to break open the foodstuffs in the cargo to stave off starvation. Governor Richard Keats was appalled at the poor conditions on board all the vessels and complained to the Colonial Office about "the Loss of Life and Misery which has been sometimes produced by the manner in some instances (shocking to humanity) Passengers have been brought from Ireland." He argued that the rescinding of the provisions of the *Passenger Act* in relation to the Newfoundland fishery had given too much leeway to vessel masters and owners, and urged "some legislative Regulation" of the passenger trade involving fishing servants.[80]

We do not know the name of the vessel that Michael and Mary Ryan sailed on, but several accounts from that period exist. The year 1825 marked the beginning of another major influx of Irish to Newfoundland, and by 1 May, eight passenger vessels had arrived from Ireland, all of which failed to comply with the provisions of the *Passenger Act*. The masters or owners, however, advised local authorities that a recent British Treasury order had dispensed with the provisions of the legislation regarding the Newfoundland passenger trade and "that therefore they might bring as many as they could stow whether shipped servants or not." In addition to cramming passengers atop cargo, many vessel owners had also initiated a system of having passengers provide their own food and water, and many passengers—ill-informed about the length of the passage and unable to afford the fare,[81] let alone provisions—found themselves without food or water early in the voyage.[82]

Lack of proper regulation continued to plague the Ireland-Newfoundland passenger trade.[83] In 1827, for example, the *Freedom* arrived from Ireland with its passengers in deplorable condition, a number either dead or dying of dysentery. Local authorities determined that had the *Passenger Act* still been in effect in relation to Newfoundland, the vessel could have been charged with carrying twice the number of passengers permitted by its tonnage and, indeed, because of insufficient space between the deck and cargo hold, would actually have been disqualified from carrying passengers altogether. In fact, the vessel had only one deck, and the passengers had literally been stowed on top of the cargo of salt within a space that measured no more than three feet in height. Furthermore, no distinct supply of provisions had been issued to the passengers. The vessel itself was filthy and had not been ventilated throughout the month's voyage, causing "an intolerable stench" in the passengers' hold. Authorities estimated that total infractions of the former legislation would have incurred penalties in the amount of £8,220.[84] John Moore, the Surveyor of Navigation who inspected the vessel at St. John's, observed that while he had had occasion in the past to fine masters severely for breaches of the "late Act," he had never seen "an Instance that would have called for more Severity, than that of this Vessel."[85] A further case of abuse presented itself on 26 August 1831, when the *Nelson*, sailing out of Killala en route to Quebec, arrived in St. John's with its passengers in a high degree of distress owing to severe overcrowding and a lack of proper provisions and water. The vessel had cleared Killala claiming 183 passengers, but had actually carried somewhere between three and four hundred on the ten-week voyage. In this case, however, as the passengers were not intended for the Newfoundland fishery, the master was charged under the *Passenger Act* and fined £350. The owner, merchant Charles McCallagher of Balina, Mayo, pleaded for leniency, stating that the master had taken on additional passengers without his permission, that poor weather had stretched the voyage beyond the capacity of the provisions, and that only a few aged, infirm, and sickly young children had died on the voyage. Generally, he blamed the tragedy on his own inexperience, but whether or not he was successful in mitigating his responsibility is not stated in the record.[86]

The specter of sick and starving passengers staggering from the holds of passenger vessels added a new component to the construction of Irishness in Newfoundland in the period after 1815: the image of contagion and disease. Vessels arriving in port with sick or dead passengers and crew were inspected by local medical officers, who came back ashore with warnings of flux, bilious and putrid fevers, and other dire offerings from the medical lexicon of the early nineteenth century. There was a constant fear of contamination spreading to the inhabitants, especially in the main port of St. John's, where many of the vessels initially landed and where a rising population and cramped quarters increased the danger of epidemics. As the influx of Irish immigrants increased from 1815 through the 1820s and early 1830s, images of filth, pollution, and disease became firmly linked with Irish passenger vessels and the Irish "lower orders" living in the town in general. In reporting on the possible connection between the arrival of the *Freedom* and the presence of typhus and other fevers in St. John's, for example, surgeon William Warner explained to local magistrates:

> The great want of attention to accomodation & cleanliness is the source whence it emanates—This disease I presume might with more propriety be called Putrid Fever, It is generated by whatever lessens the Nervous power—as bad diet, fatigue, foul atmosphere, or want of Ventilation & Cleanliness. A crowded Vessel at sea—where moisture is combined with heat and the putrid Efflu[v]i[u]m arrising from the Excremeatitious Matter of living bodies, pent up below for many days as was the Case in the Freedom—cannot fail to produce such diseases as Fluxes & Putrid fever and become the source of infection of others. I therefore consider that had not the passenger Vessels brought so many infected persons among us, that the town might have been but little diseased from the mere influence of season & the habits of the people.

Still, Warner went on to state, sanitation in the town left much to be desired, and while the seeds of the disease may have been carried in passenger vessels from Ireland, they found fertile ground in the "the present filthy state of the streets, Cook rooms, and dwellings of the lower orders."[87]

Five other doctors had been consulted on the matter, and four reached similar conclusions (the fifth declined to comment): that the current round of typhus and other fevers had spread from passengers of the *Freedom* and found a welcome breeding ground amidst "the poverty, filth & manner of living of the lower orders here."[88] One embellished this more conventional epidemiology with additional moralistic comment, stating that "the disease lay lurking [within the passengers] appearing some days after their landing with violence from the drinking of bad Spirits and too great excess."[89] Surgeon Edward Kielley agreed with his colleagues that the disease was "generally confined to the hovels of the poor," which were "absolutely reservoirs for filth and evident contagion." He found himself, however, in the awkward position of having treated some cases in "respectable families"; obviously these, he noted, had been "communicated by the imported contagion" rather than poor sanitary conditions.[90] Meanwhile, the principal inhabitants of St. John's had called a town meeting and formed a special committee to check epidemics. They sent a deputation to the governor to express their concern that "the Extremely dirty state of the Streets and Lanes of the town [had] contributed materially to augment disease," but attributed the primary cause to the poor condition of newly arriving passengers and requested that the governor use his influence to prevent future "introduction of diseased persons in Crowded Vessels," which had "in a great degree led to the present

Calamity."[91] Thus as the numbers of Irish arriving in Newfoundland increased within the context of declining standards in the passenger trade, "imported contagion" became one more facet of the perception of Irishness held by "respectable" inhabitants of the island.

It is difficult to determine how typical or exceptional the above passages were in terms of the Irish passenger trade to Newfoundland at the time. Certainly, newspaper reports and governors' correspondence of the day were more likely to deal with the exceptional than the routine (although this does not rule out the possibility of frequent abuse). A different perspective on some less eventful passages can be gained by reviewing the letterbook of Edward Kough, a merchant of New Ross who was involved in the provisions and passenger trade with ports in Newfoundland (including, over time, St. John's, Ferryland, and Placentia).

Details about the 1825 voyage of the passenger vessel *Concord,* bound for St. John's, are particularly enlightening.[92] Recruitment of passengers had begun by February, and demand for passages to Newfoundland was brisk. Potential employment in the Newfoundland fishery was the largest drawing card: "the success of these passengers in procuring employment will influence many more in emigrating from this country," Kough informed an associate, "and if you can procure orders for the shipping of youngsters, they can be got here to any number required." Women were charged a different fare than men: "for men I obtain £6.10.0 British on bail but have taken two for £10.10.0 [£5.5.0 each] Irish cash. Women £7.10.0 British on Bail four of which I have taken for £24.18.6 [£6.4.7½ each] cash."[93] Fear of the Atlantic crossing obviously played on potential passengers' minds, for a number were dismayed by the *Concord*'s small size and poor appearance (a situation that Kough sought to remedy with a coat of paint). Ultimately, however, finances dictated the fate of many emigrants, who opted for cheaper passage (as low as £4) on board vessels from Waterford, regardless of traveling conditions.[94]

The *Concord* finally sailed with seventy-nine passengers (although Kough had hoped for over one hundred). The average fare was £6.15.0 (this suggests that most passengers traveled on bail). Provisions were generous, compared with the other accounts above, and consisted of the following: 14 *pipes* of water "in addition to the casks belonging to the vessel"; 31 cwt. of bread; 10 cwt. of oatmeal; 420 stones of potatoes; 89 lb. of butter; 1 tierce of beer; 213 lb. of beef; and 1,116 lb. of pork.[95] Every two passengers were permitted to bring on board one chest containing personal effects,[96] and while the voyage out was lengthier than usual owing to contrary winds and weather,[97] no passengers complained during the voyage (according to Kough) of inconvenience or lack of room between the cargo hold and the deck. Although not all the passengers had arranged employment before leaving Ireland, Kough was certain that their purpose in going to Newfoundland was to find work in the fishery: "I am warranted in saying they went for no other purpose, as they would all have preferred shipping here for it to running the risk of obtaining Masters when they got out."

Kough and his St. John's partner, John Boyd, appear to have been more scrupulous operators than many, and the passengers of the *Concord* seem to have had a less traumatic crossing than some Irish migrants bound for the Newfoundland fishery. Still, a footnote must be added to this account, for a report received at the Colonial Office regarding this same passage indicates that the sixty male and twenty-five female passengers on board (evidently, the complement had increased slightly from Kough's initial reporting) "were literally stowed in bulk, and but for the shortness of the passage which had been pretty general this spring, many of them must have been in a distressing condition."[98] Kough and Boyd, then, were also susceptible to bringing out "as many as they could stow whether shipped servants or not."

The above accounts of the passage from Ireland to Newfoundland provide insight into a range of emigrant experiences, from the relative comfort of the Presentation sisters, traveling on the *Ariel*, to the distress and debilitation suffered by the passengers of vessels such as the *Fanny* or the unfortunately named *Freedom*. In the middle of the spectrum, there was the more benign crossing provided by Edward Kough on his vessel, *Concord*. The nuns' experience was surely atypical. But just as surely, there must have been other more responsible operators like Kough, who had recruited fishing servants for specific employers on the island and wished to deliver their passengers in fit condition to work at the fishery. By contrast, there were also those carriers who merely wanted to maximize profits by cramming their vessels for the crossing, with few scruples about sufficient provisions of food and water. We can only speculate about how representative these passage experiences were. In terms of women passengers, given the lack of personal accounts, we must also deploy our imaginations to recreate their fears and reservations, expectations of future prospects, and the tremendous effort to care for families in often primitive conditions—confined to close living quarters for a month and sometimes even two, maneuvering for cooking space on the *cabouse* or a sawed-off puncheon tub with a fire laid on sand and rocks for insulation, jostling for scarce provisions—on board ships that they hoped would transport them to better lives.

Still, despite difficult passages and an often inauspicious welcome (in terms of both physical environment and official attitudes), Irish women came to the southern Avalon in increasing numbers after the middle of the eighteenth century, and they would be integral to community formation and survival.

NOTES

1. James Joseph O'Brien, "Cape Broyle," unpublished chronicle of the old families of Cape Broyle, 1971, copy in possession of author. "Jim Joe" was a repository of the oral tradition and the acknowledged community historian of Cape Broyle during his long lifetime. In his later years, he began to transcribe much of the information he had accumulated about the community and individual families who had settled there. His writings, when compared with more traditional historical sources, such as nominal census material at the Provincial Archives of Newfoundland and Labrador (PANL), are amazingly accurate. His reporting of Michael Ryan's death corresponds with reports of the loss of the sealing schooner *Confidence* off Petty Harbour Motion in 1830; see Shannon Ryan, *The Ice Hunters: A History of Newfoundland Sealing to 1914* (St. John's: Breakwater, 1994), 285–86. Similar information about the Ryan family also appears in the Ferryland Museum Database (FMDB), except that Mary's name appears as Margaret and the date of her remarriage to Edward Coady is given as 1832; see FMDB, file 02B (Morry and Carter Families), notes on the Coady family tree. The FMDB file also notes that the Ryans and Edward Coady had initially emigrated together from Wexford. Regardless of some minor discrepancies, however, the essence of the Ryans' experience remains the same in both retellings.

2. Vice-Admiral Charles M. Pole (Web Link) was governor of Newfoundland in 1800 and 1801. He commissioned local magistrate Robert Carter to take a nominal census of Ferryland district, which detailed the names of families, fishing employers, fishing servants, and dieters who were resident in the district in the winter of 1799–1800 and the following summer.

3. See, for example: MHA, Keith Matthews Collection, 16-C-2-035, Sir John Berry, "A list of ye Planters Names with an acct. of their Concerns from Cape de Race to Cape Bonavista," 12 September 1675 (from CO 1, vol. 35 [17ii], fols. 149v-156); PANL, GN 2/39/A, Berry Census, 1675 and 1677 (from CO 1); and MHA, R 95/20, "List of Inhabitants' Names, the No. of Their Families, 1708" (from CO 194, vol. 4, fols. 253–56).

4. MHA, Matthews Collection, 16-D-1-006, Story, "An account of what fishing ships, Sack Ships, Planters & boat keepers from Trepasse to Bonavist & from thence to faire Island the Northward part of Newfoundland," 1 September 1681 (from CO 1, vol. 47 [52i], fols. 113–121v).

5. In 1679, two years previous to Story's account, for example, five sack ships from Ireland (three from Waterford, one from Youghal, and one from Dublin) had been reported in Newfoundland. In 1715, twenty vessels from Ireland were reported by local naval officers. See C. Grant Head, *Eighteenth Century Newfoundland* (Toronto: McClelland and Stewart, in association with the Institute of Canadian Studies, Carleton University, 1976), 86.

6. Head, *Eighteenth Century Newfoundland*, 89 (quoting Calendar of State Papers, Colonial, 1720, 178).

7. The traditional ship fishery at Newfoundland consisted of large vessels that transported smaller boats and large crews to Newfoundland each spring to fish for cod, returning to home ports at the close of the season in late October. A sedentary or resident fishery was also carried out by inhabitants who remained on the island in the wake of official colonization attempts and fishing personnel who opted to stay in Newfoundland for the longer term. By the middle of the seventeenth century, the bye-boat fishery had also developed; bye-boatkeepers kept their fishing shallops in Newfoundland, while they and their small crews traveled to and from Newfoundland each season as passengers on the larger fishing ships. There were variations in pattern as well as interchanges of personnel between the ship, bye-boat, and sedentary fisheries. All three sectors fished inshore in the seventeenth century. A bank, or offshore, fishery did not develop until the early eighteenth century. See: Keith Matthews, "A History of the West of England-Newfoundland Fishery," D.Phil. diss., Oxford University, 1968); and Head, *Eighteenth Century Newfoundland.*

8. MHA, MF-105, Letterbook of Capt. Michael Richards (Commander at Fort William, 1700–03), 134–55, Hearings at Fort William, 9–12 March 1702.

9. MHA, MF-105, Richards Letterbook, 215–17, "Request to y^e^. Commodore Leake," 20 September 1702.

10. CO 194, vol. 3, fols. 424–25, particularly fol. 425, Remarks of Naval Officer Cummins in relation to Newfoundland, [1705?-received at the Colonial Office via the House of Commons 25 February 1706].

11. MHA, Matthews Collection, 04/058, coll. 24, box 9, sub-series 04-056/01, file 25-B-2-1, Van Brugh to Commissioners for Trade, 6 November 1738 (from CO 194, vol. 10, fol. 93).

12. Raymond J. Lahey, James Louis O'Donel in *Newfoundland, 1784–1807: The Establishment of the Roman Catholic Church*, ed. Shannon Ryan and G. M. Story (St. John's: Newfoundland Historical Society, pamphlet 8, 1984), 5.

13. CO 194, vol. 25, fols. 107–11, particularly fol. 110, Drake, "Answers to the Queries Contained in His Majesty's Instructions," 22 November 1751.

14. Other areas of particular concern, because of their significant Irish populations, were Conception Bay and St. John's.

15. CO 194, vol. 25, fol. 110, Drake, "Answers."

16. PANL, GN 2/1/A, vol. 7 (reverse end), 96–98, Petition from the merchants and principal inhabitants of Renews to Montagu, 29 July 1778.

17. PANL, GN 2/1/A, vol. 7 (reverse end), 159–60, Montagu to Robert Carter, Magistrate, October 1778.

18. CO 194, vol. 42, fols. 167–69, Ogden to Waldegrave, 2 July 1800.

19. See: Michael McCarthy, *The Irish in Newfoundland*, 1600–1900: *Their Trials, Tribulations, and Triumphs* (St. John's: Creative Publishers, 1999), 8–9; and MHA, Matthews Collection, 04/058, coll. 24, box 9, sub-series 04-057/02, file 25-A-27-56, Cadre Smith to Commissioners for Trade, 1742, and Byng to Commissioners for Trade, 1743 (from CO 194, vol. 11, fol. 41).

20. PANL, GN 2/1/A, vol. 2, 236, Proclamation, Dorrill, 22 September 1755.

21. Harold A. Innis, *The Cod Fisheries: The Study of an International Economy*, rev. ed. (Toronto: University of Toronto Press, 1954), 153, n. 32.

22. While theories of race propagated by British anthropologists and phrenologists of the Victorian age lent "scientific" validity to Anglo-Saxon claims to superiority, English perceptions of Irish difference—of racial and cultural inferiority—long pre-date the period of this study.

23. The *Penal Laws* or *Popery Laws* were statutes legislated in both England (later, Britain) and Ireland to restrict the civil rights of Roman Catholics and, to a lesser extent, Protestant Dissenters. The English laws grew out of the English Reformation, and various acts were passed over the next two centuries that limited the rights of Catholics and Dissenters to hold office, vote, own or inherit property, bear arms, operate their own schools, and (in the case of Catholics) practice their faith fully and openly. In Ireland, Penal Laws of a similar nature were passed by an Irish Protestant parliament from the 1690s, after William of Orange defeated the Catholic-supported Jacobite cause in Ireland, through the first half of the eighteenth century. By the late eighteenth century, these disabilities were gradually being lifted in Britain and Ireland, but Catholics could still not sit in parliament or hold certain high offices until Catholic Emancipation was achieved in 1829. Some recent scholars have questioned the effectiveness of the Penal Laws, arguing that they were piecemeal and unevenly enforced, and suggesting that they could be readily circumvented by conversion to the Church of England/Ireland. But this only qualifies the effectiveness of the regime. While some were not consistently enforced, others (such as the right to vote, sit in parliament, or hold office) were strictly applied. Furthermore, regardless of the degree of enforcement, the fact that these laws existed at all must have had a debilitating effect on those they targeted. The laws may not have been *systematic*, but they created systemic discrimination in both Britain and Ireland that took generations to correct. And in Ireland, where Catholics were overwhelmingly in the majority, they also created a sense of grievance and mistrust of Irish Protestants and the British government that lasted long after the formal Penal Laws had been repealed.

In the Newfoundland context, there were no specific directions given to governors about enforcing Penal Laws, other than the "except Papists" clause that appeared in governors' instructions up to 1779 and permitted liberty of conscience to all Christian faiths other than Catholicism in Newfoundland. (The same clause appeared in instructions to governors of many British colonies until 1779–82.) In practical terms, this left the application of the remaining laws somewhat to gubernatorial discretion, and there was some variation of the level of enforcement from governor to governor. Still, the governors would have been expected to uphold the laws of the mother country, and certain key Penal Laws, such as those mentioned here in the text, were more consistently applied than others. For a discussion of the "except Papists" clause in colonial instructions, see Hans Rollmann, "Religious Enfranchisement and Roman Catholics in Eighteenth-Century Newfoundland," in *Religion and Identity: The Experience of Irish and Scottish Catholics in Atlantic Canada*, ed. Terrence Murphy and Cyril J. Byrne (St. John's: Jesperson Press, 1987), 34–52.

24. In 1762, a governor ordered local magistrates "to Continue in due force the Tax levied on the Roman Catholicks p[er] late Governor [James] Webb"; PANL, GN 2/1/A vol. 3, 149–50, Order from Governor Thomas Graves to JPs of St. John's, 29 October 1762. The reference here is obscure, but Howley explains that this was a tax on Catholic and Irish traders, which had apparently lapsed due to irregular collection during the latter stages of the Seven Years' War; Rev. Michael F. Howley, *Ecclesiastical History of Newfoundland* (Boston: Doyle and Whittle, 1888; reprint, Belleville, ON: Mika, 1971), 178.

25. Similar anecdotes also appear in: Howley, *Ecclesiastical History*, 181; Frank Galgay, Michael McCarthy, Sr. Teresina Bruce, and Sr. Magdalen O'Brien, *A Pilgrimage of Faith: A History of the Southern Shore from Bay Bulls to St. Shott's* (St. John's: Harry Cuff, 1983), 27 and 65; and RCAASJ, Michael A. Fleming Papers, 103/32, Dean Patrick Cleary, "A note of church history," 4 and 6–7. (Cleary was a Catholic parish priest at Witless Bay and kept a rough scrapbook of local events and Catholic Church history on the island that covered the period 1784–1850. It is more commonly known as "Dean Cleary's Notebook.") Visual displays of these episodes also appear in the Capt. William Jackman Museum at Renews.

26. Precisely these measures were taken in 1755 by Governor Dorrill and his Surrogate, Thomas Burnett, against Catholics who were caught flying the Irish colors, harboring a priest, and celebrating Mass in the Harbour Grace area. Fines were imposed, houses burned, and deportations ordered in Harbour Grace, Carbonear, Harbour Main, Crockers Cove, and Mosquito Cove from 15 August to the end of September 1755. See various orders in PANL, GN 2/1/A, vol. 2, 202 and 251–64, August-September 1755.

27. For example, the appointment of the first naval governor in 1729, with power to appoint justices of the peace, and the establishment of a customs house after the Seven Years' War. For a discussion of the evolution of the legal system in Newfoundland, see Chapter 6, n. 4.

28. In response to large-scale organized colonization attempts in Newfoundland in the early seventeenth century, West of England stakeholders in the Newfoundland trade became concerned that resident fishermen would have an advantage over migratory fishermen. They requested and were granted a Western Charter in 1634 that established the priority of the migratory fishery at Newfoundland and acknowledged the customary rights of a "free" fishery. As the ship fishery went into a decline at mid-century, primarily due to wars and market conditions, fishing ship interests found scapegoats in the bye-boat and resident fisheries, and effectively lobbied to have their concerns addressed in revised Charters in 1660/1 and 1670/1. However, they began to abandon their anti-settlement lobbying by the end of the seventeenth century, once they realized that their trade would only be enhanced by a resident fishery and that the various sectors of the industry—ship, bye-boat, and resident—were complementary in nature. Still, they agreed with the policy to limit local government, which would have reduced their powers as established by the Western Charters and the later *Newfoundland Act* of 1699, and lobbied against the various embryonic measures of governance introduced in the eighteenth century. See Matthews, "West of England-Newfoundland Fishery."

29. Palliser's term at Newfoundland was unusually long. One should also note that at this point, naval governors only served at Newfoundland during the fishing season. Not until the winter of 1817–18 were governors instructed to spend the winter in Newfoundland. The incumbent at that time, Governor Francis Pickmore, succumbed that same winter to the stresses of office and the harsh physical climate, an inauspicious beginning to year-long governorship of the island.

30. PANL, GN 2/1/A, vol. 4: 2–3, "Order rel[ative] to the property of Land & cutting grass in this Country," Palliser, 31 July 1766; 9, Order, Palliser, 16 August 1766; and 19, Order, Palliser, 15 September 1766.

31. PANL, GN 2/1/A, vol. 4, 41–44, Order, Palliser, 2 June 1767. Palliser's regulations would provide the backbone of the *Act 15 Geo. III, Cap. 31*, which was the British government's final major effort to bolster the ship fishery at Newfoundland. It was passed in 1776, after Palliser's term as governor had come to an end, but became known locally as *Palliser's Act* because he had formulated its spirit and intent.

32. CO 194, vol.16, fol. 188, "Annual Return on the Fisheries and Inhabitants, etc., at Newfoundland for the year 1765." Throughout the second half of the eighteenth century, Catholics formed roughly half of the island's population. Palliser's overestimate was handily bested by Governor Waldegrave, at the time of the United Irish scare, when he warned that nearly nine-tenths of the inhabitants of Newfoundland were natives of Ireland or their descendants. See CO 194, vol. 40, fols. 93–95, Waldegrave to Colonial Office, 19 June 1798. However, the perceptions of both governors were likely skewed by the increasing predominance of Irish Catholics in the administrative center of St. John's in the latter decades of the eighteenth century.

33. CO 194, vol.16, fol. 188, Annual Return, 1765.

34. PANL, GN 2/1/A, vol. 3, 272–73, Order, Palliser, 31 October 1764.

35. PANL, GN 2/1/A, vol. 4, 79, Order, Palliser, 23 October 1767.

36. PANL, GN 2/1/A: vol. 4, 201, Order, Byron, 29 September 1769; vol. 4, 285, Order, Byron, 31 October 1770; vol. 5, 60, Order, Shuldham, 24 June 1772; vol. 5, 102, Order, Shuldham, 13 July 1772; vol. 5, 143, Order, Shuldham, 12 October 1773; vol. 6, 17, Order, Duff, 12 July 1775; vol. 6, 100–101, Orders (2), Duff, 16 October 1775; vol. 7, 33–35, Circular Letter, Montagu to the Magistrates of the various districts in Newfoundland, 6 October 1777; vol. 7, 70, Order, Montagu, 3 October 1778; vol. 12, 38–41, Proclamation and Public Notice, Milbanke, 13 October 1789; vol. 12, 157, Public Notice, King, 19 September 1792; vol. 14, 282–87, Proclamation, Waldegrave, and covering correspondence to the Magistrates of Newfoundland, 27 September 1798; and vol. 16, 282–87, Proclamations (2), Gambier, 18 September 1802. After Waldegrave's 1798 proclamation, the magistrates of St. John's convinced him that dieters had become essential to the island's economy, particularly in terms of the *Western* (or bank) fishery, which began earlier than the regular fishing season, and the seal fishery, which was carried out completely in the off-season. Waldegrave modified his regulations to permit a limited number of fishing servants to remain over the winter, provided that their names, intended residences, and previous and potential employers were registered. See PANL, GN 2/1/A, vol. 14: 403–8, Magistrates at St. John's to Waldegrave, 16 October 1798; and 409–14, Waldegrave to Magistrates at St. John's, 17 October 1798.

Nonetheless, Gambier's 1802 proclamation reiterated earlier warnings that houses that kept dieters during the winter would be torn down.

37. PANL, GN 2/1/A, vol. 4, 285, Order, Byron, 31 October 1770. This provision was not repeated in the orders of succeeding governors.

38. PANL, GN 2/1/A, vol. 2, 102–3, Milbanke to "M[r] O Donnell, R. C. Priest" [note the refusal to acknowledge O Donel's ecclesiastical rank], 2 November 1790, while on board the *Salisbury*. To a large extent, Milbanke was reacting to a recent large-scale Irish factional fight that had occurred in Ferryland. His decision was influenced by the surrogate who heard the ensuing cases, Captain Edward Pellew. Pellew felt that Catholic priests should be removed from the island altogether (see Chapter 5).

39. PANL, GN 2/1/A, vol. 5, 23, Byron to William Keen, JP, Bonavista, 14 October 1771.

40. PANL, GN 2/1/A, vol. 7 (reverse end), 12–13, Proclamation, Montagu, 7 July 1777.

41. PANL, GN 2/1/A, vol. 7 (reverse end), 13–14, Montagu to Carter, July 1777.

42. No orders specifically directed at English Protestants during the period appear in either of the two main series in which governors would have recorded them: CO 194 and PANL, GN 2/1/A.

43. The 1671 Charter banned habitation within six miles of the shore and prohibited the transportation of any passengers to Newfoundland whatsoever. It was followed by an order-in-council in 1675 stipulating that all plantation at Newfoundland be discouraged and any inhabitants encouraged to remove themselves to New England or back to their home country. Another order in 1676 directed that the inhabitants be forcibly removed. After pro-settlement reports by naval commodores Berry and Russell, as well as an effective petition campaign led by planter John Downey, these orders were rescinded.

44. W. Gordon Handcock, *Soe longe as there comes noe women: Origins of English Settlement in Newfoundland* (St. John's: Breakwater Books, 1989), 31–2 (citing CO 195, vol. 1, fol. 41).

45. MHA, MF-105, Richards Letterbook, 215–17, "Request to y[e]. Commodore Leake," 20 September 1702; see also 129–30, "Instructions for y[e]. Harbour Guard relating to y[e]. Inhabitants," [February 1702?].

46. The Newfoundland situation also contrasts with that of New South Wales, where women were recruited as settlers, after an initial perception of women who ventured into the bush as whores was quickly over-written by images of women as civilizers and moral guardians who would help to regulate men's behavior and establish stable family life in frontier settlements. See Malcolm Campbell, *Kingdom of the Ryans: The Irish in Southwest New South Wales, 1816–1890* (Sydney: University of New South Wales Press, 1997), 118–20.

47. Handcock, *Soe longe*, 32 (citing CO 1, vol. 5, fol. 241).

48. MHA, Matthews Collection, 16-D-1-006, Story, "An Account," 1681.

49. Cullum and Baird provide a discussion of various efforts to discourage women settlers in Newfoundland in the seventeenth and eighteenth centuries, but they do not examine these actions in terms of ethnicity. See Linda Cullum and Maeve Baird,

"'A Woman's Lot': Women and Law in Newfoundland from Early Settlement to the Twentieth Century," in *Pursuing Equality: Historical Perspectives on Women in Newfoundland and Labrador,* ed. Linda Kealey, Social and Economic Papers, no. 20 (St. John's: ISER, 1993), 68–75.

50. PANL, GN 2/1/A, vol. 3, 232, Order, Palliser, 2 July 1764.

51. PANL, GN 2/1/A, vol. 4, 23, Order, Palliser, 2 October 1766, in the matter of *Thomas Pendergrass v. Jonathan Blakener.*

52. PANL, GN 2/1/A, vol. 7, 35–36, Order, Montagu, 20 October 1777.

53. PANL, GN 2/1/A, vol. 18, 307–8, Gower to the Magistrates of St. John's, 18 September 1805.

54. PANL, GN 2/1/A, vol. 20, 47, Holloway to the Magistrates of St. John's, 29 August 1808.

55. See CO 194, vol. 38, fols. 86–101, 110–18, 180–82, and 282–83. And see PANL, GN 2/1/A: vol. 11, 458–60; and vol. 12, 8–13, 30–31, 48, and 54–55. See also Bob Reece, "'Such a Banditti': Irish Convicts in Newfoundland, 1789—Part 1," *Newfoundland Studies* 13, no. 1 (spring 1997): 1–29. A listing at CO 194, vol. 38, fols. 94–96, provides details such as name, age, birthplace, crime, and sentence for the male convicts detained in St. John's, but contains no information on any female convicts. A further, partial listing at CO 194, fol. 38, fol. 112, does provide the names of the seventy-four male and six female convicts who were removed to Spithead on board the brig *Elizabeth and Clare,* but no details on those who remained in Newfoundland. The number of female convicts who actually arrived in St. John's is unclear, but likely included the six who sailed on the *Elizabeth and Clare* as well as one other who was deported shortly thereafter for prostitution. This leaves the possibility that all or some of the remaining five women from the original twelve, as well as a number of their male cohorts, remained on the southern Avalon where they had originally landed and where they may have melted into the predominantly Irish population.

56. CO 194, vol. 38, fols. 86–87, Governor Milbanke to Grenville, 20 September 1789.

57. CO 194, vol. 38, fols. 282–83, "Extract of a Letter from Newfoundland," 21 August 1789; italics added.

58. Although this episode was an isolated one in Newfoundland, it can be contextualized by the larger-scale transportation of female convicts to Australia from 1788 to the mid-nineteenth century. There, too, the presence of such women provoked profound anxieties in local authorities, for the women's visibility in public spaces and their sexual assertiveness were seen as polluting and contaminating—a source of social chaos. See: Joy Damousi, *Depraved and Disorderly: Female Convicts, Sexuality, and Gender in Colonial Australia* (Cambridge: Cambridge University Press, 1997); and Babette Smith, *A Cargo of Women: Susannah Watson and the Convicts of the "Princess Royal"* (Kensington: New South Wales University Press, 1988).

59. MHA, Matthews Collection, 04/048, coll. 24, box 9, sub-series 04-057/05, file 25-A-27-57, Petition of Poole merchants to Commissioners for Trade, 8 November 1752 (from CO 194, vol. 13, fol. 34).

60. PANL, MG 49, Sweetman Collection, box 5, Saunders and Sweetman Letterbook, 1788–93 and 1802–04, Pierce Sweetman at Placentia to "Dear Brother," 11 May 1788.

61. Saunders and Sweetman provided transportation back to Waterford each fall for their fishing servants, keeping only a winter crew to cut ships' timber and carry out other preparations and repairs for the next year's fishing season. By 1789 and 1790, however, Pierce Sweetman, who was running the Placentia branch of the business (with dealers in St. Mary's Bay and Trepassey), was observing the growing numbers of "unshipped" men who were staying through the winter and anticipating that many of the bills drawn for servants' wages would likely be returned to the local store for provisions by servants who had no work. See Letterbook, box 5, "PS" to "Dear Sirs" [likely, principals], 3 November 1789; "PS" to John Blackney, November 1789; and "PS" to John Blackney, 1 November 1790. Similarly, in 1802, he reported low numbers of servants wanting to return to Ireland and wondered whether he should cancel the return voyage to Waterford altogether, although he finally sent the vessel, feeling that it would not be prudent to allow too many unemployed servants to remain over the winter. See Letterbook: Pierce Sweetman in Placentia to [Francis Eamond ?], 9 October 1802; and "PS" to "My D[r]. Saunders," 21 October 1802.

62. Fishing admirals had the first choice of fishing rooms in harbors for any given season, and certain coves were repeatedly selected because they were well situated in terms of shore facilities and proximity to fishing grounds. Thus, the name "Admiral's Cove" became quite common along the English Shore—a situation that caused increasing confusion as postal operations and other government services increased and centralized. On the *Southern Shore*, there was an Admiral's Cove in Fermeuse harbor and another in Cape Broyle harbor. The Newfoundland government changed a number of community names in the twentieth century—some for practical reasons, others simply to prettify or sanitize the name. In the process, Admiral's Cove, Fermeuse, became Port Kirwan, while Admiral's Cove, Cape Broyle, maintained its original name.

63. PCA, Sister Magdalene O'Shaughnessey to Rev. Mother, Presentation Convent in Galway, 22 September 1833.

64. PCA, Sister Mary Xavier Lynch to Rev. Mother, Presentation Convent in Galway, 22 September 1833.

65. PCA, Mother Mary Bernard Kirwan to Rev. Mother, Presentation Convent in Galway, [1833].

66. PCA, Sister Mary Xavier Lynch to "My dearest Ann," 6 January 1834.

67. PCA, SisterO'Shaughnessey to "My ever dearest Sister M. Augustine," 21 November 1833.

68. Bishop Fleming to Mother Superior of Galway convent, 17 July 1833, and 5 August 1833, in Howley, Ecclesiastical History, 281–82 and 284–86.

69. In 1773, for example, Governor Shuldham instructed the vice-admiralty court at St. John's to look into the complaint of Bridget Kent in relation to the "inhuman and Barbarous treatment she received on Board the Brig —— Charles Durell Master, in the course of her passage from Waterford to Harbour Grace last Spring, and as

those Acts of Violence said to have been committed upon her, were done upon the High Seas, . . . to bring all and every the Offenders to Justice." See PANL, GN 2/1/A, vol. 5 (reverse end), 74, Shuldham to Edward White, Judge of the Vice Admiralty Court, St. John's, July 1773.

70. James Joseph O'Brien, "Cape Broyle, 1959–60," unpublished community history, [1960?], copy in possession of author, 1; and O'Brien, Cape Broyle (1971), 8.

71. Daniel W. Prowse, *A History of Newfoundland from the English, Colonial, and Foreign Records* (London: Macmillan, 1895; reprint, Belleville, ON: Mika Studio, 1972), 406. This information is also on display at the Capt. William Jackman Museum.

72. Various correspondence involving the Colonial Office, the governor and other local authorities, and merchants of both St. John's and Waterford appears at PANL, GN 2/1/A, vol. 27, 16–24, 33–46, 117–22, and 205.

73. See, for example, correspondence and documents at PANL, GN 2/1/A: vol. 27, 408–11; vol. 28, 362–64, 409–15, 433–34, 446, and 482; vol. 30, 139–40, 166–67, and 192; and vol. 31, 423–25, 473, and 490–92. Even masters and owners who had followed the spirit, if not the exact letter, of the law (e.g., provided adequate provisions and space, but failed to produce a satisfactory passenger list) were subject to fines, although some penalties were eventually mitigated. Local and Irish customs officers were also occasionally brought to task for paying insufficient attention to enforcing the regulations.

74. PANL, GN 2/1/A, vol. 27, 408–10, Thomas Coote, Chief Magistrate at St. John's, to Governor Pickmore, 28 April 1817.

75. See, for example, correspondence at PANL, GN 2/1/A, vol. 35, 288–90, 329–30, and 339–41.

76. Compare this food and water allowance with that of the Irish convicts who had been returned from Newfoundland to Spithead in 1789: 3½ lb. of bread, 2 lb. of flour, 3 lb. of pork, 3 pt. of peas, ½ lb. of butter, and 7 gal. of water *each* per week. See CO 194, vol. 38, fols. 86–101, particularly fol. 101, Advertisement for a vessel to transport the Irish convicts to Spithead, dated 17 September 1789, enclosure in Governor Milbanke to Colonial Office, 20 September 1789. In addition, Milbanke had arranged for the convicts to be supplied with forty beds, bolsters, blankets, and coverlets, and each was issued "navy slops," consisting of shirt, frock, trousers, shoes, and stockings. See CO 194, vol. 38, fols. 180–82, particularly fol. 182, "An Account of the Expense of Maintaining and Sending to England in the Brig *Elizabeth and Clare* a Number of Irish Convicts, who were landed upon the Island of Newfoundland in the Year 1789," enclosure in Milbanke to Colonial Office, 8 December 1789.

77. CO 194, vol. 51, fols. 17–23, Governor Duckworth to Colonial Office, November 1811. See also CO 194, vol. 56, fols. 63–70, particularly fol. 66, "A List of Vessels that have arrived at St. Johns Newfoundland from Ireland with Passengers," enclosure in Governor Richard Keats to Colonial Office, 1 October 1815. This correspondence with attachments also appears in PANL, GN 2/1/A, vol. 27, 16–18. See also Cyril Byrne, "The Case of the Schooner *Fanny* from Waterford to St. John's, 1811," An Nasc 3, no. 1 (spring/summer 1990): 19–22.

78. An abstract of Irish passengers on various vessels arriving at St. John's in 1811 indicated that 125 men, twenty women, and ten children disembarked at St. John's from the Fanny; however, these must have been approximations because, allowing for thirty-two deaths en route, this would have brought the total passenger complement to 187, not 184. See PANL, GN 2/1/A, vol. 22, 24, "N°. of Passengers arrived from Ireland 1811." Still, these estimates are closer than that of the original list of survivors forwarded to the Colonial Office, which contained only the names of one hundred men. See CO 194, vol. 51, fols. 17–23.

79. This proportion of male to female passengers is high, but representative of the Napoleonic War period, when there was an employment boom for male servants in the Newfoundland fishery. Total numbers of Irish passengers arriving at St. John's are available for the following years:

	Men	Women	Children	Total
1807	614 (91.6%)	56 (8.4%)		670
1811	1,026 (84.6%)	128 (10.6%)	59 (4.9%)	1,213
1812	1,541 (92.2%)	116 (6.9%)	14 (0.8%)	1,671
1815*	2,060 (92.3%)	172 (7.7%)		2,232

* Passengers were reported as "male" or "female"; whether these numbers included children is not clear.

Still, some individual vessels carried proportionally larger complements of women passengers: e.g., the *Harmony* out of Cork brought twenty-five men and ten women to Newfoundland in 1807; and in 1811, the *Joyce* arrived in August with twenty-four men, eighteen women, and thirteen children, while the *Jenny* came in October with three men, eleven women, and eight children (given the late arrivals, these two vessels were obviously not carrying servants shipped for the current fishing season). Indeed, the *Joyce*, a vessel out of New Ross, usually carried a significant number of women passengers even when it came out in the spring (thirty-six in 1812, and thirty-five in 1815). See abstracts of passenger lists at PANL, GN 2/1/A: vol. 19, 103; and vol. 22, 24 and 297. And see CO 194, vol. 56, fols. 63–70, Governor Keats to Colonial Office, 1 October 1815.

Unfortunately, there are no other abstracts of passenger lists available for the period of this study, and thus it is impossible to estimate the overall proportion of women passengers to men outside the boom period of the Napoleonic Wars. However, it is safe to assume that passenger complements were predominantly male, although not always as heavily weighted as in the above years. In 1825, for example, women made up 30 percent of the passengers on board Edward Kough's vessel *Concord* (see below).

80. CO 194, vol. 56, fols. 63–70, Keats to Colonial Office, 1 October 1815. Keats noted that the same problems did not exist on ships from England and Jersey, and that, at any rate, the volume of traffic from these countries was not comparable to that from Ireland.

81. Many Irish passengers to Newfoundland traveled *on bond* or *on bail*. They promised to pay their fares upon arrival, and provided the names of bondsmen in both Ireland and Newfoundland who would be held responsible for their fares in default of payment. Often, the security in Newfoundland was given by fishing employers in partial fulfillment of the terms of shipping papers.

82. CO 194, vol. 71, fols. 313–15, Report of A. Hogsett, Naval Officer at St. John's, 1 May 1825. The practice of having passengers provision themselves was a great cost-cutting measure, but sometimes vessel owners or masters felt a backlash. In this same report, Hogsett tells of the *Ceres*, recently arrived from Cork, which "had not been at sea more than ten days, by the Masters [Bowman] own confession, when the Passengers were quite out of Provisions and he further states that he was obliged to walk the Deck armed until he got supplied from another vessel at Sea."

83. Repercussions of the slackening of regulations governing the Newfoundland trade were also felt in the broader passenger trade, as some owners and masters of vessels clearing Ireland declared their passengers' destination to be the Newfoundland fishery when, in actuality, they were bound for elsewhere. Such was the case of the brig *Thomas Farrell*, which cleared New Ross in the spring of 1825 with one hundred men and sixty-two women reportedly destined for the Newfoundland fishery. The passengers had actually contracted with the owner for passage to Quebec, but the owner's false declaration enabled him to overcrowd the vessel and to require the passengers to provision themselves. The vessel did make a stop at St. John's as a formality, but the passengers ultimately moved on to Quebec. See Cyril Byrne, "The Brig *Thomas Farrell*," *An Nasc* 4, no. 1 (winter 1991): 6–7 (citing CO 194, vol. 71, fols. 322–23). Another intriguing episode occurred in 1833, when the brig *Good Intent* out of Youghal arrived in St. John's with a passenger list that, according to the inspecting customs officer, "so totally differs both in name and description with the Persons actually on board, that of the whole number containing in that List, not one Individual is to be found which corresponds with the names therein stated." See PANL, GN 2/2, vol. 13, 77–78, Customs Officers, St. John's, to James Crowdy, local Colonial Secretary, 24 May 1833.

84. See PANL, GN 2/1/A, vol. 36, 180–83: Governor Thomas Cochrane to J. Moore, Surveyor of Navigation for St. John's, 18 May 1827; Chief Magistrate to Cochrane, 17 May 1827; Moore to Cochrane, May 1827; as well as related correspondence and documents at vol. 36, 191, 215, 218, 283–84, 361–74, and 392–93; and vol. 37, 95–101. And see PANL, GN 2/2, vol. 2, 110–21, 132–34, 199–206, 256–76, and 462–68, various correspondence and reports in May, August, and November 1827.

85. PANL, GN 2/2, vol. 2, 110–12, Moore to W. A. Clarke, local Colonial Secretary, 17 May 1827.

86. See: PANL, GN 2/1/A, vol. 38, 163–64, 174, 177–78, and 196, various correspondence and reports through August and September 1831; PANL, GN 2/2, vol. 13, 199–202, Customs Officer, St. John's, to Colonial Secretary, 25 April 1833, enclosing memorial of Charles McCallagher, 1 January 1833; *Public Ledger*, 26 and 30 August 1831; and *Royal Gazette and Newfoundland Advertiser* [*Royal Gazette*], 31 August 1831.

87. PANL, GN 2/2, vol. 2, 258–61, Warner to the District Surgeon and Magistrates at St. John's, 1 August 1827.

88. PANL, GN 2/2, vol. 2, 256–76, various medical reports to the Magistrates at St. John's, 1–3 August 1827. Quotation from report of J. Shea, 266–67, 1 August 1827.

89. PANL, GN 2/2, vol. 2, 263–64, [?-signature indecipherable] to the Magistrates at St. John's, 1 August 1827.

90. PANL, GN 2/2, vol. 2, 268–70, Kielley to the Magistrates at St. John's, 3 August 1827. Not surprisingly, when the brig *James* arrived from Ireland less than two weeks later with several sick passengers and crew members, the alarm was raised by attending doctors and clergy, who urged that immediate measures be taken to prevent any intercourse between people of the town and the vessel's passengers and crew. See PANL, GN 2/2, vol. 2, 306–12, various correspondence and reports, 13 August 1827. See also related correspondence at PANL, GN 2/1/A, vol. 36, 266 and 344–45.

91. PANL, GN 2/1/A, vol. 36: 241–42, G. W. Busteed, Chairman of the Committee for checking Contagion, to W. A. Clarke, for submission to Governor is, 28 July 1827; and related correspondence at 242, 254–65, and 276.

92. The following account of the *Concord*'s voyage is taken from various correspondence in the MHA, MF-191, Letterbook of Edward Kough (1818–34), February-September 1825. In particular, see: Kough to James M. Henderson, Liverpool, 21 February 1825; Kough to John Boyd, 25 March and 9 April 1825; and Kough to the Inspector General of Customs for Ireland, 21 September 1825. John Boyd was Kough's associate who coordinated orders for passengers and provisions in the St. John's area.

93. The higher fares for women are intriguing. The higher bond rate could be explained by their being deemed a slightly greater risk in terms of being able to find employment and pay their passage once in Newfoundland. However, the cash fare—at least in this example—also appears to have been higher. It is possible that women's fares may have included young children traveling with them.

94. A comparison of fares to Irish wages of the period would be useful, but the information is difficult to come by on this side of the Atlantic. The secondary literature does outline some wages earned by Irish agricultural laborers of the period, but even here, the data are not consistent. Cormac O Grada estimates the mean nominal wages of agricultural laborers in 1829 at 61d. per week. See Cormac O Grada, *Ireland: A New Economic History, 1780–1939* (Oxford: Clarendon Press, 1994), 237. He does not indicate an average or mean number of weeks worked, but even assuming full employment, the maximum annual earnings would have been only £13.4.4, likely a high estimate as this type of employment was rarely continuous. Using evidence presented to the Poor Inquiry Commission of the early 1830s (appointed 1833, reporting 1836), Kenneth Connell estimates that the average daily wage of a laborer was 8½d. with a potential employment period of up to 135 days per year; the maximum average annual earnings would, therefore, have been £4.15.7½. See Connell, *The Population of Ireland, 1750–1845* (Oxford: Clarendon Press, 1950), 76, n. 2. Both Connell's and O Grada's figures, however, are based on aggregate data for Ireland, and it is difficult to determine how representative they are of the southeast counties from which the Newfoundland Irish came. Furthermore, neither discusses total family earnings, including women's and children's paid work or earnings from pigs and poultry. A more nu-

anced set of estimates is provided by Mary Cullen, using the same Poor Inquiry evidence to estimate annual family cash incomes (laborer's wages and income from pigs and fowl) for specific baronies in various counties, several from the southeast, e.g.:

Kilkenny	£7.0.0 (occasional laborer)-£9.0.0 (cottier)
Kerry	£6.10.0-£8.18.0
Limerick	£6.15.0-£9.0.0
Tipperary	£11.6.8
Waterford	£8.0.0-£10.0.0

The mean number of days worked in these specific counties was 200 days per year. Cullen also provides some family budgets (for counties outside the southeast), indicating that all or most of family cash incomes were expended on necessities—such as potatoes, rent, and turf—with small amounts left for clothing, soap, and tobacco. Saving for passages would, therefore, have been difficult. See Cullen, "Breadwinners and Providers: Women in the Household Economy of Labouring Families, 1835–6," in *Women Surviving: Studies in Irish Women's History in the Nineteenth and Twentieth Centuries*, ed. Maria Luddy and Cliona Murphy (Dublin: Poolbeg Press, 1989), 85–116, particularly 92–103. Cullen's estimates, however, do not include women's and children's earnings from seasonal agricultural work or women's earnings from cottage textiles (particularly, the woolen industry). In a documentary collection, Maria Luddy includes a Poor Inquiry report on women's and children's agricultural wages in the 1830s. Based on an earning group of a wife and four children of working age, reports from Munster indicated potential earnings ranging from lows of £1 per wife plus £1.10.0 per child (£7 total) per year to highs of £20 and £22.10.0 per year. No information was cited for Leinster. The report indicated that women's paid work in both the agricultural and cottage industries sectors was in decline. See "Report from His Majesty's Commissioners for Inquiring into the Condition of the Poorer Classes in Ireland, Appendix D (1836)," in Luddy, *Women in Ireland, 1800–1918: A Documentary History* (Cork: Cork University Press, 1995), doc. 47.3, 166–72.

In general, agricultural wages had been declining and unemployment had been rising between the sailing of the *Concord* in 1825 and the hearings of the Poor Inquiry in the early 1830s. Also, smallholders and artisans who formed part of the emigrant stream to Newfoundland would have earned higher incomes than laborers (but had higher expenditures as well). The overall picture on incomes is therefore murky. But certainly, most emigrants would have been hard pressed to save passage money for transatlantic crossings, and the feat must have been extremely difficult for family groups traveling together. The high incidence of emigrants booking their passage to Newfoundland on bond is therefore hardly surprising, given the far higher earning potential in the fishery (see Table 4.1).

95. Kough's average fare was likely higher than that of many vessels out of Waterford because Kough, unlike many others in the trade, was actually provisioning his

passengers. In 1831, because of damages to one of his ships and continuing competition from Waterford vessels, he considered having his passengers provision themselves as other carriers were doing. Whether he actually succumbed to this practice is unclear. See MHA, MF-191, Kough Letterbook: Kough to Robert Hutton and Co., 1, 9, 14, and 30 March 1831; Kough to Captain Taylor, 2 March 1831; and Kough to William Kydd, 12 April 1831.

96. The Saunders and Sweetman Letterbook at PANL, MG 49, also details arrangements for transporting fishing servants' chests to and from Waterford; these would have contained some clothing, small items of gear, and other necessities for the fishing season.

97. Kough did not specify the actual length of the voyage, although he indicated in mid-August that he still had not heard news of the *Concord*'s arrival and that relatives and friends of passengers were becoming concerned. See MHA, MF-191, Kough Letterbook, Kough to Boyd, 15 August 1825. Lengths of voyage, when stipulated in the previous accounts, ranged from one month to ten weeks. The diary of Ferryland magistrate Robert Carter mentions the traveling time of several vessels arriving in the district from Ireland, ranging from a very short passage of twelve days, through more average lengths in the twenties, to a longer passage of forty-nine days. See PANL, MG 920, Robert Carter Diary, 1832–52. The Sweetman Collection contains a notebook detailing the arrival and departure of vessels at Placentia from 1831 to 1835. Lengths of voyages from Waterford ranged from very short passages of fifteen, sixteen, and eighteen days, to exceptionally long passages of fifty, fifty-four, and sixty days. Most voyage lengths, however, fell within the range of twenty-two to thirty-eight days. The average passage time was 31.47 days, and the mean length of passage, 30 days. See PANL, MG 49, Sweetman Collection, box 2, file 12.

98. Byrne, "Brig *Thomas Farrell*."

3. CIPHERING CIPHERS

Tracing Irish Women on the Southern Avalon

> There were there 110 men, at least half of them armed, not counting women and children . . . This place is very fine. There are 17 houses, and about 116 men, not counting women and children. We found sheep and cows here.
>
> —Father Baudoin, ca. 1697

Like other seventeenth-century observers in Newfoundland, Father Baudoin demonstrated a knack for "not counting women and children" and a propensity to lump them together with the livestock.[1] English naval officers in the late seventeenth century were also somewhat relaxed about counting women, and certainly about identifying them, in their census reports to the Commissioners of Trade: a mistress of a fishing *plantation*, if she was enumerated at all, appeared only as the numeral "1" next to her husband's name in a column headed "Wife"; servants were tabulated together in another column, undifferentiated by sex. However, the census system became more systematized with the passage of the *Newfoundland Act* of 1699, and numbers of mistresses and women servants were more regularly (if not always accurately) reported by the naval commodores and governors annually from that point onwards. Still, the task of tracking Irish women immigrants to the southern Avalon is not an easy one.

Newfoundland is not exceptional for the paucity of its early census and immigration records. Historians studying early migration patterns to other parts of

North America have also encountered difficulties in ascertaining the actual numbers of people who arrived in the New World. The task is further complicated by any attempt to separate the permanent immigrant from the sojourner (a task that was, no doubt, almost as difficult for official recorders of the day). Because of Newfoundland's unique status as a fishery rather than a colony (at least in official terms) until the early nineteenth century, historians of early settlement continue to struggle with the question of how to measure accurately the transient versus the permanent elements of Newfoundland's population.

While early census material exists, summer population figures were often temporarily inflated by ship-fishermen, bye-boatkeepers, and fishing servants hired only for the summer or two summers and a winter;[2] even over-wintering populations included large numbers of transient servants and dieters (although many did settle in time). Furthermore, even as the migratory fishery entered its prolonged demise in the latter part of the eighteenth century, the ascendant resident fishery continued to employ significant numbers of fishing servants, both migrant and resident, at least until after the Napoleonic Wars, when the traditional planter fishery virtually collapsed and was replaced by household production in the industry (see below). Additionally, some migrants used Newfoundland as a stepping-stone to colonies on the mainland, relatively cheap fares to the island making it an attractive layover. This phenomenon is difficult to measure because it was not systematically recorded, although it was frequently referred to in anecdotal evidence of the period.[3]

There are other reasons why early Newfoundland census material does not provide a solid foundation for calculating the dimensions or components of migration and population growth. There are sometimes internal anomalies within individual censuses as well as inconsistencies between censuses.[4] Also, estimates in round numbers were sometimes recorded by observers when exact information was not available for particular communities or districts. Additionally, categories shifted over time and were not clearly defined. Before the 1836 census, for example, women were enumerated as either "mistresses" or "women servants," with no category to differentiate unmarried women who were not servants.[5] Indeed, the category of "women servants" is itself problematic, for it does not differentiate between domestic servants and fishing servants. Age groupings present a further complication. In annual reports up to the early 1830s, "children" were reported separately from adults, although the age demarcation was not given. From 1836 onwards, males and females were reported under specific age groupings; yet even these categories changed in 1857 (the most notable change, in terms of separating adults from children in the population, was the shift from an "under 14" category to an "under 10" category).

Precise information on Irish immigration and ethnicity is also elusive. There are no specific immigration statistics available for the period covered in this study, and the ethnic origins of the inhabitants were not recorded until the 1857 census. Even then, the category only recorded non-native-born classifications such as "Irish-born" and "English-born," not the multi-generational ethnic group. The CO 194 returns did enumerate a category of "passengers" by source area (England, Ireland, or Jersey), yet even this word is open to interpretation. Passengers in the early years of reporting were people coming to the island as seasonal workers in the fishery (either for the migratory fishery or the resident fishery); but gradually, throughout the eighteenth century, increasing numbers of passengers came to Newfoundland in the hope of remaining on the island. Thus the line between seasonal migrants and permanent immigrants became further blurred. The picture is also clouded by the fact that many Irish passengers to the southern Avalon from the turn of the nineteenth century onwards likely disembarked at St. John's. Separate passenger figures for most of the Southern Shore (Bay Bulls to Cape Race) rarely appeared thereafter, and not at all after the Napoleonic War period, although passengers to Trepassey and St. Mary's continued to be recorded separately. None of these passenger numbers were demarcated by sex.

Given the drawbacks of the early census materials, it is difficult to provide precise baseline data on the migration of Irish women to the southern Avalon up to the mid-nineteenth century. It is possible, however, to capture impressions of these movements, using the breakdowns that are available in terms of winter and summer inhabitants, masters and mistresses, male and female servants, and religion. Parish records, birth, marriage, and death notices in newspapers, name file collections, and the oral tradition provide additional insights into source areas, immigration networks, marriage and settlement patterns, and early community formation.

SOURCE AREAS

When Mary Ryan left county Wexford in 1826 to come to the southern Avalon, she was following one of the most well-traveled Irish migration streams to Newfoundland in general, and to the southern Avalon in particular. The *Historical Atlas of Canada* maps the source areas of known emigrants from Ireland to Newfoundland from 1780 to 1850. It demonstrates that, overwhelmingly, the Irish in Newfoundland came from the southeastern counties: Kilkenny (1,835) provided the greatest number of emigrants; Wexford (1,685) slightly edged out Waterford (1,625) for second place, while Tipperary (1,135) ran a respectable fourth; Cork (505) and Carlow (190) followed distantly as source areas, while the remaining known emigrants (420) came from other Irish counties.[6] The logic of the emigrant stream was intrinsically tied to the Newfoundland fishery. These counties formed the hinterland of ports that had been stopping points for the West Country fishing ships in the seventeenth and early eighteenth centuries, and which had developed a passenger and provision trade in their own right in the eighteenth century.

The *Atlas* also provides a breakdown for inhabitants of Ferryland district in 1836 who had been born outside Newfoundland. This analysis indicates that the major source regions for those who were Irish-born were similar to those of the larger Irish migration stream to Newfoundland, with a slight re-ordering of the top three source areas: Wexford first (78), followed closely by Kilkenny (73) and Waterford (71). Tipperary (34) was not as well represented as in the general Irish emigrant population, sending only half as many emigrants as either of the top three. As with the larger migration stream, Cork (16) and Carlow (7) followed in fifth and sixth place, respectively. Another 14 persons hailed from other Irish counties.[7]

Information on the source areas of Irish women emigrants to the southern Avalon is very sparse indeed. I have been able to identify only sixty-seven women who came directly from Ireland and to track only sixty-three of these to their home counties (information on towns, villages, and parishes is even more scarce and statistically negligible).[8] While data are limited, they certainly trace a picture that does not vary far from the two analyses outlined above and, indeed, correspond closely with that for the Irish-born of Ferryland district: Wexford (18) was the leading source area, with Waterford (14) and Kilkenny (13) ranking second and third, respectively; again, Tipperary (9) was a respectable fourth (indeed, better represented among women emigrants to the area than among the Irish-born in Ferryland district), while Cork (5) ranked fifth (see Table 3.1). Although it is difficult to ascertain how representative these figures are, the impression they create is that Irish women's emigration to the region was generally linked to overall Irish movements to the southern Avalon (see Figure 3.1). In other words, there does not seem to have been a separate migration stream—a distinct cluster or pocket of source areas for women emigrants—that was different in character from the larger movement that was overwhelmingly impelled by the Newfoundland fishery.

MOTIVES AND PATTERNS OF MIGRATION

Writers such as Mannion, Head, and Nemec have already described the particular blend of push and pull factors that attracted many migrants from the southeast of Ireland to Newfoundland (see Appendix B). A series of crop failures from 1726 to 1729, the severe frosts in the winters of 1739–40 and 1740–41, a devastating drought in 1741, and high unemployment triggered by the Spanish War provided an impetus for migration by the middle of the eighteenth century that happily corresponded with an increasing demand for Irish servants in the Newfoundland fishery. Furthermore, in the latter eighteenth and early nineteenth centuries, the southeastern counties, like other parts of Ireland, were experiencing the ill effects of overpopulation and land shortage. Subdivision and subletting of land were increasingly undermining the viability of holdings and eventually came under prohibition altogether, leaving few options for surplus offspring in small-holder or cottier families. Meanwhile, the domestic textile industry was struggling, particularly in the recession that followed the Napoleonic Wars. The agricultural sector was also badly hit by the post-war slump, as prices for farm produce dropped and markets for provisions declined. And although advances were made in farming technology, they created a surplus of labor that was not absorbed by any corresponding increase in town manufacturing. The southeast was not as heavily affected by these developments as the west and north, but these push factors combined with the drawing power of employment and good wages in the Newfoundland fishery to create a very specific emigration stream from the southeast to Newfoundland—one that, in its largely Catholic composition, was quite distinct from the markedly northern and Protestant character of the broader Irish emigration flow to North America up to the post-Napoleonic War period,[9] and one that, in its responsiveness to employment opportunities in Newfoundland and declining conditions in the mother country, challenges Miller's perception of an inferior Irish Catholic emigrant type.

Other written sources, historical and contemporary, confirm the attraction of Newfoundland fishery for Irish immigrants.[10] The oral tradition on the southern Avalon also acknowledges the role of the fishery in drawing the Irish to the area. Audio Sample In addition, it offers some alternative motivations: the Irish rebel running from the law; the Irish Catholic fleeing from religious persecution; the Irish cottier escaping the Great Famine. But while isolated cases such as these may have existed, these explanations are far more reflective of an inherited mythology of grievance than actual experience. The Irish rebel was more likely a deserting servant hiding from a fishing master; the religious refugee would surely have sought sanctuary someplace other than a British possession affected by the Penal Laws; and, while crop failures and regional famines may have encouraged movement to the southern Avalon, the hungry peasant of the mid-nineteenth century most likely went to the mainland, for most Irish immigrants to Newfoundland had arrived by the early 1830s. This is not to dismiss the importance of these communal myths of migration, for they provide insight into the evolution of ethnic identity and reflect a shared collective historical memory of deprivation and struggle that is in itself a significant cultural continuity with the home country and with other Irish emigrant groups.

But for immediate motivations for migration, we must return to the economic lure of the Newfoundland fishery and the opportunity provided for migration, first by West Country fishing ships, and later by Irish vessels involved in the passenger and provision trade. But how did women feature in this distinctive migration pattern? While the current literature has identified male immigrants to Newfoundland as craftsmen, farm laborers, or the sons of small farmers, it does not speculate on the socioeconomic backgrounds of female immigrants. Specific data are scarce, but some logical inferences can be drawn from the historical geography of their source areas. According to O Grada, the triangular area from Cork to Dundalk to Wexford—an area that corresponds roughly with the southeastern Irish homeland of many southern Avalon immigrants—was a high tillage zone in the relevant period, with labor-intensive agriculture and a relatively complex social structure, including farm laborers, tradesmen, artisans, and small farmers as well as middling and large farmers.[11] The inference, then, that Irish women immigrants on the southern Avalon came from agricultural or artisanal family backgrounds who were feeling the squeeze of demographic and economic pressures in Ireland is a reasonable one. It is also quite likely that many had worked in cottage textile industries. In particular, there was a high degree of women's participation in the domestic woolen industry, which flourished in southern Ireland until at least the late eighteenth century and was as important economically to that area as the linen industry was in the north. Thereafter, it declined steadily as a result of rising wool costs and competition from English textiles, and had virtually disappeared in some areas by the taking of the 1841 census.[12] On this front as well, then, Irish women were facing the specters of recession and unemployment. It is thus hardly surprising that a number of women from southeastern Ireland turned their eyes to the Newfoundland fishery as an attractive alternative to declining opportunities in Ireland.

As naval officers and governors in Newfoundland had occasion to remark, a significant number of single Irish women came to Newfoundland in search of work as servants and ultimately married among the fishermen or planters and remained.[13] One such woman was Mary Crane, who came out to Ferryland from County Cork in the late 1820s. According to family folk history, she spotted local carpenter Tade Bryan on the wharf as she was disembarking and declared then and there that he was the man she was going to marry—a prophecy that proved correct in fairly short order.[14] But romance likely took a back seat to the exigencies of earning a living for most of these women. A few became fishing servants, heading, splitting, salting, and drying cod as part of shore crews. Far greater numbers contracted themselves as household servants to merchants, planters, administrators, and their families—a type of service that was itself often an important component of the sedentary fishery (see Chapter 4). In either case, the women were hired (by oral agreement or by a written shipping paper[15]) either in Ireland or upon arrival in Newfoundland. When women were specifically recruited for work in this fashion, the law looked upon the arrangement as a formal contract, just as in the cases of men contracted as fishing servants. In a 1787 court case in Ferryland, for example, Elizabeth Cullen complained that she had been shipped in Ireland "on order" by the wife of Patrick Goff to serve James Shortall in Ferryland. But the vessel had had a long passage over, and Mr. Shortall had run out of patience and hired another servant instead. When Elizabeth finally arrived, Mr. Shortall "reshipped" her to his neighbor, Mary Sanders. Elizabeth served Sanders for a while, but they had a falling out and parted. Elizabeth went back to Shortall, but he refused to take her in, and she was forced to take lodgings with a Hannah Gaffney. Finally, Elizabeth took her original employer—Mr. Shortall, the one who had recruited her from Ireland—to court for her boarding expenses; and the court agreed with her, ordering Shortall to pay for Elizabeth's lodging and diet with Hannah Gaffney and to take her back into his own care.[16] Case File 1

Of course, not all Irish women servants signed shipping papers, but verbal employment agreements were also recognized by law. The existence of this system conjures up an image of an Irish woman servant who was far more informed and purposeful than the impoverished, immoral woman of eighteenth-century governors' proclamations.[17] Most of these women were making informed decisions to improve their lives when they left Ireland to come to Newfoundland, even those who gambled on finding work upon arrival.[18] It was their intention to lead purposeful lives on the island, not to become a burden on their new community.

In addition to single servants, numbers of women immigrated as part of family groups—particularly as wives, potential wives, or common-law partners[19] of men who were involved in the fishery.[20] Some of these men had already been working in Newfoundland and sent passage money back to Ireland or made arrangements with their employers to bring out wives or future brides. In the fall of 1830, for example, James Whelan, who was fishing at Salmonier, made the following request of his employer, Saunders and Sweetman:

> . . . I have one request to beg of you that is to give Elinor Hannigan a passage out to placentia in the Spring of the year and I shall pay you and by doing so you will oblige me very much and I shall be for ever under a compliment to you and please to let me have an Answer if you will be so obliging.[21]

The company letterbook provides further evidence of arrangements made by fishing servants to send money home or have wages paid to wives or other family members in the home country.[22] While these letters are sporadic and do not designate the use of the money, there can be little doubt that in some cases, remitted wages would have helped to pay passage for family members—male and female—to Newfoundland.

There is strong evidence of Irish women migrating as part of family units to join the fishery at Cape Broyle and Caplin Bay in the late 1700s and early 1800s,[23] and this was likely reflective of much female immigration to smaller *outharbors* in the area, where there would have been less demand for female servants than in more established and populous centers such as Ferryland, Bay Bulls, and Renews. In Cape Broyle, for example, the first permanent families—Kelly, Aylward, Grant, Walsh, Fitzgerald, Bryan, and Kent—were all Irish, and they immigrated as family units in the 1780s, 1790s, and early 1800s.[24] In some cases, male members of the family had already been involved in the Newfoundland fishery in some capacity. This was possibly the experience of Michael and Mary Ryan, whom we encountered in the previous chapter. It was certainly the case of the Bryan (also Brine and O'Brien) family. Catherine and Michael Bryan of the parish of Hook, Wexford, had likely married by 1767–68 (when their first child was born). Michael may have already been fishing at Newfoundland at that time, but he was certainly fishing at Brigus South as early as 1774, for a reference is made to his fishing plantation there in a grant of fishing premises to John Welsh and John Sullivan.[25] Catherine remained in Wexford in the early years and raised their growing family (six boys and one girl by 1787–78) while her husband was away at least for several months of the year (and possibly for years at a time, if Michael over-wintered in Newfoundland). But in 1792, Catherine and the children joined Michael on the southern Avalon. They settled in Cape Broyle harbor, although the Pole Papers indicate that by 1800, Michael was still fishing off Brigus South—by this time, as a boatmaster for merchant Richard Hutchings—and that four of his sons (Michael Jr., James, Richard, and Thomas) had joined him in Hutchings's employ.[26]

Some details survive of other family migrations from Ireland to Cape Broyle. Elenor (Nellie) Lyons and her husband, Richard Welsh, left Wexford in 1784 to come to the southern Avalon. They arrived in Petty Harbour in 1784, where their first child, Michael, was born, and they moved on to Cape Broyle the following year. In 1788 or 1789, Nellie gave birth to their second child, Thomas, the first child born in Cape Broyle harbor.[27] Mary Ann and William Leahy (or Lahey) and their two children, Michael and Margaret, came to Cape Broyle in 1812 to take advantage of the high wages in the Newfoundland fishery in the latter stages of the Napoleonic War period. They were part of the "Kehoe [or Kough] gang," recruited by George and Thomas Kough, Irish Protestant merchants from Ross with a base of operations at Cape Broyle. The Leahys were the first family to settle across the river in *Fairy Pond*.[28] Johannah Doran and her husband,

Richard Furlong, were natives of Tipperary who arrived in Cape Broyle circa 1813–15; like the Leahys, they were probably lured by the prosperity of the Newfoundland fishery. According to the local oral tradition, they were married in a church in County Galway and then walked straight to the ship that would carry them to the southern Avalon.[29] Interestingly, Sarah *Drohan*, a widow or single woman, and her children were listed in the Pole Papers as residing at Cape Broyle in 1800; it is possible that Johannah *Doran* Furlong may have been related to this group and that she and Richard may have come to Cape Broyle through family connections on Johannah's side of the family.[30] Audio Sample

Irish families also featured in the early settlement of Caplin Bay (now Calvert).

Diarist Aaron Thomas noted in his journal that an Irishman named Poor (or Power) was living in that outharbor in 1794 with a young wife, "very fair and beautiful," and four children.[31] This was likely Michael and Alice Power, who were still in the community, with seven children, in 1800.[32] The oral tradition also tells of early Irish family immigration to that outharbor, noting that among the first permanent Irish settlers in Caplin Bay was a group that arrived in the summer of 1805 from County Wexford, consisting of a Wade family, three Sweyne (or Swain) families, a Kehoe family, and a Meaney family. They initially lived at Stone Island, a headland at the mouth of the harbor close to the fishing grounds, but soon moved further inwards for protection. They were joined by a young man named Joseph Sullivan, also of Wexford, who married one of the Sweyne daughters, Mary.[33]

So despite the cool reception from naval officers and governors at Newfoundland, Irish women joined the migration stream as single servants, as prospective partners or married women, and as daughters. In various outharbors along the southern Avalon, they began to live productive lives within family units and providing essential services to the growing fishing population. And the increasing presence of Irish women would have a particular impact on community formation in the area. Given the transient nature of employment in the Newfoundland fishery, it was quite common for male fishing servants to find employment in different harbors from year to year. Figures 3.2, 3.3, and 3.4 are based on nominal census data in the Pole Papers. They trace the movements of male servants and dieters who over-wintered in Ferryland district in 1799–1800 as well as those who worked in the fishery in the area in the summer of 1800. Figure 3.2 traces non-local migrations in Ferryland district for the spring of 1800, and demonstrates a significant movement of men into and out of the district at the start of the fishing season. Figure 3.3 and Figure 3.4 illustrate further movements of male fishing personnel from harbor to harbor within the district itself between the winter of 1799–1800 and the spring of 1800.

Granted, these local migrations would have included some men who had already settled in the area—men such as Michael Bryan and his sons, encountered above, who had been living in Cape Broyle for some time but worked in Brigus South. However, many others were shifting locales, in and out of the southern Avalon or between harbors in the area, as work opportunities presented themselves.

It was the presence of women that would eventually tie most of these men to particular communities. Some Irish fishermen were joined by wives or fiancés from the home country. Yet in more significant numbers, single male servants arriving on the shore found wives not only among the small English planter group already established there, but increasingly among Irish women immigrants and, certainly by the turn of the century, among an expanding group of first- and second-generation Irish Newfoundland women living in the area. Matrilineal bridges often factored in the clustering of families in particular coves and harbors; and matrilocal or uxorilocal residence patterns played a crucial role in community formation, as many couples established themselves on land already occupied by the wife or apportioned from or adjacent to the family property of the wife. In contrast to some population movements, in which men primarily established themselves first in new communities and then sent for fiancés, wives, and children, this was a phenomenon in which a large number of men joined women, setting down roots and raising families in their wives' home communities.

This occurred in Cape Broyle, for example, with the wave of young male servants who arrived in the latter stages of the Napoleonic War period and during the final large wave of Irish immigration in the 1820s. When John Cashin came from Wexford in 1812, he first worked in Caplin Bay; but he met Mary Welsh, the first-generation Irish Newfoundland daughter of Nellie Lyons and Richard Welsh, and married her in 1814, and the couple settled in Mary's community of Cape Broyle. Philip Hays from Kilmaback, Wexford, married Bridget Brennan, first-generation Irish Newfoundland daughter of James and Anstice Brennan of Cape Broyle, in 1813; the couple remained in Bridget's home community. John Dalton arrived in Cape Broyle in the 1820s and married Mary Grant, first-generation Irish Newfoundland daughter of Richard and Margret Grant, who had come from County Tipperary in the 1780s; John and Mary settled in Cape Broyle (their daughter, Mary Dalton, would also marry an immigrant—Charlie Oldridge [or Aldridge] of the London area—around mid-century, and settle on her family's property on Dalton's Lane). Edward Hartery was also a new arrival from Ireland in 1820s; he married Elizabeth Kelly, first-generation Irish Newfoundland daughter of Catherine and Cornelius Kelly (agent at Cape Broyle for the Koughs), and they established themselves on land near the Kelly home.[34]

In nearby Brigus South, an Irish Newfoundland woman, Catherine Henley, married newcomer Michael Hayes of Ireland around 1790, and the couple settled in Catherine's home community. By a will dated 1826, Catherine's father or brother, Patrick Henley, left her a fishing plantation, lands, and houses in Brigus South. Catherine died in 1828, and her husband, Michael, applied for letters of administration of her estate in 1829, which were granted in 1830. The couple's sons, Michael and James, married local Irish Newfoundland women: Johannah Neil, most likely of Brigus South, and Elizabeth Kelly, of Cape Broyle (the same Elizabeth Kelly who had previously married Edward Hartery of Ireland, above, now widowed). The two younger couples settled in Brigus South on the lands from Catherine's estate and were still there in 1871.[35]

Irish and Irish Newfoundland widows, like Elizabeth Kelly Hartery Henley, who remained in Newfoundland and raised families on their own, or remarried and formed new families, also provided essential continuities in early settlement. The Pole Papers provide various examples of widows raising families without male partners in 1800. Margret Whelan, Elizabeth Forehan, and Mary Whelan, for example, were all widows living in Ferryland with large families (four or five children); Sarah Drohan was living in Cape Broyle with two teen-aged children; Margret Aylward of Fermeuse was widowed with five children; and Bridget Flaherty was raising a family of four young children, all under the age of twelve, alone at Fermeuse. This census also provides instances of families with children whose surnames differed from those of the listed fathers—suggesting that the mothers may have previously been either married or in common-law relationships.[36] Margret and James Neill of Ferryland, for example, were raising a family of children with surnames Murphy, Furlong, and Neill; Anstice and Edmund Dunphy were living in Brigus South with two children with the surname Buckley; Mary and James Ready of Fermeuse were raising a family of seven children—three with the surname Ready and three with Clancy; the children of Fanny and Edmund Chidley at Renews had surnames Chidley and Gearn.[37]

Anecdotal evidence provides further examples of widows who helped to establish communities on the southern Avalon. Catherine Cooney of Kilkenny, for example, married Peter Weston, magistrate and merchant in Ferryland, circa the mid-eighteenth century, and later became mother-in-law of William Carter, judge of the vice-admiralty court of Newfoundland. At Peter's death, Catherine inherited one-third of his extensive estate and, in her widowhood, became a powerful matriarch of both the Weston and Carter families. Furthermore, while these families were Protestant, Catherine remained Catholic and exercised a high degree of influence with several priests at the Catholic mission in Ferryland.[38] Mary Neill, the wife of Constantine Neill (originally of Ballymartin, Kilkenny; Mary's birthplace is not known), was widowed at Fermeuse circa 1810. She had eleven children at the time, nine of whom were eighteen years of age and younger (the older two were twenty-eight and thirty, and likely the offspring of an earlier marriage of her husband). Constantine, who died intestate, left a considerable estate worth approximately £1,800, and it was ultimately distributed one-third to the widow and two-thirds to the children. Mary stayed on in Fermeuse to raise her family and remarried (to James Dalton) circa 1814.[39]

We have already encountered Mary Ryan of Wexford, who remained in Cape Broyle with her three young sons after Michael's untimely death, eventually married James Coady of Wexford, and raised a second family with him. Another example is provided by Margret Bryan, who came out to Cape Broyle from Wexford with her parents and brothers in the 1790s (see above). Margret initially married John Kelly, another offspring of Catherine and Cornelius Kelly. John died at an early age, and Margret inherited his fishing premises at Cape Broyle, which she gave to her brothers and which were operated by family production for the next century and a half. Margret remarried; her new husband was Michael Gregory, the son of an established English planter family at Brigus South (the couple were practicing Catholics, although whether Michael's family had already converted from Protestantism is unclear).[40]

It is apparent, then, that matrilocality and uxorilocality played an intrinsic role in community formation in the area. These patterns repeated in various communities along the southern Avalon. In 1799, Thomas Power from Carrick-on-Suir married Elizabeth Connelly of Ferryland. James Murphy from Wexford married Margaret Power of Witless Bay in 1806. Patrick Corane (possibly Crane or Careen) from Wexford married Judith Cullotin of Fermeuse in 1807. Daniel Wright from Tralee married Bridget Phelan Makis of Ferryland in 1808. Matthew Meaney from Carlow married Mary Bryan of Ferryland in 1813. Richard Lacey from Waterford married Bridget Condon of Ferryland in 1814. John Bagley from Waterford married Eleanor Cahill of Witless Bay in 1817. Michael Molloy from Wexford married Mary McGee of Ferryland in 1823. Thomas Gower from Waterford married Bridget Doyle of Renews in 1825. Tobias Thomson from Waterford married Catherine Neal of Renews in 1826. Patrick Tobin from County Kilkenny married Sarah Dunn of Ferryland in 1827. Maurice Daly from Waterford married Mary Whelan from St. Mary's in 1844. Patrick Shanihan from Wicklow married Mary Kennidy of Mobile in 1844. William Grant Malone from Wexford married Esther McCarthy of Renews in 1847. William Kirney from Tipperary married Mary Murphy of St. Mary's in 1853. Michael Moore from Wexford married Anne Gready of Mobile in 1853. Edward Roben from Tipperary married Margaret Dinn of Witless Bay in 1854. John Hurly from Cork married Ellon Murphy of St. Mary's in 1858. All these couples remained on the southern Avalon.[41]

A standard demographic technique for measuring the stability of community populations is surname-sieving: tracing the persistence of surnames over time in a given locality to establish the transition to a permanent population. Gordon

Handcock uses this method in his examination of English migrations to and settlement in Newfoundland.[42] But this technique has a patrilineal-patrilocal bias that does not accommodate alternative forms of continuities in early community formation in Newfoundland. Figure 3.5 for example, shows a partial family tree for the Oldridge family in Cape Broyle. Surname-sieving would not locate any significant clustering of the Oldridge name until the late nineteenth century. But continuities in the family line date back to the late eighteenth century: through the wife of the first Cape Broyle Oldridge, Mary Dalton, a second-generation Irish Newfoundland woman on her mother's side, whose grandparents came to the island from Tipperary in the 1780s; and through their son John's wife, Kathleen Walsh, whose grandparents on her father's side had come to Cape Broyle from Wexford in the 1780s, and whose maternal roots in the community went back three generations to Michael and Catherine Bryan of Wexford. Furthermore, the Oldridge surname no longer exists in Cape Broyle, although numerous relatives through maternal links and sister marriages continue to live in the area.

Granted, this chart demonstrates an unusual case of a surname establishing itself late and subsiding quickly. Most Irish surnames would have established themselves earlier in the nineteenth century, and many persist in the area today. However, the example effectively demonstrates the limitations of surname-sieving. The technique gives the demographer something concrete to work with, for written records on men are much more readily available than those on women; but it certainly requires strenuous qualification if used in the Newfoundland context, for it mutes the matrilineal bridges and matrilocal/uxorilocal residence patterns that often predated patrilineal-patrilocal patterns in early settlement. For every marriage of a male immigrant to a "local woman," a similar family chart would extend back at least one generation, possibly more, as well as laterally among collateral kin. If these women-centered networks are taken into account, it becomes evident that the tendency towards population permanence began earlier than surname-sieving can reveal.

A final example comes from the oral tradition and a family history of the "two brothers came out from Ireland" genre. Women's agency is virtually absent in a local manuscript—primarily a retelling from the oral tradition—about the Ryan family of Biscay Bay.[43] The chronicle develops from the perspective of the men involved. We are told that the patriarch, Denis Ryan, came out from Ireland (possibly Cork) in the early 1800s and fished for four summers with Goodridge's at Renews. He had a large family, and his son Thomas and Thomas's brother-in-law Richard Hartery eventually founded the settlement of Biscay Bay. Lineage and settlement patterns in this account are traced through the patriline only. Family enterprises are described without reference to the participation of wives, sisters, and daughters.

But if we look carefully, we can see the themes of matrilocality, intermarriage, and matrilineal bridges woven into this family history. Like many other Irish fishing servants, Denis Ryan married a local woman, Susanna Moore (likely of English or mixed English-Irish ancestry) of *the Lower Coast*, Trepassey, sometime before 1810 (when their first child was born). After their marriage, the couple moved to *the Dock* in Trepassey and built on land near Susanna's family home (possibly on land owned by her family). The couple had seven children—two boys and five girls. All five daughters married and remained in the Trepassey-Portugal Cove South area to raise their families. The two sons married local women from nearby Daniel's Point and Portugal Cove South, and they, too, stayed in the area. One of the sons, Thomas, met his future wife, Bridget Hartery of Portugal Cove South, while fishing as a servant with her family. The couple married about 1850, and through this connection, Bridget's brother Richard met and married Thomas's sister Margaret. Thomas and Bridget moved to Island Pond Gulley, Biscay Bay; they were joined by Richard and Margaret shortly thereafter, and the two couples became founding families of the community that would later develop there. Thus, with this slight re-emphasis of the limited information on women in the family, it is possible to bring forward the centrality of Susanna Moore, the Ryan sisters, and Bridget Hartery in this particular clustering of families in the Trepassey/Portugal Cove South/Biscay Bay area.

Given the paucity of records on women in early settlement, it is not possible to ascertain how representative such anecdotal evidence is. But it is possible to find within these stories the cues we need to help us rethink the processes of immigration and community formation in Newfoundland—to shift the focus of family and community histories to include women in the frame.

INTERMARRIAGE AND ASSIMILATION

Irish-English intermarriages, such as those between Susanna Moore and Denis Ryan or between Margret Bryan and Michael Gregory, were common on the southern Avalon, especially in older communities with mixed populations such as Brigus South, Ferryland, Bay Bulls, Renews, and St. Mary's. Irish male servants married women of English or mixed English-Irish ancestry (widows or daughters and granddaughters of English planters). John Macaboy from the parish of Ross, Wexford, for example, married Mary Midleton of Bay Bulls in 1800; John Murphy from Cork married Mary Peterson of Ferryland in 1804; and Bartholomew Dumpty (or Dunphy) from Wexford married Mary Jordan of Brigus South in 1813. Irish or Irish Newfoundland women married English fishing servants and men from English planter families as well. Margaret Gibbons Muny (or Mooney) of Ferryland, for example, married John Prose from Dorsetshire in 1805; Mary Hennessy of Ferryland married John Moody from Greenock in 1809; Mary Power from Tipperary married Thomas Norris of Witless Bay in 1810; Mary Bryan Bull of Ferryland married John Browse (possibly Prowse?) from South Hampton in 1817; Johanna Mackey of Brigus South married James Binning from Devonshire in 1818; and Mary Dalton of Cape Broyle married Charlie Oldridge from England in the mid-nineteenth century.[44]

Most of these intermarriages brought about conversions to Catholicism and/or the raising of children in the Catholic faith; ultimately, they resulted in assimilation to Irish culture.[45] Census material for the period provides evidence of a continuing integration of much of the English Protestant population into an expanding Irish Catholic ethnoreligious group. Figure 3.6 traces roughly in intervals of decades the growth of the population wintering over on the southern Avalon from 1735 to 1857 and provides a snapshot of the population in terms of its growth and structural components. Perhaps the most striking feature is the rapidly rising proportion of Catholics in the population, as indicated by the line at the top of the graph. Late seventeenth-century census material had evidenced a strong English Protestant presence on that shore; yet only one century later, the inhabitants were almost totally Catholic.

In particular, there was a dramatic increase in the percentage of Catholics in the population between 1754 and 1805. Certainly, this period witnessed an influx of Irish into the study area, and using the standard Newfoundland formula of ethnicity—Catholic = Irish, Protestant = English—one could view this movement purely in terms of a net movement of incoming Irish immigrants and outgoing English inhabitants. Anecdotal evidence provided by Catholic priests and ministers of the Society for the Propagation of the Gospel in Foreign Parts (SPG), however, strongly suggests that the processes of intermarriage, conversion, and assimilation were at work in conjunction with Irish in-migration.

In reporting on the satisfactory "progress of religion" in the Catholic mission at Ferryland, for example, Father Thomas Ewer was able to boast to his superiors in 1796 of making considerable inroads in the Protestant population:

> The many fruitless attempts of Methodist Preachers have been successfully baffled & there is now but one of that sect in the district of Ferryland & Trepassey whose family became Catholic this year. The Protestants likewise lose ground & their minister oblidged to decamp notwithstanding his £70 a year from the Society. Their feelings at such an event are easily conceived.[46]

By 1801, the SPG still had a mission on the Southern Shore, but the missionary's report that year revealed only 225 Anglicans (with 7 actual communicants) in the district, compared with 1,579 dissenters, "particularly Papish."[47] By 1845, the Anglican congregation on that shore had shrunk further to 132 members in Ferryland, Aquaforte, and Renews.[48]

Indeed, a sense of fatalism about the increasing Catholic presence pervades the records of the SPG for the southern Avalon. As early as 1773, the Protestant inhabitants of Bay Bulls had indicated "that to their great concern they find the Roman Catholic Religion daily gaining ground."[49] In 1842, when Anglican Bishop Aubrey Spencer visited Bay Bulls and "some adjoining settlements," he found "but one single Protestant family, where the Church of England had once sixteen hundred persons in her Communion." The bishop continued on to Ferryland "with deep gratitude to Almighty God, that he had guided me to these few sheep in the wilderness, who have not followed the multitude into the strange pastures."[50] His doleful observations strongly suggest intermarriage and conversion rather than out-migration of Protestant families. In 1845, Anglican Bishop Feild reported that "all in St. Mary's Bay and along the whole coast from thence to Renews are now Romanists," while only four families in Placentia "remain of our Communion (and some of these wavering)." He concluded, "Nothing can keep the remaining members of our church steadfast in their profession but an immediate increase of Ministers."[51] Like his predecessor, Feild sketched an impression of assimilation rather than exodus.

Catholic Bishop Michael Fleming, on the other hand, happily commended his priests for the gains they had made in the battle for souls on the southern Avalon. While touring that shore in 1835, he was pleased to stop in the mixed community of Renews and confirm 140 candidates, "the great part of whom had been converted to our holy religion."[52] On the island in general, he was pleased to see the numbers who had turned from "the flock of the stranger" to "the bosom of Christianity" upon the arrival of the Catholic missionaries.[53]

But while the Catholic bishop and his priests congratulated themselves on their success in converting the Protestant population (and there is no doubt that their official presence after 1784 contributed greatly to the process), Figure 3.6 suggests that assimilation was already well under way before the arrival of Catholic clergy. There was certainly a dramatic jump in the percentage of Catholics by 1785, but it is far more likely that, with the proclamation of liberty of conscience issued in 1784, more Catholics finally felt free to openly admit their faith than that the founding of a Catholic mission had had such a dramatic and immediate effect on conversion rates. It appears that the process of assimilation had gained momentum during an earlier period, roughly from the 1740s to the 1770s. The presence of a few itinerant priests, hiding in cellars and fishing boats, would hardly have accounted for such a significant shift. A more compelling explanation can be found in the increasing numbers of Irish arriving in the area, with conversion and assimilation resulting from intermarriage.

The effectiveness of the priests in shepherding souls from "the flock of the stranger" likely correlated significantly to the growing numbers of Irish Catholics in the marriage pool.

A comparison of available records of Catholic and Protestant marriages (covering primarily the period from the turn of the nineteenth century onwards) confirms that this process gained momentum in the latter half of the study period. Very rarely does an Irish surname appear in the Anglican parish records of the area. Within the Catholic parish records, by contrast, English surnames are frequently interspersed among the Irish, indicating a high degree of assimilation of English Protestant patrilines into the expanding Irish Catholic ethnoreligious group by the early 1800s. A more in-depth breakdown of marriage patterns within the two groups adds further texture to the impression of a growing and maturing Irish Catholic population, steadily incorporating new members, vis-à-vis a beleaguered English Protestant group, increasingly middle class,[54] in retreat and turning inwards on itself or recruiting from outside the southern Avalon to maintain its pedigree.

Table 3.2 demonstrates patterns of marriage within the Catholic community on the southern Avalon, using those marriages for which the places of birth for both spouses could be identified. While data for the period up to 1800 are too sparse to be significant, and information for the period up to 1830 is less comprehensive than that for later years, it is still possible to detect a Catholic population that is growing and becoming increasingly established in the area. The table indicates that significant recruitment of marriage partners from Ireland continued up to the 1840s; within this group, the pattern of southern Avalon women marrying Irish men was two to three times more common than the reverse, once again emphasizing the importance of matrilocality in initially establishing an Irish population in the area.

By the 1830s, there was a shift in the prevailing marriage pattern to that of the wife and husband both hailing from the southern Avalon, indicating that the peak years of Irish immigration were over. This pattern markedly predominated the latter part of the period of this study, reflecting an established population that was replenishing itself internally. Throughout the time frame, there was a constant incorporation of English surnames. A number of these family lines likely had begun to be absorbed into the Catholic population in the late eighteenth century and thus already had mixed English-Irish bloodlines by the time parish records were more systematically kept. But the trend continued, and was reinforced by ongoing intermarriage with the Irish in the nineteenth century.

A similar table on English Protestant marriage patterns (Table 3.3) provides a strong contrast. Only sixty-two Protestant marriages on the southern Avalon can be traced for the study period, reflecting two significant factors about this ethno-religious group: its small and relatively declining size compared with the Catholic community; and the fact that this mostly middle-class group continued to recruit members from outside the southern Avalon (hence, many marriages were registered elsewhere, particularly in parishes in St. John's or England). From the limited data that are available, the pattern of southern Avalon wife marrying southern Avalon husband was the most common in the latter decades, but only in the 1831–45 period did it account for over half (54 percent) of the marriages; thereafter, it declined to 40 percent (compared with the climb from 53 percent to 80 percent within the Catholic population for the same periods). Overall, unions between two local spouses accounted for only 39 percent of Anglican marriages, indicating significant recruitment from outside the area. Also, unlike the expanding Irish Catholic population, the English Protestant group married almost exclusively within itself, either choosing local spouses from the same ethnoreligious group and class or securing spouses from the English Protestant middle class elsewhere to maintain its homogeneity. Thus, a limited set of local surnames—Carter, Coleman, Johnston, Morry, Payne, Saunders, Sweetland, and Weston—dominate the records, while the regular appearance of certain St. John's family names—Tessier, Livingstone, Lemessurier, Rendell, and Skinner—indicate that connections with this particular segment of the middle class in the capital were being reinforced through marriage. Endogamy within such a small group resulted in some complex webs of relationships (see Figure 3.7).

Thus the equation of ethnicity and religion in the study area must be qualified. The "Protestant=English" portion of the formula held true (for the most part) among the local elite, with the exception of some few Irish Protestant mercantile families in the eighteenth century, such as the Bengers, Dobels, Nasons, and Ludwiggs (see Chapter 9). But the "Catholic=Irish" segment faltered within plebeian culture as many English Protestants were absorbed into the Catholic community. On the southern Avalon, the Irish ethnic group subsumed the English, with the exception of a small group predominated by mercantile and administrative families. Here, again, the southern Avalon Irish experience was quite different from the initial segregation and ultimate assimilation described in much of the literature on Irish migrations to America and Britain. The Irish on the southern Avalon not only intermingled with the English population but actually became the dominant ethnic group. And it was a process in which Irish or Irish Newfoundland women played a vital part, as marriage or common-law partners of not only incoming Irish Catholic migrants but also plebeian men of English Protestant descent, thus bringing many English Protestant patrilines (families with surnames such as Glynn, Williams, Yard, Carew, Maddox, and Martin) into the Catholic population. The growing Irish ethnic group was reinforced by further Irish immigration and intermarriage over time. But even by the turn of the nineteenth century, a high proportion of the Catholic population (and hence, of the plebeian community and even the total population) was either of direct Irish extraction or had some Irish in the bloodline.

A MATURING POPULATION

Figure 3.6 also illustrates that there was a generally increasing trend in the size of the total winter population (a loose approximation of the permanent population of the area), with peaks and troughs paralleling the fortunes of the fishery. The male population line has similar sinuosities to that of the total, reflecting influxes of male fishing servants during peak periods in the sedentary fishery. The numbers of women and children wintering over, however, follow a generally more even, upward course, particularly after the American Revolutionary War period, and are reflective of a more stable resident group. Because of the processes of intermarriage and assimilation, it is logical to infer that an increasing proportion of these women and children were Irish or Irish Newfoundlanders (of full or partial Irish descent). The figure shows significant increases in all sectors in the years from 1805–15 and from 1825–35; these movements correspond with the two main periods of total Irish migration to Newfoundland and are therefore highly suggestive of Irish in-migration, particularly as there was no significant increase in total English migration to Newfoundland during the same periods. Figure 3.6 also demonstrates a maturing population with sex ratios moving closer to one by the middle of the nineteenth century. (The 1857 results are skewed somewhat by the Trepassey–St. Mary's area, where there was still a relatively high male-to-female ratio of 1.56; Ferryland district, by contrast, had reached a more mature ratio of 1.17.)

A breakdown of masters, mistresses, children, male servants, and female servants in the winter population of the southern Avalon is shown in Figure 3.8. The close alignment of the numbers of masters and mistresses wintering over, with roughly corresponding variations in the line representing children, reinforces the impression of a family settlement pattern among the planter group.[55] The steady increase in this sector from the American Revolutionary War period onwards also corresponds with anecdotal evidence about the growing influx of Irish and an expansion of Irish planter society on the southern Avalon. The line representing male servants again supports anecdotal evidence about Irish immigration to the area: note, for example, the sharp increase over the period of the Seven Years' War, when the Irish began to replace English servants in significant numbers; note also the surges during the American Revolutionary

War, the period immediately following the outbreak of hostilities with France in 1793, and the latter stages of the Napoleonic Wars, when servants for the resident fishery were in particular demand. Also, by this time, significant numbers of male fishing servants were becoming long-term residents themselves. The Pole Papers of 1799–1800, for example, provide ample evidence of servants living with their families in Ferryland district. In addition, the smaller, yet still discernible, surges in the women servants' line during the Seven Years' War, the American Revolution, and the latter stages of the Napoleonic Wars also suggest that the recruitment of women as servants (either domestic or fishing) was linked to the fortunes of the resident fishery.

The increasing number of women in the area is particularly significant, for this phenomenon permitted the re-establishment of the key social, cultural, and economic unit of rural Ireland: the family.[56] This revival had significant implications for production in the fishery and the actual survival of fishing communities along the southern Avalon.

TRANSITION TO HOUSEHOLD PRODUCTION

Figure 3.8 in conjunction with Figure 3.9 provide evidence of another area in which women played a pivotal role in the establishment of early communities: the transition to the household production unit. The two figures represent inhabitants and personnel involved in the resident fishery on the southern Avalon for roughly five-year intervals during winter and summer, respectively. The critical components to observe in each figure, but particularly in the chart representing inhabitants during the summer fishing season, are the broken line representing hired male fishing servants (who initially provided the bulk of the labor in the resident fishery) and the three solid lines representing the planter family group (masters, mistresses, and children). Both figures clearly demonstrate an overwhelming reliance on hired servants in the sedentary fishery at the middle of the eighteenth century. As the migratory fishery at Newfoundland went into decline due to almost constant wartime conditions, particularly from the American Revolutionary War onwards, the resident sector moved into ascendancy in both actual and relative terms. However, this ascendant position was not reflected in an increased hiring of servants by the sedentary fishery on the southern Avalon past the early 1790s; after this point, significant numbers of servants continued to work in this sector, but never again in the same proportion to the planter group. Rather, we can observe the solid lines representing the planter family group rising to meet and subsume the plummeting broken line representing hired male servants. By 1805, the numbers of servants converged with the planter group, with numbers of male servants dropping towards the numbers of masters and mistresses. If the resident fishery had continued to rely overwhelmingly on hired labor, this convergence would not have happened. What had occurred over this period was a significant shift towards household production, in which family members took over fishing and shore work, with women assuming much of the work of shore crews—especially salting and drying, although in some cases, heading and splitting as well (see Chapter 4). At this stage, the resident fishery consisted of two types of planter groups: planters who continued to depend primarily on the labor of hired servants, and planters who hired servants in smaller numbers to reinforce the family production unit, with the latter group predominating in most areas after 1800.

The latter years of the Napoleonic War period witnessed the final decline of the migratory fishery and consolidated the position of the resident fishery. Prosperous conditions in the sedentary fishery at this time induced a final surge in the numbers of hired servants on the southern Avalon. This reflected broader trends in the Newfoundland fishery, which saw increased hiring of servants and elevated capital investment by planters during the boom created by the re-opening of fish markets, the temporary absence of French and American competition from those markets, and inflated fish prices—all in conjunction with the local development of a viable North Shore/Labrador fishery and a spring seal fishery. But in the post-war recession, the waged-labor foundation of the planter fishery was undermined as fish prices dropped while inflationary wages and provision prices persisted. Adding to the planters' dilemma was a wage and lien system, carried over from the days of the migratory fishery, in which waged servants had a first lien on a planter's fish and oil for their wages, contracted in advance and payable in full, regardless of the outcome of the fishing season; the planter's current merchant supplier had a second lien on his fish and oil. Given this combination of factors in the post-war period, numerous bankruptcies ensued, the planter fishery based on waged labor shriveled, and the resident fishery became almost fully dependent on household production. Fishing servants continued to be hired, but mostly as a supplement to family labor.[57]

There has been a tendency to view this final transition to household production in terms of opportunities lost and failure—the traditional planter fishery in retreat, forced to rely on family labor as a last resort. But the shift to a family fishery was a positive response to changing circumstances in the fishery, reflecting a more careful management of personnel and resources. Certainly, family members, with high stakes in the outcome of the season, would generally have been more reliable workers than waged labor. Granted, significant numbers of fishing servants were hired on *shares*, or were paid with a combination of wages and shares, and therefore had more of a stake in individual voyages than those receiving wages alone. But even servants on shares would not have had the same kind of long-term commitment to the enterprise, being able to contract their services elsewhere as labor demand and the fortunes of the fishery dictated. In terms of capacity, the family production unit that incorporated the extended family would certainly have matched the output of a small-scale traditional planter fishery. And it was a rational economic response to contracting market conditions (including increasing competition, shrinking demand, and declining prices) and the vagaries of the fish resource. Even the oppressive wage and lien system of the period was not the major determinant in spelling the demise of the traditional planter fishery, for it is doubtful that a planter fishery based on hired labor would have ultimately challenged the growing logic of a family production unit, given the wide fluctuations in the trade and in fish catches.

Certainly, this is the impression created by the data from the southern Avalon.[58] While good markets and high wages stimulated production and attracted large numbers of servants to the fishery, their numbers never did reach their former proportions of the eighteenth century and remained lower than the numbers of the planter family group (Figure 3.8 and Figure 3.9). By contrast, the shift to the family production unit may be detected in the steady climb of the planter family group from the 1780s onwards, and it had certainly gained considerable momentum by the turn of the nineteenth century. This transition was not set off course by the increased hiring of servants during the late Napoleonic War period; rather, family production (with some hired servants) continued and ran in tandem with the traditional planter fishery. In the post-war recession, the resident fishery was stressed and retreated to pre-boom levels. But the transition to the family production unit accelerated and solidified, while the planter fishery based on hired labor spiraled downwards and ultimately collapsed.[59] As Figures 3.8 and 3.9 demonstrate, by 1836, the number of masters had passed that of male servants for the first time, the number of mistresses had taken a dramatic upswing towards the number of male servants, and the size of the overall family group had completely overtaken the servant group, who were now mostly supplementing family labor—continuing a process that, with perhaps slight fluctuations due to briefly abnormal conditions, had been underway since the last quarter of the previous century.[60]

The two figures suggest a precipitous drop in the numbers of male servants for the years 1845 and 1857. The censuses for those years did not methodically record the number of servants in Newfoundland—an administrative decision that was, in itself, indicative of change. Indeed, Ferryland was the only district in Newfoundland to report any servants for these two years (211 and 141, respectively), and whether these were fishing or domestic servants, male or female, was not specified.

However, the 1857 census does provide evidence of a system of family production fully in place on the southern Avalon, as demonstrated by Figure 3.10.[61] When examining the figure, there are some anomalies in the census figures that must be considered. There were two categories under which people involved in the fishery could report: "Persons engaged in catching and curing fish" and "Able-bodied Seamen and Fishermen in this Colony and its Dependencies." There were obviously variations in recording under these categories, depending on the census taker. Given the distribution of numbers for the area between Bay Bulls and Lamanche, it seems likely that women were reported under the former category while men were reported under the latter; on the shore between Brigus South and Cape Race, both women and men were recorded under the former category. For the section from Cape Race lighthouse to Cape Dog, again, only the former category was used, but it seems likely, given the low numbers, that men only were recorded. (It is impossible to accept that no women in the Trepassey–St. Mary's were involved in the fishery—Colonial Office census material, anecdotal evidence, court records, and the oral tradition argue otherwise.)

Given these limitations in the record, there is still strong evidence of an almost complete shift to household production. Figure 3.10 shows those involved in the fishery in key communities as a percentage of the population between the ages of 10 and 70 (an approximation of the working population). As can be seen, participation in the fishery in some areas was extremely high, particularly in the area between Brigus South and Cape Race, where percentages ranged from 90.71 percent (Ferryland) to 102.71 percent (Cape Broyle). The low percentages for the Trepassey–St. Mary's area have already been attributed to the census-taker's idiosyncrasy. Results for Bay Bulls and Mobile also seem low and likely reflect an anomaly in recording. Nonetheless, the overall percentage of the working population on the southern Avalon reporting in these two categories was 74.19 percent. If we remove the anomalous Trepassey–St. Mary's area, the percentage climbs to 84.94 percent of the working population of the remaining communities; and if we remove the low reportings from Bay Bulls and Mobile, the percentage climbs again to 93.71 percent. The evidence of the shift to household production on the southern Avalon is overwhelming—the culmination of a process that had already gained momentum in the late eighteenth century.

CONCLUSION

The Irish women who arrived on the southern Avalon during the study period came from the southeastern counties of the home country, primarily Wexford,

Waterford, Kilkenny, and Tipperary. Like most Irish male migrants to Newfoundland, they were responding to economic recession and land shortages in Ireland and the economic lure of the Newfoundland fishery. They came out as single servants (fishing and domestic) and as members of family groups, and it was their intention to lead productive lives within their family units and the broader fishing community. These women were not passive victims of forces beyond their control; rather, they weighed the evidence before leaving Ireland and made conscious decisions that they felt would be in the best interests of themselves and their families. And, regardless of the popular refrain of eighteenth-century governors' proclamations, most did not become a charge upon the community.

Women played an integral role in early settlement of the area, for it was their presence that was key in stabilizing community populations through the late eighteenth and early nineteenth centuries. Had British authorities had their way in stemming the flow of women immigrants, the migration stream to the southern Avalon (and, indeed, the entire English Shore) would have remained largely temporary and transient, given the nature of employment in the Newfoundland fishery. As Captain Wheler had so accurately observed in the seventeenth century, "Soe longe as there comes noe women, they are not fixed." But women had come and remained; they formed a marriage pool for incoming planters and fishermen, and thus provided the basis for permanent settlement. While male fishing servants moved in and out of the southern Avalon, and from harbor to harbor within the area, women were a more permanent element in local populations. Migrant fishermen found wives or common-law partners originally among the English planter families already on the shore, but in the later decades of the eighteenth century and beyond, among increasing numbers of Irish women, especially first- and second-generation Irish Newfoundland women after the turn of the century. Matrilocality and uxorilocality were important elements of community formation as an occupational group that had remained largely transient for more than 250 years began to settle in the area.

Irish women were also instrumental in the processes of intermarriage, conversion, and assimilation that saw the English Protestant planter society of the southern Avalon almost completely subsumed by an Irish Catholic culture. Numerous English patrilines were incorporated into the Catholic population; in time, they would consider themselves as much a part of the Irish ethnic group as those who bore Irish surnames. These processes were reinforced by continuing Irish immigration, and by the end of the eighteenth century, the population of the southern Avalon was almost completely Catholic.

From the American Revolutionary War period onwards, there was a steady increase in the planter group—a group that was becoming more and more Irish as Irish in-migration increased and as the process of assimilation of the English ethnic group continued. Initial momentum for the transition to the family production unit in the fishery can also be discerned in this period. Although the resident fishery was moving into ascendancy over the dying migratory fishery, there was no corresponding surge in the hiring of fishing servants by the sedentary fishery after the 1780s, as the planter fishery based essentially on hired servants steadily gave way to a planter fishery based on family labor, with some supplemental hired labor. The Napoleonic War period saw the final stand of the former system, and its almost complete demise in the post-war recession. The transition to the family production unit continued steadily thereafter and was overwhelmingly in place on the southern Avalon by the 1857 census.

Here, then, was another essential contribution of Irish Newfoundland women to the stability of early communities on the southern Avalon. Throughout the late eighteenth and early nineteenth centuries, women increasingly took on shore work in the emerging family production unit. Particularly in the wake of the Napoleonic Wars, when the migratory fishery had all but collapsed and the traditional planter fishery was in its death throes due to depressed fish prices that could not meet inflated servant wages and provision prices, women stepped into the breach and took the place of male fishing servants in producing saltfish for market. It was just one of many ways that Irish Newfoundland women helped to sustain settlement along the southern Avalon.

NOTES

1. Taken from the observations of Father Baudoin, a Recollet priest who accompanied French forces in their campaigns out of Placentia eastwards and northwards along the English Shore in 1696 and 1697. See Alan F. Williams, *Father Baudoin's War: D'Iberville's Campaigns in Acadia and Newfoundland, 1696, 1697*, ed. Alan G. Macpherson (St. John's: Memorial University of Newfoundland, 1987), 60.

2. Naval commodores' reports on the population and fisheries for the late seventeenth and early eighteenth centuries are available at the MHA and PANL; also, from 1699 onwards, annual returns of the fisheries, inhabitants, imports, and exports of Newfoundland were forwarded to the Colonial Office each fall after the fishing season had ended and are contained in the CO 194 Series at the CNS and PANL; a nominal census of Ferryland district for 1799–1800 (the Pole Papers) is housed in MG 205 at the PANL; and *Newfoundland Population Returns*, 1836, 1845, and 1857 are available at the CNS, MHA, and PANL.

3. For example, various proclamations were issued throughout the second half of the eighteenth century and into the early decades of the nineteenth century that banned the transportation of passengers—especially artisans, fishermen, and seamen—to the

mainland without the governor's permission, indicating that the attrition of skilled workers through step-migration to the mainland was an ongoing problem. See PANL, GN 2/1/A.

4. For example, the Pole Papers list only one female servant in the district during 1799–1800, although the annual return in the CO 194 Series for 1801 (a return for 1800 is not available) indicates that there were 136 female servants in that district.

5. Handcock provides an educated guess that "women servants" included all unmarried women over fifteen years of age, although he does not explain his rationale. See W. Gordon Handcock, *Soe longe as there comes noe women: Origins of English Settlement in Newfoundland* (St. John's: Breakwater Books, 1989), 93.

6. John Mannion and W. Gordon Handcock, "The Southeast Ireland Homeland" and "The Southwest England Homeland," in *Historical Atlas of Canada*, ed. R. Louis Gentilcore, vol. 2 (Toronto: University of Toronto Press, 1983), plate 8.

7. A chart showing source counties appears in Mannion and Handcock, "Origins of the Newfoundland Population, 1836," in *Atlas*, ed. Gentilcore, vol. 2, plate 8. The precise figures were provided to me by John Mannion from his private database. Note that the boundaries of Ferryland district were not coterminous with those of my study area, for Trepassey Bay and St. Mary's Bay were not included.

8. Given the nature of the industry that attracted these emigrants and the reliance on male shore crews in the period before the transition to household production, there were fewer female than male emigrants to the area. However, given the overall lack of attention to women in the records of the day, the numbers of female emigrants would have been far greater than the limited segment represented here.

9. A number of historians of Irish emigration have noted that more than half of those who relocated from Ireland to North America before the 1820s were Protestants, particularly Ulster Presbyterians; many were small farmers and artisans who were suffering the effects of competition from large-scale agriculture and restrictions on the linen and woolen industry. See, for example: Donald H. Akenson, *Being Had: Historians, Evidence, and the Irish in North America* (Don Mills, ON: P. D. Meany, 1985); David Doyle, "The Irish in North America, 1776–1845," in *A New History of Ireland*, ed. W. E. Vaughan, vol. 5 (Oxford: Clarendon Press, 1989); David Fitzpatrick, "Emigration, 1801–70," in *New History*, ed. Vaughan, 562–622; Cecil J. Houston and William J. Smyth, "The Irish Diaspora: Emigration to the New World, 1720–1920," in *An Historical Geography of Ireland*, ed. B. J. Graham and L. J. Proudfoot (London: Academic Press, 1993), 338–65; Houston and Smyth, *Irish Emigration and Canadian Settlement: Patterns, Links, and Settlers* (Toronto: University of Toronto Press, 1990); Graeme Kirkham, "The Origins of Mass Emigration from Ireland," in *Migrations: The Irish at Home and Abroad*, ed. Richard Kearney (Dublin: Wolfhound Press, 1990), 81–90; Kerby A. Miller, *Emigrants and Exiles: Ireland and the Irish Exodus to North America* (New York: Oxford University Press, 1985); and Janet A. Nolan, "The Great Famine and Women's Emigration from Ireland," in *The Hungry Stream: Essays on Emigration and Famine*, ed. E. Margaret Crawford (Belfast: Centre for Emigration Studies, Ulster-American Folk Park, and Institute of Irish Studies, Queen's University, 1997), 61–70.

10. See, for example: MHA, MF-191, Kough Letterbook; PANL, MG 49, Sweetman Collection, box 5, Letterbook; Rev. Michael F. Howley, *Ecclesiastical History of Newfoundland* (Boston: Doyle and Whittle, 1888; reprint, Belleville, ON: Mika, 1971); Daniel W. Prowse, *A History of Newfoundland from the English, Colonial, and Foreign Records* (London: Macmillan, 1895; reprint, Belleville, ON: Mika Studio, 1972); Keith Matthews, "A History of the West of England-Newfoundland Fishery" (D.Phil. diss., Oxford University, 1968); and Harold A. Innis, *The Cod Fisheries: The Study of an International Economy*, rev. ed. (Toronto: University of Toronto Press, 1954).

11. Cormac O Grada, *Ireland: A New Economic History, 1780–1939* (Oxford: Clarendon Press, 1994).

12. See: L. A. Clarkson, "Ireland 1841: Pre-industrial or Proto-industrial; Industrializing or De-industrializing?" in *European Proto-industrialization: An Introductory Handbook*, ed. Sheilagh C. Ogilvie and Markus Cerman (Cambridge: Cambridge University Press, 1996), 67–84; Dierdre Mageean, "To Be Matched or to Move: Irish Women's Prospects in Munster," in *Peasant Maids—City Women: From the European Countryside to Urban America*, ed. Christiane Harzig (Ithaca, NY: Cornell University Press, 1997), 57–97; and Maria Luddy, *Women in Ireland, 1800–1918: A Documentary History* (Cork: Cork University Press, 1995), part 3, "Work."

13. Much anecdotal evidence from authorities on the island discusses the arrival of significant numbers of single women, as has already been seen. Passenger lists for ships arriving at Newfoundland are not readily available; usually, passenger numbers only are cited in official reports. However, newspaper notices to passengers who had not paid their fares also create an impression of significant numbers of single women traveling alone. There were sixteen women's names among the fifty-four names of passengers arriving on the brig *Joyce* from Ireland in 1809, 1810, and 1811 who had not paid fares; only two of them appeared within a surname clustering that could be taken as a family group. Similarly, of the fifty-two non-paying passengers listed from the brig *Good Intent* from Waterford in 1817, six were women, but none were clustered with other family members. See PANL, Mildred Howard Collection (citing the *Royal Gazette and Newfoundland Advertiser*, 30 July 1812 and 14 October 1817). Granted, some of these women may have traveled with family members whose fares had already been paid, but surely many were single travelers. Their situation can be contrasted with the sixty-two women on board the brig *Thomas Farrell* out of Ross and bound for Quebec, of whom three-quarters were traveling within family groups. See Cyril Byrne, "The Brig *Thomas Farrell*," *An Nasc* 4, no. 1 (winter 1991): 6–7.

14. HE, Ferryland, correspondence with author, 8 March 1999.

15. Although I have encountered references to women's shipping papers in the court records of the area, I have not found any surviving contracts signed by women. The following is a shipping paper signed by a shoreman for Sweetman's and likely provides a rough equivalent in terms of wording:

> I hereby engage to serve R. F. Sweetman on order from the date hereof until the 20th October as an Able Shoreman Engaging to do every thing else in my power for my

Employers Interest & the good of the voyage agreeably to the custom of the fishery In consideration of my services well & duly performed without hinderance or neglect I am to be paid as Wages the Sum of Sixteen pounds Currency

My Wages to rate from 1st May next my diet being an equivalent for my labor the winter

Placenta 22 November 1839
his
Peter X Connors
mark

See PANL, MG 49, Sweetman Collection, box 1, file 59.

16. PANL, GN 5/4/C/1, Ferryland, box 1, 43, *Elizabeth Cullen v. James Shortall*, [26 September?] 1787.

17. The fact that Edward Kough (see Chapter 2) was transporting women on bail with securities on both sides of the Atlantic implies that the system was still in place in 1825, for some of these women likely had prospective employers in Newfoundland who had shipped them "on order" and stood security for their fares.

18. Not all vessel owners in the passenger trade required securities in both Ireland and Newfoundland for passengers traveling on bond. While stationed at Newfoundland ca. 1813, Royal Navy Lieutenant Edward Chappell, of the *HMS Rosamond*, noted that significant numbers of fishing servants traveled on speculation with securities only in Ireland, hoping to find employment on arrival. This may have been a more common practice with male servants, however, as their likelihood of readily finding employment in the fishery was greater than that of women, and hence the risk for vessel owners was lower. Also, Chappell's account was written during the boom period of the Napoleonic Wars, when work was plentiful, and may not have been representative of other time periods. See Chappell, *Voyage of the Rosamond to Newfoundland and the Southern Coast of Labrador* (London: n.p., 1818), 218–22.

19. A *common-law* relationship was one in which a man and woman were not married by a religious, civil, or informal ceremony, but were cohabiting and having a sexual relationship as if they were husband and wife. Common-law relationships had no legal status during the study period and were deemed a "civil inconvenience" by central authorities because they deviated from a moral order that bolstered a patriarchal system of property inheritance. See Linda Cullum and Maeve Baird, "'A Woman's Lot': Women and Law in Newfoundland from Early Settlement to the Twentieth Century," in *Pursuing Equality: Historical Perspectives on Women in Newfoundland and Labrador*, ed. Linda Kealey, Social and Economic Papers, no. 20 (St. John's: ISER, 1993), 119. Court records, census material, and early missionaries' writings indicate that common-law relationships and informal marriages were not uncommon in the area, certainly up to the early 1800s (see Chapter 8).

20. The oral tradition provides the most romantic variation on this theme: Julia, the daughter of a wealthy Irish lord, renounced family name and fortune and eloped

in the early 1800s with her father's stableboy/footman, named Ryan; they came to the southern Avalon—possibly to Caplin Bay (now Calvert) or Trepassey—to pursue the fishery. The story of "Lady Julia Ryan" is particularly intriguing to me because Julia Ryan was the name of my maternal grandmother and great-grandmother, both of Caplin Bay.

21. PANL, MG 49, Sweetman Collection, box 4, file 16, James Whelan to R. F. Sweetman, 30 October 1830.

22. See, for example, PANL, MG 49, Sweetman Collection: box 3, file 55, Capt. David Doody to Mrs. Brownrigg re: wages of Michael Mahoney to be paid to his wife, Betsy Mahoney, February 17, 1837; and box 4, file 20, Peter Carew to R. F. Sweetman re: effects of son John received by daughter Mary, February 16, 1835.

23. This pattern diverges somewhat from the one described by Handcock in relation to early English settlement in Newfoundland. Handcock says that English sailors and servants tended to marry "local women," while men of status or rank tended to bring their wives out with them. See Handcock, *Soe longe*. While most Irish male fishing servants also found wives among women residing in Newfoundland, particularly from the latter Napoleonic War period onwards, a smaller but significant number of male servants in earlier years were accompanied from Ireland by wives and young families. This was not unusual in the Irish context, for the emigration of women in family groups was actually the most common pattern of female emigration in pre-famine Ireland, and markedly so up to the 1820s. See Nolan, "Great Famine and Women's Emigration," 63.

24. James Joseph O'Brien, "Cape Broyle, 1959–60," unpublished community history (1960); and O'Brien, "Cape Broyle," unpublished chronicle of the old families of Cape Broyle (1971). While O'Brien identifies the Grants as Tipperary natives, oral informant HE, from Ferryland, says that the Grants might have been English Protestant Loyalists who immigrated to Newfoundland after the American Revolution; but she has also heard that they were Irish. E. R. Seary says that the name could be English, Irish, or Scottish. See Seary with Sheila Lynch, *Family Names of the Island of Newfoundland*, rev. ed. (St. John's: Memorial University of Newfoundland, 1984), 200–201.

25. PANL, GN 2/1/A, vol. 5, 195, Grant to John Welsh and John Sullivan, 19 October 1774.

26. This family chronicle is a composite of information from: O'Brien, "Cape Broyle" (1960) and "Cape Broyle" (1971); PANL, MG 205, Pole Papers, 1799–1800; PANL, GN 2/1/A, vol. 5, 195, Grant to John Welsh and John Sullivan, 19 October 1774; and Mannion Name File, Cape Broyle, "Bryan" (various).

27. See: PANL, MG 205, Pole Papers, 1799–1800; and O'Brien, "Cape Broyle" (1960) and "Cape Broyle" (1971).

28. See: O'Brien, "Cape Broyle" (1960) and "Cape Broyle" (1971); also, James Joseph O'Brien, "Leahy Family" (unpublished and untitled notes on the Leahy family at Cape Broyle, [1971?]).

29. O'Brien, "Cape Broyle" (1960) and "Cape Broyle" (1971).

30. PANL, MG 205, Pole Papers, 1799–1800.

31. Aaron Thomas, *The Newfoundland Journal of Aaron Thomas*, ed. Jean M. Murray (London: Longmans, Green, 1968), 155. Thomas was a seaman with the Royal Navy and was serving on the HMS Boston in 1794 when it was assigned as a convoy ship to Newfoundland.

32. PANL, MG 205, Pole Papers, 1799–1800.

33. See: Lorraine Hawco, "Ledwell [family surname], Calvert, Caplin Bay," MHA, 43-B-1-47, Geography 2000 Collection, [early 1970s]; FMDB, file 03B, Swain family, and file 015B, Sullivan family; and Calvert Come Home Year Committee, "From Caplin Bay, 1920 to Calvert, 1995" (Calvert: Calvert Come Home Year Committee, 1995), 9. Also, EW, interview by author, Calvert, 21 July 1999.

34. O'Brien, "Cape Broyle" (1960) and "Cape Broyle" (1971); also James Joseph O'Brien, "The Oldridge Family" (unpublished notes on the Oldridge family at Cape Broyle, [1971?]).

35. See: Mannion Name File, Brigus South, "Henley, Catherine"; and PANL, GN 5/2/C/1, Administration of Estate of Catherine Henley, 10 September and 2 March 1830.

36. The incidence of such family groupings is far too high to warrant an explanation that all these children were orphans taken in by local families. The lack of overlapping in children's ages within the family groupings also suggests that these were children born of consecutive relationships rather than mixtures of orphans and biological children, which surely would have exhibited some age convergences (see Chapter 8 for further discussion).

37. Neither of these lists from the Pole Papers is exhaustive.

38. Cyril J. Byrne, ed., *Gentlemen-Bishops and Faction Fighters: The Letters of Bishops O Donel, Lambert, Scallan, and Other Irish Missionaries* (St. John's: Jesperson Press, 1984), 105–6, Father Phelan at Waterford to Archbishop Troy of Dublin, 4 February 1788. See also: PANL, GN 2/1/A, vol. 6, 149–53, Governor John Montagu, Grant to Catherine Weston and daughters Catherine and Sarah, 26 September 1776; and PANL, GN 5/4/C/1, Ferryland, box 1, Catherine Weston v. William and Hannah McDaniel, 8 March and 5 October 1787, and 17 August, 15 September, and 15 October 1790.

39. Mannion Name File, Fermeuse, "Neill" (various, citing PANL: GN 5/2/A/9, 14 and 26 October 1810; and GN 5/2/A/1, 8 December 1828 and 5 January 1829).

40. O'Brien, "Cape Broyle" (1960) and "Cape Broyle" (1971). Also, NNSF, interview by author, Cape Broyle, 1972.

41. Derived from various parish records for the southern Avalon, Mannion Name File Collection, and various O'Brien writings cited above. This list is not exhaustive.

42. Handcock, *Soe longe*.

43. Francis Corrigan, "The Ryans of Biscay Bay (1850—1970): A Study of Settlement," MHA, 43-A-1-42, Geography 2000 Collection, [early 1970s], 3–7. Some of the details were also confirmed by EW, interview by author, Calvert, 21 July 1999.

44. Derived from various parish records for the southern Avalon, Mannion Name File Collection, and various O'Brien writings already cited. Again, this list is not exhaustive.

45. Today, the area has been dubbed the "Irish Loop," for better or for worse, by government road signage and tourist information. Residents pride themselves on living in the most Irish corner of Newfoundland. Families that bear English surnames consider themselves as much a part of the Irish ethnic group as those that bear Irish surnames. Indeed, until recently, many were not aware of their partial English Protestant ancestry, although there is a growing awareness of mixed lineages, particularly among younger generations.

46. Byrne, ed., *Gentlemen-Bishops*, 140–42, Father Thomas Ewer to Archbishop Troy, Dublin, 20 September 1796.

47. PANL, MG 598, SPG Collection, C Series, box 1A/18 (Nova Scotia and Newfoundland), 180, Rev. John Dingle to Rev. Doctor Morris, Secretary to the SPG, 22 November 1801.

48. PANL, MG 598, SPG Collection, E Series, Report on the Diocese of Newfoundland, Mission of Ferryland, 1845.

49. PANL, MG 598, SPG Collection, C Series, box 1 (Newfoundland), 56, petition of the Inhabitants of Bay Bulls for a clergyman, 19 October 1773. Also contained in SPG Collection, D Series.

50. PANL, MG 598, SPG Collection, G Series, vol. 1, 9–10, Bishop Aubrey Spencer to Rev. A. M. Campbell, 22 June 1842. Spencer did not indicate how few were the "sheep in the wilderness" in Ferryland, but in 1826, the clergyman stationed there, Rev. Charles Blackburn, had indicated that the Protestant population numbered only 129. See PANL, GN 2/2, vol. 1, 49–50, Blackman to Edmund. B. Brenton, Colonial Secretary, 6 November 1826.

51. PANL, MG 598, SPG Collection, G Series, vol. 1, 159, Bishop Edward Feild to Rev. Ernest Hawkins, November 1845.

52. Monsignor Michael Fleming, *Report of the Catholic Mission in Newfoundland in North America*, submitted to the Cardinal Prefect of Propaganda (Rome: Printing Press of the Sacred Congregation, 1837), 39. Copy at the RCAASJ, Fleming Papers, 103/26.

53. Michael Anthony Fleming, "The State of the Catholic Religion in Newfoundland Reviewed in Two Letters by Monsignor Fleming to Rev. P. John Spratt" (Rome, 1836), 91. Copy at the RCAASJ, Fleming Papers, 103/26. Also, Fleming, *Report*, 39.

54. Anglican parish records for Ferryland district, extant from 1823 onwards, registered the occupations of fathers in baptismal entries until the incoming minister in 1855 stopped recording this information. The occupational profile for Anglican fathers in the district between 1823 and 1855 was: 3 clergymen; 19 merchants or merchant/planters; 2 merchants/sub-collectors of customs; 1 merchant/naval lieutenant; 7 masters of merchant vessels; 1 master of merchant vessel/merchant; 1 master of merchant vessel/planter; 3 planters; 1 mercantile agent; 1 gentleman; 4 carpenters; 1 sail-maker; 1 blacksmith; 1 laborer/mason; 1 laborer; 12 fishermen; 3 not given. Intriguingly, no fishermen fathers were listed before the mid-1830s, and all but two baptisms in this group occurred in the 1840s and beyond. See PANL, Church of England Parish Records, Petty Harbor Parish, Ferryland District, box 2, Baptisms, 1823–55.

55. One exception—a larger peak in the numbers of masters in 1815—corresponds with extremely prosperous conditions in the resident fishery. A significant number of single men (or at least men without families in Newfoundland), having earned high wages as servants, may have tried their fortunes as planter fishermen during this period.

56. Campbell discusses the family-centered nature of eighteenth- and nineteenth-century rural Irish society—both the conjugal unit and the extended kinship network with its physical manifestation, the *clachan* (the traditional clustering of families in which kinship ties defined community boundaries and property was communally owned and rotated in a system known as *rundale*). Campbell observes: "The family was of crucial importance in Irish rural society, not only as the primary economic unit of rural production, but also as the foundation of cultural continuity, social stability and support." See Maclolm Campbell, *The Kingdom of the Ryans: The Irish in Southwest New South Wales, 1816–1890* (Sydney: University of New South Wales Press, 1997), 112–13. By contrast, Kevin O'Neill sees family formation as having decreasing relevance in pre-famine Ireland, arguing that declining opportunities caused a decrease in the labor demand/supply ratio, which actually discouraged family formation and led to increased emigration, particularly among farm laborers and smaller and larger farming households; only middling farming families remained relatively unaffected by the dictates of inheritance practices and the vagaries of employment demands in determining family growth. For the rest, reduced or delayed family formation was a means of population control in the face of demographic and economic pressures. O'Neill provides a very detailed and carefully researched analysis of the specific demographic responses of different household types to economic change in Ireland. However, the economic reductionism of his "market impulsion model" does not measure the social impact of these forces on Irish families and communities and does not satisfactorily address the cultural importance of family in Irish rural society or the impetus to establish or re-establish families after emigration. See Kevin O'Neill, *Family and Farm in Pre-famine Ireland: The Parish of Killashandra* (Madison: The University of Wisconsin Press, 1984). For a detailed description of rundale, see Robert James Scally, *The End of Hidden Ireland: Rebellion, Famine, and Emigration* (New York: Oxford University Press, 1995).

57. See, for example: Sean Cadigan, *Hope and Deception in Conception Bay: Merchant-Settler Relations in Newfoundland, 1785–1855* (Toronto: University of Toronto Press, 1995), particularly Parts 2 and 3; Matthews, "West of England-Newfoundland Fishery"; and Shannon Ryan, "Fishery to Colony: A Newfoundland Watershed, 1793–1815," *Acadiensis* 12, no. 2 (spring 1983): 34–52.

58. Regional variations in economic development must be kept in mind. There was no southern Avalon involvement in the North Shore/Labrador fishery, and very limited participation in the sealing industry. There was, however, a significant banking fleet.

59. It did not disappear completely. The merchant firm Goodridge's at Renews, for example, was still hiring labor for fishing and curing on a large scale by the end of the study period.

60. This transition from the late eighteenth century is supported by sporadic anecdotal evidence from the period. Head, for example, cites the "First Report on the State of Trade to Newfoundland" (Great Britain, House of Commons) as evidence that most planters were using family labor in the fishery by the end of the eighteenth century, with women and children processing the catch. See C. Grant Head, *Eighteenth Century Newfoundland* (Toronto: McClelland and Stewart, in association with the Institute of Canadian Studies, Carleton University, 1976), 218. Sweetman's were noting through the 1790s the inability of planters to meet the inflationary wage demands of fishing servants, and were complaining by 1804 that there were insufficient shore crews to split, salt, and dry fish on shore. "From the very great Scarcity of men, both with me and planters," M. Sweetman wrote to the firm's principals, "we have not been able to get a Fish in *pile* as yet." A shift to family production was implied in such observations. See PANL, MG-49, Sweetman Collection, box 5, Letterbook: James Downey, agent, to Saunders and Sweetman, 29 August and 4 and 5 October 1792; and M. Sweetman to Saunders and Sweetman, 15 June and 14 July 1804. In 1819, Lewis Anspach, an Anglican missionary in Conception Bay (but writing about Newfoundland in general), noted the participation of women in the curing process. See Rev. Lewis A. Anspach, *A History of the Island of Newfoundland* (London: Anspach, 1819), 468. In 1838, American observer Ephraim W. Tucker was impressed by the skill of women in processing fish on the Labrador coast, and wrote: "At the fish stands, while the cod fishery is in the full tide of operation, the women are seen among the most constant and dextrous in dressing the fish, thrown up by the fishermen. Some of these females will dress two or three thousand fish in a single day." See Beth Light and Alison Prentice, eds., *Pioneer and Gentlewomen of British North America 1713–1867*, Documents in Canadian Women's History, vol. 1 (Toronto: New Hogtown Press, 1980), 58–9, citing Tucker, *Five Months in Labrador and Newfoundland During the Summer of 1838* (Concord, 1839), 119–20. And Norwegian fisheries investigator Peter Stuwitz observed that women and children were involved in processing fish in the St. Mary's Bay area in 1840. See Helge W. Nordvik and Lewis R. Fischer, "Peter M. Stuwitz and the Newfoundland Inshore Fishery in 1840," *Newfoundland Studies* 1, no. 2 (fall 1985): 129–40, particularly 135 and 138.

61. A similar figure cannot be attempted for the 1845 census year as there were profound problems in terms of reporting those involved in the fishery. The 1845 census contained a category "Planters, Fishermen, and Shoremen," but the reported numbers were very low, not accounting for even half the adult male population; for some communities, none were recorded under this category at all. Given that the cod fishery was the staple industry in the area, these recordings were obviously flawed.

4. "A GOOD, HARD-WORKING STUMP OF A GIRL"

Irish Women's Work and the Construction of Identity on the Southern Avalon

Irish women from the more moderate climate of southeast Ireland found themselves in somewhat altered circumstances in terms of work routines in Newfoundland. Witness the following account from the travel musings of Aaron Thomas while visiting the island in 1794–95:

> Do you know that in this Country, in the Winter time, a girl can Milke a Cow into her Apron and carry the Milke home in it? If she Milkes the Cow in the open air the intensity of the weather will freeze the Milke as it falls from the Cow into the Apron and [it will] remain there, a hard, conglutinated, frozen mass, until melted by heat.[1]

Even allowing for Thomas's stylistic leaning towards occasional hyperbole, it is certain that Irish immigrant women would have had to modulate their skills and work rhythms to harmonize with a fishing and subsistence farming economy on the southern Avalon. Still, they also found themselves far removed from the congested farmlands of the home country, in a place where they and their families could occupy property for fishing and subsistence agriculture with minimal interference and move freely through woods and meadows, gleaning firewood and foraging for local plants and berries—a place where the game in the forests and fish in the streams were available to all comers.

As these women adapted to a new physical and socioeconomic environment, they assumed vital roles within the division of labor in early fishing settlements, and this understanding of women's place within the work cycle contributed significantly to the configuration of self-identity and the construction of Irish womanhood within the Irish plebeian community. The feminine ideal that boarded the ship in the home country and thrived within the context of immigration and early settlement was that of "a good, hard-working stump of a girl."[2]

HOUSEHOLD PRODUCTION

Transient fishermen and shoremen had made up the primary work crews of the early Newfoundland fishery in both its migratory and sedentary sectors. But by the mid-1700s, the evolution of the family work unit in the planter fishery had begun, and the momentum of this transition increased through the end of the eighteenth century and into the nineteenth. Household production became essential to survival in both the fishery and subsistence agriculture, and men and women followed the rhythms of complementary work routines. These rhythms were grounded primarily in efficiency and pragmatism rather than rigid perceptions of men's and women's work.[3]

COD FISHERY

One of the greatest adaptations required of Irish immigrants to the area was the shift from an agricultural base to a fishing economy. The cod fishery was the primary industry of the island, and the mainstay of the local economy on the southern Avalon during the eighteenth and nineteenth centuries. By contrast, Ireland, although also surrounded by the sea, had not developed a significant fishing industry outside a small-scale effort on the west coast.[4] Most immigrants from the southeast of Ireland, then, would have had to learn a new set of skills to earn their livelihood in Newfoundland. For a number of men, the transition was gradual, coming out to Newfoundland on a migratory basis as youngsters, gaining experience as they found a niche within the ranks of shore and boat crews,[5] and ultimately making the decision to remain. But women tended to be permanent immigrants, and thus they were pitched headlong into this new form of enterprise with little preparation or training. Their capacity to adjust quickly to fishing production was a critical aspect of adaptation to life in the New World and a vital contribution to the success of the settlement process.[6]

Some women, primarily widows, became fishing employers or household heads who operated fishing premises in their own right.[7] This was signified, for example, in a notice issued by Ferryland magistrate Robert Carter in 1787 that fishing servants were not to be served liquor, "unless it be by and with the Consent of his *Master or Mistress* in writing";[8] the implication was that women were employing servants in the industry, not just in their capacity as wives in planter households (in which case, under the principle of coverture, the consent of the "Master" would have been sufficient), but under the status of *feme sole*.[9] Indeed, a number of these women were mentioned by name in the records. In August, 1768, for example, Governor Palliser ordered the magistrate at Ferryland to tax twenty-four persons in the district who had kept dieters the previous winter, "as the entertaining [of] Idle People, is the cause of all disorders and mischiefs in this Country." Listed among the employers was Mary Shea, who had housed three dieters over the winter (slightly more than the average of 2.75 and the median of two hired by the total group); her fine totaled £1.2.6 (7s. 6d. per servant), and in default of payment, fish and oil of equal value were to be seized.[10] Five years later, the same Mary Shea was granted a fishing room on the northwest side of Ferryland harbor, which had already been in her possession for a number of years, "to quietly and peaceably possess the same so long as you shall employ it to the advantage of the Fishery."[11]

In 1775, Alice Thomas, a fishing employer at Renews, was sued by two fishing servants for their wages; Alice had assumed control of the premises after the death of her planter husband, Thomas.[12] Similarly, Catharine Clements was the proprietor of a fishing premises and fishing employer in Renews in the 1780s and 1790s, having also taken over the management of the premises at her husband's death.[13] Case File 2 In 1794, Jane Holly was one of several boatkeepers in Ferryland district entangled in a dispute between a former and current fishing supplier.[14] In the 1820s, Ann Ryan rented a fishing room and premises in Caplin Bay—including stages, flakes, beaches, dwelling house, gardens, and lands—from Philip Tree for £6 per year.[15] The rent of a fishing room was charged against the account of Mary Row of Renews in the Goodridge ledgers in 1839 and 1841.[16]

The names of several women—Sarah McCarthy, Mary Murphy, Dorothy Cantwell, Mary Morris, Widow Blanch (and Son)—appeared in the Sweetman ledgers for the 1820s and 1830s with credit entries for fish and oil, indicating that they were either fishing employers or heads of family production units.[17] Catherine Kenny and Sons also produced fish and oil that they sold to the Goodridge's Fermeuse establishment in 1840 and 1841.[18] Other family ventures in Renews operating under the names of "Rachel Welsh and Son"[19] and "Elizabeth Beaves and Son"[20] were most likely fishing production units as well. Furthermore, liquor licensees in the eighteenth and early nineteenth centuries were required to operate at least one fishing shallop in the fishery, so by inference, any female licensees were also boatkeepers (see section on hospitality trade, below). And these are just the women's names that have survived in the written record; they likely do not constitute an exhaustive list of all women who operated fishing premises as *femes sole* in the period.

Certainly, however, a far greater number of women managed fishing plantations with their husbands or common-law partners, with the responsibility of boarding fishing servants and dieters added to their other household and subsistence duties. And increasingly, plebeian women participated in processing fish in family production units, replacing the hired, transient, primarily male shore crews of the traditional planter fishery. As noted in the previous chapter, this assumption of shore work occurred at a critical juncture in the fishery. Without women's presence and their capacity to adapt their routines to include this additional, labor-intensive work on flakes, the beleaguered planter fishery would have been hard pressed to survive the roller-coaster effects of the French-Revolutionary and Napoleonic War periods and, more particularly, the recession that followed.

Most women who worked in family units were primarily involved in *making fish*, curing and drying the cod on shore. After the fish was headed, gutted, and split (operations usually, but not exclusively, performed by men), men or women carried away the fish in *barras* for salting. Larger fish were laid in *saltbulk* while smaller fish were pickled in puncheon tubs. After about five days, the fish was washed, again by men or women or both, using water drawn from the ocean in large tubs. They then loaded the fish (at this stage, called *waterhorse*) on barras and transported it over rocky shorelines and hills, sometimes even over steep cliff faces, to a flake or a beach for drying. This required considerable strength, given the heaviness of the *green* salted fish, but it was not unusual for women as well as men to carry barras.[21] At this point, the women's work began in earnest. Every morning (weather permitting), the fish were spread flesh-side up for drying; in the evening, the fish were gathered up in *yaffles*, or armfuls, and turned skin-side up in small piles called *faggots*. Throughout the process, women had to guard against fly-blows, waving away flies with boughs to prevent them from landing on the fish, or scrubbing away *fly-spit* containing eggs that would hatch into maggots and spoil the cure (see Audio Sample No. 36). As the fish became drier through respreading, the size of the faggots was increased until the fish could be placed in *piles*. When almost completely dried, the fish was laid in small bulks in a fish *store*; and after several more dryings on the flake, it was piled in larger bulks in the store, ready for shipping to market.

Women's skill and judgment were critical throughout this process, for if the fish did not contain the right amount of salt or moisture for its intended market, the quality was ruined. Also, as more and more fish was processed, various stacks would be at different stages of drying, requiring good organizational skills and a careful eye to detail. An examination of the relatively high wages paid to hired shore crew (see Table 4.1)—and, arguably, some women performed the equivalent supervisory duties of a *master of the voyage*—demonstrates the monetary value, and hence the importance, assigned to this work by the industry. Thus, while women did not receive wages within the family production unit, the intrinsic value of their processing work to the household was considerable. Of course, making fish had to be juggled with childcare and housework as well as other outdoor work (notably, weeding, milking, berry-picking, and haymaking). And if a rain shower threatened during the daily drying process, women had to drop anything else they were doing and run to the flakes to cover the fish with long strips of dried tree bark, kept in place by a network of boughs and rocks (see Audio Sample No. 9). Indeed, while all duties had to be balanced efficiently, none was to take priority over making the fish properly. As one elderly Cape Broyle woman observed, "If the fish wasn't spread when the men came in [from the water], there'd be some racket."[22]

In peak periods, when fish were plentiful, women worked at the fish through the night along with the men. At such times, it was not uncommon to find women on the stage involved in the pre-drying stages of processing. Some women helped the men *prong* the fish from boat to *stagehead*. More commonly, women *pewed* the cod through the open windows onto the cutting table; skill and precision were required to stab the fish in the head only, for fish that was *broken*, or damaged in the body, brought a lower price. Women also assisted in splitting fish—again, a stage that required care and dexterity to protect the quality of the finished product (note in Table 4.1 the high wages paid to hired splitters, signifying the value of this work). And a woman who was proficient at cutting cod tongues and *sculps* for local consumption was a highly regarded worker as well. But while fishing was seen solely as men's work, and women who worked at the earlier cutting and splitting stages were usually deemed to be "helping the men" (except those few women who did this work on a regular basis), making fish came to be considered within fishing families an integral part of women's work. In the eyes of the local plebeian community, women were not merely helping on the flakes and beaches; rather, "Women made fish along with the men."[23] Indeed, in peak catching periods, the curing of fish became almost exclusively the preserve of women, assisted by older children.

Furthermore, although the work performed by Irish Newfoundland women in the fishery was difficult in terms of physical labor and time management, these women did not view the task as drudgery. Indeed, according to twentieth-century informants who had split and made fish themselves, women "loved to be out at it."[24] Many women hired domestic servants (commonly called *shipped girls*) not just to help with household routines, but to "free" them from their housework so that they could join the men on the stage and flake. Others relied on older daughters or grandmothers to supervise the household and younger children in their absence, and it was not uncommon for a nursing infant to be breast-fed on the stage or flake and then settled away in a sawed-off puncheon tub while the mother worked on. Nor was the "respectability" of these women at issue. Women saw it as their right to participate in a family enterprise in which they held an equal stake, and they took pride in their capacity to contribute to the process. At the same time, the value and dignity of their work was acknowledged by the larger community. The perception of these women as essential, skilled workers in the fishery was an integral part of their own self-image and of the construction of womanhood within the plebeian community in general.[25]

SUBSISTENCE AGRICULTURE

While saltfish production was a new venture for Irish immigrant women, many would have been quite comfortable with the performance of agricultural work. Still, adjustments had to be made in adapting to their new environment, even if they were not quite as dramatic as diarist Aaron Thomas implied. Most certainly, Irish immigrants encountered less fertile soil conditions and a less temperate climate, with later springs, hotter summers, and much harsher winters than in their home counties in southeastern Ireland. With poor soil and a short growing season, there was very little development of commercialized agriculture on the island, and thus the small-scale farming or agricultural laboring backgrounds of many Irish immigrants were refocused on subsistence agriculture to support fishing incomes.

Some adjustments also had to be made in terms of produce, although there was a good deal of continuity as well as change. The potato had been introduced to Newfoundland by the middle of the eighteenth century,[26] before the major influx of Irish to the island, and grew well in local conditions. However, the potato was not as large a feature of the pre-famine Irish diet in the home country as historians once believed. Granted, the diet of cottiers and landless laborers was rather monotonous, although still nutritious, with staples of potatoes, milk, eggs, and fish until dependence on the potato increased in the decades before the famine. But outside this class, the Irish ate a varied diet, including meat (pork/bacon, mutton, some beef), milk and its by-products, cereals and grains (bread, porridge, stir-about, oatcakes), potatoes, peas, beans, cabbage, fish, fowl, and eggs.[27] Most of these items were available to the Irish in

Newfoundland either through their own production efforts or from their supplying merchants. The greatest shift in diet was a decreased dependence on cereals and grains, which could not be supported by the local climate (although imported flour and hard bread were available) and a greater dependence on root crops (not just potatoes, but carrots, turnips, and parsnips) that could more readily survive the peculiarities of the Newfoundland growing season.

Some efforts were made to stimulate local agriculture in the late eighteenth and early nineteenth centuries, but despite the increasing acreage of cleared land (much of it for meadows), the island remained dependent on outside supplies of many foodstuffs.[28] Because of this, there is a tendency in the literature to be somewhat dismissive of farming efforts along the English Shore. But subsistence agriculture did help to support growing populations in local communities, complementing the predominantly salted or dried provisions purchased on credit from the merchant (usually salt pork and beef, flour, tea, butter, molasses, dried peas, and rum) by providing a reasonable variety of fresh produce, meat, eggs, butter, cream, and milk for local consumption. Furthermore, subsistence production cushioned the impact of variations in provision prices and supplies from year to year, and helped to mitigate the hardship of bad fishing seasons.[29] Women on the southern Avalon contributed significantly to this effort, often in less than ideal circumstances, working to ensure the survival of families and communities.

Gardens and fields: Members of the plebeian household shared the work of preparing and maintaining vegetable gardens: some near the house, some in back meadows. Indeed, spring planting and fall harvesting were cooperative affairs, with men's and women's efforts complementing each other. In the earliest period of settlement, both men and women engaged in the heavy physical labor of clearing land, stone-picking, digging and fertilizing gardens, trenching potatoes, and harvesting vegetables. Indeed, one oral informant told of women pulling plows in the "old days,"[30] although spade and hoe agriculture was likely the predominant form of ground preparation through most of the period under discussion. Still, labor-intensive farming methods were hardly strange to women who had hailed from farming areas in Ireland, where genteel observers of the eighteenth and early nineteenth centuries were horrified at the physical nature of women's agricultural labor. One shocked Englishman noted in 1812:

> Females in Ireland are treated more like beast[s] of burden than rational beings, and although I never saw anyone yoked to a plough . . . I have seen them degraded in a manner disgraceful to the other sex and shocking to humanity. In the country, they are subjected to all the drudgery generally performed by men; setting potatoes, digging turf and the performance of the most laborious occupations.[31]

But women's work—often hard physical labor—was essential in family agricultural enterprises, ranging from the cottier's potato plots to the small, semi-subsistence farms that were a common feature of the pre-famine Irish countryside.[32] Rural Irish families could ill afford to defer to the sensibilities of middle-class observers. Similarly, the Irish plebeian community on the southern Avalon had not yet absorbed gender ideologies that designated women as the "weaker" or "gentler" sex. Women's farm labor was part of a comprehensive package of survival skills that they brought to all family enterprises.

As families on the southern Avalon became more established and grew in size, however, men tended to assume tasks in the gardens that required greater physical strength—digging and trenching, for example—although this was certainly not a hard and fast rule, with women continuing to participate on an as-needed basis (for example, in the case of male absence or of a small family with no extended kinship networks). Otherwise, women were generally responsible for setting vegetables, transplanting cabbage, fertilizing, thinning out crops, and weeding through the growing season, as well as harvesting greens and gathering up the root vegetables that had been dug by the men in the fall. Still, this was hard physical labor, and sometimes unpleasant by current standards: spreading cods heads between the transplanted cabbages, for example, or stable manure and caplin on potatoes as the men followed behind, trenching and covering the fertilized seeds or plants with soil, were hardly tasks for those fastidious in nature. In the early days of settlement, women may also have been involved in a practice that was common in coastal areas of Ireland: carrying seaweed on their backs from the shore to gardens for fertilizing.[33] Certainly, one of women's most specialized tasks on the southern Avalon was *growing seeds*—that is, sowing and nurturing seedling plants—and they took pride and care in doing so because strong seedlings ensured the harvest. Some women developed reputations for consistently producing good plants that were sought by others for their own gardens—a source of status in communities that lived so close to the margin.

Aside from larger gardens, every family also tended a kitchen garden. The kitchen garden supplied "a little bit of everything"[34]: some root crops, cabbage, beets, peas, rhubarb, hops, black currants, gooseberries, strawberries, flowers, and plum and apple trees. Men helped to prepare the beds in the spring of the year, digging furrows while women set their seeds. Thereafter, however, the kitchen garden became a woman's preserve in terms of both responsibility and usage.

Haymaking, by contrast, involved the entire household, although the actual curing was in the women's care. When the long grass in meadows had grown to a foot or more, the men cut it with scythes and left it in swathes overnight. The task of spreading and drying the hay was performed by women, assisted by older children, not because it was secondary in importance, but because it had to be done in daylight, when the men were fishing. The women *turned out*, or spread, the grass in the morning, turned it again later in the day, and then pronged it into cocks and left it overnight. As with the process of drying fish, the piles were initially small while the grass was green to deter rot, but steadily increased in size as the hay dried. The spreading and cocking process was repeated until the grass was sufficiently dry for storing in the family's stable loft. Men and women carried hay from meadows near the stable on their backs, in hay-cloths made of brin bags. Hay from back meadows was transported on *hay-frames* (trellis-like structures drawn by horse and cart). Men and women pronged the hay into stable lofts, where children compacted the dried grass by jumping into the piles and then stowed it as tightly as possible into every available nook and cranny to maximize storage.

Overall, work routines in the gardens were generally dictated by expedience and availability. Men and women worked together in the spring and fall at planting and harvesting, but in the summer, when men spent most of the day fishing, women assumed the greater responsibility for the gardens. Physical strength determined to some extent the division of labor after families had become more established, but women did perform hard physical work and were capable of taking over men's duties when needed.

Animal husbandry: Plebeian families on the southern Avalon kept a variety of livestock—sheep, chickens, cows, horses, pigs, and, to a lesser extent, goats—to meet household requirements for food and clothing. Of course, the number and type of animals varied with the affluence of the household, and some poorer households had none at all, but local networks of exchange (some eggs traded for butter, for example, or some cabbage seeds for wool), third-party transactions through the merchant, or even a neighbor's charity could often compensate for a lack.

Again, the rota of duties associated with men and women meshed with other work rhythms. Men were responsible for stabling and feeding animals during the winter. In the summer, horses were let out into meadows to graze, and cows, sheep, and goats ranged freely through the community. However, the family cow(s) had to be milked morning and night, and therefore had to be rounded up every evening; and as the men were usually occupied with fishing at the critical period, it was women's responsibility to locate the animals, which had sometimes roamed over a mile away, and bring them home for milking before joining their menfolk on the stages and flakes. Milking cows and goats was mostly done by women, regardless of the season, and the milk was used mainly for household purposes.

The family's hens, housed near the stable and within close range of the house, were also primarily the responsibility of women throughout the year. Women fed them twice a day (usually household scraps or a mash of boiled vegetables) and gathered eggs each morning. Both women and men slaughtered chickens for the family table, but the preparation for eating—the plucking and cooking—was women's work. Shearing sheep was often a joint enterprise. In some families, the men spanceled and held the sheep while the women clipped their wool and marked them with the family's distinguishing mark. In others, the roles were reversed, with women holding the sheep while men did the shearing. Some informants stated that both tasks were performed solely by women. Certainly, further processing of the wool was women's work (see below).

Irish women, then, were actively involved in animal husbandry and field work on the southern Avalon. Indeed, their valuable role in subsistence agriculture continued well into the twentieth century, unlike that of women in Ireland and Britain, who were increasingly marginalized from farm work (both paid and subsistence) with the spread of capitalist agriculture.[35] As with women's work in the fishery, there were no connotations of drudgery or lack of respectability attached to women's work in gardens and fields on the southern Avalon. This contrasts with mainland colonial contexts, where there was considerable pressure to remove the wives and daughters of farming families from the fields into the home and replace their labor with that of indentured servants and slaves. In mainland colonies, white women's field work was seen as aberrant, a sign of poverty and inferiority (although often a necessary evil in newly establishing areas).[36] The reverse was true within the plebeian community on the southern Avalon; there, servant girls were employed to release their mistresses from household tasks so that mistresses could contribute effectively to more important family enterprises. Indeed, a family's ability to hire servant girls and free the mistress for productive work was a sign of its increasing affluence, not its poverty, and most women did not aspire to escape outdoor work and immerse themselves in housewifery. Middle-class women on the southern Avalon did follow the pattern of withdrawing into domesticity during the period (see Chapter 9) but their aspirations to retire from productive work were not absorbed by the plebeian community.

HOUSEWIFERY

A key aspect of women's contribution to household production was the performance and management of routines necessary for the efficient maintenance of the household. This involved a whole repertoire of tasks and skills, such as cooking, cleaning, sewing, spinning, knitting, preserving fruits and vegetables, and household repair. Of course, housewifery was not as developed in the first years of settlement as it would become later in the study period. Houses were more rudimentary and had little furniture and few amenities.[37] Women initially delegated more of their time to outdoor efforts, working with the men to clear land and establish gardens in addition to performing their vital work in the fishery. Basic equipment for maintaining the household was introduced over time; spinning wheels and butter churns were luxuries that came later, if at all (some women had to rely on others to spin their wool for them, and many were still churning butter by hand well into the twentieth century). But eventually, as families became more established, as houses expanded to meet growing family requirements, and as nonessentials (such as individual dishes and bedsteads or decorative furnishings) increased, women's household duties expanded proportionately.

Still, women had to maintain a balance between productive work and housework, and the former took priority. In the British Isles, as women increasingly retired from productive work into unpaid housework throughout the nineteenth century, household cleanliness became linked with working-class respectability, and working-class women joined battle against pollution and dirt, maintaining new standards of "decency" by whitening doorsteps and black-leading grates.[38] While similar standards of cleanliness were certainly maintained by women on the southern Avalon by the twentieth century, it is unlikely that they were possible (or even aspired to) in the earlier days of settlement, although some movement in this direction may have been taking place by the mid-nineteenth century. More central to housewifery during the earlier time frame were the techniques necessary for the processing of raw materials (either produced by the family or purchased from merchants) into usable goods for the household. With this repertoire of skills and activities, women fed, clothed, and generally sustained the family work unit.

Most of the family's agricultural output was readied for household use by women. After milking the cows, for example, women prepared the milk for family consumption. The milk was strained into pans and placed in the pantry to *set* (let the cream rise); then it was placed on a hot stove to scald, and the cream was skimmed off the top. (A small amount of *scald cream* was occasionally set aside for eating as a special treat.) The skimmed milk was then cooled in the pantry and used as required for drinking or baking, while the cream was churned (often by hand) into fresh butter for the family table, a product deemed far superior to the butter imported by the merchant. Buttermilk, a by-product of the churning process, was used in baking.

Similarly, after sheep were shorn, women took over the processing of the wool, drawing on expertise developed in the domestic woolen industry of the home country. They washed, picked, and carded the fleece, spun the wool and wound it into hanks, then washed and dried it. Through the fall and winter, they knit the wool into a multitude of functional items of clothing for their families—an assortment of durable vests, mittens, sweaters, *buskins*, socks, stockings, *vamps*, caps, scarves, *palms*, and winter petticoats. Any family clothing that was not knit was sewn by women, who turned out a full complement of under- and outer-wear for family members—summer drawers and petticoats, skirts, dresses, blouses, shirts, pants, jackets and coats—sometimes using fabrics purchased from merchants, or more often, recycling older clothing or cotton sacks that had been boiled with lye soap to remove any markings and then dyed. Women also made all manner of bedding, from quilts, sheets, and pillowcases to mattresses, cushions, and pillows. In addition, they sewed items necessary for outdoor productive work, such as oilskins, *oil petticoats*, bonnets, and sails for the fishery as well as hay-cloths from brin bags for carrying loads of hay from the meadows. They also hooked mats in the winter, transforming piles of colored rags into patterned rugs (some basic, some quite intricate) by pulling them with a mat hook through a burlap backing stretched across an adjustable rectangular wooden frame.

While gardens provided much of the fresh produce for the family table, women also foraged through woods, meadows, and bogs for wild plants for dietary and medicinal purposes. Berry-picking sometimes became a family excursion, but it was most regularly done by women and children. Women made jams, jellies, and wines from a wide variety of local plants, including marshberries, cranberries, bakeapples (or cloudberries), blueberries, partridgeberries, and rhubarb. They made beer from spruce boughs, juniper bark, or hops from their kitchen gardens. The versatile hop was also mixed with potato and molasses to make *barm* for raising bread. Women also collected plants for their stock of home remedies: dogwood and cherry branches for cough medicine; wormwood to cure hoarseness; bog vein for tonic; juniper bark for tonic and tea. And while Irish women were accustomed to the role of family healer, their repertoire of cures and ointments had to be adjusted after migration to compensate for the lack of some traditional ingredients with the careful addition of unfamiliar flora from the southern Avalon.

In addition, women collected firewood—a familiar routine for Irish women, who were used to carrying heavy sacks of peat on their backs, sometimes over long distances, in the home country.[39] Men did more substantial cutting of wood during the winter, bringing their loads home by horse and cart, piling the long poles into *wharves of wood* until they could be chopped into *junks* in the woodyard. But in the summer and early fall, it was women who foraged in the woods for windfall branches, returning home with brin bags full of brambles and loads of *bresneys* and *blasty boughs* on their backs so large that "you just could see their feet coming along the road."[40] These branches were used to make fast, hot fires in the summer for baking or meal preparation. And throughout the summer, women went to the woodyard to gather loads of *chips* in their aprons to light quick fires for small cooking jobs—baking buns, for example, or frying fish.

Women were also primarily responsible for drawing water for family use, although this task was sometimes transferred to children as they got older. Water for washing floors and clothing was often taken from nearby ponds or streams, but drinking water preferably came from wells, which were usually uphill and often a quarter to a half mile away from the house. Wells were usually quite deep, and the water was drawn by lowering and raising a bucket on a string or a *gaff.* When water had to be transported over a long distance, women carried buckets with the assistance of a hoop from a puncheon tub. This was a miracle of engineering simplicity, for the hoop was not attached to the woman, nor were the buckets fastened to the hoop in any way. After filling two buckets, the woman laid them on the ground on either side of her, draping the handles outward; she then laid the hoop on top of the buckets, pulling the handles back in toward herself as she lifted them, so that the counter-pressure helped to keep the buckets away from her legs and balance the load. Still, this was hard physical labor, requiring several trips and involving loads of up to five or six gallons. Wash days were particularly demanding, as tubfuls of water had to be transported and boiled on the stove before soiled washing was added, together with soap that the women had made from *fatpork* and wood ashes from the grate.[41] On fine days in the summer, however, women often took their washing directly to the sides of ponds and rivers and did their scrubbing on the rocks.

Women did most of the baking and cooking for their families, transforming provisions from the merchant's store and their home-produced fruits, vegetables, milk, eggs, fish, and meat into a reasonably varied and nutritious diet for the household. In the days of early settlement, meal preparation was done on an open fireplace—a time-consuming task requiring large amounts of firewood and frequent trips to the woodpile as women stoked the fires in central hearths and did their cooking *on the dog irons.* There was one general exception to this assignment of cooking duties to women: when men were out fishing, they cooked a meal of stewed fish and potatoes for themselves in sawed-off puncheon tubs insulated with clay and rocks; but it was common for women to prepare the men's *grub boxes,* which contained all the items, other than fish, that the men would require for their *mug-up* on the boat, such as tea, molasses, bread, and perhaps a piece of gingerbread. All other meals and mug-ups were women's responsibility, as was the family's baking: the endless production of raisin buns, *frozies,* pies, gingerbreads, *bottomers,* and several batches of bread per week (indeed, some women with large families baked bread daily).

Women also had to turn their hands to home repair. While houses, outbuildings, and fences were generally constructed by men (although, again, the initial building of structures was sometimes shared by the sexes in the very first years of settlement), women were very much involved in their maintenance and were expected to be able to lime a house, replace fence pickets, or tar a roof along with the men in the family (or, more often the case, without them during the fishing season).

In terms of household production, then, women within the Irish plebeian community of the southern Avalon worked indoors and outdoors, through long days, in all seasons of the year to sustain their households. And the continuous roster of production and household duties had to be juggled around the requirements of child and elder care, which usually fell within the province of women's work as well.

WRECKING AND SALVAGING

One household enterprise that was more common on parts of the southern Avalon than many other areas of Newfoundland was the salvaging and recycling of items from wrecked vessels. While this type of activity is not usually found in discussions of traditional household production, it was part of the repertoire of economic coping strategies in the area and therefore deserves mention in an examination of how families survived in the years of early settlement. The greater incidence of this activity on the southern Avalon was not due to the transfer of a wrecking tradition from southeast Ireland, but to the geographical position of the shore—a long and treacherous finger of coastline abutting much-traveled shipping lanes between Europe and North America—and an unpredictable climate marked by impenetrable fogs, shifting currents, coastal ice, and sudden storms. Indeed, the southern Avalon has been the site of so many shipwrecks over the centuries that mariners have labeled the southernmost point of the shore, the area around Cape Race, *the graveyard of the Atlantic*.[42]

There is no doubt that people on the southern Avalon benefited in varying degrees from many of these shipping disasters, although it is important to differentiate between levels of participation in wrecking and salvaging activities. There were probably very few incidents of actual, deliberate wrecking of vessels. The oral tradition does ascribe this more sinister activity to certain families in particular areas (usually the more southerly portion of the shore, including Renews, Cappahayden, Trepassey, St. Shott's, and Portugal Cove South). Some people in these communities, for example, are said to have tied lanterns on the horns of cows on stormy nights to lure unsuspecting vessels onto the rocks. One particularly ruthless man from an especially notorious family of wreckers is claimed to have bitten the finger off a dead man's hand to obtain a ring that stubbornly clung to the swollen finger of the corpse. Informants asserted, however, that most local people would not have participated in deliberate wrecking activities. Certainly, none of these tales appeared in written documents of the day.

Over-zealousness in salvaging items from a wreck was the more common accusation leveled against the people of the southern Avalon. Governors' files, court records, and newspapers of the period contain various complaints against local inhabitants for mistreating shipwrecked crews and passengers and stealing items, or at least precipitously removing them, from vessels that had not been fully abandoned.[43] However, while local inhabitants were usually anxious to obtain their share of salvage, they were also, on a number of occasions, commended for their bravery in rescuing crews and passengers from distressed vessels and for their generosity in housing, clothing, and feeding victims and attending to their injuries.[44]

But humanitarian sensibilities aside, the wrecked property from a vessel was seen as a windfall, and boats often came from communities all around the site to reap the rewards. Of course, salvage operations after a vessel had been abandoned by its captain and crew or had otherwise become derelict were a common and legal means of obtaining property and/or extra income in maritime communities. Generally, local salvagers were awarded from one-third to one-half the value of recovered property.[45] There was considerable discrepancy, however, between legal definitions of salvage and what local inhabitants perceived to be their entitlement. Indeed, the government's introduction in 1860 of a system of wreck commissioners was deeply resented by most people on the southern Avalon. The legislation called for the appointment of commissioners in every electoral district to attend at the site of wrecks and oversee the salvage and distribution of wrecked property as expeditiously as possible. The statute also established various fines and penalties for taking property from a wreck and failing to report it, and gave the wreck commissioners "full power to suppress all tumults and disturbances" at the sites of shipwrecks.[46] Clearly, then, the legislators were anticipating open hostility and resistance to the measure. Certainly, within the plebeian community on the southern Avalon, the system was perceived as a scheme for taking a source of income from "the poor starving people" and hoarding all the spoils for the government. Hence, there was a tendency to race against the arrival of the wreck commissioner in a pre-emptive local salvage effort, for "what the people could steal is what they'd get."[47] Audio Sample

It is difficult to assess women's involvement in salvage activities. While it was unlikely that they actually took to boats to reach foundering vessels, there are suggestions that women joined with men in stripping wrecks that had come ashore and combing the beaches for articles washed in by the tide.[48] Gender-inclusive language was often used in contemporary documents about illicit activities at wreck sites. Complaints of local plundering, for example, were made against "the *People* at and about S^{t}. Maries" in 1777, the "local *inhabitants*" of Ferryland in 1782, the starving "*inhabitants*" and "riotous and tumultuous assembling of *people*" in Bay Bulls in 1817, and "the *inhabitants*" of the Point La Haye neighborhood in 1844.[49] Similarly, in the court cases that followed the wreck of the Spanish barque *La Plata* at Trepassey, the ship's captain discussed ensuing events in gender-neutral terms, referring constantly to the "*people*" on the beach who, he claimed, disabled and plundered the vessel. He also specifically referred to two women among the crowd: the wife of local magistrate George Simms and another woman, who took the captain and crew to their homes for food and dry clothing. While the magistrate's wife was probably not one of the "mob," the unidentified woman may have been, for it was not unusual for residents to take items from a wrecked vessel, yet still take crew and passengers into their care.[50]

Until recent years, there has been a tendency among historians to interpret collective nouns such as *people, crowd, mob,* or *inhabitants* as "men," thus coloring more neutral, contemporary reports with latter-day assumptions. Especially if the ringleaders or arrestees in such incidents were male, historians have tended to gender the entire crowd male. But since the late 1980s, compelling evidence of women's central involvement in communal actions—most notably food riots, but also other forms of confrontations involving property and work—has challenged the discipline to rethink collectivities in terms of participation of not just men, but also women and older children.[51]

Several oral informants certainly acknowledged that women were involved in this level of salvaging activity, suggesting that it was more common in "the old days" than within their own lifetimes. One story of a specific incident in the early twentieth century, although outside the study period, illustrates by next-best approximation what was likely a long-standing tradition. In the wake of a wreck at Caplin Bay, a number of cases labeled "catsup" were washed up on the beach. This was a somewhat exotic item by local standards; indeed, inhabitants were not always sure of the purpose of the articles that came ashore after wrecks (in another instance, for example, pasta noodles were mistaken for tapers for lighting candles), but they gamely took the items home and found some use for them. So the catsup was a rare item, but a valued prize nonetheless. Two local fishermen had found a cache of the cases and were apportioning the catsup between them, when Mrs. Mary Margaret ——, "a very determined woman," came marching over the beach to fight for her share of it. One of the fishermen, a mild-mannered man named Mr. Jim ——, immediately relinquished his portion to her, saying: "I wouldn't have Mrs. Mary Margaret —— on my back for all the 'cat soup' in the world."[52] As this anecdote helps to illustrate, salvaging wrecked property from the coast was something that fell within the accepted range of women's work.

And oral informants all agreed that, whether or not they were directly involved in salvaging efforts, women had no moral dilemmas about using any items brought home from a wreck, but were instead ruled by pragmatism and a desire to give some small extra comfort to their families. Recovered foodstuffs were particularly valued as a means of stretching provisions or varying the diet.[53] Furniture, shelves, deck planks, canvas, and doors provided welcome additions to household furnishings. Such items were seen as part of the bounty of the sea, a gift that it would be a "sin" to waste. One informant advised that wrecks were "better than the fall of the year [when families settled up with their merchants and obtained new supplies for the winter],"[54] and virtually everything that was removed from vessels or washed ashore found a use. Audio Sample Indeed, most homes I visited for oral history research contained at least one item, and sometimes several, from wrecked vessels—some having been in the families for generations, others having arrived as recently as the 1940s. The salvaging of items from wrecks, then, was one of numerous economic activities in plebeian households, and one in which women played roles as both salvagers and recyclers as they worked to make ends meet for their families.[55]

SEXUAL DIVISION OF LABOR WITHIN HOUSEHOLDS

Along the southern Avalon, most family members (except the very young, the very old, and the sick) were expected to contribute to household production, and both men and women worked long hours, often at difficult tasks that required physical exertion, skill, and experience. But there was a gendered division of labor, although traditional dichotomies for conceptualizing work delegated by sex—such as skilled/unskilled labor, primary/secondary contributions, or indoor/outdoor work—are not useful in differentiating men's and women's tasks in this historical context. Indeed, there was a high degree of flexibility in the allocation of work routines.

Still, some duties were more clearly delegated along sex lines than others. It was very unusual for women to actually fish in the ocean, for example, although they did fish in fresh water for trout. But women's reproductive role, together with the degree of physical strength required to row out into the North Atlantic and pull handlines or seines filled with cod, steered women landward and allocated fishing activity to the men in the family unit.[56] Yet even physical strength was not a clear criterion for the division of labor, for much of the landward work performed by women required a good deal of physical exertion. Furthermore, there was no traditional belief on the southern Avalon that women in boats were an "aberration" or that they caused bad luck.[57] The universal explanation from oral informants for women's nonparticipation in actual fishing was that they already had "enough" or "too much" to do on the land. Certainly, women were not excluded because of a lack of capacity to cope with essential work; indeed, their involvement in shore work and in other productive efforts demonstrated quite the opposite.

Just as it was uncommon for a woman's hand to guide a fishing boat, so it was unusual for a man's hand to rock the cradle. Women generally assumed the responsibility for child care, but this was not because of notions of women as the "gentler" sex and superior maternal love—cultural facets of motherhood that were gaining prominence among the middle class but had not made inroads into plebeian culture on the southern Avalon in this time period.[58] Indeed, eighteenth- and early nineteenth-century observers in Ireland noted that parents of both sexes were very fond of their children, a genuine affection that was not simply rooted in the need for large family work units and security in old age.[59] Rather, Irish plebeian women's greater role in child care on the southern Avalon was prompted by women's reproductive role and life cycle and reinforced by a division of labor that sent men out on the water daily in the summer. Still, women did employ alternative methods of child care when possible—a servant girl or older daughter; an elderly mother or aunt; even, on occasion, a sawed-off puncheon on the stage or flake—in order to free themselves for productive work. Thus the responsibility for child care did not relegate plebeian women to the domestic hearth.

Indeed, in many work assignments, there was much blurring of boundaries. Heading and splitting fish was generally considered men's work, for example, but some women did it on a regular basis. Some women performed heavier physical labor in fields and gardens that was normally associated with men, such as digging and trenching. And in those families in which men were involved in a fall fishery, the harvesting of crops had to be managed by women (with the assistance of hired servants, if sufficiently affluent). There were also sub-layers of involvement in work routines, such that while certain work was designated as men's or women's, the other sex also participated in some capacity. Many women were involved in the process of trenching potatoes, for example, by laying the seed potatoes and covering them over with sod that the men had dug. Then there were the variations in scheduling of the same work. While both men and women worked in gardens and fields, for example, it was logical for women to assume greater responsibility for this work during the summer months because they were not out on the water. Similarly, the care of the family cow was the men's responsibility in the winter, and women's during the summer. Cutting firewood was men's work in the winter, but in the summer, it was women who scoured the woods for dried alder branches and blasty boughs for cooking. The work rota had a certain internal logic and rhythm that delegated tasks as much on the basis of availability and expedience as on gendered notions of ability or strength.

Work roles were also quite fluid, as men and women occasionally crossed over boundaries as needs arose. Men might do household chores in the winter, for example, when their wives were busy at more specialized tasks such as spinning or knitting, while women might split and head fish at the peak of the season when there were insufficient hands on the stage. When women did *men's work* or men did *women's work* on a temporary basis, they were perceived to be *helping* the other. A man might help his wife scrubbing floors, for example, or a woman might help her husband splitting fish. Men might help women drying the hay if it was a poor day for fishing, while women might help men tarring a roof. Women more often assumed men's duties than the reverse, however, and in cases of men's absence (for example, at the bank fishery or, less commonly, the seal fishery), women were entirely responsible for the management of all family work at home. While women colonists in New England and Upper Canada were generally perceived by their communities as *helpmeets* to their husbands,[60] the Irish plebeian community on the southern Avalon did not make this clear-cut distinction, but assigned the status of helper to either sex within specific work contexts, based on a sexual division of labor that designated essential tasks to both men and women.

Indeed, there was no perception during this period or beyond of women's work in household production (whether reproductive or productive) as secondary. If anything, they were seen as contributing more than an equal share, for, as one local informant stated and many others implied, "Women did it all."[61] There was certainly no stigma attached to women's productive work within the plebeian community throughout the study period; indeed, there was no perception of a gender divide between productive and reproductive work, as work routines intermeshed and were shared by both sexes. Nor was a woman who did men's tasks seen as aberrant. Quite the reverse was true: a woman who could juggle all her own routines and step in and do a man's work when necessary was highly esteemed. Marriages were seen as economic partnerships in which both sexes held equal shares and carried equal risks. Work routines were roughly delegated by sex, but they were flexible. Within this schema, women were seen as essential contributors in a collective enterprise and their efforts were highly valued. In essence, a woman's versatility and capacity for hard work were integral parts of the way womanhood was defined, both by the women themselves and by the larger community.[62] Audio Sample

WOMEN IN PAID WORK, THE HOSPITALITY TRADE, AND PROTO-PROFESSIONS

While almost every adult plebeian woman (barring ill health) contributed to household production on the southern Avalon, a smaller but still significant number also performed paid work, operated businesses in the hospitality trade, or worked in proto-professional occupations such as community healing and teaching. This facet of women's work has received only passing mention in the literature on early settlement in Newfoundland (usually only a sentence or two in descriptions of women's work). But for the women involved, it was an important means of earning cash or additional credit to support themselves or contribute to family economies.

SERVICE

Service was the most common form of paid work for women during the eighteenth and nineteenth centuries. Originally, young women were shipped, particularly from Ireland by the latter part of the eighteenth century, to work as servants for planters and merchants along the southern Avalon. Various court cases throughout the study period, such as *Elizabeth Cullen v. James Shortall* (discussed in see Chapter 3), illustrate that the contracts by which these women were hired, whether oral or written, were perceived to be binding and that negotiated terms had to be honored by both employer and employee alike.

Fishing service: While most discussions of women servants in Newfoundland during the period assume that they were in domestic service, there is evidence that women were hired by local merchants and planters as fishing servants to process fish on shore. In the fall of 1797, for example, Anstice Dwyer of Brigus South sued Cornelius Kelly for her outstanding wages. Kelly was the agent for Irish merchants George and Thomas Kough, and had taken the entire *voyage* of Anstice's employer, John Sloan, before her wages had been paid. Anstice produced a shipping paper that she had entered into with Sloan—a written agreement by which she had contracted to perform the duties of heading, curing, and drying fish as well as cooking for Sloan's shore crew for wages of £9 for the season. The court ordered Kelly to pay Anstice the balance of wages she was owed in the amount of £4.10.0.[63] At the seduction trial of James H. Carter of Ferryland in 1827, testimony revealed that he had hired his alleged victim, Ellen Delahunty, to cut *sounds* with his shore crew.[64] In the fall of 1848, Ellen Leary of Ferryland sued John Butler for £2.10.0 Newfoundland Currency [Cy.] in payment for curing fifty *quintals* of fish that summer.[65]

Indeed, a number of employment disputes involving female fishing servants appear in the court records of the period (see Chapter 6). And there are other types of references to women's fishing service as well. In a diary entry for 13 July 1841, for example, Robert Carter commented on the abundance of fish being taken by local boats and noted in the margin that Mary and Betsy Kehoe were among the four servants processing it at his premises late into the night.[66] The oral tradition also acknowledges the hiring of women for shore work. A local folksong, "Betsy Mealey's Escape," relates the true story of the ill-fated voyage of Betsy and several other women who had been recruited as fishing servants for the fishery at St. Mary's Bay.[67] Some might argue that these women were merely isolated examples of an uncommon phenomenon. But given that almost all have come to light only because of difficulties they encountered with employers, it is far more likely that they signify a somewhat larger pool of women fishing servants, most operating without sufficient inconvenience to cause them to appear in court records or ballads of the day.

					£	s	d
To	Julia McCarthy	13½	days work	@ 2s.	1	7	-
"	Esther Cahill	45½	D°.	D°.	4	11	-
"	Mary Power	4	D°.	D°.	-	8	-
"	Mary Conway	47¼	D°.	D°.	4	11	6
"	Mary Ann Fowler	45½	D°.	D°.	4	10	6
"	Fanny Devine	6	D°.	D°.	-	12	-
"	Fanny Rose	12½	D°.	D°.	1	5	-
"	Catherine Cahill	22¼	D°.	D°.	2	4	6
"	Phoebe Squires	3¾	D°.	D°.	-	7	6
"	Margaret Dunphy	29½	D°.	D°.	2	19	-
"	Nancy Gerian	22¼	D°.	D°.	2	4	6
"	Bridget Meagher	4¾	D°.	D°.	-	9	6

Indeed, according to local informants, Goodridge's premises at Renews hired large numbers of women to spread fish in the nineteenth century; they were supervised by a male master of the voyage and were thus regular shore crew.[68] Audio Sample This observation is borne out by surviving ledgers of the Goodridge firm. The books for 1839 to 1841 are peppered with entries of payments to women for shore work in the fishery. Their rate of pay was 2s. per day—the lower end of the male shore crew's earnings, which ranged from 2s. to

2s.9d. per day.[69] Some of these women were employed for only several days, but others worked on the flakes for extended periods. The following excerpt from the firm's "fishery" account for 1841, for example, demonstrates that local women worked an average of 21.4 days, within a range of 4 to 47.25 days:

Given the robust participation of women in family shore crews, it is hardly surprising to find fishing concerns that still depended upon hired labor, like Goodridge's, tapping into women's expertise and experience.

Domestic service: Nonetheless, women (particularly young women) were hired in increasing numbers for domestic service during the study period. In the eighteenth and early nineteenth centuries, servant women were recruited from the British Isles, especially Ireland, and became an integral part of planter households—cooking, washing, and sewing not just for family members but also for the fishing servants who were hired each season. As the population stabilized, these shipped girls increasingly came from the ranks of local fishing families, and domestic service became a life-stage occupation by which young women earned a small income and room and board while they prepared for married life. Whether they worked for traditional planter households or the ascendant family production units, few women on the southern Avalon remained servants for life, and most went on to become mistresses of their own households.[70]

Indeed, the question of the social mobility of female servants (fishing and domestic) on the southern Avalon (and Newfoundland in general) is an intriguing one.[71] Because of the disproportionate sex ratios in the fishing population, there is reason to believe that servant girls who emigrated from the British Isles in the period of early settlement were likely more upwardly mobile than those who remained at home,[72] marrying into planter and (less frequently) mercantile families after their arrival.

Perhaps the most striking example from the area was Mary (last name unknown), an Irish servant who came out to Ferryland circa 1650 in the service of Lady Frances Hopkins. Lady Frances was a political refugee and sister-in-law of Sara Kirke, wife of David Kirke, co-proprietor and governor of the island who had headquartered himself at the colony originally established by George Calvert (Lord Baltimore) at Ferryland.[73] Mary eventually married the Kirkes' son, also named David, but her husband was captured by the French in their late-seventeenth-century incursion into the English Shore, and he died at Placentia in 1697. One or two years later, Mary married James Benger, an Irish Protestant merchant in St. John's. In 1708, she petitioned the British crown to have the Kirke property on the southern Avalon restored to her, as rightful heir to her first husband. Thus, the Benger family became major landholders in the Ferryland area.[74]

Of course, Mary's upward mobility was exceptional, and most men of the merchant-planter group married women of their own class (often women from the home country in the seventeenth and eighteenth centuries, and women from their local social circle or from St. John's in later decades). But marriage or cohabitation between servant women and smaller-scale planters was more common. A typical example of the phenomenon was Anstice Dwyer, the above-noted fishing servant who successfully sued for her wages in 1797 by producing a shipping paper that she had entered into with John Sloan. Apparently, they entered into another concordat as well, for by the taking of the 1800 census, Anstice and John were living together in a common-law relationship.[75] The oral tradition and contemporary anecdotal evidence, particularly from British authorities on the island dating back to the late seventeenth century, suggest that many servant girls like Anstice married or entered into stable cohabiting arrangements with fishermen or planters and became mistresses of their own family fishing enterprises, some of which were quite substantial operations. Many women from service or laboring backgrounds who had emigrated from Ireland to the southern Avalon had thus likely increased their opportunities for moving up in the world.[76]

Still, their lives as servants were filled with long days and hard work. The term "domestic service" had different connotations in small fishing communities than in urban areas. Like servants in the rural British Isles and other rural colonial contexts, most of these women were responsible for performing a variety of tasks both in and out of doors.[77] Women servants cooked meals, performed housework, and looked after young children, but they were also expected to feed livestock, milk cows, and work in the gardens and meadows as needed. Indeed, at the peak of the fishing season, servant girls on the southern Avalon were sometimes recruited for drying fish on the flakes as well. More commonly, however, their mistresses within the plebeian community left their female servants to keep house and care for young children while the mistresses themselves performed what was seen as the more crucial work of curing fish, milking, gardening, or making hay. Still, the servant girl was generally expected to "do a bit of everything"[78] in peak work periods and to be on call day and night. The exceptions were those few servants working for larger mercantile households, where indoor maids responsible for child care and specialized household duties were differentiated from servants hired for more general indoor and outdoor work.[79]

Long hours, hard work, low wages,[80] and lack of privacy were experiences that these women shared with domestic servants elsewhere. But some of the isolation and pressures that existed in situations elsewhere—for example, class tensions between mistress and servant, and even antagonism within stratified ranks of household servants—were not as pronounced on the southern Avalon, for the power dynamic in the relationship was muted. Many servants were working for plebeian families, in which mistresses bore their share of the heavy workload; there was little differentiation among the ranks of servants in most situations; and women servants could look forward to becoming mistresses of their own households in time.[81] Furthermore, as Chapter 6 will demonstrate, servants on the southern Avalon had reasonable access to the courts in cases of ill-treatment or non-payment of wages, and thus were likely less vulnerable to abuse than many women who entered service in other historical contexts.

PAID WASHING AND SEWING

A number of women on the southern Avalon washed and sewed for community members outside their own families, catering to the large numbers of single men in the population as well as to a small clientele from the local elite. Their work contributed to the limited cash incomes of families; indeed, for some fishing families, it was likely the only source of cash in many years. Additionally, their services were an important link in the local exchange economy as many of their customers, particularly fishermen and shoremen, "paid" them through their merchant's account book. For example, supplies issued to a washer or sewer were *contra'd* by making a credit entry in her account in the name of the appropriate fishing servant or fisherman, with a corresponding debit entry in the latter's account. Ultimately, the merchant was paid by a deduction from the fishing servants' wages or from fish and oil collected from independent fishermen in the fall.

Of course, catering to a largely transient fishing clientele, washerwomen and seamstresses found that some of their customers attempted to abscond at the end of the season without making payment. This was most unfortunate for the women involved, but the court cases that ensued provide the historian with some means of measuring their livelihood. Twenty-six court cases during the period involved or made reference to laundresses and seamstresses (the specific profile being twenty-two washerwomen and four combined washerwomen/seamstresses). Again, most of these women appeared in the court records due to unusual circumstances and surely made up only a subsection of the total numbers actually involved in these occupations.

The court records indicate a high proportion of married or widowed women working as seamstresses and washerwomen. Of the twenty-six identified, at least fourteen of the women can be readily placed in this category because they were referred to as "Mrs." in the record and/or because their husbands were suing for payment as their legal agents. This does not exclude the possibility that some of the others were also married, widowed, or living in alternative family arrangements, for the flexibility of combining paid sewing and washing with household production and childrearing made it possible for these women to juggle their paid work with their other household responsibilities.

Given the consistency in the amounts claimed in the court actions, it is obvious that most women negotiated a flat rate with their customers for their services (only one woman negotiated a piece rate for washing—4s. 6d. per dozen items—in 1818).[82] While rates are not detailed in all the cases, definite trends can be seen. Only two amounts for washing appear in the records for the eighteenth century: £5.2.0 for washing for eleven fishing servants in the summer of 1779 (or roughly 9s. 3d. per customer); and £1.5.0 for one customer in 1785 (this seems high, and may have been payment for an entire year, as opposed to a single season, or for washing and sewing services combined). In the early 1800s, the rate for washing increased, likely due to increased demand from the high numbers of transient men in the population as well as generally inflationary conditions, and fluctuated between 15s. and 25s. per customer per season (summer or winter). It then declined after the Napoleonic War period, from 18s. in 1820 to a range of 12s. 6d.-15s. in the next two decades, likely reflecting fewer transient men in the population and hence a lowering of demand as well as an economy in recession. In the early 1840s, the going rate for washing hovered around the 15s. mark per season (with two exceptions: 10s. per season, and a very low 12s. for a year's washing). These rates were by now being charged in Newfoundland Currency rather than British Sterling, reflecting a further decrease in the remuneration for these women. By mid-century, however, the rates were beginning to creep slightly upwards again to the 16-18s. range. Of course, combined washing and sewing services garnered higher rates, with amounts of £2.17.6 (1818), £1.5.0 (1832), and £1.16.0 (1835) per customer specifically mentioned in the court records. It is difficult to draw conclusions from these few examples for the combined service, other than to note that they also seem to reflect a reduction in rates as the male population became more settled and the economy cooled down.

The evidence in the court cases is supported by accounts for laundresses and seamstresses in the Sweetman and Goodridge ledgers (see Appendix C, section 2). The Sweetman evidence is sporadic and deals mostly with the 1820s. However, it again suggests the significant involvement of married women or widows in these occupations. It also indicates that the flat rate for washing generally ranged from 15s. to 18s. per season, and the charge for combined washing and sewing ranged from £1.8.0 to £1.10.0 per season, corresponding with the amounts from the court cases for the same period. The ledgers also provide us with an approximate rate for sewing only, with what would appear to be fixed rates for a season generally ranging from 3s. 6d. to 6s., and other amounts obviously reflecting charges for piece work. The Goodridge ledgers also mirror the court cases in reflecting a gradual decline in rates (likely due to lowering demand) for women's washing and sewing services. While washing rates ranged from 10s. to 17s. per season, by far the most frequent charge was 12s. Seamstresses were charging 5s. per season or piece rates ranging from 1s. to 1s. 6d., with the mode being 1s. 3d.

Many of these women had multiple customers, a fact that is reflected in both the court cases and the business ledgers. Indeed, a Mrs. Delany in Bay Bulls washed for eleven fishing servants for the summer of 1779;[83] Mrs. James Barron, a laundress and seamstress in Placentia–St. Mary's, had fourteen customers in 1823;[84] and Mary Galway of Renews sewed for ten local fishermen in 1840.[85] Most other laundresses and seamstresses had up to five customers per year, although there were several with over five. The records also suggest that women maintained long-term arrangements with some of their clients. For example, Margaret Yetman of St. Mary's had a working relationship with William Christopher for many years, seeking £62 from his estate in 1835 for washing and other services performed over Christopher's lifetime.[86]

While eighteenth- and nineteenth-century wardrobes were limited, especially among fishermen customers, the demands this work placed on these women's time were considerable, given that most of them likely had families to care for as well. Washing, in particular, was strenuous work, involving the drawing and boiling of prodigious amounts of water as well as soap-making for a process that also had to be performed for the washerwoman's own family.[87] Sewing, while not as physically arduous, required both long hours and substantial skill. But what value was attributed to such work by the local community in relation to other forms of employment?

The most accessible wage information for comparative purposes, at least for the early decades of the nineteenth century, is from the fishery. Still, it is difficult to compare the monies earned by washerwomen and seamstresses with the wages paid to fishing servants and seamen: there is no way of ascertaining, for example, exactly how many customers these women had per season, and it is difficult to find matching data in any given year for both fishery workers and washerwomen/seamstresses. The purchasing power of these women (based on the prices of provisions, as per Table 4.2) is also difficult to ascertain without knowing the numbers of their clientele. The following discussion is, therefore, highly impressionistic, based on the sporadic data at hand.

Given these limitations, Table 4.3 takes women's earnings recorded in court cases and account books for years in which fishing wages are available, and projects the amounts that would have been earned based on a clientele of three, five, or ten customers per season.[88] When compared with Table 4.1, it can be seen that only the earnings of those women who combined washing and sewing for ten customers per season would have approached the earnings of a youngster or less experienced fishing servant (although the combined service in 1818 would have netted the equivalent of an experienced fisherman's or shoreman's wage). Ten customers for both washing and sewing, however, would have been a rather large workload for women with other household duties, and probably untenable for many with large families. Overall, then, these women were not being remunerated as skilled workers, likely because their work was seen as an extension of their familial roles.

Nonetheless, some of these women may have had significant purchasing power. Table 4.3 also provides examples of the provisions that could have been bought with these women's earnings—again, based on a clientele of three, five, or ten—as well as a sample package of provisions for those with earnings on the high end. The table demonstrates that their earnings could make significant contributions to their family incomes, particularly those who may have had five or more customers and, most especially, those who combined washing and sewing services. The table also suggests that, even though the rates for washing and sewing declined after the Napoleonic War period, the purchasing power of laundresses and seamstresses did not slide dramatically, given the context of a generally cooling economy. Their work, then, had economic value, even though it was not as highly rated as fishing service, for it bolstered the resources of families living on the margin and also helped to drive the exchange economy in the study area.

AGRICULTURE—PRODUCTION FOR MARKET AND PAID LABOR

While most women's agricultural labor on the southern Avalon contributed to family subsistence, there is evidence that some women sold their agricultural labor or produce to outsiders and earned cash or credit for themselves and their families. Mary Foley of the Renews area provides a striking example, for her efforts encompassed several aspects of women's paid work. The extant records for Goodridge's (1839–41) indicate that Mary had obtained from the firm, on credit, large quantities of soap and sewing materials, suggesting that she was sewing and washing for people in the community, and/or perhaps servants in her own household, as part of the contracted terms of their employment. In addition to the usual contra entries made in her account and those of her customers, Mary paid for her supplies with various installments of agricultural produce, including potatoes, milk, cream, pigs, poultry, and eggs (see Table 4.4). Her commercial activity was well rooted in the traditional activities of rural Irish women; in particular, sales of pork/bacon, eggs, fowl, and dairy products were common means for Irish women to earn income that was essential to their families' survival.[89]

On the southern Avalon, women fattened pigs through the summer months, making meal from dabs (small flatfish found in coastal waters) in the earlier part of the summer, then switching to a boiled mash of potato peels and other household scraps later in the process so that the meat would not taste of fish. The fattened and slaughtered animals were sold to merchants and dealers, or in smaller amounts to community members for payment in cash or kind. Women also sold butter, cream, and milk to their merchants—as did Mary Foley and her neighbor Johanna Leary, who was credited with "37 days milk" by Goodridge's in 1840—or they exchanged these items within the community.[90] Poultry also provided an important source of income for women in the early days of settlement. The Goodridge accounts indicate that several women in the Renews area raised fowl for sale, enabling them to offset their debts with the firm:[91]

Mary Foley	1840	23 ducks, 1 doz. eggs
	1841	20 ducks
Ann Jackman	1840	6 ducks
Margaret Jackman	1840	6 fowls, 2 geese
Mary Knox	1841	3 fowls
Margaret Dunphy	1841	9 ducks
Nancy Shannahan	1841	6 ducks

Various other sales of poultry and eggs credited to men's accounts also likely reflected the husbandry of their wives and/or daughters.[92] This cash- or credit-producing activity was likely even more prominent in the earlier part of the study period, when larger proportions of the population were more transient and thus had to rely on purchasing such items. In 1794, for example, when diarist/seaman Aaron Thomas wanted to buy some poultry, a young servant directed him to a local Irish woman who had sold fowls to his master at 2s. 6d. "per Couple." Thomas passed himself off as a priest by showing the woman a pyx he was carrying, and he negotiated the price of his purchase down to 2s. a pair, the woman discounting the birds "for your Religion's sake."[93] Thomas also encountered a young Irish woman in Caplin Bay, a Mrs. Poor (or Power), who was very worried that her geese, ducks, and chickens had taken to laying and sitting their eggs in the woods and would likely fall prey to wild animals. According to Thomas, she did not share the same level of concern for her children, whom she had sent in search of the strays and who had become lost in the foggy woods overnight, finally making their way to the neighboring harbor of Cape Broyle in the morning. Mrs. Poor's fowl, then, were of great importance to her, and were likely a means of earning income as well as feeding her family.[94]

Indeed, the significance of poultry in the family income of Irish women has been commemorated by the local folksong "Betsy Brennan's Blue Hen." Having enumerated the many fine qualities of her champion fowl, Betsy rains down curses on the "scoundrel" who has stolen her hen and her drake:

May his whiskers turn green
When he eats a crubeen
And may pork fat and beans
Nearly make him insane;
May two dogs and a crackie
Eat all his tobaccy -
The villain who stole my poor little Blue Hen.

Making no gendered assumptions about the sex of the thief, she also launches several salvoes at a possible female perpetrator:

May the ravenous baste
Burst her blouse at the waist;
May she not get a taste
Of a dumplin' or cake;
May a man from Freshwater
Go back on her daughter,
That lifted my hen and my beautiful drake.[95] *Audio Sample*

Although this song and Thomas's earlier anecdotes are humorous, there is an underlying gravity in the concern of these women for the fate of fowl that made a significant contribution to their families' livelihoods.

Another important source of women's income in rural Ireland came from dairying, but there is no evidence that Irish immigrants brought large-scale commercial dairying practices with them to the southern Avalon. Still, a few isolated examples (some Irish, some English) of small-scale dairying exist in the records. A 1786 court case reveals that a family in Fermeuse named Welsh had been supplying the merchant house of Leigh and Co. with milk the two previous years and that Mrs. Welsh was a central figure in the business.[96] Aaron Thomas mentions in his journal that the widow Mary Keene (also Kean and Keen) was keeping fourteen cows in *the Grove* at Ferryland in 1794, which in the Newfoundland context, he said, put her "on a par with Job in point of Riches."[97] Indeed, two years previous, the widow had been ordered to mortgage the herd to Holdsworth and Co. as partial security for a debt of £125.[98] A herd of this size was surely for purposes beyond her household consumption.

Similarly, the five cows that Elenor Tobin of Witless Bay inherited from her husband, Laurence, at his death in 1852 must have produced more than her family required; and it was evident that some effort was being made to develop the herd, for a proviso of Laurence's will stated that Elenor "keep up" the stock and "not allow [it] to diminish during her lifetime."[99] The Ryan and Hartery families at Biscay Bay provide another example with their two dozen cattle and two dairies by the middle of the nineteenth century.[100] Nonetheless, dairying did not develop as a more substantial industry, doubtless due to insufficient winter feed for large herds and a limited local market. Thus, the large-scale employment of women in dairying, and the subsequent devaluation of their labor that occurred in the British Isles with the "rationalization" of the industry, were not processes that played out on the southern Avalon.

Women did, however, hire themselves out for occasional agricultural work, particularly weeding, harvesting, and haymaking. Women's paid farm labor was not as common as it was in Ireland, where, particularly up to the early decades of the nineteenth century, women regularly contributed to family incomes with wages from seasonal work in the spring and fall. Still, there is some evidence from the southern Avalon that women hired themselves for work outside family gardens and meadows. Harriet Carter, the wife of a "gentleman farmer" in Ferryland, wrote to her English uncle in the late 1820s of hiring a local woman to help her with her kitchen garden.[101] Her husband's cousin, Robert Carter, made references in his diary to occasional hired labor in his gardens, such as the following entry in 1836: "Biddy Hegarty's girl weeding part of a day, came after 10 A.M."[102] Some women also made hay for wages or sold hay from their own or family surpluses. Carter, for example, notes in an 1841 entry: ". . . bought up 2 cwt Hay from Martin Culliton's Wife."[103] The Goodridge ledgers provide further examples of women's sale of hay for cash or credit.[104] And, as noted above, field work occasionally featured on the roster of duties for domestic servants.

Clearly, then, not all women's agricultural labor was for subsistence purposes only. For some, paid labor and the sale of farm produce were part of a variety of economic mechanisms to ensure their survival. Susan Layman of Renews, for example, combined the sale of hay with laundering for the Goodridge family and work on the Goodridge flakes to pay her way in the world. Her neighbor, Julia McCarthy, sold hay, worked on the Goodridge flakes, and sewed for the Goodridge family and other community members. Yet another neighbor, Ann Jackman, sold hay to Goodridge's and worked as shore crew for a B. McCarthy.[105] Plebeian women's working careers were often much more multi-faceted than the traditional model for outport Newfoundland, which included essentially only the options of family production or service.

HOSPITALITY TRADE

The hospitality trade provided another opportunity for women to contribute to family economies through the keeping of boarders, small shops, and public houses.[106] Some women in the area kept itinerant, paying boarders—casual travelers, for example, or teachers, doctors, and priests. As with sewing and washing, this type of work appealed to married women and widows, for it could be balanced with household and child care responsibilities. But the almost universal manifestation of this service was in the boarding of fishing servants by planter households, both in the earlier boatkeeper phase of the resident fishery as well as in the evolving family production stage. Of course, the traditional planter household generally accommodated more fishing servants than the household production unit, which required fewer servants to supplement family labor. Nevertheless, in both cases, servants had to be housed and fed. In the summer months, they usually stayed in separate cookrooms or *bunkhouses*, where they often prepared their own meals. But provisions were advanced against their wages, and often charges for sewing and washing services were deducted from their pay; these transactions involved the mistresses of fishing households, not only as service providers, but often as account managers as well (see Chapter 5).[107]

Boarding services came more directly under the hand of the household mistress in the winter, when households kept dieters to perform winter work in exchange for their room and board. These winter servants were far fewer in number than the summer fishing servant population, but many resided within the household itself, and thus full board had to be provided by the mistress of the house. In exchange, the family received valuable labor such as wood-cutting and the repair of fishing premises and gear in preparation for the next fishing season.

Shopkeeping was also a source of income for a small number of women, primarily married women and widows. While merchants were the main source of provisions and supplies for local communities, shops also sold a small assortment of goods—some foodstuffs, notions, small household articles, and homemade goods. Very few of these women shopkeepers appear in the written record, although some names occasionally surface. The eight court cases that Jane Austin of Ferryland initiated against customers of her shop in Ferryland, for example, suggest that she was doing a brisk trade in the 1830s and 1840s.[108] A Mrs. Leary was running a shop in Renews when she applied for a license to sell liquor on the premises in 1854,[109] and the number and variety of amounts in Mary Morris's account with Sweetman's that were contra'd against fishermen's accounts suggest that she may have been a shopkeeper, a tavernkeeper, or both.

The oral tradition indicates that shopkeepers were often women, and that they usually sold "a bit on the side" (illicit liquor) in addition to their lawful trade;[110] thus, the tradition of female *shebeen-keeping* seems to have crossed the Atlantic with the Irish. This claim is substantiated by the 1786 regulations for retailing liquor, which included female shopkeepers in their scope.[111]

Female tavernkeepers appeared slightly more frequently in the records because of the requirement that all public houses be licensed on an annual basis. Indeed, authorities carefully monitored the retailing of liquor because of its adverse effects on fishermen and seamen, and hence on the orderly operation of the fishing industry itself. They were especially concerned about the practice of crediting migrant fishing servants and seamen with liquor "to the Amount of the whole or great Part of their Wages, "causing" all kinds of Disorders, debauchery's, Excesses and Idleness"[112] and leaving many fishing servants with insufficient monies to pay their passage home at the end of the fishing season or support themselves during the winter. Not surprisingly, then, orders and regulations to stem the flow of liquor to seamen and fishing servants emanated from various governors on a regular basis, particularly up to the early nineteenth century, when the migratory and traditional planter fisheries were still in operation.[113]

Witness the wording of a license issued to Elizabeth Sutton of Trepassey in 1794:

> I James Wallace Kn^t^. Governor of the Island of Newfoundland do allow and Licence Elizabeth Sutton of Trepassey Widow to keep a Common Ale House or Victualling House and to utter and sell Victuals, Beer, Ale, Cyder and other exciseable Liquors to be drunk in any part of Trepassey where she may chuse to reside for One whole year from the Twenty Ninth day of this present Month of September and no longer so as the true assize in bread, Beer, Ale, and other Liquors hereby allowed to be sold be duly kept, and no unlawfull Game or Games, Drunkness, or any other disorder be suffered in her House, Yard Garden or Backside, but that good Order and rule be maintained and kept therein according to the Laws of the Realm of England in that behalf made, and that she does not Harbor or entertain at improper times or Seasons, Seamen, Marines, or Soldiers belonging to His Majesty's Ships of War and that she do not secret, Harbor nor entertain with undue quantities of Liquors, Seamen and employed in the Merchants Service or Servants employed in the Fishery during the Fishing Season under such Penalties as the Court of Sessions can legally inflict exclusive of being deprived of her Licence.[114]

Although records on the liquor trade are spotty, at least nine women on the southern Avalon received similar liquor licenses during the study period.[115] And, as noted above, the brisk third-party activity in Mary Morris's account with Sweetman's suggests that she may have been another acknowledged liquor retailer in the period.[116]

This representation, while significant, seems to pale in comparison with the sixty-four male names that appear as license holders in the same records, and suggests that women participated only marginally in the liquor trade. Indeed, there has been a tendency in the historiography to interpret women's operation of public houses primarily as an option in widowhood, for this was certainly the life-stage in which a woman was most likely to have a liquor license issued in her own name. The sale of liquor did help some widows and their families stave off difficult times, and authorities were cognizant of the often marginal nature of widows' livelihoods when granting licenses. Governor Pole, for example, acknowledged Elizabeth Sutton's need for a means of support as "a Widow with a small helpless Family" in the preamble of her license renewal in 1800.[117] But the peculiarities of the licensing regulations and the principle of coverture likely masked a much more robust level of participation by married women in the trade.

Certainly, early regulations for the selling of liquor suggest significant female involvement, for they were as gender-inclusive as they were pervasive. Take, for example, the fairly representative instructions issued by Governor Jonathon Elliot (Web Link) to the justices of the peace in 1786 for issuing liquor licenses. In order to ensure the stability and respectability of the licensees, he required that:

> . . . every *Person* who shall be allowed to keep a Public House in this Island do give full & ample security for *his* or *her* good Behaviour, and that no *Person* whatever be allowed to keep such Public House who does not, or shall not every Season, keep one Fishing Shallop at least; and Whereas further to encourage the Fishery and that it may be the Interest of every Individual resorting to this Island to promote the same His Majesty has been pleased to direct that every *Person* who shall keep on *his, her* or *their* own Account any Shop or Store for selling or retailing any Goods or Commodities whatever be obliged to keep one fishing shallop at least.[118]

Obviously, then, authorities anticipated the participation of women in the liquor trade. However, the requirement that the license holder have at least one fishing shallop employed in the fishery, together with the legal principle of coverture, dictated that a license would be issued in the name of a living husband, whether or not the business was a family enterprise or even being run primarily by the wife.[119]

Elenor Evoy (later Welsh) of Ferryland provides an example of this type of masked participation by women. Elenor was obviously involved in the trade through the 1790s and early 1800s, even though a liquor license was issued in her name only in the year 1799, after she had been widowed. Prior to that, the license for the Evoys' public house had been issued in the name of her first husband, Michael Evoy. By 1800, she had remarried, and the name of her second husband, James Welsh, appeared on various licenses for the district thereafter.[120] But it is likely that the license related to the same establishment and that a vital element of continuity in the enterprise was Elenor herself, who most likely had been an integral part of the business before Michael died and continued to operate the public house, as the more experienced partner, in her new marriage with James. Certainly, court records indicate that she rose to the defense of the business, in both physical confrontations and court proceedings, during both marriages—at least once without the benefit of any spousal support (see Chapter 5).

Another illustration of the point is provided by the case of Thomas Leary of Renews and his wife. In the fall of 1854, Mrs. Leary applied for a liquor license to operate a public house in the absence of her husband, who was away at sea. The local constable advised her, however, that she would be denied a license, as "her husband was the proper person to make application." When Thomas returned from sea, he was apparently too ill to make his way to Ferryland to apply for the license, but evidently this did not postpone the sale of liquor at the Leary premises. On 2 January of the following year, a summons was issued against Thomas for illegally selling liquor, and he appeared in court two days later as the "proper person," in the eyes of the law, to answer the charge. However, the circumstances of the matter strongly suggest that it was Mrs. Leary who was primarily operating the business, and had probably been doing so at least since the previous fall. This was apparently not an obstacle to the Learys' obtaining a liquor license. Perhaps in the spirit of the season, or more likely with seasoned pragmatism, the local magistrates issued the license, and even backdated it to the day before the summons had been issued.[121] Case File 3

Indeed, the ever-practical magistrates were often willing to issue liquor licenses after illicit sellers had been detected (usually either by local constables or through local informants). This happened in the case of at least two female licensees. In 1794, for example, Margret Keney (or Kenny) was fined for selling liquor without a license, but the lack was rectified the following year, when she was issued a license by magistrate Robert Carter.[122] And again, Elizabeth Sutton of Trepassey serves to illustrate the point, for she let her liquor license lapse by refusing to pay the licensing fee in 1802. In September, the visiting surrogate, Micajah Malbon, issued the following instructions to the local constable:

> It is my direction that you go to the house of Elizabeth Sutton of Trepassey aforesaid who lately kept a public house known by the sign of the Ship, and give her Notice to immediately take down the said sign and to desist from selling Ale Beer Spiritous

> liquors or other strong waters, as on the contrary her house will be pulled down and the penalty of £10 will be enforced against her.

But by November, another surrogate, Lieutenant McKillop (also McKellop), had issued her a new license for her house.[123] Case File 4 Authorities could be accommodating, then, but they were equally reasonable with male applicants, and it is certain that female publicans were held to the same standards of scrutiny and security as male tavernkeepers.

These cases also suggest an additional way that the licensing system masked the involvement of women in the trade: that some women sold liquor without having the benefit of a license either in their own or their husbands' names. While Elizabeth Sutton, Margret Kenney, and Mrs. Leary eventually complied with regulations, others did not. Mary Keating and her husband, for example, were deported from Ferryland in 1773 for keeping a “disorderly house” in which they entertained “riotous friends.”[124] As noted above, the oral tradition acknowledges that women shopkeepers often sold “a bit on the side” and that women who took in boarders would usually “have a drop” for their lodgers.[125] There were also long-standing traditions of smuggling liquor (particularly West Indian rum) and distilling illicit liquor in the area.[126] Audio Sample Smuggled rum was certainly sold on the side in local shops and public houses, and while locally distilled liquor was made mostly for personal consumption or sharing with family and neighbors, some of it was sold by local establishments or by other enterprising individuals.

In effect, then, there was much more female participation in the liquor retailing trade than a casual perusal of liquor licenses would suggest. Indeed, the entire hospitality trade was a thriving concern for many women in the area and provided considerable scope for them to contribute to family economies.

COMMUNITY HEALING AND MIDWIFERY

Most women on the southern Avalon managed the first-line medical treatment of their own families, combing their gardens and meadows, the forests and barrens, for medicinal herbs and plants and applying a host of home-remedies—tonics, herbal teas, poultices, salves, and charms—to illnesses and injuries that occurred on a regular basis. The skill and compassion required for effective healing were seen to be feminine characteristics, and the medical arts were handed down from one generation of women to the next.

But some women also nursed members of the community outside their families on a fee-for-service basis. Indeed, this nursing tradition—and, in particular, the dependence of visiting fishermen on the medical ministrations of local women—stretched back to the days of unofficial settlement. As early as 1677, for example, the English Board of Trade was advised that, "In case the masters or servants of the ffishery are visited with sickness, as oftentimes it soe falls out, heere are noe other Nurseries for them but the Planters houses wch are allwayes at their service and their wives to attend them."[127]

Court records of the area indicate that this tradition continued into the early nineteenth century. For example, when Redmond Ellward (or Aylward) was fatally injured in Cape Broyle in 1787, Honour Tobin was called in to attend him in his final days (and ultimately to lay him out as well).[128] That same year, a servant named Stokes was turned off a fishing room in Cape Broyle by the master of the voyage because his hands had become "benumbed" due to rheumatic fever; magistrate Carter arranged for a local woman (unidentified) to lodge and nurse him.[129] Case File 5 In 1818, Mary Sweeny of Ferryland brought Patrick Fowler to court for refusing to pay for her nursing care of his servant James Aylward. According to Mary, Fowler had agreed to pay her 20s. per week for his servant's board, lodging, and medical attendance. Aylward had been under her care for seven weeks, but when she presented Fowler with the appropriate charge of £6, he had refused to pay her. The court ordered that Fowler compensate Mary for her services.[130] Case File 6

This is the only case that details a fee based on a specific time period (20s. per week). Other records mention amounts without time frames (for example, an 1831 claim of £8 against an estate for nursing the deceased; a claim of £1.17.6 for "nursing and attendance" in 1847), so it is difficult to determine how representative Mary Sweeny's fee was for the period. Still, it is evident that some women's expertise in healing was acknowledged and rewarded financially—again, providing cash for some families in a local economy that saw little cash from year to year. In the case of Mary Sweeny, her remuneration of 20s. per week (2s. 10d. per day), if projected into a 173-day earning period equivalent to that of the fishing season,[131] would translate into £24.3.9—well within the wage range of £16-30 for most fishermen in the area that year. Mary, then, was obviously being paid for her time as a skilled practitioner according to contemporary pay standards.

However, while women who attended transient fishermen charged for their service, as communities stabilized and networks of reciprocal exchange developed between neighbors, women who provided nursing services for other community members more commonly were either paid in kind or rendered their services without charge. The oral tradition tells of women who were particularly adept at making salves or stitching wounds—much-valued talents in communities where pups and open wounds from mishaps with fishing hooks, knives, and saws were pervasive. Some women were known for providing particularly effective remedies for maladies such as persistent coughs, toothache, warts, frostbite, indigestion, constipation, or *poor blood* (vitamin and/or mineral deficiency). They were consulted by community members on a regular basis, and while payment was rarely solicited, some foodstuff or service was usually proffered in exchange, unless the patient was too ill or poor to provide it.

One such woman was Johanna (Jackman) Johnson, who lived in Renews in the mid-nineteenth century.[132] Although some of her nursing experiences may have taken place just beyond the study period, they reflect a tradition rooted in the eighteenth and early nineteenth centuries. A display at the Capt. William Jackman Museum in Renews describes Johanna as "a local doctor of sorts" who is "credited with curing many ailments and saving the life of a man who had accidentally shot himself." A surviving great-granddaughter expanded on this very succinct biographical note in an interview.[133] According to family folklore, Johanna had "nerves of steel." Salves for healing cuts and sores were her specialty, but she was also equal to larger challenges. When Phil Jackman's gun accidentally discharged and "blew the side off him," for example, Johanna attended him, packing his wound continuously with a medicinal paste concocted of a flour base; she saved his life, using a whole barrel of flour in the process. Johanna was noted for being able to keep her head in an emergency. On another occasion (in the 1870s), she saved the life of a Miss Walsh (later, Mother Patrick of the Presentation order), who was walking over the harbor ice with her brother when she fell through a weak spot. Johanna rushed to her assistance and held her "by the bun of the head" until rescue arrived. In addition to a caring nature, then, resourcefulness, courage, and calm in the face of crisis were hallmarks of the early community nurse.

Similar characteristics were sought in midwives, many of whom were also acknowledged healers in their communities.[134] Midwives attended at the delivery of babies and cared for mother and child during a nine-day lying-in period. They also attempted to handle complications that arose in the birthing process or the post-natal period. Indeed, many were trusted practitioners who were perceived by women to be "as good as any doctor."[135] Some, but not all, performed light housework (washing, baking bread) as part of their service. Like women who provided broader healing services, midwives were more likely to leave their patients' bedsides with a block of butter or some fresh eggs in their aprons than coins in their purse, and they performed their work *pro bono* when circumstances required.[136] Still, because of their acknowledged expertise in a process that was fraught with danger for mother and child, the community perceived them to be entitled to some form of payment, if the patient could afford it.

Certainly, the local courts acknowledged midwives' claims for fee payment and recognized midwifery expenses as legitimate claims in bastardy cases. Thus, some evidence of midwifery fees appears in the court records, although the amounts of the claims are not always detailed.[137] A small clustering of cases around the turn of the nineteenth century indicates that 2s. 4d. per day, or £1.1.0 for a lying-in period of nine days, was a standard fee at that time.[138] (Extra amounts were charged if the mother required additional nursing due to some childbed illness or if the child required extra attendance beyond the regular lying-in period.) In 1822, a midwife charged 40s. for a lying-in period in a bastardy case, almost double the earlier fee.

A comparison of fishing wages with midwifery fees (see Table 4.5) can make no claims to representativeness, given the scarcity of data, but it does suggest that midwives during the period were deemed to deserve payment as skilled workers. Midwifery fees at the end of the eighteenth century and turn of the nineteenth century were roughly equivalent, on a per diem basis, to a fisherman's wages in 1798. The proportion declined to 40 to 67 percent of fishermen's earnings in 1802, but this was at the onset of a period of vastly inflated wages in the fishery due to the effects of the Napoleonic Wars. By contrast, a midwife's daily earnings represented from 160 to 239 percent of the daily wages earned by fishermen in 1822. The comparison, again, is impressionistic. Certainly, these fees may have been inflated by the fact that they were being charged in bastardy cases; most likely, amounts charged outside the framework of litigation were lower, if fees were charged at all. Yet these substantial rates were allowed by the local courts, and suggest that a midwife's services were assigned considerable value vis-à-vis the main industry of the period.

In addition to occasional monetary rewards, the roles of midwife and community healer attracted respect and status in the plebeian community.[139] There is sometimes a tendency to look upon these practitioners as low-status stopgaps in areas where "real" doctors were not available. But access to professional medical men during the period was not as limited as one might initially suppose. Court records indicate that there were several professional medical men operating in the area from the late eighteenth to the mid-nineteenth centuries, although the numerous cases initiated by these doctors suggest that, aside from local elite families whom they also attended, the bulk of their practice was taken up with the large male fishing servant population.[140]

In this regard, male practitioners had an advantage over most female attendants through much of the period, because doctors' fees for attending fishing servants were secured by a system of holding back set amounts from servants' wages each season (Greenwich hospital fees, known locally as *doctoring fees*).[141] However, female medical attendants were often called upon by both visiting fishermen and the local community, not just out of necessity, but by choice. Granted, their willingness to provide service for little or no pay and their reputation for attending regardless of adverse weather conditions or long distances made them a very attractive alternative. Still, their ability to deal with many complications "as good as any doctor" lent them a similar status in the eyes of community members. Like Johanna Jackman Johnson, they were seen as "local doctor[s] of sorts."

Indeed, some of these women attained the designation of "doctress" in official reports of the day. An example by next-best approximation, from nearby Fortune Bay on the south coast, is provided in a report from Lieutenant Douglas of the British transport ship *HMS Phyllis*, which was wrecked off Cape Ray on 13 October 1795. The officer reported that the survivors were brought into Great Jarvis in advanced stages of frostbite. There, a "*native* doctress" amputated the frozen limbs of one injured man and effected a "miracle" cure.[142]

On the southern Avalon itself, in Trepassey, a local doctress was also operating at the turn of the nineteenth century, rather to the dismay of the visiting surrogate and a local male practitioner, who felt that he was being deprived of a significant portion of his doctoring fees. In 1802, surrogate Micajah Malbon issued the following warning to Margaret Curry:

> I hereby give you Notice that you immediately desist from following your practice as a Doctress at Trepassey or any other place on the Island of Newfoundland as if I find upon my return you continue to follow the practice I will cause your house to be pulled down and have you conveyed out of the Island.[143]

Likely, the surrogate felt that Curry had stepped beyond gendered bounds, operating not simply as a midwife or nurse, as befitted her sex, but as a "professional" medical attendant on local fishing servants. The gender order had been inverted, and the surrogate hoped to use the threat of deportation to set the world aright and bring Curry back in line. His effort was not immediately successful, however, simply because some fishing servants continued to use her services rather than those of the male doctor for the district, Michael Davenport Dutton.

This did not sit well with Dutton, who was losing potential clients to his female competitor. The following year, he sued local merchant and boatkeeper Clapp and Co. for all moneys that had been stopped from servants' wages for medical services to pay Mrs. Curry. It is evident from the ensuing court hearing that Mrs. Curry had been the medical practitioner of choice for Clapp and Co. in the past; it is also evident that she had continued to practice doctoring, despite Malbon's order to desist, for, while some servants were now being seen by Michael Dutton, others were still going to Mrs. Curry. One servant, for example, explained that he had asked Mr. Clapp to allow him to continue to see Mrs. Curry "on account of D^{r}. Dutton misbehaving to one of his fellow servants by making him an Improper Charge." Another testified that he had applied to Mr.

Clapp to employ Mrs. Curry as his doctor because Mr. Dutton had refused to attend him and his family.

When Dutton had approached Clapp for the doctoring fees, Clapp had told him the moneys had been stopped for Mrs. Curry, and that Dutton must look to the servants he had treated for any payment. As the dispute played out in local court, another visiting surrogate, John McKillop, expressed his opinion that, while it was customary for an employer to appoint a particular medical practitioner for his or her servants, Clapp had not, in this case, appointed a "proper person" in Mrs. Curry. Ultimately, the matter was decided by the chief justice for the island, Thomas Tremlett, who ordered that Dutton's claim be recovered from the servants' current wages with their present masters.[144] There is no further evidence of Mrs. Curry's medical activities in the court records, and one can only assume that after this matter, she either stopped her doctoring or, perhaps more likely, went underground with her practice. Case File 7

But while Mrs. Curry was not considered by the court to be a "proper person" to provide medical services, it is important to note that she was operating within (and being paid by) the local community as an acknowledged medical practitioner. And fishermen and their families were not consulting her because she was a cheaper alternative, for the full amount of doctoring fees was being held back from their wages for her services. Rather, many went to her by choice because, like many other female practitioners of the day, she had established trust with her skill, accessibility, and fair dealing. Furthermore, while the increasing male professionalism of medical practice throughout the nineteenth century eroded the status of community healers in many areas, the high regard in which midwives and community nurses were held within the plebeian community of the southern Avalon remained constant throughout the period under study.[145]

SCHOOL TEACHING

Another proto-professional occupation open to women on the southern Avalon was school teaching. This occupation provided a limited number of Irish Newfoundland plebeian women with the opportunity to earn not only a regular salary but also community status and prestige, for, as one oral informant observed, "You had to raise your cap to the teacher."[146] But as they made inroads into the echelons of "respectable" folk, schoolmistresses came up against middle-class assumptions about women's place and the value of women's work that were not as intrusive in the lives of plebeian women who remained in the household production unit.

The Newfoundland government passed its first *Education Act* in May of 1836,[147] and the newly appointed boards of education for the districts of Ferryland and Placentia-St. Mary's immediately began to make provisions for establishing public schools along the southern Avalon. There is no evidence of formal schools operating in the area before this time, other than a Sunday school established in Ferryland in the 1820s by the Society for the Propagation of the Gospel.[148] Communities may have had earlier, informal arrangements for schooling their youth. For example, the governor reported to the Colonial Office in 1815 that the children in Bay Bulls district were "taught by the women in the summer and by a man in winter."[149] And some wealthier families hired private tutors. For example, Kearnon Mulloney was tutoring the children of Henry Coryear in 1818,[150] and Sarah Garland received payment of £2.5.0 from Alan Goodridge in 1841 for "1_ years Schooling p. Boys."[151] But traces of teachers before the days of public schooling are few in both the written record and collective historical memory.

The newly established educational system in 1836 was non-denominational, as were the two school boards that were appointed for the area, although their membership came predominantly from the English Protestant middle-class community.[152] Still, the initial by-laws and resolutions adopted by the two boards were ecumenical in spirit, requiring that nothing of a sectarian nature be taught in the school, that no religious textbooks be used, and that no religious instruction be given on school premises or during school hours.[153] In 1843, however, legislation was passed that divided the education grant to support separate Protestant and Catholic systems, and thereafter Irish schoolchildren on the southern Avalon came under the jurisdiction of Catholic boards.[154]

From the beginning, female teachers were a significant presence in southern Avalon schools.[155] As seen below, for example, women constituted slightly more than half of the first teaching roster for Ferryland district in 1836–37, particularly after certain male candidates did not survive the screening process:[156]

Note that most of the surnames were Irish, or represented English lines that had married into the Catholic community (with two exceptions), reflecting the predominating ethnoreligious group within the school populations of the specific communities.[157] There was only one school in the St. Mary's region, taught by schoolmaster Lawrence Neill, but of the total of six teachers for the Placentia-St. Mary's district, three were male and three were female.[158] By 1860, the teaching roster for the entire area was divided evenly between the sexes, although there was a marked predominance of male teachers in Bay Bulls district (four out of five) and of female teachers in Ferryland district (six out of eight in public schools, in addition to eight nuns teaching at convent schools).[159]

There was nothing in the legislation and by-laws of school boards in the area up to 1860 that overtly differentiated teaching levels and salary scales by gender.

Place	**Initially appointed or under consideration in 1836**	**Roster, 4 October 1837**
Renews	John Dwyer	John Dwyer, *pro tem,* pending judgment on complaints received against him
Fermeuse	Thomas Larassey	Thomas Larassey
Aquaforte	-	Jane Winsor
Ferryland	Elizabeth Coulman	Elizabeth Coulman
Caplin Bay	Robert Fitzharris	Nicholas Fitzgerald Elizabeth Coulman
Cape Broyle	-	Ann Coryear (school at Riverhead if suitable school room found)
Brigus	Catherine Power	Catherine Power
Athlone	-	Jane Cashin
Toad's Cove	-	-
Mobile	-	-
Witless Bay	Nicholas Fitzgerald	[Nicholas Fitzgerald?]
Bay Bulls	James Murphy	Jos^{h} Murphy [likely the same person, with an error in name transcription]

Nonetheless, it is evident that certain gendered assumptions underwrote many board policies, and the boards had broad powers in terms of hiring, setting teachers' salaries, and the overall management of schools. Available evidence suggests that schoolmasters consistently tended to be paid more than schoolmistresses, regardless of class size and subjects taught, a differential that was magnified when one considers that masters in outharbors were permitted time off in the summer to go fishing if required (see Table 4.6).[160] This differential was grounded in the middle-class assumption that men were primary income earners and required higher salaries than women, who were seen as secondary income earners.

It also reflected the desire to offer a more advanced curriculum to boys to prepare them for careers outside the home, as well as the notion that male teachers (the teachers of choice for boys' schools) were more capable of teaching higher-level subjects, leaving women to prepare female students for nonprofessional careers. Certainly, when sex-segregated schools were established in several communities in the study area,[161] male teachers were hired to teach boys and female teachers to instruct girls. However, many of the board schools in the area remained coeducational throughout the period, and with the exception of students in two commercial schools that were operating in Ferryland and Bay Bulls in the late 1850s, most of the scholars along the southern Avalon, male and female, remained at elementary levels of reading, writing, spelling, and ciphering, with very few venturing into intermediate subjects such as history, geography, navigation, or industrial arts. Indeed, of the 107 students at the Bay Bulls commercial school in 1859, none were taking geography, English grammar, or navigation.[162] Thus any rationale for salary differentials between masters and mistresses based on subjects taught rested on shaky grounds. Indeed, one of the most comprehensive curricula of the day was offered by the Presentation nuns in their convent schools, and Bishop Mullock ventured the opinion in 1859 that "it would be a very great improvement if the incompetent Masters, who only receive a small salary in the small outports," were replaced by school mistresses trained by the nuns at their main convent in St. John's (although a proselytizing agenda may have inspired some of his enthusiasm).[163]

The assumptions that governed the differences in salaries and training requirements for male and female teachers remained an unstated principle until after the middle of the nineteenth century. They were more formally introduced in the requirements for teacher certification that were legislated in 1876; the resulting Syllabus for Grading Teachers stipulated that for Grade I (highest level) certification, female teachers, unlike male teachers, did not have to pass examinations in the advanced subjects of algebra, Euclidean geometry, and practical mathematics, but were required to be able to give instruction in domestic economy, needlework, knitting, and netting.[164]

The arguments made by the inspector of Catholic schools in 1880 for increasing the pay of male teachers also provide some insight into the underlying perceptions that likely governed the earlier period. "Qualified Female Teachers," he noted, "may be obtained for such [currently low] salaries—£25 or £30 a year—but it is unreasonable to expect that Male Teachers, possessed of any energy and ability, will give their services at so low a rate." If something was not done soon about the situation, he warned, most schools would be filled with female teachers, a predicament which he felt was untenable. While female teachers were acceptable (indeed, better) teachers for young children and girls, most of the schools in the outports were coeducational. Given the deficiency of female teachers in certain advanced subjects such as arithmetic and science because of their natural lack of proclivity in such areas, he asserted, something must be done to attract more male teachers to these schools to ensure a better standard of education in situations where boys must, out of necessity, attend school with girls.[165]

Thus schoolmistresses on the southern Avalon, as elsewhere in Newfoundland, became enmeshed in gender ideology that ranked their abilities as secondary, and their work of lesser value than that of their male counterparts. Although they had improved their lot in terms of cash income and prestige within the plebeian community, these benefits had to be traded off against a subordinate status within their own occupational group as they skirted the edges of middle-class respectability.

CONCLUSION

Women in the Irish plebeian community on the southern Avalon were essential contributors to the collective enterprises of household production and survival. They performed vital work in the fishery, in subsistence agriculture, and other forms of household production. Many also contributed to family economies through paid work, the hospitality trade, and proto-professional occupations such as midwifery and teaching. A significant number combined household production with various types of paid work within a broad repertoire of economic coping strategies, as demonstrated by women's accounts in the Goodridge ledgers. Ellen Fowler, for example, washed and cooked for six customers in 1839. Mary Ann Fowler worked on the flakes, sold oakum to Goodridge's, and hired out her punt to the vessel *Pelter* for the 1841 fishing season. Margaret Dunphy worked on the flakes and sold poultry. Mary Knox also sold fowl and did paid washing and sewing. Esther Cahill was a laundress and a shore worker for Goodridge's. Margaret Leary washed for the Goodridge family and cooked for the firm's boat crews. All made important contributions to their family incomes through cash, extra credit, or exchange.

The multi-faceted role of Irish Newfoundland women in family economies on the southern Avalon was rooted in the traditional work routines of rural Ireland. In the southeastern homeland, at least up to the early nineteenth century, women performed a variety of tasks that were vital to the survival of their families. They participated in both paid and subsistence agricultural work: stone-picking, planting, manuring,weeding, and harvesting. They gathered peat for fuel and seaweed for fertilizer and food, carrying it home on their backs, sometimes over long distances. They distilled and sold spirits, sold butter and eggs, and raised pigs and poultry for sale in local markets. Until the decline of the domestic woolen industry by the middle of the nineteenth century, they also earned scarce cash income as domestic spinners and knitters. Indeed, on many small farms, it was women's cash earnings that paid the rent. Thus, in both Ireland and Newfoundland, Irish women were vital co-producers in family enterprises.

Certain work routines within the plebeian community on the southern Avalon were divided along sex lines, but mutually exclusive gender dichotomies that differentiate men's and women's work in terms of physical strength/weakness, outdoor/indoor work, paid/unpaid work, skilled/unskilled labor, or primary/secondary work are too rigid for examining the sexual division of labor in the area. Granted, physical strength generally dictated that men hauled handlines and seines in the fishery, but other work assignments delegated to women—such as carrying barras of fish up cliff faces, shouldering massive loads of boughs and bresneys, transporting five to six gallons of water over long distances, digging, fertilizing, and weeding gardens—were hardly based on notions of a "weaker sex." Granted, men worked primarily outside the household, but women's duties were carried out both in and out of doors. And a significant number of women worked for pay. Some women—laundresses, seamstresses, teachers—found their work undervalued because it was seen as an extension of women's familial role. But others, such as fishing servants, midwives, and doctresses, were perceived as skilled workers or virtual professionals, even though cash payment only occasionally materialized for community healers.

As the family production unit in all its facets evolved on the southern Avalon, women's work was perceived by the local community to be as skilled and as important as men's. Women were not seen as "helpmeets," but as essential members of family work units. Furthermore, there was no pressure exerted within the plebeian community to move women away from outdoor work into the household and its close environs. Within the small elite community, by contrast, women's outdoor work was increasingly stigmatized through the period. Gentry women retreated into their households and focused on childrearing and the supervision of domestic servants, who now performed the more labor-intensive household tasks. As their families embraced English, middle-class feminine ideals, the withdrawal of these women from productive work, even the supervision of outdoor work, was perceived as a mark of increasing affluence, gentility, and respectability (see Chapter 9).

However, women from Irish plebeian culture on the southern Avalon were positioned differently in the division of labor than English women, for there was no stigma attached to their outdoor, manual labor or paid work, and there was no cultural capital ascribed to their economic idleness. Granted, plebeian women, like middle-class women, hired domestic servants to relieve them of certain work routines, and their ability to do so was a sign of some degree of affluence. However, they did not hire servants in order to escape outdoor work and retire into genteel domesticity, but rather to *escape* their households to perform productive work on flakes and in the fields. Indeed, far from regretting the time spent away from home and family, many looked forward to the break from housework. A woman who was "too sickly" or "too grand" for outdoor work was an object of pity or scorn within the plebeian community.[166] The capacity to contribute to the household's output was a vital part of the Irish Newfoundland woman's self-image, a defining component of her identity.

Resourcefulness, resilience, physical hardiness, efficiency, flexibility, courage, tenacity: these made up a package of survival skills that defined the Irish plebeian woman in the days of early settlement on the southern Avalon and constructed a feminine ideal that has survived in the collective memory of the culture. The "good, hard-working stump of a girl" of the home country transplanted successfully along the southern Avalon, and indeed, outlasted her Irish counterpart, whose status eroded with the increasing marginalization of women from agricultural work and the devaluation of women's labor as the nineteenth century unfolded. On the southern Avalon, women's work maintained its social and economic value within the plebeian community well into the twentieth century. And the construction of Irish womanhood as hard-working, essential partners in family enterprises had repercussions in the broader social, economic, and political life of their communities (see Slide Show).

NOTES

1. Aaron Thomas, *The Newfoundland Journal of Aaron Thomas*, ed. Jean M. Murray (London: Longmans, Green, 1968), 187.

2. A saying from Irish peasant lore signifying the ideal qualities of a wife; a similar sentiment was expressed in the saying "Good looks don't boil the pot." See Janet A. Nolan, *Ourselves Alone: Women's Emigration from Ireland, 1885–1920* (Lexington: University Press of Kentucky, 1989), 20.

3. Much of the following material on household production, unless otherwise specified, comes from the oral tradition and student papers in the MHA (see bibliography). Most of the work routines were still in existence within the memory of many oral informants and, indeed, some had been carried out by a number of the people interviewed. When asked, these older informants were firm in their belief that these routines had been established in the period under study.

4. Cormac O Grada notes that there was a small Irish fishing industry on the west coast, but that it remained undeveloped due to lack of infrastructure and equipment. A bounty system initiated in 1819 brought some prosperity to the industry, but Westminster pulled the plug on the scheme in the late 1820s within the context of a broader economic policy of *laissez-faire*. See O Grada, *Ireland: A New Economic History, 1780–1939* (Oxford: Clarendon Press, 1994). Anne O'Dowd briefly discusses the significant contribution of women to family fisheries in these west-coast communities, noting that they performed various aspects of shore work, such as gutting, curing, and cleaning gear for storage; some also marketed fish. See O'Dowd, "Women in Rural Ireland in the Nineteenth and Early Twentieth Centuries: How the Daughters, Wives, and Sisters of Small Farmers and Landless Labourers Fared," *Rural History* 5, no. 2 (1994): 171–83.

5. The labor force in the fishery was differentiated by skill and experience: e.g., on shore—ordinary shoreman, splitter, header, salter, and *master of the voyage*; and in boats—seaman (migratory fishery only), fisherman, *captain*, *midshipman*, *foreshipman*, and boatmaster.

6. Note that this section deals only with women's participation in the fishery as boatkeepers and within their own family production units. Women's involvement as paid fishing servants will be discussed below in the section on service. This is a rather artificial separation that is made for organizational purposes only, and is not meant to divert attention from the range of women's involvement in the industry, particularly in the eighteenth and early nineteenth centuries.

7. Pope observes that a number of women in Kirke's seventeenth-century colony at Ferryland were also single heads of fishing enterprises, and that many others were partners in household production. Using census data, he compares the numbers of servants in households with and without mistresses, and finds that those with mistresses had at least one fewer servant than those without, suggesting that a planter's wife performed the equivalent work of a male servant. See Peter Pope, "The South Avalon Planters, 1630–1700" (Ph.D. diss., Memorial University of Newfoundland, 1992), 306–13.

8. PANL, GN 5/4/C/1, box 1, 23, Notice, Magistrate Robert Carter to "all Merchants, Traders, Boatkeepers and Innkeepers in the District of Ferryland," 8 January 1787; italics added.

9. The English common-law doctrine of coverture dictated that the legal personality of a married woman was subsumed in that of her husband. Upon marriage, she became a *feme coverte*; a single woman, by contrast, maintained her own legal identity as *feme sole*.

10. PANL, GN 2/1/A, vol. 4, 95–96, Order, Palliser, 2 August 1768.

11. PRL, 340.9 N45, Ferryland, Grant of a Fishing Room to Mary Shea, 15 September 1773; also appears in PANL, MG 31, Carter Family Papers, file 32.

12. PRL, 340.9 N45, Ferryland, *Lawrence Dunn and J. Whealon v. Alice Thomas*, 5 October 1775.

13. See: PANL, GN 2/1/A, vol. 10, 49–51, Petition of James Rows, ca. 14 August 1784, and Order, Governor Campbell, 27 August 1784; PRL, 340.9 N45, Ferryland, *Catharine Clements v. James Rouse*, 31 August 1785; and PANL, GN 5/4/C/1, Ferryland, box 1, *Graham Little v. James Bryan*, 11 April 1791.

14. PANL, GN 5/4/C/1, Ferryland, box 1, *Thomas Gibbs and Co. v. William Knox, John Rice, and Henry Studdy*, 11 August 1794.

15. PANL, GN 5/1/C/1, Ferryland, 97–98, Philip Tree, Mortgage to John Teague, 29 November 1823.

16. PANL, MG 473, Alan Goodridge and Son Collection, 1839 ledger, fol. 413, and 1841 ledger, fol. 292.

17. PANL, MG 49, Sweetman Collection, boxes 2 and 3.

18. MHA, Alan Goodridge and Sons Limited fonds, 1840–1909, 1840 ledger, fol. 363; and PANL, MG 473, Goodridge Collection, 1841 ledger, fol. 266.

19. MHA, Goodridge fonds, 1840 ledger, fol. 381.

20. After the death of Thomas Beaves of Renews, his account with merchants Hunt, Stabb, and Preston was continued under the head "Elizabeth Beaves and Son," and the firm tried to attach Elizabeth's fishing premises to pay her late husband's debts. See PANL, GN 5/1/C/1, Ferryland, 124–25 and 162, *Hunt, Stabb, Preston and Co. v. the Estate of Thomas Beaves*, 6 November and 11 December 1820.

21. Several informants from Calvert told of a local woman of the early twentieth century, Mrs. Mary Johnny Kavanagh, who illustrates the point by latter-day example. She regularly carried one end of a barra over a steep hill from the shore to her family's flake, while two young teenaged sons usually manned the other end. The physics of the barra dictated that in order to share a load equally, both carriers had to hold the handles by the ends. However, if one person decided to take the brunt of the load, he or she would grip the handles closer to the platform bearing the fish. One day, Mary Johnny was carrying a load with an adult male member of the work unit. He was a very slight man, not nearly as hardy as she. As they climbed the hill to the flake and he was clearly faltering, she was heard to say, "Ah, ya poor little bugger, sure I'll have to 'catch that in' for ya now." (This specific anecdote was told by VF, interview by author, St. John's, 26 March 2001.)

22. QSF, interview by author, Cape Broyle, 22 July 1999.

23. This distinction was acknowledged by community members, and was carefully drawn by oral informants, but it was not always made by outside observers. In describing Newfoundland women, for example, Anglican missionary Anspach noted, "the very valuable *assistance* which they afford during the season for curing and drying the fish . . ." (italics added). See Rev. Lewis A. Anspach, *A History of the Island of Newfoundland* (London: Anspach, 1819), 468. Norwegian observer Peter M. Stuwitz was perhaps more inclusive in his 1840 remarks on the inshore fishery at St. Mary's: in the processing of fish, he noted, the men's families, women and children included, "participate" and "also work with them." See Helge Nordvik and Lewis R. Fischer, "Peter M. Stuwitz and the Newfoundland Inshore Fishery in 1840," *Newfoundland Studies* 1, no. 2 (fall 1985): 135 and 138.

24. Quotation from NO, interview by author, Ferryland, 24 August 1999; but virtually the same sentiment was also expressed by KO, EO, QSF, NSF, and QO.

25. While family production in the fishery was pervasive by the end of the study period, it was not universal—e.g., some men fished in areas too far from their own harbors to return daily, and their catch was processed by male boat crews. But the exclusion of women from the processing in these cases had nothing to do with concerns about respectability or the difficulty of the work; indeed, in the prolonged absence of men, these women had to shoulder additional duties in terms of caring for children, households, gardens, and livestock. In the early twentieth century, women's work in processing continued, although small inroads were being made by discourses on female respectability and domesticity. However, women's participation declined significantly with the introduction of fresh-frozen technology at mid-century. See: Ellen Antler, "Women's Work in Newfoundland Fishing Families," *Atlantis* 2, no. 2 (1977): 106–13; and Miriam Wright, "Women, Men and the Modern Fishery: Images of Gender in Government Plans for the Canadian Atlantic Fisheries," in *Their Lives and Times: Women in Newfoundland and Labrador: A Collage*, ed. Carmelita McGrath, Barbara Neis, and Marilyn Porter (St. John's: Killick Press, 1995), 129–43. But until women were sidelined by the modernizing industry, they saw themselves as not only obligated, but entitled, to take part in family processing, unless they had acceptable family or outside work reasons for their absence.

26. C. Grant Head, *Eighteenth Century Newfoundland* (Toronto: McClelland and Stewart, in association with the Institute of Canadian Studies, Carleton University, 1976), 142 and 187, n. 5. Head notes that the first mention in the written record of the use of potatoes in Newfoundland appears in a 1754 despatch from the governor to the Colonial Office.

27. The potato was introduced into Ireland in the late sixteenth century. While Irish historians had long assumed that reliance on a potato diet was widespread by the early decades of the seventeenth century, M. Drake and K. H. Connell have more recently argued that the transition came later, in the 1770s–1780s. L. M. Cullen states, however, that Drake and Connell have been misled by the evidence of contemporary observer Arthur Young, whose remarks about the dependence on a potato diet applied only to cottiers and laborers. Other areas, especially in the north and southeast, maintained much more varied diets into the nineteenth century. Nonetheless, the population explosion within the cottier and laboring class increased the aggregate dependence on the potato steadily and dramatically after the turn of the nineteenth century. See: Kenneth H. Connell, *The Population of Ireland, 1750–1845* (Oxford: Clarendon Press, 1950); Louis M. Cullen, *The Emergence of Modern Ireland, 1600–1900* (New York: Holmes and Meier, 1981); and L. M. Cullen, "Irish History Without the Potato," in *Nationalism and Popular Protest in Ireland*, ed. C. H. E. Philpin (Cambridge: Cambridge University Press, 1987), 126–38. See also Deirdre Mageean, "To Be Matched or to Move: Irish Women's Prospects in Munster," in *Peasant Maids—City Women: From the European Countryside to Urban America*, ed. Christiane Harzig (Ithaca, NY: Cornell University Press, 1997), 57–97.

28. See: Head, *Eighteenth Century Newfoundland*; and Sean Cadigan, *Hope and Deception in Conception Bay: Merchant-Settler Relations in Newfoundland, 1785–1855* (Toronto: University of Toronto Press, 1995). Newfoundland had originally been supplied by West Country merchants, joined in the eighteenth century by American and Irish traders. By the end of that century, direct links had been forged with suppliers in the West Indies and Canada as well.

29. Sometimes poor growing and fishing seasons corresponded, as in the 1820s and 1830s, with devastating consequences for many communities.

30. XF, interview by author, Brigus South, 22 June 1999.

31. Edward Wakefield, quoted in Hasia Diner, *Erin's Daughters in America: Irish Immigrant Women in the Nineteenth Century* (Baltimore, MD: Johns Hopkins University Press, 1983), 13.

32. For a discussion of women's vital contribution to family economies in prefamine rural Ireland, see: Joanna Bourke, *Husbandry to Housewifery: Women, Economic Change, and Housework in Ireland, 1890–1914* (Oxford: Clarendon Press, 1993); L. A. Clarkson, "Love, Labour, and Life: Women in Carrick-on-Suir in the Late Eighteenth Century," *Irish Economic and Social History* 20 (1993): 18–34; Mary Cullen, "Breadwinners and Providers: Women in the Household Economy of Labouring Families, 1835–6," in *Women Surviving: Studies in Irish Women's History in the Nineteenth and Twentieth Centuries*, ed. Maria Luddy and Cliona Murphy (Dublin: Poolbeg Press, 1989), 85–116; Mary Daly, "Women in the Irish Workforce from Pre-industrial

to Modern Times," *Saothar* 7 (1981): 74–82; Diner, *Erin's Daughters*; *Maria Luddy, Women in Ireland, 1800–1918: A Documentary History* (Cork: Cork University Press, 1995); Mageean, "Irish Women's Prospects"; and Nolan, *Ourselves Alone.*

33. This practice is generally noted in the literature cited in the previous note. Luddy also cites some contemporary reports on women's farm work in Munster that indicate that women in that county performed this task. An 1822 report, for example, noted that in Waterford, "The females near the sea coast manure the fields with sea weed, which they carry on their backs: this dangerous and laborious employment the reporter has never seen performed by men." See Luddy, *Documentary History*, 163–66, particularly 164, doc. 47.2, *First Report of the General Board of Health in the City of Dublin* (Dublin, 1822), Munster Women and Farm Work ca. 1818. And in Cork, according to an 1836 report, "the young women assist the men in bringing the seaweed on their backs in baskets from the sea shore . . ." See Luddy, Documentary History, 166–72, particularly 168, doc. 47.3 *Report from His Majesty's Commissioners for Inquiring into the Condition of the Poorer Classes in Ireland*, appendix D HC 1836(43), xxxi.

34. This wording was used by most informants.

35. See, for example: Bourke, *Husbandry to Housewifery*; Anna Clark, *The Struggle for the Breeches: Gender and the Making of the British Working Class* (Berkeley: University of California Press, 1995); Daly, "Women in the Irish Workforce"; David Fitzpatrick, "The Modernisation of the Irish Female," in *Rural Ireland: Modernisation v. Change, 1600–1900*, ed. Patrick O'Flanagan, Paul Ferguson, and Kevin Whelan (Cork: Cork University Press, 1987), 162–80; Mageean, "Irish Women's Prospects"; Kerby A. Miller, David Doyle, and Patricia Kelleher, "'For love and liberty': Irish Women, Migration, and Domesticity in Ireland and America, 1815–1920," in *Irish Women and Irish Migration*, ed. Patrick O'Sullivan, Irish World Wide Series, vol. 4 (London: Leicester University Press, 1995), 41–65; Nolan, *Ourselves Alone; Jane Rendall, Women in an Industrializing Society: England, 1750–1880*, Historical Association Studies (Oxford: Basil Blackwell, 1990); Rita Rhodes, *Women and the Family in Post-famine Ireland: Status and Opportunity in a Patriarchal Society* (New York: Garland, 1992); K. D. M. Snell, "Agricultural Seasonal Unemployment, the Standard of Living, and Women's Work, 1690–1860," in *Women's Work: The English Experience, 1650–1914*, ed. Pamela Sharpe (London: Arnold, 1998), 73–120; and Deborah Valenze, *The First Industrial Woman* (New York: Oxford University Press, 1995).

36. See, for example: Carol Berkin, *First Generations: Women in Colonial America* (New York: Hill and Wang, 1996); Berkin and Leslie Horowitz, eds., *Women's Voices, Women's Lives: Documents in Early American History* (Boston: Northeastern University Press, 1998); Kathleen M. Brown, *Good Wives, Nasty Wenches, and Anxious Patriarchs: Gender, Race, and Power in Colonial Virginia* (Chapel Hill: University of North Carolina Press, 1994); Elizabeth Jane Errington, *Wives and Mothers, Schoolmistresses and Scullery Maids: Working Women in Upper Canada, 1790–1840* (Montreal: McGill-Queen's University Press, 1995); Beth Light and Alison Prentice, eds., *Pioneer and Gentlewomen of British North America 1713–1867*, Documents in Canadian Women's History, vol. 1 (Toronto: New Hogtown Press, 1980); Mary P. Ryan, *Womanhood in America: From Colonial Times to the Present* (New York: New Viewpoints,

1975); and Laurel Thatcher Ulrich, *Good Wives: Image and Reality in the Lives of Women in Northern New England, 1650–1750* (New York: Knopf, 1982).

37. The structure that likely provided the initial shelter for many new arrivals on the southern Avalon until a permanent home could be built was the *tilt*—a primitive, single-roomed hut built of vertical studs or logs and covered with bark or boughs, a form of shelter that had been traditionally employed by the migratory fishermen at Newfoundland. The more permanent housing style built by the Irish in Newfoundland was the one-and-a-half story hip, a local variant of housing styles found in both the West Country and southeast Ireland. The house was a small wooden structure (often about 16' by 24', although one surviving example in the study area measures only 13' by 20') with kitchen and parlor (locally, known simply as *the room*) on the first floor, two bedrooms upstairs, and a central hearth and stairway. Many also had a *back kitchen* or *linhay* serving as a pantry at the rear of the house, either with a flat roof or a roofline that extended down from the main roof in saltbox style. There were some variations: a three-room version, with a kitchen, parlor, and bedroom on the first floor; and a full two-story variant. The walk-in hearth or settle fireplace (with a bench at either side of the hearth) was common. So too was the smaller, open fireplace with a fire set on dog irons in the hearth. These central fireplaces were used for both cooking and heating throughout the period under study; after 1860, the wood stove began to replace the fireplace for cooking purposes. By the end of the study period, a housing form similar to the Cape Cod was developing, with two storys and four (rather than two) bedrooms to accommodate increasing family size, suggesting a growing expectation of privacy. See: Gerald L. Pocius, "English Styles and Irish Adaptations: The Emergence of Newfoundland House Forms on the Southern Shore" (paper presented to a joint meeting of the Irish Newfoundland Society and the Newfoundland Historical Society, 29 January 1981); Pocius, "Architecture on Newfoundland's Southern Shore: Diversity and the Emergence of New World Forms," *Society for the Study of Architecture in Canada Bulletin* 8, no. 2 (June 1983): 12–19; Pocius, *A Place to Belong: Community Order and Everyday Space in Calvert, Newfoundland* (Athens: University of Georgia Press, 1991), Chapter 6; Shane O'Dea, "Simplicity and Survival: Vernacular Response in Newfoundland Architecture," *Society for the Study of Architecture in Canada Bulletin* 8, no. 2 (June 1983): 4–11; and John Mannion, *Irish Settlements in Eastern Canada: A Study of Cultural Transfer and Adaptation* (Toronto: University of Toronto Press, 1974).

38. This combat imagery is borrowed from Jane Rendall, *Women in an Industrializing Society*, 88–90. Other writings on the link between cleanliness and respectability include: Bourke, *Husbandry to Housewifery*; Dot Jones, "Counting the Cost of Coal: Women's Lives in the Rhondda, 1881–1911," in *Our Mothers' Land: Chapters in Welsh Women's History, 1830–1939*, ed. Angela V. John (Cardiff: University of Wales Press, 1991), 109–33; Elizabeth Roberts, *A Woman's Place: An Oral History of Working-Class Women, 1890–1940* (Oxford: Basil Blackwell, 1984); and Ellen Ross, *Love and Toil: Motherhood in Outcast London: 1870–1918* (New York: Oxford University Press, 1993).

39. Nolan, *Ourselves Alone*, 50.

40. QSF, interview by author, Cape Broyle, 22 July 1999.

41. Later in the period, lye could be purchased for the soap-making process, and soap itself was sometimes purchased from local merchants, especially by washerwomen with multiple customers.

42. This description of the coast comes from Frank Galgay and Michael McCarthy, *Shipwrecks of Newfoundland and Labrador,* vol. 1 (St. John's: Harry Cuff, 1987), 1. Various wrecks in the area are described throughout this volume, as well as in vols. 2, 3, and 4 (St. John's: Creative Publishers, 1990, 1995, and 1997).

43. For example, the murder of the crew of a vessel wrecked off St. Peters and theft of items belonging to the vessel was the subject of various letters, depositions, and orders found in PANL, GN 2/1/A, vol. 3, 57–59 and 80–86, September-October 1759. In 1777, the people of St. Mary's were accused of doing nothing to help the survivors of a shipwreck in their harbor and of stealing items from the doomed French vessel. Governor Montagu observed that "every part of the Conduct of the People at and about S^{t}. Maries concerned in this transaction appears to me the most inhuman and Barbarous proceedings I ever heard of in a Christian Country." See PANL, GN 2/1/A, vol. 6 (reverse end), 134–38, and vol. 7 (reverse end), 3–4, May 1777. In 1782, Capt. Lane of the *HMS St. Johns* complained that a large portion of a cargo that had been saved by him and his men from a vessel wrecked at Ferryland had been illegally carried away by local inhabitants. See PANL, GN 2/1/A, vol. 9, 363–64, Governor Campbell to Capt. Lane of *HMS St. Johns,* 14 October 1782. In 1816, a notice respecting the loss of the *HMS Comus* off St. Shott's was posted in the district of Trepassey, requiring "Persons saving any of the Materials to give information thereof to M^{r}. Jackson of Trepassey when they would be entitled to one third of the Value thereof as Salvage & cautioning persons against concealing any of the said Stores etc." See PANL, GN 2/1/A, vol. 27, 308, Notice, 16 November 1816. Obviously, two Trepassey men chose to ignore the order, for the Court of Sessions offered a reward for their capture or information leading to their capture for stealing the sails and rigging from the disabled vessel. See PANL, Mildred Howard Collection, vol. 1, citing *Royal Gazette,* 26 November 1816. In 1817, the *Royal Gazette* reported that when the brig *Guysborough* entered Bay Bulls harbor in distress, it was met by a "riotous and tumultuous assembling of people . . . with apparent intent to plunder" the provisions on board. See PANL, Mildred Howard Collection, vol. 1, citing Royal Gazette, 11 March 1817. A report by the magistrates on the event noted: "The Inhabitants of the district of Bay of Bulls being destitute of supplies and their Merchants having none of the necessaries of Life in their Stores, met and sent Messengers to the Owners of the Cargo to request part of it might be delivered to them, at the same time threatening to break open the Hatches of the Vessel and take it by force if their demand should not be complied with." See PANL, GN 2/1/A, vol. 28, 309–15, and vol. 29, 297–300, correspondence and case summary, April and ca. December 1818. That same year, John Hayes of Ferryland district was sentenced to thirty-nine lashes for assaulting a constable who tried to prevent him and others from removing goods from the wrecked vessel *Rapid.* See PANL, GN 5/1/C/1, 13–14, *King v. John Hayes,* 8 November 1817. In April of 1830, complaints were made about certain inhabitants of Witless Bay who plundered two vessels wrecked near the

harbor. See Mannion Name Files, Witless Bay: "Carew, Al"; "Mullowney, Thomas and Patrick"; "Nash, W. M."; "Norris, James"; and "Power, Matthew." In 1831, a notice was posted in a local newspaper directing those persons who had recently engaged in the "most barbarous and outrageous plunder of the property of the crew" of the brig *William and Ann*, wrecked south of Renews, to relinquish the goods or face prosecution. See PANL, Mildred Howard Collection, vol. 1, citing *Royal Gazette*, 17 December 1831. In 1836, Robert Carter, magistrate at Ferryland, attended at a wreck site in Toad's Cove, where a West Indian vessel laden with molasses had been dismantled and relieved of its cargo. See PANL, MG 920, Robert Carter Diary, 5 January 1836. In 1844, a local newspaper reported that when the brig *William* went ashore in a thick fog in St. Mary's Bay and lay stranded on Point La Haye Beach, "the inhabitants of the neighbourhood plundered the vessel of everything they could lay their hands on." See PANL, Mildred Howard Collection, vol. 1, citing *Royal Gazette*, 9 July 1844. In 1845, various parties at Ferryland were charged with plundering a wrecked vessel. See PANL, GN 5/4/C/1, box 2, *Regina v. William Williams, John. Dullanty, and John Reed*, 1, 2, and 10 June 1845. In 1850, two men from Chance Cove were accused of taking shingles and provisions (beef, butter, porter, sugar, chocolate, and oatmeal) from the lost schooner *Matilda*. See PANL, GN 5/4/C/1, box 2, 1848–66 file, Complaint of Donald Henry Green, Master of the *Matilda* of Halifax, 5 January 1850. In 1853, several men at Renews were charged with cutting the masts of the stranded vessel Hugh and removing its cargo. See GN 5/4/C/1, box 2, *Regina v. William Neal, Francis Gearin and Martain McCarthy*, 3 December 1853. In 1857, the captain of the Spanish barque La Plata accused the people of Trepassey of cutting the vessel's masts and stealing its cargo after the captain had deliberately run it ashore on the beach to ride out a storm. See Galgay and McCarthy, Shipwrecks, vol. 4, Chapter 4, 31–42.

44. Galgay and McCarthy provide several examples from the area in *Shipwrecks*, vols. 1–4. See also PANL, GN 2/1/A, vol. 27, 304–9, October-November 1816, respecting the billeting of survivors of the wrecked vessels *Comus* and *Harpooner* by residents of Trepassey. The oral tradition also notes that local inhabitants often endangered themselves to save crews and passengers from foundering vessels and did their best to provide comfort and hospitality to those in distress, although clearly this was not always the case, as the previous note attests.

45. This was customary practice according to Harry Newson, *The Law of Salvage, Towage, and Pilotage* (London: William Clowes, 1886), 71, and matches the impression given in various local court cases.

46. Statutes of Newfoundland, 23 Vict., Cap. 5, *An Act to Provide for the Protection of Property Wrecked on the Coast of Newfoundland*, passed 14 May 1860.

47. Quotation from XT, interview by author, Calvert, 19 July 1999; similar thoughts were expressed by AG and ESF.

48. Articles washed ashore on the beach clearly fell under the jurisdiction of the 1860 legislation that governed salvaging activities. Wrecked property was defined in section XXII as "all wrecks of the sea, or any goods or chattels, jetsam, flotsam, lagan, or derelict, or any boat, vessel, apparel, anchor, cable, tackle, stores, or materials, or any goods, merchandize, or other article or thing . . . found floating, or sunk at sea, or

elsewhere, in any tideway, shore, or coast of this Island, or cast, thrown, or stranded upon the shore or coast thereof; and whether the same be found above or below high water mark, and whether wholly in water or partly on land, or partly in the water." Thus, beach-combing activities performed by women did qualify as salvage operations.

49. See n. 43, above.

50. Galgay and McCarthy, *Shipwrecks*, vol. 4, Chapter 4, particularly 36–37.

51. For a general discussions of this issue, see E. P. Thompson, *Customs in Common* (London: Merlin Press, 1991), 305–36.

52. Related by EW, interview by author, Calvert, 21 July 1999, with the request that the parties' names remain anonymous.

53. Older informants reminisced happily, for example, about the bounty from the *pork wreck* of 1918 (the wreck of a Belgian relief vessel that carried large quantities of food stuffs, including salt pork) as well as the cases of raspberry and strawberry jam that washed ashore from the wreckage of the *Torhamvan* in 1926.

54. AG, interview by author, Ferryland, 21 July 1999.

55. One final aspect of women's participation in this activity can be noted, although it does not relate directly to women's work. The oral tradition holds that children (particularly those in the area from Renews to St. Shott's) ended their prayers every evening with the request, "Please God, send us a wreck before morning." A utilitarian attitude towards events that would be judged by modern-day standards as tragic was thus instilled early in life. Many oral informants saw this as a particularly female influence on younger generations, for "it was women who taught children their prayers." (Several informants—EW, ESX, KO, AG—used this exact phrasing.)

56. I have found no evidence of women fishing for cod during the study period. However, some local women have fished in the ocean in modern times. An oral informant from Calvert, for example, had joined her husband from her middle years to retirement in handlining for cod, having also raised a family of fifteen children and worked in the family saw mill through her earlier married life. Audio Sample Another, younger Calvert woman (formerly of Cape Broyle) is currently fishing for crab with her husband.

57. Compare this with the perception of women as "pollutants on the water" and *jinkers* (jinxes) in an English Newfoundland community on the northeast coast of the island described by James C. Faris in *Cat Harbour: A Newfoundland Fishing Settlement* (St. John's: ISER, 1972), 73. This suggests the possibility of ethnic differences in constructing womanhood, but much more research would have to be done in this area before drawing conclusions.

58. For discussions of the idealization of motherhood, with all its cultural aspects—e.g., the definitions and values, the extra social and emotional requirements attached to the construct—as well as the gap between middle-class ideals and the realty of plebeian/working-class mothers' lives, see: Ross, *Love and Toil*; Rendall, *Women in an Industrializing Society*; Errington, *Wives and Mothers*; and Ryan, *Womanhood in America*.

59. Connell, *Population of Ireland*.

60. See, for example: Berkin, *First Generations*, 28; and Errington, *Wives and Mothers*, Chapter 2.

61. EC, interview by author, St. Mary's, 10 September 1999.

62. In her examination of Vila Chã, Sally Cole similarly discusses how women's productive work was linked to self-definition within the fishing community (*pescadores*): women proudly identified themselves as *trabalhadeiras* (hard-working women), and men sought *trabalhadeiras* as marriage partners. This attitude was not shared, however, by the agricultural community (*lavradores*), where women's productive work was stigmatized. See Cole, *Women of the Praia: Work and Lives in a Portuguese Coastal Community* (Princeton, NJ: Princeton University Press, 1991), especially 40–46 and 80–81.

63. Mannion Name File, Brigus South, "Dwyer, Anstice," re: *Anstice Dwyer v. Cornelius Kelly*, 27 October 1797.

64. GN 5/1/C/1, Ferryland, 142–45, *Catharine Delahunty v. James H. Carter*, 4 October 1827.

65. GN 5/4/C/1, Ferryland, box 2, *Ellen Leary v. John Butler*, 5 October 1848.

66. PANL, MG 920, Robert Carter Diary, 13 July 1841.

67. This song has been attributed by some compilers to John Quill, a shoemaker in St. John's. Betsy had apparently been born on Meeting House Hill in that town. The song also appears as "Betsey Mealy" and "A Newfoundland Heroine." See James Murphy, comp., *Songs and Ballads of Newfoundland, Ancient and Modern* (St. John's: n.p., 1902), 44–46; Gerald S. Doyle, ed., *The Old Time Songs and Poetry of Newfoundland* (St. John's: Gerald S. Doyle, 1927), 63; and Ronald Martin, ed. and comp., *Poems of Action, Sentiment and Reflection* (St. John's: n.p., 1945).

68. The Goodridge fish business was first established in Renews ca. 1807 by Henry Goodridge of Devon, who most likely operated it from the West Country. His youngest son, Alan Goodridge, came to Renews in 1828 on his schooner the *Viola* and settled in the community to run the business from there. Alan Goodridge and Sons moved its main premises to St. John's in the 1850s, but maintained a branch in Renews. Alan died in 1884. The Renews branch liquidated in 1920.

69. MHA, Goodridge fonds, 1840 ledger; and PANL, MF 473, Goodridge Collection, 1839 and 1841 ledgers. The women were clearly identified as shore workers in the 1840 and 1841 ledgers. In the 1839 ledger, some entries denoted payment for unspecified "work" only, but given that these entries usually appeared in September, October, and early November (the latter months of the fishing season) and that the rate of pay was 2s. per day, it is most likely that they related to shore work in the fishery. Other forms of women's paid work (haymaking, cooking, or washing, for example) were specified as such in the ledger.

70. By contrast, Berkin and Horowitz write that it was not unusual for wives of tenant farmers and poorer landowners in colonial America to continue to do housework and field work for wages after marriage; see Berkin and Horowitz, eds., *Women's Voices*, 117. Similarly, the wives of small farmers, recent immigrants, squatters, and tenant farmers in Upper Canada often did seasonal field labor and domestic work for others; see Errington, *Wives and Mothers*, 17, 83, and 126. Light and Prentice also note

that a significant number of married and older women could be found in service in British North America; see Light and Prentice, eds., *Pioneer and Gentlewomen*, 5. The system of farming out young women before marriage, however, appears to have been common throughout colonial North America.

71. The following discussion is largely speculative, as the impoverished state of Irish emigration records and southern Avalon parish records for this period makes the process of linking statistically significant numbers of immigrant women to their pre-migration status impossible.

72. Certainly, the literature on British female domestic servants of the period suggests that they were not upwardly mobile. See, for example: Edward Higgs, "Domestic Service and Household Production," in *Unequal Opportunities: Women's Employment in England, 1800–1918*, ed. Angela John (Oxford: Basil Blackwell, 1986), 125–50; and Bridget Hill, *Women, Work, and Sexual Politics in Eighteenth-Century England* (Oxford: Basil Blackwell, 1989).

73. The English government made several proprietary grants of Newfoundland territory in the early seventeenth century in the hope of stimulating colonization. In 1637, David Kirke was named co-proprietor and governor of the entire island and moved his family and some one hundred colonists to the Ferryland site that had been established in 1827 by Lord Baltimore. Numerous complaints were lodged against Kirke by colonists and migratory fishermen, but his undoing ultimately came from his royalist sympathies during the English Civil War. He was replaced as governor by John Treworgie in 1651 and recalled to England to answer the various charges against him. Some say he died in an English prison in 1654; others claim that he returned to Newfoundland and died there several years later. Nonetheless, his wife, Sara, and family stayed on in Ferryland and managed his considerable estate there. The Kirkes were still substantial planters in the area when the French attacked in 1696 (Web Link). See: Gillian Cell, *English Enterprise in Newfoundland, 1577–1699* (Toronto: University of Toronto Press, 1969); Eileen M. Dinn and Carla S. Krachun, "Kirke, David," in *Encyclopedia of Newfoundland and Labrador*, ed. Joseph R. Smallwood, vol. 3 (St. John's: Harry Cuff, 1991); and Pope, "South Avalon Planters."

74. Traces of Mary's story appear in PANL, MG 247, Carter-Benger-Nason Papers. This anecdote also survives in the oral tradition, and I am especially indebted to HE, Ferryland, for her summary of Mary's life history in correspondence dated 8 March 1999. Additionally, Agnes Field disdainfully mentions Mary in her discussion of the "mesalliances [between local men and Irish servant girls by which] the type of Newfoundland settler steadily got worse." See Field, "The Development of Government in Newfoundland, 1638–1713" (master's thesis, University of London, 1924).

75. PANL, MG 205, Pole Papers, 1799–1800.

76. It is important to note that many male fishing servants in Newfoundland were also upwardly mobile, moving from the status of inexperienced youngster into the ranks of skilled labor in the fishery, with many becoming planters (either boatkeepers or the heads of household units) in their own right. Audio Sample

77. See, for example: Errington, *Wives and Mothers*; Mona Hearn, *Below Stairs: Domestic Service Remembered in Dublin and Beyond, 1880–1922* (Dublin: Lilliput

Press, 1993); Higgs, "Domestic Service"; Hill, *Women, Work, and Sexual Politics*; Bridget Hill, Servants: *English Domestics in the Eighteenth Century* (Oxford: Clarendon Press, 1996); Rendall, *Women in an Industrializing Society*; K. D. M. Snell, "Agricultural Seasonal Unemployment, the Standard of Living, and Women's Work, 1690–1860," in *Women's Work: The English Experience, 1650–1914*, ed. Pamela Sharpe (London: Arnold, 1998), 73–120; and Valenze, *First Industrial Woman*.

78. Quotation from QSF, interview by author, Cape Broyle, 22 July 1999, and from ESX, interview by author, Calvert, 19 July 1999; but most oral informants made a similar observation.

79. For example, while diarist Robert Carter and his family hired local women for gardening and haymaking, on several occasions, they recruited servant girls from St. John's, who were more likely hired for specialized work indoors. See, for example, PANL, MG 920, Robert Carter Diary, 8 November 1836, and 14 May 1837.

80. Wage rates for household servants are difficult to gauge from the limited data available. Wages mentioned in court cases are ambiguous: "per year" sometimes means *per season* or *per summer*, and complainants are often suing for the "balance of wages" without specifying the full wage amount. Still, the total amounts mentioned—£2 per season/year (1826), £2.12.3 per season/year (1829), £3.6.6 Cy. per summer (1836), £3 per year (1840), £5 per summer (1846)—are quite low in comparison to fishing wages (see Table 4.1). Amounts mentioned in the Goodridge ledgers—e.g., £2.2.0 for a summer's wages and £9 Stg. for a full year's wages in 1840; £1.7.6 for "Wages p. Girl last winter & a P^{r} of Shoes," £1.4.0 for two months' wages, and 13s. 3d. for 25 days' wages in 1841—are also much lower than the wages either women or men were earning from the firm for shore work (2s. and 2s.–2s. 9d. per day, respectively).

81. Some historians point to the transition from paternalism to the contractual wage relationship that accompanied industrialization as a major source of tension in master/mistress-servant relations. See, for example, Hill, *Servants*, and Hearn, *Below Stairs*. In addition, some have noted that tensions, particularly between mistresses and servants, arose from middle-class efforts to "improve" the morals and habits of their servants—interference that was usually resented by the laboring class. See, for example: Valenze, *First Industrial Woman*; and Rendall, *Women in an Industrializing Society*. These explanations, however, have more explanatory power in historical contexts other than the southern Avalon.

82. All calculations of wages, piece rates, and provision prices in this study have been rounded to the nearest pence.

83. PANL, GN 2/1/A, vol. 8, 101–2, Order, Governor Edwards to John Dingle, JP, Bay Bulls, 27 October 1779, in response to a complaint laid by Donald Delany against the men's employer, Mr. Brookes, for non-payment of his wife's account.

84. PANL, MG 49, Sweetman Collection, box 3, file 18a, 21.

85. MHA, Goodridge fonds, 1840 ledger, fol. 342.

86. PANL, GN 5/2/C/3, 1835–47 journal, 1–2, *Margaret Yetman v. Philip and Briget Brown, James and Mary Whealan, and Tomas Dee,* Administrators to the Estate of the late William Christopher, 26 October 1835; also in GN 5/2/C/8, 1835–42 journal, 12–13.

87. The Goodridge ledgers indicate that a number of washerwomen were purchasing soap by 1839–41.

88. This was roughly the upper part of the range encountered in the written records. Mrs. James Barron, with her fourteen customers as noted above, appears to have been somewhat exceptional.

89. See: Nolan, *Ourselves Alone*; Luddy, *Documentary History*; and Mageean, "Irish Women's Prospects." Luddy cites an 1836 report that some fifty rural women of county Cork regularly transported eggs into the city of Cork for ultimate sale in English markets:

> . . . these individuals are generally young women of blameless morals and great industry; the distance they have to travel bare-footed with such a load as 300 eggs in a basket on their backs is to many no less than 50 miles; some will take so many as 350 of these eggs, others not more than 200; they generally bring as heavy a load back from the city, and make ten or a dozen such journeys every year; the time devoted to such a journey is generally a week; their profits are inconsiderable, perhaps about £3 in the year.

See Luddy, *Documentary History*, 169, doc. 47.3, *Report . . . [on] the Condition of the Poorer Classes in Ireland*, appendix D HC 1836 (43). The profits of £3 per year may have seemed "inconsiderable" to the report's author, but such earnings would have made a substantial contribution to a laboring family's income and may have been the only cash income earned by the family (see Chapter 2, n. 94).

90. MHA, Goodridge fonds, 1840 ledger, fol. 338.

91. MHA, Goodridge fonds, 1840 ledger, fols. 336–37 and 342; and PANL, MG 473, Goodridge Collection, 1841 ledger, fols. 246 and 306.

92. See, for example, PANL, MG 473, Goodridge Collection, 1841 ledger, fols. 246 and 306. Note that formal business ledgers do not show private transactions—either for cash or barter—between individuals.

93. Thomas, *Newfoundland Journal*, 114–16.

94. Thomas, *Newfoundland Journal*, 155.

95. Johnny Burke, "Betsy Brennan's Blue Hen," in *Doryloads*, ed. Kevin Major (St. John's: Breakwater Books, 1974), 79–81. It is evident that songwriter Burke has borrowed liberally from the Irish ballad "Nell Flaherty's Drake," customizing his offering with local vernacular and rejigging the tragedy from a killing to a theft. See: Nolan, *Ourselves Alone*, 31, from whose interpretation of the Irish song I have borrowed; and Kevin Danaher, *Irish Country People* (Cork: Mercier Press, 1966), 14.

96. PRL, 340.9 N45, Ferryland, —— *Welsh v. Leigh and Co.*, 25 September 1786.

97. Thomas, *Newfoundland Journal*, 109.

98. PANL, GN 5/4/C/1, Ferryland, box 1, 9–10, *Arthur Holdsworth and Co. v. Mary Keen*, 9 October 1792.

99. PANL, GN 5/1, Registry of Wills, vol. 2, 147, Will of Laurence Tobin, planter, Witless Bay, 11 July 1848. See also Mannion Name File, Witless Bay, "Tobin, Elenor."

100. Francis Corrigan, "The Ryans of Biscay Bay (1850–1970): A Study of Settlement," MHA, 43-A-1-42, Geography 2000 Collection, [early 1970s].

101. PANL, MG 31, Carter Family Papers, file 26, Harriet Carter to her uncle (likely George Williams), ca. late 1820s or early 1830s.

102. PANL, MG 920, Robert Carter Diary, 21 July 1836.

103. PANL, MG 920, Robert Carter Diary, 14 April 1841.

104. MHA, Goodridge fonds, 1840 ledger, fol. 341, Ann Jackman's account credited 6s. 11d. for 1 3/8 cwt. hay; PANL, MG 473, Goodridge Collection, 1841 ledger: fol. 247, Susan Layman's account credited £1.8.3 for 8.0.11 [cwt.?] of hay @ 3s. 6d.; fol. 248, Mary Neill's account credited 11s. 4d. and £1.14.1 for 3.1.0 and 9.3.0 [cwt.?] of hay, respectively; and fol. 248, Julia McCarthy's account credited 6s. 8d. for 1.3.17 [cwt.?] of hay.

105. See MHA, Goodridge fonds, 1840 ledger, fol. 341, Ann Jackman's account. And see PANL, MG 473, Goodridge Collection, 1841 ledger: fol. 247, Susan Layman's account; and fol. 248, Julia McCarthy's account. See also Appendix C.

106. This experience mirrors that of women in mainland colonies. See, for example: Light and Prentice, eds., *Pioneer and Gentlewomen*; Berkin and Horowitz, eds., *Women's Voices*; and Ryan, *Womanhood in America*.

107. Also note that a number of mistresses would have been assisted in sewing and washing by female servants.

108. See discussion on debt collection in Chapter 6.

109. PANL, GN 5/4/C/1, Ferryland, box 2, *Regina v. Thomas Leary*, 2 and 4 January 1855.

110. Quotation from ESX, interview by author, Calvert, 19 July 1999; but a similar observation was offered by numerous oral informants. In this regard, most oral informants mentioned a woman in Shore's Cove, Cape Broyle harbor, who operated her business in the early to mid-twentieth century; while outside the study period, the example serves to demonstrate the tradition. This woman ran a shop attached to her home and sold rum that her husband and his brothers smuggled from St. Pierre on a regular basis. Many informants felt that she was the "brains" behind the whole operation, and some suggested that she had inherited that role from her mother-in-law.

111. PANL, GN 2/1/A, vol. 11, 62–65, Instructions from Governor Jonathon Elliot to the Justices of the Peace, 25 September 1786.

112. PANL, GN 2/1/A, vol. 3, 251, Order, Governor Palliser, 2 October 1764.

113. In addition to the above, see the following governors' orders in PANL, GN 2/1/A: vol. 1, 17, Order, Rodney, 14 August 1749; vol. 1, 113 and 236, Orders, Drake, 21 August 1750, and 13 August 1751; vol. 4, 84–85, Order, Palliser, 31 October 1767; vol. 4, 202, Order, Byron, 30 September 1769; vol. 5, 100, Notice, Shuldham, 4 July 1772; vol. 10, 166, Instructions to Justices, Campbell, 14 September 1785; vol. 11, 62–65, Instructions to Justices, Elliot, 25 September 1786; vol. 12, 153–55 and 181, Orders, King, 15 September and 16 October 1792; vol. 17, 16–17, Proclamation, Gambier, 21 October 1802; and vol. 35, 268, Proclamation, Cochrane, 20 February 1826.

114. PANL, GN 2/1/A, vol. 12, 268, liquor license granted by Governor James Wallace to Elizabeth Sutton of Trepassey, 30 September 1794.

115. Lists of liquor licenses issued for the district for various years appear in PANL, GN 2/1/A, and GN 5/4/C/1, Ferryland, box 1. However, there are many gaps in the records. Only the following years are covered with any degree of comprehensiveness: 1750, 1795–1805, 1818–19, 1831, 1837, and 1840–41. References to license holders for other years of the study period are sporadic.

116. There is no indication in the ledgers of Mary's precise residence; she may be from the southern Avalon, or she may be serving here as an example by next-best approximation (see Appendix C, section 8).

117. PANL, GN 2/1/A, vol. 16, 7–8, liquor license granted by Governor Pole to Elizabeth Sutton, 12 October 1800.

118. PANL, GN 2/1/A, vol. 11, 62–65, particularly 63, Instructions from Elliot to Justices of the Peace, 25 September 1786; italics added. These instructions were received by the Ferryland magistrates and entered into the local court records. See PANL, GN 5/4/C/1, box 1, 18–19. The wording is similar, although the local records indicate that a license could be issued only to a person who would keep *or give security for keeping* at least one fishing shallop in the ensuing season. Similar wording appears in many of the orders cited above. To some extent, governors may have used this phrasing to maintain the appearance of enforcing *Palliser's Act* and its intent to privilege the fishery. However, it was also a genuine attempt to ensure the stability of liquor licensees, not a mere formality. When Governor King realized that the system was being abused, for example, he issued an order in 1792 requiring that all fishing boats of licensees be numbered and clearly identified by the owners' names on a conspicuous part of the boat. See PANL, GN 2/1/A, vol. 12, 181, Order, King, 16 October 1792.

119. Of course, at the husband's demise, the public house (and, presumably, the fishing shallop, to meet legal requirements) often reverted to the widow. By inference, then, these widowed tavern owners were also fishing employers. This criterion for respectability was eliminated by the new colonial legislature, for the first local act to regulate the retail of liquor, passed in 1839 (3 Vict., Cap. 6), contained no requirement for the employment of a boat in the fishery, and justices of the peace were given the discretion to determine who was "fit and proper" to hold a license. This act, however, and its successor acts in the 1850s (13 *Vict.*, *Cap.* 9, and 19 *Vict.*, *Cap.* 7) did remain gender inclusive in their wording.

120. PANL, MG 205, Pole Papers, 1799–1800.

121. PANL, GN 5/4/C/1, Ferryland, box 2, *Regina v. Thomas Leary*, 2 and 4 January 1855. An episode slightly outside the time frame also adds to the argument that women's involvement was masked by the licensing regulations. In 1867, Peter Winser of Aquaforte was charged with selling liquor in his shop without a license. The main witness for the crown, James Croft, testified that it was actually Mrs. Winser who had sold him the incriminating half pint of rum. Winser paid a small fine and obtained a license in his own name, but it is likely that his wife was working in the shop and selling liquor to the customers. See PANL, GN 5/4/C/1, Ferryland, box 2, *Regina v. Peter Winser*, 18 October 1867.

122. See: PRL, 340.9 N45, Ferryland, *Rex v. Margret Keney*, 14 July 1794; and PANL, GN 2/1/A, vol.13, 225–26, Robert Carter to Governor Waldegrave, 20 October

1797, enclosing various accounts, including a list of liquor licenses that had been issued for Ferryland district for 1795.

123. PRL, 340.9 N45, Trepassey–St. Mary's, *Re: Elizabeth Sutton*, 28 September and 18 November 1802. Also, PANL, GN 2/1/A, vol. 17, 35, Governor Gambier to McKillop, 30 October 1802.

124. PRL, 340.9 N45, Ferryland, *Mary Keating v. Stephen Kennely*, 14 September 1773; see also Mannion Name File, Ferryland, "Keating, Mary."

125. Quotation from ESX, interview by author, Calvert, 19 July 1999; numerous informants provided the same information.

126. Locally distilled liquor, called *moonshine* by the twentieth century, was made with molasses, hops, and oats boiled in a pot from which a coiling tube extended; the coil was passed through cold water, causing the vapors from the boiling mixture to condense. The liquid that exited the end of the tube would "tear the guts out of you." (QSF, interview by author, Cape Broyle, 22 July 1999.) Being "pure alcohol," it was also highly flammable; indeed, "If it wouldn't burn, it wasn't any good." (AG, interview by author, Ferryland, 21 July 1999.) Oral informants say that "everybody had their own little still" (VF, XT, QO, and AG) or knew who to borrow one from, although the practice appears to have been more common in some communities—e.g., Caplin Bay, Renews, St. Mary's—than others. Liquor distillation had deep roots in Ireland, and the illicit form of the activity resurfaced in the modern era with the re-introduction of duties on Irish spirits in 1661. The practice remained common in northwestern Ireland well into the twentieth century, although large-scale, legally operating distillers in the southeast were making inroads into local markets by the late eighteenth century because favorable government regulations permitted them to provide a cheaper, legal product. See Kenneth Connell, *Irish Peasant Society: Four Historical Essays* (Oxford: Clarendon Press, 1968), Chapter 1. Still, there can be little doubt that the long-standing tradition of illicit distilling made the trans-Atlantic crossing with the Irish and was reinstated on the southern Avalon by people who could not afford, or chose not to afford, excised liquor.

127. PANL, GN 2/39/A, box 1, William Poole to Board of Trade, 10 October (or possibly September) 1677 (typed transcript from CO Series).

128. PANL, 5/4/C/1, Ferryland, box 1, 28–33, —— *Hogan v. Patrick Shea*, 26 August 1787.

129. PANL, 5/4/C/1, Ferryland, box 1, 38–39, *Dennis Stokes v.* ——*Butler*, [3 July] 1787.

130. PANL, GN 5/1/C/1, Ferryland, 50, *Mary Sweeny v. Patrick Fowler*, 7 October 1818.

131. Wages in the fishery were generally paid for a season that ran from May 1 to October 20, or 173 days. (There were slight variations in dates—e.g., from mid-May to the end of October.)

132. Johanna Jackman's ancestors had come to Renews from the Isle of Wight in 1637, but, like many other local English lines (including her in-laws, the Johnson family), had begun to intermarry with the Irish population in the early 1800s and continued to do so as the nineteenth century unfolded.

133. QO, interview by author, Renews, 31 August 1999.

134. In her discussion of Martha Ballard, a midwife in Maine from 1785 to 1812, Laurel Thatcher Ulrich notes that the midwife was just one of a network of female "social healers" (compared with the "professional" medical men) who provided general health care to the community, although the midwife was herself the most visible and experienced of these women healers. See Ulrich, *A Midwife's Tale: The Life of Martha Ballard, Based on Her Diary, 1785–1812* (New York: Knopf, 1990), 61–66.

135. Quotation from EO, interview by author, Calvert, 26 August 1999; many informants expressed the same view.

136. Janet Mcnaughton provides a much more detailed description of traditional midwifery in Newfoundland in "The Role of the Newfoundland Midwife in Traditional Health Care, 1900 to 1970" (Ph.D. diss., Memorial University, 1989). Although she focuses on twentieth-century midwives, her observations on traditional obstetrical practices and the status of midwives in their communities correspond with information from the southern Avalon for the eighteenth and nineteenth centuries.

137. Note that these were fees for medical attendance, not witness fees, as were often allowed in bastardy and fornication matters in courts in colonial America.

138. The standard fee charged by Maine midwife Martha Ballard from 1785 to 1812 was 6s. per delivery, although wealthier patients often paid more. Like southern Avalon midwives, she often received payment in kind or in a combination of cash and kind, and sometimes she forgave fees altogether. Unlike southern Avalon midwives, however, she generally did not attend the mother in the lying-in period unless there were complications. Thus, she was actually paid a higher rate for her time than midwives on the southern Avalon. Martha also provided general medical services and, for one case, received the sum of $8.50 for 17 days' attendance, or $0.50 per day; this compared favorably with the standard charges of contemporary physicians in her area from $0.50 to $1.00 per visit. See Ulrich, *A Midwife's Tale*, 188–89, 197–200, and 247–48.

139. Oral informants spoke with great appreciation and affection for the midwives who had birthed them. A typical example was Mrs. Mary Johnny Kavanagh of Caplin Bay, who, in addition to her work in raising a large family and her involvement in household production, also worked as a laundress for local middle-class families and was a highly respected midwife. According to the oral tradition, she never refused to come out to a birth, and on one stormy night when the horse drawing her carriage could go no further, she set out and walked the remaining distance herself. Similar discussions of irrepressible midwives and the respect they enjoyed in their communities appear in the literature. See, for example: Ulrich, *Midwife's Tale*; Light and Prentice, eds., *Pioneer and Gentlewomen*, 145–49; Susan E. Merritt, *Her Story II: Women from Canada's Past* (St. Catharines, ON: Vanwell, 1995), 18–26; and Catherine M. Scholten, "'On the Importance of the Obstetrick Art': Changing Customs of Childbirth in America 1760–1825," in *Women's America: Refocusing the Past*, ed. Linda Kerber and Jane Sherron de Hart (New York: Oxford University Press, 1982), 51–65.

140. Such is the impression created by the large numbers of male fishing servants (or their employers, who held back *doctoring fees* from their wages) among the debtors in these court actions. Granted, this may also simply reflect the disproportionately

high numbers of male servants in the population. It is also possible that doctors were targeting the ready pool of local doctoring fees with their lawsuits, ignoring claims less likely to result in payments. Or perhaps fishing servants/employers were simply more recalcitrant bill-payers. Still, their overwhelming (almost exclusive) presence as defendants in court actions initiated by local doctors does suggest that, outside the local elite, the main focus of the doctors' attentions was the transient fishing servant population.

141. Even this system was not foolproof, however, as the court records contain numerous cases in which fishermen disputed payment of the fees. In 1836, an insurance fund for sick and disabled seamen, fishermen, shoremen, *sharemen*, sealers, and other fishing servants was established by legislation, with fees being held back from employees' wages for medical treatment. See 6 *Wm. IV, Cap.* 1, *An Act for the Relief of Sick and Disabled Seamen, Fishermen, and other Persons,*" passed 30 March 1836.

142. Report of Lieutenant Douglas, *HMS Phyllis*, cited in Galgay and McCarthy, *Shipwrecks*, vol. 4, 11; italics added. Within the context of eighteenth-century Newfoundland, the term *native* was often used to distinguish local inhabitants of European extraction from visiting migratory fishermen. Douglas was likely referring in his report to a local woman of European extraction, not an aboriginal woman.

143. PRL, 340.9 N45, Trepassey–St. Mary's, Notice of Micajah Malbon, Surrogate, to Margaret Curry, 27 September 1802.

144. PRL, 340.9 N45, Trepassey–St. Mary's, *M[ichael] D[avenport] Dutton v. Clapp and Co.*; the initial court hearing was undated, but the hearing before Chief Justice Tremlett was dated 27 September 1803.

145. See, for example, Ulrich, *Midwife's Tale*, 214; and Scholten, "'The Obstetrick Art,'" 53.

146. ESX, interview by author, Calvert, 19 July 1999.

147. 6 *Wm. IV, Cap.* 13, *An Act for the encouragement of Education in this Colony,* passed 6 May 1836.

148. CO 194, vol. 70, fol. 227, Governor's Annual Return and Additional Information respecting Newfoundland, 1825.

149. CO 194, vol. 57, fol. 12, Governor's Annual Return and Additional Information, 1815.

150. PANL, GN 5/1/C/1, Ferryland, 45, *Kearon Mulloney v. Henry Coryear,* 11 May 1818.

151. PANL, MG 473, Goodridge Collection, 1841 ledger, fol. 306.

152. In Ferryland, for example, ten out of twelve members appointed to the board in May 1836, and ten out of thirteen in December 1836, came from the English Protestant group. Similarly, in Placentia–St. Mary's, ten out of thirteen of those appointed in August 1836, and nine out of thirteen appointed in December 1836, came from this group. See *Journal of the Legislative Council* [*JLC*], 1836 (St. John's: Ryan and Withers, Queen's Printer, 1837), appendix, "Education Returns" (unnumbered and unpaginated).

153. See *JLC*, 1836, appendix, "Education Returns": Bye-laws, Rules, and Regulations adopted by the Ferryland Board of Education, 16 October 1836; and Resolutions passed at a meeting of the Placentia–St. Mary's Board of Education, 22 August 1836.

See also PANL, GN 21/1/A, Department of Education, Minute Book of the Protestant Board of Education for the District of Ferryland, 1836–37 and 1843–78, Minutes, 26 September and 8 October 1836 (note that, while the series is identified as relating to the "Protestant Board," the board was non-denominational until separate Catholic and Protestant systems were created in 1843). These ecumenical requirements did not become statutory until 1838, with the passing of 2 *Vict., Cap.* 5, *An Act to amend . . . An Act for the Encouragement of Education in this Colony*, passed 25 October 1838.

154. See 6 *Vict., Cap* 6, *An Act for the Encouragement of Education in this Colony*, passed 22 May 1843.

155. This was not the case everywhere on the island. In Conception Bay schools, for example, there were no female teachers appointed by the non-denominational board from 1836 to 1843. The Roman Catholic board in the district appointed only one female teacher during the period 1843–57: Mary Hearn, at Bryant's Cove. See PANL, GN 21/6/2, Department of Education, Minute Books of the Roman Catholic (again, actually non-denominational until 1843) Board of Education for the District of Conception Bay, 1836–57.

156. PANL, GN 21/1/A, Department of Education, Minute Book of the Ferryland Board of Education, Minutes, 26 September, 8 and 14 October, 1836, and 5 April and 4 October 1837. Note that Nicholas Fitzgerald's name does not appear on the final roster of 4 October 1837, but there is no indication elsewhere in the minutes that he has been replaced. Also, Robert Fitzharris was originally to be offered the school in Caplin Bay, but he had a drinking problem. He was to provide a certificate swearing that he would abstain from all intoxicating liquors (Minutes, 8 October 1836), but obviously he did not or could not comply, and his name did not appear on the final list.

157. An exception was the appointment of Elizabeth Coulman, an English Protestant woman who was hired to teach the predominantly Irish Catholic school population of Caplin Bay and Ferryland. The predominance on the board of English Protestant merchants from Caplin Bay and Ferryland may have been a factor in her hiring, for they may have wished to have a genteel woman of their own ethnoreligious group teach their daughters and younger children. Elizabeth's direct relationship to the locally powerful Carter family, and the fact that she had several relatives on the board, may also have influenced their decision. Nonetheless, she would have been a well-educated and certainly qualified to fill the position. Jane Winsor was also of English Protestant descent with middle-class ties, but this ethnoreligious group predominated in her community of Aquaforte, so her hiring fits the pattern of the other appointments.

158. *JLC*, 1836, appendix, "Education Returns."

159. *JLC*, 1860 (St. John's: Joseph Woods, 1860), appendix 36, "Second Year's Report upon the Inspection of Catholic Schools in Newfoundland, 1859" (Michael J. Kelly, Inspector), 352–418. Note that the inspector did not provide a full return for the St. Mary's area, and that four schools in that bay were not accounted for.

160. The Ferryland board, for example, confirmed that all schoolmasters under its jurisdiction would "be allowed from 15th June to 1st September to their own benefit to

employ themselves as they chose, subject to the discretion of two Commissioners"—the stipulated time frame implying that the anticipated employment of choice for those masters who took advantage of this clause would be fishing. See PANL, GN 21/1/A, Department of Education, Ferryland Board of Education, Minutes, 4 October 1837. Classes were held year-round at this period, with short Christmas, Easter, and summer breaks, although most children would not have attended on such a regular basis. Note also that teachers' salaries were supplemented by student fees, but although a scale of fees was legislated, schools boards (and, later, teachers) had the authority to remit them in cases where students could not afford them—a common situation in many outports at the time. Thus the teachers' remuneration from pupil fees was very irregular and usually quite small.

161. During the study period, sex-segregated schools were established in St. Mary's (by 1838), Renews (1840), Admiral's Cove in Fermeuse (1854), Ferryland (1858–59), and Witless Bay (1860). Just after this period, separate schools for boys and girls were established in Cape Broyle (1865) and Bay Bulls (1866). See Frank Galgay, Michael McCarthy, Sister Teresina Bruce, and Sister Magdalen O'Brien, *A Pilgrimage of Faith: A History of the Southern Shore from Bay Bulls to St. Shott's* (St. John's: Harry Cuff, 1983). See also the various education returns in the appendices of the JLC.

162. JLC, 1860, appendix 27, 383.

163. JLC, 1860, appendix 27, "School Return for the Presentation Convent Schools for the year ending December 31, 1859," provided by Bishop John T. Mullock, 399. The sisters offered a curriculum based on that of the Irish National School System: reading, writing, arithmetic, English grammar, geography, history, drawing, maps, sewing, marking, needlework, and embroidery, with an industrial department that provided classes in weaving, spinning, and knitting. The obvious differences in relation to the desired curriculum for boys' schools was the omission of navigation and the addition of various domestic arts. This emphasis on preparing young women for motherhood and domesticity will be discussed again in Chapter 8.

164. *JLC*, 1878 (St. John's: J. C. Withers, Queen's Printer, 1878), appendix 40, "Syllabus for Grading Teachers," 417–19.

165. *JLC*, 1880 (St. John's: J. C. Withers, Queen's Printer, 1880), appendix 52, "Report on the Public Schools under Roman Catholic Boards for the year ended December 31, 1879," 399–517, especially 408–9.

166. Quotations from QSF, interview by author, Cape Broyle, 22 July 1999; similar sentiments were expressed by most informants.

5. "SHE MADE THE CANNONBALLS, AND HE FIRED THEM"

Irish Newfoundland Women and Informal Power in Family and Community

On 22 July 1822, Ellen Veal (also Vail) appeared before the justice of the peace at St. Mary's to lodge a complaint of assault against her neighbor Mary Bowen. Two days earlier, Mary had been entertaining her friends Ellen (Nell) Tobin and Mary Molly in her home. The women were chatting companionably while Mary Bowen nursed her baby and puffed contentedly on her pipe. Suddenly, Ellen Veal appeared in the doorway and demanded to know why Mary "shoud have caried Lyes and storys up the harb[or]" about her deceased husband and a Mrs. Bishop, and why she was spreading rumors that her daughter had received a pair of shoes from James Barry (with all that may have implied). Ellen had heard this scandalous news from Catherine St. Croix, who had, in turn, heard the gossip from the same Nell Tobin who now sat comfortably in Mary's house. Mary told Ellen to stop making "an oration" of the matter and ordered her to leave the house or she would "turn her off." Ellen "swore God if She did, she woud break the Bucket over her head" and stood her ground. Mary put aside her nursing child, and tried to push Ellen away, but Ellen resisted; she broke off the pipe in Mary's mouth, and battle commenced. Witnesses Nell and Mary could not swear who had struck the first substantial blow, but all agreed that the defendant won the upper hand in the resulting fracas, for Ellen retreated with "blood running."[1] Case File 8

This court case illustrates plebeian women on the southern Avalon deploying power—through verbal wrangling, physical brawling, and gossip—in ways that clashed with hegemonic discourses on femininity in contemporary Britain. Within the English common-law tradition by the eighteenth century, women were viewed as dependents and virtual possessions of fathers or husbands, incapable of controlling their own property, skills, and labor. Most restricted was the married woman, the *feme coverte*, who could not own property in her own right, enter into contracts without her husband's permission, sue or be sued. Meanwhile, Enlightenment thought was underscoring the division between the public (rational, active, individualist, masculine) sphere and the private (emotional, passive, dependent, feminine) domain. Female domesticity was glorified as women's lives were channeled towards marriage and motherhood. Late eighteenth-century and early nineteenth-century evangelicalism reinforced the dichotomy of "public" man and "private" woman as it shaped middle-class ideals of female domesticity, respectability, passivity, and dependence.[2]

Newfoundland was a British fishing station and, later, a colony during the study period, and these discourses were certainly infiltrating Newfoundland society through its British legal regime and an emerging local middle class of administrators, churchmen, court officials, and merchants, many of whom maintained strong ties with Britain.[3] But how did these constructions of womanhood play out within the essentially plebeian Irish community on the southern Avalon, where community formation was still in its early stages and where gender relations were very much contested terrain?

In day-to-day life, Irish women in the area exercised considerable authority in their families and communities, and continued to function in public spaces throughout the period. This was true of married women as well as those who were single or widowed, for although the law of coverture dictated that a husband and wife became one legal entity in the person of the husband, the vital roles of plebeian women as co-producers and reproducers in family economies ensured that their identity in most everyday contexts was not subsumed in marriage. In this, they were similar to their counterparts in rural Ireland, at least in eighteenth- and early nineteenth-century rural Ireland, where women derived considerable status from their role as co-producers in a mixed farming and domestic textile economy. Within both settings, married women exercised relative autonomy in the running of their households and also had significant influence over matters outside the home. While a façade of patriarchal authority was usually maintained in both cultures, women frequently directed male decision-making behind the scenes. Clarkson describes this family power structure in Ireland as "matriarchal management behind a patriarchal exterior." [4] The oral tradition on the southern Avalon offers a more homespun equivalent: "She made the cannonballs, and he fired them."[5]

The strong family matriarch has been identified in other maritime cultures as well. Hector St. John de Crèvecoeur, for example, observed the ability of women in eighteenth-century Nantucket whaling families "to transact business, to settle accounts, and in short, to rule and provide for their families" while their husbands were at sea.[6] Laurel Thatcher Ulrich notes that wives of New England fishermen and merchant sea captains stood as deputies for absent husbands—keeping accounts, defending shore property from encroachments, acting as attorneys, supervising the planting and harvesting of crops, and attending to other family concerns.[7] Sally Cole discusses the autonomy and decision-making power of *pescadore* women of Vila Chã, Portugal, which grew out of their vital roles as fishers, marketers, and household managers.[8] However, women's authority in these contexts was linked to long-term absences of men in terms of their fishing activities. This has no explanatory power for the southern Avalon, where most men fished near their homes and also remained in their home communities in the off-season. There, the authority of Irish Newfoundland plebeian women emanated from something other than the status of proxy husbands or fathers.

THE FAMILY

Within fishing families, there were gendered spheres of authority that were linked to the sexual division of labor, with some overlapping where work routines coincided. Men made decisions about fishing, for example, but both women and men in family production units exercised authority over the curing process. Indeed, women usually shouldered greater responsibility in processing when men spent more time on the water in the height of the fishing season. As both men and women shared gardening and haymaking responsibilities, most married couples jointly discussed matters such as the timing of planting and harvesting or the types of crops to be grown. The dominant authority in matters respecting home and family, however, was generally the woman. Most men "didn't know what end went foremost" around the house, and left household affairs and child rearing to the women, occasionally intervening in disciplinary matters when their help was solicited by their wives.[9]

In terms of the day-to-day management of household resources, women's authority was paramount in many families.[10] Of course, this was self-evidently true of women who enjoyed the status of *feme sole*, but married women were also the primary household managers within the plebeian community on the southern Avalon. In carrying out this responsibility, women had to balance the requirements and contributions of large households that, in some cases, included domestic and fishing servants as well as family members. Their power as household managers extended to the allocation of any amounts (usually small) of cash the family may have accumulated. In addition, women who were part of a family production unit in the fishery often oversaw, from behind the scenes, the tabulation of the family's account with the supplying merchant. While the male "head of the family" generally went to the merchant's store to settle up in the fall, he was often acting on the advice of a wife or mother who had actually kept track of the various supplies issued to the family and the amounts of fish and oil provided to the merchant in return. Thus, the family matriarch usually had an accurate idea of the balance of the family account, and if her husband or son did not conclude the negotiations with the merchant to her satisfaction, she would send him back to have the account adjusted accordingly. Indeed, it was not unknown for the woman herself to pay a visit to the merchant's premises to fine-tune the balance.

It is difficult to say how far back into time this practice of account-keeping extended; it was represented by informants as common practice within the family production unit, certainly in the latter decades of the study period; but it may have been in evidence in the traditional planter fishery as well. In a 1793 court case, for example, in which a servant was suing Trepassey boatkeeper James Warne for outstanding wages, Warne's wife was required to testify because it was she who kept the household accounts.[11] Evidence of women keeping accounts and dealing with merchant suppliers certainly appears in the literature on colonial America, so southern Avalon women would not have been out of step with their contemporaries elsewhere in exercising this duty.[12]

According to the oral tradition, women's general ability to manage the household's resources—to make very little stretch a long way during hard times, and to put a bit aside in good times—was critical to family survival. Indeed, most informants felt that it was more important for a woman to be a *good manager* than for a man to be a *good provider*, for no matter how successful a man's economic activity was, a poor female manager could squander the proceeds and leave the family very badly off; by contrast, the wife of a bad provider could make ends meet if she judged consumption and allocated resources carefully. The female household manager could, therefore, "make or break" a family, and the wife who could see her family through the "long and hungry month of March"[13] was prized indeed. Audio Sample

A woman's powerful status within the household extended into widowhood. Even when a man bequeathed the family home and property to a child or children, it was done so with the understanding that his wife not only would be looked after, but also would continue to have a substantial say in the running of the household. The mother was usually still *the boss*, and inheriting children would continue to respect her wishes after her husband's death. Audio Sample

Of course, women on the southern Avalon did not universally experience this substantial degree of informal power within the family. There were some "who didn't have any say; they just kept the children coming, washing and cooking for them, and died before their time."[14] And a woman who did exercise strong influence within the family was still expected to maintain some façade of deference to patriarchal authority for the outside world. If a woman stepped beyond this limit, if she was too domineering in public, she was labeled a *real boss.* Kathleen Brown discusses the equivalent figure in colonial Virginia: the *scold,* who subverted gender hierarchies by attempting to dominate her husband.[15] Yet the term *boss* did not carry quite the same stigma as *scold,* for the southern Avalon label often carried with it a degree of grudging respect—an acknowledgment of strength of character, particularly for women who had to take over in the absence or default of male authority. Audio Sample Nonetheless, most marriages were partnerships, according to oral informants. While the patriarchal family was the ideal in hegemonic discourse, there was a significant gap between this rhetoric and the reality of power relations within plebeian families in the area. Brown's conceptualization of a gender hierarchy that was fairly fixed, yet occasionally besieged by women, therefore seems too rigid for discussing gender relations on the southern Avalon in the period of early settlement.

The concept becomes even more problematic with evidence that the scope of plebeian women's informal power extended beyond the family to the community. Oral informants agreed that most women had considerable influence over how the family was represented in the larger community by the men—at public meetings, for example, or at the merchant's store. The veneer of patriarchal authority was maintained in the presence of a male family representative. As one informant explained: "Well, the man was *supposed* to be in charge [laughs]. That was the way it was given down. But a woman had to have a voice too, you know."[16] Audio Sample Another pointed out that a man going to a meeting "would be well-informed [by his wife] before he went" as to what his opinions should be.[17] So women would generally let their views be known, even in matters outside the home, and their husbands generally respected their advice. And there were other areas of community life in which women deployed informal power as well, suggesting that gender was very much in the process of negotiation during the study period.

THE ECONOMIC SPHERE

As we have already seen, Irish plebeian women on the southern Avalon were an intrinsic part of the economic life of their fledgling communities, as mistresses and servants in fishing households, as washerwomen and seamstresses, as shopkeepers and tavernkeepers, or as proto-professionals. And increasingly, Irish Newfoundland women moved into the essential role of shore crew for the household production unit in the fishery, working on stage head and flake to produce saltfish for the marketplace. Their presence at these public sites of economic production and their vital and recognized contribution to the process was an important source of power for these women, even into the twentieth century

Further evidence of women's participation in the public economic sphere can be seen in mercantile journals and ledgers, which indicate that women were a significant part of the exchange economy of the area. Surviving Goodridge ledgers for the years 1839 to 1841 provide a comprehensive picture of women's involvement at Renews, albeit for a limited time frame.[18] Women's accounts also appear in the Sweetman records.[19] Unfortunately, these books are not intact, even for limited years, and many accounts are merely loose leaves in files; but the entries reinforce the conclusions that can be drawn from the Goodridge records.[20] Appendix C provides a detailed (but by no means exhaustive) overview of the types of women's accounts and economic activity revealed by these mercantile records. The following discussion will draw from these examples, with links to appropriate sections in the Appendix.

Although women's names appear far less frequently than men's in the ledgers, a significant number of women held accounts in their own names and in a variety of capacities. The intact Goodridge ledgers provide some indication of the frequency of this phenomenon. Thirty-nine women headed accounts with the firm in 1839, forty in 1840, and forty-four in 1841. In each successive year, there was an attrition of some customers and the addition of others, such that the total number of women holding individual accounts for the entire three years was actually sixty-eight. Still, there was a good deal of continuity in women's presence in the ledgers, for half of them were repeat customers, with fourteen heading accounts in two years and another twenty appearing in all three ledgers. This was a significant level of participation by women in the local economy, given the modest population of the area, and particularly the small number of local adult women. (In 1836, there were 146 women aged fourteen and over in Renews; in 1845, the total was 153. Adding adult women from nearby Fermeuse, a community which also dealt with Goodridge's, the totals for the two years were 247 and 272, respectively.)[21]

Only one of these female account holders was identified as a widow, although this was most likely also the status of Catherine Kenny, who headed the account of "Catherine Kenny and Sons," and Rachel Welsh of "Rachel Welsh and Son." Two others were specifically identified as married women, who were operating accounts separate from those of their still-living husbands. It is highly unlikely, however, that the remaining female account holders were all single, given population figures; some may have been widows, but it is likely that a number were married women holding accounts with the firm as if they were *femes sole*.[22] This is reinforced by the fact that few (and often no) supplies of basic foodstuffs appeared in the majority of these accounts. Most listed supplies of soap and materials necessary for washing and sewing, along with extras such as sugar, shoes, and senna tea. The inference can thus be drawn that many of these account holders were married women whose food supplies were debited to the accounts of male household heads, but whose separate economic activities warranted separate accounts in the merchants' books.

Still, some women were obviously household heads in their own right (see Appendix C, section 1). Rachel Welsh and Jane Careen were two such independent householders, for family supplies and credit were advanced in their names. In addition, women such as Catherine Kenny, Mary Morris, Sarah McCarthy, Mary Murphy, and Dorothy Cantwell headed household units that were producing oil and saltfish for market. A larger number of women account holders were washerwomen and seamstresses (see Appendix C, section 2). Supplies for washing and sewing were advanced to them and then contra'd against the accounts of their customers through the merchants' ledgers. In addition, a significant number of women in the Renews area paid for supplies advanced to them through work on the Goodridge's flakes (see Appendix C, section 3). And many combined a package of paid services—shore work, sewing, washing, cooking, and the sale of poultry, hay, or oakum—which attracted payment either directly from the firm or in third-party transactions involving mutual customers of the women and the merchants (see Appendix C, section 4). Occasionally, wages of women servants or of servants employed by women appeared—some in direct payment from the firm, others in third-party transactions through the employer's account with the merchant supplier (see Appendix C, section 5). Payments of rent to and from women were also sometimes transacted through the merchants' ledgers (see Appendix C, section 6).

Women, like men, obtained supplies on credit and settled up in the fall. Julia McCarthy of Renews provides a good example. Her accounts with Goodridge's for 1839 to 1841 are shown in Table 5.1. Julia had a number of local customers, including some of the Goodridge family, for whom she washed or sewed for piece rates. Her supplies were generally paid by a contra entry that credited her account while debiting the account of her customers. In addition, in 1841, Julia received credit for working on the Goodridge's flakes and for selling hay to the firm. In 1838, Goodridge's gave her an abatement in order to balance her account. In 1840, Julia was fortunate enough to break even. In 1841, however, she had a debt of 3s. 5d. that was carried forward to the next year. In no year, then, did she receive any cash, but she was able to keep her head above water with the paid work she performed. In this respect, she was like most of the firm's customers, both men and women.

Nonetheless, twenty accounts headed by women did contain entries of cash payments made either to the women themselves or to others on their behalf. The total number of payments involved was twenty-nine, and most were made in the autumn, after settling up.[23] With the exception of two large cash amounts paid to and on behalf of Mrs. Alan Goodridge (£32.2.7 and £9.17.5, respectively), all other cash amounts were £2 and under, and nineteen were under £1. Still, the fact that these women were able to earn cash through their economic enterprises was significant in an economy that saw little cash in circulation. And several women, rather than drawing cash, had their profits applied towards the debt of a male relative, likely a husband or father.[24]

A number of women who dealt with Goodridge's had credit balances in the fall of the year (three in 1839, six in 1840, and six in 1841). Similarly, the Sweetman records indicate credit balances for eight women in both 1802 and 1843 (the only years for which itemized lists are available). Some of these balances were quite substantial (see Appendix C, section 7). The majority of women, however, barely broke even or carried over some level of debt to the following year. This was a classic feature of the truck system in Newfoundland, and, indeed, it was not unusual to see "bad debts" appear among the entries in accounts for both men and women. Some of the entries in the Goodridge ledgers—seven in 1839, seven in 1840, and nine in 1841—related solely to women's bad debts, without any other indication of economic activity (similar entries for men were far more numerous). But in only two cases (one in 1839, one in 1841) were the amounts written off completely by the firm (one other debt, in 1840, was paid by a male relative). In every other case, balances were carried forward, indicating that the firm had some expectation of women being able to pay their debts over time.

Although women account holders were not as numerous as men, then, they were present in the records in significant numbers and participated in the exchange economy in ways that were sometimes distinctive, but more often typical of the merchants' broader clientele. Furthermore, any discussion of women's participation in the exchange economy must include the invisible presence of women in the accounts of male household heads. Fish and oil credited to many of these accounts were produced by family work units that relied upon the labor of women. And many of the goods appearing under the names of male household heads were used by women in household production, using labor and producing goods that were assigned no market value and therefore not included in formal business accounts of the day. Furthermore, merchant books did not record networks of informal trade that involved women—the exchange of eggs for butter, for example, or milk for wool: what Johanna Miller Lewis describes as an "underground economy" which helped women in many early colonial communities keep their families clothed and fed.[25]

Some useful comparisons can be drawn with women's participation in the exchange economy of late eighteenth-century Horton, Nova Scotia.[26] Elizabeth Mancke finds women appearing in Horton's merchant ledgers primarily as consumers (almost always through men's accounts) of unfinished goods for household production, concluding that "women consumed to produce and men produced to consume."[27] This gender differential was not quite so clear-cut on the southern Avalon. Granted, women there did *consume to produce*, often through accounts in men's names, but they also *produced to consume* as part of family work units that provided the chief commodity of the local exchange economy. And a number engaged in some form of independent economic activity, performing services for customers in order to purchase goods, often small luxuries, for themselves and their families.

Mancke interprets the predominance of men's names in the Horton business accounts as an indicator of women's subservient social status. While the same can be said in relation to the southern Avalon in terms of formal legal status, especially of married women, the ledgers may not have been an accurate portrayal of how gender relations played out on the ground. In setting up their books, merchants or their agents and clerks would have been mindful of the law of coverture, which dictated that a husband was responsible for his wife's debts. But this concession to patriarchal authority in the books did not necessarily reflect the reality of family power relations. Furthermore, both Goodridge's and Sweetman's were obviously willing to extend credit to women in their own names when they performed some autonomous form of economic activity, regardless of their marital status. Mancke also finds that account balances in women's names in Horton tended to be small: none over £10, and most under £3. In the Goodridge records, by contrast, thirty-three accounts contained balances of £3 or more, of which nine were over £10. Furthermore, some very high balances (debit and credit) appear in women's accounts in the Sweetman books (see Appendix C, section 7). Even allowing for some inflation in prices and earnings between the eighteenth and nineteenth centuries and possible differentials based on region, these findings are still highly suggestive of a higher level of independent economic activity for women on the southern Avalon than in Horton.

Finally, Mancke interprets various examples of women's receipt of third-party payments for goods or services as confirming women's subordinate social condition through servitude and wages. But the economic agency of their southern Avalon counterparts is apparent. Indeed, the incomes these women made from selling their goods and labor were essential contributions to their family economies, or, if single, to their own survival. Granted, their participation in activities such as washing, sewing, and service indicated their lower social status, but one must be careful in viewing their positioning solely through the lens of gender, for they were in no more servile a position than many fishermen in the area. Indeed, in one way, they were more independent, for the income from paid washing and sewing had a value that, unlike most aspects of the truck system, could be negotiated with their customers and was not "fixed" (or perceived to be fixed) by the merchants. While rates among different providers in a community were often similar in any given year, this can be attributed to competition rather than the heavy hand of the local merchant.

In general, then, while gender ideology increasingly provided a powerful impetus in many contexts to remove women from the workplace and marketplace or to devalue the contributions of those who remained, plebeian women on the southern Avalon remained active and essential in the economic sphere throughout the study period as producers of goods and services and as an integral part of the truck system that underwrote the resident fishery. Their participation in productive work, particularly saltfish production, and their significant contribution to the exchange economy (sometimes highly visible, sometimes muted in the merchant account books of the day) enhanced the power and status of these women in their own community.

THE SPIRITUAL REALM

The spiritual life of any group is a site of continuous negotiation between the natural and supernatural worlds. The process is enigmatic; the issues, profound; the stakes, unfathomable. Those who are chosen as mediators must, therefore, necessarily enjoy considerable authority and respect within their communities. In various cultures and at various times, women have acted as negotiators and guides through the spiritual landscape, and there is certainly evidence that religion—in both orthodox and informal observance—was an alternative source of female power for the Irish women of the southern Avalon, particularly before the encroachment of ultramontanism[28] and the devotional revolution of the mid- to late nineteenth century (see Chapter 8).

These women played an essential role in keeping the Catholic faith alive as the scarcity of priests in the area persisted well beyond the penal regime into the middle of the nineteenth century. Catholic women, for example, performed religious rites and assumed other forms of religious authority during the period under consideration. Indeed, Bishop Michael Fleming complained to his superiors in the 1830s that before the establishment of the Catholic missions in the 1780s, "The holy Sacrament of Matrimony, debased into a sort of 'civil contract,' was administered by captains of boats, by police, by magistrates, and *frequently by women*.The Sacrament of Baptism was equally profaned." He also expressed his dismay that midwives had taken the authority upon themselves to dispense with church fasts for pregnant women.[29] And Fleming may have been unaware that midwives and other women continued to baptize babies at birth to "tide them over" until formal church baptisms took place—a stopgap that reduced the urgency for observing the formal church rite (which sometimes took place months, or even years, after the births).[30] In addition, Dean Cleary tantalizingly referred to an incident (in the 1830s or 1840s) in which "the pious women" of St. Mary's took "the sacred fire from the altar to burn a house"—perhaps a rite of exorcism of some sort—at the behest of their priest, Father James Duffy.[31]

Furthermore, the oral tradition indicates that, just as women were the financial managers, so too were they the spiritual overseers of Irish Catholic households. Women, more than men, maintained the rituals and kept the faith alive before the priests came. Indeed, as one informant stated and most others implied: "If it was left to the men, sure there'd be no religion at all."[32] Every informant agreed that women played a more vital role in transmitting this facet of Irish Catholic culture to following generations, for "it was women who taught children their prayers."[33] These references suggest that women played an important custodial role in relation to the Catholic faith and, by extension, the identity of the ethnoreligious group in the period of early settlement.

In addition, female figures were prominent in the Irish Catholic hagiolatry of the area, harking back to the powerful position of goddesses and female druids in the pagan Celtic belief system, a status that carried over into early Celtic Christianity. Indeed, to this very day, the Virgin Mary, St. Brigid[34], and "good St. Anne"[35] are a triumvirate to be reckoned with on the southern Avalon. The cult of St. Anne was more likely a nineteenth-century phenomenon in the area, arising out of the devotional revolution in the Irish Catholic Church, but devotion to Brigid and Mary was of much longer standing. And while some male saints were invoked on specific occasions (St. Anthony was solicited to help find lost items, for example; and St. Jude, the saint of hopeless causes, was called upon in a variety of predicaments), their influence was not as pervasively felt in everyday life as that of Mary, Brigid, and Anne. Although these women were revered by both sexes (men and women, for example, plaited St. Brigid crosses from straw and erected them over doorways on her feast day for protection throughout the year, and Mary's capacity as a powerful intervener between Christ and man was acknowledged by the entire community), they were (and are) particularly cherished by women—not as the sanitized feminine ideals presented in the church calendar of saints, but as women who once lived worldly lives and who could therefore empathize with the experiences of other women. When asked if women prayed especially to Mary, Brigid, and Anne, one woman informant in the area advised me, "Oh God, yes, sure I'm still at it."[36]

While Irish women and female saints played an important role in the preservation of Catholicism in the study area, women were also central figures in an informal system of beliefs and practices that had been transported from the home country. On the southern Avalon, as in Ireland, there was an alternative pre-Christian religious system operating in tandem with (and sometimes overlapping) formal Catholic practice.[37] Today, there is a tendency to look at these ancient beliefs and practices as quaint folk traditions, grist for the mill of the modern-day tourism industry. But, as Sean Connolly points out in his discussion of the derivative traditions in Ireland, this "body of beliefs and practices . . . made up a very real part of the mental world of large numbers of Irish Catholics" in the eighteenth and nineteenth centuries.[38] On the southern Avalon, women were important navigators of this mental landscape.[39]

A belief in the occult powers of certain persons was part of the ancient belief system, and women featured prominently as mediators between the natural and the supernatural worlds. Women were proficient in reading tealeaves and telling fortunes. Certain women (and men) had special healing powers—the ability to stop blood with a prayer, for example. A widow's curse, by contrast, had the power to do great harm: to wither crops or drive fish from nets, to cause physical injury or even death.[40] Audio Sample Indeed, a woman's ability to rain down invective on her enemies—as was so ably demonstrated by Betsy Brennan in the loss of her hen (see Chapter 4), or by Jane Holehan of St. Mary's, who allegedly caused the milk of her neighbor's cow to dry up (see Chapter 6)—was a formidable weapon in her repertoire of conflict resolution skills, for the repercussions of ritual cursing were not to be taken lightly.[41] And women's special powers were woven into the very physical landscape, for places like *Mrs. Denine's Hill*, *Peggy's Hollow*, and the *Old Woman's Pond* (named for the women who had died there) had supernatural qualities that could cause horses to pull up in their tracks and grown men to lose their way.

The Irish inhabitants of the southern Avalon also believed in supernatural beings, and women were again central, either as symbolic figures or intermediaries in deflecting evil from family and other loved ones. The *bibe*, or banshee, for example, was a female figure—an ancient crone whose wailing cry in the night was the harbinger of death. So too was the *old hag* who rode the chest of many a nightmare sufferer through a troubled night. Sheelagh (or Sheila)—in popular belief, the wife or companion of St. Patrick—was blamed for the fierce ice storms and heavy snowfalls that battered the island on or soon after her feast day of 18 March—a consistent weather phenomenon that is still known today as *Sheelagh's Brush* or just *Sheelagh*.[42]

Women also featured prominently in fairy lore. On the southern Avalon, the belief in fairies was pervasive. The natural environment was filled with evidence of the existence of the little people, for *fairy paths*, *fairy caps*, and *fairy pipes* proliferated in the woods and meadows just beyond the garden gate. Fairies had the power to replace human children with changelings and render all humans, young and old, senseless, or *fairy-struck.* Audio Sample Infants were most vulnerable to their power, for the little people could enter homes and snatch babies from their very cradles. Women played a vital role in protecting their families from these troublesome creatures who moved so easily between the natural and supernatural worlds. It was women, for example, who made and blessed the bread that had special powers to keep the fairies from stealing their children—the same bread that could help people who were *fairy-led*, or lost in back-meadows or woods, find their way home.[43] It was primarily a woman's responsibility to ensure that loved ones, particularly children, who moved beyond the safety of the hearth had a piece of blessed bread, or *fairy bun*, on their person. Bread made on Good Friday had special protective powers, and most women ensured that they made a batch on that day specifically for this purpose—a combination of practices from formal Catholicism and the pre-Christian belief system.

Connolly notes that this overlapping of systems was quite common in Ireland. Some customary observances maintained their original content but acquired Catholic labels; others were modified to fit the Catholic faith (for example, the dedication of ancient holy wells to Christian saints). In some cases, Catholic rituals were incorporated into magical practices (for example, the use of relics to verify oaths, or a prayer to stop blood). Occasionally, the Catholic Church was complicit in this process. The adoption of St. Brigid into the Catholic calendar of saints, for example, demonstrates formal religion's willingness to co-opt aspects of the pre-Christian belief system.[44] The feast day of the *holy woman of Kildare* was celebrated by the church on 1 February, which corresponds with *Imbolc*, the ancient Celtic feast of fertility celebrating the coming of spring, the return of light after winter's darkness, and the beginning of the lactation of the ewes. The name of the Celtic goddess of fertility was Brigid. Thus, Catholic saint and Celtic goddess were conflated in one entity by the church itself. But more often, it was the Catholic laity who intermixed the two systems, seeing them not as conflicting, but rather as mutually reinforcing as the congregation molded the old and the new into a spiritual mèlange that lent meaning to their lives.

This mixing of belief systems can also be seen in many practices on the southern Avalon, including those in which women featured prominently. Women used a Christian symbol, the sign of the cross, to give protective power to fairy buns and made special batches of blessed bread on Good Friday, the most sacred day in the Catholic calendar. Women healers put pieces of paschal candles in their cures to give them extra potency.[45] The accuracy of women's predictions, particularly the identification of future spouses, was greatest on

St. John's Eve and All Souls' Night (All-Hallows Eve) in the Catholic calendar, which corresponded to Midsummer's Eve and the Celtic feast of *Samhain* in the ancient calendar, celebrations of fertility and the harvest.[46]

Women also combined formal and informal systems when they anointed their homes with holy water and blessed candle wax to protect their households from general danger and to ward off specific threats such as thunder and lightning. Holy water was any water blessed by a priest or holy person, but it was ideally obtained from a holy well, reminiscent of the ancient belief in the power of holy and magical sites.[47] Blessed candle wax was obtained from the priest on Candlemas Day, 2 February. In his 1819 history of Newfoundland, Anglican missionary Rev. Lewis Anspach wondered at the devout observance of this holy day by Catholics, "who most eagerly crowd to their respective chapels to receive a few drops from the lighted blessed candles on their hats and clothes, and a piece likewise blessed by their priest, which they carry home and preserve with the most religious care and confidence, as a protection against the influence of evil spirits."[48] The Catholic Church promoted the candles blessed on Candlemas Day as a symbol of Christ, deriving from the use of candles in the catacombs of Rome by early Christians who risked their lives to practice their faith. According to Catholic teaching, the bleached beeswax of the candles[49] represented Christ's "spotless body," the wick, "his Soul," and the flame, "the union of the nature of God with the nature of man."[50] However, within the Irish community on the southern Avalon, Candlemas was always associated with Mary and a fervent belief in her power to ward off evil. Thus, when women dripped blessed candle wax at the windowsills of their homes, it was Mary's blessing and protection that they sought; and when they dabbed the wax into their children's shoes, they said a prayer to Mary to guide their children's footsteps. Audio Sample

According to local belief, Candlemas was the day when Mary was *churched*.[51] This was an unlikely event in the life of a Jewish woman, but it demonstrates the awe with which Mary was regarded by the Irish community that a feast day for venerating Christ was co-opted to honor his mother instead. A further demonstration of the importance of female saints to the Irish community was the effort to tie Brigid, the *Mary of the Gael*, to the event, even though the two women were not contemporaries. According to local informants, Brigid walked before Mary as she was on her way to be churched, with rays of light pouring from her head to distract attention from Mary's shame. This, they say, is why St. Brigid's feast day is celebrated the day before Candlemas, on 1 February (which, as noted, was also the Celtic feast of *Imbolc*, celebrating fertility, the return of light after the long winter darkness, and the goddess Brigid, who was herself sometimes portrayed with rays of light pouring from a headdress of candles).

Here, then, was not only a conflation of Celtic and Catholic systems, but a conflation of time itself. The tradition of making Brigid and Mary contemporaries already existed in Ireland in other variations. One very compelling version held that Brigid was a midwife to Mary and wet nurse to Jesus, making her a favorite of pregnant women nearing their time of delivery (note, again, the connotations of fertility that hark back to the goddess Brigid). Another portrayed Brigid weaving a web from her ewes (again, a link to the Celtic goddess) to protect the infant Jesus from harm during the flight into Egypt.[52] Shirley Toulson describes such contemporizing of Brigid and Mary as a "venture into the spiritual, timeless world that makes nonsense of chronology," a convention that wreaks havoc with history's love of time lines.[53] But it was a tradition, with women at its core, that helped Irish Catholic communities on the southern Avalon and in Ireland make sense of their spiritual and natural worlds.

Perhaps the most striking example of the combination of ancient and Catholic practices was the wake. Here, women also played an essential role in the rituals associated with death.[54] The corpse was usually laid out by a woman or group of women, who bathed the body and then poured the water on the ashes in the fireplace, a ritual that suggests spiritual as well as physical purification. The women were sometimes assisted by a man, especially in shaving the face if the deceased was male; but the cleansing process was decidedly regarded as women's work in which a man might occasionally help. The women then dressed the body in a *habit* that had in most cases been made by a female relative of the deceased, but otherwise by another woman of the community with good sewing skills. A woman would also have made the shroud that covered the coffin and the small white cloth that would be placed on the face of the corpse before the coffin was closed. (Pragmatic and reconciled to the inevitability of death, most adult women kept a habit and ceremonial cloths in readiness for the next funeral in the family.) Throughout the laying out of the corpse, men would cluster outside, waiting for this part of the ritual to be completed before entering the wake-house—a spatial separation that suggests that they were remote from this process of ritual cleansing and preparation.

As in Ireland, the wake itself was a mixed gathering at which stories and practical jokes abounded, *"God be merciful" pipes* were at the ready, and liquor was usually in good supply.[55] The body was constantly attended until the interment, and women as well as men *sat up* with the corpse overnight to guard its spirit, although the practice varied: in some instances, only men stayed up; in others, only women; more commonly, however, both sexes were in attendance. It was during the overnight vigil that practical jokes were most likely to occur, usually with men as perpetrators and women as victims. The oral tradition abounds with stories of women being terrified by the sight of a corpse smoking a pipe, or its chin whiskers moving, or a body sitting up or rolling over in a coffin (thanks to some strategically tied string). Protestant middle-class observers of the period often denigrated such practices; Robert Carter, a merchant and surrogate in Ferryland, for example, stipulated in his will that there be "No Wakings of my Bodie, I protest against such practices, its very Indecent."[56] Similarly, modern-day observers might view such rituals and jokes as callous or distasteful. But they actually had important functions in helping mourners cope with the loss of loved ones and, in a broader sense, re-affirming life, even in the face of death. Audio Sample

Both women and men attended the mass for the dead and the prayers at the graveside, although, as the nineteenth century progressed, women's presence at the actual burial was being discouraged by the Catholic Church (with limited success on the southern Avalon) as being an unsuitable activity for the "gentler" sex. Another ritual performed by both sexes, but primarily by women, was keening—a ritualistic crying, both at the wake-house and the graveside, to mourn the departed, placate his or her spirit, and mark his or her transition to the afterlife. Anspach observed the practice among the Irish at Newfoundland with some awe and trepidation, describing it as "crying most bitterly, and very often with *dry* eyes, howling, making a variety of strange gestures and contortions expressive of the violence of their grief."[57] But while keening often struck the outside observer as primitive and strange, it was an accepted and effective mechanism for expressing grief within the Irish community.

Furthermore, this characteristic wailing traditionally punctuated a ritual eulogizing, sometimes in rhyming form that required a fair degree of literary finesse. Anspach did not record this aspect of keening (which is not to say that it did not occur in Newfoundland), but observers in contemporary Ireland commented on this more formal element and the musical quality of the lament. They also noted women's central role in the ritual. A Protestant minister, James Hall, who was generally unsympathetic to Irish Catholic death rites, conceded that "some of the women rhyme extempore and offhand with wonderful facility, particularly when they have got a little (but not too much) whiskey," and others described the "plaintiveness" and "melancholy sweetness" of the crying accompaniment.[58] Indeed, Angela Bourke points out that the Irish word *caoineadh*, from which the English word *keening* derives, actually suggests, in one of its meanings, a stylized tradition of women's poetry. As late as the eighteenth century, she notes, it was common for women to lead their communities in this public demonstration of grief, and the various emotions expressed in their rhythmic lament—denial, anger, bargaining, sadness, and acceptance—are recognized by modern-day psychoanalysts as necessary stages of the mourning process.[59] While such emotions would have ebbed and flowed in the keening process and not manifested in the precise stages outlined above, this ritual crying did provide an important outlet for communal mourning. It was a practice, however, that was seen as pagan and heathenish by the Catholic Church, both in Newfoundland and in Ireland, and was aggressively discouraged. By the middle of the nineteenth century, ritual keening was increasingly being represented as self-indulgent caterwauling. (One male informant, when asked about the role of women's keening, told me, "Yes, some of them were real bawlers, alright."[60]) Thus, while most of the other rituals related to death persisted well into the twentieth century, this one did not. Its disappearance marked a general campaign by Catholic clergy to dismantle the alternative belief system in the area.

Indeed, there was a concerted effort by the Catholic Church to stop ancient customary practices in both Ireland and Newfoundland. Connolly points out that, as early as the eighteenth century, higher church authorities in Ireland were trying to discourage popular supernaturalism because it threatened their ambitions for a monopoly on mediation of the supernatural world and provided alternative mechanisms for meeting the emotional and psycho-social needs of their flock. But many in their congregation were reluctant to part with their customary practices, which helped to explain and control "what would otherwise have appeared as a meaningless pattern of good and bad fortune."[61] Thus, while the church unleashed the full battery of its "machinery of discipline"—the confessional, public denunciation, exclusion from the sacraments, and even excommunication—it found that these measures were effective only to the extent that the congregation was willing to reinforce them through the shunning of non-compliers. Until the people themselves wished to abandon the ancient system, it would persist; the clergy could only lead the people where they, the people, wanted to go.[62]

The tide turned for the Catholic Church in Ireland in the second half of the nineteenth century as adherence to formal religious practices increased markedly. Emmet Larkin attributes this transition to the devotional revolution spearheaded by Paul Cardinal Cullen, with its increased church discipline and intensification of devotional practices.[63] Certainly, these reforms spurred an evangelical revival in the Catholic Church in Ireland. But Connolly very compellingly argues that a more significant impetus came from the dramatic shift in the profile of the Irish population that occurred during the Great Famine. Before mid-century, the overwhelming majority of the population was made up of laborers, cottiers, and smallholders—groups that clung tenaciously to the older belief system. After the famine, this class had been decimated due to death and emigration, and the small farmer class emerged as the backbone of the population, with aspirations to greater respectability that more closely meshed with the wishes of church authorities.[64] Once again, the priests were leading the people where they wanted to go; the composition of their flock had simply changed.

The Catholic population of Newfoundland also experienced the impact of the devotional revolution through the religious personnel regularly recruited from Ireland, but it did not experience the massive demographic and economic transitions that Ireland underwent at mid-century. As the nineteenth century progressed into the twentieth, many Catholics within rural plebeian culture continued their customary practices in concert with formal religion, and women's roles in this alternative system—both as symbolic figures and as interpreters of the supernatural world—persevered beyond the period of this study. But this alternative female power was perceived by church authorities as competing with, not complementary to, the church's own status as interpreters of the supernatural. It would be discouraged as part of an effort to impose church and middle-class notions of respectability on the congregation in general, and feminine ideals of domesticity and dependence on Catholic women in particular (see Chapter 8).

THE INFORMATION HIGHWAY

Oh I often hear men ask why a woman talks so fast
Nor how she comes by every bit of news
She's from morning, noon and night, from day until midnight
And the way she use her tongue it beats the news . . . .
There's no use of you beginnin' for to stop a woman's chinnin'
Whatever you does she's equal to whatever it is
When I am working hard I will find her in the yard
And she's talking to her neighbors o'er the fence.
—"A Woman's Tongue Will Never Take a Rest," local song

The female gossip, whispering through the garden fence, idly destroying reputations and disrupting lives, has been a tenacious image within western culture.[65] Yet the word gossip in the English language did not always have such associations. Indeed, the term was originally gender-neutral and had connotations of friendship and intimacy, for its etymology can be traced to a late Old English word meaning god-parents or other close friends invited to celebrate a christening.[66] By the Middle Ages, however, the word gossip had been feminized and denigrated.[67] Yet we have only recently begun to understand why gossip has so persistently been associated with women and why it has garnered such a high degree of moral and social opprobrium.

Sociologists and anthropologists have been examining and debating the social significance of gossip for some time.[68] Early writings in these disciplines argued that gossip was an effective method of social control or group preservation, serving to validate communal norms and values and to maintain solidarity by acting as a deterrent to deviant behavior, particularly within small, pre-urban, morally homogeneous groups. These functionalist interpretations of gossip came under attack, however, in the latter decades of the twentieth century. They did not take into account individual motivations for gossip, critics argued, such as the increase in status of the conveyor of gossip as the bearer of secret and important information. Nor did they represent the dynamics of gossip as a means of distributing information. Yet while new theories addressed these weaknesses, they still did not provide historical insight as to why gossip has been stigmatized and why it has so persistently been linked with women. To address this lack, feminist scholars in anthropology and sociology have brought forward their own explanatory model: that gossip provides a subversive form of female solidarity that threatens male domination in patriarchal societies; it is thus feared by men, who take measures to discredit and defuse it as a shameful, malicious, female practice.[69]

Karma Lochrie follows a similar line of thought in her study of medieval uses of secrecy. Lochri suggests that from the Middle Ages to the present, the representation of gossip as a discourse of malice, secrecy, and deception and its association with femininity have served to maintain women's status as a marginalized group. Gossip, she argues, was and continues to be perceived as "a resistant oral discourse" of the "other," and the association of gossip particularly with women "serves . . . to reinforce gender ideology and valorize traditional institutional forms of discourse and authority."[70]

Feminist scholars in sociolinguistics have also developed constructs of dominance and difference in their writings on women's language.[71] In discussing the trivialization of women's talk, Dale Spender observes that men engage in similar forms of talk with comparable functions, but magnify its importance to preserve their advantaged gender position. She argues:

> It is not surprising to find that there are no terms for man talk that are equivalent to chatter, natter, prattle, nag, bitch, whine, and, of course, *gossip*, and I am not so naïve as to assume that this is because men do not engage in these activities. It is because when they do it is called something different, something more flattering and more appropriate to their place in the world. This double standard is of great value in the maintenance of patriarchal order.[72]

However, there has been a tendency among feminist sociolinguists to examine women's gossip only in terms of an articulation of a women's subculture—an expression of women's concerns and values, a means of establishing and maintaining networks of support and cooperation—that is intimate, personal, and very much rooted in the private domain.[73] Such writings try to retrieve some of the positive aspects of women's talk. But the danger here is in interpreting women's gossip in terms of an essentialist, homogeneous women's culture that addresses uniquely female concerns and needs; in short, it denies gossip some of its very public functions.

Such interpretations, for example, do not help us understand the complexity of community relations that led to the 1822 confrontation between Ellen Veal and Mary Bowen at St. Mary's—the case that introduced this chapter. Mary, Catharine St. Croix, and Nell Tobin were obviously a part of a unit that transmitted gossip and sexual innuendo about Ellen, her daughter, and her husband. Yet the very next year, Nell Tobin herself had fallen out with the St. Croix family, contradicting the notion that female bonding is intrinsic to gossip.[74] Furthermore, the gossip deployed in the Veal-Bowen affair did not offer female resistance to patriarchal domination, but rather attempted to enforce hegemonic norms on sexuality, both male and female; indeed, the gossip was as divisive as it was cohesive in terms of female friendships. Thus, while female networking and female resistance are aspects of women's gossip, they do not represent the entire multi-faceted configuration. As Cole has noted in her study of the women of the Praia, gossip should not be examined as a separate sphere for women, but as an integrated part of the social, economic, and political relations of their communities.[75] It is important to acknowledge diversity and divisiveness as well as commonality in women's experiences, and to anchor such discussions in the contexts in which women have lived.

The southern Avalon in the late eighteenth and early nineteenth centuries was a rural, pre-industrial society—a cluster of small populations, each spatially condensed, which facilitated networking even as it mitigated against privacy. In this context, women's gossip in some respects operated differently than it does in the modern urban women's networks often studied by sociolinguists. Here, it is helpful to revisit some of the older, functionalist arguments about gossip in traditional societies, so as not to lose the helpful insights that they offer. Did women's gossip on the southern Avalon serve to stabilize the community when limited formal mechanisms for group preservation and social control existed, and when even informal mechanisms such as kinship ties may have been diluted by the process of emigration?[76]

In her study of the somewhat comparable society of colonial Virginia, Kathleen Brown uses functionalist arguments to portray women's gossip as a source of alternative female power. Through gossip, she says, women created "informal political networks" in which they could "wield influence over the behavior of their neighbors," regardless of sex or status. As "conduits of information" about the character and lives of local personalities, women helped to maintain community standards in colonial Virginia in ways beyond the scope of, and often in competition with, more formal legal institutions.[77] This interpretation of women's talk is shared by Melanie Tebbutt, who perceives gossip as an "arena for moral and political debate" in which the values of the community were shaped. Women's gossip, she notes, "expressed the politics of everyday living, and as such was an important vehicle for . . . [women's] informal power."[78]

Does this conception of women's gossip as a female political network for maintaining communal norms apply to the southern Avalon during the study period? Empirical evidence on women's gossip in the area is limited. Of course, this is historically true of much of women's language, because it was usually verbal in nature and persistently trivialized.[79] However, some insights can be derived from an examination of the fourteen court cases from the study period involving women in which gossip was a factor: eight defamation of character/slander cases; five cases of assault involving or provoked by gossip; and one case of theft which was pursued because of information obtained through gossip.

A breakdown of the cases in terms of gossip producer, object, and targeted behavior provides the profile shown in Table 5.2. It suggests that women were the predominant gossip producers, while men and women were equally targeted by gossip—women being the objects in six of the cases, men in seven, with a mixed-sex target in the remaining case. All gossipers were from the plebeian community, as were all their targets, with the exception of one. This lends some credence to arguments that gossip was frequently deployed to reinforce standards of behavior within a closed group. Certainly, there was no evidence of the involvement of elite women in these networks. This is not to suggest that middle-class women did not gossip, but that they maintained their own information networks that did not manifest itself in the court records.[80] Here is an example of class and ethnicity cutting across gender lines to preclude the formation of a homogeneous women's subculture on the southern Avalon.[81] This is also not to suggest that plebeians did not talk about the elite or vice versa, but rather that the power of such talk to do harm was defused by the outsider status of the target. A local merchant, for example, would feel obliged to defend his reputation against scurrilous remarks from someone in his own circle and might initiate a court action for libel; unflattering talk from the plebeian community, by contrast, would more likely be dismissed as merely the grumblings of the "lower orders."

The court records do reveal one object of a woman's gossip from outside the plebeian community: Christopher Valence (also Vallance), who was the largest employer in Cape Broyle in 1800, operating two banking vessels and two shallops, with twenty-four fishermen and eight shoremen.[82] Valance took his former employee, Henry Currier (also Coryear)[83], to court in 1809 for trespass. This obviously incited Henry's daughter, Elenor, to stir up ill feeling in the community towards Valence, for in the very next case on the docket, Valence was charging Elenor with "abusive & threatening language . . . & reporting falsehoods of him tending to aggravate the Inhabitants of Cape Broyle against him."[84] As with many of the court records for the area, details of the case are slim, but the evidence suggests that Elenor may have been playing against Valence's elevated status to rally support for her father within the fishing community. Thus, even when gossip was aimed against an outsider in terms of class, it still functioned to identify and maintain the boundaries of the group.

The breakdown of targeted behaviors in the above profile also points to the monitoring function of gossip. Theft, sexual immorality, witchcraft—these represented substantial threats to community order and suggest that there was a quasi-legal aspect of gossip networks that supplemented the formal legal system. Certainly, the frequency with which female witnesses gave testimony in court hearings (see Chapter 6) indicates that the legal system was at least partially dependent on women's information networks for intelligence on events in the community. Indeed, in one of the cases profiled in Table 5.2, a woman's gossip actually instigated a formal charge of theft. When Ann Bowen of St. Mary's brought her neighbor Mary Money to court for allegedly stealing her brown and blue serge gowns from her garden fence in 1823, she was acting on information she had received from Ansty White. Ansty had told Ann that she had seen Mary's children dressed in clothing of the very same fabric and color; indeed, she had gone to the Money house, inspected the clothing, and satisfied herself that they had certainly been made from Ann's missing gowns. Furthermore, Ansty appeared at the court hearing as Ann's only witness. Yet while the defendant produced two witnesses (a merchant's clerk and her own servant) who testified that she had purchased the material and that she had made the children's clothing several months previous to the theft, the local magistrate did not dismiss the charge out of hand, indicating that he gave some credence to the statements of Ann and her gossiping neighbor, Ansty, or perhaps feared some backlash himself from local gossips. At any rate, he chose the course of discretion and deferred the matter for the decision of the visiting surrogate.[85]

While there is evidence of women's gossip acting in tandem with the legal system, however, it is likely that it more often operated in place of more formal legal institutions. This would be particularly true of all the instances of gossip that did not appear in the court records, but which served on a more day-to-day basis to define and maintain standards of behavior in the community. On occasion, gossip also likely functioned in competition with the formal legal system when elite and plebeian perspectives on justice clashed.

The above cases certainly suggest the deterrent effect that the fear of gossip could have on community members. In all of these cases, people's characters had been called into question, and the fact that these objects of gossip risked further exposure by bringing charges of defamation/slander, or by assaulting the gossip producer and thus airing the slander in court by a more circuitous route, suggests that the victims were highly concerned about the impact of the gossip on their personal reputations. Indeed, when Margret Dinn called Elenor Piddle a "whore" and a "perjured villain" in the presence of Elizabeth Feagan and Catharine Lannahan, and suggested that "she coud say many other things besides against her character," Elenor had an additional incentive to bring charges against the gossiping Margret, for her own husband "threaten'd to breake her bones, if she did not apply to the Court" to clear her good name.[86]

While men and women were targeted by gossip in equal numbers in these cases, there is some evidence that they were targeted in different ways. Brown observes from the language of slander cases in colonial Virginia that gossip helped to perpetuate "gender-specific standards of behavior." A man's reputation, for example, would be tarnished by questioning his honesty and calling him a *perjured rogue*. By contrast, a woman's reputation rested on her sexual morality, and was challenged by terms such as *whore* and *jade*.[87] Ulrich also notes the frequency with which words like *whore, jade, bawd, strumpet,* and *trull* were used by village gossips against women, and how powerful a form of defamation this was in colonial New England. The only rough male equivalent was the term *rogue*, she notes, although this also had a more general connotation of dishonesty. "For a woman," she argues, "sexual reputation was everything; for a man, it was part of a larger pattern of responsibility."[88] Such language appeared in only one record of a slander case on the southern Avalon: the *Piddle v. Dinn* matter, above, in which Margret Dinn called Elenor Piddle both a *whore* and a *perjured villain*. This was a mixture of the labels so clearly demarcated by gender in the records of Virginia and New England. However, the female epithet *whore* was invoked in other types of cases, particularly assault matters.[89] In addition, the breakdown of behaviors attributed to gossip victims suggests a gender dichotomy similar to the findings of Brown and Ulrich: almost all accusations of sexual immorality were leveled at women (one man featured in a multiple accusation); by contrast, four of the five accusations of theft were aimed at men.

Of course, these fourteen cases reveal only a tiny fraction of the gossip that was exchanged on the southern Avalon during this period. However, additional insight on female gossip can be drawn from oral informants in the area. As the song at the beginning of this section demonstrates, the oral tradition supports the perception of gossip as a female preserve: women in groups *gossiped* about personal and private affairs; men in groups *discussed* weightier matters, such as politics, the effect of the weather on fishing or crops, the best fishing grounds, or the price of fish and supplies. Audio Sample This viewpoint was expressed by both male and female informants, indicating that the perception of men's talk as important and women's as trivial has been internalized, a view that may have extended back into the study period.

Still, there was an acknowledgment of the positive functions of gossip. In this regard, most informants differentiated between *useful* gossip, in which women of good character were seen to participate, and the type of spiteful venom spewed by the real *prate-box*. Here was a perceived motivation for female gossip beyond nosiness, idleness, or pure malice. Indeed, when pressed, informants set forth a variety of useful functions of female gossip in the period, which can be summarized as follows: a proscriptive role at a time when there were few formal mechanisms for maintaining order in the community; a leveling function in small communities where it would not do for individuals to set themselves above others or get "too much of a notion of themselves";[90] a means by which women could express themselves and occasionally give vent to their frustrations, particularly about husbands or perhaps the merchant or parish priest; a mechanism for sharing information among people who had a genuine interest in each other's lives; and a means of instructing the young in preferred modes of behavior by making examples of those who had strayed from communal standards. One informant revealed that her paternal grandmother and her circle of female friends had even developed their own form of pidgin English so that when they were discussing sensitive or private matters, they could not easily be understood by *outsiders* (that is, men and young children). When the informant's father, then a young boy, occasionally intruded on a gossip session, the speaker would say something like, "I-vra ca-vra no-vra sa-vra di-vras ou-vra lou-vra be-vra cau-vra dere-vras li-vra boy-vra wi-vras [I cannot say dis out loud 'cause dere's a little boy with us]."[91] Here, in various local perceptions of the functions of gossip, are all the elements of subversion and resistance, social control and group preservation, social leveling, and networking and cooperation spoken of in the academic texts.

But informants also revealed that women sometimes gossiped because they were simply jealous of what other people had. Thus, any discussion of women's gossip that overlooks the role of envy and rivalry cannot claim to be comprehensive. So argues Cole in her discussion of the concept of *inveja*—a form of envy that resulted in behaviors such as gossip and the use of the *evil eye* in the maritime community of Vila Chã. According to Cole:

> *Inveja* describes the opposition between households that perceive themselves to be competing for resources, both social and economic. Because it is women who are ultimately responsible for managing the household's resources in order to ensure its survival, *inveja* is a powerful presence . . . in the lives of women.[92]

As the principal household managers on the southern Avalon, plebeian women would also have felt the pressures of competition for resources in their small communities, a compelling reason to try to ensure that others did not get "too much of a notion of themselves." Such an interpretation provides some breadth to our understanding of women's gossip, allowing it to transcend gender stereotypes that hold that women always connect while men usually compete.[93]

Women's gossip, then, was a multi-faceted phenomenon on the southern Avalon. This brings the discussion back to the interpretation of women's gossip as an alternative source of power. Whether it manifested itself as female solidarity or resistance, as a political network that served to identify, maintain, and sometimes challenge group boundaries, or as a mechanism by which women competed for scarce resources, women exercised power in their community through the information network of gossip. The stigmatization of women's talk largely reflected men's desire to defuse its power: for gossip gave women a forum for asserting themselves in groups that often excluded men; it had a powerful socializing function outside the scope of patriarchal institutions; it had the capacity to transform private affairs into public discussions, to make or break reputations.[94] To some extent, women may even have been complicit in its trivialization, in order to negotiate maneuvering space and maintain gossip networks without formal legal sanction. However, efforts to underplay the impact of women's talk were not an unqualified success, as demonstrated by the slander cases surviving in the records and the general concern in the community about becoming the target of gossip. Despite efforts to belittle it, then, gossip was not a separate sphere for women on the southern Avalon, but rather an integral part of the power relations of the larger community.

WHAT'S IN A NAME?

One of the most obvious indicators that a married woman's identity was subsumed in the person of her husband was her identification by her husband's name. In middle-class culture on the southern Avalon, as elsewhere, women were increasingly addressed only in terms of their husbands' identities: even to people within their own social circle, for example, Sarah Randell became *Mrs. Robert Carter* after marriage, Anne Saunders became *Mrs. Matthew Morry Jr.*, Harriet Skinner became *Mrs. Arthur Hunt Carter*, and Jane Killigrew became *Mrs. John Goodridge*. Indeed, in writing his diary entries, magistrate Robert Carter never once used a married woman's first name—not even that of his own wife—choosing to follow the more formal style of address that, at first glance, might seem merely an affectation, but which also reflected the long arm of coverture.

This can be contrasted with forms of addressing women within the Irish plebeian community, where married women maintained strong associations with their natal families and their pre-marital identities. It was not unusual, for example, for a married woman to use and be addressed by her maiden name, even though she had legally taken her husband's name at marriage (a practice that was common in Ireland in the period as well).[95] Certainly women continued to be addressed by their own first names after marriage, sometimes with the addition of *Mrs.* in deference to increasing age (for example, *Mrs. Maggie*). When more than one woman in the community had the same name, the last name of a husband might also be used when speaking *of* the person, not *to* them, in order to differentiate them (for example, *Mrs. Maggie* ***Wade*** as distinguished from *Mrs. Maggie* ***Sullivan***). In small communities, where there were many common first names and surnames, married women with the same names were often differentiated by the addition of their husbands' first names to their own (for example, *Maggie* ***Tim*** as opposed to *Maggie* ***Johnny***, or *Mary* ***Bill*** as opposed to *Mary* ***Tom***).

This latter practice could be construed as an indicator of patriarchal domination—a reflection that these women were perceived to be the possessions of their husbands. Given the other circumstances of these women's lives, however, such an interpretation seems rather facile. Certainly, these women's own names were not lost altogether; unlike middle-class women and the "respectable" working class in urban areas, Irish women on the southern Avalon were never referred to within the plebeian community as *Mrs.* ***Thomas*** *Hearn* or *Mrs.* ***Stephen*** *Kavanagh*, for example, but [*Mrs.*, which was optional with increasing age] ***Mary*** *Tom* or [*Mrs.*] ***Kitty*** *Stephen*. And more distinctive names carried no reference to husbands' names at all (for example, [*Mrs.*] *Julianne*).

Furthermore, the interpretation of *wife as possession* in the system of nomenclature is even more roundly challenged by another practice in the area: sometimes the wife's name was added to the husband's for identification purposes. An example from Brigus South in the late nineteenth century provides an example just past the end of the study period. In that community, there was a surfeit of men bearing the name Ned Power, so they were differentiated by the addition of their wives' first names to their own: ***Sarah's*** *Ned*, ***Annie's*** *Ned*, ***Bride's*** *Ned*, etcetra. One year, a telegraph operator from St. John's, whose name also was Ned Power, came to work in the community. The newcomer was single, but the system did not collapse in the face of this anomaly, for he was promptly dubbed ***Nobody's*** *Ned* by the local residents.[96]

The practice of maintaining personal identity through a form of address is noteworthy, for, in combination with other facets of Irish Newfoundland women's experience, it reinforces a perception of independence and status within their communities. The only encroachment on the practice was the increasing tendency in court records, especially from the late 1830s onwards, to identify married women using their husbands' names. In earlier records, it was difficult to determine a woman's marital status unless it was revealed by the context of the case. But from the mid-nineteenth century onwards, identification forms such as "Sarah Aylward, Wife of James Aylward," "James Kenney and Ellen his Wife," or even more anonymous forms such as "Mrs. Ryan," "John Bavis and his wife," and "the widow of John Doyle" appeared in the record books. However, this more likely reflected the increasing preoccupations of middle-class magistrates or efforts by recording clerks to gentrify their entries than a change in perceptions or practice within the plebeian community itself.

COLLECTIVE ACTIONS AND PRIVATE WARS

Another manifestation of women's influence within the plebeian community during this period can be seen in their public participation in collective actions to enforce communal standards and in individual verbal and physical interventions to sort out day-to-day power struggles within the community. Traditional treatments of the worlds of political activity and public confrontation have tended to treat them as male preserves, but more recent literature has begun to accommodate the presence of women in these spheres of activity and influence.[97]

There is no surviving evidence of any solely female collective action during the period, and women's involvement in incidents involving both sexes has tended to be disguised by later misreadings of the sexually indeterminate language of the day. Such was the case with wrecking and salvaging activities (discussed in Chapter 4), which had strong undertones of plebeian redistributive justice that can be linked to the current discussion. Similarly, women's participation in the two most prominent collective actions during the period—the Ferryland riot of 1788 and the Father Duffy affair at St. Mary's in 1834–35—has been muted by subsequent historical interpretations. As in the case of wrecking activity, gender-neutral collective terms like *mob* and *crowd* have been gendered male, particularly when arrestees in the incidents were men.[98] But it is difficult to believe that women did not participate in some capacity, and thus it is a legitimate exercise to attempt to interlineate or superimpose their presence, and to retrieve the neutral connotation of collectivities that were reported in contemporary accounts.

The Ferryland riot was a clash between rival Irish factions hailing from Munster and Leinster.[99] While Irish faction-fighting has often been presented as an almost recreational outlet for grievances that had been nursed for centuries, and certainly ancient grudges provided an enabling mythology, there were usually more immediate causes for particular incidents than the "pure devilment and divarsion" attributed by Prowse.[100] The Ferryland affray was triggered by a jurisdictional dispute between the Prefect Apostolic, James O Donel (from Munster), and a renegade priest, Patrick Power (from Leinster). Power was one of several "strolling priests" whom O Donel had tried to dislodge from the newly established Catholic mission in Newfoundland.[101] Power had removed himself to Caplin Bay, where he proceeded to stir up the district by charging that O Donel was favoring Munster priests over Leinster candidates in his recruiting for the mission. Tensions simmered and then erupted in a large-scale faction fight on the Ferryland downs in the winter of 1787–88.

This was certainly not the first incident of Irish faction-fighting in Newfoundland, for Irish Catholic missionaries admitted that the "ancient feuds between the lay people of Munster and Leinster" had been in evidence in Newfoundland "those 40 years past."[102] But the 118 men who were convicted in the ensuing court cases in September found themselves the recipients of harsh justice—stiff fines (ranging from £1 to £20, with a mode of £5), forfeited wages, floggings, transportation, and banishment—at the hands of the magistrates who represented leading families of the local gentry. As Christopher English has argued, these penalties reflected not only the long arm of the British state, but also "the determination of a small elite to maintain order and their own social and economic prominence" within the growing fishing population.[103]

While the severity of the response to the riot was provoked by class tensions, the motivations behind ensuing events were shaded with ethnoreligious undertones.[104] In the wake of the trials, Anglo-Protestant magistrates, merchants, and traders in Ferryland immediately seized the opportunity to lobby for the removal of the recently arrived Catholic priests from the area. They forwarded a memorial to Governor Elliot, voicing their fear "for the safety of our persons, and property" and requesting military protection.[105] The visiting surrogate at Ferryland, Capt. Edward Pellew, supported their request; he denounced "Pope, Popery, Priests, & Priestcraft" in the courthouse[106] and informed the governor that the Protestant community had "reasonable grounds" for their fears.[107] One might wonder, then, why these same concerned Protestant inhabitants sheltered the main instigator, Patrick Power, housing him and feeding him for the next four years until he wore out his welcome with mounting debts. O Donel, in the meantime, defended his mission by advising the governor that the "Seneschals of sedition if any there are cou'd be rather found among the Envious Merchantsof Ferryland than among the popish Priests as the voice of prejudice now runs."[108] The dispute reveals a power struggle between Protestant establishment and the institutional presence of the Catholic Church that most certainly had ethnoreligious nuances, but there is no evidence that these undercurrents bled into the plebeian community (which, at the time, would still have contained a sizeable minority of English Protestants, particularly in Ferryland itself).

The other major fracas during the study period involved the destruction in 1835 of a large flake on the beach of St. Mary's that purportedly formed part of the mercantile premises of Slade, Elson and Company.[109] This exercise in collective action involved perceptions of grievance based on both ethnicity and class, as the largely Catholic plebeian community, led by the newly appointed parish priest, Father James Duffy, took action against an English Protestant merchant firm and its agent, John Hill Martin (who was also the representative for the district in the House of Assembly and a local justice of the peace).[110] In his capacity as magistrate, Martin had refused Duffy permission to build a chapel on a portion of the beach in question; and in his capacity as agent for Slade, Elson, Martin had claimed that title to the beach had been sold to the firm and proceeded to erect a large flake over the entire area. However, the community had long considered the beach to be a commons. An area that had traditionally been used for mending nets and repairing boats and gear, it also served as a right-of-way to the Catholic cemetery and the neighboring community of Riverhead. Martin offered Duffy an alternative site for the chapel on wet, marshy ground, but Duffy declined the offer and organized work teams from his congregation to proceed with the construction of the chapel on the beach.

The ensuing events can be briefly summarized as follows. Duffy petitioned Martin to remove the company flake on the grounds that it constituted a public nuisance. Martin refused and, before leaving for a legislative session in St. John's, ordered the clerks at Slade, Elson to refuse supplies to Duffy. Duffy countered by ordering his congregation to destroy the flake, and on 13 January 1835, a large assembly of people proceeded to chop the flake to pieces with hatchets and burn the debris.[111] Martin, acting on the advice of Chief Justice Henry Boulton, initiated an action in the supreme court for riot, rebellion, and destruction of property against Duffy and eight other male ringleaders. Duffy was arrested and made to walk to Ferryland, where he was charged before local magistrates who, according to Catholic Bishop Fleming, "could not restrain themselves from giving expression to their satisfaction at having 'caught' a priest."[112] Meanwhile, two constables were sent from St. John's on board the brig *Maria* to arrest the remaining ringleaders, but they met with fierce resistance from the community and failed in the attempt. The governor made arrangements with the colonial secretary to send a ship of war with a garrison of soldiers to re-establish order in the area, but Bishop Fleming appealed to the Catholic community for quiet and to the ringleaders, in particular, to surrender. Duffy and the eight fishermen named in the arrest warrants walked to St. John's and turned themselves in, but although two efforts were made to try them (in 1836 and 1837), no witnesses appeared for the prosecution, and the charges were finally stayed.

Women are not immediately obvious in written histories or oral retellings of the Ferryland riot or the Father Duffy affair. No local *Macha Mong Ruadh* or *Grainne Ni Maille* is hailed for leading her people into battle against the enemy, and no reference is made to women within the ranks.[113] But it is difficult to believe that, with such major disturbances in their communities, plebeian women remained completely in the background. Rosemary Jones, in her analysis of the *Ceffyl Pren* tradition in Wales, suggests that there are various forms of female participation in collective actions that frequently go unremarked in traditional treatments of these incidents, such as: informal gossip channels that detect and define aberrant social behavior; social boycott to bring psychological and economic pressure to bear on an offender; spokesperson roles; initial seizure and/or subsequent verbal and physical abuse of an offender; inflammatory roles; and the transmission of the tradition to successive generations.[114] One could add to this list various forms of support services such as providing food, tending injuries, and harboring fugitives.

It is highly probable that as the men from Leinster and Munster faced off in Ferryland in 1788, Irish Newfoundland women played an incendiary role or heaped abuse on those from the "wrong" province of the home country. Certainly, in his reporting of the incident, surrogate Edward Pellew noted that "many *People* came and assembled" on the downs, hailing not just from Ferryland but also from the large harbors on either side.[115] With such a massive gathering, it is not difficult to envision women at least on the sidelines. And, in fact, it is even possible that some women participated in the affray, for it was not unusual for women in eighteenth- and early nineteenth-century Ireland to participate in faction fights, often wielding stockings filled with rocks as weapons.[116] The fact that no women were charged in court in the wake of the riots does not disprove such involvement, for authorities were generally reluctant to arrest and prosecute women participants on such occasions because they felt it might diminish the legitimacy of their own police action.

Were there women present in the fighting on the Ferryland downs, then, and was their presence simply trivialized and downplayed by the arresting authorities? And what of other levels of participation? Surely, in the aftermath of the battle, women were involved in tending wounds and hiding ringleaders from authorities (twelve remained at large for some time). As the dispute between Power and O Donel dragged on, these women, as members of the Catholic community, chose to side with either Father Power or the bishop's candidate, Father Thomas Ewer, thereby boycotting the pastoral services of the perceived interloper.[117] And, as mothers, they likely helped to pass on a sense of rivalry between the two provinces to the next generation. Granted, the experiences of men and women in the episode were differentiated by gender, but it is highly unlikely that women were not involved at all.

Similarly, while modern retellings of the Father Duffy affair speak only of the men of St. Mary's, it is quite probable that plebeian women were also involved in the action against Slade, Elson. Doubtless, they played an inflammatory role and provided support services. And while the truck system would not have allowed fishing families the luxury of boycotting their supplying merchant, certainly the episode became one more item on a long list of grievances passed from one generation to the next (by women as well as men) that demonized merchants in Newfoundland fishing communities.[118]

Furthermore, while the nine people who led the incident were all men, a more careful reading of the contemporary historical records suggests that women were directly involved in the episode. The deposition of William Lush, chief clerk for Slade, Elson and witness to the incident, did not specify gender in describing the perpetrators. He stated that in addition to the ringleaders, "*divers other persons* amounting to the number of 80 or upwards [note that there were only 64 adult men living there as of the 1836 census] . . . were unlawfully riotously and tumultuously assembled" and that "the greater portion of the *people* then assembled" were employed in destroying the flake. He himself heard Father Duffy "order the *persons assembled*" to carry out the demolition. When Lush "spoke to *several persons* then assembled and requested that they would desist," they replied that they could not disobey the orders of their priest. And he heard several others state that "James Duffy had told the *congregation in chapel* to break up and burn the flake and that those who might refuse to do so should have the curse of God and *the congregation* on them."[119]

In reporting to the acting colonial secretary in St. John's on the subsequent efforts that were made to arrest the ringleaders, Martin similarly spoke of "the outrageous proceedings of the *People*" on the arrival of the brig *Maria* at St. Mary's. Martin had ordered his local constable, Burke, to assist the St. John's constables in effecting the arrests before the presence of the *Maria* was made known. However, Burke advised that its arrival

> was already known to the *People*, many of whom had been expecting her—that in coming from his own house he had observed a constant, and unusual quick *passing of lights from house to house*, and which extended *throughout the Harbour*, that he was persuaded that the *People* were on the alert, and he could speak from his own knowledge to the fact of their determination not to suffer any man [referring specifically here to the male ringleaders] amongst them to be taken—and moreover it would, in his opinion, be impossible to take any of them on that night, for if a Constable approached any one of their houses a signal would be made that would bring to it *every person* concerned in the destruction of the flake, and, perhaps, many not

concerned as *all the People of the Harbour* were in some way or other, related to each other.[120]

These references to the participants in the action were gender-neutral and suggest that women as well as men contributed to the destruction of the flake and were called upon to ostracize non-participants. Women were also likely part of the signaling system that "extended throughout the Harbour," as well as the menacing presence of the mob that served to protect the ringleaders and prevent their arrest.

This gender-inclusive language contrasts with the accounts of proceedings given by the constables and seamen of the *Maria*, who had to explain their failure to arrest the ringleaders. A seaman from the yacht said that on 13 December, he had been removed from the vessel by "two *armed men*" and brought to a larger group of "30 *armed men*," who questioned him about the numbers of the arresting party and threatened to "make a Sacrifice of him" if he did not answer truly. When Martin sent a man to verify the seaman's story, his informant reported encountering "50 *armed men*" armed with guns, swords, pews, and hatchets. Martin ordered local constable Burke to assist the St. John's constables, but Burke advised him that during the night, "his house was beset by a *great number of men* who threatened to shoot him" if he joined the arresting party. Burke felt in such danger that he preferred to relinquish his post rather than "assist on so perilous an occasion"; Martin obliged him by promptly dismissing him from his office. On 14 December, "groups of *men* numbering from 20 to 30, some of them armed," were seen "hovering about," and when a small boat was seen leaving the Maria, a group of "*upwards of 60 men*" (apparently, every male adult in the community) ran to where it was likely to land, only permitting the party to come ashore when it was ascertained that there were no constables among them.[121]

These accounts very specifically indicate that an overwhelming (and, apparently, ever increasing) presence of *armed men* prevented the arrest of the ringleaders. Yet even here, one is left to wonder whether the participation of women in the mob was discretely omitted. Certainly, if the arresting party was trying to justify to the chief justice and governor its inability to complete its assignment, the menace of a mob of armed men may have provided greater mitigating power than the opposition of a mixed crowd of men, women, and children. It is intriguing that, at the end of his report, Martin suggested that the "place seemed less hostile" by 15 December, and his description of local resistance returned to the more sexually indeterminate terms of *mob* and *crowd*, once again allowing for an interpretation of events that included the presence of women.

A less renowned incident that also likely involved Irish plebeian women occurred in Ferryland district the following year during the election of a local member to the fledgling House of Assembly. Diarist Robert Carter recorded the battle between his cousin, Lieutenant Robert Carter, R.N., scion of a prominent local English Protestant mercantile family, and Patrick Morris, an Irish Catholic merchant (originally from Waterford) residing in St. John's, with strong southern Avalon connections because of his involvement in the passenger trade to that area. (Web Link) Here was one of the few occasions when ethnoreligious tensions flared in the study area as the large Irish Catholic population in the district rallied solidly behind Morris. Again, the contemporary account is quite gender-neutral in its language. Carter observed that the day before the polls opened, Father James Duffy led a parade around Ferryland harbor "with a green flag, his horse's head Stuck with spruce boughs and one in his hand." On the first day of polling, feelings were running high. "Large bodies of *people* assembled from the North and South," Carter wrote on 14 November. "The *crowd* very great in and around the Court. Great show of disapprobation by the *friends* of Morris to those of Carter but the *people* were kept in order through Rev. J. Duffy's influence over them." Indeed, throughout the course of the polling, the district was "tolerably quiet considering all," according to Carter, and certainly did not experience the election violence that plagued Conception Bay and St. John's in the middle decades of the century. However, the menace of the crowd was still acutely felt by English Protestant middle-class families in the district, especially as the episode followed so shortly after the incident at St. Mary's. In the aftermath of the voting, Carter reflected on the ultimate victory of Morris and his fellow liberal reformers, "elected by the populace at the Instigation of the Priests, the representatives of the dregs of the People" in his view. "May the Home Government take upon them the rule of this Island or devise some means to put down the amazing excitement now raging between different sects of religions," he wrote. "Protestant and Tory are used as synonymous terms, and down with Tories, and on all occasions by the rabble. God send us his divine protection."[122]

The involvement of women in the episode again must be read into the sexually indeterminate language of the contemporary account, based on a tradition of Irish plebeian women's participation in collective actions. Although women could not vote, they likely featured prominently in enforcing solidarity within the ethnoreligious group and in intimidating rival factions. This was certainly the case in Ireland. There, Catholic women were urged in chapel to attend at polling stations and mark those individuals who voted against their priests' instructions. They discouraged supporters of rival candidates from attending the polls by threats and physical attacks upon their property and persons, and they participated in election riots, not only in a symbolic role, bedecked in green sashes with green bushes in their hands, but also in physical confrontations with opposing factions.[123] There is every reason to believe that Irish Catholic women on the southern Avalon, with a strong stake in the interests of the plebeian community and their ethnoreligious group, participated in similar ways in intimidating the supporters of Lieutenant Carter.

Female intimidation and incitement clearly played a role in an episode involving the Irish population in a neighboring bay: the effort to run Sweetman's agent, James Hogan, out of Placentia in the winter of 1845–46. "[A] Storm has been raised against me," Hogan wrote to his principals in January. "My life is sought in open day, their is a gang here determined to have my life." Hogan complained that this group was inventing and circulating "heaps of calumny of the worst description . . . to exasperate the people." His tormentors had ordered the people of the harbor not to ship themselves to him, had attacked his house, "roaring and abusing me threatening my life," and had made several attempts to beat and murder him as well as seamen on board the *Juliet*. This was primarily a local campaign to replace an agent who was seen to be dealing unfairly with fishing families; but there were also factional undertones, for Hogan was from Wexford, and his enemies were apparently threatening to roust all his fellow countymen with him. Prominent in the events were several local women: "Mich^{ls} [gang leader Michael Baldwin] wife, Norah and Mary among other women haloo them on and encourage them," Hogan wrote; and further, "in the riots lately both Norah and Mary & Baldwins wife Encouraged the gang on the street publicly singing out Now the Y. Bellys (*Yellow Bellies*) and Paddy meaning me should hide themselves."[124] Here, then, was direct evidence of plebeian women in a conspicuously incendiary role in a communal action of the period—a role similar to that played in collective actions by their contemporaries in Ireland.

A more celebrated example of plebeian resistance, at least in community folk history, is the existence of a band of outlaws in the Renews area known as the *Masterless Men*. According to the oral tradition, in the mid-eighteenth century, Peter Kerrivan and some companions jumped ship at St. John's and deserted from the British Navy. They made their way to the *Butterpots* near Renews, where they lived off the land, occasionally trading with nearby fishing communities. Over time, they were joined by a number of fishing servants who had deserted from service, escaping the harsh conditions imposed by their fishing masters. Despite repeated efforts by the navy to round them up, the band proved elusive, living in portable shacks suitable for quick escape and leaving false trails in the woods. Most remained at large until the traditional fishery, with its abusive masters, collapsed and they were able to move back into a normal existence in various settlements along the coast.

Once again, women do not figure in the narrative proper. But the oral tradition does mention in passing that the Masterless Men married women from local settlements and raised families in the woods. Peter Kerrivan himself is said to have had four sons and several daughters.[125] At the Capt. William Jackman Museum in Renews, there is a depiction of the legend along one wall, painted by local artist Dana McCarthy; the mural shows a man and a woman hiding and smiling as two soldiers blunder off in the opposite direction. The oral tradition, then, admits to the existence of *Masterless Women*, even if it does not celebrate them.

While this band are hailed as local folk heroes, scholars are more skeptical of the possibility of long-term survival of such a group, particularly through the island's harsh winters. Nonetheless, the isolated barrens and Butterpots of the area were an ideal place for runaways to hide from authorities,[126] and the tendency of local residents to harbor deserters was noted in the written record. In 1797, for example, John Dingle, a justice of the peace from Bay Bulls who had temporarily removed to Trepassey after a French attack on his home community in 1796, notified Governor Waldegrave that he had just received news "that several men had been seen lurking in the woods, and that they were judged to be runaways." He then described the difficulty in apprehending deserters, given the recalcitrance of the inhabitants:

> . . . it was then late at night, and the *Inhabitants* of this place were mostly in Bed-knowing that deserters seldom want a resting place, & thinking that the *Inhabitants* might afford them Shelter, M^{r}. Hunter [a local merchant] and myself considered it as a proper step to apply immediately to M^{r}. Justice Follett [local justice of the peace] for a Warrant to collect together a large body of constables and armed assistants, and to search the houses of the said *inhabitants* without delay. This was accordingly done and I have the satisfaction to say that the Merchants, and their followers, in their researches, used their utmost endeavours to secure the said deserters,-but I am sorry to add, none were found.
>
> We now thought that by such proceedings as I have mentioned, the said deserters had fled to the westward, but for these two days past, reports are propogated, that the same fellows are still lurking in the skirts of this Town, and these reports, for what I can learn, are not without foundation—M^{r}. Hunter and myself, have had a consultation on the best plan for apprehending them, and we consider that it will be to no purpose to send the Constables into the woods after them—These civil Officers are frequently so timid, where such desperate men are the object, and the *common people* in general are more inclined to shelter than give up deserters.[127]

In 1802, Dingle, now back in Bay Bulls, again wrote Governor Gambier respecting the frequency with which deserters from the navy made their way through that community and on to the south, where they found sanctuary and employment with the "inhabitants." He reminded Gambier of the 1797 incident in Trepassey, "when a desperate gang, deserters from the Newfoundland Regiment, were lurking about that place" and the "inhabitants" had refused to cooperate with authorities in rounding them up.[128] If the harboring of deserters was as effective as Dingle's letters imply, the entire plebeian community—women as well as men—had to be part of the network of sanctuary and the conspiracy of silence.

While the written record is somewhat closefisted with specific evidence of women's involvement in larger-scale collective actions, it is more generous in relation to smaller-scale events. Certainly, the court records for the southern district indicate that plebeian women were involved in very public and physical efforts to enforce community standards and to protect personal and family interests. In some of these cases, the women acted individually; in others, they were part of a small collectivity.[129]

The records reveal various instances of women's use of physical violence to defend family property against perceived encroachment.[130] The women of the Berrigan family, for example, were a vital force in the family's struggle to maintain possession of their fishing room in Renews harbor in the 1830s and 1840s. Case File 9 In May of 1835, local merchant and magistrate John William Saunders initiated an action of ejectment against Thomas Berrigan Sr. to recover possession of fishing premises occupied by the Berrigan family on the south side of the harbor. The records do not specify the reason for the action. It is likely that Berrigan was a tenant of Saunders and was being ejected for non-payment of rent, given that Saunders had already launched a successful rent recovery action against Berrigan in 1832.[131] However, the property in the earlier action was not described in the records, and given that family fishing premises often comprised multiple pieces of property, it is not possible to conclude with finality that both suits involved the same property. Furthermore, the presence of Saunders' storekeeper among the plaintiff's witnesses in the 1836 action also suggests that the suit may have been related to a debt for which Berrigan may have entered into a mortgage with his supplier as security.[132] At any rate, Berrigan entered a demurrer in the second action, but the matter proceeded to trial in November of 1836, and the jury, on hearing the case, decided in Berrigan's favor.[133]

But the matter did not end there, for Saunders pursued his claim, to the peril of several court officials and, ultimately, himself. By the fall of 1838, Saunders had convinced the court to issue a writ of possession, but he would soon discover that the Berrigans would not relinquish the premises without a fight. In September, charges were brought by deputy sheriff Philip Wright against Anastatia, Edward, Alice, and Bridget Berrigan and Walter Barron for "violently" assaulting him at Renews on 16 August as he tried to execute the writ of possession. Anastatia was identified in the records as the wife of Thomas Berrigan Sr.; the relationship of the other Berrigan women was not explained, but they were likely daughters, sisters, or relatives by marriage. At the hearing, the defendants were required to enter into sureties to keep the peace for twelve months and to appear in court to stand trial in the next term.[134]

There is no surviving record of an 1839 hearing, but on 31 December 1842, Anastatia, Bridget, and Alice Berrigan were again before the court, along with William Berrigan, to face charges of assaulting yet another deputy sheriff, John Stephenson. Once again, the Berrigans had allegedly obstructed and "violently" assaulted a court official as he attempted to execute another writ of possession for the contested property. Once again, warrants were issued for the arrest of the parties, and on 31 January 1843, they were required to enter into bonds to keep the peace for twelve months and to appear at trial in the next quarter sessions to answer Stephenson's charges. (Anastatia was sick and unable to attend this particular hearing at Ferryland; her bond was sworn before the resident justice of the peace at Renews, Alan Goodridge.) At the general quarter sessions on 23 February 1843, a grand jury returned a bill of indictment for "Riot and assault" against the defendants, but a petty jury returned a verdict of not guilty.[135]

The final trace of the matter in the court records appears in proceedings initiated on 13 and 14 June 1843. John William Saunders swore a complaint that he himself had been threatened, assaulted, and prevented from taking possession of the fishing room at Renews by various parties, including James Gearing Sr., Benjamin Wilcox, and yet another lineup of the Berrigan forces: Thomas Sr., Thomas Jr., Edward, and the ever-present matriarch, Anastatia. Saunders claimed that, by this time, he felt that his very life was in danger from the frequent threats and assaults of the Berrigan faction and asked for the protection of the law. This may have been formulaic pleading, but Saunders' frustration was obviously mounting as he exhausted all legal remedies available to him. The charge against Gearing was dropped for lack of evidence, but the remaining parties were once again arrested and ordered to enter into bonds to keep the peace for twelve months.[136]

The matter then disappears from view, and we are left to speculate whether or not the Berrigans were successful in holding fast to their fishing premises. But for the present discussion, the most significant point is the presence of the Berrigan women in the midst of the struggle. There were variations in the members of the Berrigan family involved in each case, but Bridget and Alice were involved in two of the three incidents, while the family matriarch, Anastatia, was present every time. Their participation was not unusual within the historical context of this fishing-based economy. As essential members of their household production unit, the Berrigan women were defending a family enterprise in which they felt they had an equal stake, using verbal attack and physical force to protect their source of livelihood in the face of perceived injustice at the hands of their landlord/supplying merchant and the formal legal system. Additionally, given that the family was assisted by neighbors in protecting their property and that petty juries on two separate occasions found in the Berrigans' favor, it is likely that their defiance enjoyed some support within the plebeian community.

A comparable incident was reported in Renews in 1853–54. Deputy Sheriff Francis Geary complained that when he tried to execute a writ of ejectment against John Bavis, he was assaulted by Bavis and his wife. A warrant was issued for John's arrest, but when four constables showed up at the house to take him into custody, his wife stood in their way and swore that he was not going anywhere. Meanwhile, a mob had gathered outside the house with bludgeons in their hands, threatening to rescue Bavis if the officers tried to take him by force. The constables were outnumbered and forced to retreat, with the mob following after them, shouting and hissing at them.[137] Again, a woman played a key role in a public, collective action to protect family property and, in this case, her husband's person as well; and the family's resistance to the officers of the crown had the backing of the plebeian community, reinforcing what they perceived to be decent treatment for the Bavis family, regardless of what formal laws and court orders had to say on the matter.

Women were not always acting from a defensive position in property disputes that appear in the court records. In at least one case, a woman was the aggressor in both a property dispute and a related assault. In 1835, Jane Hayley of Cape Broyle was brought before the magistrate by Henry Coryear of the same place. Henry complained that Jane "had dispossessed him of a piece of Ground Granted to him and driven off his Servant with a Hatchet threatening further Violence if molested." Ultimately, Jane relinquished the claim and agreed to pay court costs; but her use of verbal threats and physical confrontation to dispute possession of the property provides further evidence of women deploying power in the community in the period of early settlement.[138]

Plebeian women rose to the defense of more than real property. Maintaining one's good name was important within the community, as Ellen Veal vividly demonstrated in the episode that introduced this chapter. Elenor Evoy of Ferryland provides another example, for she was involved in several incidents in which her family business and personal reputation were at stake. Case File 10 She and her husband, Michael, owned one of the public houses in the district in the 1790s.[139] Indeed, although the liquor license for her tavern was officially in Michael's name up to his death in 1798, it is likely that Elenor had much to do with the running of the establishment, and she may have been the sole operator. Certainly, it was Elenor who defended the integrity of the business against aspersions cast by Michael Ryan of nearby Caplin Bay. In July of 1795,

Ryan complained to the magistrates that Elenor, along with several other local women, had assaulted him and battered him with stones outside the Evoy public house. In their defense, the defendants claimed that Michael had "several times behav'd Rude to them, and as a Punishment they were Determin'd to Hustle him." The women were given small fines and reprimanded.

The following week, Elenor filed a petition in which she gave her own version of the episode, claiming that Michael had provoked the rock-throwing incident outside her establishment with his rude comments. She herself had not cast any stones, she claimed, but had simply advised him to move on for his own good. In response, he had threatened to beat her and defamed her character, accusing her of keeping a bawdy house. Elenor took particular offense at this slur against herself and her business and asked the magistrates for redress. Michael explained that he had spoken "from passion" because the girls were tormenting him, but he was fined £5 pounds (later reduced to 5s.) and ordered to keep the peace.[140] Throughout the proceedings, there was no mention of Elenor's husband; it is evident that it was *her* reputation and *her* business that were being defended, and the magistrates acknowledged her right to do so, despite the principle of coverture, which should have required her husband's attendance in the courtroom as her legal personality.[141]

By 1799, Michael Evoy had died and Elenor's name appeared on the liquor license for the first time. By the taking of the Carter census in 1800, however, Elenor had married a James Welsh (also Walsh), and the liquor license thereafter appeared in his name. Still, Elenor, as the experienced tavern-keeper, likely continued to run the business. One night in late March of 1803, Elenor and her new husband James, his brother, Sylvester, and Elenor's son (by her first husband) Patrick Evoy broke into the house of another publican family in Ferryland—Adam and Ann McLarthy—and assaulted and "ill-used" them. According to the several informations laid, Elenor and James took on Adam McLarthy while Sylvester and Patrick harried Ann in the passageway of the house. The records are not specific about the cause of the assault, but given that the McLarthys also owned a local public house, the episode very much has the appearance of a turf war between two rival firms, and the women—Elenor and Ann—were right in the thick of the fray. This time, Elenor and her cohorts were fined and ordered to keep the peace. Elenor's fine was 50s.—significantly less than the £5 each imposed on James and Sylvester, but more than the 20s. levied against her son Patrick (whose role was more that of an accessory).[142]

The court records reveal other instances of women's involvement in family feuds. On 27 June 1823, Ellen (Nell) Tobin (the same Nell Tobin who had witnessed the Ellen Veal-Mary Bowen affray the previous year) brought a complaint of assault against Ann St. Croix. Ellen attested that she had confronted Ann at a Mrs. Linehan's house that same day and "asked her the reason why she so abused my Sister-and [was] often in the habit of th[r]owing rocks at me and my Brother." In response, Ellen claimed, Ann "took a stick from out of the fire and struck me several times on the face." Three days later, in a related case (the records are sketchy, but the matching surnames in this small community suggest a link),[143] Bridget St. Croix (presumably a relative of Ann) complained that on the previous evening she had encountered Thomas Tobin (possibly Ellen's brother and the victim of Ann's rock-throwing episodes), who had "accosted" her and said, "now you vagabond [w]hore I have you." Bridget told him that she "woud not be wishing for him for a pair of Shoes to touch me." Thomas responded to her provocation by grabbing the broomstick she was carrying and striking her several times. He left her with the dire warning "that he would watch us day and night—to be revenged."[144]

The cause of the dissension between the two families is not clear. It may have dated back to an 1820 episode in which Catherine St. Croix had accused Martin Tobin of stealing two cotton shirts, although this may have been merely an earlier symptom rather than the cause of the tensions.[145] But what is certain is that women of the Tobin and St. Croix families were very much involved in their families' quarrels in ways that conflicted with hegemonic ideals of female passivity and fragility. Case File 11

Another case involving bad feelings between families involved the Dooleys and Kenneys of Renews. On 12 September 1850, Maurice and Mary Dooley and their stepson complained to the magistrates that James Kenney and his wife, Ellen, had repeatedly threatened their lives, and they asked for the protection of the law. Warrants were issued for the arrest of the Kenneys, and they were brought into court by Constable Sullivan and required to enter into security to keep the peace for twelve months.[146] The motive for the harassment in this case was not stated in the records, but it is highly probable that Ellen Kenney and Mary Dooley, like Elenor Evoy and the Berrigan women, were attempting to assert or protect their families' interests.

There is also a record of one case of assault involving a woman's defense of her children, although the fact that she had struck other children in the process landed her in hot water with the local court. On 24 October 1820, Ann Prichet was charged with beating and wounding two children belonging to Bryan Dunn. Ann admitted that she had given "two strokes" to one of the children, but argued that she had been acting in defense of her own children, who were being "ill used" by the others, and in response to "provoking words to herself." The court acknowledged that Ann had not been acting out of "malice," but ordered her to pay a fine of 5s. plus court costs, as well as to give security that she keep the peace for twelve months. Ann refused to provide the security and was committed to the local jail, indicating that the magistrates were not deterred by her sex in treating her like any other recalcitrant defendant.[147]

In general, plebeian women on the southern Avalon were not reluctant to use physical violence in sorting out their daily affairs. There were 111 complaints of assault involving women (all from the plebeian community) brought before the local courts during the period, and while fifty related to male assailants of female victims, sixty-one involved female aggressors.[148] Furthermore, these female assailants were not particular about the sex of their victims: thirty-two were women and twenty-eight were men (with child victims in the remaining case). Most episodes involved the use of threatening language and/or physical assault, with a variety of motivations: defense of personal reputation, employment disputes over wages or ill-treatment, defense of family business, enforcement of community standards, and defense of family property. Given the unfortunate economy of local court clerks in recording details, there was also an assortment of cases in which the motivation for the assault remains a mystery.

In 1839 and 1840, for example, Margaret Ryan of Caplin Bay appeared before the magistrate to respond to two separate complaints by neighbors: first, of assaulting and threatening Catharine Reddigan and, later, of using violent and threatening language against John Rossiter and his family.[149] In 1841, John Crotty, a fisherman at Cape Broyle, complained of being assaulted and beaten by Johanna Morrissey and asked for the court's protection.[150] In 1851, Mary Buckley accused Mary Ann Pendergast of striking her on the head with a water bucket, causing a "severe cut on her Head" and making the "Blood to flow copiously from the wound" and all over her clothing.[151] In 1844, Arthur H. O. B. Carter brought charges against Bridget Dullanty for throwing stones at him, "severely wounding" him, and "thrusting a stick at him."[152] This was Bridget's second offense; she had already been convicted of an assault against a party named Cose in 1837.[153]

Certainly, there was a variety of such cases, and while we do not always know the motivations for the defendants' actions (and doubtless not all were noble), the physical assertiveness of these women and the court's matter-of-fact handling of these matters suggests that these women's violence was no more shocking to the community than men's, indicating a certain fluidity of gender relations within the plebeian community and demonstrating that these women felt they had the right to use verbal and physical intimidation in the public sphere. Examining colonial New England, Ulrich arrives at a different conclusion respecting women's violence, noting that when women used physical force, "they broke through a powerful gender barrier. Violent men were still men; violent women became superwomen, amazons, viragoes."[154] On the southern Avalon, however, the gender "barrier" was more a highly permeable membrane through which plebeian women easily moved in their daily transactions, despite hegemonic discourses on "women's place."

Of course, there were also seventy-one reported female victims of assaults, ranging from threatening language and ill treatment to more serious physical and sexual assaults. The breakdown by sex of the accused in these cases was thirty-two women and fifty men (with multiple defendants in several cases). In feminist scholarship, male violence against women—actual or potential—has been implicated as a mechanism of patriarchal control. Yet it is evident that on the southern Avalon, the use of physical violence was not gender-specific, and cannot be readily examined as a milieu characterized by a pattern of male aggressors and female victims.[155] Furthermore, it is important to note that plebeian women in the area evidently felt that it was their prerogative to take their abusers to court. Only three were represented in actions initiated by their husbands (who had also suffered an assault or destruction of property during the incidents); the remaining sixty-eight victims provided depositions and appeared in court themselves when summoned to give testimony against their assailants. These women perceived themselves as individuals with rights that deserved the protection of the legal system, and they were not deterred by notions of female respectability and self-sacrifice from pursuing these rights in a public forum.

CONCLUSION

Brown's and Ulrich's frameworks for discussing gender in colonial America, with concepts of fixed gender hierarchies or gender barriers occasionally stormed by exceptional women, are too rigid for examining the complexity of gender relations on the southern Avalon in the late eighteenth and early nineteenth centuries. Gender in any context is constantly under negotiation and renegotiation—a dynamic process, in which gender hierarchies are constructed, legitimated, contested, and either maintained or redefined.[156] And I would suggest that there are contexts in which the process is likely to be more vigorous, the negotiations more aggressive. A period of immigration and early settlement—such as unfolded on the southern Avalon from the mid-eighteenth to mid-nineteenth centuries—provides just such a hyper-dynamic situation, when understandings of gender are in greater flux.

Furthermore, while feminine ideals of domesticity and passivity were powerful proscriptive conventions, they were not automatically adopted by plebeian and working-class communities. Thus, while middle-class constructs of femininity were increasingly influencing Newfoundland society, they did not easily insinuate themselves into Irish plebeian culture on the southern Avalon. Women's essential role in community formation and economic life, their powerful position in an alternative belief system, their strong sense of individual personhood, and their deployment of informal power in the community mitigated against the adaptation of gender ideologies that did not fit local realities. And because the southern Avalon remained a pre-industrial society into the twentieth century, plebeian women's status did not undergo the erosion experienced by their counterparts in the industrializing British Isles.

In rural Ireland, women were increasingly marginalized from agricultural work in the nineteenth century, particularly from the post-Napoleonic War period onwards—a trend that was exacerbated not just by mechanization, but also by a shift in production from labor-intensive tillage to pasturage. The mechanization of dairying and the contraction of the domestic textile industry also reduced women's income-earning capacity, and the result was a critical decline in their status as essential producers in their family economies. This slide, gaining momentum from 1815, became precipitous at mid-century. The collapse of the potato culture by the 1840s and 1850s led to a decimation of the cottier and laborer class that had relied so heavily on female productive work. It also brought to a virtual halt the extensive practice of subdivision and partible inheritance that had permitted virtually universal and early marriage. The remaining farming class in Ireland was more inclined to practice impartible inheritance and primogeniture: one son inherited, and represented an eligible partner for one daughter of another farming family, who was, in turn, expected to bring with her a sizeable dowry. Marriage became increasingly restricted as families' hopes and financial resources focused on the inheriting son and the first-married daughter. The remaining children became "surplus"—particularly daughters, whose wage-earning opportunities were fewer than their brothers' in the changing socioeconomic milieu. As a result of massive economic and demographic reorganization in nineteenth-century Ireland, then, there was a significant depreciation of women's worth as both producers and reproducers—a decline to which many responded by emigrating.[157]

Similarly, in England in the eighteenth and nineteenth centuries, accelerating enclosure and the loss of customary rights, the masculinization of farm labor and dairying under capitalist agriculture, and the mechanization and industrialization of cottage industries led to the devaluation of women's labor and the channeling of women's work into sweated labor in cottage manufacturing or into dead-end, low-paying jobs in factories. This was a process in which working-class men were complicit: with increasing competition between the sexes for work, male trade unionists spearheaded a quest for a male breadwinner's wage by espousing female domesticity and denigrating women's paid work; meanwhile, male Chartists incorporated female domesticity and passivity into their bid for working-class "respectability" and the vote (an effort which many working-class women initially supported, until the process led them to a double shift of paid work and housework because the male breadwinner's wage remained elusive).[158]

The devaluation of women's economic contribution in both Ireland and England was accompanied by a decline in women's status, and they struggled to assert agency within the confines of increasingly patriarchal family and work contexts. Along the southern Avalon, however, the economy continued to rely on family production in its main industry, supported by a multi-faceted package of subsistence agriculture and supplementary income-earning ventures in which women still played a prominent and essential role. In addition, the very broad (almost universal) male franchise in Newfoundland likely warded off any political incentive within the plebeian community to pressure women into lives of genteel respectability.

Thus, while gender ideology and feminine ideals of domesticity, fragility, and dependence increasingly circumscribed the lives of many women elsewhere, Irish plebeian women on the southern Avalon enjoyed considerable status and exercised significant authority both in family and community during this period. Within families, they shared in decision-making over mixed-sex work processes and were the sole authorities in routines performed by women. They were also the primary household managers, juggling resources with consumption demands and monitoring family accounts with local merchants. Women also shouldered responsibility and wielded power outside the home in the day-to-day life of community. They remained active and essential in the economic sphere: in subsistence production, the fishery, and other forms of economic activity, and as an integral part of the exchange economy that supported the resident fishery. They also acted as custodians of the Catholic faith and as interpreters of the supernatural within an alternative belief system—roles that not only gave them considerable status but also placed them in the vanguard of preserving the ethnoreligious identity of the Irish Catholic community.

Plebeian women also deployed power through their information networks. Women's gossip—whether it manifested itself as a means of group identification and preservation, a site of female resistance, or an expression of competition among women in their roles as household managers—was a component of power relations within the larger community. And in collective actions and individual interventions, women publicly flexed their muscles (often literally as well as figuratively) as they negotiated space for themselves and their families in the social, economic, and political life of their community. Thus, while plebeian women were barred from the exercise of formal power by their gender and class, within the plebeian community, their access to informal power was considerable, indicating that gender relations were very much a shifting territory in the days of early settlement, and that perhaps women not only made the cannonballs, but fired them too.

NOTES

1. PANL, GN 5/4/C/1, St. Mary's, 116–17 and 119–20, *Ellen Veal v. Mary Bowen*, 22 July and 1 August 1822. In the 1 August hearing, both parties were found culpable and required to enter into bonds of £5 each to keep the peace and be of good behavior for twelve months. Note that although some of the last names above were of English derivation, these family lines had been incorporated into the Irish Catholic population.

2. See, for example: Constance Backhouse, *Petticoats and Prejudice: Women and Law in Nineteenth-Century Canada* (Toronto: Osgoode Society, 1991); Linda Cullum and Maeve Baird, "'A Woman's Lot': Women and Law in Newfoundland from Early Settlement to the Twentieth Century," in *Pursuing Equality: Historical Perspectives on Women in Newfoundland and Labrador*, ed. Linda Kealey, Social and Economic Papers, no. 20 (St. John's: ISER, 1993), 66–162; Anna Clark, *The Struggle for the Breeches: Gender and the Making of the British Working Class* (Berkeley: University of California Press, 1995); Leonore Davidoff and Catherine Hall, *Family Fortunes: Men and Women of the English Middle Class, 1780–1850* (Chicago: University of Chicago Press, 1987); Sonya O. Rose, *Limited Livelihoods: Gender and Class in Nineteenth-Century England* (Berkeley: University of California Press, 1992); Jane Rendall, *Women in an Industrializing Society: England, 1750–1880*, Historical Association Studies (Oxford: Basil Blackwell, 1990); and G. S. Rousseau and Roy Porter, eds., *Sexual Underworlds of the Enlightenment* (Chapel Hill: University of North Carolina Press, 1988).

3. Up to the early nineteenth century, most were Anglo-Protestant, and many returned to Britain after stays of varying lengths on the island. Even those who remained in Newfoundland maintained strong family, commercial, and/or professional connections with Britain. There was a smaller Irish mercantile and professional elite in Newfoundland as well; but, while this group achieved increasing prominence in St. John's in the nineteenth century, their counterparts on the southern Avalon—a small, predominantly Protestant group of Irish merchant-planters—had wound up their interests in the area by the late eighteenth century.

4. L. A. Clarkson, "Love, Labour, and Life: Women in Carrick-on-Suir in the Late Eighteenth Century," *Irish Economic and Social History* 20 (1993): 30. By contrast, Errington notes that Upper Canadian farming families were distinctly hierarchical and patriarchal, the image of the "good wife" presented as "caring, quiet, [and] submissive"—although Errington's reliance on middle-class sources may have skewed

her findings somewhat. See Elizabeth Errington, *Wives and Mothers, Schoolmistresses and Scullery Maids: Working Women in Upper Canada, 1790–1840* (Montreal: McGill-Queen's University Press, 1995), 33 and 39.

5. This phrase was first encountered with EW, interview by author, Calvert, 21 July 1999, but it also resurfaced, or a similar opinion was expressed, in most interviews conducted.

6. Hector St. John de Crèvecoeur, *Letters from an American Farmer* (London: J. M. Dent, 1912), 146–47.

7. Laurel Thatcher Ulrich, *Good Wives: Image and Reality in the Lives of Women in Northern New England, 1650–1750* (New York: Knopf, 1982), 39–42.

8. Sally Cole, *Women of the Praia: Work and Lives in a Portuguese Coastal Community* (Princeton, NJ: Princeton University Press, 1991).

9. Quotation from QSF, interview by author, Cape Broyle, 22 July 1999; similar information was imparted by all informants.

10. Carol Berkin also notes the essential role of women as household managers in colonial America, where they were "expected to manage resources, time, and the available labor to best advantage, balancing production against maintenance, the needs of daily consumption against long-term supply, and the particular capabilities of servants and children against their assigned chores." See Berkin, *First Generations: Women in Colonial America* (New York: Hill and Wang, 1996), 28.

11. PRL, 340.9 N45, Trepassey–St. Mary's, 15, *Thomas Murphy v. James Warne*, 20 November 1793.

12. See, for example: Kathleen M. Brown, *Good Wives, Nasty Wenches, and Anxious Patriarchs: Gender, Race, and Power in Colonial Virginia* (Chapel Hill: University of North Carolina Press, 1994); de Crèvecoeur, *Letters*; and Ulrich, *Good Wives*.

13. March was a critical period in Newfoundland fishing households, when the winter's diet was virtually gone and the spring supplies had not yet been advanced by merchants. This expression, and the terms *good/bad manager* and *good/bad provider*, were used by most informants in discussing this issue. A similar theme on the importance of women's household management strategies to family survival appears in literature on urban working-class families. See, for example: Bettina Bradbury, *Working Families: Age, Gender, and Daily Survival in Industrializing Montreal* (Toronto: McClelland and Stuart, 1993); Elizabeth Roberts *A Woman's Place: An Oral History of Working-Class Women, 1890–1940* (Oxford: Basil Blackwell, 1984); and Ellen Ross, *Love and Toil: Motherhood in Outcast London, 1870–1918* (New York: Oxford University Press, 1993). However, these women occupied a more marginal place in family economies, despite their essential economic coping strategies, because, with the increasing separation of home and workplace in industrializing areas, women's contribution was perceived as secondary as the rhetoric of the male breadwinner and female domesticity intruded in their lives.

14. ESF, interview by author, Cape Broyle, 25 August 1999.

15. Brown, *Good Wives, Nasty Wenches*, 28–29. Thompson also notes the use of the ducking stool and scold's bridle in eighteenth-century England. See E. P. Thompson, *Customs in Common* (London: Merlin Press, 1991), 501.

16. AG, interview by author, Ferryland, 21 July 1999. Similar thoughts were expressed by other informants.

17. EW, interview by author, Calvert, 30 August 1999. Other informants provided similar information.

18. PANL, MG 473, Goodridge Collection, 1839 and 1841 ledgers; MHA, Goodridge fonds, 1840 ledger.

19. PANL, MG 49, Sweetman Collection, various files in boxes 2 and 3. Place of residence was often not given, so it is difficult to identify which of the women whose names appear in these accounts were strictly from the study area. Those who were not, however, were from neighboring areas and thus still serve to illustrate the points raised here by next-best approximation.

20. Other sources confirm these findings. Similar entries appear in a business journal found in the White-Maher house in Ferryland before its demolition in the 1960s; the journal is currently in the possession of HE of Ferryland. Although the business is not identified, the customer names are from the local area, and while the journal entries are dated 1881–82, they reflect the continuation of a system of exchange that was in place during the study period. Further evidence of women's involvement in the exchange economy can be found in the court records, such as third-party transactions in merchant and boatkeeper accounts entered in evidence as well as outstanding accounts presented by women themselves for payment.

21. *Newfoundland Population Returns*, 1836 (St. John's: n.p., 1836); and *Newfoundland Population Returns*, 1845 (St. John's: Ryan and Withers, 1845).

22. The more fragmentary Sweetman records also hint at this. Contrast, for example, the accounts of "*Mrs.* Jas. Mullaly" and "*Mrs.* Ths. McCarthy" with those of "*Widow* Lamb" and "*Widow* Conway."

23. There were exceptions, such as Mary Plece (also Please or Pleace) and Ann Huffman, household servants with the Goodridge family, who appeared to receive cash wages semi-annually.

24. For example: Catherine Shannahan's 1839 profit of 19s. 8d. from her work as a laundress was applied towards the account of Mathew Shannahan (1839 ledger, fol. 384). Margaret Leary had 10s. from her 1840 profits paid to "Thomas" at St. John's (1840 ledger, fol. 339). Washerwoman Mary Butler had 1s. 10d. from her earnings applied towards the account of William Butler and was still able to draw cash in the amount of £1.10.0 in November (1840 ledger, fol. 340). Mary Neill's 1841 profit of 10s. 4d. from selling hay to Goodridge's was applied towards the account of William Neill (1841 ledger, fol. 248). Nancy Gerian earned sufficient wages from her work on the Goodridge flakes in 1841 to have 14s. 2d. applied towards the account of Thomas Gerian and still receive cash in the amount of 5s. (1841 ledger, fol. 306).

25. Johanna Miller Lewis, "Women and Economic Freedom in the North Carolina Backcountry," in *Women and Freedom in Early America*, ed. Larry D. Eldridge (New York: New York University Press, 1997), 195. Lewis discusses evidence of women's economic activity in the business books of Rowan County, North Carolina; she observes, however, that working for a living was usually a life phase experienced by women before marriage or in widowhood, in contrast to my southern Avalon findings.

More like their southern Avalon counterparts were women in frontier Pennsylvania, who were essential members of their family production units after marriage and appeared regularly in merchant account books, regardless of marital status. Some maintained their own accounts, while most others transacted their purchases through husbands' and fathers' names, even borrowing cash on account. See Judith Ridner, "'To Have a Sufficient Maintenance': Women and the Economics of Freedom in Frontier Pennsylvania, 1750–1800," in *Women and Freedom*, ed. Eldridge, 167–90.

26. For the comparative context of Horton, see the discussion in Mancke, "At the Counter of the General Store: Women and the Economy in Eighteenth-Century Horton, Nova Scotia," in *Intimate Relations: Family and Community in Planter Nova Scotia, 1759–1800*, ed. Margaret Conrad, Planter Studies Series, no. 3 (Fredericton: Acadiensis, 1990), 167–81.

27. Mancke, "At the Counter of the General Store," 171.

28. In Roman Catholicism, *ultramontanism* was an emphasis on the supremacy of the pope in Rome, who lived *ultramontanus*, or "beyond the mountains [south of the Alps]" from the perspective of northern Europe. This doctrine advocated centralization and a move away from the ecclesiastical peculiarism of churches of individual nations. Its influence was increasingly felt in the Irish Catholic Church through the nineteenth century, particularly from mid-century onwards, and the transition was marked by an increasingly patriarchal influence on the Irish Catholic congregation.

29. Monsignor Michael Anthony Fleming, "The State of the Catholic Religion in Newfoundland Reviewed in Two Letters by Monsignor Fleming to Rev. P. John Spratt," (Rome, 1836), 90; italics added.

30. This information comes from the oral tradition.

31. RCAASJ, Fleming Papers, 103/32, "Dean Cleary's Notebook," 29.

32. The direct quotation came from EO, interview by author, Calvert, 26 August 1999, but most informants made a similar observation.

33. This observation echoed through numerous interviews. Just as women are credited by oral informants for maintaining the Catholic faith in the past, so too are they primarily blamed, especially by older informants, for current-day lapses in religious practice. To illustrate the enormity of the problem of declining maternal guidance in the spiritual realm, one elderly woman in Calvert exclaimed in exasperation: "Sure now they [children] blesses themselves back-foremost!" IV, interview by author, Calvert, 23 August 1999.

34. The cult of St. Brigid has spread with the Irish diaspora. Brigid (ca. 455–525), or the *Mary of the Gael*, was possibly a female druid before she converted to Christianity. She founded a mixed religious community (not unusual for the Celtic world) at Kildare, and some sources indicate that she may have been ordained a priest, and possibly a bishop, by Mel, bishop of Ardagh. She is said to have had intimate relationships with both a male bishop, Conlaed, and a female member of her community. When she was brought into the formal Catholic calendar of saints, however, her life story was sanitized. She was made into a model of Christian womanhood, virtue, and piety, and her mixed community was transformed into an exclusively female order of nuns. See: Peter Berresford Ellis, *Celtic Women: Women in Celtic Society and Literature*

(London: Constable, 1995), 27–29 and 146–50; and Shirley Toulson, *The Celtic Year: A Month-by-Month Celebration of Celtic Christian Festivals and Sites* (Shaftesbury: Element, 1996), 73–81.

35. St. Anne was Christ's maternal grandmother. She, too, is represented by the Catholic Church as a model of self-sacrificing Catholic womanhood—particularly for wives and mothers—and is the patron saint of housewives in the Catholic calendar of saints.

36. ESX, interview by author, Calvert, 19 July 1999.

37. In the following discussion, information on the pre-Christian religious system in Ireland is taken primarily from: Sean J. Connolly, *Priests and People in Pre-famine Ireland, 1780–1845* (Dublin: Gill and Macmillan, 1982); Sean Connolly, "Popular Culture in Pre-Famine Ireland," in *Talamh An Eisc: Canadian and Irish Essays*, ed. Cyril Byrne and Margaret Harry (Halifax: Nimbus, 1986), 12–28; George Casey, "Irish Culture in Newfoundland," in *Talamh An Eisc*, ed. Byrne and Harry, 203–27; Danaher, *Irish Country People* (Cork: Mercier Press, 1966); Deirdre Mageean, "To Be Matched or to Move: Irish Women's Prospects in Munster," in *Peasant Maids-City Women: From the European Countryside to Urban America*, ed. Christiane Harzig (Ithaca, NY: Cornell University Press, 1997), 57–97; Padraic O'Farrell, *Superstitions of the Irish Country People* (Dublin: Mercier Press, 1978); and W. G. Wood-Martin, *Traces of the Elder Faiths of Ireland*, vol. 2 (London: 1902; reprint, Port Washington, NY: Kennikat Press, 1970). Information on the corresponding system on the southern Avalon comes primarily from oral interviews conducted in 1999 and 2000, although Casey's "Irish Culture" was again useful in this regard. Some additional information on customary practices associated with death derives from undergraduate papers at MUNFLA, particularly: Zita Johnson, "Calendar Customs and Rites of Passage at Renews," MUNFLA ms. 68-011D, unpublished research paper, Memorial University of Newfoundland, 1967–68, 30; and Andrew O'Brien, "Wake, Funeral and Burial Customs in Cape Broyle," MUNFLA ms. 68-016C, unpublished research paper, Memorial University of Newfoundland, 1967–68, 7–10.

38. Connolly, *Priests and People*, 100.

39. The following discussion focuses on aspects of the system that had a particular female component. It does not include the myriad other beliefs and practices in which men and women participated equally (e.g., the belief in good luck charms and omens of misfortune).

40. Belief in the power of a widow's curse persisted in the area into the twentieth century, as demonstrated by the anecdote on the audio clip, collected from ESF, interview by author, Cape Broyle, 25 August 1999 (with the request that the parties' last names remain anonymous).

41. This was true of the derivative tradition in Ireland as well. Patricia Lysaght observes that ritual cursing was often a means employed by women in exacting revenge against enemies and authorities who had caused them harm. It was not a ritual to be entered into frivolously, as the curse, once uttered, had to fall somewhere, and if undeserved by the intended recipient, would recoil on the invoker. See Patricia Lysaght, "Women and the Great Famine," in *The Great Famine and the Irish Diaspora in*

America, ed. Arthur Gribben (Amherst: University of Massachusetts Press, 1999), 21–47. Wood-Martin also notes the potential for curses to return to the utterer; see Wood-Martin, *Traces of the Elder Faiths*, 57–58.

42. The association of Patrick with Sheelagh can be traced to Ireland, although the weather belief is purely local. See: Casey, "Irish Culture," 219; and Bridget McCormack, *Perceptions of St. Patrick in Eighteenth-Century Ireland* (Dublin: Four Courts Press, 2000), 48–49. McCormack observes that Sheelagh was noted for her tempestuous nature and that a possible archetype for her tradition was the *sheela-na-gig*, a female icon associated with protection, productivity, and fertility in the Middle Ages, but transmuted into a talisman to fend off the "sin" of lust by the early modern Catholic Church.

43. The bread was blessed by making the sign of the cross over the dough before baking, lightly touching down on the dough four times to mark each extremity of the cross. The custom persists today, especially among older women and even among some middle-aged women. They no longer believe in fairies, but they continue the practice as an act of benediction on their families, in the belief that it will help to ward off harm in a more diffuse sense.

44. See note 34, above.

45. Paschal candles were used by the Catholic Church at Easter time to celebrate the end of mankind's banishment from heaven (and hence the return of light after a long period of darkness) with the resurrection of Christ after crucifixion and his ascension into heaven.

46. Another propitious day for predictions was the first of May, or *Bealtinagh* in the ancient Irish calendar, when a ritual fire was lit at the seat of the high king at Tara to celebrate the first day of summer. The first of May is not a significant holy day in the Catholic calendar. But in the legend of St. Patrick, he is said to have lit the first paschal fire on the Hill of Slane on the night of *Bealtinagh*. The fire could be seen from Tara, and the druids warned high king Laoghaire that if this fire was not quenched, it would consume all of Ireland. Laoghaire was unable to subdue Patrick, and hence, the *fire of Christianity* replaced the *fire of paganism* in Ireland. Of course, the chronology here is skewed, for Easter never occurs as late as 1 May, but the symbolic power of the narrative for the emerging Catholic Church was profound, and provides yet another example of the intersection of ancient and Catholic belief systems. See John B. Bury, *The Life of St. Patrick* (1905; reprint, Freeport, NY: Books for Libraries Press, 1971), 104–8 and 301–3.

47. Father Duffy's Well, near Salmonier, St. Mary's Bay, provides a local example from this period. Father Duffy led his congregation at St. Mary's in the destruction of a merchant's fish flake in the mid-1830s. When he and eight other ringleaders were walking to St. John's for their trial, they found themselves weary and thirsty, with no source of water in sight. According to the oral tradition, Father Duffy struck the ground with a stick and water sprang forth at his touch. A more recent manifestation of a holy well is the grotto at Renews, built in the 1920s on the site of the Mass Rock, where Catholics gathered in penal times. It was modeled on the Grotto of Our Lady of Lourdes in France and contains a piece of rock from that shrine. Belief in the spiri-

tual and curative powers of the water from both sites was pervasive on the southern Avalon as late as the 1960s and 1970s, and continues among the older generation today.

48. Rev. Lewis A. Anspach, A *History of the Island of Newfoundland* (London: Anspach, 1819), 474.

49. Candles made of tallow or fat were not deemed appropriate for this service, although they were most likely used in small chapels in remote areas such as the southern Avalon.

50. Rev. Leonard Boase, ed., *Catholic Book of Knowledge*, vol. 3 (London: Virtue and Company, 1961; reprint, Chicago: Catholic Home Press, 1962), 262.

51. Churching was the formal church blessing of a woman after childbirth. It was viewed as a ritual of purification rather than thanksgiving within the Catholic congregations in both Newfoundland and Ireland. Churching and shaming will be discussed further in Chapter 8.

52. In Christian belief, after the birth of Jesus Christ in Bethlehem, Herod, the king of Judea, was visited by three wise men seeking the new "king of the Jews" whose birth had been foretold by the stars. To remove this potential threat to his crown, Herod decreed that all male children in Bethlehem aged two or under be slain. Christ's father, Joseph, was warned by an angel of the impending slaughter and moved his family to Egypt until after Herod's death, when they returned to Joseph's old home of Nazareth.

53. Toulson, *The Celtic Year*, 80.

54. Hasia Diner notes a similarly central role of women at Irish wakes; see Diner, *Erin's Daughters in America: Irish Immigrant Women in the Nineteenth Century* (Baltimore, MD: Johns Hopkins University Press, 1983), 27–28.

55. Wakes of those who had died young or under tragic circumstances were perhaps more somber affairs; certainly, they were in the twentieth century.

56. PANL, MG 31, Carter Family Papers, file 33, Will of Robert Carter Sr., 29 March 1795.

57. Anspach, *History*, 472–73.

58. These quotations appear in Connolly, *Priests and People*, 157–58. Diner also notes that a number of contemporary observers in Ireland wrote about "a class of professional keeners, elderly women who made a living mourning the dead." See Diner, *Erin's Daughters*, 28.

59. Angela Bourke, "The Irish Traditional Lament and the Grieving Process," *Women's Studies International Forum* 11, no. 4 (1988): 287–91.

60. XT, interview by author, Calvert, 19 July 1999.

61. Connolly, *Priests and People*, 119.

62. Connolly, *Priests and People*, chap. 3, particularly 119–34.

63. Emmet Larkin, "The Devotional Revolution in Ireland, 1850–75," chap. 2 in *The Historical Dimensions of Irish Catholicism*, ed. Larkin (New York: Arno Press, 1976).

64. Larkin also acknowledges this demographic shift, but places much greater weight on Cullen's efforts in dramatically increasing adherence to formal Catholic practices.

65. The epigraph is from a local song, "A Woman's Tongue Will Never Take a Rest," collected in Cape Broyle in 1968. See Andrew O'Brien, "Songs from Cape Broyle," MUNFLA Tape 68-16/490, Memorial University of Newfoundland, 1967–68.

66. Melanie Tebbutt, *Women's Talk? A Social History of "Gossip" in Working-Class Neighbourhoods, 1880–1960* (Aldershot: Scolar Press, 1995), 19–20. Tebbutt writes that traces of this older meaning survived in nineteenth-century dialect in Somerset, where gossiping still referred to a christening feast or general merrymaking.

67. Karma Lochrie, *Covert Operations: The Medieval Uses of Secrecy* (Philadelphia: University of Pennsylvania Press, 1999), chap. 2.

68. The discussion in this paragraph derives from a theoretical review by Jörg R. Bergman, *Discreet Indiscretions: The Social Organization of Gossip*, trans. John Bednarz Jr. (New York: Aldine de Gruyter, 1993), 63–67 and 139–53. The authorities he cites include: F. E. Lumley, B. Malinowski, W. F. Ogburn, and M. F. Nimkoff (social control); Max Gluckman and E. L. Epstein (group preservation); Robert Paine (information management); Jörg R. Bergman (a social form of "discreet indiscretion"); and M. Weigle, V. Aebischer, R. Borker, D. Jones, C. Benard, E. Schlaffer, A. M. Waliullah, and B. Althans (a subversive form of female solidarity).

69. Bergman dismisses this "so-called 'feminist' literature" as lacking in explanatory power. He argues that women are seen as gossipy simply because the traditional division of labor has put them in a position to be gossip producers to a greater extent than men. Particularly as washerwomen, maids, and servant girls, he argues, women have had far greater access than men to the private affairs of others, and therefore have been perceived as more likely to be the producers of gossip. Unfortunately, this does little to explain the association of gossip with all women, regardless of occupational group. Furthermore, Bergman himself lists a variety of traditionally male occupational groups—barbers, postmen, small shopkeepers, landlords—who have access to private information and are known to be gossipy (he rather naively rules out others, such as doctors, lawyers, priests, and psychotherapists, because they are prevented by professional codes of ethics from revealing the information). See Bergman, *Discrete Indiscretions*, 63–67. Given this plethora of potential male gossips, Bergman's explanation still begs the question: Why in Western culture has this "morally reprehensible" behavior historically been associated with women?

70. Lochrie, *Covert Operations*, 57, and chap. 2 in general.

71. See, for example: Jennifer Coates and Deborah Cameron, eds., *Women in Their Speech Communities: New Perspectives in Language and Sex* (London: Longman, 1988); also Deborah Cameron, ed., *The Feminist Critique of Language: A Reader*, rev. ed. (London: Routledge, 1998).

72. Dale Spender, in Tebbutt, *Women's Talk*, 1; citing Spender, *Man Made Language* (London: Routledge and Kegan Paul, 1980 and 1985), 107.

73. See, for example: Jennifer Coates, "Gossip Revisited: Language in All-Female Groups," in *Women in Their Speech Communities*, ed. Coates and Cameron, 94–122; and Deborah Jones, "Gossip: Notes on Women's Oral Culture," in *Feminist Critique*, ed. Cameron (1990), 242–50; reprinted from *Women's Studies International Quarterly*

3 (1980): 193–8. Jones breaks gossip down into four categories of women's language: house-talk, scandal, bitching, and chatting.

74. PANL, GN 5/4/C/1, St. Mary's: 134, *Ellen Tobin v. Ann St. Croix*, 27 June 1823; and 135, *Bridget St. Croix v. Thomas Tobin*, 30 June 1823. This parting of the ways is discussed below.

75. Cole, *Women of the Praia*, 121.

76. With few exceptions, Irish immigration to Newfoundland did not follow channels of kinship to any great degree. See John Mannion and Fidelma Maddock. "Old World Antecedents, New World Applications: Inistioge Immigrants in Newfoundland," in *Kilkenny: History and Society-Interdisciplinary Essays on the History of an Irish County*, ed. William Nolan and Kevin Whelan (Dublin: Geography Publications, 1990), 345–404.

77. Brown, *Good Wives, Nasty Wenches*, 95–100.

78. Tebbutt, *Women's Talk*, 1 and 11.

79. Tebbutt, *Women's Talk*, 1.

80. For example, diarist Robert Carter and his family were estranged from Mr. and Mrs. Wright (likely Thomas Wright, merchant at Ferryland, and his wife, Sarah) for an extended period over a matter that began with "some curtness" on Mrs. Wright's part to Carter's daughter, Eliza, in January of 1834, but escalated when Mrs. Wright began "spreading scandal" about the Carter family. Fences were mended, however, for in August of 1836, Carter noted, "Mrs. and Mr. Wright called to-day after staying away more than 12 months." PANL, MG 920, Robert Carter Diary, 28 January and 22 March 1834, and 9 August 1836.

81. The sense of difference between women of the local elite and the plebeian community is discussed further in Chapter 9.

82. PANL, MG 205, Pole Papers, 1799–1800.

83. Appendix A describes a middling group between the elite and plebeian communities on the southern Avalon whose allegiance was primarily with the plebeians, with whom they shared much in terms of work and leisure routines and world view, but who were still connected to the local elite by ethnoreligious and patronage ties. Henry Currier (or Coryear) was one of this group. In the 1800 census, he was listed as a boatmaster for Christopher Vallance; he was also listed as a small-scale employer, with one fishing servant and two dieters in the winter of 1799–1800. Like many fishermen who came out to Newfoundland, however, he was upwardly mobile, and likely moved into the vacuum created by the numerous bankruptcies in the traditional planter fishery in the late and post-Napoleonic War period. By 1817, for example, he was in possession of three plantations, which he devised by deeds of gift to his children. See PANL, GN 5/1/C/9, 31–33, Deeds of Conveyance, 15 March 1817. By 1818, he had hired a clerk for his business and a private tutor for his family at a salary of £15 per year plus washing. See PANL, GN 5/1/C/1, Ferryland, 45, *Kearon Mulloney v. Henry Coryear*, 11 May 1818. So Currier had obviously come up in the world. In the 1809 episode, however, his daughter was still appealing to the family's plebeian connections.

84. PANL, GN 5/4/C/1, Ferryland, box 1, *Christopher Valence v. Elenor Currier*, March 1809.

85. PANL, GN 5/4/C/1; St. Mary's, 132–33, *Ann Bowen v. Mary Money*, 9 March and 1 April 1823. The final deposition of the case has not survived in the records.

86. PANL, GN 5/4/C/1, St. Mary's, 103 and 107, *Elenor Piddle v. Margret Dinn*, 5 September and 13 October 1821.

87. Brown, *Good Wives, Nasty Wenches*, 99–101. Julie Richter also notes that in colonial Virginia, nothing damaged a woman's reputation more than being called a whore. See Richter, "The Free Women of Charles Parish, York County, Virginia, 1630–1740," in *Women and Freedom*, ed. Eldridge, 295.

88. Ulrich, *Good Wives*, 96–97.

89. See, for example, PANL, GN 5/4/C/1, St. Mary's, 135, *Bridget St. Croix v. Thomas Tobin*, 30 June 1823; also, PRL, 340.9 N45, Ferryland, *Bridget Murphy v. Catherine Dauton and Mary Whealon*, 28 September 1795.

90. KO, interview by author, St. John's, 15 May 1998.

91. IT, interview by author, Calvert, 19 July 1999.

92. Cole, *Women of the Praia*, 122, and 108–24 in general.

93. The perception of women as natural bonders and men as natural competitors has been given "scientific" endorsement by writers such as biological anthropologist Robin Dunbar in *Grooming, Gossip and the Evolution of Language* (London: Faber and Faber, 1996). Dunbar argues that grooming, once the primary means of bonding by primates, became unfeasible in human social groups as these groups became larger. Language therefore evolved to replace grooming as the most important method of networking. Furthermore, he says, the chief networkers in primate species have been female because they are more likely to remain in the group in which they are born and give it coherence over time. Language permits group members to exchange essential information about the physical and social world, to identify and form ties with other group members, and to provide support in times of crisis. This type of communication, so necessary to the survival of the group, is more associated with the type of cooperation that typifies the female world. The male world is much more competitive, focused on mating or acquiring resources (status) that will attract mates. Thus when people talk, Dunbar argues, "the women are engaged in networking, while the men are engaged in advertising" (177).

94. This line of argument appears in Tebbutt, *Women's Talk*, 176; see also 7–9 and 220. Jones makes a similar point in "Gossip," 245. Thompson also notes men's fear of the power of women's tongues to incite and shame in *Customs in Common*, 333 and 501.

95. Diner, *Erin's Daughters*, 18.

96. This anecdote was originally told by Monsignor Francis A. Coady, who had served as a priest on the southern Avalon, to Dr. Cyril Byrne, Coordinator of Irish Studies at Saint Mary's University, Halifax. Dr. Byrne related it to me by email dated 8 September 2000.

97. This literature includes: Temma Kaplan, "Women and Communal Strikes in the Crisis of 1917–1922," in *Becoming Visible: Women in European History*, ed. Renate Bridenthal, Claudia Koonz, and Susan Stuard (Boston: Houghton Mifflin, 1987), 429–49; Rosemary Jones, "Women, Community, and Collective Action: The 'Ceffyl

Pren' Tradition," in *Our Mothers' Land: Chapters in Welsh Women's History, 1830–1939*, ed. Angela V. John (Cardiff: University of Wales Press, 1991), 17–41; Rusty Bittermann, "Women and the Escheat Movement: The Politics of Everyday Life on Prince Edward Island," in *Separate Spheres: Women's Worlds in the Nineteenth-Century Maritimes*, ed. Janet Guildford and Suzanne Morton (Fredericton: Acadiensis Press, 1994), 23–38; Sean Cadigan, *Hope and Deception in Conception Bay: Merchant-Settler Relations in Newfoundland, 1785–1855* (Toronto: University of Toronto Press, 1995), chap. 4; Maria Luddy, *Women in Ireland, 1800–1918: A Documentary History* (Cork: Cork University Press, 1995), 245–50; Thompson, *Customs in Common*, 305–36; and Ulrich, *Good Wives*, 184–201. Absent from the southern Avalon, however, was the practice—common in the British Isles—of men's use of female disguise either to signal the seriousness of the issue, such that the "weaker" sex would actually cross over gender "boundaries" to involve themselves, or to mitigate their own responsibility and pass off the actions as the work of mere "frail" women. This may reflect the fact that within the plebeian community on the southern Avalon, constructions of womanhood did not incorporate frailty or weakness; nor did most middle-class magistrates harbor such perceptions of plebeian women (see Chapter 6 and 8).

98. Most of the literature cited in the previous note refers to the general reluctance of authorities to arrest women in these types of actions.

99. The following account is a summary of information taken from the following sources: PANL, GN 2/1/A, vol. 11, 388–95, 437–41, and 459, various correspondence 1788–89; PANL, GN 5/4/C/1, Ferryland, box 1, *Rex. v. Various*, 17–30 September and 1, 20, and 25 October 1788; Cyril J. Byrne, ed., *Gentlemen-Bishops and Faction Fighters: The Letters of Bishops O Donel, Lambert, Scallan, and Other Irish Missionaries* (St. John's: Jesperson Press, 1984), various correspondence, 62–117; Christopher English, "Collective Violence in Ferryland District, Newfoundland, in 1786," *Dalhousie Law Journal* 21, no. 2 (fall 1998): 475–89; Raymond J. Lahey, *James Louis O'Donel in Newfoundland, 1784–1807: The Establishment of the Roman Catholic Church*, ed. Shannon Ryan and G. M. Story (St. John's: Newfoundland Historical Society, pamphlet 8, 1984), 13–20; and Gerald J. Barnable, "The Ferryland Riots of 1788," *An Nasc* 7 (summer 1994): 4–9.

100. Daniel W. Prowse, *A History of Newfoundland from the English, Colonial, and Foreign Records* (London: Macmillan, 1895; reprint, Belleville: Mika Studio, 1972), 402. Prowse is actually quoting "an old Irishman" of his acquaintance.

101. Byrne, ed., *Gentlemen-Bishops*, 98–101, Father James O Donel to Archbishop Troy, Dublin, 24 December 1789.

102. Byrne, ed., *Gentlemen-Bishops*, 69–72 and 110–11, O Donel to Governor Elliot, 1788, and Fathers Patrick Phelan (Harbour Grace), Edmund Burke (Placentia), and Thomas Ewer (Ferryland) to Cardinal Antonelli, Propaganda Fide, 14 December 1790.

103. English, "Collective Violence," 487.

104. It should be noted, however, that although elements of ethnicity and class obviously underscored this event and the later Father Duffy affair, sectarianism was not a primary rallying point in either episode. Despite official concerns about the

volatility of the Irish population on the southern Avalon, in terms of ethnoreligious tensions, the district was far less explosive than other areas on the island with mixed Irish and English populations. St. John's and Conception Bay, for example, witnessed significant ethnoreligious strife. But while these other districts held distinct Irish and English populations, along the southern Avalon, the English Protestant group was almost totally assimilated into the Irish Catholic ethnic group, doubtless contributing significantly to the quiescence of the district. The only large-scale manifestation of ethnoreligious boundaries on record related to the election of 1836 (see below). Sporadic incidents of livestock-maiming may also have had ethnic as well as class undertones (Appendix A). And there was the slightest hint of an assertion of ethnicity in the report of an 1803 court case, in which Nicholas White of Ferryland was charged with assaulting Margret Gibbon on the public road and "tearing her cap for having an orange-Coloured Ribband in it." White admitted the assault but pleaded intoxication. He was fined 20s. and ordered to keep the peace and be of good behavior. See PANL, GN 5/4/C/1, Ferryland, box 1, *Rex v. Nicholas White*, 6 May 1803.

105. PANL, GN 2/1/A, vol. 11, 388–89, Petition from the merchants and principal inhabitants of Ferryland to Elliot, undated (likely received by the governor in early October 1788, given its placement in the letterbook and the fact that the governor responded to it on 9 October 1788).

106. Byrne, ed., *Gentlemen-Bishops*, 73–76, O Donel to Troy, 16 November 1788.

107. PANL, GN 2/1/A, vol. 11, 391–93, Pellew to Elliot, 9 October 1788.

108. RCAASJ, O Donel Papers, 100/3/3, O Donel to Elliot, 1788.

109. This account is taken from the following sources: CO 194, vol. 94, fols. 1–24; PANL, GN 5/4/C/1, Ferryland, box 1, 80–81, *Slade, Elson and Company v. Rev. James Duffy et al.*, 29 October and 3 November 1835; Bishop Michael Fleming, reports and letters cited in Rev. Michael F. Howley, *Ecclesiastical History of Newfoundland* (Boston: Doyle and Whittle, 1888; reprint, Belleville, ON: Mika, 1971), 323–28; Michael McCarthy, *The Irish in Newfoundland, 1600–1900: Their Trials, Tribulations, and Triumphs* (St. John's: Creative Publishers, 1999), 143–61; and Sister Elizabeth Whelan, "History of the Community of St. Mary's," unpublished research paper, 4 April 1972, housed at the CNS, chap. 3, 19–31.

110. Governor Henry Prescott (Web Link) reported to the Colonial Secretary in 1836 that the entire community was Catholic save Martin, his two clerks, and one servant. See CO 194, 94, fols. 3–10, Prescott to Lord Glenelg, 4 January 1836.

111. This was not the first time that mercantile premises in the harbor had been targeted by the plebeian community. In 1826, magistrate John H. Martin had written Governor Cochrane of an attack on the premises of William Rideout, in which the perpetrators had stolen stores and attempted to burn the premises to the ground. See PANL, GN 2/2, vol. 1, 29–32, Martin to Cochrane, 13 February 1826.

112. Bishop Michael Fleming, cited by Howley, *Ecclesiastical History*, 327.

113. These were powerful and celebrated Irish female leaders of the past. *Macha Mong Ruadh*, or "Macha of the Red Hair," forcibly seized the throne of Ireland from her uncles after the death of her high-king father in 377 BC and ruled for seven years. She lends her name to Armagh (in Gaelic, *Ard Macha*, or "Macha's Height"), the

primal seat of Christianity in Ireland. *Grainne Ni Maille* (ca. 1530–1603), or, in its anglicized form, "Granuaile," or "Grace O'Malley," was a Mayo chieftain's daughter who became the commander of 200 fighting men and three raiding ships that controlled the Connacht coastline and harried English shipping in the sixteenth century. She also led trading missions to south Munster and was involved in insurrectionary activities against the English. In the 1590s, she went to London and negotiated a private truce with Elizabeth I. See Ellis, *Celtic Women*, 79–80 and 214–20.

114. See Jones, "Women, Community and Collective Action." Temma Kaplan's "Women and Communal Strikes," although dealing with urban working-class women of a later period, is a useful discussion of female consciousness activated in defense of family and community.

115. PANL, GN 2/1/A, vol. 11, 391–93, Pellew to Elliot, 9 October 1788; italics added.

116. Janet A. Nolan, *Ourselves Alone: Women's Emigration from Ireland, 1885–1920* (Lexington: University Press of Kentucky, 1989), 32.

117. Power was excommunicated by Archbishop Troy of Dublin. See Byrne, ed., *Gentlemen-Bishops*, 88–89, Edict, Troy, 4 March 1789. Still, he maintained considerable support in the district until he left in 1791. In March of 1790, Ewer, acting on O Donel's instructions, renewed Power's excommunication, extending the decree to all who would continue to support Power; Power reciprocated by excommunicating Ewer and all his flock. See Byrne, ed., *Gentlemen-Bishops*, 102–4, O Donel to Troy, 13 June 1790. This brought about an interesting impasse and ironic repercussions, as noted by community historian Gerald Barnable: "Thus are all Ferryland parish people the descendants of excommunicated Catholics." See Barnable, "Ferryland Riots," 8.

118. Another possible facet of female participation in the incident was suggested to me by one of my oral informants while speculating on the reference in "Dean Cleary's Notebook" to the women of St. Mary's taking fire from the altar and burning a local house at the request of Father Duffy (see above). I have interpreted this action as possibly a rite of exorcism, but my informant suggested that it may have been an act of retaliation in relation to the Father Duffy affair. EW, interview by author, Calvert, 30 August 1999. In either interpretation, there are strong ritualistic overtones in women's use of "sacred fire."

119. CO 194, vol. 94, fols. 19–24, Deposition of William Lush sworn before Peter Weston Carter, JP of the Central District, 13 November 1835, and before Chief Justice Henry Boulton, St. John's, 24 November 1835; italics added.

120. CO 194, vol. 94, fols. 11–18, Martin to Joseph Templeman, 22 December 1835; italics added.

121. CO 194, vol. 93, fols. 11–18, various accounts summarized in Martin to Joseph Templeman, 22 December 1835.

122. The episode is documented in PANL, GN 920, Robert Carter Diary, 13–23 November and 31 December 1836, and 1 January 1837; italics added.

123. See various original documentary reports in Luddy, *Documentary History*, 245–50. Here, for example, is an excerpt from the outraged report of *The Tipperary Advocate* of an 1865 clash between rival factions. Note the portrayal of women's involvement as aberrant, maniacal, out of control:

In that yelling crowd of Langanites and O'Beirnites, all entangled and struggling in one heaving billow, young and old, lusty and infirm, male and female, were to be found shouting, whistling, groaning, dancing, foaming with irrepressible rage. . . . here there was a fearful looking scene—well looking, well dressed girls, one a perfect Amazon, bared their arms, wound their shawls tightly around them, and rushed with the mêlée. That woman there, with the black chenille net and lilac muslin gown, is a perfect maniac . . . there is a little girl of sixteen, her features distorted and her whole frame quivering with frenzied agitation; now she beats the wooden planks and bites everything within her reach!

124. PANL, MG 49, Sweetman Collection, box 4, file 37, Patrick Hogan to Principals, 2 January 1846.

125. Note again the specificity in tracing sons compared with the vagueness in tracing daughters in the oral tradition.

126. As late as 1833, Robert Carter referred to "a gang supposed to be robbers having passed Westward at the back of the Harbours." See PANL, MG 920, Robert Carter Diary, 29 September 1833.

127. PANL, GN 2/1/A, vol. 13, 163–65, Dingle to Waldegrave, 28 July 1797; italics added.

128. PANL, GN 2/1/A, vol. 16, 288–94, Dingle to Gambier, [15 September?] 1802. Note that Dingle's warnings occurred within the context of the United Irishman Rebellion and the 1800 mutiny in the Newfoundland Regiment, at which time it was felt that every man to the south of St. John's had taken the United Irishmen's oath (see Chapter 2).

129. The oral tradition is very reticent about female physical violence. Oral informants generally observed that, while women were frequently involved in verbal confrontations, they did not get into physical fights. One informant (VN, interview by author, Ferryland, 9 May 2000) did mention that she used to hear the "old people" talking about women fighting on the beach with splitting knives; however, this was the only example offered. Given overwhelming evidence to the contrary in the court records, however, I am inclined to interpret this reserve as a reflection of the scruples of a later period.

130. Similar incidents involving plebeian women in periods of early settlement have been described in: Cadigan, *Hope and Deception*; Bittermann, "Women and the Escheat Movement"; Ridner, "Sufficient Maintenance"; and Ulrich, *Good Wives*.

131. PANL, GN 5/2/C/1, Box 2, 12, *John William Sanders and Co. v. Thomas Berrigan*, 17 September 1832.

132. The former scenario is the more likely of the two, although either is possible, given the complex evolution of the ejectment action up to the time the Berrigan matters were being heard. In older English law, the ejectment was a trespass action that could be taken only by a leaseholder for damages resulting from having been wrongfully dispossessed of property. By the fifteenth century, the lessee could also seek to recover the remaining term of his lease. This allowed the action to be extended to determine freehold title as well via a legal fiction: *imaginary* lessees were created and one sued the other for ejectment; but in reality, the court was determining the freehold rights of the two "lessors." By the seventeenth century, the most

common form of ejectment action was that of "lessor v. lessee." However, it was still used to determine entitlement to freehold as well. Thus, the ejectment of a lessee or the ejectment of a mortgagor in default are both possible interpretations of the *Saunders v. Berrigan* matter. See: David M. Walker, *The Oxford Companion to Law* (Oxford: Clarendon Press, 1980), 395; Bryan A. Gardner, *Black's Law Dictionary*, 7th ed. (St. Paul, MN: West Group, 1999), 534–35; and John A. Yogis, *Canadian Law Dictionary*, 3rd ed. (Hauppauge, NY: Barron's Educational Series, 1995), 77.

133. PANL: GN 5/2/C/4, Writ no. 8, *J. W. Saunders Esqr. v. Thomas Berrigan*, issued 25 September for return 1 November 1836, Action in Ejectment; GN 5/2/C/3, 1835–47 journal, 62 and 64–65, *John W. Saunders v. Thomas Berrigan*, 3 and 5 November 1836; and GN 5/2/C/8, 74 and 76–77, *John W. Saunders v. Thomas Berrigan*, 3 and 5 November 1836.

134. PANL, GN 5/4/C/1, Ferryland, box 1, *Regina v. Anastatia Berrigan et al.*, 3 and 20 September 1838.

135. PANL, GN 5/4/C/1, Ferryland, box 2, *Regina v. William Berrigan, Anastatia Berrigan, Bridget Berrigan, and Alice Berrigan*, 31 December 1842, and 31 January and 23 February 1843.

136. PANL, GN 5/4/C/1, Ferryland, box 2: *Regina v. James Gearing Sr., Benjamin Wilcox, Edward Berrigan, Anastatia Berrigan, Thomas Berrigan Sr., and Thomas Berrigan Jr.*, 13, 14, 20, and 27 June 1843; and *Regina v. Thomas Berrigan Jr.*, 5 February 1844.

137. PANL, GN 5/4/C/1, Ferryland, box 2, *Regina v. John Bavis and his Wife*, 29 December 1853, and 5 January 1854.

138. PANL, GN 5/4/C/1, Ferryland, box 1, 67, *Henry Coryear v. Jane Hayley*, 8 and 16 April 1835. Fences were not completely mended between the parties, however, for the following year, Coryear brought Hayley back to court on the matter of an outstanding debt in the amount of £1.16.10 Cy. See PANL, GN 5/4/C/1, Ferryland, box 1, 83–84, *Henry Coryear v. Jane Hayley*, 4 January 1836.

139. Lists of liquor licenses issued for the district for various years appear in PANL, GN 2/1/A, and GN 5/4/C/1, Ferryland, box 1.

140. PRL, 340.9 N45, Ferryland, *Michael Ryan v. Elenor Evoy et al.* and *Elinor Evoy v. Michael Ryan*, 21 and 28 July and 3 August 1795.

141. In fact, Elenor was no stranger to the courthouse. The previous Christmas season, she had been in a fracas with Moses Rowe and successfully sued him for damages to her cloak and handkerchief in the amount of 2s. See PRL, 340.9 N45, Ferryland, *Elenor Evoy v. Moses Rowe*, 29 December 1794.

142. PANL, GN 5/4/C/1, Ferryland, box 1, *Rex v. James Welsh, Rex v. Sylvester Welsh, Ann McLarthy v. Patrick Evoy*, and *Rex v. Elenor Welsh*, 1 April 1803.

143. The entire district of St. Mary's, which included the community of St. Mary's as well as other pockets of inhabitants in adjacent coves and harbors to the north and south, had only 236 inhabitants wintering over in 1825. See CO 194, vol. 70, fol. 227, Governor's Annual Return of the Fisheries and Inhabitants, 1825.

144. PANL, GN 5/4/C/1, St. Mary's: 84, *Catharine St. Croix v. Martin Tobin*; 134, *Ellen Tobin v. Ann St. Croix*, 27 June 1823; and 135, *Bridget St. Croix v. Thomas Tobin*, 30 June 1823. The disposition of the 1823 cases is not revealed in the existing records.

145. PANL, GN 5/4/C/1, St. Mary's, 84, *Catharine St. Croix v. Martin Tobin*, 22 January 1820.

146. PANL, GN 5/4/C/1, Ferryland, box 2, *Regina v. James Kenney and Ellen, his Wife*, 12 September 1850. Although the first names of the Dooleys appear as James and Ellen in the record book, the initial draft of the proceedings (contained in a file folder with the journal) shows that the complainants were actually "Maurice Dooley, Mary his Wife and Step Son." Apparently, the clerk mistakenly transcribed the first names of the defendants for those of the complainants in the final entry.

147. PANL, GN 5/1/C/1, Ferryland, 117, *Rex v. Ann Prichet*, 24 October 1820.

148. Note that some incidents of assault involved multiple complaints being brought. Three cases, for example, were general affrays involving both men and women. The number of complaints made was therefore greater than the number of actual incidents reported. Also, there was not necessarily a one-to-one correlation between numbers of aggressors and numbers of victims. In some cases, for example, a single victim reported multiple assailants or, alternatively, one assailant allegedly attacked multiple victims. For a discussion of the significance of the number of cases found, see Appendix B.

149. PANL, GN 5/4/C/1, Ferryland, box 2, *Regina v. Margaret Ryan*, 13 August 1839, and *Regina v. Margaret Ryan*, 22 July 1840.

150. PANL, GN 5/4/C/1, Ferryland, box 2, *Regina v. Johanna Morrissy*, 28 December 1841.

151. PANL, GN 5/4/C/1, Ferryland, box 2, *Regina v. Mary Ann Pendergast*, 16 and 19 August 1851.

152. PANL, GN 5/4/C/1, Ferryland, box 2, *Regina v. Bridget Dullanty*, 18 April 1844.

153. PANL, GN 5/4/C/1, Ferryland, box 1, 100, — *Cose v. Bridget Dullanty*, 6 May 1837.

154. Ulrich, *Good Wives*, 191.

155. This finding differs significantly from Judith Norton's in her examination of assault cases in the planter townships of Nova Scotia in the first fifty years of settlement. Norton notes: "Women were particularly vulnerable in early Nova Scotia. In the forty-five recorded incidents of abuse or assault identified in the early court records, twenty of the victims and five of the assailants were females." See Judith Norton, "The Dark Side of Planter Life: Reported Cases of Domestic Violence," in *Intimate Relations*, ed. Conrad, 185.

156. See: Denise Riley, *"Am I That Name?": Feminism and the Category of Women in History* (Minneapolis: University of Minnesota Press, 1988); and Joan Wallach Scott, *Gender and the Politics of History* (New York: Columbia University Press, 1988).

157. For a discussion of this decline in women's status in rural Ireland, see, for example: Mary Daly, "Women in the Irish Workforce from Pre-industrial to Modern Times," *Saothar* 7 (1981): 74–82; Diner, *Erin's Daughters*; David Fitzpatrick, "The Modernisation of the Irish Female," in *Rural Ireland: Modernisation v. Change, 1600–1900*, ed. Patrick O'Flanagan, Paul Ferguson, and Kevin Whelan (Cork: Cork University Press, 1987), 162–80; Luddy, *Documentary History*; Ma-

geean, "Irish Women's Prospects"; Kerby Miller, David Doyle, and Patricia Kelleher, "'For love and liberty': Irish Women, Migration and Domesticity in Ireland and America, 1815–1920," in *Irish Women and Migration*, ed. Patrick O'Sullivan, Irish World Wide Series, vol. 4 (London: Leicester University Press, 1995), 41–65; Janet A. Nolan, "The Great Famine and Women's Emigration from Ireland," in *The Hungry Stream: Essays on Emigration and Famine*, ed. E. Margaret Crawford (Belfast: Centre for Emigration Studies, Ulster-American Folk Park, and Institute of Irish Studies, Queen's University, 1997), 61–70; Nolan, *Ourselves Alone*; and Rita Rhodes, *Women and the Family in Post-famine Ireland: Status and Opportunity in a Patriarchal Society* (New York: Garland, 1992). Joanna Bourke also notes the shift in women's economic activities through the nineteenth century, which culminated during the period from 1890 to 1914 in the withdrawal of most Irish women into the home. She suggests, however, that this movement into full-time housework was a rational choice in the face of declining opportunities and did not necessarily entail a loss of status for women. Many found housework fulfilling, she argues, and a source of creativity and pride. Women's domestic role helped minimize the risk of poverty because they could "invest" time in children, who would care for them in their old age, and because their family contribution in terms of housework had greater value as they aged than the labor of aging men, who were more likely to enter poorhouses due to unemployment. Housework removed rural women from monotonous and physically challenging agricultural chores, she argues. And remittances from children who had emigrated increased the value of women's reproductive labor. Bourke has certainly located Irish women's agency in the shift to full-time housework. However, her celebration of their withdrawal into domesticity founders under the weight of the costs of the transition, many of which she suggests herself: declining employment and educational opportunities; reduced access to cash resources; increased female dependence on male income earners; decreased participation in all aspects of life outside the non-domestic sphere; a tendency for women to have less leisure time than men because housework was a continual task; and an increased tolerance of wife abuse justified by the wife's unsatisfactory performance of household tasks. Her argument that women escaped economic dependency on relatives through marriage (273–74) is untenable in the face of their increased economic dependence on husbands. Furthermore, she appears to accept the sexual division of labor and wage and education differentials in her study period as givens, without reflecting on the processes by which women's options were channelled so narrowly that they "chose" domesticity. See Joanna Bourke, *Husbandry to Housewifery: Women, Economic Change, and Housework in Ireland, 1890–1914* (Oxford: Clarendon, 1993).

158. See, for example: Clark, *Struggle for the Breeches*; Leonore Davidoff, "The Role of Gender in the 'First Industrial Nation': Farming and the Countryside in England, 1780–1850," in Davidoff, *Worlds Between: Historical Perspectives on Gender and Class* (Cambridge: Polity Press, 1995), 180–205; Bridget Hill, *Women, Work, and Sexual Politics in Eighteenth-Century England* (Oxford: Basil Blackwell, 1989); Theodore Koditschek, "Gendering of the British Working Class," *Gender and History* 9,

no. 2 (August 1997): 333–63; Rendall, *Women in an Industrializing Society*; K. D. M. Snell, "Agricultural Seasonal Unemployment, the Standard of Living, and Women's Work, 1690–1860," in *Women's Work: The English Experience, 1650–1914*, ed. Pamela Sharpe (London: Arnold, 1998), 73–120; and Deborah Valenze, *The First Industrial Woman* (New York: Oxford University Press, 1995).

6. "HUMBEL" PETITIONERS AND "LITIGEOUS" PERSONS

Southern Avalon Women and Encounters with Formal Justice

Historians of women have demonstrated that the British legal system in the eighteenth and nineteenth centuries was a patriarchal regime dominated by male legislators, judges, lawyers, and juries.[1] Women were subject to the authority of the law, but had no formal political voice or access to elected or appointed office at any level. Discriminatory laws, designed by male legislators and enforced by male jurists, reinforced women's subservient status in society. The married woman was most subordinate of all. Under the principle of coverture, her legal identity was absorbed by that of her husband. She could not hold property in her own right, enter into contracts, sue or be sued in a court of law. She did not even have the right to control her own body. Certainly, she had no legal status in civil actions in the courthouse. At best, the historiography tells us, she could rely on personal influence in the home and discretionary forms of justice to provide her with indirect access to the formal legal system.[2]

However, while women's status within the legal system was indisputably secondary, they were not denied access entirely. Yet there is a tendency in the literature to focus almost exclusively on two tragic images: the female victim of crime, and the female casualty of discriminatory matrimonial laws—both, vulnerable in a system stacked against them.[3] Presenting the female crime victim as powerless, however, overlooks the agency of many of these women in taking their abusers into public court settings in pursuit of justice. And using the experiences of married women to generalize about the reception of all women also distorts the picture, leaving the reader with the impression that women were virtually excluded from the legal system altogether. Granted, the majority of women passed through the married state in adulthood; but many also spent adult years as single women and widows, life-stages in which they would have had greater access to the legal system. Furthermore, coverture was not always strictly enforced at the local level, and it is therefore important to investigate how formal justice played out on the ground within specific historical contexts.

So let us adjust our focus to examine women's encounters with the formal justice system on the southern Avalon, with an eye to their capacity to negotiate the complexities of the system and the response of authorities to their efforts.[4] At the start, however, some parameters must be established. Women in Newfoundland had no formal political voice throughout the study period and therefore had no input into the making of statutory law (a deficiency they shared with all inhabitants of the island, regardless of gender or class, until representative government was granted in 1832). Women on the island did not hold office, either local or central (a disability shared with Catholics until 1829). They did not sit on petty or grand juries. They were subject to virtually the same statutory regime as women in other British jurisdictions.[5] Yet they were present in the court system, as civil litigants, as complainants and defendants in criminal matters, as witnesses, and as petitioners.[6] Far from being excluded from the system, women on the southern Avalon, especially plebeian women, were a vital part of local court life, and the courtroom was more often a site of their empowerment than their oppression.[7]

CIVIL LITIGATION

When generalizations are made from married women's experiences about access to the court system, the image of the female civil litigant rarely surfaces because married women had no formal legal status separate from their husbands' until the late nineteenth century. On the southern Avalon, however, the involvement of women in civil litigation, although not as frequent as men's, was quite extensive from the mid-eighteenth to the mid-nineteenth century. Their participation fell primarily within the categories of debt collection, employment disputes, landlord-tenant matters, and trespass.[8]

DEBT COLLECTION

Women or their estates appeared quite frequently in litigation involving debt, emerging as creditors or debtors in 104 cases during the study period. Table 6.1 provides a breakdown of creditor/debtor status in these cases, and indicates that there were 76 women creditors (individual and joint) and 36 women debtors (individual and joint), giving a total of 112 female parties to the collection actions recorded.[9] This suggests that women were twice as likely to be creditors as debtors, a finding that is somewhat at variance with the stereotypical image but not altogether surprising, given the extent of their participation in the economic life of their communities. The causes of action varied, although the greatest activity (when specified) occurred in the areas of washing and/or sewing services, merchant or shop accounts, estate matters, landlord-tenant matters, and bonds/book debts/mortgages/bills of exchange, as indicated by Table 6.2. The majority of the debts (64.4 percent) were amounts under £10, but there were a significant number of big-ticket actions, with two of the cases involving amounts in excess of £200 (see Table 6.3).

There was only one recidivist debtor among the cases surveyed, but there were several repeat creditors. Collection actions became something of an occupational hazard for Jane Austen (also Austin), for example, as she sued eight different debtors during the 1830s and 1840s for goods sold and delivered from her shop in Ferryland (all for amounts under £4).[10] Margret Kenny of Ferryland was busily tidying up her affairs in the Ferryland area at the turn of the nineteenth century, possibly just after joining her husband, who had entered the Newfoundland Regiment at St. John's. During 1799–1800, she sued five local individuals: four actions, with unspecified causes, were for amounts in the £3–5 range; the fifth and final action was for £20 for rent and damages in relation to a plantation in Ferryland, but she was non-suited, the court finding her to be a "litigeous person" and ordering her to pay 40s. to the defendant.[11] Catherine Weston, an Irish Catholic woman who had married into a powerful English Protestant merchant-planter family, initiated three separate suits (through her attorney) for the collection of amounts ranging from £50.18.3-3/4 to £109.4.5 in the period from 1787 to 1790.[12] Another gentry woman, Ann Sweetland, initiated two smaller actions to recover monies for the sale of ground (40s.) and rent arrears (£6.19.6) in 1798.[13] The estate of Mary Ludwigg (or Ludwick), an Irish Protestant woman who had considerable property and financial interests in the area, appeared as creditor in the 1750s and 1760s in four separate matters involving mortgage arrears of substantial amounts (£60, £109, and £167.4.0) and the adjustment of book debts with another wealthy Irish Protestant landowner and businessman in the area.[14] And

Ferryland washerwomen Mary Bryan appeared in court personally to sue two of her customers in 1803 for amounts which, though unspecified, would likely have fallen in the 12–15s. range normally paid to laundresses at that time.[15]

As the above examples suggest, ethnicity and class were often factors underlying the types of action that were brought. All the women who sued for washing and/or sewing services as well as nursing/midwifery services were from the plebeian community, predominantly from Irish backgrounds or English families that had been assimilated by the time their respective suits were initiated. Women of the local elite (English Protestant and Irish Protestant) were much more prominent in estate matters and collections involving rent, book debts, mortgages, and bonds. The latter were almost exclusively the creditors and debtors in suits involving amounts of £100 and over (Hannah McDaniel was the only exception; see below). Plebeian women were overwhelmingly involved in suits under £10; however, they were also a robust presence in the middle band, being represented in roughly two-thirds of the suits involving amounts from £10 to £49 and one-half the suits involving amounts from £50 to £99.

Marital status was also a factor that determined whether these women had legal status in their actions. While all the debts in question were owed to or by women (either individually or jointly with husbands), not all these women appeared personally in the collection actions. In accordance with the principle of coverture, husbands often represented their wives in such matters. In the fall of 1818, for example, Mrs. Dollard was owed money for washing services provided to John Neile's fishing servants (one Comerford and others) at Fermeuse; but it was her husband, John, who sued the employer for some fish allegedly left on Neile's fishing room by Comerford to pay his debt—although Mrs. Dollard had herself initially gone to Neile's premises and demanded that Comerford pay her.[16] Case File 12 In the eyes of the law, husbands also assumed responsibility for their wives' debts upon marriage. For example, when Mrs. William Coleman ordered two blankets from merchant Samuel G. Carter and neglected to pay her account, it was Mr. Coleman who was sued and ordered to pay the debt, even though he claimed (and the plaintiff could not disprove) that he had no knowledge of the order.[17] Case File 13 The husband's responsibility even extended to debts contracted before marriage. In 1818, for example, the court ordered John Power to pay a debt of £3.5.3 that had been incurred by his wife, Margaret Neill, before they had wed. Indeed, although Margaret had property (a bed) from her previous marriage, it was attached only when it was demonstrated that John did not have sufficient property of his own to secure payment of his wife's debt.[18] Case File 14

Still, of the 112 total female creditors and debtors examined here, only 20 (18 percent) were represented by husbands acting as legal agents (either for the wife only or for the couple) under the law of coverture. Another 8 (7 percent), all women of local merchant-planter families, were named parties in the actions but were represented by guardians, brothers, or attorneys in the courthouse, reflecting a general tendency for elite women to avoid the public courtroom, regardless of marital status. The remaining 84 female creditors and debtors (75 percent) represented themselves. The relatively low number of actions in which husbands acted for wives suggests that there may have been a disproportionate number of single or widowed women among the litigants; but it also hints that the principle of coverture may have been occasionally relaxed in southern district courts.

Unfortunately, a lack of comprehensive parish registers makes it impossible to track such a phenomenon, but the proportions are suggestive. This was certainly the case with Hannah McDaniel, who acted as petitioner and attorney for her family when financial difficulties arose over an alleged debt to the Weston family (see below). And even in cases in which wives were not named as legal agents, women sometimes acted as important witnesses when disputes arose as to the validity or amount of a debt (see below). Furthermore, while formal law recognized the husband as the legal agent in collection actions (and whether or not this principle was relaxed by local courts), the control of household finances often played out differently on the ground, for in many fishing families, it was the wife who managed whatever small amounts of cash were on hand. Thus, while a wife from the plebeian community may have been required by law to send her husband to court to collect money owed to her, this did not necessarily signal a relinquishment of control over that money in the same way that it did for many middle-class women.

Certainly, the local courts did not apply the principle of coverture as a blanket treatment in inappropriate circumstances. In 1818, for example, Hunt, Stabb, Preston, an English mercantile firm operating out of Renews, discovered that they had relied too heavily on the application of coverture when they brought a collection action against the estate of Thomas Beaves to recover a balance of £70 (raised to £78.9.0 the following month). Case File 15 The plaintiffs stated that when Beaves had died in 1810, he had been indebted to the firm in the amount of £65; the remainder of the debt had been incurred by his widow, Elizabeth, since that time, under the head of "Elizabeth Beaves and Son." In her defense, Elizabeth argued that the firm had made no claim to her in relation to her husband's debt since his demise. The debt was of such long standing, she continued, that the firm had exceeded the statutory time limit for collection. She herself had maintained credit balances in her account with the plaintiffs since her husband's death until 1817, when she, too, had fallen into debt in the economic malaise following the Napoleonic Wars. The firm had proceeded to sell, at public auction, her fishing room, house, and gardens—property that had been left to her by her mother—and had itself purchased the premises for £28 to be applied towards her husband's debt. The sale had been made without her consent, Elizabeth claimed, and without lawful authority, and she asked that she be put back in possession of her property.

The magistrates reserved judgment until various documents were produced, and the evidence did little to ingratiate Hunt, Stabb, Preston to the court. Since 1810, the firm had been registering various accounts with the court in relation to Thomas's debt to continue them, and thus to prevent the applicability of the statutory limitation period. And it had done so without Elizabeth's knowledge. The court found that regardless of the "ingenuity" with which the firm had attempted to carry over Thomas's debts, "this Court is ever awake to prevent their effect being extended beyond legal bounds," and the statute of limitations was therefore, as Elizabeth had argued, a bar to the debt. Furthermore, the court found that the property sold under auction had indeed been left to Elizabeth by her mother's last will and testament. Elizabeth's late husband had never exercised any right to the property; furthermore, Hunt, Stabb, Preston had never demanded it as security, operating under the misapprehension that all real property of the wife was, under the principle of coverture, the property of the husband, and thus would automatically be attachable for his debts. On the basis that "property acquired of the Wife either before or after Marriage over which the Husband has exercised no manner of right or control is not liable to the debt of the Husband," the court rendered judgment that "the Action against the property of the Widdow cannot prevail."[19] The principle of coverture, then, was tailored by the local courts to the particular circumstances of a case, and occasionally was set aside altogether.

EMPLOYMENT DISPUTES

Twenty-five employment disputes involving southern Avalon women appear in the records from the study period. These cases involved seventeen female complainants and seven female defendants acting as legal agents, as well as two instances in which female claimants were represented in court by men (one husband, one former employer against a current employer), and two instances in which husbands were the actual defendants but their wives were an integral part of the dispute. As Table 6.4 indicates, there were three main causes of action: refusal by a servant or a master/mistress to honor a shipping or apprenticeship agreement; dispute over the calculation of wage balances; and alleged ill treatment.

In several cases, there were multiple causes of action. All three major causes overlapped, for example, when Frida Tobin had a falling out with her mistress, Mary Bony (or Bonia) and brought her to court in the fall of 1818. Case File 16 Frida complained that Mary had struck her several times "without any provocation," then refused to pay her wages. Frida's shipping papers, contracting her for the season from 7 April to 31 October 1818 were produced in court. The defendant admitted that she had assaulted Frida, but insisted that she had not refused to pay her wages. The court ultimately found in the servant's favor and ordered Mary to pay the balance of Frida's wages, a fine of 2s., and court costs.[20] Similarly, there were multiple causes in a hearing held the very next day on a complaint brought by Catherine Lancrop of St. Mary's against her employer, John Doody Jr. Case File 17 Catherine had been shipped by Doody the previous year, but he had still not paid her passage money from Ireland as per their agreement. Doody had also struck her and drawn blood; indeed, the assault was so severe, said Catherine, that she "lay some time for dead." Doody still owed her the balance of her wages at the time of the court hearing. The court decreed that he pay her passage money and her wages, and Doody was also fined 40s. for the assault on Catherine and ordered to pay court costs.[21]

In all, there were only five actions involving alleged ill treatment of servants. Four involved mistress/female servant relationships; only one involved a master/female servant dyad. While the type of service in which these servants were employed was not stated in any of the cases, it is likely that they were mostly domestic servants, given the more frequent appearances of mistress/servant dyads.[22] In 1795, for example, Mary Whealon of Ferryland complained that her mistress, Margret Wallace, had assaulted her, and sought the protection of the court. Margret admitted that she had thrown stones at Mary, but argued that she had been provoked by her servant's abusive language.[23] In 1835, Nancy Addis of Brigus South complained that her mistress, Mary Power, had beaten her with rocks in her fist and threatened to do her further violence.[24] It is apparent that the physical abuse in most of these cases did not seem severe by the standards of the day, for the offending employers received lenient treatment—small fines or peace bonds—or had their charges dismissed outright. Only the mistreatment of Catharine Lancrop by John Doody attracted a fine of any substance (40s.); and while this case involved the only master/female servant dyad, the more significant fine was likely due to the relative severity of the abuse rather than any affront to sensibilities about a man's striking a female servant.

The most common form of complaint in the employment dispute category was non-payment of wages, being cited in a total of sixteen cases involving eleven female complainants, three female defendants, one female servant represented by her husband as complainant in court, and a wife of a male defendant who, although not named in the style of cause, was integral because her household accounting was in question.[25] This breakdown indicates that the women involved in these cases were more often servants (complainants) than employers (defendants). Most of the cases pitted employees against their employers, or the legal representatives of either, but there were three exceptions. In 1830, Catherine Delahunty tried to sue her son's employer, Thomas Norris, for the balance of her son's wages for "being on the Cut tails" on Norris's boat that summer; the court ordered, however, that she had no cause of action.[26] The other two variants involved claims for unpaid wages entered by female fishing servants against their masters' supplying merchants. The 1797 claim of Anstice Dwyer, who sued the agent of her employer's suppliers for the balance of the wages she had earned as shore crew, has been discussed in Chapter 4. Margret Neile (or Neill) launched a similar action when she worked "in the Service of James Linch curing fish on shore" in Ferryland during the fishing season of 1818. Linch's supplying merchants, John and James Munn, had taken his fish and oil for payment of their account, before Linch had paid Margret her outstanding wages. Margret successfully sued the Munns for the balance of £3.[27] Both Anstice and Margret were exercising the privilege of all fishing servants in Newfoundland to *follow the fish* and have their wages paid before the accounts of current supplying merchants.

Indeed, disputes involving wages were taken quite seriously by the local courts, and when servants complained that their wages had been miscalculated or any balance left unpaid, the courts closely examined shipping agreements and account books of employers to verify balances. This reflected a customary priority accorded in the island's fishing economy to the payment of servants' wages, owing not so much to an altruistic principle that the servants be justly treated as to a pragmatic concern that servants have sufficient funds to pay for their passage home after the fishing season (a practice that was given statutory force by *Palliser's Act* in 1776). Certainly by the late eighteenth century, the payment of wages was not left to the whim of masters or mistresses, and servants of both sexes enjoyed a high success rate in obtaining outstanding balances from recalcitrant employers (both female and male). Of the sixteen cases examined here, ten resulted in court judgments in favor of the servant complainants, while another three were settled out of court (likely with satisfactory compensation to the servant).

Nine of the cases examined specifically referred to employment agreements.[28] Of these, six involved complaints between employer and employee, but three involved mothers' interventions in the employment agreements of their sons.[29] Hannah McDaniel appeared in 1797 as co-defendant with her son John to answer a complaint by John's employer, Michael Malone, that John had refused to fulfill his shipping agreement on his mother's counsel. Hannah and John successfully argued that Malone had tried to force John to work outside the agreed geographical range of the shipping agreement, and a settlement was reached.[30] In the 1830s, Elizabeth Madden and Jane Fitzpatrick used the courts to question the operation of their sons' shipping or apprenticeship agreements and the proper fulfillment of the contracted terms by their sons' employers.[31]

Just as women were given equitable treatment by the courts in terms of wage payment, so too were they afforded similar treatment in terms of employment contracts. Employers and employees of both sexes were expected to honor the terms of the shipping agreements to which they were party. When Anstice Dwyer sued Cornelius Kelly for her wages in 1797, for example, her proof of claim lay in a shipping paper hiring her as shore crew and cook. When Frida Tobin had a falling-out with her mistress Mary Bony, Frida's shipping paper was produced in court to reinforce her claim for wages. Catherine Lancrop's shipping agreement supported her claim for wages and passage money from her employer, John Doody. As noted earlier, oral agreements were also deemed to be binding legal contracts. When Bridget Whealon charged her employer with abusive treatment, for example, evidence was entered that Bridget had been hired verbally for one year at a wage of £3; the court found that, despite the beatings and scoldings of her mistress, she must return to service and honor her agreement.[32] Case File 18 Employment contracts, whether they involved men or women, and whether oral or written, were usually enforced to the letter by authorities during this period.

In general, while the servants on the southern Avalon occupied the lower social and economic strata, their work was essential to the economy, and thus they were not without recourse in terms of ensuring a reasonable standard of living. The various cases examined here suggest that certainly from the late eighteenth century onwards, servants in the area were not expected to tolerate irregular treatment from masters and mistresses or arbitrary justice from local courts. While there was obviously a certain level of acceptance within the community of moderate corporal punishment of servants, more severe abuse would attract the displeasure of the magistrates or visiting surrogate. Furthermore, local courts were very accessible in terms of wage claims, by female as well as male servants. And shipping agreements were sacrosanct, with both employers and employees, male and female, strictly held to the terms of the oral or written contracts they had negotiated.

LANDLORD–TENANT MATTERS

Female landlords: Twenty female landlords were involved in disputes affecting their properties on the southern Avalon during the period of this study (see Table 6.5).[33] The women were the named legal agents in all the matters but two: one in which a husband sued for rent owed on property he possessed "by virtue of his wife"; and another in which a brother represented the interests of himself, his brother, and his sister. In two other matters, the female landlords were the named parties but were represented by others in the courtroom: a case in which a minor was represented by her male guardian; and another in which an adult woman was represented by a male attorney. Over half the matters arose in the eighteenth century, reflecting a strong presence of women from the traditional planter society in this category. Most of these eighteenth-century matters involved English women, but at least four of these earlier landlords were Irish. An Irish presence predominated in this category in the nineteenth century.

Eleven of the matters involved actions for rent recovery and/or eviction in relation to houses, gardens, and fishing rooms. These eleven complainants met with varying success: four won their suits (all rent recoveries only), while another two were settled by the parties; two other female landlords were non-suited; one matter went to arbitration, and the result was not recorded; one matter was continued with no further indication of the outcome; and the remaining matter appeared in the records only in the form of the writ issued. Three other matters involved actions for debt recovery in which creditors were attempting to attach the rents of female landlords to satisfy arrears on mortgages or bonds. One of these matters resulted in the full attachment of rents, and another in the partial attachment of the rents. In the third case, however, the female landlord successfully warded off her creditor until the parties finally settled the matter out of court.

Female landlords also surfaced in litigation involving estates. In 1792, for example, the children of Morris Brazil—two sons and a daughter—successfully initiated an action for repossession of a plantation, possibly in Cape Broyle, that had been attached by their father's creditors back in 1784, proving that their father's debt had been paid and that the rental of the plantation should now accrue in their favor.[34] In the same year, Mary Kennedy successfully sued her brother William Tucker for an equitable distribution of rents earned from the property of their late father—a landmark case in local law on intestacies that will be discussed in greater depth in Chapter 7.[35]

Two other estate matters involved disputes over the possession of fishing premises. In 1752, for example, two sisters of James Dunn, a Renews planter, successfully pressed their claim before the fishing admirals in the harbor for possession of their intestate brother's plantation and the right to receive the rents from its current tenant.[36] Another matter involved a 1772 dispute over possession of a fishing room on the south side of Petty Harbour. William Coombs, who had leased "Langworthys Room" from the widow Barbara Murphy of Ferryland, was challenging her right to possession of the property, arguing that it had not been occupied or used for the fishery for over twenty years. However, the governor confirmed Barbara's interest, provided that she would erect fishing premises on the property within two years and employ *green* men on the room.[37] Barbara must have complied—or, technically, Coombs did, in fulfillment of the terms of his building lease—because in a separate court matter two years later, "Barbary" Murphy was mentioned as being still possessed of the room, with Coombs, still her tenant.[38] Case File 19

The remaining matter in this category involved a female landlord and her agent. Frances Power (likely the widow of Patrick Power, an Irish merchant-planter at Renews) petitioned the governor in 1789 to investigate an alleged fraud on the part of her agent, James Sparkes. She had left the rental of her plantation in Renews in his hands, but he had remitted no rents since 1786. Sparkes had recently died, but she had received information that he had forged a lease of the plantation to himself for a term of twenty-one years, and that the plantation had been sublet to merchants Wills and Witburn. Governor Edwards instructed magistrate Robert Carter to "make strict enquiry into the Matter," and if proved, to put Frances Power "into quiet and peaceable possession" of the plantation and to have the rents that had been collected since Sparkes's death remitted to Frances.[39]

While female landlords did not appear nearly as frequently in the southern Avalon court records as male landlords, they were still a significant presence and demonstrated their willingness to litigate during the study period.[40]

Female tenants: Women tenants also defended their interests before the authorities on at least seven occasions during the study period (see Table 6.5).[41] Six were involved in eviction actions based on default or expiration of lease and/or rent arrears, while the seventh appeared in court on a matter of rent arrears only. All but one of the female tenants were from the plebeian community, the exception being a member of an English Newfoundland merchant family; and five out of the seven were Irish Newfoundland women. Five were single or widowed and named as legal agents in the writs issued; one woman was named as co-defendant with her husband; and another represented her family's interests due to her husband's incapacity. The records indicate that evictions were ordered in only two cases. In a third case, the landlord plaintiff was non-suited. In the remaining four matters, either orders for continuance were given, or the tenant was granted time to pay rent arrears. None of these latter four matters reappeared in the records—either a reflection of the incomplete nature of the records or an indication that a satisfactory resolution was found between landlord and tenant outside the courtroom.

In the two matters in which the female tenants were unsuccessful in staving off evicting landlords, the women still managed to buy some time for themselves and their families. For example, Mary Bryan of St. Mary's petitioned the governor in October of 1780 to extend her family's tenancy of a fishing plantation held in her husband's name. Case File 20 Unfortunately, her husband had been deemed "insane," and she and her family were about to be turned off the plantation. The landlord, John Richards, had re-let the plantation to a Mr. Townshend the previous February, without giving the required notice of twelve months, as stipulated by the lease with her husband. The governor, mindful that "the Poor woman and her family must naturally be distressed if turned out of their House . . . at this time of Year," instructed the local magistrate to settle the matter "as amicably as you can—tho I think Mr. Townshend has a right to possess it in time to carry on his fishery next year." Ultimately, then, the change in tenancy occurred. However, the purpose of Mary's petition had been to extend the life of her husband's lease by pleading improper notice. Allowing for the fact that Mary had been aware of the new tenant since the previous February, she and her family were effectively being given more than the required twelve months' notice through the governor's intervention. Thus, she was successful in lobbying for extra time to make alternative living arrangements.[42]

In a more prolonged matter that ran from 1837 to 1841, Catherine Dullenty, the widow of John Dullenty, tried to ward off eviction from her home and adjoining gardens, first by William Carter, then by the executors of his estate. In fact, the action was initiated for "trespass and eviction," but Catherine's family had obviously been in possession of the property for some time, so this was not a straightforward case of trespass. While the records are not specific, it is possible that either Catherine (and/or her late husband) had no written lease, or that the lease had expired and not been renewed, or that after the death of Catherine's husband, Carter had deemed the lease to be void. It is also possible that Catherine was disputing Carter's ownership of the property and was refusing to pay rent. Recorded details are sparse, but the matter was complex, involving several previous owners and the interests of several estates, and it was continued every year by agreement of the parties. Catherine Dullenty appeared in court throughout, but as the matter increased in complexity, she was assisted by Renews merchant Peter Winser (also Winsor) for the final hearings of the matter in 1840–41. Initially, a special jury sworn in October 1840 found primarily in Catherine's favor, allowing her the house and surrounding gardens, with a larger garden being awarded to Carter's estate. However, a year later, estate executor Robert Carter re-applied for a writ of possession, and the court ordered that the previous verdict be "set aside due to irregularity." (Details are insufficient to determine whether there was legitimate cause for this reversal or whether this was a case of middle-class magistrates rallying around one of their own.) On 1 November 1841, the court ordered Catherine's eviction from the land and awarded damages to the plaintiff in the amount of £40.0.0 (inflated considerably from the £9.0.0 originally sought in 1837).[43]

Also worthy of note is the 1841 action against Mary Gaulway of Renews for rent arrears (£7.0.0 Cy.) owed to William Strachan, a minor, brought by his guardian, J. W. Saunders (the complainant in the Berrigan ejectment discussed in Chapter 5). The case was, in and of itself, uneventful, as Mary admitted in court that she was in arrears, and judgment was awarded in Strachan's favor.[44] What is intriguing is that the following year, the same Mary "Gulloway" brought charges against the same J. W. Saunders for assault.[45] Both sides presented several supporting witnesses, but unfortunately, no details of their testimony remain in the records. Ultimately, a special jury found Saunders not guilty. But the hard feelings between the parties may have emanated from the earlier action for rent arrears, and one might speculate whether Mary had initiated a grudge match in the local court, rallying support from several members of the plebeian community who may even have had their own bones to pick with the local merchant and magistrate.

While these female tenants met with varying success in these actions, the fact that they appeared in court or petitioned the governor to defend their interests challenges the stereotype of the powerless female tenant at the mercy of the rapacious landlord. It is possible that informal evictions occurred without the support of the court system, but it is not likely that the number would have been high, primarily because most local inhabitants had no landlords—either holding grants to fishing premises in their own names or, much more frequently, simply occupying the land with the tacit approval of authorities (Web Link). And had informal attempts at eviction been attempted in the area, they would most likely have created a sense of outrage within the plebeian community, resulting in collective actions that would ultimately have found their way into the written record. Certainly, there were not the pressures on the land (overpopulation, subdivision, changing market demand triggering a shift from tillage to pasturage) that prompted large-scale evictions in Ireland in the nineteenth century.

TRESPASS

Women also defended their property through the law of trespass (see Table 6.5). Seven such matters were brought before the authorities during this period: in four, women were the named parties (although one was represented by a male attorney); in the remaining three, husbands acted as legal agents for their wives. Three of the matters involved women of the eighteenth-century English planter society, while the remaining four involved women of the plebeian community.

Two of the actions related to fishing properties, both involving eighteenth-century planter women. The widow Catharine Clements, for example, became embroiled in a suit and counter-suit with James Rows (Rouse) over fishing premises at Renews. Case File 2 Rows initially sought Governor Campbell's intervention in 1784, and the matter was revived by Catharine in surrogate court the following year. Rows claimed that the property had originally been granted to his father in 1732 by Captain Thomas Smith, and that his father had built fishing works on it and carried on a fishery there for many years. Rows admitted that the room had been left to decay since his father's death (which would have made his family's right of occupation tenuous, given that grants at this time stipulated that waterfront property must be utilized in the fishery). He indicated, however, that he had recently inherited the property from his deceased mother and had attempted to rebuild a flake there, but he had been prevented from doing so by Mrs. Clements' master of the voyage, Stephen Poor, and her son-in-law, Arthur Jackman.

Catharine was in possession of an adjoining property, known as Pottersby's Plantation, which she employed in the fishery, and claimed that the beach area in dispute had long been used first by her late husband and then by herself for drying fish. Rows had applied to the fishing admirals for redress but received no satisfaction, and he therefore applied to the governor for the right of quiet possession of the property and restitution for the trespass. His petition was supported by an affidavit from Robert Carter, justice of the peace. The governor accordingly ordered that Rows be put in possession of the premises, again with the standard proviso that he use it for the purposes of the fishery. However, the fishing admiral at Renews in 1784, Richard Bully, was of the opinion that Mrs. Clements' claim was more valid by reason of more recent possession. He therefore ordered that Rows's flake be torn down. When Mrs. Clements revived the matter in court in 1795, both parties presented witnesses to support their claims, and the matter remained unresolved. Indeed, in 1806, the property was still under dispute between the parties.[46]

The remaining actions of trespass during the period related to smaller properties. In 1784, for example, Edmond Dunfey (or Dunphy) of Brigus South acted as agent for his wife, Anstis, in successfully suing James Connoly for trespass on land that had been in his wife's possession for approximately fifteen years. Connolly was ordered to return the hay he had cut on the land, mend the fences he had broken, and pay a fine in the amount of 5s.[47] In St. Mary's, in 1804, Mary Stokes brought Martin Doyle to court for trespass on her property while she had been absent in Trepassey. The property had been decreed to Mary by a former surrogate, Captain Malbon. Martin had apparently obtained the key to Mary's house from her sister under false pretenses, and the current surrogate, Timothy Bird, ordered that Martin give up possession of the house within a week.[48] In 1836, Mary Brien brought an action of trespass against William Carter, charging that he had entered her premises near Freshwater in Ferryland and unlawfully seized and carried away property valued at £5.7.6 Cy.[49] There are no details in the record as to why Carter had removed the property; if it was for payment of debt, there is no evidence in the records of any collection action initiated by him, or of any registered mortgage or bond. At any rate, Mary lost her suit in what could be described as a "stacked" courtroom, with magistrate Robert Carter, James Carter, and Lieutenant Robert Carter, along with local constable Richard Sullivan, providing evidence for the defendant, and James H. Carter acting as foreman of the jury.[50]

Overall, women claimants experienced mixed results in trespass matters: four won their suits; one (who took on the powerful Carter family) did not; and the results of the remaining two cases are unknown. But the success rate was reasonable, indicating that women property holders on the southern Avalon were able to use the law of trespass as an avenue to seek remedy for encroachment.

CRIMINAL MATTERS: FEMALE COMPLAINANTS AND DEFENDANTS

By a wide margin, the most prominent presence of women in the courtrooms of the southern Avalon was in relation to criminal matters, as both complainants and defendants. Indeed, the breakdown of alleged victims and perpetrators in these cases was almost even, with seventy-five women complainants and seventy-six women defendants. The familiar image of the female crime victim, therefore, does not reveal the full complexity of women's encounters with criminal justice in the period of early settlement on the southern Avalon.

The charge most frequently leveled both by and against women in criminal matters was that of assault. These cases, ranging from threatening language to more serious physical and sexual assaults, have already been discussed in the previous chapter.[51] As noted, women were aggressors (sixty-one in total) almost as frequently as they were victims (seventy-one in total) by a proportion of .86:1.[52] All defendants and complainants were from the plebeian community, and all but three of the assault victims provided depositions and/or appeared in court themselves to give testimony against their assailants. These complainants were women who felt that they were entitled to the protection of the legal system and were not deterred by notions of female respectability from asserting their rights in the public sphere.

Furthermore, the testimony of these women was often accepted by the court without corroboration—a phenomenon that applied equally to male and female complainants in assault matters. Here it must be noted that local courts had a propensity to deal fairly leniently with most offenders of both sexes by meting out fines and binding defendants to keep the peace; jail sentences were only employed very occasionally. These relatively light sentences may have eased local magistrates' minds in accepting the uncorroborated testimony of complainants, permitting them to err on the side of caution to ensure order in their communities.[53] But they also reflected the penal philosophy of the age. Until the end of the eighteenth century, jails functioned mainly as holding areas before trial, transportation, or execution in British jurisdictions. The use of incarceration as a method of actual correction did not gain prominence in penal ideology until the early nineteenth century,[54] and even then, alternative sentencing continued as a stopgap in districts such as the southern Avalon that did not have the facilities or funds to accommodate multiple prisoners or even individual inmates for lengthy stays.[55]

But while local courts rarely moved beyond the realm of fines and peace bonds in dealing with common assaults, the weight of the penalty varied with the circumstances, as the following cases help to illustrate. In 1818, Margret Leary complained that Edward Connolly had assaulted her; a witness to the incident, Edward McDaniel, testified that he had seen the defendant enter Margret's home and "klench his fist and chuck the plaintiff on the breast and Stagger her." Furthermore, he had "used very odious language and threatened her." Connolly claimed that he had been provoked because Margret had been gossiping about him, but he was ordered to pay a fine of 40s., plus court costs in the amount of 27s. 10d.[56] A more serious assault the following year still attracted only a fine and peace bond. Catharine Payne complained that Peter Winsor had come into her house and ordered her to quit same (this was likely an attempted eviction), and that upon her refusal, he had "struck her a blow with his fist on the face and Seizing her by the arms, used all his strength to drag her out—and failing therein, he Seized her by the neck, and held and drag[g]ed her with such violence as nearly suffocated her." He had used such force in the struggle that the marks and bruises were still evident on her face and body. Winsor admitted to the assault and was ordered to pay a fine of £5 and court costs of £2.7.8, and to give security in the amount of £30 to keep the peace for three months.[57] Case File 22 The higher fine and hefty peace bond in this case likely reflected the severity of the second assault (although it should be noted that the fine may have been upgraded to fit the financial circumstances of the defendant, who was a substantial merchant-planter and justice of the peace). Still, the category of punishment did not vary from that for the lesser assault in 1818. Indeed, only one incident of common assault against a woman during the period resulted in a prison sentence—and a short one, at that. In August of 1841, Charlotte Flood of Ferryland complained that several times in the absence of her husband, William Mitchell had assaulted and beaten her and repeatedly threatened to kill her, her husband, and her child. Mitchell was tried in October and found guilty, yet he was sentenced to only twenty-four hours' imprisonment, despite the seriousness of the assault and despite his previous record (he was already in custody for threatening the local doctor, and had been convicted of two previous assaults in the past year alone).[58] Case File 23 Generally, then, fines, peace bonds, and, very occasionally, minimal jail time were the punishments of choice for assault in the local courts. Heavier sentences (including longer imprisonment, whippings, and deportation) were reserved for cases involving extreme violence, particularly sexual assault and domestic violence (see Chapter 8).

The other criminal matters that involved women in the area all related to theft and/or receiving charges: a total of seventeen charges involving four female complainants and fifteen female defendants (one of whom was represented in court by her husband). Seven of the cases involved the theft or receiving of items of little or no monetary value—mostly clothing and blankets, as well as boughs from a flake and a dead sister's trunk full of personal effects (all four female complainants filed charges in this category). Nine other incidents, all of which involved female defendants, involved fairly substantial items: housing materials (two); shop goods (three); provisions (one); a boat (one); eight quintals of fish (one); and a composite of saltfish, coal, hay, and shop goods (one). In the remaining case, the nature and value of the stolen items were not recorded.

Just as in assault cases, the local courts were accessible to female complainants in theft cases, and there is no indication that their allegations—even those involving minor matters—were treated with any less attention than complaints brought by men. Ann St. Croix of St. Mary's, for example, took Elizabeth Feagan to court in 1821 on what appeared to be little more than a comedy of errors. Elizabeth had apparently burst into Ann's house and taken the blanket from her bed, swearing "by the X [cross] of Christ" that it was the same blanket that had been stolen from the defendant's fence the previous day. Elizabeth claimed that she had realized her mistake by the next day and sheepishly returned the blanket. Still, the local magistrate agreed to hear evidence in the matter, including the testimony of a witness who had sold the blanket to Ann originally, and ordered that Elizabeth pay a fine of 1s. and court costs.[59]

Just as in assault cases, both male and female defendants, when convicted of minor thefts, were treated similarly and accorded the court's standard correctives of financial penalties and orders to keep the peace and be of good behavior. In both categories, however, a gender divide did arise in the area of sentences for matters deemed more serious by the courts. While magistrates and surrogates were willing to unleash the full battery of punishments at their disposal—whippings, imprisonment, and transportation[60]—against male defendants convicted of thefts and riotous or particularly violent behavior, they trod more gently in applying these options to women.

This was especially the case with corporal punishment. In 1751, for example, Governor Francis Drake issued a decree in a case heard at Trepassey in which five men and one woman were charged with entering the house of Robert Rose and cruelly beating Patrick and Simon Fennassy "to the Effusion of their blood." The various male perpetrators were sentenced to thirty-nine lashes each and ordered to give security to keep the peace. By contrast, the woman who had accompanied them, Ann Stevens, was found to be an accessory only, and while she too was ordered to give security to keep the peace, no corporal punishment was ordered in her case. Drake's judgment did stipulate that "if she is *guilty of any further crime* she is to be whipped & sent from the Harbour; if she can't find security she is to be sent from the harbour." Had she been a man, however, the governor likely would not have fired this warning shot.[61]

Another example of official leniency towards women occurred in the theft charges brought against John and Margret Kenny and various servants in Ferryland in 1795. It was evident from the testimony provided by the Kenny's servant, Margret Riely, that Margret Kenny had masterminded most of the thefts, scheming with her husband and various servants to steal hay, coal, and saltfish from the Holdsworth premises, and a poker, shovel, and two decanters from the premises of Leigh and Co. Yet, in the range of punishments meted out to the various parties, Margret's fell in the middle in terms of severity. The spate of thefts garnered fines for all the convicted parties, with John's and Margaret's being the largest (£3) as befitted their central position in the crime ring. However, while John and one of the servants were also sentenced to a whipping and imprisonment (remitted when they joined the Newfoundland Regiment), Margret was sentenced to neither—despite the obvious fact that she had been the linchpin in the series of crimes.[62] Case File 24

Indeed, no case survives in the court records from the southern Avalon in which a whipping sentence was actually meted out to a woman defendant. By contrast, corporal punishment was allotted to male defendants, particularly in the eighteenth and early nineteenth centuries, and especially in relation to property crimes and violent crimes against the person. Several of the ringleaders of the Ferryland riot, for example, were sentenced to whippings, along with stiff fines and transportation.[63] Often, the severity of the punishment detailed in the records seems quite shocking to present-day sensibilities. In 1790, for example, Thomas Quinn, Pat Lundergan, and William Dullahunty were convicted of stealing six quintals of fish. Quinn was sentenced to twenty-four lashes on the bare back, then eight lashes at the "point beach", eight more at the "Northside Room", and a final eight strokes back at the courthouse. To add an element of mortification, he was to walk from one site to the next with a fish hung around his neck. He and his two cohorts were to be imprisoned until deported.[64]

While much has been made in the traditional historiography of the harsh justice handed down by visiting fishing admirals and naval surrogates, two local magistrates assisted the visiting surrogate in this 1790 decision. In the following years, local justices demonstrated that they were ready to hand out severe punishments on their own to prevent violent crimes, protect property, and discipline servants. The most extreme sentences, however, occurred in the decade immediately following the Ferryland riot, and may have reflected the residual fear of English Protestant magistrates as they attempted to send a message to the growing Irish Catholic plebeian community.[65]

Still, the local courts balked at sentencing women to corporal punishment. However, they were more willing to order imprisonment and transportation for female defendants who came before them. Women were not imprisoned in the same numbers as men, but they formed a smaller proportion of the population until sex ratios equalized in the 1850s. Furthermore, men were not jailed with any great regularity either, even after the paradigm shift in the use of incarceration, because the district continued to lack adequate facilities or funds to house prisoners. Still, the courts employed the jails on occasion for both sexes, especially in cases of violent behavior or larger property crimes.

The longest prison term allotted to women in the area was imposed on Bridget Hegarthy and her daughter Mary Reed (also Read) of Ferryland. In 1842, Benjamin Sweetland, clerk and storekeeper for merchant James H. Carter in Ferryland, told the court that he had reason to believe that the two women had taken an amount of salt beef and pork from Carter's premises and asked the court for a warrant to search Hegarthy's home. No sign of the salt meat was found, but when the constable and the storekeeper went down into the cellar, they found a whole assortment of other shop goods: boots and shoes, shirts, men's braces, ladies' hose, yards and yards of materials, chests of tea—everything from a needle to an anchor. Based on the evidence at hand, a petty jury had no difficulty in convicting the two women of larceny. The court also tried to bring Bridget's husband, Charles Hegarthy, into its net with a charge of possession of stolen goods, but the jury found him not guilty. Evidently, Charles had had no knowledge of the matter; the enterprise was a mother-and-daughter affair only. The two women were imprisoned for twelve months for this particular caper.[66]

This was a stiff jail term for the Ferryland court, regardless of the sex of the convicted. Of course, the extent of the theft was significant, and the magistrates in the matter (all members of local mercantile families) were likely making clear to the plebeian community their intention to protect merchant interests in the area.[67] Also, this particular mother-and-daughter team was already known to local authorities. In 1833, Bridget (whose last name at the time was Murphy) had been charged with receiving stolen goods; the chief witness against her had been her daughter, Mary Read. Mary told the court that Bridget had received stolen goods from her on several occasions, "well knowing the same were the property of Patrick Connors and stolen from the House of the sd. Patrick Connors by directions of her said Mother."[68] Indeed, Bridget seems to have remained on the dubious side of the law. She came under suspicion again in 1844 for stealing building materials from a house belonging to the estate of William Carter, although in fairness to Bridget, it must be noted that on this occasion, there was insufficient evidence to convict her.[69] Case File 25

However, long-term incarceration was rarely imposed by the local courts. Shorter jail terms were more frequently employed to hold persons before deportation, or as an alternative when defendants refused or were unable to pay fines or give security to keep the peace. When Bridget Dullanty of Ferryland, for example, was convicted of assaulting Arthur H. O. B. Carter and "severely wounding" him, she was ordered to pay a fine of 10s. or, in default thereof, to be imprisoned for one week in the local jail. This sentence was somewhat stiffer than the usual peace bond imposed in similar circumstances and may have been precipitated either by the complainant's status as a member of the prominent Carter family, the severity of the attack, or by the fact that this was a repeat offense for the defendant. At any rate, Bridget opted to pay the fine.[70] Ann Prichet chose the alternative in 1820 when she was convicted of beating her neighbor's children; she refused to pay her fine of 5s. and provide security to keep the peace, and was incarcerated for an unspecified period of time.[71] The local magistrates, then, were not deterred from employing jail terms as punishment against female defendants as circumstances demanded.

Indeed, on at least one occasion, a local court imprisoned female defendants while leaving a male defendant at large for what appeared to be similar offenses. At St. Mary's on 27 October 1837, Anastatia Goff and Mary Daley were tried by jury for an assault and battery of Mary White of Salmonier the previous May. The two were convicted, and the following day, each was sentenced to four days' imprisonment and a fine of £1 plus court costs.[72] In the very next case, before the same jury, William Lush was charged with an assault and battery of Judith Grant the previous April; a charge of common assault was added to the indictment the following day. Lush was convicted and sentenced to pay a fine of £10.10.0, but no prison term was ordered.[73] As is often the case with many of the records, details of the cases were scarce, so it is difficult to interpret the difference in treatment of the defendants in the two cases. The charges in both cases were similar, although Lush was charged with an additional count of common assault. The fine levied against the male defendant was much heavier—£10.10.0 versus £1—yet only the women served jail time. Perhaps the assault and battery perpetrated by the women was more violent. Possibly the local jail could not accommodate both male and female prisoners at the same time (a preoccupation of grand jury presentments of the day), and prison time was allotted on the pragmatic basis of "first come, first served." Or perhaps the local court was tailoring the sentences to the particular circumstances of the defendants: possibly the women were unable to pay a larger fine, and thus the prison time was combined with a lower fine to add weight to the sentence. Certainly, however, there was no leniency shown towards these women in terms of incarceration.

While imprisonment was employed with some discretion, transportation (technically, deportation) back to England or Ireland was regularly employed in the eighteenth and early nineteenth centuries—a reflection of a still stabilizing population with many recent immigrants whom authorities were happy to send home on fishing and passenger vessels plying between the British Isles and Newfoundland if they landed on the wrong side of the law. Again, this option was used mostly in cases of property crimes or violent or riotous behavior, all of which were seen as serious threats to the social order. Again, men were more frequently deported than women, largely reflecting the higher proportion of transient men in the local population in the period when transportation to the home country was still a viable option. Nonetheless, the local courts occasionally found cause to remove troublesome female defendants as well.

In some cases, there were gendered undertones in the targeting of women for deportation, particularly in the perception of the nature of the danger they posed to the moral and social order. We have already observed, for example, the threat of transportation being issued against the doctress Mrs. Curry, who inverted the gender order with her medical practice on fishing servants at St. Mary's (see Chapter 4). The sentence was also levied against two female *complainants*, both known prostitutes, in sexual assault matters in the eighteenth century (see Chapter 8).

However, women, like men, also earned deportation sentences for property crimes, particularly up to the early 1800s. In September of 1751, for example, Margaret Penny of Bay Bulls was accused of receiving goods stolen by Thomas Power of Waterford. A witness had seen Power revealing the illegal contents of his chest to Penny in her house; the two had apparently then concealed the chest under some hay in Penny's cellar. Both parties were sentenced to be transported back to Ireland.[74] Similarly, in 1804, when Mary Power of Ferryland district was convicted of breaking and entering into Joseph Smith's store and taking "Sundry Merchandise," the court ordered that she be "Transported from this Island, never to Return."[75] Doubtless, had Bridget Hegarthy and Mary Read committed their theft from the Carter stores fifty years earlier, they, too, would have found themselves on a ship bound back to Ireland.

FEMALE WITNESSES

Women appeared as witnesses in the court records of the southern Avalon almost as frequently as men, although the presence of witnesses in general (male or female) was not extensive, as the majority of cases at the local level were decided simply on the evidence of the parties involved. Still, the value of women's testimony to the local courts was manifest as they appeared in a variety of matters, ranging from slander and seduction to debt, eviction, and assault (see Table 6.6). Their testimony sometimes detailed extraordinary events, but often merely reflected the gleanings of day-to-day experience, illustrating once again the role of women's information in helping to maintain social order and the extensive overlapping between private and public domains in the period of early settlement.[76]

Female witnesses appeared in largest numbers as crown witnesses in cases of assault against their own person. (This was true of male witnesses in the system as well.) These women victims/witnesses have already been discussed as complainants above, but two findings are worth reiterating here. First, these women felt they had recourse to the judicial system to protect their rights. Second, their evidence was usually accepted by the court, often without corroboration, although to some extent this may have simply reflected the pragmatism of local magistrates as they tried to maintain law and order with limited means at their disposal.

Women also appeared as witnesses in a variety of other matters, most especially in cases involving assault against others, property and account disputes, theft, and defamation. Indeed, in an 1833 assault case, a woman not only testified for, but also acted as the legal representative of, one of the defendants. In *Rex v. Matthew Meany and Martin Curreen*, co-defendant Meany did not appear in court at all, but was instead represented at the hearing by his wife, Margaret, who successfully defended him against a charge of assault and battery against Thomas Ryan.[77]

The testimony of female witnesses often carried significant impact, reinforcing the value of women's information in identifying and controlling behavior unacceptable to the community. When Patrick Kelly alleged in 1806 that John Flyn had assaulted him in the house of Michael White "some time in the Winter," for example, his complaint was "provd by Ellenor White to be just," and Flyn was fined 40s. and bound for £20 to keep the peace.[78] In a Cape Broyle case in 1787, the evidence of a woman who had attended an assault victim at his deathbed prevailed over the testimony of several male witnesses of the attack that had purportedly led to his demise. In that instance, a man named Hogan charged that Patrick Shea had beaten his uncle, Redmond Ellward (or Aylward), causing his death. Hogan brought forward several male witnesses who had been in the Shea house at the time of the attack and testified that Shea had struck Ellward on the side, causing his victim to cry out "Murder, murder!" They claimed that Ellward had to be helped to bed, complaining of a pain in his side and experiencing difficulty in breathing as a result of Shea's beating.

Furthermore, they said, when Ellward remained restless in the bedroom, Shea had gone upstairs and likely hit the older man with "a clift of whitling [split of wood]" he had taken from the woodbox.

However, the court gave considerable weight to the deposition of Honour Tobin, who had been brought in to nurse Ellward and, ultimately, to lay him out when he died several days later. She testified that, while she had found Ellward quite ill, she had not found any marks of violence on him other than a cut on his forehead, which had apparently come from a fall against an iron pot. Furthermore, during the two days that she tended him, he had been conscious but had never mentioned any attack by Patrick Shea. (By contrast, the credibility of a doctor who had attended the sick man shortly after the attack was somewhat diminished by the fact that he had detected no wounds or bruises whatsoever on Ellward and had only become aware of the alleged assault later through the community grapevine.) Relying heavily on Honour's testimony, the court decided that there was insufficient evidence that Ellward's death had been directly caused by Shea's attack and acquitted him.[79] Case File 26

Women witnesses provided evidence in cases involving thefts of property ranging from clothing and housewares, to poultry and livestock, to housing materials. Indeed, women's intimate knowledge of the lives of their employers and neighbors sometimes gave them an edge in detecting property that had been separated from its rightful owners: when one family's ducks appeared on another family's dinner table, for example, or when a merchant's stores appeared in a neighbor's house. Women's ability to move between private and public domains gave their testimony considerable weight in such cases.

In one quite extensive matter in 1795, the testimony of Margret Riely, a servant in Ferryland, was instrumental in stopping the veritable crime spree of her employers, Margret and John Kenny.[80] Riely's position inside the Kenny household had enabled her to overhear schemes being hatched by the Kennys and several servants (their own and others') to steal various items from two mercantile firms operating in the community: Holdsworth's and Leigh and Co. Riely's watchful eyes had seen suspicious-looking bundles being spirited into the Kenny house or outbuildings, usually under cover of darkness: a bundle of hay arriving after midnight on the backs of John Kenny and his servant; bags of coal being delivered at night throughout the winter by a Holdsworth's servant; a bag of dried fish appearing in the early hours of the morning carried by one of the Kennys' dieters and a servant of John Baker, agent for Holdsworth's; fire irons and decanters entering under the "packet" of a servant of Arthur Hunt, agent for Leigh and Co. On the strength of Margret Riely's testimony, five of the seven people charged in the action were found guilty by a jury and sentenced to punishments ranging from fines to imprisonment and whippings.[81] Case File 24

Female witnesses also featured in disputes over accounts—usually in relation to their own families' accounts, but occasionally in relation to employers' accounts or matters outside their households. For example, when a dispute arose in 1848 between John Connell and John Power of Brigus South as to the amount of saltfish Power had transported to St. John's on Connell's behalf, the combined weight of the testimony from the defendant's two female witnesses (Catharine Dooley and Sarah Greene) overrode that of the lone male witness for the complainant (Robert Power), and the plaintiff was non-suited and ordered to pay court costs. The evidence offered by the two women related to the amount of fish that had been cured by Connell, then weighed and transported by Power. Given the specificity of their testimony, they were obviously knowledgeable about the fishery and must have been present at the wharf during the consignment of the fish to Power, perhaps as fishing servants or members of a household production unit in the fishery. Certainly, the court accepted their expertise, and the defense prevailed.[82]

Wives also acted as important witnesses when disputes arose over the validity or amount of a debt. Although they were not the legal agents named in the formal charges, it was evident that they saw themselves as having an equal stake in protecting their families' interests. Indeed, in several cases, it was apparent that the wife was primarily responsible for keeping the household accounts. In 1827, for example, when Walter Shelly sued Michael Keanon to recover £5.5.8 Stg. due on a "note of hand," it was Eleanor Shelly (most likely Walter's wife, although possibly another female relative) who proved the debt in court.[83] In 1793, when James Warne, a boatkeeper at Trepassey, was sued by his servant Thomas Murphy for outstanding wages, it was *Mrs.* Warne's accounting that Murphy complained about, claiming that she had overcharged him by £6 and not settled with him a £3 bill of exchange he had given her. Mrs. Warne attended the court hearing with books in hand to prove the accuracy of her accounting, and the court determined that Murphy's charge was "Malicious and illfounded." Indeed, Murphy was not only disappointed in his suit, but was confined to jail on bread and water for three days and fined 40s.[84] Case File 27 Similarly, when a man named Welsh of Ferryland initiated an action against Leigh and Co. in 1786 for not crediting his account properly for milk, calves, and hogs, Mrs. Welsh appeared in court to provide supporting evidence in relation to the accounting (without success in this case, as the Welshes were ordered to pay Leigh and Co. the full balance on the books of £71.2.9¾).[85]

The presence of women witnesses in the courtroom demonstrates the court's reliance on women's testimony as a credible source of information and a useful resource for the efficient operation of the local justice system. Sometimes, the court was tapping women's more intimate knowledge of the day-to-day affairs of their neighbors and their capacity to bring private issues into the public arena.

But not all the matters on which they testified were private, and a number of women (such as Catharine Dooley and Sarah Greene in the fish consignment case at Brigus South) gave evidence from their status as persons involved in public spheres of activity. Clearly, women were not reticent in coming forward—at least not those from the plebeian community[86] (here again, there was a class difference, with women from the local elite recorded only in the capacity of witnesses to documents—a function that did not require their actual presence in the courthouse). Certainly, there was a willingness on the part of the court to weigh the evidence of female witnesses along with that of male witnesses.

Of course, just as in the case of male deponents, some of the testimony of female witnesses was deemed inaccurate or frivolous. In an 1819 defamation case, for example, Jane Holehan accused Catherine Walsh of spreading rumors that Jane had dried up her cow's milk by force of witchcraft. Case File 28 The visiting surrogate, likely unconvinced of the seriousness of the charge, issued a summons to the defendant but relegated the matter to be heard by the local magistrate, William Phipard. In the hearing a month later, Jane produced two witnesses—one male and one female—to substantiate her complaint, but the female witness, Ellen Piddle, was somewhat vague in her testimony. Magistrate Phipard, finding the case "labouring under such inconsistencys" as to be impossible to adjudicate, dismissed the matter, with costs to be paid by the defendant.[87] In this instance, the court was likely happy to divest itself of a matter that the magistrate saw as trifling, although the capacity for defamation within the plebeian community may have been quite real.[88] In general, however, the court seemed as open to the legitimacy of women's testimony as men's testimony, and female witnesses were an integral part of the local justice system.

FEMALE PETITIONERS

Court records, official correspondence, and newspapers reveal fifty-seven instances of individual petitioning by women on the southern Avalon during the study period. Petitioning required a degree of legal astuteness on the part of these women—not only in terms of drafting the petitions (although some may have been helped by outside parties) but also (and more importantly) in terms of having an awareness of their rights and an understanding of how to make formal institutions work to their advantage. As Table 6.7 indicates, women petitioned central authorities and local magistrates and administrators (most wore two hats)[89] on a variety of concerns, the documents ranging from applications in estate and property matters to requests for relief and redress.

Women's petitioning has been examined in other historical contexts as a means by which women transcended the legal constraints on their participation in public life. Campbell takes this approach, for example, in her examination of women's petitioning of the New Brunswick legislature in the mid-nineteenth century, finding a high level of female involvement in two general categories: petitions seeking some personal or community advantage, and those seeking changes in the law (specifically, prohibition). Through this mechanism, she argues, women helped to shape the political culture of the day.[90] All the women's petitions on the southern Avalon during the study period were comparable to Campbell's first category (seeking personal advantage or redress). There were no women's petitions requesting changes in the law during the study period, but then there was no local campaign equivalent to the temperance movement discussed by Campbell. In as much as southern Avalon women were aware of their rights and able to use petitioning to protect them, however, they were participating in the public and political domain.

Rosen has also examined women's petitioning, within the context of colonial New York. She presents the practice as a means by which women could seek redress from a legal system that otherwise excluded them to a large degree. In late seventeenth- and eighteenth-century New York, she observes, only a small proportion of women sought conflict resolution through the formal court system. Petitioning, by contrast, was an "alternative path to justice" for a group that found themselves marginalized from the rights-based legal system of the period. However, the petition was essentially a plea to the "discretionary justice" of governors and other authorities of the day, she argues. While it helped colonial women to transcend the legal constraints of the court system, it reinforced their deference and subservience and "only partially mitigated [their] lack of freedom."[91]

However, Rosen may be reading too much into the deferential tone of women's petitions. In terms of language, they were using the conventions of the day—formulae followed by most petitioners, regardless of class or gender. Caution must be used in drawing connections between a protocol used as a means to an end and the internalization of social attitudes. Some of her other observations also do not apply tidily to the southern Avalon context. There, both men and women petitioned for discretionary justice, so the mechanism was not gender-specific. Furthermore, petitioning was not the only recourse for women to obtain justice on the southern Avalon. Indeed, it was often as much a part of or complement to the formal legal system as it was an alternative to formal justice. Most of the petitions examined here (thirty-eight petitions, or 67 percent) were either submitted to local magistrates as direct entrées into the court system (sixteen) or used to initiate probate or administration of estates (twenty-two). Another four (7 percent) fell amidst the flurry of petitions for land grants from both men and women in the late 1820s and early 1830s as imperial authorities gradually relaxed the impediments to holding title to (as opposed to merely occupying) property (see Appendix A).

Only fifteen petitions (or 26 percent) were directed to local magistrates or central authorities (the governor or chief justice) in pleas for discretionary justice comparable to those described by Rosen. Yet even these do not all fall neatly into such a categorization: four either arose from or were segued into cases in the local courts; and another eight sought resolution of disputes that quite likely would have gone to court had the matters not been resolved, given women's general willingness to initiate such actions. Magistrate Robert Carter noted in his diary in April of 1840, for example, that he went to Fermeuse "to view some Land petitioned for yesterday by Mary Oneile—part claimed by Wm Brothers towards Admirals' Cove." The grant was awarded to Mary later that year, despite Brothers' adverse claim, but she likely would have pursued the matter in court if necessary, for she had already petitioned the court previously on matters related to her late husband's estate.[92] That same year, Carter noted that he had written James Jackman and "ordered him to desist from interfering with Land petitioned for by Margaret Dunphy at Renews."[93] Again, while Margaret sought the magistrate's intervention, she likely would not have hesitated to initiate a suit against Jackman if necessary, for six years later, she sued her employer, Nicholas Power, for outstanding wages.[94] It is far more probable, then, that women were petitioning authorities to mediate disputes as a preliminary step in conflict resolution, rather than as their sole recourse to justice. Indeed, as has been seen, far from being excluded from formal legal processes, women were a visible presence in the courtrooms of the southern Avalon. Furthermore, unlike colonial New York, where the legal system became more exclusionary of women as it became more formalized, along the southern Avalon, as the court system evolved in the late eighteenth and early nineteenth centuries, formal justice appeared to become even more accessible to women, for women's participation in court matters increased in both absolute and proportionate terms.

If anything, as the formal court system developed, women's petitioning on the southern Avalon dwindled away, except in probate and administration matters, which surged in the 1820s, 30s, and 40s. The floodgates for the latter had been opened by the 1824 *Judicature Act (5 Geo. IV, Cap. 67)*, which gave the chief justice the power to grant administration of intestacies in addition to his existing power to grant probate.[95] These estate petitions themselves demonstrate that women were able to embrace changes in the legal system and use them to their advantage. But petitioning on other matters appears to have been a disproportionately eighteenth-century activity, with only ten individual petitions appearing after the turn of the century on issues other than estate matters (four of which were standard petitions for land grants, not pleas for discretionary justice).

By contrast, women's appearances in the courtrooms of the district rose after the passage of the first *Judicature Acts* of 1791 and 1792 (see note 4, above), so they were increasingly using the mechanisms of criminal charges and civil litigation rather than petitioning to seek resolution of conflicts.

It is tempting to interpret the decline in women's petitioning on matters other than probate/administration matters in terms of class—a transition in traditions, as the Irish plebeian community, with less formal literacy, swelled towards the turn of the century. It is clear that women from the English Protestant gentry had been active eighteenth-century petitioners, especially in property disputes and estate matters, but their participation dropped off sharply in the 1800s as they were increasingly represented in such matters by men in their circle (see Chapter 9). However, this does not explain the decrease in overall petitioning, as Irish women also proved to be adept petitioners in all categories, authoring eighteen out of twenty-two petitions for probate/administration, eleven out of nineteen petitions on property matters, seven out of eight petitions for redress for assault, and two out of three relating to employment disputes. Again, the likely explanation of the decline in petitioning on non-estate matters is the greater degree of access to the court system and its apparatus for conflict resolution, and a greater willingness on the part of Irish plebeian women to access this more public route.

Of course, the woman who was most constrained by the formal legal system was the married woman, the *feme coverte*, with no formal legal identity separate from her husband's. For the married woman, then, the petition could indeed be an important alternative for redress of grievance or resolution of conflict. Although the marital status of southern Avalon female petitioners was not always indicated, available information indicates that at least fourteen (25 percent) of the women involved in the petitions examined were married—a fairly substantial level of participation—while another nineteen (33 percent) were widowed.[96] Still, it must be noted that married women's petitioning did not always signal a lack of access to the legal system. Some of the petitions did emanate from or evolve into court matters involving married women (especially from the plebeian community), either directly or as star witnesses in court matters headed by their husbands' names. Indeed, authorities sometimes waived the principle of coverture completely, and permitted married women to represent not just themselves but also their husbands and/or their families. This was the case in at least five of the petitions examined, and all five petitions came from women of the Irish Newfoundland plebeian community.

We have already encountered Elenor Evoy, whose 1795 petition to the court emanated from a desire to defend her family business and reputation (see Chapter 5), as well as Mary Bryan's successful effort to borrow time on the lease held by her husband who had become mentally incapacitated (see above). The other three petitions in this category issued from one of the most interesting petitioners from the Irish Newfoundland ethnic group, and the most prolific petition writer over all: Hannah McDaniel, alias Carney, of Ferryland. Hannah and her husband, William, took on some big guns in the area—the Westons and Carters, merchant-planters and magistrates—in a matter that dragged on for years in the late eighteenth century. The family was being sued first by Peter Weston, and then by his widow and executor, Catharine Weston, in relation to a debt in the amount of £109.4.5 that had originally been owed to the Westons by Hannah's father.

Hannah initially appealed to Governor Campbell for intervention in 1784. In a petition that she most likely wrote herself, she explained that, because of the debt, Peter Weston had tried to attach a piece of property belonging to her mother, and that the property was eventually attached, or "hemmed in," by Weston's son-in-law, William Carter. Hannah argued that, while her mother had dealt with the Weston house for over seven years, she had never received a satisfactory accounting of "them old Arrears." Hannah's mother, Mary Shea, had previously petitioned Governor Montagu on the matter and received from the Admiral "a few Lines under Hand to Indemnify her," which had, unfortunately, been "mislaid." The property had since passed into Hannah's possession at her mother's death. In a deliberate play to Governor Campbell's chivalry, Hannah ended her petition with the following plea: "Your Excellency will take petitn^{rs} Case into Consideration being apoor woman with avery great Charge seven helpless Children to support maintain & nourish ~ that never knew anything about these Accounts before." Campbell was sympathetic and ordered that "Hannah McDonnell and her husband" (an interesting reversal in gender protocol) retain peaceful possession of the property "so long as they shall Continue to employ it for the use of the Fishery."[97]

By March of 1787, however, the McDaniels were brought before the local magistrates by Catherine Weston, as executor of her late husband's estate. The summons was issued on 8 March to both Hannah and William, and ordered them both to appear in court the following morning. But Hannah initially appeared alone and advised that William had "gone in the woods"; her tardy co-defendant joined her in court that afternoon. At this juncture, the Weston camp was attempting to attach the *rent* for the property, which had since been let by *William* McDaniel to two local fishermen, Matthew Ronane (also Ronan) and John Grace, for £22 per year. However, the McDaniels had now crafted the following argument: that they were not truly married, that Hannah's last name was actually Carney (also Kearney), and that they were merely cohabiting (even though they had produced seven children over the years). Therefore, *William*, who was not legally Hannah's husband, had no claim to the fishing premises she had inherited from her mother, and had no right to lease them; the rents should therefore not be attached to pay the debt. This was a tidy argument, demonstrating an awareness of the laws of coverture. The local magistrates, however, treated the relationship as an informal marriage within the context of the flexible local marriage regime (see Chapter 8) and decided that William and Hannah were merely trying to "stave off from paying the said Debt." They ordered that the rents for the property be paid to Catherine Weston until the debt had been paid in full. The couple refused to comply, so a court order was issued to the lessees of the property advising them to withhold the rent from the McDaniels until further notice.[98]

The matter was then referred to Governor Elliot, although whether by the magistrates or by Hannah through another petition is not directly stated in the records. Yet the logical source of an appeal would have been the McDaniel family, now deprived of its rent. Furthermore, the governor's directions that his ensuing order "be entered in the Records of the District and the Paper . . . *to be delivered to the Petitioner*" suggest that Hannah had again plied her pen to represent her family's interests. If so, she was rewarded for her efforts, as Elliot concurred with Campbell's earlier decision that the Weston claim was not valid, although more from pragmatism than point of law, reasoning that "it would be the means of creating endless confusion throughout the Island if the Governor for the time being was to enter into the merits upon which his Predecessors had founded all their decisions." He directed the local magistrates to ensure that Hannah and William enjoyed quiet possession of the property.[99]

The *Weston v. McDaniel* matter resurfaced in 1790. On 17 August, Catherine Weston had another writ issued in relation to the debt of £109.4.5. This time, the action was taken against William McDaniel only, with the implication that the principle of coverture applied to the debt and the property inherited by Hannah. (Again, no evidence appeared in the records to disprove the McDaniels' claim that they were merely cohabiting, but the magistrates were apparently still disposed to treat the relationship as an informal marriage.) The sheriff served the writ on William and demanded payment or security for the debt. William refused, and the sheriff attached the property, described as "affishing Room, Dwelling houses, Stage and Flake."

Neither of the parties named in the action appeared at the 15 September hearing of the matter: Catherine was represented by local merchant and magistrate Henry Sweetland, and William was represented, once again, by his wife Hannah. Hannah produced the previous decisions of Governors Campbell and Elliot as evidence; nonetheless, the court found in favor of Catherine Weston and ordered that William pay the debt and court costs. The final reporting of the matter in the court records is a cryptic note dated 15 October 1790, stating that the proceedings had been rescinded by consent of the parties and that the writs of attachment and execution had been destroyed.[100] We are left to speculate by what means the parties came to a settlement, although one cannot help but think that Hannah's persistence had worn the Weston camp down. Ultimately, the much-disputed property was sold to William Carter by both William and Hannah in 1795 for £30.[101]

But the court had not heard the last of Hannah McDaniel, alias Carney. In 1791, she wrote a petition to the chief justice of the Island, John Reeves, in relation to a bond her husband had given six years previously to one Mr. Baker of Ferryland (most likely, John Baker, agent for Holdsworth's) as security for a debt of £100 Stg. William had agreed to pay £20 per year towards the debt, she said, but Baker was taking more than this amount each year from the rent of a fishing room that Hannah had leased to try to maintain her family. Furthermore, he was unfairly charging compound interest and was also trying to pressure Hannah to sell the premises to discharge the debt. As in her 1784 petition, Hannah appealed to the chivalry of the chief justice as she asked for relief for herself and her "poor helpless charge of six Children." Again, the petition was obviously written in her own words:

> The Humbel Petition of Hanna M^c^Daniel otherwise Carney most humbly sheweth- That petitioner begs leave to inform your honor that one M^r^. Baker in Ferryland has a bond of Petitioners husb^d^ of One Hundred pounds Sterling these six years in his hands, & was to pay but Twenty pounds a year in part payment of said sum by Agreement, and in stead of that sum there was Twenty seven pounds ten shillings payd aforesaid Baker these two years past that is seven pounds ten shillings more then she Contracted. Compound was because the afores^d^ M^r^. Baker wanted to distress petitioner & her poor helpless charge of six Children. Petitioner set [let] a fishing Roome to maintain herself & familey—The aforesaid Baker took all this rent to himself tho his Compound agreement was to Receive but Twenty pounds a year and not allow Petitioner a hundred [weight of] Bread out of his store towards mantaining her heavey charge—The aforesaid Baker several Different times wanted petitioner to sell her Room to pay himself & likewise wanted her to sign him a Bond for the Intrest of the aforesaid sum after paying more than Compound agreed upon yearly the tinnant that ouccupies petitioners room pays the aforesaid Baker the rent of said Roome without the Petitioners order or Consent—Your Petitioner cannot get no Good of ye said M^r^. Baker There fore Petitioner hopes your honor will Take it into consideration & vindicate the Cause then your Petitioner in Duty bound [obliterated] will be for Ever bound to pray~

Chief Justice Reeves agreed with Hannah that Baker had no right to stop the full amount of the rent and that the wording of the bond gave him no right to charge interest, nor to dispose of the skiffs that had apparently been put in his possession as security only. He ordered that Baker apply the £20 per year taken from the rent directly against the principal and that he provide a complete accounting to the McDaniels upon full payment of the bond in order "to prevent the Court being troubled unnecessarily with McDaniel's Complaints."[102]

However, the court would be troubled by Hannah's worries one last time. In 1797, Michael Malone of Ferryland brought Hannah and her son John to court because John had reneged on his apprenticeship agreement with Malone "by the Counsel of his mother." According to Malone, John had "absented himself from his service and refused to serve out his time according to agreement." The hearing of the matter revealed, however, that John had been shipped specifically to fish out of the harbor of Ferryland for Malone for a season's wages of £15; but Malone had hired his boat to Martin Molloy and Thomas Clements of Renews, and he felt that he had the right to transfer the service of John McDaniel along with the boat. Hannah disagreed, and so did the court, finding that Malone "could not dispose of his servant, as he had done with his private property, without the servants consent." Given that John had shipped himself specifically to fish out of Ferryland, he could not be compelled to serve in any other harbor. Molloy and Clements ultimately agreed to fish out of Ferryland; John McDaniel thereupon agreed to serve them, and the matter was resolved to the McDaniels' satisfaction, with court costs of 16s. to be paid by the plaintiff.[103] Case File 29

By the time of the 1800 nominal census, Hannah was no longer in the district. Her family was still there, however, which suggests that she had probably died (there are no parish records available for the 1790s to confirm this). And thus the court was deprived of one of its most adept petitioners and litigators, for it is evident that the McDaniels, and Hannah in particular, were extremely adept at maneuvering within the legal system; these were not just poor simple fisher-folk being out-gunned by members of the community's elite. It is also worth noting that it was Hannah, not her husband, who wrote the petitions, framing them in her own words (with detailed explanations and her own idiosyncratic expressions interspersed among the stock petitioner's phrasings). So Hannah was likely literate and certainly able to muster arguments to her cause. She appeared to have a basic appreciation of legal principles. She also effectively played the role of a poor distressed woman with hungry children to her advantage, especially to officials in St. John's who had no familiarity with her circumstances.

Throughout the McDaniels' legal battles, it was Hannah, more than William, who represented the family's interests. What is more, she herself even directly represented William in the courthouse on occasion—a relaxation of the principle of coverture, given that the magistrates were eager to treat their relationship as a marriage. Even in the final sale of the long-disputed property to the Carters, Hannah joined with William as a signatory to the deed as one of the executors of her mother's estate. Her experience contrasts with that of Catherine Weston, who was represented in the proceedings by Henry Sweetland, likely because it would not have been deemed proper or respectable for a woman from a powerful merchant-planter family to appear in the courthouse. But it was Hannah, the woman from the plebeian community, who was more empowered by her ability to represent herself in the public sphere and by the community's acceptance of her presence there.

One other form of women's petitioning was evident during the period, in the form of community petitions for relief from distress. Petitions for relief poured into the local colonial secretary's office from the English Shore from the late 1810s into the 1830s as poor crop-growing conditions coincided with low fish catches and depressed fish markets to create acute hardship in many areas around the island.[104] While numerous petitions arrived from the south coast and the northern districts year after year, however, there were very few such petitions from the southern Avalon. One came from the district of Bay Bulls in May of 1822, and a presentment from the grand jury of Ferryland sought relief for the district in 1826.[105] But nothing further was entered into the records by the colonial secretary until the winter and spring of 1832–33, suggesting that the fishery or potato crop in the area may not have suffered as badly and/or that local relief measures (for example, charitable subscriptions, funds from liquor licenses) in this less heavily populated area were a sufficient stopgap for such hardship as did exist. But by the winter of 1832–33, after three consecutive poor growing seasons, requests for relief from the southern Avalon joined those from the northern districts and the south coast, as fishing families found themselves without seed potatoes to plant and local merchants and administrators declared their inability to extend any further relief from personal or communal resources. Still, the level of distress on the southern Avalon must not have been as pervasive as in other areas at the time: no petitions for community relief appeared from Trepassey–St. Mary's district; only two arrived from Ferryland district (Renews and Fermeuse), and two from Bay Bulls district (Bay Bulls and Witless Bay).[106]

Requests for assistance from around the island generally came in the form of appeals from missionaries, magistrates, and/or *ad hoc* relief committees, often accompanied by petitions from distressed residents themselves. Generally, these petitions were signed by household heads—primarily men and widows—with families to support. Such was the case with the petition forwarded from Fermeuse in April 1833, under a covering letter from local merchant Thomas Congdon. Congdon indicated that the petitioners would require 200 barrels of seed potatoes, as they had none for planting that season. The petition itself, written in a hand different from Congdon's (and possibly by one of the petitioners), showed a familiarity with the ornate conventions of petition-writing of the period:

> Humbly Sheweth that your petitioners in consequence of the great failure of their potato crop last season, together with the quantity which have rotted in their Cellars in Consequence of the early set[t]ing in [of] the past severe Winter before the potatoes were properly secured, or from the Want of maturity in the growth of the crop put in—are totally destitute of seed or the means of providing any for the coming season.
>
> That your petitioners are all people with large families depending on them for support, consequently look forward with Fearful anxiety to the approach of another [bad growing season] Which must bring inevitable starvation on a large portion of them, unless it may by the aid of your Excellency, under the blessing of Divine Providence be averted.
>
> In tender consideration of our great necessities and the fearful consequences that may result from them We humbly pray that your Excellency may be graciously pleased to grant us such relief as in your Excellencys Wisdom and Humanity may seem meet and your petitioners as in duty bound will forever pray ~

The petition was signed by twenty-three family heads, including two women: Mary Fahey and Catherine Tobin.[107] This was fairly representative of the petitions received from all districts.

Less typical was the petition received from Witless Bay in May that same year. In this instance, eight widows and two men (one described as a "cripple" and the other as "old and infirm") were the only signatories (all by their mark). The language was much plainer and appealed to the governor's chivalric instincts in relation to widows and their children:

> We your Excellency's humble petitioners, poor Widows with large families, being deprived of all possible means of procuring Seed Potatoes, do most respectfully lay our distress before your Excellency, hoping you will take it into your gracious consideration, and send us that relief which your Excellency may think proper to bestow. And your petitioners as are duty bound will ever pray~

No reference was made in the text to the men who had to be supplied due to incapacity; their situation was obviously conflated with that of the "poor Widows with large families" by the petition's author. The family size and specific needs of each petitioner were entered, with the total need assessed at thirty-one barrels of seed potatoes. A marginal note by the colonial secretary, however, indicates that only twelve barrels were actually sent.[108] Perhaps the governor was suspicious of the high level of widowhood in such a small community (although a couple of fishing disasters could have accounted for this).[109]

In general, however, there seemed to be an official reluctance to send seed potatoes to the southern districts, including the southern Avalon and Placentia Bay. Relief committees in all districts of the island were instructed to assess need carefully and to keep precise records of all seed potatoes and other relief (such as bread and molasses) distributed. The instructions to the southern districts, however, always included firm admonitions that the seed potatoes were to be considered a loan only, to be repaid in kind at the fall harvest. When additional relief was provided in the form of bread and molasses, the colonial secretary took pains to explain that the governor had limited the quantities supplied "as only to be sufficient to support life~ & not to create a desire to depend on the bounty of Gov^{t}. in future."[110] Such cautionary language is not as evident in the correspondence with the northern districts, and the reproving tone seems somewhat unwarranted, given the limited number of requests from the southern Avalon compared to the overwhelming dependence of the northern districts on relief distribution for many years. Perhaps authorities questioned the validity of the claims from the south, given that some areas in the southern districts were coping without assistance. However, there is also a possibility that there was some residual mistrust of predominantly Irish Catholic districts among Anglo-Protestant governors and civil servants of the day.

At any rate, this was a very different form of petitioning from the individual women's petitioning examined above, emanating from an extended period of poor growing and fishing seasons—a combination of natural circumstances that brought high levels of distress to numerous Newfoundland communities and ignored gender in its impact. Male and female household heads joined in what were, indeed, deferential requests to a central authority for relief from impending starvation. These were extraordinary efforts in exceptional times, not comparable to the individual petitioning described earlier, in which women were acting in a quest for individual justice, whether through the formal legal system or as an effective alternative to it.

CONCLUSION

Southern Avalon women found various ways to gain access to the legal system between the mid-eighteenth and mid-nineteenth centuries, even if their way was sometimes impeded by the law's assumption of women's secondary status. Their participation was not as extensive as men's, but they were present in the system in substantial numbers and in a variety of capacities: as civil litigants, complainants and defendants in criminal matters, witnesses, and petitioners.

Indeed, women's involvement with the legal system—especially that of plebeian women—increased as the courts became more formalized in the late eighteenth century and the early decades of the nineteenth century.

For the most part, local magistrates placed men and women who appeared before them on a fairly equal footing. Yet not all women had ready access to the courtroom. The greatest bar to women's participation was the common-law principle of coverture, although it should be noted that the status and authority of married women in plebeian families likely permitted them a good deal of behind-the-scenes involvement in any legal matters confronting their families. Still, the local courts generally recognized coverture, although they also made a significant number of exceptions.[111]

Husbands were usually recognized as the legal agents of their wives in civil matters involving debt, for example. Nonetheless, the court occasionally permitted married women to initiate actions: Jane Austen and Margret Kenney, for example, sued various debtors in their own right, even though their husbands were alive; and the high percentage (75 percent) of female creditors and debtors who appeared on their own behalf in court suggests that the principle was waived on other occasions as well. It is worth noting here that most local magistrates were also members of mercantile families who—if Goodridge's and Sweetman's were representative—permitted married women to hold accounts in their own names if they carried out economic activities independently of their husbands. The principle of marital unity, then, was often tempered by local circumstances in a number of spheres, as a certain laxness towards coverture permeated various realms at the level of daily practice.

Magistrates also generally held that husbands were entitled to the property of their wives after marriage, although again they made exceptions. For example, the local court excepted any property of the wife over which the husband had not exercised any control or act of possession, as occurred when the firm of Hunt, Stabb, Preston tried to attach property belonging to Elizabeth Beaves to pay her late husband's debts. And there were other occasions on which the principle of coverture was not applied. Mary Bryan, a married woman from St. Mary's, represented her family's interests in 1780 in relation to a property matter, although there was cause for relaxation of the principle in that matter, as her husband had been deemed "insane." A more clear-cut example was that of Hannah McDaniel, who represented herself and her husband in a protracted property and debt dispute in the 1780s and 1790s.

There were other cases in which wives represented their husbands in the courthouse. As noted above, Margaret Meaney appeared for her husband and successfully defended him against assault charges in 1833. And when John Fowler initiated an action against Richard Shallow for recovery of a property at Renews, it was Shallow's wife who appeared in court and defended the family's claim to the land. At the initial hearing, she stated "that she was taken by surprise in the matter" and asked the court to "grant her time [and] she would produce several material Witnesses to prove her occupancy of the property in possession for a period of over thirty years." The court gave her only until the next morning, but she managed to find two witnesses to establish her claim, and a judgment was initially given in her favor, although a new trial was later ordered on the grounds that the judgment was "contrary to law and Evidence."[112] So married women were no strangers to the courtroom.[113]

Furthermore, while English common law held the father to be legal guardian of the children of a marriage, local courts sometimes tempered this principle in terms of parental spheres of influence. In 1800, for example, Trepassey doctor Michael Dutton complained to the magistrate that he had frequently seen the children of the Welch family taking boards from a fish stage in the harbor. Although the "Welch family" were the named defendants, and the culprits were specifically identified as "the Children of John Welch," it was Mrs. Welch who appeared in court and received the surrogate's warning that her children were to cause no complaint in the future. In this case, it seems that the court went directly to the mother as the parent most likely to be able to enforce the court's judgment.[114] Furthermore, in matrimonial matters, the courts did not always uphold the rights of fathers as legal guardians of children. In Chapter 8, for example, several cases involving child custody will be discussed in which wives—even those who had technically "deserted" the marriage—were given custody of the children of the marriage.

In some of the cases in which mothers represented their children's interests, the women had assumed the status of legal guardian in widowhood, as the law permitted. Catherine Delahunty of Ferryland, for example, was a widow when she sued James H. Carter for the seduction of her daughter Ellen in 1827,[115] and Thomas Norris for her son's outstanding wages three years later.[116] Although the records are not clear, Jane Fitzpatrick, who tried to have her son's apprenticeship agreement with Robert Pitt voided in 1837, was also likely widowed or separated from her husband, for parish records indicate that her husband had either died or left between the birth of her daughter in 1826 and the birth of another son in 1828.[117] Elizabeth Madden was likely also single, separated, or widowed when she intervened in her son's working arrangements with local employer Michael Curragan in 1836.[118] However, such was not the case when Hannah McDaniel appeared as co-defendant with her son John for having advised John to renege on his shipping agreement with Michael Malone in 1797. John's father, William McDaniel, was very much alive, for he was listed with the family in the 1800 nominal census. In this case, the complainant and the court chose to prosecute the parent who had provoked the alleged breach of contract, regardless of legal guardianship.[119]

Did women themselves seek differential treatment from the legal system? Occasionally, women appealed to the chivalric impulses of governors or magistrates in framing their requests or defenses. This was particularly true in women's petitioning, in which a variation of the phrase "poor distressed woman with a large family, [x number of] children to feed" appeared with some regularity. Whether this form of suasion was an accurate reflection of the woman's circumstances (as was likely when the women of Witless Bay were seeking seed potatoes in 1833), or a ploy to win the sympathy of authorities (as was likely in Hannah McDaniel's petitioning) probably varied from case to case.[120] Sarah Turpin's petition in 1780 from Bay Bulls, requesting the intervention of the governor in relation to the "Rude Behaviour of Fishermen at Bay of Bulls to women who pass along while their Jigging of Squids," was also likely intended to touch on gentry sensibilities and notions of propriety and respectability.[121]

In most civil and criminal matters, however, there was no evidence in the court records that female plaintiffs sought preferential treatment because of their sex, nor were there impassioned pleas from female defendants for mercy for the "gentler sex." For the most part, women took their chances, and their lumps, in the same manner as male participants in the system, and the court dealt with them on this basis. There was an exception, however, in the area of more severe punishment. Here, authorities did tend to treat women differently: there were no cases in which women were sentenced to whippings, and imprisonment and transportation were not applied to women with the same frequency as they were to men, although they were certainly employed against women who were perceived as extreme threats to the moral and social order.

What is most striking about the matters examined above is the degree of agency exhibited by women on the southern Avalon in their encounters with the formal justice system. This experience appears to diverge from that of women in many other British colonial jurisdictions. Rosen, for example, in her examination of the legal system in colonial New York, states: "Clearly the courtroom . . . was considered primarily a male, not a female, place."[122] Yet this image of exclusion does not come into such sharp focus on the southern Avalon. A closer comparison can be seen in the women of colonial Virginia, as described by Richter, who "knew how to use the county court system to protect their freedom, interests, and families."[123] Yet even Richter interprets women's presence in the system primarily in terms of *the extension of their roles as wives and mothers*—the "public use of household authority." They were not stepping outside the gender roles that had been assigned them by colonial Virginia society, she says, and thus were not perceived as a threat to the social order.[124]

Yet, as argued in the previous chapter, understandings of gender on the southern Avalon, particularly within the plebeian community, were still very much under negotiation in the period of early settlement. It is not likely that these women, or the communities in which they lived, saw their lives solely in terms of marriage and motherhood. Indeed, describing women's public actions only in terms of the extension of their roles as wives and mothers is surely a gender pitfall. Similar actions by men (be they court matters, petitioning, food riots, or other articulations of plebeian justice) are never seen purely in terms of *the extension of their roles as husbands and fathers.*[125] It is gendered reporting that pre-supposes that the public woman is an aberration—that some rationale for her public presence must be found rooted in the domestic sphere, that the reasons for her public acts are always different from those which motivate men, and that these reasons must always be selfless.

The evidence from the southern Avalon suggests that plebeian women often acted from self-interest and in pursuit of their individual rights, just as they also frequently acted (as did men) in the interests of their families—families for which they felt they had equal responsibilities. Moreover, the formal legal system, at least at the local level, was not hostile to their presence on these terms and exhibited a fair degree of flexibility in accommodating not just single and widowed women, but also those married women who presented themselves when the letter of the law refused to acknowledge them. This reception, too, seems to have been at variance with the experiences of women in many other British jurisdictions of the day.

NOTES

1. See, for example: Constance Backhouse, *Petticoats and Prejudice: Women and Law in Nineteenth-Century Canada* (Toronto: Osgoode Society, 1991); Carol Berkin and Leslie Horowitz, eds., *Women's Voices, Women's Lives: Documents in Early American History* (Boston: Northeastern University Press, 1998); Linda Cullum and Maeve Baird, "'A Woman's Lot': Women and Law in Newfoundland from Early Settlement to the Twentieth Century," in *Pursuing Equality: Historical Perspectives on Women in Newfoundland and Labrador,* ed. Linda Kealey, Social and Economic Papers, no. 20 (St. John's: ISER, 1993), 66–162; Karen Dubinsky, "'Maidenly Girls or Designing Women?': The Crime of Seduction in Turn-of-the Century Ontario," in *Gender Conflicts: New Essays in Women's History,* ed. Franca Iacovetta and Mariana Valverde (Toronto: University of Toronto Press, 1992), 27–66; Susan M. Edwards, *Female Sexuality and the Law: A Study of Constructs of Female Sexuality as They Inform Statute and Legal Procedure,* ed. C. M. Campbell and Paul Wiles (Oxford: Martin Robertson, 1981); Judith Fingard, *The Dark Side of Life in Victorian Halifax* (Porter's Lake, NS: Pottersfield Press, 1989); Deborah A. Rosen, "Mitigating Inequality: Women and Justice in Colonial New York," in *Women and Freedom in Early America,* ed. Larry D.

Eldridge (New York: New York University Press, 1997), 313–29; and Laurel Thatcher Ulrich, *Good Wives: Image and Reality in the Lives of Women in Northern New England, 1650–1750* (New York: Knopf, 1982).

2. Rosen uses the term "discretionary justice" to describe a diluted form of justice dispensed by authorities on an *ad hoc* basis to women who were essentially excluded from the formal, rights-based legal system in colonial New York. See Rosen, "Mitigating Inequality."

3. Writers such as Mary Anne Poutanen, Donald Fyson, and Karen Dubinsky have recently argued that women were far from being passive victims in their contacts with the formal legal system. However, their work still focuses on prostitutes and female victims of violence and sexual aggression. Even Fyson's more broadly ranging study finds that women most often appeared in court on assault matters, rarely appeared in matters involving service contracts or property, and were much more likely to be complainants than defendants overall. See: Poutanen, "Reflections of Montreal Prostitution in the Records of the Lower Courts, 1810–1842," in *Class, Gender, and the Law in Eighteenth- and Nineteenth-Century Quebec: Sources and Perspectives*, ed. Donald Fyson, Colin Coates, and Kathryn Harvey (Montreal: Montreal History Group, 1993), 99–125; Dubinsky, *Improper Advances: Rape and Heterosexual Conflict in Ontario, 1880–1929* (Chicago: Chicago University Press, 1993); and Fyson, "Criminal Justice, Civil Society, and the Local State: The Justices of the Peace in the District of Montreal, 1764–1830" (Ph.D. diss., Université de Montréal, 1995). Carol Berkin and Leslie Horowitz, by contrast, discuss a much wider-ranging participation involvement of women in the legal realm of colonial America. See Berkin and Horowitz, eds., *Women's Voices*.

4. Throughout the seventeenth century, formal justice on the island had been a makeshift affair, dispensed by fishing admirals, the captains of the first fishing vessels to reach every harbor at the start of the fishing season. This system, with a right to appeal decisions to the visiting naval commodore, was given legislative sanction by the *Newfoundland Act* of 1699. In 1729, in grudging acknowledgment of the over-wintering population, the naval governor at Newfoundland was permitted to appoint justices of the peace and surrogates to hear fishery disputes in the absence of fishing admirals and seasonal governors. As the century progressed, the legal regime in Newfoundland was expanded to include customs officers (1739) and courts of vice-admiralty (1736), *oyer and terminer* (1750), and common pleas (1789). However, challenges were raised as to the jurisdiction of these new courts vis-à-vis the jurisdiction of the fishing admirals that had been established by statute the previous century. To resolve the issue, a court of civil jurisdiction was introduced in 1791, and its jurisdiction was broadened to include criminal matters the following year (see the *Judicature Acts* of 1791 and 1792, or *31 Geo. III, Cap. 29, and 32 Geo. III, Cap. 46*, respectively). Renewed thereafter by annual legislation, the court, with expanded duties, was made permanent in 1809. (Web Link)

At the local level, justice was meted out most frequently by resident justices of the peace, who were empowered to take depositions, and hold petty and quarter sessions. (By 1792, defendants in criminal matters and civil matters involving amounts over £10 were entitled to jury trials.) These civil magistrates provided a year-round presence in the outports, hearing a wide variety of civil and criminal matters (often but not exclusively of a summary nature) and maintaining a customary legal regime, their decisions often tempered by local exigencies. Surrogate courts, in which naval officers (appointed as justices by the governor) were assisted by local magistrates, were convened once a year in the outports—usually in the autumn quarter session to coincide with the end of the fishing season. After 1791, local civilians (such as Robert Carter in Ferryland) also served as surrogates. As Christopher English points out (see below), the system was quite accessible to working people and provided "speedy . . . and inexpensive justice" outside the capital of St. John's.

The *Judicature Act* of 1824 (5 *Geo. IV, Cap.* 67) revamped the supreme court and provided for the incorporation of towns and the registration of title to real property. It also abolished the system of surrogate courts—a reflection of the demise of the migratory fishery and the establishment of a more permanent population. The island was divided into three districts, where circuit courts were held at least once a year to hear all matters of civil and criminal jurisdiction other than treason and felonies not within the benefit of clergy. Either a judge or assistant judge of the supreme court presided, assisted by local magistrates. Local justices of the peace continued to dispense summary justice in general and quarter sessions.

Recent scholarship provides two interpretations of this early development of law in Newfoundland. Christopher English argues that the justice system developed somewhat unevenly up to the early decades of the nineteenth century. Until the local population became more permanent after the Napoleonic Wars, state authority was rudimentary, and the legal system was limited by minimal local requirements. See: English, "The Development of the Newfoundland Legal System to 1815," *Acadiensis* 20, no. 1 (autumn 1990): 89–119; English and Christopher P. Curran, "A Cautious Beginning: The Court of Civil Jurisdiction, 1791," in *Silk Robes and Sou'westers: The Supreme Court, 1791–1991* (St. John's: Jesperson Press, 1991); English, "The Reception of Law in Ferryland District, Newfoundland, 1786–1812" (paper presented to a joint session of the Canadian Law and Society Association and the Canadian Historical Association, Brock University, 2 June 1996); and English, "From Fishing Schooner to Colony: The Legal Development of Newfoundland, 1791–1832," in *Law, Society, and the State: Essays in Modern Legal History*, ed. Louis A Knafla and Susan W. S. Bunnie (Toronto: University of Toronto Press, 1995), 73–98.

Jerry Bannister challenges the notion that the island's legal system was piecemeal and primitive in the eighteenth century, arguing that, despite limited institutions established under statutory law, a very effective judicial regime developed, with civil magistrates and naval authorities acting in cooperation as they drew upon statute law, prerogative writ, common law, and the *custom of the country*. This did not reflect Newfoundland's delayed development compared to other North American colonies, he says, but simply the evolution of a different type of legal regime that was well suited to the particular historical context. See Bannister, *The Rule of the Admirals: Law, Custom, and Naval Government in Newfoundland, 1699–1832* (Toronto: University of Toronto Press, with the Osgoode Society for Canadian Legal History, 2003).

5. Even after obtaining a local legislature, Newfoundland continued to adopt much of the legislation passed by the British parliament. Two notable areas of exception, however, were inheritance and divorce law, as Chapters 7 and 8 will discuss.

6. Krista Simon also describes the presence of women in civil and criminal matters in the court life of nearby Placentia in "A Case Study in the Reception of Law in Newfoundland: Assessing Women's Participation in the Courts of Placentia District, 1757–1823" (Honors diss., Memorial University of Newfoundland, 1999).

7. The local courtroom appeared to be very much communal space in the eighteenth and early nineteenth century, attended by people of both sexes and all ages. According to Lieutenant Chappell, who visited Ferryland around 1813, a day in court could sometimes assume almost a carnival atmosphere:

We arrived at Ferryland about ten o'clock in the forenoon, and were surprised to find all the people of the place in their best attire, as if it had been the day of the Sabbath. Men, women, and children, were flocking in a body towards a large edifice upon the side of a hill. Conjecturing this to be a place of worship, we ascended with the crowd, and entered the building pell-mell with them. Here we were astonished at seeing our worthy Captain [Donald Campbell] placed in a high-railed pew; by the side of a short squab man, in a green coat, with a pair of large spectacles upon his nose. On the Captain's left hand, ten or eleven decent-looking men were huddled together in a sort of pound, with scarcely sufficient room to turn themselves. A moment's observation convinced us, that we had entered the *Surrogate Court* of Justice; that the people in the pound were Jurors; and that the little man in green was the *Magistrate of Ferryland* [emphasis in original].

For the entire court proceedings that day, see Lieut. Edward Chappell, *Voyage of the Rosamond to Newfoundland and the Southern Coast of Labrador* (London: n.p., 1818), 224–28.

8. Occasional overlapping of cases occurs in the discussion that follows: for example, a case of a female landlord's collection of rent arrears will appear in the sub-sections on both debt and landlord-tenant matters.

9. Unless otherwise specified, all tables in this chapter have been assembled from the database described in Appendix B. In judging the significance of the number of cases discussed here, the reader should remember the incomplete state of the court records and the low population figures for the area, as noted in Appendix B.

10. See PANL: GN 5/2/C/3, 1835–47 journal: *Jane Austen v. William Harvey*, 6 November 1839; and *Jane Austen v. William Sheehan*, 22 October 1840. Also, GN 5/4/C/1, Ferryland, box 1: 79, *Jane Austin v. Edmund Keef*, 26 October 1835; 91, *Jane Austin v. —— McKay*, 31 October 1836; and 91 and 93, *Jane Austin v. W. Battcock*, 31 October 1836 and 16 January 1837. Also, GN 5/4/C/1, Ferryland, box 2: *Jane Austen v. Martin Conway*, 11 November 1841; *Jane Austen v. Cornelius Kelly, Jr.*, [November] 1844; and *Jane Austen v. John Payne*, 20 October 1845.

11. All these debt collection cases are cited from the St. John's court records in Mannion Name File, Ferryland, "Kenny, Margaret" (Mannion uses the modern spelling of her first name, but the form Margret appears consistently in the Ferryland

court records). Margret Kenney (or Keney) also had the dubious honor of being the only repeat debtor among the group. Margret was a rather colorful local character. She first appeared in the Ferryland court records in 1792, when she was successfully sued by William Young for £1.4.0. In 1794, she was also charged and convicted of selling liquor without a license, although this lack was rectified the following year when she was granted a liquor license for Ferryland district by local magistrate Robert Carter. In June of 1795, Margret was sued by Margret Duggan for nonpayment for unspecified services performed (most likely work in Kenny's house or tavern). Margret Kenny advised the court that she had already provided free room and board to the other woman for three or four months, having taken her into her house "thro Compassion," as Duggan had found herself in "a distressed situation." The two women "haveing caluminated each other, and proceeded to scolding," the exasperated magistrate dismissed the matter without costs and declared their claims against each other settled; he also ordered that they "behave peaceable in future on pain of being prosecuted according to Law, if any further Complaints." Later that year, Margret and her husband as well as several male servants were charged and convicted of theft and receiving stolen goods; Margret was fined while her husband was not only fined but sentenced to imprisonment and a whipping, a sentence that he mitigated by joining the Newfoundland Regiment. Whether this episode affected her capacity to continue holding her liquor license, or indeed whether she was issued the 1795 license after her husband had left for the Newfoundland Regiment, is not clear from the records. By the turn of the century, Margret had likely joined her husband in St. John's, where his regiment would have been headquartered, for her various debt collection efforts emanated from the St. John's court, and neither of their names appeared in the Pole Papers, 1799–1800. See PRL, 340.9 N45: 18, *William Young v. Margret Keney*, 3 December 1792, and *Rex v. Margret Keney*, 14 July 1794. See PANL, GN 2/1/A, vol. 13, 225–26, Carter to Governor Waldegrave, 20 October 1797, enclosing various accounts, including a list of liquor licenses that had been issued for 1795. And see PANL, GN 5/4/C/1, Ferryland, box 1: *Margret Duggan v. Margret Kenny*, 4 June 1795; *Arthur Hunt* [agent for Leigh and Co.] and *John Baker* [agent for Holdsworth's] *v. John Kenny, Margret Kenny, William Power, William Broadfoot, Timothy Fowler, Patrick Burne, and Richard Dunphy*, Thursday, 6 [8?] October 1795. See also further discussion below.

12. PANL, GN 5/4/C/1, Ferryland, box 1: 25–26 and 50–52, *Catherine Weston v. Hannah and William McDaniel*, 8 and 9 March and 5 October 1787; 3 and 5, *Catherine Weston v. John Kearney*, 17 August and 15 September 1790; and 3–5 and 8, *Catherine Weston v. William McDaniel*, 17 August, 15 September, and 15 October 1790.

13. PANL, GN 5/4/C/1, Ferryland, box 1: *Anne Sweetland v. John Whelan*, 8 June 1798; and *Ann Sweetland v. Patrick Harvey*, 7 August 1798.

14. PANL, GN 2/1/A: vol. 1, 357, Governor Drake, Order to Thomas Cloney, Ferryland, re: debt to Ludwigg estate, 26 September 1752; vol. 3, 331, Governor Palliser, Order re: *William Ludwick, for the estate of Mary Ludwick, v. James Keen*, 28 September 1765; vol. 4, 12, Palliser, Order in *William Ludwick, for the estate of Mary Ludwick, v. Richard Ball*, 4 September 1766, re: debt to Ludwick estate; and Order re: adjustment

of book debts in *William Ludwick for the estate of Mary Ludwick v. Richard Benger*, 4 September 1766.

15. PANL, GN 5/4/C/1, Ferryland, box 1: *Mary Bryan v. Adam McLarthy*, 14 November 1803; and *Mary Bryan v. Thomas Norris*, 14 November 1803.

16. PANL, GN 5/1/C/1, Ferryland, 59 and 61, *John Dollard v. John Neile (also Neale)*, 16 and 30 October 1818. Similarly, in 1820, Patrick Pritchett sued William Summers for 18s. for washing services provided by Pritchett's wife. See PANL, GN 5/1/C/1, Ferryland, 119, *Patrick Pritchett v. William Summers*, 30 October 1820.

17. PANL, GN 5/1/C/1, Ferryland, 24–26, *Samuel G. Carter and Co. v. William Coleman*, 19 January 1818.

18. PANL, GN 5/1/C/1, Ferryland, 26, *Samuel G. Carter v. John Power*, 19 January 1818. Similarly, the court permitted Robert and James Carter to retain monies they had collected from Jeffery Jass to pay a debt of £8.16.0 that had been incurred by Jass's wife, the former Jane Dullanty, before their actual marriage. PANL, GN 5/1/C/1, Ferryland, 27, *Jeffery Jass v. Robert and James Carter*, 21 January 1818.

19. PANL, GN 5/1/C/1, Ferryland, 124–5 and 162, *Hunt, Stabb, Preston and Co. v. the Estate of Thomas Beaves*, 6 November and 11 December 1820.

20. PANL, GN 5/4/C/1, St. Mary's, 47–48, *Frida Tobin v. Mary Bony*, 28 September 1818.

21. PANL, GN 5/4/C/1, St. Mary's, 52, *Catherine Lancrop v. John Doody*, Jr., 29 September 1818. Two other cases straddled two of the categories. Jane Costeloe brought her servant Bridget Whealon to court in 1795, for example, for desertion, having "Eloped from her service," thus failing to honor a verbal employment contract. Bridget countered with a defense of maltreatment, arguing that she had been forced to leave to avoid the constant beatings and scoldings administered by her mistress. See PRL, 340.9 N45, Ferryland, *Jane Costeloe v. Bridget Whealon*, 3 August 1795. And when Anstice Dwyer of Brigus South sued Cornelius Kelly, agent for George and Thomas Kough, in 1797 (see Chapter 4), the issues of outstanding wages and shipping arrangements converged.

22. This assumption, however, must be qualified. It is clear, for example, that Frida Tobin (see above) had been hired for the fishing season; thus, she might have been an actual fishing servant, although it was also common to take on extra domestic help during the fishing season. Furthermore, it should be noted that many domestic servants were also expected to help with making fish at the height of the season.

23. PRL, 340.9 N45, Ferryland, *Mary Whealon v. Margret Wallace*, 21 July 1795.

24. PANL, 5/4/C/1, Ferryland, box 1, 71, *Nancy Addis v. Mary Power*, 1 September 1835.

25. As noted earlier, some of the suits for "unspecified" small amounts included in the section above on debt collections may actually have been wage claims (see Table 6.2). Thus, the actual total number of wage claims for the period may be underrepresented in the current discussion.

26. PANL, GN 5/4/C/1, Ferryland, box 1, 28, *Catharine Delahunty v. Thomas Norris*, 15 November 1830.

27. PANL, GN 5/1/C/1, Ferryland, 62, *Margret Neile v. John and James Munn*, 2 November 1818.

28. Richter discusses a small number of indentured servants in colonial Virginia who sought protection from the court from masters who had violated the terms of their indentures. See Julie Richter, "The Free Women of Charles Parish, York County, Virginia, 1630–1740," in *Women and Freedom*, ed. Eldridge, 297–98.

29. Rosen observes some incidents of women's petitioning on behalf of daughters who were servants, but does not mention women's intervention in their sons' service contracts. See Rosen, "Mitigating Inequality," 322.

30. PANL, GN 5/4/C/1, Ferryland, box 1, *Michael Malone v. Hannah and John McDaniel*, 9 June 1797.

31. In 1836, Elizabeth Madden complained to the magistrates that Michael Curragan (or Corrigan) had refused to employ her son on the terms that had been agreed upon between the parties; the matter was settled out of court. See PANL, GN 5/4/C/1, Ferryland, box 1, 89, *Elizabeth Madden v. Michael Curragan*, 3 August 1836. In 1837, Jane Fitzpatrick requested that her son James be released from his apprenticeship agreement with Robert Pitt, because Pitt had not properly fulfilled his contract with her son; in this particular case, however, the magistrates deemed the matter to be beyond their jurisdiction. See PANL, GN 5/4/C/1, Ferryland, box 1, 93, *Jane Fitzpatrick v. Robert Pitt*, 9 January 1837.

32. See *Dwyer v. Kelly, Tobin v. Bony, Lancrop v. Doody, and Costeloe v. Whealon*, above. A further illustration comes from just outside the study area. When Jane Kelly of Placentia complained to Governor Campbell that her employer, John Cullin, with whom she had served for fourteen years at an agreed rate of £14 per annum, had turned her out without her wages, the governor instructed the local magistrates to enquire into the matter and "cause Cullin *to fulfill the Engagement which it may be proved he made with the Woman*, Or if it should be of so Extreme a nature as to require the Interference of the Governor, to provide for her till the Governor has an opportunity of deciding upon this matter" (italics added). See PANL, GN 2/1/A, vol. 10, 85–86, Campbell to Alexander Williams and John Brown, JPs, Placentia, 12 October 1784.

33. This section deals with female landlords as litigants only. The names of female landlords, however, also arose in the records in other matters in which they were not litigants, particularly estate matters. In a protracted dispute between John Nunan and the Carter family over the Richard Nason estate at Ferryland, for example, William Holly deposed in 1850 that his father, Michael, had rented property—a house, gardens, meadows, and fishing premises—from two landlords: the Nason estate and Mrs. Morry of Caplin Bay. See PANL, MG 247, Carter-Benger-Nason Papers, file 18, William Holly deposition, 13 August 1850. The property in dispute had, in fact, been inherited by Nunan from his aunt, Anstice Gorman, who had, in turn, inherited it from the late Richard Nason (see Chapter 7). Women landlords also appeared in merchant ledgers (see Appendix C, section 6).

34. While the family was represented in court by one of the sons (William), all Brazil's children were to share the proceeds of the rent equally. See PANL, GN

5/4/C/1, Ferryland, box 1, 25–26, *William Brazil [for the estate of Morris Brazil] v. Robert Sparke and George Yard*, 13 October 1792.

35. PANL, GN 5/4/C/1, Ferryland, box 1, 25–26, *Mary Kennedy v. William Tucker*, 13 October 1792.

36. PANL, GN 2/1/A, vol. 2, 121–22, Decree of Surrogate Edward Le Cras, 3 September 1754, confirming decision at a court of fishing admirals in Renews, 2 October 1752. The opposing claimant in the matter was Bazil Fielding of Mosquito Cove, Consumption (or Conception) Bay.

37. PANL, GN 2/1/A, vol. 4, 283–84, Order, Governor Byron, 29 October 1770.

38. PANL, GN 2/1/A, vol. 5, 133–37, Depositions before and Opinion of Jonathan Pitt, Admiral, and Nicholas Mudge, Rear Admiral, at Petty Harbour, 12 September 1772, as well as Order of Governor Shuldham, 18 September 1772.

39. PANL, GN 2/1/A, vol. 8, 97, Governor Richard Edwards to Robert Carter, JP, Ferryland, 22 October 1779.

40. It is likely that the property interests of a number of elite women were masked in the records by the names of male trustees.

41. As with female landlords, female tenants also surface in records on other matters in which they were not litigants. The will of Thomas Norris Sr., for example, left his son Thomas Jr. "a potato garden in Ferryland under lease to Catherine Dellahunty." See John Mannion Name File, Ferryland, "Norris, Thomas" (will probated 10–11 December 1840). The bondsmen for the administration of the estate of Robert Jordan in Brigus South offered as security a small piece of property being rented by the widow of Joseph Power (likely, Catherine Power) for 30s. per year. See Mannion Name File, Brigus South, "Jordan, Robert, Estate of" (administration 14 December 1829). In the lengthy dispute between John Nunan and the Carter family in relation to the estate of Richard Nason at Ferryland, several current and former women tenants on the disputed properties were mentioned in various depositions, including Margaret Aylward, who sublet her premises after moving to St. John's, and Kitty Bryan and her husband Timothy, who occupied a meadow for which the leasehold interest had originally been purchased by Kitty's mother, Ellen Sanders, from Michael Poor. See PANL, MG 247, Carter-Benger-Nason Papers, files 18, 22, 26, 28, and 29. Women tenants also appeared in merchant ledgers (see Appendix C, section 6).

42. PANL, GN 2/1/A, vol. 9 (reverse end), 26, Governor Edwards to Isaac Follet, JP, Trepassey, 10 October 1780.

43. PANL, GN 5/2/C/3, 1835–47 journal, *William Carter v. Catherine Dullenty*, 10 November 1837, 3 and 7 November 1838, 30 October and 8 November 1839, 31 October 1840, and 27 October and 1 November 1841. The same records appear in PANL, GN 5/2/C/8, 1835–42 journal. Various writs and summonses in relation to the matter appear in PANL, GN 5/2/C/4.

44. PANL: GN 5/2/C/3, 1835–47 journal, *William Strachan, by his Guardian J. W. Saunders, v. Mary Gaulway*, 28 October 1841; GN 5/2/C/8, 1835–42 journal, *William Strachan, by his Guardian J. W. Saunders, v. Mary Gaulway*, 28 October 1841; GN 5/2/C/4, *William Strachan, by his Guardian J. W. Saunders, v. Mary Gaulway*, Sum-

mons no. 21, issued 25 October for return 28 October 1841, and Writ no. 20, issued 2 November 1841, returnable "1st day of term."

45. PANL, GN 5/2/C/3, 1835–47 journal, *Regina v. John William Saunders Esquire for assault and Battery of one Mary Gulloway*, 6 October 1842.

46. See PANL, GN 2/1/A: vol. 10, 49–51, Petition of James Rows, Renews, to Governor Campbell, [14 August 1784], together with Affidavit of Robert Carter, JP, Ferryland, 14 August 1784; and vol. 19, 75, Governor Gower to William Carter, Surrogate at Ferryland, 1 October 1806. And see PRL, 340.9 N45, Ferryland, *Catharine Clements v. James Rouse*, 31 August 1785. In another case involving a woman's fishing property, Henry Brook successfully petitioned the governor on behalf of Betty Pottery of Sidmouth, Devon, to have William Simmonds cease building on a fishing room in Bay Bulls upon which she had already erected various fishing works. The governor ordered that Betty could continue to occupy the room provided she used it for the purposes of the fishery and could produce a fishing certificate for the men employed by her (as stipulated by the seventh and ninth articles of the *Newfoundland Act* of 1699). See PANL, GN 2/1/A, vol. 4, 109–10, Order, Governor Palliser, 1 September 1768.

47. PANL, PRL 340.9 N45, Ferryland, *Edmond Dunfey v. James Connoly*, 26 August 1784.

48. PRL, 340.9 N45, Trepassey–St. Mary's, *Mary Stokes v. Martin Doyle*, 20 April 1804.

49. PANL: GN 5/2/C/3, 80–81, *Mary Brien v. William Carter*, 10 November 1836; and GN 5/2/C/8, 1835–42 journal, 92, *Mary Brine v. William Carter*, 10 November 1836.

50. Two other cases involving women fell within this category. In 1817, Walter Vallis of Capeland (Caplin) Bay brought an action of trespass against Patrick Tobin for clearing and enclosing a piece of land that had allegedly been left to the Vallis family by John Bryan in compensation for board and nursing services from Vallis's wife. The matter was held over until further evidence was made available. See PANL, GN 5/1/C/6, Ferryland, 7, *Walter Vallis v. Patrick Tobin*, 17 October 1817. In St. Mary's, Mary McMahon sued John Quilty in 1833 for damages of £20 for trespass on her property, and she fenced off the disputed land while awaiting the decision of a court-appointed arbitrator on the matter. The arbitrator ultimately ordered that Mary accept the compensation that had already been offered by the defendant prior to the court case: a transfer of the ground upon which her house was built and an additional piece of land (measuring 57 yds. by 55 yds. by 35 yds. by 47 yds.) plus a right-of-way through Quilty's garden to a well. See PANL, GN 5/2/C/1, box 1, 317–18, *Mary McMahon v. John Quilty*, 8 October 1833. Case File 21

51. Matters involving sexual assault and wife-beating will receive greater attention in Chapter 8.

52. This contrasts with Donald Fyson's finding that women in the district of Montreal in a comparative period were much more likely to be complainants than defendants (by a proportion of 3, no. 1) in criminal matters, with an overwhelming majority of their complaints relating to violence against their persons. See Fyson, "Criminal Justice," and "The Biases of *Ancien Régime.* Justice: The People and the Justices of

the Peace in the District of Montreal, 1785–1839," in *Power, Place and Identity: Studies of Social and Legal Regulation in Quebec*, ed. Tamara Myers, Kate Boyer, Mary Anne Poutanen, and Steven Watt (Montreal: Montreal History Group, 1998). André Lachance discusses the low number of criminal charges laid against women in New France, attributing it to the conformity of women to domestic roles in the private sphere. See Lachance, "Women and Crime in Canada in the Early Eighteenth Century, 1712–1758," in *Crime and Criminal Justice in Europe and Canada*, ed. Louis A. Knafla (Waterloo: Wilfrid Laurier University Press, 1985).

53. These sentences were light compared with the harsher alternatives that courts had at their disposal. However, the financial hardship imposed by the fines was hardly insignificant, given wage levels and limited access to cash resources during the period, and thus their punitive effect was usually considerable.

54. See: David Taylor, *Crime, Policing and Punishment in England, 1750–1914* (New York: St. Martin's Press, 1998), chap. 8; and Terry Carlson, "Dealing with Offenders: An Historical Perspective on Corrections in Newfoundland," in *Ties That Bind: An Anthology of Social Work and Social Welfare*, ed. Gale Burford (St. John's: Jesperson, 1997), 91–125.

55. In 1788, in the wake of the Ferryland riot, the merchants and principal inhabitants of Ferryland petitioned the governor for permission to apply the fines levied against the rioters towards the building of a jail and courthouse in the community, and the governor acceded to the request. See PANL, GN 2/1/A: vol. 11, 388–9, Petition from the Merchants and Principal Inhabitants of Ferryland to Governor Elliot, [October 1788]; and vol. 11, 394–95, Elliot to Memorialists in Ferryland district, 9 October 1788. But by the 1830s and early 1840s, lock-up facilities in the district were still inadequate, according to numerous presentments from grand juries on the southern Avalon. See PANL: GN 5/2/C/1, box 1, 227–28, Ferryland presentment, 29 October 1830; and 323, Ferryland presentment, 21 October 1833 (also in GN 5/2/C/1, box 2); GN 5/2/C/3, 11–14, Ferryland presentment, 3 November 1835 (also in GN 5/2/C/8); 77, Ferryland presentment re: need for jail at Renews, 9 November 1836; also St. Mary's presentment 27 October 1837; Ferryland presentment, 7 November 1838; Ferryland presentment, 6 November 1839; and Ferryland presentment, 27 October 1840. And see PANL, GN 2/2: vol. 1, 86–90, Ferryland presentments, May 1826; and vol. 2, 226–32, Judge Augustus W. Desbarres to Governor Cochrane, enclosing Ferryland presentments, 18 June 1827.

56. PANL, GN 5/1/C/1, Ferryland, 60, *Margret Leary v. Edward Connolly*, 27 October 1818.

57. PANL, GN 5/1/C/1, Ferryland, 81, *Rex. v. Peter Winsor*, 16 May 1819.

58. See PANL: GN 5/4/C/1, Ferryland, box 2, *Regina v. William Mitchell*, 2 and 9 August 1841; GN 5/2/C/3, 1835–47 journal, *Regina v. William Mitchell*, 28 October 1841; GN 5/2/C/8, 1835–42 journal, *Regina v. William Mitchell*, 28 October 1841; and MG 920, Robert Carter Diary, 31 July 1841.

59. PANL, GN 5/4/C/1, St. Mary's, 101, *Ann St. Croix v. Elizabeth Feagan*, 9 April 1821.

60. Although *transportation* is the term used in the records, the offenders were actually deported to their home countries.

61. PANL, GN 2/1/A, vol. 1, 224 and 227, Complaint of Robert Rose, Trepassey, and Governor Drake's decree, 12 August 1751; italics added.

62. PANL, GN5/4/C/1, Ferryland, box 1, *Arthur Hunt* [agent for Leigh and Co.] and *John Baker* [agent for Holdsworth's] *v. John Kenny, Margret Kenny, William Power, William Broadfoot, Timothy Fowler, Patrick Burne, and Richard Dunphy,* Thursday, 6 [8?] October 1795.

63. PANL, GN 5/4/C/1, Ferryland, box 1, 17–30 September 1788.

64. PRL, 340.9 N45, Ferryland, 13–14, *Garret Dawson v. Thomas Quin et al.*, 14 October 1790.

65. In 1792, for example, Andrew Fling was convicted by local surrogate Robert Carter and local magistrates Peter Romney and Nicholas Brand of stealing a gallon of rum from the store of Messrs. Richard Tydel and Co. The rum's value was only 10d. Still, Fling was sentenced to twenty-four lashes on the bare back on the north side of the harbor, twenty-four on the south side, and twenty-four at the flag staff before the courthouse, then to be imprisoned until deported—a very harsh punishment for such a minor theft. See PRL, 340.9 N45, Ferryland, 17, *Rex v. Andrew Fling*, 3 December 1792. This same trio of justices ordered another whipping that same year for a personal affront to one of the magistrates. A local fisherman, John Dillon, was owed money from the estate of William Coman of Ferryland, but the money was stopped by magistrate Nicholas Brand. Dillon went to Brand "and abused him bid[d]ing him kiss his arse." Brand threatened to call for local constable Cox, but Dillon countered, "to the Divil I bob you and Cox too." He met Brand the next day and again insulted him, "telling him to the Divil I bob you." The local justices ordered that he receive thirty-nine lashes on the bare back at the flag staff before the courthouse, and then be imprisoned until deported to Ireland on a Vagrant's Warrant. See PRL, 340.9 N45, Ferryland, 16, *Rex v. John Dillon*, 14 November 1792. This was an unusually harsh sentence for such a minor assault; a similar affront to a member of the plebeian community would only have merited a small fine and a peace bond at most. Again, these justices from the local elite were likely trying to rein in the local Irish fishing population in the wake of the Ferryland riot.

66. PANL, GN 5/4/C/1, Ferryland, box 2: *Regina v. Bridget Hegarthy, and Mary Reed*, 16, 17, 18, and 21 February 1842; and *Regina v. Charles Hegarthy, Bridget Hegarthy, and Mary Reed*, 21 February 1842.

67. The sitting magistrates were Robert Carter, Peter Winser, John W. Saunders, and Matthew Morry.

68. PANL, GN 5/4/C/1, Ferryland, box 1, 48, *Regina v. Bridget Murphy*, 3 April 1833. There is no indication that Mary was charged in this matter for actually stealing the goods. She may have been a minor at the time, or it is possible that the charge against her was dropped in exchange for her evidence.

69. PANL, GN 5/4/C/1, Ferryland, box 2, *Estate of William Carter v. Patrick Costelloe and Bridget Hegarthy*, 25 November 1844.

70. PANL, GN 5/4/C/1, Ferryland, box 2, *Regina v. Bridget Dullanty*, 18 April 1844.

71. PANL, GN 5/1/C/1, Ferryland, 117, *Rex v. Ann Prichet*, 24 October 1820.

72. PANL: GN 5/2/C/3, 1835–47 journal, *Regina v. Anastatia Goff and Mary Daley*, 27 and 28 October 1837; and GN 5/2/C/8, 1835–42 journal, *Regina v. Anastatia Goff and Mary Daley*, 27 and 28 October 1837.

73. PANL: GN 5/2/C/3, 1835–47 journal, *Regina v. William Lush*, 27 and 28 October 1837; and GN 5/2/C/8, 1835–42 journal, *Regina v. William Lush*, 27 and 28 October 1837.

74. Mannion Name File, Bay Bulls, "Penny, Margaret."

75. PANL, GN 5/4/C/1, Ferryland, box 1, *Rex v. Mary Power*, 30 November 1804.

76. Writers on women in colonial America have also discussed the importance of women deponents as sources of information in colonial courts. In particular, they note that women were somewhat akin to expert witnesses in fornication and adultery trials; such matters, however, were not heard in Newfoundland courts. Midwives in colonial America also provided expert testimony in bastardy cases. While a number of bastardy cases did appear in the southern Avalon courts (see Chapter 8), there is no indication that midwives testified, although their fees for lying-in periods were allowed as legitimate expenses of the complainants. For a discussion of women witnesses in colonial America, see: Berkin and Horowitz, eds., *Women's Voices*, 161; Kathleen M. Brown, *Good Wives, Nasty Wenches, and Anxious Patriarchs: Gender, Race, and Power in Colonial Virginia* (Chapel Hill: University of North Carolina Press, 1994), 98; Richter, "Free Women," 290–91; Catherine M. Scholten, "'On the Importance of the Obstetrick Art': Changing Customs of Childbirth in America 1760–1825," in *Women's America: Refocusing the Past*, ed. Linda Kerber and Jane Sherron de Hart (New York: Oxford University Press, 1982), 54–55, 103; and Ulrich, *Good Wives*, 54–55. Paula M. Humfrey observes that in England, a large number of female servants acted as witnesses in the Court of Arches, the principal court of the ecclesiastical Province of Canterbury, particularly in matrimonial and testamentary suits. See Humfrey, "'I saw, through a large chink in the partition . . . ': What the servants knew," in *Women and History: Voices of Early Modern England*, ed. Valerie Frith (Toronto: Coach House Press, 1995), 51–80.

77. PANL, GN 5/2/C/1, box 1, 323–24, and GN 5/2/C/1, box 2, 29, *Rex v. Matthew Meany and Martin Curreen*, 21 October 1833. The record notes that, while Curreen appeared in person, Meany "appeared by his Wife Margaret Meany." Richter notes that wives sometimes represented their spouses in court in Virginia; but her examples deal only with civil (not criminal) matters, in which wives acted under power of attorney in the absence of their husbands, or in one case, because the wife had greater experience in civil litigation through the handling of a former husband's estate. See Richter, "Free Women," 304–5.

78. PANL, GN 5/1/C/1, Trepassey–St. Mary's, *Patrick Kelly v. John Flyn*, 16 June 1806.

79. PANL, GN 5/4/C/1, box 1, 28–33, —— *Hogan v. Patrick Shea*, 26–28 March 1787.

80. Humfrey notes that the ability of female servants "to manipulate what they knew and were willing to reveal about themselves and others was a real determinant of power in their lives." See Humfrey, "What the servants knew," 54.

81. PANL, GN 5/4/C/1, Ferryland, box 1, *Arthur Hunt and John Baker v. John Kenny, Margret Kenny, William Power, William Broadfoot, Timothy Fowler, Patrick Burne, and Richard Dunphy*, Thursday, 6 [8?] October 1795.

82. PANL, GN 5/4/C/1, box 2, *John Connell v. John Power*, 12 October 1848.

83. PANL, GN 5/2/C/1, box 1, 140, *Walter Shelly v. Michael Keanon*, 4 October 1827.

84. PRL, 340.9 N45, Trepassey–St. Mary's, 15, *Thomas Murphy v. James Warne*, 20 November 1793.

85. PRL, 340.9 N45, Ferryland, ——*Welsh v. Leigh and Co.*, 25 September 1786.

86. One exception was Elizabeth Feagan, who was called as a witness in a defamation case, *Elenor Piddle v. Margret Dinn*, at St. Mary's in 1821. According to the court records, Elizabeth "came forward as one of the Witnesses, prayed that an Oath may not be administerd, that she was on the eve, of being confind, but stated to the Court that she did hear Margret Dinn call the Plaintiff a Whore, etc.—co-oberating with the affidavit of Catharine Lannahan." See PANL, GN 5/4/C/1, St. Mary's, 103 and 107, *Elenor Piddle v. Margret Dinn*, 5 September 1821. It is possible that the court was reluctant to take her deposition because a woman on the eve of giving birth was perceived as not being *compos mentis*. Certainly, the imminence of labor did not deter her from giving an unsworn statement that corroborated the affidavit of another witness, so why the court did not avail itself of a sworn affidavit is puzzling. Still, the wording of the record seems to indicate that the reluctance was more on Elizabeth's part. Perhaps she was aware that the matter would be held over for later determination by the visiting surrogate and felt that she would be unable to attend at that time. Or perhaps she was merely happy to have an excuse not to involve herself in an official capacity in a dispute between her neighbors.

87. PANL, GN 5/4/C/1, St. Mary's, 72 and 83, *Jane Holehan v. Catherine Walsh*, 8 October and 26 November 1819.

88. Belief in hags and bibes was real on the southern Avalon. However, the term *witch* was infrequently invoked, and usually in reference to older (often eccentric) women who were thought to have special powers to charm, whether for good or evil (including women with special healing or ritual cursing abilities). The term did not carry with it the connotations of satanic worship and unmitigated evil ascribed to it by early modern Christianity, as was the case in colonial New England. It is quite likely, however, that the community may have believed that Jane had placed a curse on Catherine's cow, and that Jane had taken exception to this allegation.

89. By the late eighteenth century, local magistrates were spearheading and administering initiatives for relief, local improvements (defense works, jails, roads), and regulation changes (liquor licensing, vagrancy), as well as keeping the governor's office informed of the general state of peace and order in the district. When Newfoundland was granted representative government, magistrates were incorporated into the network of local administration and assumed key local positions as commissioners of roads, education, relief, wrecks, etc.

90. See Gail G. Campbell, "Disenfranchised but not Quiescent: Women Petitioners in New Brunswick in the Mid-Nineteenth Century," in *Separate Spheres: Women's*

Worlds in the Nineteenth-Century Maritimes, ed. Janet Guildford and Suzanne Morton (Fredericton: Acadiensis Press, 1994), 39–66.

91. Rosen, "Mitigating Inequality," 313–14 and 325.

92. PANL, MG 920, Robert Carter Diary, 10 April 1840. On 24 October 1840, he noted, "Delivered Geo Simms, Mary O Neile Grant to be registered & paid him 5/ Currency rec[d] from her for it." See also Mannion Name File, Fermeuse, "Neill, Mary."

93. PANL, MG 920, Robert Carter Diary, 15 September 1840.

94. PANL, GN 5/4/C/1, Ferryland, box 2, *Margaret Dunphy v. Nicholas Power*, 14 September 1846.

95. English, "Fishing Schooner," 84.

96. Rosen also discusses a high level of married women's petitioning in colonial New York; however, she generalizes from married women's experience to present petitioning as virtually the only recourse to justice for all women in her study area. See Rosen, "Mitigating Inequality." Intriguingly, Campbell finds, by contrast, that most married women petitioners in New Brunswick were involved only in petitions for law reform (specifically in relation to temperance); they rarely petitioned the legislature on personal concerns, unless they were widowed. See Campbell, "Disenfranchised but not Quiescent."

97. PANL: GN 5/4/C/1, Ferryland, box 1, 50–52, copy of Order, Campbell, 10 September 1784, with attached Petition from Hannah McDaniel, [September 1784?], entered in the Ferryland court records October, 1787; and GN 2/1/A, vol. 11, 245–47, copy of Order, Campbell, 10 September 1784, attached to Order, Governor Elliot, 5 October 1787. While the petition from Hannah's mother, Mary Shea, to Governor Montagu has not survived in the records, the grant from surrogate Captain James Howell Jones (conditional on the governor's approval), dated 15 September 1773, survives in PRL 340.9 N45 and in PANL, MG 31, Carter Family Papers, File 32.

98. PANL, GN 5/4/C/1, Ferryland, box 1, 25–26, *Catherine Weston v. Hannah and William McDaniel*, 8 and 9 March 1787.

99. PANL, GN 2/1/A, vol. 11, 245–47, Order, Elliot, 5 October 1787; italics added. A copy of the order also appears in PANL, GN 5/4/C/1, Ferryland, box 1, 50.

100. PANL, GN 5/4/C/1, Ferryland, box 1, 3, 4–5, and 8, *Catherine Weston v. William McDaniel*, 17 August, 15 September, and 15 October 1790.

101. PANL, MG 31, Carter Family Papers, file 32.

102. PANL, GN 5/4/C/1, Ferryland, box 1, Petition of Hannah McDaniel, alias Carney, [September/October 1791?], together with Decision of Chief Justice John Reeves, received 12 October 1791.

103. PANL, GN 5/4/C/1, Ferryland, box 1, *Michael Malone v. Hannah and John McDaniel*, 9 June 1797.

104. See numerous petitions throughout the period—especially the late 1820s and early 1830s—in PANL, GN 2/1/A and GN 2/2.

105. See PANL: GN 2/1/A, vol. 32, 424–26, Memorial of the distressed Inhabitants of Bay Bulls to Governor Charles Hamilton, 6 May 1822, and Hamilton to John L. McKie, JP, Bay Bulls, 8 May 1822; and GN 2/2, vol. 1, 81–85, Assistant Judge Desbarres

to Acting Chief Justice Edward B. Brenton, 29 November 1826, enclosing presentments from the grand juries of Ferryland (83–84) and Placentia (85).

106. See PANL, GN 2/1/A and GN 2/2.

107. PANL, GN 2/2, vol. 12, 213–17, Thomas Congdon to James Crowdy, local Colonial Secretary, 15 April 1833, enclosing Petition of certain Inhabitants of Fermews, to Governor Cochrane, 15 April 1833.

108. PANL, GN 2/2, vol. 12, 73–74, John McKie, JP, Bay Bulls, to Crowdy, 21 May 1833, enclosing Petition from Inhabitants of Bay Bulls [district] for Relief, 20 May 1833.

109. In 1825, there were only twenty-five mistresses in total in the harbor (see CO 194, Governor's Annual Return of the Fishery and Inhabitants); in the 1836 census, women fourteen years of age and over totaled 135; see *Newfoundland Population Returns*, 1836 (St. John's: s.n., 1836).

110. GN 2/1/A, vol. 39, 21, Crowdy to the Committee of Relief for Bay Bulls, 15 January 1833. Similar instructions were sent to Bay Bulls magistrate John McKie in 1822, and to merchant R. F. Sweetman respecting the distribution of relief in Placentia in 1833. See GN 2/1/A: vol. 32, 425–26, Governor Hamilton to McKie, 8 May 1822; vol. 39, 155, Crowdy to Sweetman, 14 November 1833; and vol. 39, 174–75, Crowdy to Sweetman, 26 November 1833.

111. Berkin notes that the principle of marital unity was also not universally or uniformly applied in the courts of colonial America, although some clung to the English laws that had been transported across the Atlantic. See Carol Berkin, *First Generations: Women in Colonial America* (New York: Hill and Wang, 1996), 155.

112. PANL, GN 5/2/C/1, box 1, *John Fowler v. Richard Shallow*, 12 October 1860. The outcome is not recorded in the Ferryland records, as the matter was moved to the supreme court in St. John's.

113. And there were gray areas, such as the 1830 complaint of breaking and entering and theft against Robert Fitzhenry by the Rossiter family. The record contains no formal style of cause that would easily identify the plaintiff, but usually in such cases, the injured party, not the Crown, appeared as plaintiff (the Crown only initiated actions in larger-scale larceny charges). But as the complaint stated that Fitzhenry broke into a locked room in "the dwelling house of John Rossiter" and stole two blankets therefrom, one would expect John Rossiter to be the complainant of record. However, the charge was not brought by John Rossiter, but by "the affidavits of Elizabeth and Mary Rossiter"—obviously related women, although the relationship is not explained. Additionally, all three Rossiters—John, Elizabeth, and Mary—were identified as "Prosecutors" in the record. See PANL, 5/4/C/1, Ferryland, box 1, 21, *Rossiter v. Robert Fitzhenry*, 3 August 1830.

114. PRL, 340.9 N45, Trepassey, *Michael Davenport Dutton v. Welch family*, 20 September 1800.

115. PANL, GN 5/2/C/1, box 1, 142–45, *Catharine Delahunty v. James H. Carter*, 4 October 1827. This case will be discussed in greater detail in Chapter 8.

116. See *Delahunty v. Norris*, above.

117. The latter was branded "illegitimate" in the parish records; see PANL, Church of England parish records, Petty Harbour parish, box 2, Ferryland District, 1820–60. See also *Fitzpatrick v. Norris*, above.

118. See *Madden v. Curragan*, above.

119. See *Malone v. McDaniel*, above. See, also, PANL, MG 205, Pole Papers, 1799–1800.

120. Rosen also notes the "common rhetoric" of poverty in women's petitions, although she argues that, especially in the case of widows, it was likely a "reflection of [their] societal reality." See Rosen, "Mitigating Inequality," 318.

121. PANL, GN 2/1/A, vol. 9 (reverse end), 27, Governor Edwards to John Dingle, JP, Bay Bulls, October 1780, enclosing a proclamation in response to the petition (the original petition and proclamation were not entered in the records but were referred to in the governor's covering letter).

122. Rosen, "Mitigating Inequality," 323. See also the literature cited at the beginning of this chapter.

123. Richter, "Free Women," 290.

124. Richter, "Free Women," 308–9 and 309, n. 2.

125. Indeed, the interpretation of men's actions in terms of familial roles, in combination with other motivating factors, is only beginning to appear in recent literature on masculinity.

7. "WHILST GRASS GROWS OR WATERS RUN"

Women and Testation Practices on the Southern Avalon

By the eighteenth century, British inheritance law and customary practice favored the male line of descent.[1] Women's property rights tacked a precarious course in English common law between the Scylla of primogeniture and the Charybdis of coverture. The system of primogeniture dictated that in a case of intestacy, the eldest son should inherit the father's real property, although in the absence of sons, daughters would inherit jointly in preference to male collateral kin. The widow held dower rights—a life interest only in one-third of her deceased husband's real property, with no right to alienate (for example, sell or mortgage) the property from the estate, which would ultimately revert to the legitimate heir(s). Among the aristocracy and upper middle class, however, a system of *tail male*—the entailing or settling of an estate on a succession of male heirs—was widely practiced from the seventeenth through the nineteenth centuries, despite the *rule against perpetuities*,[2] and further reduced women's access to real property. Furthermore, such property that women did hold came under the control of their husbands at marriage under the principle of marital unity, although they could recover in widowhood any freehold property that had been theirs before marriage and had not been disposed of (with their consent) by their husbands.

Previously, in the late medieval and early modern period, the common law had been tempered by equity, manorial law, and ecclesiastical law. Manorial law, for example, often favored partible inheritance among sons rather than primogeniture; it also made provision for *freebench*, which was a widow's right to a proportion (ranging from one-third to all) of her late husband's *copyhold* (land held at the will of the lord or according to manorial custom) for either the duration of her life or until her remarriage. Ecclesiastical law dealt with leasehold property and chattels (moveable goods or personal property) and advocated a form of community property in marriage and equitable distribution of parental wealth among children. Intestacy law was influenced by ecclesiastical principles, for instance, in its distribution of chattels: one-third to the widow and two-thirds to the children of the deceased, with equal distribution of a widow's goods to all children. Furthermore, ecclesiastical courts often reduced the land-inheriting heir's share of moveable goods in favor of the other children to effect a more equitable distribution of the overall estate. Meanwhile, equity had jurisdiction in all types of property matters, and it occasionally mitigated some of the harsher aspects of common law in specific circumstances. Equity also permitted the protection of women's property from the repercussions of coverture by a system of marriage settlements and trust agreements. These options, however, were generally pursued by the well-to-do only. Furthermore, women often did not participate in such arrangements and, in effect, forfeited control of their property to male relatives, at least until their widowhood.

The balance of power among these legal systems was shifting between 1300 and 1800, but with the increasing secularization and centralization of the state in the sixteenth and seventeenth centuries, the momentum turned in favor of common law. In a process "euphemistically called the 'rationalization' of the law," according to Amy Erickson, common and statutory law came to dominate other systems: equity was incorporated into common law, while ecclesiastical and manorial law were relegated to the status of *custom* only—something less than actual *law*.[3] By the eighteenth and nineteenth centuries, in a general climate of conservatism in relation to women's rights and status, a system of inheritance that already favored the line of male descent had become even more restrictive in terms of women's property rights and economic security.

Yet within England, the law was frequently tailored to local conditions and customs. For example, widows often inherited more real property than the law entitled them to, albeit usually with a life interest only. Certainly, they inherited a substantial amount of personal property and cash from both probated estates and intestacies. Women also acted as executors, guardians, and trustees, giving them some status in the disposition of family property. In addition, pre-mortem endowments were made to younger children, both male and female, through marriage settlements and deeds of gift. Among the aristocracy and middle class, primogeniture and tail male were generally favored; but within plebeian or working-class communities, daughters frequently inherited on a relatively equitable basis with sons, sometimes with *sole use* provisions to prevent the property from falling into the hands of sons-in-law. This *share and share alike* principle most often manifested itself in communities in which family members performed productive work together within household economies.

Similar adaptations of English inheritance law also took place in Newfoundland, as Trudi Johnson concludes in her examination of the impact of the local inheritance regime on matrimonial property law.[4] Johnson argues that the reception of male-centered English inheritance law was mitigated in Newfoundland by local circumstances and customary practices. While English laws in general were tempered by island conditions,[5] the application of property and inheritance law was particularly tenuous, given the uncertainty of the nature of property in Newfoundland until the nineteenth century—the result of a traditional fishing regime that had reserved large portions of land from private use for the benefit of the migratory ship fishery. Even lands designated for private use could not be held by freehold title. From the passage of the *Newfoundland Act* of 1699 throughout the eighteenth century, local merchants and residents increasingly occupied waterfront properties as the sedentary fishery became more established, and British authorities permitted uninterrupted possession provided that the properties were employed for the purposes of the fishery. But the formal recognition of private property did not really begin to evolve until the early nineteenth century (1810s to 1830s), when authorities gave in to the demands of an increasing and stabilizing population for greater certainty in land titles. However, while the definition of property remained uncertain until that time, this ambiguity did not translate into a casual attitude towards land among residents of Newfoundland. The location of the fishing room—its proximity to fishing grounds and sources of supply and trade, its physical suitability for erecting stages and flakes, its access to wood and water—was vital in the fishing economy.[6] Of equal importance was nearby land for houses and gardens to maintain the fishing household within a tenable distance of the fishing room. Fishing families in Newfoundland thus clung to their holdings tenaciously. As Johnson points out, the continuous possession of property was critical, for it provided "a measure of economic security in a society with precarious economic conditions. The land was valued, not as an indicator of wealth, but by its proximity to the sea, the very source of livelihood. The transfer of possession, therefore, was crucial."[7]

The importance of property to Newfoundland fishing families was reflected in the evolution of a system of usage and customary practices in which title by quiet possession and partible inheritance featured prominently and were recognized by the local community. Johnson notes that local inheritance practices were frequently guided by a concern for the future economic security of all members of the family. The principle of primogeniture was often tempered by concerns for the support and maintenance of widows and daughters, and a concern for more equitable distribution influenced testation practices. This did not mean that all beneficiaries inherited equally. Sons were far more likely to receive fishing premises and gear, with the expectation that they would care for widows and dependent siblings. Widows and daughters, however, would also receive some form of maintenance: often cash, livestock, or personal effects, but sometimes real property bequests that were usually protected from sons-in-law or any future husband of the widow by the establishment of life interests.[8]

On the southern Avalon, women appeared less frequently than men in estate matters recorded by the local courts and in governor's correspondence. Yet they were quite a conspicuous presence in the records, and evidence of their participation supports many of the conclusions drawn by Johnson.[9] Johnson notes that there were five principal means by which property was designated to family members: deed of gift, deed of conveyance, intestacy, wills, and marriage settlements. Irish Newfoundland women generally appeared only in the first four categories in the records from the southern Avalon, and various examples will be discussed below. Marriage settlements and trust agreements were the province of the well-to-do, and while there were several Irish Protestant merchant-planter interests on the southern Avalon in the eighteenth century, few of the women in these families ever came to Newfoundland. Several examples of such agreements involving stay-at-home daughters appear in the Carter-Benger-Nason Papers, but they involve properties in Ireland only and have therefore been omitted from this discussion. The women of the Benger family were exceptional, since they did reside in Ferryland in the eighteenth century (see Chapter 9), but details of their marriage settlements have not survived in public repositories.

WILLS, DEEDS OF GIFT, AND DEEDS OF CONVEYANCE

Because wills, deeds of gift, and deeds of conveyance were all methods by which property was bequeathed to family members, and were sometimes used in combination by testators in a system of pre-mortem and post-mortem endowments, they will be discussed together here. A combing of wills from the study period garnered the names of sixty-five women on the southern Avalon: ten testators and fifty-five legatees, of whom nine served in the capacity of executor (see Table 7.1). Thirty female beneficiaries inherited real property, sometimes in combination with cash and/or personal effects, while twenty-four female legatees received chattel interests only. The name of one other beneficiary surfaced in a court case, but the nature of the property she inherited was not specified in the record. Another twenty-three women appeared in deeds of gift and deeds of conveyance from the period. Of these, four were transferors, while the remaining nineteen were recipients of property. All but two of these transfers involved real property, sometimes in combination with moveable goods or personal property. Only two deeds marked arm's-length conveyances between non-related parties: one involving a female transferor, and the other, a female purchaser. The remaining twenty-one were testamentary transfers between family members, typical of customary inheritance practices of the period. Of the nineteen female transferees, seventeen received real property, sometimes in combination with personal effects, while the remaining two received personal property only.

Sons on the southern Avalon were favored in terms of receiving fishing premises, family homes, and other significant pieces of real property, while daughters generally received lesser properties (such as gardens and small meadows), cash, livestock, furniture, and personal effects. In his 1797 will, for example, William Gregory of Brigus South left all his real property, including house, fishing premises and boats, gardens, and meadows to his sons, John, Thomas, Simon, James, and Richard. His two daughters, Elenor Norris and Mary Holly, were already married, and their father doubtless expected that their husbands would provide their livelihoods. Still, he left them each £40 pounds and a gold ring.[10] In 1820, two Neill brothers, Michael and John, in Admiral's Cove (Fermeuse), executed virtually identical deeds of conveyance in which their respective sons were granted fishing rooms and plantations, while their daughters received only livestock (both daughters were named Bridget, and each received two cows and a horse from her father).[11] By his will in 1834, Michael Neill of Admiral's Cove (Fermeuse)[12] initially left the bulk of his £600 estate to his five sons. He gave his eldest, Constantine, the fishing room and plantation that he had inherited from his own father; and he gave his remaining four sons—John, Michael, Owen, and James—the house and fishing premises he currently occupied, with the proviso that they care for his "beloved wife Mary" so long as she remained unmarried. (These provisions for the sons were actually confirming transfers that had originally been designated by deeds of gift dated 16 April 1833; the deeds are referred to in the will, but they have not survived in the records, or perhaps were never entered.) His surviving daughters were to divide equally all their father's livestock—"horses, cows, heifers, calfs, Bulls, bullocks, pigs, sheep"—together with the hay and fodder currently housed with them. By a codicil dated the same day, however, he revoked the livestock bequest to his daughters and delegated the animals to the benefit of his wife and all unsupported children. He also stipulated that his wife have £100 immediately for her own use, and that his daughters each receive £100 upon marriage.[13] These testamentary documents all exemplified a clear-cut division of property along the lines of gender—real property to sons, other forms of property to widows and daughters—with an effort to provide some form of support to all family members.

However, women did inherit real property quite frequently; but when real property was bequeathed or transferred to a wife or daughter, it was often only for the woman's lifetime or, in the case of widows, until remarriage. This was essentially a means of keeping the property in the family and protecting it from the repercussions of coverture in the event of daughters' marriages or a widow's remarriage. It should be noted, however, that while testators sometimes stipulated that property remain within or revert to the male line of descent, they were more frequently content that property devolve to their daughters and their daughters' legitimate heirs, keeping it among lineal descendants of both sexes. Often, the *sole and separate use* formula was also employed in these documents to remove the property from the control of sons-in-law. A life interest was specifically created for women in seventeen of the thirty will bequests involving real property and in thirteen of the seventeen gifts/conveyances involving real property examined.

Edmund Dunphy of Brigus South, for example, transferred his house, furniture, personal effects, and four gardens to his wife and daughter, both named Mary, in equal shares, with the stipulation that after his wife's death, the entire property was to devolve to his daughter "in Trust only for the Heirs of her body lawfully begotten," with the further provision that "[in] default of such Heir the said premises will & shall revert to the next lawful heir."[14] Similarly, Matthew Ronan of Ferryland left his entire property, moveable and immoveable, including a house, gardens, meadows, cattle, and farming utensils, to his wife "for her sole benefit, use and interest," with the proviso that it descend from her to her grandson, Martin Cullaton.[15] Robert Carter Sr. of Ferryland transferred to his daughter Mary Sanders a life interest in a plantation in Ferryland, with the stipulation that the property devolve to her issue upon her death.[16] In this case, however, the restriction applied to both male and female beneficiaries, for, when Mary's son Robert Sanders, in turn, gifted his share of the property equally to all his children (three sons and two daughters) in 1818, he cited his grandfather's intention that the property should remain in the family, and stipulated that no child of his own could ever dispose of his or her interest in the property to outsiders.[17]

Similarly, the three deeds of gift by which Henry Coryear transferred his various properties in Cape Broyle harbor to his children in 1817 contained restrictive covenants for his son as well as his daughters: Elenor, Ann, and Sarah received his house, adjoining gardens and meadows, and household furniture, while Elizabeth and Mary received a plantation in Cape Broyle currently occupied by Patrick Kelly, with the provision that the properties were to devolve to "their Heirs lawfully begotten of their respective Bodies"; John received Henry's main fishing premises in Shores Cove, Cape Broyle, but also with the stipulation that the property should pass on to "his heirs Male lawfully begotten."[18]

Sons, then, were also often limited in their flexibility to dispose of real property through sale, mortgage, or future bequests outside the direct line of descent, as testators created *general tails* and tails male to maintain property, particularly fishing premises, as a means of livelihood for future generations of the family.[19]

Even when women were given only a life interest in real property, they were occasionally given some discretionary power in relation to its ultimate disposition. In a deed of gift executed on 10 October 1759, for example, John Bole of Ferryland transferred all his plantations, goods, chattels, and personal estate in Newfoundland to his brother Henry's widow, Elizabeth Bole (now Seale). She was to have a life interest only, and upon her death, the property was to devolve to her children by the late Henry—Mary and Elizabeth Bole—and then on to their children. If one of the daughters died before her mother, the survivor of the two was to inherit everything. John's intention was obviously to maintain the property among lineal descendants of the Bole family and protect it from any claims arising from future spouses of Elizabeth or her daughters. The deed contained a provision, however, that gave Elizabeth some say in the final distribution of the property, for John stipulated that the daughters would inherit only if they were "dutyful to their mother"; "if they should disoblige their mother," he declared, "then she is at liberty to leave the said estate and Plantations to whom she shall think proper."[20]

Similarly, in his 1833 will, Simon Nowlan of Bay Bulls left all his plantations, gardens, and meadows to his wife Elizabeth with the proviso that the property was not to leave the Nowlan family. Nonetheless, Simon left Elizabeth with some discretionary power to leave the property at her death "to one or as many of the family as she thinks proper (and as an endowment)," although the chosen heir was still "not to sell, set, mortgage, transfer or make over to any person or persons whatsoever, but to have it go successively in the family (of Nowlan)."[21] Another example was the 1848 will of Laurence Tobin, a planter at Witless Bay. Laurence left his fishing room and equipment to four of his sons, and the remainder of his property—land, houses, furniture, and cattle—to his wife, Eleanor, with the condition that she should leave her portion to two sons, Phillip and James, only if she felt they deserved it. "Should they or either of them transgress or do any thing contrary to the will of my wife so as it can be made appear," he declared, "I leave it invested in her my wife to give their or his part to any of my other sons she consider more deserving of it."[22] Still, most of these women were restricted to redistributing the estate property within the family.

On rare occasions, women legatees inherited real property with no strings attached. In a memorandum of gift in 1809, for example, Matthew Ronan gave a piece of land to his niece Elizabeth Collitan, "her Heirs, Executors, administrators and assigns . . . [for] their use and benefit from hence and for ever without any encumbrance or consideration whatever."[23] Similarly, in an 1815 deed of gift, Nicholas Bleake (also Bleacke) gave two-thirds of his land to his son Mickel and one-third to his daughter Catherine to hold absolutely and forever, "whilst Grass Grows or Waters Run."[24] This type of unconditional bequest of land to female legatees was unusual for wills in the area; but it was an uncommon form of bequest to male legatees as well, for testators frequently employed restrictive covenants respecting land, regardless of the sex of the beneficiaries.

Although sons (and often eldest sons) were generally favored in wills, it was not unusual for other family members to have been accommodated by previous arrangements such as deeds of gift or conveyance. This appears to have been how Robert Carter Sr. allotted his estate to his various offspring in the eighteenth century. As noted above, he transferred property to his daughter Mary, likely before her marriage to Daniel Saunders, and protected the gift from the repercussions of coverture. By his 1795 will, he left the bulk of his remaining estate to his eldest son, William, with an annuity to his wife and small bequests of personal property and cash (one guinea each) to his son Robert and daughters Ann Sweetland and Joan Tessier.[25] These small bequests to younger children from Carter's extensive estate suggest that they had already received their endowments by earlier deeds of gift or marriage settlements (Mary's absence in the will suggests that she may have died before her father). Pre-mortem endowments may also have been the method by which Laurence Tobin distributed his estate, for, while his widow and four of his sons received the bulk of the estate, the remaining four sons and five daughters received token amounts of cash: 1s. or 5s. Such was also probably the case with the estate of Thomas Norris Sr. In his 1840 will, Norris left his house, gardens, meadows, fishing premises, and four rental properties to his eldest son, Thomas Jr. His other three children—a son and two married daughters—received only 5s. each according to the will. While it is possible that these male testators had each fallen out with large portions of their families, it is far more likely that they had already made arrangements for their other children prior to executing their last testaments.[26]

Sometimes the widow and younger children were favored by a final will, the older heirs having already received their portions. In his 1856 will, for example, Matthew Morry Sr. of Caplin Bay left his second wife, Ann Carter Morry, a life interest in his extensive estate—including a house, furniture, cattle, book debts, fishing rooms and appurtenances, a *Western boat* and *coasting schooner*, and all his lands, plantations, and tenements. Her interest in the house, garden, furniture, and cattle were to devolve at her death to Morry's daughter by his first marriage, Priscilla, and her lawfully begotten children.[27] The testator had had several sons and daughters by his earlier marriage, but most likely he had already provided for them with pre-mortem transfers. It is also likely that previous arrangements had been made for the major items that would not pass from Ann to Priscilla by the will—fishing premises, boats, gear, book debts, plantations, and tenements—to revert to the older children, particularly the eldest son, Matthew Morry Jr.

However, eldest sons were not always favored in testation practices. For example, in his 1810 will, Robert Carter, Mariner (of the second generation of the family in Ferryland), stipulated that after payment of his debts, the remainder of his estate should be divided equally among his wife and three children: Robert, Elisabeth, and James.[28] Carter's son Robert also followed the principle of equitable distribution in the disposition of his estate. By his will, which was probated in 1853, he basically followed the intestacy law in bequeathing to his wife, Sarah, a life interest in his dwelling house, stables and garden, and in one-third of his plantations, fishing rooms, tenements, and other properties (unstated but implied was that two-thirds would be distributed among the children of the marriage). If she remarried, Sarah was still to receive a life interest in one-third of the bequeathed property. At her death, all her property held by virtue of the will was to revert to the estate and be distributed equally to all their children (sons and daughters). In the meantime, Sarah was to act as executor of the will and was also granted the power—in her widowhood only—to dispose of any of the property she held by the will, if such a transfer was necessary for her support. The latter was an exceptional provision in terms of women legatees with life interests.[29]

In his 1848 will, Edward Power of Brigus South also apportioned his significant estate quite equitably among his two sons and two daughters (his wife, Brigid Doyle, had clearly predeceased him, as he stipulated his desire to be buried next to her at Brigus).[30] Although his main fishing premises were left to his sons, the family home and other significant real properties were left to his daughters. Indeed, Power's will was such a model of the *share and share alike* principle that it is worth summarizing the main bequests here:

- To his sons, Joseph and Nicholas, during the term of their natural lives, the fishing room with stores, stages, flakes, cook rooms, to pass within the family forever. If the sons were ever to argue over the property, one-half was to be evaluated and sold to the other or to the next closest heir.
- To Joseph, during the term of his natural life, a house and garden with potato field as well as ground near Power's fishing room that he had bought from Charles Hutchings.
- To Nicholas, during the term of his natural life, a spot of ground on Power's old fishing room, 60 feet by 40 feet, for building a house, should he require it, as well as the cultivated ground at the back of the old fishing room and the land between the old room and the sea.
- To his daughters, Sarah and Ellen, during the terms of their natural lives, his dwelling house, furniture, goods, the small garden adjoining the house, the garden at the rear of the store adjoining Mark Grace's ground, and the

land and farm on *the Hill* held by an 1832 government grant, along with any buildings and farming utensils, with the proviso that if the daughters were to marry or decide to live apart, the property was to be divided equally between the two in accordance with the judgment of the two sons.

- To Sarah, during the term of her natural life, his fishing room known as *Lookout Room* in Brigus South.
- To Ellen, during the term of her natural life, his fishing room on Brigus Island known as *Webber's Room*.
- To his grandson Edward (son of the late Peter Power), his meadows and gardens currently let to James Doyle in Brigus at a rent of 30s. per annum; Joseph to act as trustee.
- Land occupied by Martin Leary to be divided equally between his two sons and two daughters.
- To Joseph, one cow.
- To Nicholas, one cow and his horse named Star.
- To Nicholas and Joseph, the remainder of all cattle and horses.
- To Ellen and Sarah, all farm produce to be shared equally.
- The land never to be sold or mortgaged out of the family.
- Any disagreements to be referred to Robert Carter, justice of the peace, Ferryland.

In addition to the equitable distribution of the real and moveable property among his children, the other striking feature of Power's will is the life interest created for all children, regardless of sex, in the land bequeathed. Every gift of real property contained the restriction that the bequest was for the natural life of the legatee only. And in devising the main fishing premises to his sons, Power took extra precautions, stipulating that after their deaths, the property was "to descend to their children and their children's children in succession for Ever." If disagreements arose between the sons over the property or any part thereof, it was not to be sold to strangers but "delivered up to one or other of my Descendants at such a valuation as two disinterested and respectable Persons may set thereon." The right of first refusal was to be given "to the senior in possession and upon his refusal to take it then to the next senior and so, on through the several of my descendants alive in rotation untill some of them accept the offer." As a final precaution, he added a clause at the end of the will providing that no land was to be disposed of in any way outside the family, but was to devolve to his lineal heirs, male or female:

> *I further Will and Declare*, and all the Gifts and bequests aforenamed are made upon *this express and positive Condition*, that is to say, That no part or parcel of the above named landed Property shall ever be mortgaged, sold, or in any way whatever dis-

> posed of or made away with, but be and remain the Property of my descendants in rotation, so long as any of them shall survive, or be alive, and when any of the above named Parties shall die, His Heirs, and their respective proportion shall become and be the property of the next akin alive and among those equally near, to be justly and equitably divided among the Heirs of my descendants for Ever.

Although the rule against perpetuities acted as a legal bar to Edward's vesting property interests into the remote future, his wishes were respected by family members through the years, and much of his property at Brigus South continued to be held by his direct descendants in the late twentieth century.

When a male testator had no sons, he generally left his property to his widow (if she had survived him) and daughters rather than to a more distantly related male heir. Peter Weston of Ferryland, for example, made his wife, Catherine, and two daughters, Catherine and Sarah, co-heiresses of his extensive estate—including several houses, fields, gardens, stores, wharfs, fishing rooms, stages, and flakes in Ferryland harbor—leaving a nephew, William Ludwig, only 1s. Stg.[31] William Murray of Ferryland similarly divided his estate between his wife and daughter, except for one piece of ground that was left to the parish priest in payment for masses for the souls of himself and his former wife; his current wife, Mary, received a £15 annuity from a rental property, while his daughter, Mary Barron, received the remainder of his £50 estate, including property, furniture, and personal effects.[32] And the will of John Jenkins of Renews divided his entire estate between his five daughters, with the share of one daughter who had predeceased him being devised to her surviving heirs.[33]

Occasionally, special bequests were made to other female relatives. For example, John Gregory, formerly of Brigus South and then of Ferryland, left the sum of £4 to his sister Mary Holly for attending him in his final illness.[34] Robert Carter's 1810 will (see above) stipulated that his mother-in-law, Mrs. Howe, receive £400 pounds from his estate in repayment of sums of money loaned to him over time.

Women on the southern Avalon, then, were a substantial presence as beneficiaries in testamentary documents of the study period.

WOMEN'S WILLS AND DEEDS OF GIFT OR CONVEYANCE

While women were much more likely to be the recipients of property than testators and transferors, a small number of them executed testamentary documents during this period. As noted above, evidence of ten women's wills and four women's deeds of gift or conveyance exists in the records examined. And although women beneficiaries came from both the English and the Irish populations on the southern Avalon, with English women predominating, women testators and transferors came predominantly from the Irish community: eight of the ten testators and three of the four transferors were Irish or Irish Newfoundland women.

One of the two English-Newfoundland female testators in the area was a widow, Mary Keen (or Kean), and by the time she began disposing of her property in the 1790s, her descendants had already begun to marry into the Irish community.[35] Two wills purportedly executed by the widow Keen (on 16 February 1795 and 9 February 1798, respectively) surfaced in an 1817–18 court case in St. John's in which her granddaughter's husband, Thomas Meagher, was being sued by his creditors Hunters and Company for an outstanding debt of £551.1.6. The plaintiff was hoping to attach a fishing plantation at Ferryland that Meagher had mortgaged to the company as security for his original debt of £800.4.2. The plantation had initially been Mary Keen's, but Meagher had gained possession of the property through his marriage to Mary's granddaughter, Joan Ryan. Nonetheless, Meagher hoped to cast some doubt on his right to have mortgaged the premises by the production of the two purported wills. The 1795 will devised Mary's fishing plantation at Ferryland jointly to her bachelor son, James, and her granddaughter, Joan Ryan, with the proviso that the entire property devolve to Joan upon James's death. The 1798 document was purportedly executed in anticipation of Joan's marriage to Thomas Meagher, and stipulated that if the marriage took place, the property was to go to Thomas, his children, and their successors forever, provided that Thomas and his family live with Mary and that he act in concert with her for the general good of the property. Neither will was probated, although the St. John's court noted that both were entered in the surrogate court records for Ferryland (the Ferryland entries have not survived).

The court's attention in 1817–18 focused on the second will and its creation of an interest for the Meagher children, for if it was legitimate, it would have acted as a bar to the mortgage and an obstacle to Hunters's right to attach and sell the property. Ultimately, the second will was deemed a fraud upon presentation of proof that one of the witnesses' signatures was not legitimate. It appears, however, that Mary Keen did write at least one, and possibly two, testamentary documents, even though the second was not validly witnessed.[36]

Two other female testators appearing in the records were actually women who lived in Ireland. One of these women, Elizabeth Ludwigg (or Ludwick) of Waterford, was the widow of William Ludwigg, son of John and Mary Ludwigg and scion of a wealthy Irish Protestant merchant-planter family with extensive holdings in Ferryland in the eighteenth century. Although William lived at times in Ferryland, it is likely that Elizabeth never joined him there, choosing instead a life of genteel domesticity in the home country. Most of the Ludwigg properties on the southern Avalon were disposed of in the eighteenth century, but at least one remained in the family, for at Elizabeth's death in 1800, she left a fishing room, stage, and flake at Ferryland to William Coman, a merchant from Waterford City operating on the southern Avalon.[37]

Another Irish testator also held property in Ferryland through her ties to an eighteenth-century Irish Protestant merchant-planter in the study area. Anstice Gorman of Youghal, County Cork, was a servant to the family of Richard Nason and Dorcas Benger Nason, and had an illegitimate child, Thomas, by Richard. Both the Nason and the Benger families had extensive holdings on the southern Avalon, particularly in Ferryland, and although most members of the families had returned to Youghal or removed to America by the nineteenth century, they maintained many of the southern Avalon holdings as rental properties. In his 1818 will, Richard noted that his children had already been provided for by various marriage settlements and deeds of family agreements, which the will confirmed. His wife, Dorcas, had predeceased him. The remainder of his estate, including his dwelling house and garden as well as the title, rents, and rent arrears in relation to several properties in Cork and his extensive holdings in Ferryland, he left to his "faithful servant," Anstice Gorman, and their son, Thomas. Furthermore, Anstice was named executor of his will, and Richard stipulated that if any of his legitimate children disputed the will's contents, they were to be cut off with only 1s., regardless of any prior arrangements made on their behalf.[38] Thus Anstice and Thomas became substantial landlords in Ferryland. Thomas died in 1826, and Anstice herself died on 5 March 1828. By her will, executed the month before she died, she left all the property of any nature that had been bequeathed to her by Richard Nason, including her Ferryland property, to her nephew John Nunan.[39]

All other female testators/transferors in this category were Irish Newfoundland women. Johnson notes that women's testation practices in Newfoundland, like men's, followed the customary practice of partible inheritance. Unlike male testators, however, they showed a greater concern with the distribution of personal property.[40] These trends were certainly reflected in the 1815 will of Hester Brothers of Fermeuse, in which she carefully apportioned all her real and personal property to her nieces and nephews, a task that was complicated by the fact that the names of the testator and three beneficiaries were the same:

> Know all men by these presents that this my last dying will [and Testament - obliterated in original] is to leave Half my House and Gardens to John Brothers son William and the other half to his Daughter Hester Brothers and likewise Hester Brothers is to

> have my Bed and she is to have my ring and one Silver spoon, Michael Brothers daughter Hester is to have one Silver spoon and half dozen plates and one Candlestick, James Brothers Daughter Hester is to have one Silver spoon and one half dozen plates, and one Candlestick, James Brothers is to have one Table and —— [unreadable] Desk, the said William Brothers or Hester Brothers is not to demand the House or Gardens while their Father lives.[41]

But most of the remaining women's wills and deeds examined were simple, single-heir dispositions. In 1804, Mary Whealan bequeathed one-half of the property that had been left to her by her husband to her son, John Magil, as well as the use of the other half until it was required by its proprietor, Bridget Whealan.[42] Similarly, Mary Berrigan, a widow at Renews, left to her grandson William Berrigan her right to her dwelling house, fishing room, and garden by a will executed in 1826.[43] Often, widows made these dispositions to children or grandchildren in exchange for support in their old age.[44] This was likely the purpose of the two previous examples, and it was certainly the stated intent of the following family transfers. In 1816, Elizabeth Foran of Ferryland granted to her son Patrick Foran her title to her house, meadows, and gardens, as well as a rental property in Ferryland "for his present attention to me, in contributing to my support and maintenance and my expectation of his like attention to me in the future."[45] Similarly, in 1831, Margaret Aylward of Admiral's Cove (Fermeuse), a widow who had been living with her son John for the last fourteen years of her life, repaid his family for their support in her old age by leaving all her property—a house, potato garden, and furniture worth in total about £10—to John's son, also named John.[46]

Only one female testator/transferor created a life interest with her gift. In 1817, Mary Whealan granted property on the north side of Ferryland currently occupied by her son John McGill to her granddaughter Mary McGill to hold during her natural lifetime and then to pass on to her granddaughter's lawfully begotten heirs.[47] Whether this deed was intended to override Mary's 1804 will favoring John (see above) or was related only to a portion of her property is difficult to determine.

In one other instance, a widow who had remarried executed a deed of gift to transfer property held from her previous marriage to the children of that marriage in order to protect their inheritance from the repercussions of coverture. In 1814, Mary Neill Dalton (also Daulton), the widow of Constantine Neill of Fermeuse then married to James Dalton, transferred to her two oldest sons, Owen and Constantine Neill, her house, meadows and gardens, boats, nets, and seines equally, with the provision that "they are not to put the four youngest out of the House until they are able to do for themselves."[48] Although the deed was executed after her second marriage, there was no indication in the records that its effectiveness was ever challenged by the recording magistrates or her second husband.

Evidence of the remaining two women testators exists only through allusions in court cases. The will of Mary Shea of Ferryland did not survive in the records, but it was referred to in the dispute that arose between her daughter, Hannah McDaniel, and Catherine Weston in the late eighteenth century (see Chapter 6). This reference indicates that she possessed at least one fishing room at the time of her death, which had been granted to her by Governor Montagu, and that she had left the room to her daughter Hannah, presumably by a will that was probated, as her "executors," Hannah and William McDaniel, sold the property to William Carter in 1795. In addition, a fragmentary reference to the will of Catherine Carroll of Witless Bay parish, dated 25 August 1843, appears in the records of her parish priest, Reverend Cleary, to whom she left £2 to offer up masses for her soul.[49]

GENDER, ETHNICITY, CLASS, AND TESTATION PRACTICES

The fairly equitable inheritance practices in the area were still tempered by gender difference. Among legatees, the disparity appeared in the nature of property inherited. Although estates were often distributed among male and female heirs on a fairly equitable footing, male heirs still tended to be favored with bequests of major fishing premises, with widows and daughters, by contrast, inheriting properties that were of less importance in the fishing economy. Among testators, the most obvious gender difference manifested itself in sheer numbers. Overwhelmingly, the testators or transferors in the documents encountered were men, reflecting an inheritance regime that—while flexible within the local context—still favored male ownership (or possession) of property. Another obvious gender difference was in the marital status of the testators: while male testators were single, married, and widowed, most women's testamentary documents, at least those that have survived, were written by widows.[50] Most of these were disposing of relatively small estates, often in exchange for support in their old age, and they tended to be less preoccupied with maintaining properties in the patriline, although this may simply have been a reflection of the lesser significance of the properties they were transferring.

In terms of ethnicity, the provision for the saying of masses for the souls of testators and family members seems an obvious difference between English

Protestant and Irish Catholic testamentary documents. Yet it was not a preoccupation of Irish testators on the southern Avalon, and only three examples appear in the records examined.[51] This may have reflected a lack of disposable cash for such purposes, or it may be further evidence of the less rigid hold of formal Catholicism on the population during most of the period.

Both English and Irish testators in the area shared a preference for fairly equitable testation practices, with accommodation being made for all family members, albeit with a favoring of sons in terms of primary fishing premises. While this was a deviation for the English population (particularly the middle-class English), who had come from a legal tradition of primogeniture and impartible inheritance, it was less a departure for the Irish population, for whom communal property and partible inheritance had been long-standing customary practices. This suggests a possible addendum to Johnson's thesis: that an extensive Irish influence on the island may have been part of the blend of local circumstances that tempered the reception of English inheritance law in Newfoundland.

Aside from a variance in inheritance traditions, the most discernible ethnic difference in testation practices on the southern Avalon appeared in the status of women in testamentary documents. By far, English and English-Newfoundland women predominated as legatees in written documents, while Irish or Irish Newfoundland women predominated as the authors of wills (all but two) and deeds of gift or conveyance (all but one). Although there are insufficient surviving records to draw firm conclusions, it is possible that English women, who hailed mostly from the old planter society and a rising middle class that had extensive estates to manage, were less likely to write testamentary documents because the disposal of their property had already been laid out in trust agreements, marriage settlements, and the restrictive clauses and life interests of wills and family transfer agreements written by men. Still, most would have had property in their widowhood; but a number of these women retired in their widowhood to England or St. John's, and any testamentary documents written by them thereafter do not appear in the southern Avalon records.[52]

Overall, English families did figure more prominently in the testamentary documents examined in terms of the size of their estates. But there were some substantial Irish estates involved as well—not only the interests of eighteenth-century Irish Protestant merchant-planter families (such as the Ludwiggs, Nasons, andBengers) and substantial Irish Catholic planter families (such as the Neills), but also the interests of families that had begun in fishing service or small-scale family enterprises and accumulated considerable property after coming to the area (such as the Murrays, Powers, and Tobins). Indeed, the Irish plebeian community was respectably represented among the wills and deeds of gift or conveyance during the period and demonstrated the same concern to provide equitably for family members. However, they were proportionately under-represented in the documents examined, which is perhaps to some extent a reflection of the relative literacy levels of the two groups. Of course, it is quite possible that some of the local Irish executed wills and deeds that were never recorded in the court records, but whose families abided by their testamentary wishes nonetheless. The majority of Irish plebeian estates during the period, however, would have been left intestate.

INTESTACIES

At least forty-one women's names appeared in court records in relation to intestate estates on the southern Avalon (see Table 7.2). Of these, thirty-four were potential beneficiaries: thirteen (nine widows, one mother, one mother-in-law, two of unspecified relationship) petitioned to be appointed estate administrators by the court; another twenty-one women were recorded solely as beneficiaries of the estates in question, as widows, daughters, sisters, and cousins of the deceased. All but three of the thirty-four were from the Irish community. The administration of seven women's estates (two valued at £10, one each at £20, £40, £50, and £100, and one of unspecified value) were also included in the records of the period. All but one—Catherine Jackman of Renews, with an estate valued at £10—were Irish Newfoundland women. Inventories of the estates were not available in all the records of the above matters, but of those that were recorded, the estate administration always included the distribution of real property, often in combination with goods and personal effects.

As noted earlier, the English law of intestacy stipulated that in relation to chattel interests and personal property, the surviving spouse inherited one-third of the estate, and the legitimate children of the deceased inherited the remaining two-thirds. If no spouse or children survived the decedent, the estate devolved to the next of kin. This rather straightforward formula for distribution was complicated in Newfoundland by the treatment of real property as chattels real in the case of intestacies.[53] Because of the tentative definition of real property that was rooted in the traditional privileging of the migratory ship fishery, the applicability of English inheritance laws to Newfoundland was open to interpretation well into the nineteenth century. Often, local courts treated an interest in the land as chattels real in the case of intestacies, favoring a division of one-third to the widow and the remaining two-thirds among the children (or equal division among children if there was no surviving widow) over the English principle of primogeniture.

Indeed, this interpretation was made law by the fledgling Newfoundland legislature in 1834 with the passage of the *Chattels Real Act (4 Wm. IV, Cap. 18)*. Declaring that primogeniture and impartible inheritance were inappropriate for Newfoundland circumstances, the act provided that real property in intestate estates should be distributed, like personal property, as chattel interests. Debates leading up to the passage of the legislation indicated that the spirit and intent of the legislation was to accommodate the more inclusive inheritance regime that had developed through local practice. Nonetheless, colonial courts continued for years to be entangled in interpreting the Act alternately as declaratory—merely confirming a situation that had long existed by custom and usage—or as new law that had not applied to intestacies prior to 1834.[54]

Even before the passage of the *Chattels Real Act*, however, southern Avalon courts had tended to favor the distribution of real property in intestate estates as chattels real. One such case occurred in 1792, when Mary Kennedy sued her brother, William Tucker, over the distribution of the rent from property of their late father, who had died intestate roughly six years previously. William had taken over the property, which had earned a rent of £11 per year for five years, then £8 the following year. William had originally paid Mary £4 from the yearly rent, as the "intended bequest" of his father, but when the rent had dropped to £8, he had declared himself his father's sole heir and paid his sister nothing. The court declared that "Lands & Plantations, in Newfoundland, are nothing more than Chattel Interests, and should, in case of Intestacy, be distributed as such." William and Mary were therefore to share the proceeds equally (presumably there was no surviving widow), and William was ordered to reimburse his sister half the previous year's rent (£4)—a sum that was to be withheld from William's wages with Matthew Morry—plus, over time, an additional £7.10.0 to make up the deficiency in her share of the rent from the previous five years. Further, the court advised Mary that she did not have to honor the rental arrangement entered into by her brother and could take possession of half the plantation herself if she so desired. Case File 30 This case, involving an Irish Newfoundland woman on the southern Avalon, would prove to be a landmark case in the evolution of Newfoundland law on the treatment of interest in real property as chattel interest in the case of intestacies.[55]

The local courts upheld this principle in various cases, including those involving widows and the attachment of real property for debt. In the late 1810s, for example, Hunt, Stabb, Preston, an English mercantile firm operating out of Renews and struggling to keep its head above water in the post-war depression, learned to their chagrin (and considerable financial disadvantage) that their interpretation of the law of property and inheritance from the home country was not always shared by the magistrates in Ferryland. In a collection action against the estate of Catherine Jackman, for instance, they found themselves stymied by the court's application of the law of intestacy regarding real property they were hoping to attach. In 1813, Catherine had entered into a mortgage with the firm, offering her house, outhouses, and two head of cattle as security for a debt of £143.15.8, to be repaid at £20 per year until fully paid. Several years later, Catharine died, and the firm tried to foreclose on the mortgage, claiming that the debt had now risen to £160. Catharine's children (two sons) intervened, arguing that their father had died intestate in 1807, and as the debt had been contracted by their mother since that time, the mortgagees had the right to attach only the widow's third of the intestate estate. Hunt, Stabb, Preston contended that the father, Arthur Jackman, had died insolvent, and a large portion of the current debt to the firm had been incurred by him; thus, his entire estate should be responsible for that debt. But the sons argued that only their mother's debt had been secured by the mortgage and that only her share of the property had been encumbered. The court agreed with the sons and ruled that only the widow's third could be disposed of for the benefit of her creditors.[56] Case File 31

The same firm was frustrated again by the court's interpretation of the law of inheritance and coverture in their effort to collect a £50 balance on the account of William Brandy, a dealer with their house who had drowned in June of 1818. The firm invoked the principle of coverture and tried to take possession of a house and garden that, they claimed, Brandy had owned by virtue of his marriage to the widow of John Doyle. The twice-widowed Mrs. Brandy objected to their claim, arguing that her previous husband had died intestate, leaving a daughter, and that this daughter now had the full right to her father's property as his only heir. The court, however, disagreed with both interpretations. Invoking the law of intestacy, it ordered that Doyle's real property should have been distributed as a chattel interest: one-third to his widow and two-thirds to his child. The second husband, Brandy, had therefore been entitled to only one-third of the property by virtue of his marriage to the widow Doyle, and Hunt, Stabb, Preston could only attach this portion to pay his debt.[57] Case File 32

Of course, the vast majority of intestate estates, which involved most of the Irish plebeian community, would not have been processed by the courts. The chattels portion of most would have been low in monetary value; and although many estates would also have included dwellings, gardens, and fishing premises, the distribution was effected in accordance with previously expressed wishes of the deceased and/or customary practices, and was acknowledged by family members and the local community. It is likely that these unrecorded divisions followed the *share and share alike* principle that was reflected in written wills—widows assuming possession of homes and gardens for the remainder of their lives, sons taking over fishing premises and often family homes on the understanding that widows and dependent siblings be cared for, and remaining personal property and real properties of lesser value being distributed among the remaining children. Certainly, this method of partible inheritance was familiar to the Irish community and was likely transported from the old country to the new, where it was reinforced by local circumstances. In particular, given the large numbers of male fishing servants—usually non-inheriting sons in Ireland—who married into local families in the period of early settlement, it is likely that parents made special efforts to ensure that Irish Newfoundland daughters and their families would have the wherewithal to support themselves. Apportioning a piece of family property for a daughter and her new husband, for example, was a form of pre-mortem endowment, whether it was accomplished by formal deed or not. In addition, the significant role of women in economic production and their overall status also likely reinforced a tendency towards partible inheritance. By contrast, in Ireland, a move to impartible inheritance coincided with the decline in women's economic and social status, particularly from the mid-nineteenth century onwards.

CONCLUSION

As inheritance law evolved at the local level, the legal system accommodated local customary practices that advocated a more gender-inclusive system of partible inheritance than did the English tradition revolving around the male line of descent. On the southern Avalon, as elsewhere in Newfoundland, testation practices were marked by a more equitable distribution of property than that advocated by English common law.

Widows, for example, were often left with substantial property and autonomy by their husbands' wills. And while bequests were usually (although not always) restricted by life interests, widows exercised considerable independence and power in relation to family property during their lifetimes, and sometimes had discretionary power in relation to the ultimate disposition of the estate. Certainly, they were not thrown at the mercy of their children by virtue of exclusionary testation practices—a process described by Nanciellen Davis in the context of nineteenth-century New Brunswick as "patriarchy from the grave."[58] While sons were favored in terms of property related to the fishery, daughters also inherited real property—sometimes with life interests, but sometimes without (particularly in cases where children were designated as residual legatees after a widow's death). Furthermore, lineal female heirs were generally preferred over male collateral kin in the disposition of land, even among the middle class. Chattels were also often quite equitably divided between heirs of both sexes, in a manner that reflected a concern to provide some means of support for all family members.

Of course, women's experiences within the inheritance regime were tempered by gender, ethnicity, and class. Women were far less frequently testators than men, and generally only in widowhood. English Protestant women predominated as legatees, as the extensive estates of the middle class were carefully disposed of throughout the period. Still, the Irish were a respectable presence in the wills of the period. Intriguingly, Irish women were more frequently testators than English women, perhaps reflecting the "passive" nature of English women's property in the area, or possibly indicating that many of the latter retired outside the region in their widowhood, and thus their wills have been recorded elsewhere.[59]

By far, however, Irish women predominated over English women in intestacies, both as intestates and as beneficiaries. In those matters that were formally administered, women were the beneficiaries of the customary practices and, ultimately, statutory law in Newfoundland that provided that real property be treated as chattels real in intestate estates. This removed land in intestate estates from the repercussions of primogeniture and stipulated a division along the same lines as chattels: one-third to the widow for her lifetime, ultimately to devolve to the children of the marriage; two-thirds equally divided among the children. Most of the intestate estates within the Irish community, however, would never have come before the courts. As such, their distributions were left to customary practice which, in the period of early settlement, likely favored security for widows and dependent children and a continuation of the practice of partible inheritance that was still common in Ireland in the late eighteenth and early nineteenth centuries.

As with the court system, then, the inheritance regime on the southern Avalon, in both its formal and its customary aspects, allowed considerable scope for women's inclusion.

NOTES

1. The following discussion of English inheritance law borrows primarily from Amy Louise Erickson, *Women and Property in Early Modern England* (London: Routledge, 1993), with some additional insights from: Maxine Berg, "Women, Property and the Industrial Revolution," *Journal of Interdisciplinary History* 24, no. 2 (autumn 1993): 233–50; Trudi D. Johnson, "Matrimonial Property Law in Newfoundland

to the End of the Nineteenth Century" (Ph.D. diss., Memorial University of Newfoundland, 1998); Derek Mendes da Costa, Richard J. Balfour, and Eileen E. Gillese, Property Law, 2nd ed. (Toronto: Edmond Montgomery, 1990); A. H. Oosterhoff, *Text, Commentary, and Cases on Wills and Succession*, 3rd ed. (Toronto: Carswell, 1990); and Alan M. Sinclair and Margaret E. McCallum, *Introduction to Real Property Law*, 4th ed. (Toronto: Butterworths, 1997).

2. The rule against perpetuities in English common law restricted the vesting of interest in land beyond a period of twenty-one years after a life in being at the creation of the interest. This prevented a person from tying up his or her property for an indefinite period after death. Nonetheless, the spirit and intention of a tail could be kept alive through the testamentary practices of succeeding generations.

3. Erickson, *Women and Property*, 6.

4. Johnson, "Matrimonial Property Law."

5. This view is also held by Christopher English and Christopher P. Curran; see "A Cautious Beginning: The Court of Civil Jurisdiction, 1791," in *Silk Robes and Sou'westers: The Supreme Court, 1791–1991* (St. John's: Jesperson Press, 1991).

6. C. Grant Head, *Eighteenth Century Newfoundland* (Toronto: McClelland and Stewart, in association with the Institute of Canadian Studies, Carleton University, 1976).

7. Johnson, "Matrimonial Property Law," 11.

8. Johnson, "Matrimonial Property Law," 159–233. See also Raymond Gushue, "The Law of Real Property in Newfoundland," *Canadian Bar Review* 4 (May 1926): 310–14. Ryan, Berkin, and Karlsen note that English rules of inheritance were also refashioned in colonial America, and that male testators sometimes left significant shares to wives and daughters. See: Mary P. Ryan, *Womanhood in America: From Colonial Times to the Present* (New York: New Viewpoints, 1975); Carol Berkin, *First Generations: Women in Colonial America* (New York: Hill and Wang, 1996); and Carol F. Karlsen, "The Devil in the Shape of a Woman: The Economic Basis of Witchcraft," in *Women's America: Refocusing the Past*, ed. Linda Kerber and Jane Sherron de Hart, 3rd ed. (New York: Oxford University Press, 1991), 57–72. Karlsen argues, however, that in the context of colonial Puritanism, the refashioned system left female beneficiaries open to accusations of witchcraft because they "stood in the way of the orderly transmission of property from one generation of males to another" (70). Quite exceptional in colonial America was New Netherland, which was governed by Dutch law before and for several decades after its conquest by the English. Under Dutch law, married women maintained their separate legal identity, and marital property was held jointly, with estates commonly being distributed by joint wills. Widows were thus entitled to one-half of the marital estate and also had the right to administer the other half for legitimate heirs. See: Linda Briggs Biemer, *Women and Property in Colonial New York: The Transition from Dutch to English Law, 1643–1727* (Ann Arbor, MI: UMI Research Press, 1983), 1–6; and Carol Berkin and Leslie Horowitz, eds., *Women's Voices, Women's Lives: Documents in Early American History* (Boston: Northeastern University Press, 1998), 79 and 166.

9. Both Johnson and I see greater flexibility in local testation practices than Cadigan, who sees the inheritance regime as a bulwark of the patriarchal family structure. See Sean Cadigan, *Hope and Deception in Conception Bay: Merchant-Settler Relations in Newfoundland*, 1785–1855 (Toronto: University of Toronto Press, 1995), 65–68.

10. PANL, GN 5/1/C/9, 19–20, and 24 (23–24 and 28), Will of William Gregory, 1 October 1797, likely entered in the Ferryland court records in 1814 or 1815, given its placement in the records. Note that much of the GN 5/1/C/1 and GN 5/1/C/9 series at PANL contain two sets of page numbers. The alternate set will appear in parentheses throughout the citations for these series.

11. Both deeds were dated 3 May 1820, and appear in PANL, GN 5/1/C/1, Ferryland, 90 (94).

12. This may have been the same Michael Neill who had executed the previously mentioned 1820 will, with a larger family, although there were various branches of the Neill family at Admiral's Cove—all large families of the same collateral kinship group with the same Christian names running throughout.

13. Mannion Name File, Fermeuse, "Neill, Michael," Will and Codicil of Michael Neill, both dated 4 October 1834; probated 12–15 November 1834.

14. PANL, GN 5/1/C/1, Ferryland, 56–57 (60–61), Deed of Gift, 24 April 1820.

15. PANL, GN 5/1/C/1, Ferryland, 95 (99), Will of Matthew Ronan, undated in copy in court records, but the Proof of Will was sworn 20 November 1824.

16. This transfer is cited in an 1816 agreement reached between Mary's surviving children, Robert Sanders and Ann Sanders Morry (as represented by her husband, Matthew Morry Jr.). See PANL, GN 5/1/C/9, 30–31 (34–35), Agreement between Robert Sanders and Matthew Morry, Jr., 9 January 1816. The date of the conveyance is not given; however, it likely took place prior to Mary's marriage to Daniel Sanders and preceded Robert Carter's will of 1795, in which Mary was not mentioned. See also PANL, MG 31, Carter Family Papers, file 33, Will of Robert Carter, dated 29 March 1795.

17. PANL, GN 5/1/C/1, Ferryland, 50–53 (54–57), Deed of Conveyance, 10 November 1818.

18. PANL, GN 5/1/C/9, 31–33 (35–37), three Deeds of Gift, 5 March 1817.

19. A general tail was an estate tail whereby the interest in the land could be inherited by lineal descendants of either sex. Again, such tails would have been restricted by the rule against perpetuities in common law, but they were often respected by following generations nonetheless, and thus their intent was carried out in practice.

20. CNS Archives, MF 236, "Will" of John Bole, Ferryland, 10 October 1759. Although the repository lists this document as a will, its wording strongly suggests that it was a deed of gift.

21. PANL, GN 5/1, vol. 1, 171–72, Will of Simon Nowlan, 4 July 1833; probated 2 November 1833. Also John Mannion Name File, Bay Bulls, "Nowlan, Simon."

22. PANL, GN 5/1, vol. 2, 147, Will of Laurence Tobin, 11 July 1848. Also Mannion Name File, Witless Bay, "Tobin, Laurence." Tobin's remaining children (four sons and five daughters) received small amounts of cash: 5s. to all but one son, who received 1s.

23. PANL, GN 5/1/C/1, Ferryland, Memorandum of Gift, 12 July 1809; entered in the Ferryland court records 1 March 1820.

24. PANL, GN 5/1/C/9, 34 (38), Deed of Gift, 15 October 1815.

25. PANL, MG 31, Carter Family Papers, file 33, Will of Robert Carter, 29 March 1795.

26. Mannion Name File, Ferryland, "Norris, Thomas"; Will of Thomas Norris, 6 May 1840; probated 10–11 December 1840.

27. PANL, MG 237, Matthew Morry Papers, file 3, Will of Matthew Morry Sr., 25 April 1856.

28. PANL, GN 5/1/C/9, 8 (12), Will of Robert Carter, 3 June 1810.

29. The will of Robert Carter appears at PANL, GN 5/1, vol. 2, 145–46, but is undated. Carter died in 1852. A subsequent court case in which Sarah Carter appeared as executror of the estate referred to the probate of the will in 1853. See PANL, MG 247, Carter-Benger-Nason Papers, files 18, 20, and 33, various papers respecting *John Nunan v. Robert Carter and James H. Carter in re: estate of Richard Nason.*

30. See: PANL, GN 5/1, vol. 2, 227, Will of Edward Power, 7 October 1848; also Mannion Name File, Brigus South, "Power, Edward."

31. Weston's will created a life interest only for his wife, with her third of the property to devolve to the two daughters, or the survivor of them, upon Catherine's death. When the will was submitted for probate, however, Governor Montagu effectively neutralized the restrictive covenant on the wife's share by granting "to Catherine and daughters Catherine and Sarah, their heirs, administrators or assigns [this wording gave Catherine the right to transfer her interest in the property outside the family] the quiet and peaceable and uninterrupted possession" of the property. See PANL: MG 31, Carter Family Papers, file 29, Will of Peter Weston, 28 September 1775; and GN 2/1/A, vol. 6, 149–53, Montagu, Grant to Catherine Weston and daughters Catherine and Sarah, 26 September 1776.

32. PANL, GN 5/1, vol. 1, 173–74, Will of William Murray, 17 August 1833; administration 19 February 1834. Also, Mannion Name File, Ferryland, "Murray, William."

33. PANL, GN 2/1/A, vol. 1, 122–23 and 126–27, Petition of John Griffin, Renews (seeking mother's share of estate) and decree of Governor Drake, court hearing at Renews, 29 August 1750.

34. PANL, GN 5/1/C/1, Ferryland, 46–48 (50–52), Will of John Gregory, 4 July 1816; Proof of Will executed 1 November 1819; entered in Ferryland court records 1 November 1819. These parties were the son and daughter of William Gregory, mentioned above.

35. The other English testator was Rose Steer, originally of Dartmouth but living as a widow in Caplin Bay by the mid-1820s. Rose left substantial cash bequests to her relatives, both in St. John's and back in England: £50 each to her mother, two sisters, and brother, £100 to a niece, and the remainder of her cash and personal effects to another niece. See PANL, MG 237, Matthew Morry Papers, file 12, Will of Rose Steer, 20 June 1825. Note that these female legatees are not included in the tally at the beginning of this chapter, because they have no connection with the southern Avalon in terms of residence or property holdings.

36. See: PANL, GN 5/2/A/1: box 2, 143, 162–65, and 221, *Hunters and Company v. Thomas Meagher*, 18 September, 13 October and 3 November 1817; and box 3, 102 and 149–53, *Hunters and Company v. Thomas Meagher*, 27 August and 22 September 1818. See also Mannion Name File, Ferryland, "Meagher, Thomas."

37. Mannion Name File, Ferryland, "Ludwigg, William," citing an entry on his wife, Elizabeth Ludwigg, from the Registry of Deaths, Dublin, 1800.

38. PANL, MG 247, Carter-Benger-Nason Papers, file 7, Will of Richard Nason, 1 April 1818.

39. PANL, MG 247, Carter-Benger-Nason Papers, file 13, Will of Anstice Gorman, [?] February 1828. John Nunan would become involved in a protracted dispute with the Carter family over the title and rents of these properties that was still ongoing in the 1850s (see MG 247 in general).

40. Johnson, "Matrimonial Property Law," 213–14.

41. PANL, GN 5/1/C/1, Ferryland, 44–46 (48–50), Will of Hester Brothers, 20 November 1815; entered in the Ferryland court records 23 October 1819.

42. PANL, GN 5/1/C/9, 3, Will of Mary Whealan, 19 March 1804.

43. PANL, GN 5/1, vol 1., 474, Will of Mary Berrigan, 13 March 1826; administration 15 October 1845. See also Mannion Name File, Renews, "Berrigan, Mary."

44. The transfer of property to children by aging parents, with the proviso that the parents be properly cared for in their old age, was a common practice in rural Ireland. Often, the provision for elder care was stated specifically in a written deed, so that the parents' intent would not be open to misinterpretation.

45. PANL, GN 5/1/C/1, Ferryland, 82–83 (86–87), Deed of Gift, 25 March 1816; entered in Ferryland court records 3 December 1816.

46. Mannion Name File, Ferryland, "Aylward, Margaret," Will of Margaret Aylward, 5 March 1831; administration 24–28 October 1833.

47. PANL, GN 5/1/C/1, Ferryland, 72 (76), Deed of Conveyance, 3 November 1817. In addition, Mary Keen's purported second will (see above) created a life interest for Thomas Meagher, stipulating that the property was to be held by him, his children and their successors forever. As noted, however, the will was deemed invalid by the court, although it may actually have been written by Mary with testamentary intent.

48. PANL, GN 5/1/C/9, 15 (19), Deed of Gift, 24 May 1814.

49. Mannion Name File, Witless Bay, "Carroll, Catherine"; citing entry in Dean Cleary's records re: Will of Catherine Carroll, 25 August 1843 (died October 1843).

50. This can be seen from the documents, but it was also in keeping with English common law, which stipulated that married women could not make wills. Young, unmarried women would usually not have had sufficient property or motivation to write testamentary documents.

51. The will of John Carroll of Ferryland left sums of money to Father Murphy and Father Brennan for the repose of his soul, as well as those of his deceased parents and sisters. He also bequeathed money for the building of the Presentation convent at Ferryland. See: PANL, GN 5/1, vol. 2, 318, Will of John Carroll, 30 December 1857; and Mannion Name File, Ferryland, "Carroll, John." See also the wills of William Murray and Catherine Carroll, discussed above.

52. Such was the case with Sarah Carter, wife of Robert Carter (mentioned above), who moved to St. John's after her husband's death and wrote her will in St. John's in 1866. See PANL, MG 31, Carter Family Papers, file 45(b), Will of Sarah Carter, 7 September 1866. This will is not included in the computations in this chapter because it falls outside the time frame of the study.

53. *Chattels real* refers to an interest in real property that was less than freehold interest—such as leasehold interest in land.

54. See: Johnson, "Matrimonial Property Law," chap. 6; and Gushue, "Law of Real Property."

55. PANL, GN 5/4/C/1, Ferryland, box 1, 25–26, *Mary Kennedy v. William Tucker*, 13 October 1792. Johnson also discusses this landmark case in "Matrimonial Property Law," 145–46.

56. See PANL, GN 5/1/C/1, Ferryland: 113, Mortgage, Catharine Jackman to Hunt, Stabb, Preston and Co., 27 March 1813; and 47, 110, 126, and 161, *Hunt, Stabb, Preston and Co. v. the Estate of Catharine Jackman*, 6 June 1818, and 25 April, 7 November, and 5 December 1820. See also: Mannion Name File, Renews, "Jackman, Catherine"; and PANL, Mildred Howard Collection, Estate Notice, Catherine Jackman, *Royal Gazette*, 18 May 1815.

57. PANL, GN 5/1/C/1, Ferryland, 109 and 123–24, *Hunt, Stabb, Preston and Co. v. the Estate of William Brandy*, 25 April and 6 November 1820.

58. Nanciellen Davis, "Patriarchy from the Grave: Family Relations in Nineteenth-Century New Brunswick Wills," Acadiensis 13, no. 2 (spring 1984): 91–100.

59. Davidoff and Hall use the concept of passive property to describe property held by women from which they could obtain income but over which they could exercise no control. See Leonore Davidoff and Catherine Hall, *Family Fortunes: Men and Women of the English Middle Class, 1780–1850* (Chicago: University of Chicago Press, 1987).

8. "TO FIX [THEIR] CHARACTER . . . IN VIRTUE AND INNOCENCE"

The Regulation of Irish Women's Sexuality on the Southern Avalon

An important indicator of patriarchal domination in a society is the degree to which it seeks to regulate women's bodies in terms of marriage, sexuality, and reproduction. So what efforts were made to constrain Irish womanhood on the southern Avalon—by plebeian culture, by the local middle-class community, by the Catholic Church—and how effective were Irish women in negotiating control over their own sexuality in the period of early settlement? The court records of the southern district and the diary of Robert Carter Jr., a magistrate in Ferryland, provide a backdrop as a striking scene from the life of an Irish Newfoundland woman, Peggy Mountain, emerges from their pages.[1]

Peggy was the focus of an episode in the mid-1830s that began as a matrimonial matter in the local court but escalated into a public shaming incident. In early December of 1834, she brought her husband, Michael, before the local magistrates for desertion. Peggy was pregnant, and the court ordered that Michael support her and the expected baby; arrangements were to be made with a Patrick Welsh to take her into his home for the winter, at Michael's expense. Michael initially indicated his willingness to comply "as well as his ability would allow," but the very next day, he reneged on his promise, "by order of [Catholic parish priest] Father [Timothy] Browne." The priest's influence was obviously very strong, for Michael held his ground, even when the magistrates ordered that he be put in jail on bread and water for a month for contempt of court. Meanwhile,

Peggy was temporarily placed at a local public house owned by Michael Devereaux, but Father Browne, "under threat of the highest nature he could inflict," ordered that the woman be removed, and as there was no other shelter available, she was placed in the local jail. Carter was taken aback by the activities of Father Browne, noting: "The Priest is inveterate against a poor unfortunate female under his displeasure and against whom he appears to direct his greatest malice and enmity . . . How such conduct will end let time decide."

Matters came to a head rather quickly. Peggy was very ill, and while her food allowance from the magistrates was generous, the accommodations were extremely uncomfortable, and the jailer reported that there were no coals for heating her cell.[2] Still, the priest did not relent, but spoke out against Peggy in the chapel and wrote an open letter against her that was read publicly at the jailhouse. In the meantime, the local magistrates arranged for a Mrs. Cahill to attend Peggy in the jail. Peggy finally gave birth to a daughter on a night so cold that the ink froze in Carter's office and the bread froze in his storeroom. The child survived only a few hours. Peggy was then moved to Mrs. Cahill's house, but again, the priest ordered that she be removed, and finally Carter himself took her in. Several days later, she left for St. John's in the *Water Lily* and slipped quietly out of the annals of the southern Avalon.

This vignette raises as many questions as it answers. Why was the priest so angry at Peggy? Did he blame her for the breakdown of the marriage? Did he suspect that the coming child was not her husband's? What threat did he perceive in Peggy's continuing presence in the community? Although we are never told the specific reason for the shaming and ostracism of Peggy Mountain, we are left with a very strong impression that central to the issue was the priest's anxiety over "aberrant" female sexuality. Especially intriguing is the sharp contrast between the responses of the local magistrates and the priest to Peggy Mountain's circumstances, for these offices represented two important mechanisms for patrolling the boundaries of women's sexuality:[3] the legal system and formal religion.

As Newfoundland was a British fishing station and then colony in the period of this study, an examination of hegemonic discourses on female sexuality in eighteenth- and nineteenth-century Britain provides context for the discussion.[4] Within the English common-law tradition by the eighteenth century, patriarchal concerns about inheritance and the legitimacy of heirs had produced a legal regime that viewed women as virtual possessions of fathers or husbands. Women—like children, servants, and other dependents—were deemed to be incapable of controlling their bodies, their skills, and their labor. In particular, the chastity value of wives and daughters—their capacity to produce legitimate heirs—required protection. At the same time, Enlightenment thought was challenging the association of sinfulness with sexuality that had been the legacy of seventeenth-century Puritanism. Yet men and women did not have equal access to the emerging sexual freedom of the age. Enlightenment men acknowledged female sexuality, but feared that in an uncontrolled state, it would pose a threat, not only to property and legitimacy, but to the very foundation of the social order itself, because of its capacity to debauch the abstracted, rational (male) individualist who was at the core of civic virtue. The safest channel for female sexuality was, therefore, marriage and motherhood; female domesticity was glorified, while the division between the (masculine) public and (feminine) private domains intensified.

These discourses developed further within the context of late eighteenth-century and early nineteenth-century evangelical Christianity as it molded middle-class ideals of female domesticity, fragility, passivity, and dependence. Female sexuality was further constrained as middle-class ideology fashioned a dichotomized construction of woman as either frail, asexual vessel, embodied in the domesticated wife and mother, or temptress Eve, embodied in the prostitute. Yet both constructions—respectable wife/mother and "fallen woman"—were necessary to satisfy an "uncontrollable" male sexuality; and even the sexually passive wife and mother required regulation within the context of marriage and family in order to safeguard property and legitimacy. The ideology of separate spheres intensified. Women who occupied spaces deemed to be public, or who demonstrated a capacity for social or economic independence, even physical hardiness, were increasingly seen as deviant.

Overt female sexuality was particularly problematic, for it "disturbed the public/private division of space along gender lines so essential to the male spectator's mental mapping of the civic order."[5] Furthermore, as the nineteenth century unfolded, male sexuality, although discursively constructed as "uncontrollable," was increasingly cordoned off into a biological function separate from rational masculinity, while female sexuality, by contrast, took a central position in the construction of womanhood. Woman became consumed by her sex, and legal, medical, and scientific discourses embellished the construction of woman as "the unruly body," problematic by her very biological nature and requiring increased monitoring and regulation.

Such understandings of femininity were spilling over into Newfoundland society through its British legal regime and emerging local middle class. And in the Newfoundland context, these perceptions of female sexuality and respectability took on ethnic undertones, as official discourse constructed the Irish woman immigrant as vagrant and whore, a "problem" requiring special regulation. The unmarried Irish female servant required particular monitoring, for her social, economic, and sexual agency flouted middle-class feminine ideals of fragility, economic dependence, and sexual passivity. But how did these constructions of womanhood play out on the southern Avalon of Newfoundland, where community formation was still in its early stages and where gender relations were still contested terrain? And how were they received within the essentially plebeian Irish community of the area?

In Britain, middle-class ideals of female domesticity, respectability, and sexual restraint were adopted and refashioned by the working class during the nineteenth century to support their own bid for respectability in the Chartist movement and to satisfy the male-centered agenda of trade unionism. Furthermore, the British middle class encouraged this development of a working-class respectability—one that imitated middle-class ideals while maintaining sufficient difference to preserve class boundaries. Similar processes took place in Ireland, where women workers were sidelined by the spread of capitalist agriculture, while the aspirations of an increasingly "respectable" farming class meshed with Catholic Church discourses on femininity in restricting female sexuality. But did such processes occur on the southern Avalon?

IRISH WOMANHOOD WITHIN PLEBEIAN CULTURE ON THE SOUTHERN AVALON

As earlier chapters have demonstrated, Irish plebeian women enjoyed considerable status and authority based on their vital contributions to early community formation and the social and economic life of the area. Their presence provided the basis for population permanence, and matrilocal or uxorilocal residence patterns featured strongly in shaping the contours of settlement. These women played an essential role in the almost total assimilation of the old English planter society into the Irish Catholic community, and they further reinforced the identity of their ethnoreligious group as spiritual guides in both formal Catholicism and a concurrent, ancient system of beliefs and customary practices. They were also an integral force in economic life: as service providers to the fishing population, as mistresses of fishing premises, and increasingly, as essential members of the shore crews of family production units in the fishery. Their vital economic role was reflected in customary testamentary practices that adhered to a relatively gender-inclusive system of partible inheritance, contrasting with the English practice of primogeniture. Women also participated in the politics of interpersonal confrontation, wielding power through verbal wrangling and physical violence in collective actions and individual interventions that were commonplace mechanisms for informal conflict resolution during the period.

It is evident, then, that within the plebeian community of the southern Avalon, Irish womanhood was not engulfed by the constraints of feminine ideals of passivity, fragility, and dependence. Nor was it readily channeled into formal marriage.

Yet marriage was a key site for the regulation of female sexuality within the English common-law tradition and British middle-class ideology. In marriage, a woman was accessible to male sexual needs and could fulfill her destiny as reproducer of the race; yet her sexuality could be safely constrained within her roles of respectable wife and mother. Indeed, a woman's entire person was subsumed within marriage. With the adoption of the principle of *marital unity* in English common law, husband and wife became one legal entity in the person of the husband. Furthermore, the husband had sole rights to his wife's services, both domestic and sexual (the latter again reflecting a concern for patrilineal inheritance and the legitimacy of potential heirs). But while the formal marriage was institutionalized as the proper means of ordering society, within plebeian and working-class communities in the British Isles, informal marriages (for example, broomstick weddings,[6] smock weddings[7], handfasting[8]) and common-law relationships (for example, *living tally*) were not only tolerated by local communities, but seen as legitimate forms of family relationships.[9] The acceptance of these arrangements reflected a less intense concern about property, legitimacy, and inheritance than existed among the middle and upper classes, although the latter groups brought increasing pressures to bear to reform marriage law and standardize marriage practices from the eighteenth century onwards.

Within the predominantly Irish plebeian community on the southern Avalon, such informal arrangements were similarly seen as acceptable. Indeed, this level of comfort was rooted in cultural tradition, for a different understanding of gender had evolved in Gaelic Ireland than in England: one in which traditions of communal property and partible inheritance contrasted with English preoccupations with private property and patrilineal inheritance; one in which the chastity requirement for wives and daughters was muted; one in which tolerance of informal marriage and divorce, illegitimacy, and closer degrees of consanguineous marriage deviated from English norms of sexual behavior.[10] Of course, this system of understanding was eroded over time by the incursions of English law and custom and an increasingly centralized and patriarchal Catholic Church. Yet even through the early decades of the nineteenth century, the Catholic Church in Ireland was struggling to control the still prevalent practices of cohabitation and informal marriages—with limited success in most rural areas, since non-compliers were operating within local community norms.[11]

There is no surviving evidence that customary marriage mechanisms—such as the *couple beggar*, the *runaway match*, the elopement, or the abduction—were transferred from Ireland to the southern Avalon,[12] although it could be argued that the "strolling priests" that plagued Prefect Apostolic (later Bishop) James O Donel in the early years of his mission at Newfoundland may have fit the bill of couple beggars.[13] While marriage according to the rites of the Church of

England was the legal standard until 1824, marriages solemnized by Catholic clergy were acknowledged, and those performed by laymen, such as justices of the peace, were permitted in the absence of authorized clergy.[14] So there was a range of options available to the Irish plebeian community of the southern Avalon in the early years of settlement. Certainly, some marriages were performed by magistrates and ship captains; and in the absence of Catholic clergy, some semblance of a religious ceremony was performed by lay-people, including women. But a number of couples simply cohabited, in both long- and short-term arrangements. In 1789, Father Thomas Ewer, the Catholic priest stationed at the new Catholic mission in Ferryland, complained of the irregularity of marital arrangements in his parish.[15] What Ewer was observing were frequent incidents of common-law relationships and informal marriages, separations, and divorces in the area—part of a marital regime that kept fairly loose reins on female sexuality and, in effect, freed a number of women from the repercussions of coverture.

It is difficult to calibrate the extent of such relationships on the southern Avalon, given the lack of recording in this early period. However, the 1800 nominal census of 166 family groupings in Ferryland district suggests the existence of up to thirty-three such relationships (20 percent of the total), either at the time of the census or in the recent past (see Appendix D for discussion). References to informal arrangements also appeared occasionally in court hearings and governors' correspondence. As part of the process of obtaining a grant in 1750 to Pigeon's Plantation in Ferryland, for example, Elizabeth Gobbet, who had lived with Elias Pigeon before his death, had to swear to the court at Ferryland that she was not currently married to one John Allen, but that they were "only keeping company together."[16] In a 1757 petition for maintenance, Elinor Coombs of Bay Bulls complained to Governor Edwards that her husband of one year, Michael, had been "persuaded" by Ellen Williams "to Quit his Wife and live with her which he at present Continues to do."[17] In 1759, Henry Tucker petitioned the governor for title to a plantation in Ferryland that had belonged to his deceased mother. The property was then in the possession of one Thomas Power, with whom his mother had been living "in the state of incontinency without being married to him."[18] In 1787, Hannah (Carney) and William McDaniel attested to the local court that they were not actually married but living together under common law.[19] In 1802, Mary Stokes of St. Mary's sued William Kearney for her deceased mother's possessions because William and her mother had not been married but merely living "in adultery."[20] Such arrangements were not uncommon, and they were accepted by the local population (unless individual, material advantage could be gained by censure in formal petitions and civil actions), especially when children were cared for in stable family relationships and did not become a charge on the community.

Even Irish plebeian women who entered into formal marriages on the southern Avalon were not readily constrained by gender ideology because of the power they derived from their vital role as co-producers in family economies. Like their counterparts in eighteenth-century rural Ireland, married women had considerable input into family and community decision-making, wielding power both within and outside their households. In both cultures, the bounds of female "respectability" were reconciled with women's social and economic agency, and women (married and single) worked and socialized—even fought, smoked, and drank—in public areas.

In general, then, middle-class anxieties about regulating female sexuality did not easily insinuate themselves into Irish plebeian culture on the southern Avalon because they did not mesh with the exigencies of day-to-day life. And plebeian women's status during this period did not erode dramatically on the southern Avalon as it did in rural Ireland, where the marginalization of women from agricultural work and the collapse of both the domestic textile industry and the potato culture—processes that had begun by the early nineteenth century—led to a depreciation of women's economic and social status. Along the southern Avalon, by contrast, women's value as essential producers in the fishing economy, as well as reproducers of family work units within that economy, remained intact and forestalled any masculinist project within plebeian culture to circumscribe their lives.

But what efforts were made by local middle-class administrators, merchants, and churchmen to rein in plebeian womanhood on the southern Avalon? To examine the question, let us return to two key players in the Peggy Mountain story: the court system and the Catholic Church.

IRISH PLEBEIAN WOMANHOOD AND THE COURT SYSTEM

Within the British legal tradition, the court system—a patriarchal regime dominated by male legislators, judges, lawyers, and juries—was one of the chief mechanisms for the regulation of female sexuality.[21] However, it is important to recognize women's agency within this framework and to anchor their experiences in specific historical contexts. We have already seen that plebeian women were a significant part of the court life of the southern Avalon, using the courtroom as one of several alternative venues for conflict resolution. Their visibility in the formal court system and the pragmatic treatment they often received at the hands of magistrates in the area suggest that the legal milieu—at least at the local level—may not have been as inhospitable to women as it was in many other British jurisdictions. And a sharpening of our focus to matters dealing specifically with female sexuality still reveals a fair degree of *laissez faire* on the part of local magistrates in monitoring plebeian womanhood in the study area.[22]

SEDUCTION AND PATERNITY SUITS

Seduction law in the eighteenth and early nineteenth centuries fit comfortably with constructions of female sexuality as passive and woman as virtual possession. The tort was based in the English common-law principle that a master could sue for the loss of a servant's services due to injury. The action, usually taken against a recalcitrant suitor or an employer who had compromised a female servant, could only be initiated by a woman's legal guardian (usually her father), not the woman herself. The guardian, not the woman, was considered to be the injured party in the action, and damages were evaluated in terms of *the guardian's* loss of a daughter's domestic services during pregnancy and lying-in, not in terms of *her* pain and suffering or reduced social and economic expectations.[23]

The seduction action was not uncommon in other British and American jurisdictions. It is intriguing, then, that only one case survives in the court records for the southern Avalon. On 4 October 1827, Catharine Delahunty complained that James H. Carter had seduced her daughter Ellen, and she asked for compensation for the loss of Ellen's services in the amount of £100. (As Ellen's father had been dead for sixteen years, her mother was the proper legal personality to initiate the suit.) Ellen herself appeared at the trial as a witness. She told the court that, for the past year, Carter had persistently courted her attention, first by offers of work—knitting socks, cutting sounds on the stage head—and then by more romantic dint of arranging assignations in the forest to cut firewood. According to Ellen, on their second excursion into the woods, Carter had "used some liberties"; she had resisted his advances, but he had succeeded in having "connexion" with her. The couple went on several more woodcutting expeditions, and eventually, Ellen became pregnant. Her mother claimed that Ellen had been unable to carry out her duties from the seventh month of her pregnancy onwards, that her recuperation from childbirth had been slow, and that her capacity to work thereafter had been reduced as a result.

Ellen's sister, Catharine Kelly, appeared as a witness for the defense, claiming that she had recently had to warn Ellen against "walking with Robert Brine . . . a married man." Her mother countered with character witness Martin Conway, who swore that he had "never seen Ellen Delahunty conduct herself differently from what well behaved Girls in her situation in life do." The effort by the defendant to present Ellen as an "unchaste" woman would not have disproved Catharine's suit, as the action was for compensation for loss of household services only; however, he may have been hoping to lower the valuation for Ellen as "damaged goods." Certainly, the jury awarded far less than the £100 pounds sought by Catharine, but the assessed damages—£ 30 Cy.—were still substantial for the period, and a significant award for this particular court.[24] Indeed, given that seduction suits generally garnered higher damages than paternity suits, and given that James Carter was a member of a wealthy middle-class family in Ferryland, Catharine and Ellen demonstrated a fair degree of legal savvy in proceeding in this manner. No local awards under the bastardy law approached £30 during the period. Case File 33

Still, the bastardy action provided another option for pregnant women who wished to make reluctant fathers live up to their paternal responsibilities. Unlike the seduction suit, the bastardy action was initiated by the woman herself. Backhouse says that in Canada, such proceedings were neither as prevalent nor as successful as seduction actions. But on the southern Avalon, the bastardy suit was the more common approach—suggesting, again, a degree of female agency within the local legal milieu. Court records reveal nine bastardy cases for the period. Granted, this number is not overwhelming, and suggests that either there were other, informal community mechanisms operating on reluctant fathers, or that single mothers on the southern Avalon had better social and economic prospects (for example, reasonable expectations of work, future marriage, or family support) on the southern Avalon than elsewhere.[25] Audio Sample Perhaps the mere threat of legal action encouraged some fathers towards financial or marital commitment. Still, it is significant that, when less formal methods failed, these nine women were willing to take the public and political action of bringing the purported fathers of their children to court, and that in doing so, they acted as autonomous legal entities rather than legal dependents.

The final disposition of these cases appears in only six of the nine records: in all six, support for the child was ordered; and in three of these cases, the mothers were also awarded lying-in expenses. In April of 1791, for example, Catherine Oudle (also Audle), a single woman of Ferryland, appeared before the magistrates and named John Murry Sr., a fisherman of Ferryland, as the father of her unborn child. Case File 34 The court immediately ordered Murry to appear before them and give a bond for the maintenance of the child. Catherine gave birth to a boy on 22 April, and on 25 April, the court issued an order of filiation and maintenance. Murry may have disputed the paternity of the child, for the wording of the order indicates that he "hath not shewd sufficient Cause why he should not be the reputed Father of the Child." Nonetheless, the mother's affidavit prevailed, and Murry was ordered to pay the following support and expenses:

> . . . the sum of ten shillings . . . toward the Laying in of the s^{d}. Catherine Audle & ye maintenance of ye s^{d}. Child, to the time of making this Order . . . the sum of two shillings weekly & ever[y] week from this present time for the maintenance of the s^{d}. Child—so long as the Child shall be chargeable to the s^{d}. Harbour . . . And . . . weekly & ever[y] week ye sum of two shillings & sixpence, in Case the s^{d}. Catherine Audle shall not Nurse or take Care of the Child herself.[26]

That same year, Manus Butler admitted to fathering the child born to Elizabeth Carney (likely of Ferryland) the previous August. Case File 35 The court was very thorough in its support order for £9.19.6, detailing expenses for a midwife's attendance (£1.1.0), nursing services for a childbed illness suffered by Elizabeth (£2.2.0), and the nursing and clothing of the child from its birth the previous August to the May court hearing date (£6.16.6). The following week, the magistrates ordered continuing maintenance for the child in the amount of 3s. 6d. per week.[27]

There is no indication that either the mother's character or her sexual history was called into question in these cases. In addition, the mother's word seemed sufficient to establish paternity, although in three of the nine cases, the fathers also admitted the claim. In four of the cases, the purported fathers had already left the district, although this was usually before the bastardy claim was actually made, reflecting again the transience of the male fishing population. In one more dramatic case, a reluctant father, William Walsh, ran from the courtroom and later successfully resisted arrest by brandishing a large knife at the two constables who had been sent to fetch him back. While Walsh was not apprehended, several of his companions were later fined for helping him escape justice.[28] Indeed, the court took pains to arrest absconding fathers or, if unsuccessful, to attach any wages remaining in the hands of employers in the district. Of course, the magistrates were primarily concerned that mother and child not become a financial burden to the community, as evident in the stock phrasing of various sworn complaints "that the said bastard Child is likely to become chargeable to the Port of ——."[29] But the bastardy law provided women with some recourse to financial assistance and the opportunity to act as independent agents in the court. Furthermore, local magistrates were receptive to their claims and made reasonable efforts to have fathers acknowledge their responsibilities.[30]

INFANTICIDE AND CONCEALMENT OF BIRTH

The vast majority of defendants in infanticide and concealment of birth cases in British and colonial courts shared a similar profile: they were young, unmarried, plebeian or working-class women, very often servants. Most of these women, already caught in difficult socioeconomic circumstances, acted out of fear of the social disgrace and reduced employment prospects that unwed motherhood would bring. Courts were generally disinclined to prosecute, and juries, reluctant to convict on infanticide charges. The lesser charge of concealment was more often successfully tried, but even in these cases, the court often demonstrated a certain tolerance, or at least an understanding, of the desperation and limited options that motivated the mothers' actions (although sentences for mothers convicted of concealment in Newfoundland were generally heavier than those meted out in Canada).[31]

Remarkably, no cases of infanticide or concealment of birth survive in the court records from the southern Avalon.[32] It is unlikely that local courts would have turned a blind eye to such matters. However, as noted earlier, illegitimacy was not stigmatized within the Irish plebeian tradition on the southern Avalon. Family or community support often cushioned the hardship of illegitimate births, and single plebeian mothers were thus in a stronger position to survive socially and economically than those elsewhere, especially in urban areas. Furthermore, given the responsiveness of local magistrates, plebeian women had access to the court system to seek financial assistance from reluctant fathers. These factors may have lowered the fear of unwed motherhood and provided some preventative to infanticide on the southern Avalon.

PROSTITUTION

The manifestation of female sexuality that most invoked patriarchal anxieties about the moral order was prostitution. More than any other woman, the prostitute, with her blatant sexual agency, flouted middle-class constructions of female passivity and threatened the rationality and self-control that defined middle-class masculinity. Furthermore, by conducting her business in public, she transgressed the careful ordering of public and private spheres. Yet, ironically, courts in British jurisdictions often treated prostitutes with a degree of tolerance, seeing them as a necessary social evil; they were an essential component of servicing an "irrepressible" male lust that was beyond the capacity of "respectable" wives and mothers. Thus, only the most outrageous examples drew harsh disciplinary responses from the legal system.[33]

Intriguingly, no evidence survives in the court records of the southern Avalon of any specific charges laid against women for prostitution or even the catchall charge, vagrancy. On the surface, this suggests that there was a dearth of concern among local constables and magistrates about women of "ill repute." There were, however, two sexual assault cases in which the court did take action against female complainants who were deemed to be threats to the moral order. In 1773, for example, Mary Keating accused Stephen Kennely of attempting to sexually assault her. He had come into her house, she claimed, and "sat upon the Bed after her husband went out . . . [and] treated her in a barbarous and cruel manner wanting to get his will of her." Kennely would have killed her, Mary claimed, had not one John McGraugh prevented him. However, a number of Ferryland's "principal Inhabitants" (a term that referred to those of higher socioeconomic rank) testified that the Keating house was a "disorderly house" where they entertained "riotous friends"; the defendant, Kennely, by contrast, was represented as "a man of an Honest Character." On the basis of these character profiles, the magistrates ordered that Mary and her husband be "turned out of the country."[34]

The court took similar action against Catharine Power of Renews, a woman "notorious" for her drunken and promiscuous behavior, when she complained of a sexual assault in 1806. Catharine alleged that William Deringwater (or Drinkwater) had entered her house sometime between 10:00 PM and midnight while she was sleeping and had assaulted and "ill treat[ed]" her. The jury, however, was not convinced by the "unsoported solitary deposition" of this "woman of infamous character." Furthermore, a defense witness swore that he had put Catherine to bed intoxicated earlier in the evening, and three others testified that Deringwater had been at his own home at the time of the alleged assault. The court acquitted the defendant and ordered that the plaintiff, Catharine, be sent back to Ireland at the first opportunity.[35] Case File 36

The most intriguing aspect of each of these two cases is the order for removal of the complainant. As noted earlier, local courts issued sentences of transportation to the home country with some regularity in cases involving property crimes, especially in the eighteenth century. However, in terms of breaches of the peace or crimes against the person, an order of deportation was generally issued only in the most extreme cases of violence or riotous behavior. The banishment of Mary Keating and Catharine Power therefore suggests that the behavior of these women of "infamous character" was similarly seen as an extreme threat to the moral and social order—that, despite a generally relaxed attitude towards the conduct of plebeian women, there were some boundaries set for their sexual behavior by the middle-class magistrates and "principal inhabitants" of the southern Avalon.

RAPE

While plebeian women on the southern Avalon were often aggressors as well as victims of physical violence in the study period, the status of rape victim was exclusively a female preserve in eighteenth- and nineteenth-century courts. Incidents of rape, like other forms of male violence against women, are seen as indicators of unequal power relations between men and women. It is again intriguing, then, that only eight cases involving complaints of rape or assault with intent to commit rape survive in the local court records from the period. Of course, such incidents were likely under-reported; however, women's ability to fend for themselves in physical confrontations and the respect they generally enjoyed within the plebeian community may have acted as deterrents to sexual assault. Of the eight reported cases, three resulted in guilty verdicts and three were dismissed; in another, the defendant was cleared of the rape charge but found guilty of a common assault; any record of the disposition of the remaining case has not survived. Two of the three dismissals emanated from *Keating v. Kennely* and *Power v. Deringwater* (discussed above), but there is insufficient detail in the records on the third case to determine the reason for discharge.[36]

Although this conviction rate seems middling in comparison to that for other assault matters in the area, the rate was quite high in comparison to rape convictions in other British jurisdictions of the day. Certainly, in the cases resulting in guilty verdicts, there appears to have been a level of responsiveness to women complainants on the part of the magistrates and juries. Corroboration was obviously not essential to proving the charge, for in only one of the three cases—the attempted rape of Mary Jenkins—did the complainant provide a supporting witness. In the Jenkins matter, the main offender had absconded and could not be brought to trial, but two of his companions were deemed accessories and ordered to pay fines (£1 each) and actual compensation to the victim (£2 each)—an unusual resolution of an assault case for this particular court. Even the witness for the complainant—a timid shoemaker who had been present in the house at the time of the attempted rape—was fined for not rendering assistance (an early "good Samaritan" ruling).[37] Case File 37 In the other two cases ending in convictions (in 1829 and 1841), the defendants were given prison terms of twelve months and one month, respectively.[38] Both attacks—but particularly the 1829 assault, in which the defendant violently beat an Aquaforte woman on the public road "with an intent . . . against her will feloniously to ravish and carnally know [her]"—appeared to have warranted sentences beyond the court's usual range of small fines and orders to keep the peace for lesser assaults.

In many jurisdictions, the treatment of female sexuality as a precipitating factor in sexual assault made the rape trial an ordeal for victims. Consistently and effectively, "a model of female sexuality as *agent provocateur,* temptress or seductress"[39] was deployed by the defense as the sexual, moral, and social history of the complainant and her previous relationship with the accused were minutely examined to determine how she had "contributed" to her own "downfall." On the southern Avalon, however, the character and history of the woman complainant were called into question in only two cases—the alleged assaults of Mary Keating and Catharine Power discussed above—reflecting the persistent attitude in the justice system that women of "ill repute" could not be raped. Yet only in the case of Mary Keating did the court make its finding solely on the basis of the previous character of the parties involved (although it is possible that it may have come to the same decision in *Power v. Deringwater*—even without testimony of the four defense witnesses—based on the flagrant "immorality" of Catharine Power).

LOSS OF CONSORTIUM

Under English common law, a husband had legal rights to his wife's body, with exclusive rights to her domestic and sexual services. If denied her sexual services, a husband could seek a writ of *habeas corpus* to force his wife to return to the matrimonial bed. He could also initiate various court actions against a third party and demand compensation for loss of consortium: criminal conversation (having sexual relations with the wife); enticement (encouraging the wife to leave her husband); and harboring (providing the wife with refuge after she had run away). Wives had no similar recourse under the law.

There are only two brief documentary references to matters respecting loss of consortium on the southern Avalon during the study period. In the 1773 court records for Ferryland district, a court order directed Simon Pendergrass to pay Edward Farrel £5 in compensation for having had "criminal correspondence" with Farrel's wife—a relationship that had apparently been going on "for some time."[40] The other matter was fleetingly referred to in the letterbooks of the colonial secretary's office in Newfoundland. In October of 1760, Governor James Webb ordered William Jackson, justice of the peace for the district of Trepassey, "to take up and send hereunder custody one Clement O'Neal, who has carried with him ye Wife of Jos^{h}. Fitzpatrick as Likewise all his Moveable Effects."[41] Given the phrasing of the order and the peculiarities of punctuation stylings of the period, it is difficult to tell whether O'Neal and his effects were to be taken into custody, or whether O'Neal had caused offense by taking away both the wife *and* the effects of Fitzpatrick. (If the latter, it would be interesting to know which was deemed to have caused the greater injury to Fitzpatrick, the loss of his wife or his other "possessions.")

While details are sketchy, there does appear to be a difference in the way the two cases were handled, possibly reflecting a difference in attitude between the authorities involved (local versus central). The Ferryland court seems to have dealt fairly leniently with the 1773 case: a small payment was ordered to compensate the plaintiff, Farrel, for a rather long-term encroachment on his conjugal rights. The other order, issued by the governor after a hearing in St. John's, had a more ominous and punitive tone: O'Neal was to be arrested and (possibly) his effects attached; not stated but implied was that Mrs. Fitzpatrick was to return to the matrimonial home and bed. While the evidence is meager, it is possible that the local magistrates had a laxer attitude towards the issue of consortium than authorities more removed from local circumstances. Certainly, the scarcity of consortium cases from this period corresponds with the prevalence of informal marital arrangements, the acceptance of informal separation and divorce, and the lack of preoccupation with primogeniture and legitimacy in the study area—all elements of a marriage regime that kept relatively loose control over female sexuality.

WIFE-BEATING

The southern district court records from the period reveal only four cases involving domestic violence against women. As with incidents of rape, domestic violence was likely under-reported, although the low numbers may have been a further indicator of plebeian women's significant status within their families and their ability to hold their own in physical struggles. At any rate, the magistrates on the southern Avalon appeared to be sympathetic to the woman complainant in each of the reported cases. In two matters, the alleged abusers were made to enter into peace bonds and ordered to return for trial; unfortunately, the final judgments in these two cases were either not recorded or have not survived. The other two matters resulted in what were essentially court orders for separation and maintenance. There is no indication in the records that in their handling of the four cases, the magistrates made any effort to encourage the complainants to return to their husbands.

Indeed, in a 1791 matter involving extreme domestic violence, the court moved quickly to protect the wife and children and remove them from the abusive situation. Margarett Hanahan (also Hanrahan) complained on 31 January that upon returning home the previous evening, she had discovered her husband, Thomas, trying to suffocate their youngest child, and that he had later "ill-used" and flogged their older child with a bough "to oblidge it to make water." When Margarett had tried to interfere, Thomas had threatened her with a hatchet. The court observed the marks of violence on wife and children and sentenced Thomas to thirty-nine lashes on the bare back as well as imprisonment until he could provide security for a peace bond. The magistrates also granted Margarett's request to be separated from her husband. And two and a half months later, the court ordered the husband to leave the district—effectively issuing an order for divorce over 175 years before the Supreme Court of Newfoundland had jurisdiction to grant divorces.[42] Case File 38 Given the flexible marital regime at the local level, Margarett was certainly free to move into an informal family arrangement; indeed, she did precisely this, for by the taking of the 1800 census, she and her two children were living with John Ellis in Ferryland, and her assumption of John's surname suggests that the couple had gone through an informal marriage ceremony or that their relationship was otherwise accepted locally as a legitimate form of marriage.[43]

In none of the southern Avalon cases were women forced to remain in abusive marriages or be deemed to have deserted and forfeited all rights to maintenance and child custody. Furthermore, the outcome of *Hanahan v. Hanahan* indicated the court's willingness to punish excessively violent husbands in kind. The cases were few, but their disposition certainly contrasted with eighteenth- and nineteenth-century cases in Britain and other British colonial jurisdictions, where courts generally dealt with wife-beaters rather leniently and encouraged women to return to abusive situations for the sake of preserving the marriage, regardless of the violence of the assault—an approach that frequently placed battered women in even greater danger and certainly discouraged the reporting of domestic violence.[44]

DESERTION, SEPARATION, AND MAINTENANCE

Local magistrates were not often called upon to hear matters involving separation and maintenance. Indeed, Newfoundland courts did not obtain jurisdiction in matrimonial causes until 1947 and could not grant divorces until 1967.[45] They did, however, exercise a *de facto* jurisdiction in granting separations, or *divorces a mensa et thoro* ["from bed and board"], and support for deserted spouses and children.[46] On these bases, at least seven matrimonial cases were brought before the magistrates on the southern Avalon during the study period.

Only one of these actions was initiated by the husband, and it was exceptional for the area in that it was the only matter in which a husband was awarded a form of child support. In 1750, Philip Moloy (also Molloy) of Ferryland petitioned the court for redress after his wife had turned him and his child (whether a child of this marriage is not specified) out of the house. After examining Mrs. Moloy and several local inhabitants, the court ordered that "the Wife do pay him three Pounds which is to be in full of all Demands he shall pretend to have on the House and Goods in Consideration that he has a Child to maintain."[47]

In the remaining six cases, wives maintained custody of the children of the marriage—perhaps a further reflection of the more transient nature of the male population through much of the period, but again demonstrating the stabilizing role of women in early communities. All six of these cases were initiated by wives, on grounds of desertion, neglect, and/or ill treatment, and the local magistrates again demonstrated pragmatism and responsiveness to the women involved, sanctioning *de facto* separations and awarding maintenance for wives and children. In a 1791 case, for example, the court ordered that Philip Forestall provide support to his wife and child in the amount of 3s. 6d. per week and stipulated that monies be stopped from his wages for this purpose. The magistrates also directed the local constable to put Mrs. Forestall in possession of the family home. Effectively, the court was acknowledging a separation that was already playing out on the ground and was taking steps to ensure that wife and child were provided for. There was no indication in the records that Mrs. Forestall was encouraged by the magistrates to reconcile with her husband.[48]

Indeed, none of the wives in these six matters were pressured by the court to return to their spouses, and support was ordered whether it had been the wife or the husband who had deserted or committed marital infidelity. Furthermore, women who had separated from their husbands were not expected to live the remainder of their lives in sexual denial or forfeit all rights to child custody and support.[49] On 14 March 1791, for example, Mary Dunn brought a complaint that her husband, Timothy (or Tim), had refused to support their child and asked for the court's assistance. The court ordered that £5 be retained from Tim's wages for the maintenance of the child.[50] The recording of the case is sparse, and there is an automatic inclination to interpret the situation in terms of a husband's desertion of wife and child. It is possible, however, that Mary may have been the one to leave the marriage, especially given that maintenance was awarded for the child only. Certainly, the nominal census taken for the district several years later, in 1800, indicates that Mary was cohabiting with a William Hennecy. She was then using the name "Mary McCue"—possibly her maiden name, or the surname of an intervening husband/partner. In the 1800 household were Mary's child by Tim, Martin Dunn (born in 1786 or 1787), and four Hennecy children (the first of whom was born in 1788 or 1789—two to three years before Mary's day in court).[51]

The two sets of records together raise the possibility that Mary may have already left Timothy Dunn at the time of her 1791 action (unfortunately, parish records do not exist for the time frame, making the tracking impossible). If this was the case, Mary's desertion did not influence the court's decision to award her support for Timothy's child. Nor does any hint of moral judgment survive in the records regarding Mary's later living arrangements. Under the English legal regime inherited by Newfoundland, a woman who committed adultery, even after separation, would no longer be entitled to support from her husband and would often lose custody of any children of the marriage.[52] Yet there is nothing in the records to indicate that this happened in Mary's case (although this may also have merely been a reflection of Tim Dunn's lack of interest in pursuing the matter).

Similarly, Ann St. Croix of St. Mary's was not penalized for her post-separation relationship with another man. On 16 October 1821, Ann brought her husband, Benjamin St. Croix, to court for neglect and ill treatment and sought an order for support for herself and their seven children. Ann was only thirty-three years old, much younger than her seventy-seven-year-old husband—a fact that the court clerk obviously felt worthy of note, as he underscored their ages twice in the court records. The unhappy couple had already been living apart since 1819, and the court recognized this *de facto* separation. It also ordered Benjamin to give up the use of his house and garden to Ann and the children, to pay her £6 at the end of the current fishing season, and to pay £5 annually for the future support of the children, who were to remain in Ann's care.[53]

Meanwhile, in the two years since the couple had ceased cohabiting, Ann had obviously taken alternative measures to support herself and her large family. Indeed, she may have already moved into another, informal marital relationship with one Edward Power, a fisherman of St. Mary's. Whether this was the case, or whether her newfound freedom from Benjamin had simply put her in a celebratory mood, is unclear, but on 17 July 1822, almost nine months to the day after her court-sanctioned separation from her husband, Ann gave birth to a male child who, she claimed, had been fathered by Power. That October, she went back to court to seek support for the child from her new paramour, but he had already left the area and was not expected to return. Nonetheless, the court ordered that the balance of his wages with his employer, in the amount of £4.15.4, be retained for the support of the child, and that from this amount, 40s. be paid for lying-in expenses, and 3s. per week support until the wages were depleted.[54] Furthermore, there was no hint of moral judgment about Ann's extra-marital relationship with Power, and she was not deemed to have thus jeopardized her original claim for child custody or support from Benjamin St. Croix. Case File 39

Neither was the wife's character during the marriage an issue in awarding support, as an estranged husband in Biscay Bay, near Trepassey, learned in 1804. In a maintenance hearing on 13 August 1804, Mary Kearney told the court that her husband, Andrew, had "turned her to Door" about fifteen months earlier and that she had since been supported by her brother. Andrew testified that, since their marriage, Mary had "behaved very Ill frequently getting drunk and totally neglecting her household affairs." Furthermore, six months after the nuptials, Mary had been delivered of a male child who, according to Andrew, was not his. Yet, despite the husband's insinuations of Mary's slatternly nature and sexual immorality, maintenance for Mary was ordered in the amount of 3s. per week for life, provided that she had no children by any other man. Furthermore, the order was issued despite the fact that Mary obviously had some alternative means of support (her brother); thus, the court was acting not out of concern that Mary would become a charge on the community, but in recognition of her right to maintenance from her husband who had turned her out of the matrimonial home. Case File 40 Indeed, this is the only case on record from the southern Avalon in which the court had the husband sign a written maintenance agreement (Andrew's signature was joined by that of Michael Kearney, possibly his father or brother, as extra surety).[55]

As we saw at the beginning of the chapter, Peggy Mountain was also not penalized by the local court for what was likely an extra-marital indiscretion. The magistrates acknowledged the *de facto* separation of the couple, and ordered her husband to pay support for wife and expected child. They also made various efforts to find alternate accommodations for Peggy, and ultimately, after repeated interference by the parish priest, magistrate Robert Carter himself took her in for several days. Throughout his diary entries about the incident, Carter's tone was usually sympathetic, never judgmental.

What is most striking in the above discussion of the legal environment of the southern district is its relatively benign regime over female sexuality when compared with other jurisdictions in Britain, Canada, and even Newfoundland (particularly St. John's). Christopher English has offered some explanations for the court's pragmatism in its dealings with both men and women in the late eighteenth and early nineteenth centuries. He notes that the *Judicature Acts* of 1791, 1792, and 1809 had provided that English law be received in Newfoundland only "'so far as the same can be applied.'"[56] The local magistrates were men with stakes in the community, he argues, who dispensed justice based on an understanding of local issues and a familiarity with local inhabitants. If English law was deemed deficient or inappropriate for Newfoundland situations, local magistrates simply made new law.[57] These are useful insights into how the legal regime manifested itself on the ground in many outports during the period.

However, local magistrates and administrators on the southern Avalon were also part of the emerging middle class with its middle-class ideals of femininity. Certainly, the behavior of women within their own class was carefully monitored, particularly by the nineteenth century. Although there were some eighteenth-century women from the local elite who had led public and independent lives, most women of this class were retiring into lives of genteel domesticity by the following century (see Chapter 9). Wives and daughters socialized only with other middle-class families in the area or in St. John's (some, such as the Carters, also wintered in England). They married members of their own class. They did not labor on flakes or in fields, as did plebeian women; rather, their work entailed the rearing of children and the supervision of domestic servants. They did not appear personally in the courthouse; in such matters that did involve them, such as probate or debt collection, they were represented by men from their own circle. Certainly, their names did not appear in any of the cases involving assault, bastardy, slander, rape, or domestic violence. (This is not to suggest that such incidents did not occur among the middle class, but merely that they were not played out in public.) These women's lives were increasingly circumscribed by the parameters of middle-class ideology; indeed, the gentility and respectability of these women helped to maintain class boundaries in small fishing communities, where contact between middle-class and plebeian men was more frequent, and social distance therefore less clearly demarcated.

Yet, while middle-class contemporaries in Britain were trying to encourage a modified form of respectability among the working class—one that involved a reformulated construction of female respectability—middle-class magistrates and administrators on the southern Avalon had reason to pause in trying to impose similar restrictions on plebeian women. These men were predominantly either merchants or agents themselves, or were connected by kinship or marriage to local mercantile families who made their money by supplying local fishing families in return for their fish and oil. And the resident fishery had become overwhelmingly dependent on household production, in which the labor of plebeian women—work that took place in public spaces, on stages and flakes—was essential. In addition, these women, in their various economic capacities, were an intrinsic part of the exchange economy and the truck system—the system of supply and credit that underwrote the resident fishery. The working woman was not a "social problem"; she was an economic necessity. It was therefore not in the interests of local magistrates to encourage the withdrawal of plebeian women into the private sphere.[58]

Now let us turn to the final key player in Peggy Mountain's drama. Why was the contrast in the responses of the priest and the magistrates to Peggy's situation so stark?

IRISH PLEBEIAN WOMANHOOD AND THE CATHOLIC CHURCH

> Woman [Eve] destroyed life's gathered crown:But woman [Mary] gave long-lasting joys of life.
>
> —Columbanus (Irish missionary, seventh century)

Father Browne was also a man with a stake in the local community. He, like the magistrates, was familiar with local circumstances and personalities, for he had been at the mission in Ferryland for twenty years. Yet he did not try to accommodate Peggy, as the local justices did. Instead, he hounded her out of the community, because her "aberrant" sexuality deviated from his perceptions of female respectability.

Father Browne's reaction was certainly not out of line with church efforts to monitor women's sexuality. When the Catholic Church was finally permitted to operate openly in Newfoundland after 1784, the priests were overwhelmed by the numbers of informal family arrangements in their new mission. In Father Ewer's 1789 report on Ferryland district, it was the indecency of women's having multiple partners that became the particular focus of paternalistic concern (or, perhaps, blame), as he noted:

> The magistrates had for custom here, to marry, divorce & remarry again different times, & this was sometimes done without their knowledge, *so that there are women living here with their 4th husband each man alive & form different familys in repute.* I would wish to know if these mariages are but simple contracts confirmed & disolved by law, or the sacrament of matrimony received validly by the contracting partys. If the latter it will be attended with much confusion in this place, with the ruin of many familys & I fear the total suppression of us all as acting against the government.[59]

British authorities in Newfoundland had acknowledged the validity of local marriage customs, given the lack of access to formal marriage rites in this period. But the Irish Catholic Church, having grown far from its Celtic Christian roots by the late eighteenth century, was not so indulgent and, while realizing that it must tread carefully around local regulations, was determined to untie such bonds that yet "remain[ed] to be separated from adultery."[60] With the priests, then, came a concerted effort to bring women into formalized marriages within the precepts of the Catholic Church; and as their efforts met with increasing success (as revealed by the parish records available from the 1820s onwards), the options of cohabitation and informal separation and divorce disappeared.

The dichotomized construction of woman as respectable wife and mother or temptress Eve was part of Catholic discourse. And even the respectable woman was seen to have inherited from her foremother the proclivity to tempt man—a further rationale for the monitoring of her sexuality by the morally and intellectually superior male members of the church.[61] Women—especially women in their sexual prime—were constructed as "occasions of sin." Thus, with the priests came the practice of churching women after childbirth—a perfunctory, shady ritual, usually a few prayers mumbled at the back door of the priest's residence over a woman who had to be "purified" for the "sin" of conceiving a child.[62] With the priests also came more systematic shaming of adulterous wives and unwed mothers, reflecting a sexual double standard that laid the "sin" of pre- and extra-marital sexual relationships overwhelmingly at the feet of "unchaste" women. Particularly in terms of illegitimacy, mothers were punished more harshly than fathers, suffering public humiliation, even ostracism, as they were denounced from the altar and denied (either for a limited period of public penance, or indefinitely) churching and the sacraments.[63] Here, then, was a reinforcement of the chastity requirement of middle-class ideology.

Church efforts to control "unruly" womanhood and protect female "virtue" gained momentum after Bishop Michael Fleming took over the reins in Newfoundland in the 1830s. The need to patrol and protect female chastity, for example, underscored his appeal to the ringleaders of the Father Duffy affair to surrender quietly to authorities, as he begged them to "contemplate the establishment of a military Section among your wives and daughters at a season when of necessity your avocations will require the abandonment of your families, of your homes and firesides to the unbridled licentiousness of soldiers without the presence of a single magistrate, a single local tribunal to restrain them."[64]

The monitoring of female sexuality and virtue was also the primary motivation in Fleming's decision to bring the Presentation nuns to Newfoundland from Galway in 1833. In his 1837 report to *Propaganda Fide,* he expressed his abhorrence of the way in which "the children of both sexes should be moved together pell-mell" in the island's schools, declaring coeducation to be "dangerous" and "impeding any improvement of morals."[65] In a later letter to Father O'Connell, he explained his urgency in sponsoring the sisters' mission, even at considerable personal cost:

> I felt the necessity of withdrawing female children from under the tutelage of men, from the *dangerous associations which ordinary school intercourse with the other sex* naturally exhibited; for whatever care could be applied to the culture of female children in mixed schools, they must lose much of that *delicacy of feeling and refinement of sentiment which form the ornament and grace of their sex.* Besides, viewing the *great influence that females exercise over the moral character of society—the great and useful and necessary influence that the example and the conversation of the mother has in the formation of the character of her children, as well male as female—I judged it of essential importance to fix the character of the female portion of our community in virtue and innocence,* by training them in particular in the ways of integrity and morality; by affording them the very best opportunities of having their religious principles well fixed, by imparting to them, while their young minds were daily receiving the elements of a general and useful education, a course of religious instruction that should teach them the true value and the proper use of those mental treasures by which they were being enriched; for I felt that which all must feel—namely, that when *once the future mothers are impressed with the truths of religion*—once they are *solidly instructed in the Divine precepts of the Gospel,* once their young minds are enlarged and enlightened, and strengthened by educational knowledge, *the domestic fireside is immediately made the most powerful auxiliary to the school,* and instruction and true education, the basis of which is virtue and religion, are instilled into the little ones at their mother's knee, and they go abroad by-and-by, into school or into society, with all the elements that fit them to become virtuous citizens.[66]

In separate schools, the nuns could prepare young Catholic women for motherhood and domesticity, and lead them to their destiny as moral guardians of their families. A curriculum that included knitting, netting, and needlework (the *three N's* of women's education) would ease the transition from work on flakes and in gardens to pursuits more properly reflecting womanly respectability.[67] Thus "solidly instructed in the Divine precepts of the Gospel," they would abandon the ancient customary practices that were an alternate source of female power.

In this last ambition, the church was acting as more than a vehicle of middle-class gender ideology. The status of Irish women as mediators of the supernatural world was in competition with the church's own authority within the spiritual realm. Church efforts to diminish the power of the alternative belief system, and consequently women's role as spiritual guides within this informal system, can be seen as part of a larger agenda of the Irish Catholic

Church in the nineteenth century to broaden its range of influence—institutionally, geographically, socially, economically, and politically—in Ireland and abroad.[68]

The Presentation sisters did not actually arrive in communities on the southern Avalon until the 1850s and 1860s, and thus the impact of their role in domesticating young women in the area fell primarily outside the period of this study.[69] But the effort to rein in unruly womanhood had begun with the arrival of sanctioned Catholicism, and was articulated as early as Father Ewer's expression of concern about women's living arrangements. Furthermore, the endeavor intensified as the nineteenth century unfolded. The church's efforts fit perfectly with middle-class ideology of the day. And while a conflict existed for local magistrates between ideology and economic reality, there was no such conflict for the church in the pursuit of its civilizing mission on the southern Avalon. Within the framework of Catholic orthodoxy, the denial of female sexuality, the celebration of selfless motherhood, and the increasing pressure on women to transform their homes into spiritual havens, removed from the outside world, were impelling women to retire into domesticity and respectability.[70] (One oral informant, a St. Mary's woman in her 80s, tells the story of a great-uncle chastising her grandmother for singing around the house: "What are you doing sitting there singing," he demanded, "when you should have your bades [rosary beads] in your hand?"[71]) These pressures would intensify as the repercussions of the devotional revolution in the Irish Catholic Church in the latter part of the nineteenth century[72] were felt through the regular recruitment of religious personnel from Ireland.[73]

Still, church constructions of femininity met with resistance from the plebeian community because they clashed with the realities of plebeian women's lives. But some inroads were being made by the 1830s. Father Browne's success in hounding Peggy Mountain out of Ferryland suggests a widening of the wedge. A further indicator was the virtual withdrawal of plebeian women from the courtroom in matters specifically related to female sexuality. Although they continued to appear in the court records on matters such as debt, wages, common assault, and property, their willingness to pursue matters such as sexual assault, domestic violence, bastardy, separation, and maintenance seemed negligible after the 1830s; only four such cases survive in the records after this period—one sexual assault (1841), one case of domestic violence (1843), and two bastardy suits (both 1854)—despite a growing population. Women were increasingly reluctant, then, to air these matters in public, a reluctance that can be linked more to church attributions of shame and guilt to female sexuality than to magisterial hostility. Increasingly wary of public court actions, plebeian women were left with the weaker options of either handling these matters privately, or not pursuing them at all.

CONCLUSION

Middle-class feminine ideals of domesticity, passivity, and respectability bled into Newfoundland society through the island's English legal regime and an emerging local middle class of administrators, churchmen, and merchants. But these constructs of female respectability did not easily insinuate themselves into Irish plebeian culture on the southern Avalon, where women had played such a significant role in community formation, where women held property and inhabited public spaces such as courthouse and stagehead, where they had a joint custodial role in terms of culture and the spiritual life of their communities, and where they played vital roles in subsistence and the production of saltfish for the marketplace. Furthermore, while local administrators and magistrates on the southern Avalon were part of the emerging middle class, and certainly espoused domesticity and dependence for women of their own social rank, they had reason to tread lightly in efforts to impose restrictions on plebeian women. As members of local mercantile networks, they were dependent on the public presence of plebeian women in the economic life of the region. These local magistrates *cum* merchants therefore had a vested interest in forestalling the equation between plebeian female respectability and the private sphere. The Catholic clergy, by contrast, saw the regulation of "unruly" womanhood as part of their civilizing (and consolidating) mission in Newfoundland and pursued this goal with increasing zeal as the nineteenth century progressed. While church ideals on femininity conflicted with plebeian realities, their efforts were already making inroads as the *Water Lily* slipped its moorings at Ferryland and carried Peggy Mountain into historical obscurity.

NOTES

1. See PANL: GN 5/4/C/1, Ferryland, box 1, 57–60 and 64, *Margaret Mountain v. Michael Mountain*, 23, 29, and 30 December 1834, 2, 12, and 19 January, and 23 February 1835; and MG 920, Robert Carter Diary, 30 and 31 December 1834, and 1, 5 and 12 January, 14–16, 19–21, 23, and 28 March, and 6 and 9 May 1835. Note that the name *Margaret* appears in the court records, but throughout his diary entries, Carter refers to her by the more familiar form *Peggy*.

2. Magistrates Carter, Thomas Wright, and Benjamin Sweetland ordered that she be allowed 5 lb. bread, 3½ lb. pork, ½ lb. butter, 1 qt. flour, 1 pt. of molasses, ¼ lb. tea, and 3 lb. fish per week. See PANL, GN 5/4/C/1, box 1, 60, Order, 19 January 1835.

3. This concept is borrowed from Susan M. Edwards, who discusses "the patrolling of the boundaries of thought on the nature of the sexuality of women" in Edwards, *Female Sexuality and the Law: A Study of Constructs of Female Sexuality as They Inform Statute and Legal Procedure*, ed. C. M. Campbell and Paul Wiles (Oxford: Martin Robertson, 1981), 173.

4. The literature upon which the following discussion is based includes: Constance Backhouse, *Petticoats and Prejudice: Women and Law in Nineteenth-Century Canada* (Toronto: Osgoode Society, 1991); Linda Cullum and Maeve Baird, "'A Woman's Lot': Women and Law in Newfoundland from Early Settlement to the Twentieth Century," in *Pursuing Equality: Historical Perspectives on Women in Newfoundland and Labrador*, ed. Linda Kealey, Social and Economic Papers, no. 20 (St. John's: ISER, 1993), 66–162; Anna Clark, *The Struggle for the Breeches: Gender and the Making of the British Working Class* (Berkeley: University of California Press, 1995); Joy Damousi, *Depraved and Disorderly: Female Convicts, Sexuality, and Gender in Colonial Australia* (Cambridge: Cambridge University Press, 1997); Leonore Davidoff, "Regarding Some 'Old Husbands' Tales': Public and Private in Feminist History," in Davidoff, *Worlds Between: Historical Perspectives on Gender and Class* (Cambridge: Polity Press, 1995), 227–76; Leonore Davidoff and Catherine Hall, *Family Fortunes: Men and Women of the English Middle Class, 1780–1850* (Chicago: University of Chicago Press, 1987); Karen Dubinsky, "'Maidenly Girls or Designing Women?': The Crime of Seduction in Turn-of-the Century Ontario," in *Gender Conflicts: New Essays in Women's History*, ed. Franca Iacovetta and Mariana Valverde (Toronto: University of Toronto Press, 1992), 27–66; Dubinsky, *Improper Advances: Rape and Heterosexual Conflict in Ontario, 1880–1929* (Chicago: University of Chicago Press, 1993); Edwards, *Female Sexuality and the Law*; Bridget Hill, *Women, Work, and Sexual Politics in Eighteenth-Century England* (Oxford: Basil Blackwell, 1989); Angela John, introduction to *Unequal Opportunities: Women's Employment in England, 1800–1918*, ed. Angela John (Oxford: Basil Blackwell, 1986); Susan Kingsley Kent, *Sex and Suffrage in Britain, 1860–1914* (Princeton, NJ: Princeton University Press, 1987); Theodore Koditschek, "Gendering of the British Working Class," *Gender and History* 9, no. 2 (August 1997): 333–63; Lynda Nead, *Myths of Sexuality: Representations of Women in Victorian Britain* (Oxford: Basil Blackwell, 1988); Mary Anne Poutanen, "The Homeless, the Whore, the Drunkard, and the Disorderly: Contours of Female Vagrancy in the Montreal Courts, 1810–1842," in *Gendered Pasts: Historical Essays in Femininity and Masculinity in Canada*, ed. Kathryn McPherson, Cecilia Morgan, and Nancy M. Forestell (Oxford: Oxford University Press, 1999), 29–47; Roy Porter, "Mixed Feelings: The Enlightenment and Sexuality in Eighteenth-Century Britain," in *Sexuality in Eighteenth-Century Britain*, ed. Paul-Gabriel Boucé (Manchester: Manchester University Press, 1982), 1–27; Jane Rendall, *Women in an Industrializing Society: England, 1750–1880*, Historical Association Studies (Oxford: Basil Blackwell, 1990); Sonya O. Rose, *Limited Livelihoods: Gender and Class in Nineteenth-Century England* (Berkeley: University of California Press, 1992); G. S. Rousseau and Roy Porter, introduction to *Sexual Underworlds of the Enlightenment*, ed. Rousseau and Porter (Chapel Hill: University of North Carolina Press, 1988),

1–24; Mary Lyndon Shanley, *Feminism, Marriage, and the Law in Victorian England, 1850–1895* (Princeton, NJ: Princeton University Press, 1989); and Carol Smart, "Disruptive Bodies and Unruly Sex: The Regulation of Reproduction and Sexuality in the Nineteenth Century," in *Regulating Womanhood: Historical Essays on Marriage, Motherhood, and Sexuality*, ed. Carol Smart (London: Routledge, 1992), 7–32.

5. Judith Walkowitz, *City of Dreadful Delight: Narratives of Sexual Danger in Late-Victorian London* (Chicago: University of Chicago Press, 1992), 23.

6. In some English and Welsh communities, couples were married by the simple expediency of placing a broom slantwise across the threshold of a house and jumping over it before witnesses. If either party touched or moved the broom, the marriage was deemed invalid. An informal divorce was just as easily effected by the couple (or, in some areas, the husband only) stepping backwards over the broom before witnesses. See: Hill, *Women, Work, and Sexual Politics*, 206 and 218; and Stephen Parker, *Informal Marriage, Cohabitation, and the Law, 1750–1989* (New York: St. Martin's Press, 1990), 18 and 27.

7. As the name suggests, a smock wedding was an informal ceremony in which the woman was married only in her smock. Because she brought nothing but her smock to the marriage, according to custom, she could maintain her separate identity and hence her own property, financial rights and obligations, and rights to her children. See Parker, *Informal Marriage*, 24 and 69.

8. Handfasting was practiced particularly in the Scottish highlands and in Wales. Couples joined hands and pledged to live together for a year and a day. If the two were compatible, the marriage was extended for life. If the couple wished to part, they merely turned their backs on each other and left the house through separate doors. See: Hill, *Women, Work, and Sexual Politics*, 206 and 218; and Parker, *Informal Marriage*, 18.

9. See, for example: Clark, *Struggle for the Breeches; Hill, Women, Work, and Sexual Politics*; Parker, *Informal Marriage*; Sean J. Connolly, *Priests and People in Pre-famine Ireland, 1780–1845* (Dublin: Gill and Macmillan, 1982); Rendall, *Women in an Industrializing Society*; Ellen Ross, *Love and Toil: Motherhood in Outcast London, 1870–1918* (New York: Oxford University Press, 1993); and James G. Snell, *In the Shadows of Law: Divorce in Canada, 1900–1939* (Toronto: University of Toronto Press, 1991). Carol Berkin and Leslie Horowitz also note the frequency of informal separations and marriages in colonial America. See: Berkin, *First Generations: Women in Colonial America* (New York: Hill and Wang, 1996); and Berkin and Horowitz, eds., *Women's Voices, Women's Lives: Documents in Early American History* (Boston: Northeastern University Press, 1998).

10. Kathleen Brown discusses the differences in systems of knowledge about gender between England and Gaelic Ireland in *Good Wives, Nasty Wenches, and Anxious Patriarchs: Gender, Race, and Power in Colonial Virginia* (Chapel Hill: University of North Carolina Press, 1994), 33–37. See also Peter Berresford Ellis, *Celtic Women: Women in Celtic Society and Literature* (London: Constable, 1995), chaps. 4 and 5.

11. As with other customary practices, the Catholic Church in Ireland was only able to lead its congregation where it wanted to go and would only make inroads on

informal marriage practices when the community desired stricter regulation. Connolly argues that this tightening of control coincided with the demographic shift that occurred during the Great Famine. In pre-famine Ireland, frequent subdivision of land had permitted a less rigid marital regime among the landless majority of the population. However, with the collapse of the potato culture and the decimation of the landless class at mid-century, the small farmer emerged as the dominant social group in Ireland. Farmers practiced more cautious management of family land and greater control over marital arrangements in order to ensure the careful transfer of property to the following generation (reflected in the increasing incidence of the arranged match in post-famine Ireland and the wholesale shift to impartible inheritance). Church efforts to regulate sexual activity and marriage simply meshed with the social and economic requirements of this rising farmer group—hence, their increasing success after mid-century. See Connolly, *Priests and People*, chap. 5.

12. The elopement is self-explanatory, but the other methods require clarification. Couple beggars were suspended priests who made their livings by performing marriages outside church jurisdiction. They were frequently employed by couples who had difficulty in meeting the requirements of a formal marriage (e.g., lacking parental consent, being too closely related or of mixed religious backgrounds) or who simply could not afford the formal ceremony. The runaway match was another option for a couple who could not obtain parental or clerical consent to their marriage. The pair would spend a night together at the home of a sympathetic relative or friend and, being thus "compromised," would force the issue. Reluctant parents often relented and consented to a more formal marriage, and the church usually acquiesced after a period of penance had been observed. The abduction employed similar pressure tactics: the reputation of a young woman who had been abducted was in jeopardy, and most parents and the church would ultimately agree to the couple's marriage. Some abductions were genuine and were employed as a means of obtaining the fortunes of the daughters of well-to-do farming families. Others were staged, with a suitable display of maidenly reluctance on the part of the abductee. See Connolly, *Priests and People*, 200–10.

13. There were several priests on the island when O Donel arrived who were functioning without faculties from any bishop, including Father Patrick Power, who attempted to establish himself as parish priest in Ferryland in opposition to O Donel's appointee, sparking the Ferryland riot (see Chapter 5). These missionaries claimed to be operating under ancient papal authorization that was outside the jurisdiction of any bishop. Aside from their lack of compliance, O Donel found their morals and habits to be egregious, and often wished himself to be rid of these "strolling priests." See Cyril J. Byrne, ed., *Gentlemen-Bishops and Faction Fighters: The Letters of Bishops O Donel, Lambert, Scallan, and Other Irish Missionaries* (St. John's: Jesperson Press, 1984), 1–142; the quotation comes from 98–101, O Donel to Archbishop Troy, Dublin, 24 December 1789.

14. In 1824, Catholic clergy were put on equal footing with Anglican clergy in terms of celebrating marriage; in 1833, authority to celebrate marriage was also extended to Dissenting ministers. For a discussion of early marriage law in Newfound-

land, see Trudi D. Johnson, "Matrimonial Property Law in Newfoundland to the End of the Nineteenth Century" (Ph.D. diss., Memorial University of Newfoundland, 1998), 120–32.

15. Byrne, ed., *Gentlemen-Bishops*, 77–79, Ewer to Troy, 30 November 1789.

16. PANL, GN 2/1/A, vol. 1, 115, 136 and 141, Petition and Deposition of Elizabeth Gobbett, "commonly call'd Elizabeth Allen," 27 and 31 August 1750, and Patent granted to her by Governor Drake, 31 August 1750.

17. PANL, GN 2/1/A, vol. 2, 396, Order in response to Coombs' Petition, Edwards to JPs at Bay Bulls, 14 October 1757.

18. PANL, GN 2/1/A, vol. 3, 44–45, Order, Edwards to the fishing admirals and magistrates of Ferryland, 13 October 1759.

19. PANL, GN 5/4/C/1, Ferryland, box 1, 25–26, *Catharine Weston v. Hannah and William McDaniel*, 8 March 1787.

20. PRL, 340.9 N45, St. Mary's, *Mary Stokes v. William Kearney*, 30 September 1802.

21. See: Backhouse, *Petticoats and Prejudice*; Cullum and Baird, "'A Woman's Lot'"; Dubinsky, "'Maidenly Girls'"; and Edwards, *Female Sexuality*.

22. See Appendix B for a discussion of court cases in the author's database. The reader is urged not to clump the numbers of cases in this section in a total that will have little significance. We cannot read the same meaning into a woman's objectification in being deported for prostitution, for example, as we do into another woman's agency in bringing her husband to court for abuse or desertion. Furthermore, in many of the following categories (e.g., seduction, infanticide, prostitution, loss of consortium, domestic violence, and rape), low numbers are positive indicators of women's status.

23. See Backhouse, *Petticoats and Prejudice*; and Dubinsky, "'Maidenly Girls.'"

24. PANL, GN 5/2/C/1, Ferryland, box 1, 142–45, *Catharine Delahunty v. James H. Carter*, 4 October 1827.

25. Illegitimacy was deemed a serious breach of moral standards in most British and colonial jurisdictions; it was frowned upon by local communities and condemned and regulated by civil and religious leaders alike, with single mothers bearing the brunt of the social shame. See, for example: Backhouse, *Petticoats and Prejudice*; Berkin and Horowitz, eds., *Women's Voices*; Cullum and Baird, "'A Woman's Lot'"; Elizabeth Jane Errington, *Wives and Mothers, Schoolmistresses and Scullery Maids: Working Women in Upper Canada, 1790–1840* (Montreal: McGill-Queen's University Press, 1995); Allyson N. May, "'She at first denied it': Infanticide Trials at the Old Bailey," in *Women and History: Voices of Early Modern England*, ed. Valerie Frith (Toronto: Coach House Press, 1995), 19–49; and Richter, "The Free Women of Charles Parish, York County, Virginia, 1630–1740," in *Women and Freedom in Early America*, ed. Larry D. Eldridge (New York: New York University Press, 1997), 290–312. Still, bundling (parent-approved, pre-marital sex) and pre-marital pregnancy were tolerated within plebeian communities, provided couples were moving towards a stable family arrangement. See Hill, *Women, Work, and Sexual Politics*, 174–95. The Irish literature also indicates that illegitimacy brought tremendous social shame to

both the mother and child; however, much of the discussion is weighted towards the nineteenth century, when women's overall status was in decline, and contrasts with Brown's and Ellis's discussions of Gaelic Ireland's tolerance of illegitimacy (see note 10, above). Irish historians point to the low illegitimacy rates in late eighteenth- and early nineteenth-century Ireland compared with contemporary European rates, and suggest that this was due to early and universal marriage before the Great Famine as well as a sexual chasteness that ran contrary to the sexual ribaldry reflected in Gaelic literature and customs. However, illegitimate birth records do not take into account pre-nuptial conceptions, which are extremely difficult to trace, but may have been more frequent than many Irish historians have allowed for (Connolly, for example, optimistically sets them at one out of ten births, compared with two out of five for England; Mageean, however, notes that the numbers may have been quite high, and thus the extent of premarital sexual activity in Ireland is masked by the statistics). In such cases, local community mechanisms likely came into play to encourage the couple to marry before the child's birth. See: Kenneth H. Connell, *Irish Peasant Society: Four Historical Essays* (Oxford: Clarendon Press, 1968), chap. 2; Connolly, *Priests and People*, 186–218; Hasia R. Diner, *Erin's Daughters in America: Irish Immigrant Women in the Nineteenth Century* (Baltimore, MD: Johns Hopkins University Press, 1983), 21–24; Deirdre Mageean, "To Be Matched or to Move: Irish Women's Prospects in Munster," in *Peasant Maids—City Women: From the European Countryside to Urban America*, ed. Christiane Harzig (Ithaca, NY: Cornell University Press, 1997), 78–79; and Janet A. Nolan, *Ourselves Alone: Women's Emigration from Ireland, 1885–1920* (Lexington: University Press of Kentucky, 1989), 28 and 35.

26. PANL, GN 5/4/C/1, Ferryland, box 1, *Catherine Oudle [also Audle] v. John Murry, Sr.*, 3/4 (both dates appear in the record) and 25 April 1791.

27. PANL, GN 5/4/C/1, Ferryland, box 1, *Elizabeth Carney v. Manus Butler*, 16 and 23 May 1791.

28. PANL, GN 5/4/C/1, Ferryland, box 1, 86–88 and 95, *Margaret Mackey v. William Walsh*, 29 April and 9 May 1836, and 15 February 1837.

29. The urgency of this issue was noted by local colonial secretary Edward B. Brenton to attorney general James Simms in 1826 after two recent cases had come before the magistrates involving mothers who had abandoned their illegitimate children. Brenton asked what measures could be taken against "these unnatural parents so as to compel them to support their children or to punish them for the desertion of them." Simms replied that the English law would not apply, interwoven as it was with a system of parochial poor law that did not exist in Newfoundland. The property of offending parents could be attached, but the mothers in these cases appeared to be "as destitute of property as of principle." Only legislative enactment would be effectual to check such offenses, he felt. See PANL, GN 2/1/A, vol. 35, 329–31: Brenton to Simms, 28 April 1826; and Simms to Brenton, 29 April 1826. The issue was given priority by the newly formed House of Assembly in Newfoundland with the early passage (on 12 June 1834, in its second session) of *4 Wm. 4, Cap. 7, An Act to provide for the Maintenance of Bastard Children*. By the terms of this act, a woman about to be delivered of an illegitimate child could swear to its paternity before a justice of the peace.

The purported father was to provide security for maintenance of the child or, in default, be jailed. If he felt he had been wrongfully charged, "or if the Person charging him be a Woman of ill-fame, or a common Whore," he had recourse to appeal in the next quarter sessions. (Note the discrimination against the "unchaste" woman in the statutory law; whether this scruple was closely adhered to by the local courts in bastardy actions is uncertain, but as noted, there was no reference to the previous character of the mother in any of the southern Avalon cases herein.) To ensure further that the child would not become a charge on the community, any two magistrates could, at their discretion, require either the mother or the father to provide security in the amount of £20 Stg., to be disbursed by the magistrates for the care of the child. Ultimately, then, both mother and father were deemed financially responsible for the child. Of the nine cases examined on the southern Avalon, five were heard before the passage of this legislation, four after its enactment.

30. Absent among southern Avalon prosecutions, and Newfoundland cases in general, were the fornication prosecutions that were still common in England and colonial America up to the late eighteenth century. In these other jurisdictions, both male and female parties to sexual intercourse outside marriage had been punished by seventeenth- and early eighteenth-century courts. But by the middle of the eighteenth century, perceptions of women as moral guardians had constructed fornication as a "woman's crime," although this assumption was itself being challenged by the end of the century as the concept of seduction gained greater currency. See Laurel Thatcher Ulrich, *A Midwife's Tale: The Life of Martha Ballard, Based on Her Diary, 1785–1812* (New York: Alfred A. Knopf, 1990), 148–49. As noted above, however, the seduction action had its own pitfalls for women in terms of their being perceived as sexually passive and lacking in legal agency.

31. See, for example: Backhouse, *Petticoats and Prejudice*; Berkin and Horowitz, eds., *Women's Voices*; Cullum and Baird, "'A Woman's Lot'"; May, "'She at first denied it'"; and Laurel Thatcher Ulrich, *Good Wives: Image and Reality in the Lives of Women in Northern New England, 1650–1750* (New York: Alfred A. Knopf, 1982).

32. By contrast, Connell notes that infanticide rates were more significant than illegitimacy rates in Ireland, but again, he is working with data from the nineteenth century, when women's economic and social options were in decline. See Connell, *Irish Peasant Society*, chap. 2.

33. See: Backhouse, *Petticoats and Prejudice*; Edwards, *Female Sexuality*; Randolph Trumbach, "Modern Prostitution and Gender in *Fanny Hill*: Libertine and Domesticated Fantasy," in *Sexual Underworlds*, ed. Rousseau and Porter, 69–85. Poutanen notes, however, an increased targeting of female vagrancy, particularly prostitution, in Montreal through the early decades of the nineteenth century as uncertainties and unrest arising from changing socioeconomic conditions induced an emerging male bourgeoisie to demand greater state control of the street life of the city. See Poutanen, "Contours of Female Vagrancy."

34. PRL, 340.9 N45, Ferryland, *Mary Keating v. Stephen Kennely*, 14 September 1773; see also Mannion Name File, Ferryland, "Keating, Mary."

35. PANL, GN 5/4/C/1, Ferryland, box 1, *Catharine Power at the Suit of the Crown v. William Deringwater, alias Drinkwater,* 20 September 1806.

36. In 1831, a jury acquitted John Power of assault with intent to commit rape after hearing the testimony of two witnesses: alleged victim Mary Ann Lanine and Bridget Lanine. Whether the two women substantiated or contradicted each other's testimony is not clear from the record, but at the end of the day, Power was a free man. See PANL, GN 5/2/C/1, box 1, 267–68, *Rex, on the prosecution of Mary A. Lanine, v. John Power,* 14 October 1831.

37. PANL, GN 5/4/C/1, Ferryland, box 1, *Mary Jenkins v. John Power, James Callinan [also Callanan], and Patrick Cahill,* 24 February 1794 (this is the date that appears in the records, but the year was more likely 1795, as the record falls between matters heard on 17 November 1794 and 20 May 1795).

38. PANL: GN 5/4/C/1, Ferryland, box 1, 2, *Rex v. Timothy Callahan,* 21 August 1829; GN 5/2/C/1, Ferryland, box 1, 227 and 229–30, *Rex v. Timothy Callehan,* 29 October 1830; GN 5/4/C/1, Ferryland, box 2, *Mary Place v. John Higgins,* 17 February 1841.

39. Edwards, *Female Sexuality,* 50. See also: Backhouse, *Petticoats and Prejudice*; Cullum and Baird, "'A Woman's Lot'"; and Dubinsky, "'Maidenly Girls.'"

40. PRL, 340.9 N45, Ferryland, Order, William Parker, Surrogate, to Simon Pendergrass, 8 October 1774; see also Mannion Name File, Ferryland, "Farrell, Ed."

41. PANL, GN 2/1/A, vol. 3, 115, Order, Webb to Jackson, 6 October 1760.

42. PANL, GN 5/4/C/1, Ferryland, box 1, *Margarett Hanahan v. Thomas Hanahan,* 31 January, 1 February, and 11 April 1791. Christopher English has interpreted the judgment as a "virtual divorce"; see English, "The Reception of Law in Ferryland District, Newfoundland, 1786–1812," paper presented to a joint session of the Canadian Law and Society Association and the Canadian Historical Association, Brock University (2 June 1996), 40–42.

43. PANL, MG 205, Pole Papers, 1799–1800. This option was also pursued by other separated or deserted women in the area (see below).

44. See, for example: Backhouse, *Petticoats and Prejudice,* chap. 6; Anna Clark, "Humanity or Justice? Wifebeating and the Law in the Eighteenth and Nineteenth Centuries," in *Regulating Womanhood: Historical Essays on Marriage, Motherhood, and Sexuality,* ed. Carol Smart (London: Routledge, 1992), 187–206; Margaret R. Hunt, "'The great danger she had reason to believe she was in': Wife-Beating in the Eighteenth Century," in *Women and History,* ed. Frith, 81–102; Judith Norton, "The Dark Side of Planter Life: Reported Cases of Domestic Violence," in *Intimate Relations: Family and Community in Planter Nova Scotia,* 1759–1800, ed. Margaret Conrad, Planter Studies Series, no. 3 (Fredericton: Acadiensis, 1995), 183–4; Hill, *Women, Work, and Sexual Politics; and Shanley, Feminism, Marriage, and the Law.*

45. Christopher English, "From Fishing Schooner to Colony: The Legal Development of Newfoundland, 1791–1832," in *Law, Society, and the State: Essays in Modern Legal History,* ed. Louis A Knafla and Susan W. S. Bunnie (Toronto: University of Toronto Press, 1995), 84.

46. Again, the priority of ensuring that deserted families did not become a charge on the community was evidenced by the early passage (12 June 1834) by the new local

legislature of 4 *Wm.* 4, *Cap.* 8, *An Act to afford Relief to wives and Children, Deserted by their Husbands and Parents.* Here was an acknowledgment of women as legal entities with responsibilities under the law, for the act stipulated that "any Person, being such Husband, Father or *Mother*" who had absconded or was about to leave "his or *her* usual place of abode" without making provision for a wife, child, or children left behind was to be apprehended and required to enter into security to provide reasonable support for the deserted family members. Upon refusal or neglect of this requirement, justices or magistrates were empowered to attach wages or seize goods and chattels belonging to the offender of sufficient value to provide sufficient maintenance. The act stated that upon "willful" refusal or neglect on the part of the offender, the said "Father, Husband or *Wife* shall be deemed a Rogue and Vagabond" (epithets usually reserved for male recusants in colonial courts) and could, at the discretion of the justices or magistrates, be imprisoned for a month on bread and water (the option chosen by the Ferryland magistrates against Michael Mountain). Further, the act provided that if "any person being a Father, Husband or *Mother,* and being able to work," failed to provide support "by his or her neglect of work, or by spending his or *her* money in Ale Houses, Taverns, or in any other wasteful and improper manner," s/he would be "deemed to be an idle and disorderly *person,*" and the justices or magistrates were empowered to sentence the offender to prison and hard labor, "or, not being a female, to Labor on the Public Roads," for a period not exceeding fourteen days. (Italics added throughout.) As in the case of bastardy actions, any person who felt him- or herself wrongly charged could appeal the decision in the next quarter sessions. While this legislation did not explore the possibility of a wife's deserting a husband, and denied women offenders the dubious honor of serving their time on road work (perhaps too public a spectacle, although other forms of hard labor were permitted), it was relatively gender-inclusive, recognizing the financial accountability of both men and women in the support of their families. Of the southern Avalon cases discussed herein, only *Mountain v. Mountain* was heard after the passage of this Act.

47. PANL, GN 2/1/A, vol. 1, 115, *Re: Petition of Philip Moloy,* 27 August 1750.

48. PANL, GN 5/4/C/1, Ferryland, box 1, *Re: Forestall,* 13 June 1791.

49. Again, this contrasts with cases in most British jurisdictions, in which the character of the wife, both during marriage and after separation, was at issue in awarding child custody and support. Within the English common-law tradition, wives had to prove their "worthiness" to the court. Those who committed adultery or deserted the marriage, except under the most extreme circumstances (e.g., the husband's adultery in combination with violent abuse, incest, sodomy, or bestiality), lost entitlement to custody and maintenance. Indeed, a wife who had sexual relations with a man other than her husband even after separation was no longer entitled to support. See, for example: Backhouse, *Petticoats and Prejudice*; Cullum and Baird, "'A Woman's Lot'"; Errington, *Wives and Mothers*; Hill, *Women, Work, and Sexual Politics*; Joan Perkin, *Women and Marriage in Nineteenth-Century England* (Chicago: Lyceum Books, 1989); and Merril D. Smith, "'Whers Gone to She Knows Not': Desertion and Widowhood in Early Pennsylvania," in *Women and Freedom*, ed. Eldridge, 211–28.

50. PANL, GN 5/4/C/1, Ferryland, box 1, *Mary Dunn v. Timothy Dunn*, 14 March 1791. The records do not indicate whether this was a lump-sum settlement or an annual maintenance.

51. PANL, MG 205, Pole Papers, 1799–1800.

52. Cullum and Baird, "'A Woman's Lot.'"

53. PANL, GN 5/4/C/1, St. Mary's, 111, *Ann St. Croix v. Benjamin St. Croix*, 16 October 1821.

54. PANL, GN 5/4/C/1, St. Mary's, 130–31, *Ann St. Croix v. Edward Power*, 17 July 1822.

55. PRL, 340.9 N45, *Mary Kearney v. Andrew Kearney*, 13 August 1804.

56. 49 *Geo. III, Cap. 27.*

57. English, "Reception of Law," 44. See also English and Christopher P. Curran, "A Cautious Beginning: The Court of Civil Jurisdiction, 1791," in *Silk Robes and Sou'westers: The Supreme Court, 1791–1991* (St. John's: Jesperson Press, 1991). Berkin also notes the tailoring of English laws to local circumstances in some American colonies, although she notes that others preserved the older laws, even after England itself had abandoned them. See Berkin, *First Generaions*, 155.

58. In this regard, resident magistrates may have been more pragmatic and utilitarian than governors, chief justices, and visiting surrogates, who were not directly involved in the fishery. This may, to some extent, explain the difference in my observations and those of Cadigan in relation to the court's perception of women's "place" in Conception Bay, particularly in the debt collection cases of Butler and Lundrigan of the 1820s, which resulted in harsh corporal punishments and provided much fodder for the reform movement in Newfoundland. Cadigan argues that the purpose of the whippings imposed by surrogates on these men was to punish them for the roles their wives played in physically resisting the attachment of their properties for debt. The two men were being disciplined, Cadigan writes, not so much for their contempt of court in a socially turbulent time, as has always been believed, but because of their inability to keep their womenfolk in line—their failure as patriarchs—as the court tried to impose a gentry-bourgeois model of patriarchy on the local fishing population. See Cadigan, "Whipping Them into Shape: State Refinement of Patriarchy among Conception Bay Fishing Families, 1787–1825," in *Their Lives and Times: Women in Newfoundland and Labrador: A Collage*, ed. Carmelita McGrath, Barbara Neis, and Marilyn Porter (St. John's: Killick Press, 1995), 48–59. It is possible that the involvement of visiting surrogates rather than local magistrates in these two cases was a factor in their outcome. Still, it is difficult to understand why, if the intention of the court was to make examples of these two men as failed patriarchs, the surrogates permitted the message to be so completely lost on the local community. Why play into the hands of local reformers by leaving the entire population suffering from the "misapprehension" that the punishments were for contempt of court? And can we interpret the attitudes of two surrogates as representative of the broader local legal regime? Certainly, similar actions by wives on the southern Avalon did not attract corporal punishment for their husbands. The Butler and Lundrigan matters aside, however, Cadigan still observes a much greater effort by courts in Conception Bay to impose

standards of female respectability and domesticity than I have found in my study area—again, possibly reflecting differences in ethnic mix and economic development in the two areas.

59. Byrne, ed., *Gentlemen-Bishops*, 77–79, Ewer to Archbishop Troy, 30 November 1789; italics added. Prefect Apostolic O Donel had already expressed similar concerns to Leonardo Antonelli, Cardinal Prefect of Propaganda Fide. See Byrne, 55, O Donel to Antonelli, [December] 1785. The clergy were also worried about the close degrees of consanguinity in Newfoundland marriages. See, for example, Byrne, 329–33, Bishop Thomas Scallan to Cardinal Francesco Luigi Fontano, Prefect of Propaganda Fide, 6 October 1822.

60. Byrne, ed., *Gentlemen-Bishops*, 55, O Donel to Antonelli, [December] 1875.

61. The concept that women, as descendants of Eve, had inherited her capacity for temptation was espoused by most Protestant sects as well. Of the Christian churches, only the Quakers believed that the burden of Eve's "sin" had been transmuted by Christ's death and resurrection. See Berkin and Horowitz, eds., *Women's Voices*, 125–26.

62. There was no real association of churching with thanksgiving in the study area. Nor did oral informants link it with "uncleanliness" associated with blood and the birthing process. The overwhelming perception of the rite was that it was a form of absolution for the shame of women's participation (albeit necessary) in the sexual act for the purpose of procreation.

63. The information on perceptions of women as occasions of sin, churching, and shaming comes from the oral tradition of the area, with informants relating what the Irish Catholic community understood the church's attitudes and interpretations to be. These perceptions tend to correspond with the literature on the declining status of women within the Catholic Church in Ireland. The Irish historiography, for example, also notes that the greatest disgrace for illegitimacy was borne by the mother and, to a lesser extent, the child, particularly as the nineteenth century progressed. Indeed, that century was marked by a decreasing tolerance of illegitimacy and increasing sexual restriction. The Catholic Church in Ireland was extremely active in patrolling sexuality and found that its efforts met with increasing success as its desires meshed more closely with the more "respectable" farming class that dominated post-famine Irish society. As on the southern Avalon, however, church discourse fashioned a sexual double standard. See, for example: Connolly, *Priests and People*; Diner, *Erin's Daughters*; Mageean, "Irish Women's Prospects"; Kerby Miller, David Doyle, and Patricia Kelleher, "'For love and liberty': Irish Women, Migration, and Domesticity in Ireland and America, 1815–1920," in *Irish Women and Irish Migration*, ed. Patrick O'Sullivan, Irish World Wide Series, vol. 4 (London: Leicester University Press, 1995), 41–65; and Nolan, *Ourselves Alone*. Lynne Marks notes that Protestant churches in Upper Canada also carefully monitored the sexual behavior of their congregations, but, by contrast, their efforts were aimed more at establishing a single sexual code for both men and women rather than reinforcing the sexual double standard of secular discourses. See Marks, "No Double Standard?: Leisure, Sex, and Sin in Upper Canadian Church Discipline Records, 1800–1860," in *Gendered Pasts*, ed. McPherson, Morgan, and Forestell, 48–64.

64. Michael McCarthy, *The Irish in Newfoundland, 1600–1900: Their Trials, Tribulations, and Triumphs* (St. John's: Creative Publishers, 1999), 157–58, citing Bishop Fleming, Pastoral Letter, 10 May 1836.

65. Mons. Michael Anthony Fleming, *Report of the Catholic Mission in Newfoundland in North America*, Submitted to the Cardinal Prefect of Propaganda (Rome: Printing Press of the Sacred Congregation, 1837), 3–4.

66. CNS, Michael Anthony Fleming, "Letter on the State of Religion in Newfoundland," 11 January 1844, addressed to the Very Rev. Dr. A. O'Connell, Dublin (Dublin: James Duffy, 1844), 18; italics added.

67. For a discussion of the nuns' efforts, see Frank Galgay, Michael McCarthy, Sr. Teresina Bruce, and Sr. Magdalen O'Brien, *A Pilgrimage of Faith: A History of the Southern Shore from Bay Bulls to St. Shott's* (St. John's: Harry Cuff, 1983), particularly chap. 9, "Ministry of the Presentation Sisters on the Southern Shore."

68. For a discussion of the development of an institutionalized Catholic Church in Newfoundland under Bishop Fleming, and its increasing influence on the social and political life of the colony, see John E. Fitzgerald, "Conflict and Culture in Irish-Newfoundland Roman Catholicism, 1829–1850" (Ph.D. diss., University of Ottawa, 1997).

69. Ironically, convent living provided those women who entered the orders with some latitude, even as the church's espousal of female domesticity and passivity sought to confine women's independence. Convent life meant freedom from the domestic authority of fathers and husbands, release from domestic routines, and the opportunity to perform socially useful work (teaching, nursing, social work) without the loss of "respectability" this normally would have entailed for women who remained single. Also, convents were all-female institutions with considerable autonomy in running their day-to-day affairs, although they were increasingly brought under the control of the male church hierarchy after the Middle Ages. See Caitriona Clear, "The Limits of Female Autonomy: Nuns in Nineteenth-Century Ireland," in *Women Surviving: Studies in Irish Women's History in the Nineteenth and Twentieth Centuries*, ed. Maria Luddy and Cliona Murphy (Dublin: Poolbeg Press, 1989), 15–50.

70. This impetus is noted in the Irish literature cited above. Campbell also observes a similar phenomenon in New South Wales. He notes that the Catholic Church discouraged women's involvement in rough agricultural work and "unfeminine labour." Middle-class ideals of domesticity and fragility were espoused, and the *Holy Family* (Christ and his parents, Mary and Joseph) was held up as a model for all Irish families. The Irish mother, located firmly within the home, was glorified. Indeed, the church actually invented a link between female domesticity and a "traditional" and distinctive Irish way of life—a linkage that had been far from the reality of many Irish women's lives. See Malcolm Campbell, *The Kingdom of the Ryans: The Irish in Southwest New South Wales, 1816–1890* (Sydney: University of New South Wales Press, 1997), 130–32.

71. QC, interview by author, St. Mary's, 11 September 1999.

72. Brian Clarke provides insight into these processes in industrializing Toronto. He argues that Irish Catholic women gained some moral authority in their homes at a

time when their economic contribution to the household was increasingly discounted. Recruited by the church to promote an increase in devotional practices, these women were exhorted to create spiritual havens for husbands and children, removed from the materialism of the outside world. Still, their moral authority was very much grounded in the cult of domesticity, and Catholic women were located very firmly in the home, with some mediating influence between household and parish. It was also an influence rooted in constructions of "female virtues" of piety, purity, obedience, humility, dependence, self-sacrifice, and service, as epitomized by church images of the Virgin Mary. Like Mary, Catholic women could create their own "holy family" by instructing their loved ones at the domestic hearth. Clarke observes that this image of "true womanhood" was quite convenient for Irish Catholic men, and while it gave Catholic women some authority in the home, it gave them very little influence outside it. Also, although they participated significantly in parish fund-raising, selling their baked and hand-crafted goods at bazaars and fairs, women's contribution was seen as an extension of their roles as wives and mothers, and they were subservient to male clergy, sodalities, and finance committees. See Clarke, *Piety and Nationalism: Lay Voluntary Associations and the Creation of an Irish-Catholic Community in Toronto, 1850–1895* (Montreal: McGill-Queen's University Press, 1993), chap. 4.

73. Because the Catholic population of Newfoundland was predominantly Irish, a strong link was naturally forged with the Catholic Church in Ireland. From the latter eighteenth century through the nineteenth century, Irish religious orders monopolized the spiritual stewardship of the island's Catholic congregation. Irish Augustinian friars and Irish Franciscan Recollet priests spearheaded this ministry; Presentation Sisters from Galway and the Sisters of Mercy from Dublin arrived in the colony in 1833 and 1842, respectively, to educate Catholic girls; and the Irish Christian Brothers came out to teach Catholic boys in 1875. Although these orders eventually admitted native Newfoundlanders, generations would pass before a substantial complement could be drawn from the local population. Furthermore, there was an early perception that local people would not make "proper" priests, nuns, or brothers. Recruitment of personnel from Ireland was thus quite significant, even into the twentieth century. See Byrne, ed., *Gentlemen-Bishops*; Arthur P. Monahan, "Canada," in *A History of Irish Catholicism*, ed. Patrick J. Corish (Dublin: Gill, 1971), 1–34; Rev. Michael F. Howley, *Ecclesiastical History of Newfoundland* (Boston: Doyle and Whittle, 1888; reprint, Belleville, ON: Mika, 1971); Sister M. Williamina Hogan, *Pathways of Mercy in Newfoundland, 1842–1984* (St. John's: Harry Cuff, 1986); Paul O'Neill, *Upon This Rock: The Story of the Roman Catholic Church in Newfoundland and Labrador* (St. John's: Breakwater Books, 1984); and A. L. O'Toole, *Challenged: The Story of Edmund Rice and the Christian Brothers in North America Since 1825* (Bristol: Burleigh Press, 1975).

9. THE "OTHER" WOMAN

While women on the southern Avalon during the period were predominantly of the Irish Catholic plebeian community, there were English Protestant and Irish Protestant women living in the area as well. They are not the focus of this study, and certainly an add-on chapter cannot to justice to their experiences, but they deserve some attention here. Indeed, women of the local elite have already been mentioned, albeit very peripherally as a foil to women of the Irish Catholic plebeian community. Thus a brief discussion of their lives is warranted to elucidate the various comparisons that have been made.

ENGLISH GENTRY WOMEN

These gentlewomen were the wives and daughters of local mercantile and professional men.[1] Their husbands, fathers, and brothers were merchant-planters, mercantile agents, ship owners and captains, naval officers, doctors, and Anglican clerics-men who also served as magistrates and local administrators (school board members, road commissioners, relief commissioners, customs collectors, and directors of hospital boards), and whose names appeared regularly on the grand jury lists and presentments for the area. From the mid-1830s onwards, they also formed the pool from which representatives to the island's House of Assembly were elected. This local gentry, in the broad sense of the word, was tied economically to the plebeian community through interdependence in the fishery. Nonetheless, they maintained social distance through their separate ethnoreligious pedigree, exclusive patterns of marriage and socializing, and different forms of consumption, housing, dress, and behavior (for a fuller discussion of class on the southern Avalon, see Appendix A).

This group increasingly adopted middle-class ideologies and lifestyles from the late eighteenth century onwards, and the construction of middle-class womanhood became one of the defining elements of their class identity. Middle-class men, by necessity, had to associate with the outside community on a daily basis. Some of their activities—their orchestration of supply and credit, their legal and administrative functions—reinforced the power dynamic between middle-class and plebeian communities. But the regular intermingling of men from both social groups on waterfront premises, in gardens and fields, in stores and public houses, tended to blur the boundaries of class somewhat within the small fishing villages of the area. Thus, the removal of middle-class women from the public sphere, the increasing separateness of their lives, and, in particular, the contrast between their lives and those of plebeian women were instrumental in reinforcing class distinctions on the southern Avalon.

This contrast, however, was less stark in the mid-1700s than it was a century later, for female roles among the local elite were not static over the study period, and the life experiences of these women changed in several respects over the span of a hundred years. The most obvious difference was their residence patterns, for most wives and daughters of merchant-planters, vessel owners, and naval officers operating in the area up to the late eighteenth century remained in the home country; in fact, few ever set foot on the southern Avalon. One of the earliest exceptions was Anne Wylley Carter, who came out to Ferryland from Sidmouth, Devon, with her husband, Robert, in the mid-eighteenth century. Indeed, according to the oral tradition, it was Anne who decided that the family would settle on the southern Avalon, for, while Robert had intended that Ferryland be merely a stopover on the way to the mainland, Anne "put her foot down and refused to go further."[2] Her instincts served her well, for the couple founded a local dynasty that carved out an extensive commercial, administrative, and judicial niche in the area and became one of its most wealthy and powerful families during the period of this study.

Anne's life would have been quite different from the lives of her granddaughters, or even those of her daughters later in the century. Despite the Carters' relative affluence, their original accommodations would have been fairly rudimentary in what was essentially still a fishing outpost with more temporary residents than long-term inhabitants. Still, they likely built or moved into a multi-roomed house more commodious than a fishing family's residence—perhaps a dwelling vacated by an outgoing merchant-planter—that likely combined the functions of residence and business.[3] Nonetheless, housewifery would have been less time-consuming until the family become more firmly established and until amenities increased and their housing became more elaborate. Anne's household production duties likely included outdoor as well as indoor work, although, unlike plebeian women, she would not have done shore work in the fishery, and her work outside the home would have been largely supervisory. More similar to plebeian women, but unlike her nineteenth-century descendants, she also would have taken significant responsibility for household management in terms of balancing the needs and resources of not only her family, but also large numbers of fishing and domestic servants. Indeed, it is quite likely that she perceived herself as an able planter and businesswoman in her own right. Because there were few other gentry families in the area, Anne's duties as hostess would have been less elaborate than those of nineteenth-century women. And because her opportunities for contact with other people of her class would have been limited, it is likely that she intermingled with the plebeian community more frequently than her female descendants and was more involved in the day-to-day life of the community.

Indeed, according to the oral tradition, Anne was no shrinking violet. She is credited with leading the women of Ferryland, for example, in defending the harbor against the French in 1762, towards the end of the Seven Years' War. A French force had arrived in Bay Bulls in June and moved northwards, taking St. John's, Carbonear, and Trinity. The Carters rallied the inhabitants of Ferryland and moved them with arms and provisions to the Isle aux Bois (also Isle du Bois), a small island with fishing premises at the mouth of the harbor. Robert Carter then outfitted a fleet of shallops and sailed northwards to meet the French at Bay Bulls. In the absence of the men, according to local collective memory, Anne and the other local women stationed themselves at the gun battery on the island and thwarted the attempt of two French warships to raze the settlement, fending them off with cannon fire.

Like most women of her day, regardless of class, Anne outlived her husband. She inherited from Robert's estate an annuity of £30 and the use of his household furniture during her widowhood, with the proviso that she would forfeit both upon remarriage. The couple's eldest son, William, received the bulk of the estate, while three other children were left small cash amounts (one guinea each) and personal property (such as clothing and books).[4] It is most likely that children other than the primary heir had already received their portions from the estate through a series of deeds of gift, marriage settlements, and trusts that were characteristic of their class. Within this system, female heirs were usually beneficiaries of passive property, from which they could obtain income but over which they could exercise no control. Anne's annuity, administered by her son William as executor of the estate and subject to forfeiture upon her remarriage, was a typical example.[5]

Still, as noted earlier, testation practices in Newfoundland did not always conform to an English norm of primogeniture and impartible inheritance, even among the local elite. Although Robert Carter Sr. opted to follow the English tradition, his second son and namesake did not. Robert Jr. would follow the local preference of "share and share alike" in the disposition of his estate. By his last will and testament, made shortly before his death in 1810, he left the remainder of his estate (after payment of a debt to his mother-in-law) to his wife, Eliza, and three children—Robert, Elisabeth, and James—in equal shares.[6]

Robert Jr. was a mariner, and he had married Elizabeth (or Eliza) Harris Howe, the daughter of a Devonshire glazier, in Dartmouth in 1789. Eliza typified a new generation of gentry women who were adopting local residence in greater numbers. She came out to the area with her husband, and while she may have returned to England on occasion, she was still residing in Ferryland in the 1820s, traveling back and forth occasionally to St. John's, where she ended her days in 1851.[7] By the time of Eliza's marriage, the lives of elite women on the southern Avalon had begun to change. More and more, the household was becoming the primary setting for their activities, as they withdrew from outdoor work. Houses had become larger, with two to three stories, multiple rooms, and elaborate furnishings requiring sharper attention to housewifery, as a more conspicuous display of consumption honed class distinctions.[8] Increasingly, these women's lives revolved around the management of household servants and rearing of children, the entertainment of social peers, and regular visits to St. John's and England to maintain family contacts, to arrange for the schooling of their sons (Eliza's sons, for example, were educated at Teignmouth in Devon), and to check out the latest fashions in furnishings and dress. More and more, their economic inactivity was becoming a hallmark of status and affluence.

Still, it was acceptable for women in difficult financial straits—widows, for example—to engage in certain genteel forms of economic activity, like teaching or inn-keeping.[9] Such was the fate of Mrs. Tree, the widow of an American loyalist captain who had accompanied her husband to Ferryland from Boston. The couple had lost considerable property during the American Revolution, and her husband's estate being thus diminished by the time of his death, Mrs. Tree turned to running an inn by the 1790s to maintain her lifestyle.[10] Eighteenth-century diarist Aaron Thomas described his encounter with the "corpulent" and convivial Mrs. Tree at her establishment, the London Inn, where he found her to be "in a very comfortable situation, . . . [with] a large and roomy House and Genteel Furniture." He reported:

> A Gentleman may have as good a Dinner and Rest at this House as any in Newfoundland. I Din'd here the day I made the Tour on Four Covers, Viz. a Boiled Leg of Pork, Fowls, Lamb, Ducks, Pudings, Green Pease and other Vegitables, served up with Sauces and Gravys. Had an Epicure been one of the Guests he could not a found fault with a single Dish.[11]

While Mrs. Tree was in reduced circumstances, having to run a "House of Entertainment," she was certainly more comfortably appointed than the woman at Thomas's next stop, for, when Mrs. Tree could not accommodate his request to sell him some fowls for his journey, Thomas searched around the settlement and eventually found himself, "amidst the rugged Barren and Houses," at the door of an Irish household:

> There was no person at home except a Weoman, the Mother of the Family, and she was ill in Bed. After thumping for some time at the door I heard a voice in the adjacent place (I cannot call it a Chamber). I went into it and beheld the Weoman in Bed, apparently very ill. . . . She related, at large, how many weeks she had been in Bed, how old she was, how many Children she had got, the age of her Husband, the part of Ireland she came from, how hard the times was, how slow the Fish bite at present and that there was nothing to be got but Flint Biscuits in Newfoundland.[12]

One suspects that her table would not have exhibited the same range of epicurean delights as Mrs. Tree's.

So the widow Tree still enjoyed a certain degree of material prosperity, but she was straddling the boundary of genteel "respectability" and plebeian "vulgarity"—a condition that she recognized herself, as she lamented her lack of proper society to Thomas. "I should like to go to Britain with you for the sight of a *Friend* would be very entertaining to me, having never *yet seen one*," she told him; and then, inviting him to join her in a drink, ". . . my Friends are my Irish Fishing Servants now in the Kitchen who, I am confident, will be as noisy and as merry and as *friendly* with you as your best *Friends* in England, providing you pay for the *Liquor* [emphasis in original]."[13] Thus, she found her position somewhat compromised by her need to work, her status rather tarnished when compared with other widows of her class who had been better provided for by their husbands' estates: Anne or Eliza Carter, for example, or Catharine Weston and Ann Sweetland—women who did not have to go out into the world to support themselves, women whose financial affairs and litigation in relation to property and estate matters were generally handled by male relatives or other men in their circle.[14]

Indeed, throughout the period, marriage was the most acceptable means of support for women of this class, and it increasingly became their only respectable option as their withdrawal into domesticity became an indicator of their class status. Of course, these unions had to be carefully arranged, for marriages among the elite were social and economic partnerships between families, rather than arrangements between individuals, as in the plebeian community. Strategic alliances helped to expand networks and consolidate family holdings; as such, they were instrumental in the formation and reinforcement of class in the area. Because the economic and social stakes were higher, then, these marriages were more heavily orchestrated than plebeian marriages. In the process, genteel women were more subject to commodification, being treated as marriageable possessions by which kinship networks, contacts, and capital could be expanded.[15] Unregulated marriages, by contrast, threatened to erode carefully established socioeconomic networks. A small island in Ferryland harbor stands testament to the importance of "proper" marriage choices for women of the local elite. The island is called *Nancy's Portion* and lies just off the shore of Isle aux Bois. It is a small hummock of land with no beach area—useless for grazing sheep or drying fish. According to the oral tradition, it was the only endowment of Judge Carter from his large estate to his daughter Nancy, who had "married beneath herself" and thus incurred her father's wrath.[16]

With pressures on their young to enter into suitable marriages, the middle class on the southern Avalon became a largely endogamous group in terms of ethnicity and class by the early nineteenth century, either marrying within their own local circle or recruiting partners from middle-class families in St. John's or areas in England such as Dartmouth and Topsham, where traditional links to the fishery continued to be maintained. An examination of the partial Carter and Morry family trees in Appendix E, for example, demonstrates a common pool of families from which marriage partners were drawn—Carter, Morry, Sanders, Sweetland, Lemessurrier, Tessier, Rendell, Skinner, Williams—all middle-class families with significant interconnections in their private and public lives.

Daughters were provided with numerous opportunities to meet acceptable future husbands, as these families socialized exclusively amongst their social peers at home and when visiting St. John's and England. While there was a high degree of mixing of middle-class men in terms of their economic and administrative functions as well as social networks (for example, dinners, clubs, trout fishing, hunting and shooting parties), there were various mixed-sex gatherings as well: walks, picnics, boat rides, teas and dinners, dances, carriage and sleigh rides, and carefully arranged long-term visits with families in the marriage pool.

But outside this closely supervised social whirl, the lives of elite women became increasingly circumscribed as the first half of the nineteenth century unfolded. More and more, middle-class assumptions of femininity shaped their lives. Women were no longer expected to carry out the traditional tasks of housewifery, but rather to oversee their execution by household servants.

Withdrawal from outdoor work was complete, as women's activities came to revolve around the domestic hearth. Daughters received a general liberal education, and a wide range of interests—from gardening to politics—was encouraged, but their training was directed towards their future roles as wives, mothers, household mistresses, and diverting hostesses—in contrast to the business or professional orientation of their brothers' education.

Like their counterparts in the home country and in mainland colonies, they were expected, as potential wives, to develop "an aura of respectable leisure" and to contribute to a "culture of hospitality" that would reflect well on future husbands.[17] While plebeian daughters cooked and cleaned, made fish, tended gardens, foraged through woods and meadows for firewood and edible plants, middle-class women went on picnics, sketched pictures, wrote poetry, and cultivated appropriate feminine accomplishments as they strived towards British middle-class ideals.[18] And their gentility and respectability, their everyday behaviors and dress—and, ultimately, the behavior and dress of their children—helped to maintain class boundaries in small communities where the nature of economic activity necessitated substantial mixing of men of both classes.

Typical of this generation of women was Sarah Rendell Carter, a St. John's woman who married Robert Carter (grandson of Robert and Anne Wylley Carter, son of Robert Jr. and Eliza Howe Carter) on 25 April 1815.[19] Sarah was a daughter of a St. John's mercantile family that was part of the Carters' social and economic network. No diaries or letters written by Sarah survive in public repositories, but her husband's journal for the period from 1832 to the day before he died in 1852 still exists, and its entries permit us to steal a glimpse of what life was like for the wife of this local magistrate and businessman.

The diary begins long after the couple had married, and well after the birth of their seven children,[20] so it provides no insight into Sarah's efforts to adjust from town living to life in a fishing community, and from a sheltered girlhood to married life. It does not tell us how the couple were introduced; most likely, she met Robert on one of his numerous trips to the capital, although it is possible that the couple were first introduced on the southern Avalon, for an excursion to Ferryland to stay with family friends would have made a suitable holiday for a young woman of the St. John's middle class, provided she was properly chaperoned.[21] However they met, it is clear that the couple did not immediately set up their own household upon marriage, for on 15 September 1833—more than eighteen years after they had wed—Robert noted the day as the fifth anniversary "of residing at the Northside of the Harbor in my own home." It is likely, then, that the couple had lived for some time in Robert's family home with his widowed mother, Eliza.[22] Given the powerful position of widows in stem family households, we can only speculate whether Eliza's presence eased Sarah's transition into married life or made it more difficult for her to establish herself as household mistress.

Robert's phrase "*my* own home" is very telling, for Sarah seems to have been such a peripheral part of his life. She is a shadowy, amorphous figure in her husband's diary—referred to, when she is mentioned at all, as "Mrs. Carter" or "Mrs. C," never by her first name, and certainly never by any term of endearment.[23] Indeed, Sarah seemed to spend much of her time in St. John's with her family, and frequently traveled to England to visit relatives and to bring her sons, Robert and James, to and from school in Teignmouth, where their father had been educated before them.[24] Their daughters, by contrast, were educated at home, where they learned the domestic skills and genteel arts that would make them attractive potential wives.

The couple led far more separate lives than did plebeian couples of the period. Even on significant occasions such as Christmas Day or wedding anniversaries, Sarah did not appear to be in Ferryland. Note, for example, the following entries:

25 December 1833	. . . John Pollard and Henry Prim dined with *me* this day.
25 December 1839	. . . M^{r}. Bowman [the newly arrived Anglican minister] & family dined with *me* this day.
25 April 1836	The 21st Anniversary of my wedding day. My wife in England, sailed in December. Not a letter from England to this date, from her or any other of my friends there.[25]

The diary intimates that the couple had not anticipated remaining in Ferryland permanently when they first married, and perhaps as the likelihood of Robert's leaving became more remote, Sarah simply carried on her life elsewhere as much as possible. Certainly, Robert did not have as much opportunity to travel as his wife—likely because of business and magisterial commitments—and a strong sense of claustrophobia occasionally surfaces in his writing:

12 October 1832	This day I accomplished my 42nd year, having passed in Newfoundland very nearly 29 years of that time, in which time I have seen many changes but have observed the trade to be of that nature as never to allow any one concerned in the fishery to rise to affluence in any Outport, useless to regret it as my property lays here and cannot be now realized.[26]
12 October 1840	This day I complete my Fiftieth year of Age—thirty seven of which have been spent in this Place except having gone occasionally to England but not that for 14 years past.
25 April 1841	This is the 26th anniversary of my Wedding day the chief part of which period has been passed in Ferryland very contrary to my Expectations when I married ~

That April, Sarah again seemed to be absent. However, she was home on some anniversaries, as in 1835, when Robert recorded: "Walked out over the Downs with Mrs. Carter, Eliza and Fanny. This is the 20th anniversary of my marriage. Had no party last year or this."[27]

Yet even when Sarah was at home in Ferryland, her existence seemed frequently to run on a separate track from that of her husband. Unlike plebeian women, who often joined their menfolk in productive work, Sarah's household duties were all indoor and largely supervisory. Even this managerial role must have been limited by her frequent absences—and also, occasionally, by lengthy illness. Through the first half of 1834, for example, Robert's diary is peppered with entries such as: "Mrs. Carter very ill," and "Mrs. Carter ill in bed all day—Did not go out." The entries become increasingly terse—"Mrs. Carter confined to her room to-day"; "Mrs. Carter in her bedroom"; "Mrs. Carter in her room"—and one wonders whether she was availing herself of the fainting couch.[28] Still, she managed to step forth on occasions that spring and other years, usually to join her husband and children in the round of social activities typical of their circle:

16 March 1834	Mrs. Carter, self and son, with J.H.C. [his brother, James Howe Carter] drank tea at Caplin Bay.
25 March 1834	Mrs. Carter, self and Eliza invited to dine with the Judge, the former did not dine there but came up in the evening, not having returned from sleighing in time to dress.
31 July 1834	Went to Isle du Bois to tea:—Mrs. C. and Fanny my brother, Mr. Shears, S. Prowse and other children.
12 August 1835	A party to dinner at Isle du Bois at my invitation, ladies and gentlemen, which passed off very comfortably. . . . Danced in the evening.

How much time Sarah spent socializing exclusively with other women in the area is not evident from Robert's writing. Indeed, his diary creates the impression that women socialized more frequently in mixed activities, although this may be because of his inattention to (or unawareness of) the details of women's lives that did not intersect his own. But certainly, her participation in mixed gatherings and in the extension of hospitality to guests was one of the necessary methods by which Sarah, as a middle-class woman, contributed to her family's status. Hospitality was a means of reinforcing the family's public reputation for affluence and power by opening up for scrutiny the circumstances of their domestic lives.[29] The genteel woman was a central image in the tableau, for the figure of the "lady" was important in "constructing social space" through a form of socializing peculiar to the middle class.[30]

As the diary progresses, however, Sarah is mentioned with less and less frequency, and one wonders how much time she was spending away from Ferryland. Perhaps the sorrow of her daughter Emily's death in early 1837 kept her increasingly away from home. Certainly, Robert's socializing took on more homosocial aspects: dinners and shooting parties with male relatives and friends, even a dinner club formed in January of 1842, with six members to meet weekly at Three Corner Pond.[31]

At any rate, it is obvious that Sarah's geographic mobility was much greater than that of plebeian women of the area, while her productive and managerial roles were more limited. But like many women of the period, regardless of class, Sarah outlived her husband by several decades. In her widowhood, she was perhaps more influential than she had been as a wife in terms of the powers she was granted under her husband's will to act as executor and dispose of real property as necessary for her support (see Chapter 7). Whether she exercised these powers or relinquished the practical control of such matters to male relatives is unclear; certainly, she left court appearances on estate matters to male attorneys. She spent her final years in St. John's and died at her Cochrane Street home in 1879 at the age of 87.[32] Following the principle of equitable distribution typical of nineteenth-century Newfoundland testation practices, she left all her property to her five surviving children equally, with the express provision that the shares of her married daughters "shall be for their sole and separate use and not subject to either the debts or control of their respective husbands."[33]

A slightly younger contemporary of Sarah Carter was Harriet Maria Skinner Carter, the daughter of Harriet Williams and Colonel Thomas Skinner, commander of the Royal Newfoundland Regiment at St. John's. Harriet's family was also part of the St. John's circle with whom the Carter family socialized, and on 27 May 1826, she married Arthur Hunt Carter (a first cousin of Sarah's husband, and the son of vice-admiralty judge William Carter and Catherine Weston) and began her married life in Ferryland.[34] Perhaps the marriage was a love match, or perhaps its chief purpose was to shore up St. John's–Ferryland connections. At any rate, monetary gain was not Arthur's primary motivation, for Harriet's uncle George Williams congratulated Harriet from his home in England on having for a husband "a man of sense and liberality who has chosen a wife for her personal merit in despite of the disadvantage of fortune."[35]

In fact, Harriet had not come to the marriage completely empty-handed. She was supposed to be receiving the income from an annuity of £17—a portion of the rental from a St. John's property in the estate of her maternal uncle, Monier Williams.[36] The annuity was actually held by her father, in right of his wife (who was deceased), and had at one point been signed over to another party as security for debt. However, Harriet's brother, Lieutenant Thomas Skinner, had cleared the debt for his father in 1824, with the understanding that the rental thenceforth be paid to Harriet. This was another typical example of the passive property of which middle-class women were beneficiaries. Atypically in this case, however, the annuity did not pass over to Arthur in right of his wife upon their marriage, since it technically remained in her father's name (or so Arthur later argued to the trustees in his bankruptcy). Still, it was primarily Arthur who corresponded with various interested parties in relation to the rental income throughout the years, and it is therefore likely that Harriet had ceded practical control of this and other financial matters to her husband. This appeared to be the assumption of her English uncle George Williams, who approached her in 1833 to consent to a potential sale of the rental property "when you have consulted with M^r^. Carter (your husband)."[37] Unfortunately for Harriet and Arthur, the benefit of the annuity was never fully realized, as there were ongoing disputes among the beneficiaries of the Monier Williams estate over the disposition of the property, the amount of the rental, and the arrears owed by tenants. As late as 1847 (well after Harriet's death), Arthur was still trying to collect the balance of arrears.[38]

The annuity, although small, might have provided some comfort to the couple in the tenuous financial situation in which they found themselves soon after their wedding. Arthur himself was described in the Anglican parish records as a "gentleman," reflecting the moneyed status of his family, but by the late 1820s and early 1830s he had encountered financial difficulties and was undergoing bankruptcy examinations.[39] Still, he threw himself enthusiastically into farming and agricultural experiments, and successfully applied for a grant of land at Merrymeeting River, Ferryland, which he had already staked and clear-burned.[40] Harriet boasted to her English relatives that he was "indefatigable in his exertions on his new estate."[41]

Harriet had received the liberal education typical of young women of her class, and she carried out a correspondence with her uncle George Williams in England that demonstrated not only a high degree of literacy, but also an interest in international politics and agricultural experimentation (especially in introducing new plant species into Newfoundland).[42] Indeed, George placed a good deal of stock in Harriet's observations about farming as a viable alternative to fishing on the island. In 1827, he commented in a letter to Arthur on Harriet's acumen:

> I mean to . . . acknowledge the gratification I had from the details which your intelligent wife gave of your country, and its present condition. It would not be the worst proof that Bathurst and the rest of them who set themselves up to govern our colonies gave of their fitness for the affair if they were to seek such sources of information as this of my cousin Harriett, for the dull fellows in whom they put their trust seem only to mislead them. . . . Harriets account of the prosperous farms that are growing up around you makes me almost languish for a lot myself of 300 Acres, and I really think I shall make some effort towards it.[43]

Although Harriet's optimism about the agricultural potential of the Ferryland area may have been misplaced, apparently her uncle treated her opinions with respect. Harriet and Arthur sent local plant specimens and produce to George, and he in turn sent them seeds and seedling plants to introduce into their Ferryland holding. There is one reference to Harriet's sending out servants to pick berries, and her uncle remarks upon the delicious taste of "the Capillaire berries [creeping snowberries], the fruit of her research."[44] It is evident from most of the correspondence, however, that while Harriet was intellectually interested in agricultural experimentation, she was generally removed from the actual process—that the operation and management of the farm was in Arthur's hands and that he and hired servants provided the labor.

In a letter to George, undated but written circa 1830, Harriet admitted, "I am not very strong myself not half so hardy as I ought to be to make an *active Farmers wife* [emphasis in original]."[45] Arthur had been detained by bad weather during a recent trip to St. John's and was so behind in his farm work that he had given over the care of the family's kitchen garden to Harriet, a responsibility that seemed to overwhelm her somewhat, although it would certainly have been a comfortable domain for women within the plebeian community (or, for that matter, Arthur's grandmother, Anne Wylley Carter). Harriet attributed her general feeling of weakness to the fact that she was still nursing her fourteen-month-old daughter, and looked forward to regaining her strength after the child was weaned. One cannot help but compare this lengthy recovery from childbirth with the immediate return to productive work by plebeian women after a nine-day lying-in period.

Turning from matters agricultural, Harriet demonstrated great enthusiasm for the "very pretty gown" of the latest spring fashion that she had recently received from her uncle and her English cousins: "it was the first of it's kind imported into Ferryland," she wrote, "which I am sure you will think added not a little to its value." This was not the only reference in the correspondence between the two in relation to dresses or materials being sent out to Harriet,[46] and she was quite grateful for the gifts, because she was aware of the importance of her dress and her behavior in maintaining social distance in the small community of Ferryland and also in preserving her family's position among their social peers. She wrote:

> . . . my dear kind Uncle I feel truly obliged for the trouble you have taken to put me in possession of the material and information to be *fashionable.* Dress seems every day becoming a subject of increasing importance & without attending in some measure to it we can hardly "pass blameless" thro' the crowd . . . [emphasis in original]

Indeed, Harriet was conscious of her social status and seemed to remain aloof from women of the primarily Irish plebeian community. She was even reluctant to hire local female help for the kitchen garden, for example: "The people here I am sorry to say are not at all too honest, and if we hire a woman . . . for a day or two, it is impossible to leave her a moment if we wish the seed to be put in our own ground." This same sense of class and ethnic difference had been articulated some thirty-five years earlier by the gregarious Mrs. Tree. Her experience in the hospitality trade may have made her less fastidious about the company she kept, but her sardonic comments about her Irish "friends" revealed that a sense of separateness from the plebeian community already existed—a distance that was even more pronounced within the next generation of middle-class women in the area.

Still, while Harriet's circumstances differed in many respects from those of most Irish women on the shore, some of her concerns would have been shared with other women in the population. She wrote about family health matters, for example:

> . . . my little girl . . . 14 months old . . . had the whooping cough all the winter and the small pox was in Ferryland since the beginning of Lent, my children had not been vaccinated against Cow-pox and no virus was to be obtained until lately, however Thank God they both escaped the former [smallpox] and have since taken the latter disease [cowpox] I hope, effectually [for immunization to smallpox].

In general, however, common experiences such as marriage, childbirth, or potential widowhood did not create gender solidarity across class boundaries on the southern Avalon. Women such as Harriet and Sarah Carter were isolated from women of the plebeian community by education, mannerisms, life-style, and the less explicitly productive, more social nature of their contribution to family economies.

In this last regard, these nineteenth-century middle-class women were even more removed from the larger community than was their husbands' grandmother, Anne Wylley Carter, and one senses their isolation and constant longing to be elsewhere—in St. John's or England, closer to a larger society of their own social peers. Sarah eventually escaped to St. John's, but Harriet's concerns about her inability to endure her new lifestyle were confirmed all too soon. She had five children in fairly quick succession in the late 1820s and early 30s—the last, her namesake, born in August of 1834—and then died the following year at the age of thirty-six.[47] The parish register did not record the cause of her death; neither did her diarist cousin-in-law. She may have fallen victim to a disease such as diphtheria or scarlet fever, or she may have died of complications from giving birth—a common fate for women of the period, and one that ignored ethnicity and class.[48]

Representative of the next generation of middle-class women on the southern Avalon was Mary Ann Simms Carter, who married Robert and Sarah

Carter's son Robert in the late 1840s. Mary Ann was the daughter of George Simms, a justice of the peace in Trepassey and colleague of her future father-in-law. Indeed, Robert Carter's diary indicates that she and her parents were occasional visitors to the Carter home in the late 1830s and 1840s; doubtless, the hospitality was reciprocated, and it is also likely that Mary Ann was part of the larger social gatherings attended by members of both sexes. Mary Ann and Robert wed on 1 June 1847, and the couple had ten children over the course of their marriage.[49]

Mary Ann left a tracing of one brief period of her life in the form of a scrapbook, a collection of pencil sketches and poetry assembled in her early womanhood (teens and early twenties) before her marriage to Robert.[50] It suggests a genteel and sheltered upbringing, from the inscription on the flyleaf—"Mary Ann Simms/Given to her at Christmas/By her Affectionate Papa. . . . /1839"—to the tranquil drawings of country scenes (some, far too pastoral to be of the area and possibly done in England or copied from prints) and the various moral sayings surrounded by embossed floral borders. Most of the scrapbook, however, is taken up with handwritten poetry, the titles reflecting properly feminine concerns of the heart and hearth: "Remembrances," "On the hearts Struggles," "Secret,[51] " "Song of the Spirit of Love," "Friendship," "Domestic Love," "Woman," "The Path of Life." Typical of the contents of genteel young women's scrapbooks of the period, these offerings were generally not original verse, but copies of poems from other sources that were in fairly wide circulation among members of Mary Ann's class. They served not only as a show of refinement but also as a means of expressing feelings suitable to particular occasions.

Most telling are a series of highly emotional poems entered in 1844 by Mary Ann and a number of friends. Although they are mostly transcriptions, their tone strongly suggests that she was leaving Trepassey, possibly in preparation for marriage. In Mary's hand, "The Brides Farewell" (taken from "The Bride of the Greek Isle," by Felicia Hemans) intimates her desolation at leaving the shelter of her childhood home:

Why do I weep?-to leave the vine
Whose clusters o'er me bend?
The myrtle - yet, oh! call it mine!
The flowers I loved to tend?
A thousand thoughts of all things dear,
Like shadows o'er me sweep
I leave my sunny childhood here
Oh! Therefore let me weep!

The poem goes on to bid farewell to a cherished sister, who has been a close companion "by stream, by shore, in song, in prayerful sleep"; a doting father, "whose eye o'er all my youth hath smiled"; a loving mother, whose "lips . . . have lulled me with your strain, eyes . . . have watched my sleep." Each verse ends with the entreaty: "Let me weep!"

There follows a series of poems that suggest that what was likely an arranged marriage to consolidate two powerful local families was having a profound effect possibly on disappointed romantic partners and certainly on a circle of close girlhood friends. Immediately following "The Brides Farewell" come the following verses (from "Lines Written in an Album, at Malta" by Lord Byron, 1809), signed "John":

As o'er the cold sepulchral stone
Some name arrests the passer-by;
Thus, when thou view'st this page alone,
May mine attract thy pensive eye!

And when by thee that name is read,
Perchance some succeeding year,
Reflect on me as on the dead.
And think my heart is buried there.

Another hand takes over with this unsigned offering:

To Mary
Lines addressed to a young Lady on bidding her farewell
10 Sep 1844

Adieu, dear Maid, stern fate decrees
That we must shortly sever
And if we ne'er should meet again
Adieu adieu for ever.

I'd say could I with impious thoughts
Accuse the warp of heaven
Why has the wish to call thee mine
Without the power been given?

And similar outpourings came from "AM^cLH" or "A.M^c", who penned several dramatic leave-takings on 11 July 1844—"The Parting Kiss," "Lines on the evening of Separation," and "To x x x x ~" (from "To Emma," also by Byron):

Since now the hour is come at last,
When you must greet your anxious lover;
Since now our dream of bliss is past,
One pang, my girl, and all is over.

The poem goes on to describe various romantic encounters, and ends:

This is the deepest of our woes,
For this our tears these cheeks bedew
This is of love, the final close
Oh! God, the fondest, last adieu!

While it would not have been unusual to write such lines upon leaving a friend's parlor after a visit, the clustering and tone of these verses suggests an emotional parting. One facet was shared by these and all the other love poems appearing in the album: none were signed or initialed by Mary Ann's future husband, Robert Carter.

The scrapbook entries end in 1844, as if signaling the end of Mary Ann's youth. The image that remains with the reader is one of a genteel young woman, much loved and indulged by family and friends, who was suddenly thrust from her childhood paradise into the reality of a marriage of convenience. Whether or not she was happy in her marriage—as, indeed, some parties to arranged marriages were—the public record does not reveal. But her pathway there—from cosseted child to cultured and romantic young woman, from obedient daughter to dutiful wife and mother—was one that was followed by many other young women of her class in the period.

Mary Ann represents the final generation of elite women during the study period. Her experiences before entering into marriage were quite different from those of young women of the plebeian community at the mid-nineteenth century; indeed, her life also differed significantly from that of her husband's pioneering great-grandmother. The overall impression created by the experiences of the Carter women is one of decreasing influence and increasing withdrawal into genteel domesticity as one generation succeeded the next. Of course, the movement was not simultaneous for all middle-class women of the area, and for a number, domesticity and economic idleness may well have remained more a social ideal than a reality. Mrs. Tree, for example, could not afford the luxury of economic inactivity, her lived experience a contradiction of the model that was being constructed by gender ideology of the day. But it was an ideal that was aspired to by these women and their families in a way that was not embraced by women of the plebeian community in this time frame. The various references to female acquaintances in Robert Carter's diary indicate that a significant number of women were moving steadily towards the ideal by the latter decades of the study period, as they found themselves increasingly circumscribed by the domestic sphere.

"EXCEPTIONAL" WOMEN

This discussion of women of the local elite, seen primarily through the lives of the Carters, has created an image of a group that was homogenous in terms of ethnicity, but real life is rarely so tidy. While class did tend to be linked with ethnicity along the southern Avalon, with most of the gentry being English Protestant and most of the plebeian community being Irish Catholic (or in the process of being assimilated into that ethnoreligious group through intermarriage), there were exceptions, particularly in the earlier part of the period. For example, in the eighteenth century there were various Irish Protestant merchant-planters operating in the area, some of whose wives and daughters lived at least part of their lives on the southern Avalon.

The Benger family provides a good example. We have already encountered Mary Kirke, the widow of David Kirke Jr., who married James Benger, a merchant from Waterford, and became the matriarch of a significant mercantile and landholding family in Ferryland (see Chapter 4). Their son, John, became a merchant-planter and justice of the peace in the area. He married a St. John's woman, Serah, and the couple had six children: three girls and three boys. Serah resided in Ferryland with her husband (although she doubtless visited her relatives and friends in St. John's on occasion). Meanwhile, John Benger had formed a partnership with Richard Nason of Youghal, and the two held various properties in Ferryland, Aquaforte, Fermeuse, and Renews that they used in their trade or rented to various tenants. Their alliance was reinforced when John's daughter, Dorcas Benger, married Richard's son, Richard Nason Jr., in 1754. The parties entered into a marriage settlement. Although details are not available, it is possible that certain properties on the southern Avalon were transferred to Richard Jr. at that time, since Richard Jr. and Dorcas's brother, John Jr., were managing the properties during the second half of the century.[52]

The oral tradition suggests that the marriage between Dorcas and Richard was not a happy one and that Dorcas was one of the unfortunate women for whom an economic union between families did not develop into a companionate marriage. Dorcas bore eight children and died in Ferryland, likely when she was in her late forties or early fifties.[53] Richard moved with his children back to his family home in Youghal, passing the sole management of the properties over to his brother-in-law, John. He ultimately left his Ferryland properties to his Irish mistress, Anstice Gorman, and their son Thomas Nason by his will of 1818; because Thomas predeceased his mother, the properties devolved entirely to Anstice and ultimately to her nephew John Nunan.[54]

Meanwhile, Dorcas's sister Rachel had married another merchant-planter, William Dobel, of Boston, in 1765; the couple had six children, all born in Ferryland. Their marriage, from various accounts, appears to have been somewhat happier than that of Dorcas and Richard Nason. Rachel and William left Ferryland in 1782, and William left the management of his Ferryland properties to John Benger Jr. (it is likely that at least some part of the properties had come to William by way of a marriage settlement with the Bengers as well). The couple lived in Ireland for two years and then settled on an estate on the banks of the Delaware River, near Philadelphia, where they were joined by Rachel's unmarried siblings, Thomas and Mary. William died there in 1788, and Rachel "did not long survive the loss of so kind & indulgent a Husband whom she soon followed."[55]

Another Irish Protestant mercantile and landholding family on the southern Avalon were the Ludwiggs, also from Waterford. John Ludwigg operated out of the area and was justice of the peace there in the late 1720s and early 1730s. Whether his wife, Mary, joined him on the southern Avalon is unclear, but she did inherit his interests in various properties in the area and, in turn, left them to her children, William and Mary Fitzwalter, who remained in Ireland and disposed of the properties by the early 1800s.[56] Thus, there were some Irish Protestant gentry women living or holding interests on the southern Avalon, although most of these families had moved by the turn of the nineteenth century and were winding up their interests in the area.

While the local gentry of the eighteenth century were almost wholly Protestant (be it English or Irish), they were not exclusively so. William Coman, for example, was a Catholic merchant from Waterford City with substantial holdings in the Ferryland area in the eighteenth century. And at least one Irish Catholic woman married into the ranks of the local elite. Catherine Cooney of Kilkenny married Peter Weston, an English Protestant merchant-planter, who would ultimately become a justice of the peace in Ferryland. Their daughter Ann married William Carter, who would become a vice-admiralty judge for the island. Thus Catherine became the matriarch of two powerful local families. She and both her daughters co-inherited considerable property at Peter's death, and she was still administering her portion at the turn of the century, initiating various suits against recalcitrant debtors and tenants (although she was usually represented in actual court hearings by men from her circle).[57] Like her contemporary Anne Wylley Carter, then, Catherine had a hand in the management of her financial affairs and also wielded some power in the broader life of the community. Indeed, when Catholic Prefect Apostolic James O Donel was having difficulty in establishing his nominee, Father Ewer, at Ferryland in the late 1780s because he could not unseat the maverick priest Patrick Power (see Chapter 5), it is likely that Catherine was key in rallying sympathy for the renegade within her social circle. Irish Catholic Church authorities felt that the matter could be resolved if Catherine could be convinced to switch allegiance and use her considerable influence to persuade the gentry community to withdraw their support of Power—a sure indication of her authority because this group was largely Protestant. In 1788, Father Phelan, the Franciscan Superior at Waterford, wrote to Archbishop Troy of Dublin:

> I was advised to write to Doctor Lanagan [Bishop of Ossory] in favour of Mr Ewer & had that interest been gain'd, Power must, all at once, fall to the ground: Viz a lady of great influence lives in Feriland by name, a Widow Weston a Roman Catholik & a native of Kilkeny [Power's home county]. I wrote to Dr. Lanagan & requested he'd write to this Lady, & recommend Mr. Ewer to her as being the only clergyman qualified to officiate, and also to withdraw her protection from Power &c. The Doctor has not answered me, & it's very probable he has not wrote to Feriland: this makes me suspect he is for Power.[58]

Typical of her generation of gentry women, Catherine was more powerful than her daughters and granddaughters. And, like the Benger women, she demonstrates that not all members of the elite on the southern Avalon had an English Protestant pedigree, particularly in the eighteenth century.

However, the ethnoreligious homogeneity of the group began to firm up by the late eighteenth and early nineteenth centuries, as many Irish merchants voluntarily wound up their affairs on the southern Avalon or went bankrupt.[59] Yet even this consistency varied somewhat geographically, for in St. Mary's district, a number of Irish names had begun to creep into the grand jury lists by the late 1830s, indicating that at least several members of that ethnic group had become significant property and business owners by that time. This contrasted markedly with Ferryland district, where only a couple of Irish names—Cashin and O'Neil—had sufficient family status and property to be considered "principal Merchants and Gentlemen" of their communities by the latter part of the study period.[60] Neither, however, became part of the Carters' social network.

One more set of exceptions must be noted to the relationship between class and ethnicity in the area. Just as the southern Avalon elite was not entirely English Protestant, neither were all English Protestants in the area part of the local elite. This was particularly true in the eighteenth century, when English Protestant servants were still coming out to the area to work in the fishery. Skilled artisans at that time—carpenters, blacksmiths, coopers, sail-makers—also tended to be English Protestant. As noted earlier, however, Irish servants increasingly replaced English servants in the fishery, and the English plebeian community was increasingly assimilated into the Irish Catholic ethnoreligious group. Still, there were holdouts into the nineteenth century, such as the Halls, Perrymans, and Paynes of Aquaforte, or the Boons and Butlers of Ferryland. The women in these families, like Irish women in the plebeian community, were involved in economic production and, like other plebeian women, participated in community life, sometimes in interpersonal confrontations that brought them to the attention of authorities. Several incidents will illustrate the point.

On Wednesday, 22 June 1842, Ellen Payne of Aquaforte lodged a complaint with the court that, on the previous Friday and Saturday, Sarah and Catherine Payne had violently beaten her and had forcibly removed her six-month-old child from her custody.[61] The records are frustratingly sparse, but it is highly probable that these women were related to each other, either by blood or marriage. This could possibly have been a situation in which the two perpetrators felt that the mother was unfit and were taking matters into their own hands as the next nearest female relatives of the child. Although Catherine and Sarah were ordered to give security to keep the peace for twelve months for this particular episode, Ellen's problems with her assailants did not end there. In August of 1851, she again complained to the court that she had been "assaulted, abused, threatened and beaten" by Catharine and Sarah, who had now been joined by Elizabeth Frost and Barbara Sisk (or Sesk), also of Aquaforte.[62] Again, the motivation for the incident is missing from the record, but the episode suggests a collective shaming or disciplinary action by a group of women against another in their community.

A more explicit example of an attempt by English Protestant plebeian women to enforce community standards again involved women of Aquaforte, including the irrepressible Sarah Payne.[63] The incident unfolds through the recording of two back-to-back court cases in 1854. On 13 July 1854, Mary Ann Perryman of Aquaforte appeared in court to name Marmaduke Clow of Ferryland as the father of her unborn child and to seek support. The very act of confronting him in open court in an effort to make him admit financial responsibility was itself a public assertion of informal power. Marmaduke, however, denied that he was the father.[64] The next day, he was waylaid at Ferryland by Mary Ann's neighbors from Aquaforte, Peter and Sarah Payne, who began to abuse him by John Morry's wharf. Peter was carrying a hatchet and thrust it into the wharf in a threatening fashion. When Marmaduke tried to escape, Sarah Payne grabbed him and struck him several times. Peter and Sarah took turns threatening him with the hatchet, and Sarah varied the routine by throwing rocks at Marmaduke.[65]

The fact that Marmaduke was a court official (acting clerk of the peace) and had sufficient connections to have Henry Morry of the local mercantile elite stand bond for him may have caused concern that the alleged father was going to escape formal justice. Also, the fact that Marmaduke was not originally from the southern Avalon (he hailed from Port-aux-Basques) may have added motivation to the Paynes' concern about his adherence to local norms of behavior.[66] Meanwhile, if Mary Ann Perryman's claim was true, Marmaduke's upcoming nuptials to Mary Johnson likely gave him strong motivation to deny paternity. Unfortunately, the final disposition of the case is not indicated in the records, but it is worthy of note in terms of the efforts of these women to enforce community standards by shaming a man into assuming his alleged paternal responsibilities. Although evidence on English Protestant women of the plebeian community is sparse, given their relatively low numbers at the time the court records began, these anecdotes suggest a willingness to involve themselves in the politics of interpersonal confrontation. Certainly, they were essential producers in family economies, like their Irish counterparts, and they likely enjoyed a similar degree of authority and status as a result of their productive activity and the generally more equitable gender relations that pervaded the plebeian community during the study period.

CONCLUSION

The core of the elite community on the southern Avalon was formed by a group of families with English Protestant ethnoreligious ties that held key mercantile, professional, and administrative positions in the community. Elite women were thus members of the most powerful families in the area. They traveled more than plebeian women, received broader educations, enjoyed greater access to amenities and consumer goods, and had better housing and dress. Yet in many respects, they had less influence in their homes and communities than plebeian women had in theirs, particularly by the early nineteenth century. Unlike plebeian women, who continued to negotiate status and influence for themselves in flakes and fields, in courthouse and tavern, and in the everyday running of their households, middle-class women were increasingly marginalized from the public sphere of economic production, from community politics, and even from the financial aspects of household management. Widowhood gave some an entrèe into economic activity, but most confined their public appearances to church-going and properly chaperoned travel and social events, where they conveyed status and gentility through their dress, their mannerisms, and their networks of acquaintances and friends.

This was a process that unfolded over several generations: the relatively public and active lives of Anne Wylley Carter or Catherine Weston, for example, contrasted with the more circumspect activities of the elusive Sarah Carter and her frail cousin-in-law Harriet. But even these earlier gentry women eschewed field and shore work, and were absent from the courtroom and the public house. Increasingly, the activities of middle-class women played out in the domestic sphere or in public gatherings that were highly social in aspect. Totally absent in the study area were the types of activities that gave middle-class women elsewhere a "respectable" admittance to the public sphere—church fund-raising and philanthropic work, for example, or anti-slavery and temperance movements. Along the southern Avalon, the lives of these women focused increasingly inward on domestic concerns, particularly on the rearing of children and the supervision of servants. While their economic idleness became a hallmark of their class, this inactivity disempowered middle-class women and relegated their lives more and more to the mediation of patriarchy.

NOTES

1. The following discussion will be based primarily (although not exclusively) on women in the Carter family of Ferryland, for two main reasons. First, the family epitomizes the local elite in the study area in terms of their range of activities and life experiences. Second, a fair number of documentary sources are available on the family, making their lives more readily accessible to the modern-day historian. Among these sources are the Carter Family Papers (PANL, MG 31), the Carter–Benger–Nason Papers (PANL, MG 247), the Robert Carter Diary (PANL, MG 920; also available at the Ferryland Museum and at MHA, MF-053 [typed transcript, 1832–37 only]), and the Mary Ann Simms Scrapbook (PANL, MG 708).

2. HE, Ferryland, correspondence to author, 8 March 1999.

3. Pocius describes the house of contemporary merchant Arthur Holdsworth in Ferryland. Built around 1770, it measured 60 feet by 24 feet and was constructed of stone. The ground floor consisted of a parlor, counting house, and shop; the second level contained four rooms; the house was topped with an attic fitted as warehousing space for dry goods. The property contained several other buildings: a stable, cooper's shop, barking house, and a row of fishermen's cottages. This house, together with other structures, including another large, two-story structure with hipped attic and chimneys, is shown on the "Holdsworth Map" drawn when the plantation was surveyed for sale ca. 1835. See Gerald L. Pocius, "Architecture on Newfoundland's South-

ern Shore: Diversity and the Emergence of New World Forms," *Society for the Study of Architecture in Canada Bulletin* 8, no. 2 (June 1983): 13 and 15.

4. PANL, MG 31, Carter Family Papers, file 33, Will of Robert Carter Sr., 29 March 1795. Another child, Mary Sanders, had already received her portion, likely before her marriage, and may have predeceased her father. See Chapter 7.

5. This type of annuity typically came from a rent charge on land that had been purchased with the cash portion the wife had brought into the marriage. The rent provided a source of income for the couple and a means of maintaining the wife in widowhood, with the advantage of keeping the main estate intact for the heir. Erickson describes it as "a form of inheritance designed to create dependence." See Amy Louise Erickson, *Women and Property in Early Modern England* (London: Routledge, 1993), 25 and 70.

6. PANL, GN 5/1/C/9, 8 (12), Will of Robert Carter, 3 June 1810.

7. See: PANL, MG 920, Robert Carter Diary; and FMDB, file 02B, Morry and Carter Families.

8. For example, in PANL, MG 31, Carter Family Papers, there are two sketches of quite elaborate houses. One is labeled "The Judges old house in Ferryland" (possibly belonging to vice-admiralty judge William Carter) and shows the façade of a large, two-and-one-half story stone structure with four portals (suggesting four separate residential units), a central archway for carriage entrance to the stores, six glazed windows on the main floor and twelve on the second, and a high A-framed attic (no chimneys, but this was obviously an oversight). See file 61. The other is a cartoon sketch and shows the façade of a two-and-one-half story structure with two end chimneys for heating, a high A-framed attic, a shed extension at the back, a side extension with a door and three windows, and an ornate entranceway flanked by two glazed windows on either side. In the same garden, there is a smaller outbuilding, possibly a separate servants' quarters, and the property is surrounded by a picket fence. The sketch is not dated, but the paper contains a watermark: John Hayes 1822. See file 66. Pocius provides a description of the substantial home built by the Sweetland mercantile family in Caplin Bay in the early nineteenth century. The house was a full-Georgian structure, typical of those built in Nova Scotia and New England, with imported frame, two and one-half stories, large rooms, large central hallway, and end chimneys, indicating upper-floor hearths for heating. He also describes the contemporary home of the Morry family, a much smaller, but still substantial, "Georgian-influenced" two-story structure with kitchen and parlor on the first floor separated by a central stairway, and two end chimneys, indicating that the upper story was heated by separate hearths, rather than by warm air rising from below. See Gerald L. Pocius, *A Place to Belong: Community Order and Everyday Space in Calvert, Newfoundland* (Athens: University of Georgia Press, 1991), 204 and 223–24.

9. Of course, teaching was not an option on the southern Avalon until the 1830s. Eliza Coulman, Anne Wylley Carter's great-granddaughter, was the first teacher for Ferryland and Caplin Bay under the newly appointed school board in 1836.

10. In the 1800 family census for Ferryland that forms part of the Pole Papers, a widow by the name of Bridget Tree appears as the head of a household with her son,

Philip, aged 28, still living at home. Doubtless, this was the merry widow of Thomas's journal. Nonetheless, there was no record of her holding a liquor license—yet another example of the hidden participation of women in this trade. In 1795, the year of Thomas's writing, a liquor license for Ferryland district was issued to "Frances" Tree—doubtless a clerical error. See PANL, GN 2/1/A, vol. 13, 225–26, Robert Carter to Governor Waldegrave, 7 September 1797 (reporting retrospectively). There are no surviving licensing records for 1796 and 1797. By 1798 and 1799, the licensee is listed in the masculine form of the name, as "Francis" Tree. See PANL, GN 5/4/C/1, Ferryland, box 1, List of liquor licenses issued for 1798 and 1799. The widow had a son Francis, who may have been living with her in the late 1790s, although he had established his own household with wife and one-year-old child by the 1800 census. It is likely, then, that the license was being issued in his name, even though his mother ran the inn. Another possibility is that the license continued to be issued in the name of the widow's late husband, which was also Francis. At any rate, the name—in either the masculine or feminine form—no longer appears on the lists of licensees after 1799. There is no way to ascertain whether the widow died shortly after the taking of the census in 1800, whether she ceased operating the business, or whether she carried it on informally after the former license-holder had left her household.

11. Aaron Thomas, *The Newfoundland Journal of Aaron Thomas*, ed. Jean M. Murray (London: Longmans, Green, 1968), 110.

12. Thomas, *Newfoundland Journal*, 114.

13. Thomas, *Newfoundland Journal*, 113.

14. Various examples can be found in the court records for the area and in PANL: MG-31, Carter Family Papers; MG 247, Carter–Benger–Nason Papers; and MG 920, Robert Carter Diary.

15. This was the case with middle-class women in the home country as well. See Leonore Davidoff and Catherine Hall, *Family Fortunes: Men and Women of the English Middle Class, 1780–1850* (Chicago: University of Chicago Press, 1987).

16. The oral tradition does not identify which of the judges Carter this story describes. Several generations of Carters held positions in the judiciary during the period: the original Robert Carter was a surrogate and justice of the peace, his son William was a vice-admiralty judge, and his grandson Robert was a magistrate. The story most likely relates, however, to the first Robert Carter, local surrogate, who fought the French in St. John's and whose wife, Anne, spearheaded the defense of the Isle aux Bois. Robert was the original grantee of the island as a result of this service. He and Anne had a daughter Anne (possibly the disobedient Nancy) who married Sam Hill of Topsham; perhaps this was an unsuitable match. After Sam died, Anne married Henry Sweetland, a merchant-planter from Devon, who certainly would have been an acceptable choice. She later married Matthew Morry Sr., thus forging an alliance with another significant mercantile family in the area. Her father's will, described above, leaves the bulk of his estate to his first son, but he likely doled out portions earlier by marriage settlements and trusts—perhaps transferring *Nancy's Portion* at the time of her first marriage. Neither William, the vice-admiralty judge, nor Robert, the magistrate, had a daughter named Anne or Nancy.

17. See Kathleen M. Brown's discussion of gentry hospitality in colonial Virginia in Brown, *Good Wives, Nasty Wenches, and Anxious Patriarchs: Gender, Race, and Power in Colonial Virginia* (Chapel Hill: University of North Carolina Press, 1994), 296. See also: Carol Berkin, *First Generations: Women in Colonial America* (New York: Hill and Wang, 1996); and Davidoff and Hall, *Family Fortunes.*

18. The Robert Carter Diary (PANL, MG 920) provides some insights into the pursuits of middle-class daughters in the period. The Mary Ann Simms Scrapbook (PANL, MG 708) provides a more vivid view, and is discussed in greater detail below. See also a poem by Tom Flood (a local versifier) transcribed by Ann Carter, 10 November 1843, in the Carter Family Papers (PANL, MG 31, file 63). It is a temperance poem, which obviously appealed to Ann's sensibilities, with a moral lesson about the evil effects of drink upon a fresh-water fisherman, who falls in a pond and drowns after imbibing too much rum:

The moral of this mournful tail
To all is plain and clear
A single drop to[o] much of rum
May make a watery bier.

And he who will not sign the pledge
And keep the promise fast
May be in spite of fate a stiff
Cold water man at last.

19. FMDB, file 02B, Morry and Carter Families; and HE, notes provided during interview by author, Ferryland, 20 July 1999.

20. Anglican parish records for the area are available from 1820 onwards. They list the baptisms of the three youngest children only (Mary, Harriet, and Emily) between 1825 and 1828. According to FMDB, file 02B, Morry and Carter Families, the first three children (Robert, Eliza, and Fanny) also arrived in quick succession between 1814 and 1817. (Robert's birth date of 1814 precedes the date of his parents' marriage; either this is a transcription error, or his birth was pre-nuptial.) The birth or baptism of the middle child, James, is not recorded, so he was likely christened elsewhere. Harriet died in her infancy, and Emily succumbed to scarlet fever just before her ninth birthday.

21. Throughout Carter's diary, there is a constant traffic of visitors, male and female, between St. John's and the Ferryland-Caplin Bay area. Women, married or single, traveled with suitable companions to ensure that they would not be compromised, either physically or socially. On one occasion, however, one of the Carters' female friends was forced to return to St. John's unaccompanied, and Carter expressed his concern at such an impropriety: "Miss Anna Hoyles left us by the *Snipefish* to return to St. John's against my wishes, there being no other female or other respectable passenger, but Cullin is a steady man and from appearances must have reached St. John's by sunset." See entry dated 6 October 1833.

22. Robert's father died in 1810, but his mother lived until 1851. It is evident that she spent her final years in St. John's, for Robert wrote to her there on a regular basis.

23. Granted, the use of *Mr.* and *Mrs.* by spouses in addressing each other in public was a middle-class affectation in general. See Davidoff and Hall, *Family Fortunes*. But it seems odd that Robert Carter did not relax this convention in his private journal, even when discussing more emotional matters such as the death of a child or Sarah's frequent and long absences. Perhaps he saw the diary as "public" space, in that it might be read by others after his death. Still, the sense of distance between the spouses is palpable, and this may have been an arranged marriage in which the spouses did not develop any great degree of affection for each other.

24. The diary contains numerous references to the sons' departures and homecomings. Robert also noted on 12 October 1832 that it was his forty-second birthday and that he had passed nearly twenty-nine years in Newfoundland, indicating that he had been in England until he was thirteen years of age.

25. Italics added throughout. Sarah did not return in 1836 until 6 August, although several letters did arrive from her in May and July. She brought their son, Robert, home from school with her. This particularly lengthy stay occasioned the strongest show of sentiment in Robert's diary in relation to his wife: "Thankful beyond all things for safe return of my wife and child" (7 August 1836). Various other entries in the diary also suggest Sarah's absence on other anniversaries.

26. The cod fishery at Newfoundland was, indeed, severely depressed at this time.

27. See entry dated 25 April 1835.

28. See entries dated 27 and 28 February, 10, 13–17, 22, and 25 April, and 25 July 1834. The comments about Sarah's lingering illness all appear at the end of entries about weather and other local news, almost as an afterthought. But Robert was not a man without feelings. He was moved, for example, to devote an entire entry to the death of his dog: "Poor Snap died of his wounds last night having been dreadfully marred about the head by large dogs a few nights ago, poor faithful little fellow." He is buried at the top of the rock back of the kitchen." See entry dated 2 August 1836. He was also terribly upset when his daughter Emily died of scarlet fever, providing an almost daily charting of her condition to the exclusion of almost any other news until the end: "Poor dear little Emily a little better but my hopes are very faint that she will recover" (12 February 1837); and finally, "Wind N.E. a good deal of snow falling. All hopes of my dear Emily's recovery fled. At 4 P.M. dear Emily breathed her last—dear little soul" (13 February 1837). See virtually all entries from 28 January to 18 February 1837 (the day of Emily's funeral).

29. See Brown's discussion of gentry hospitality in colonial Virginia in *Good Wives*, 271.

30. Cecilia Morgan, *Public Men and Virtuous Women: The Gendered Languages of Religion and Politics in Upper Canada, 1791–1850* (Toronto: University of Toronto Press, 1996), 227. Errington also observes that gentry women in Upper Canada were "public representatives of their class" and were expected to take an active role in social functions and philanthropic work as a means of reinforcing their husbands' status

and influence. See Elizabeth Jane Errington, *Wives and Mothers, Schoolmistresses and Scullery Maids: Working Women in Upper Canada, 1790–1840*, (Montreal: McGill-Queen's University Press, 1995), chaps. 6 and 7; quotation from 132. See also: Berkin, *First Generations*; Jessica Kross, "Mansions, Men, Women, and the Creation of Multiple Publics in Eighteenth-Century British North America," *Journal of Social History* 33, no. 2 (1999): 385–408; and Mary P. Ryan, *Womanhood in America: From Colonial Times to the Present* (New York: New Viewpoints, 1975).

31. The club was initiated on 17 January 1842, and later diary entries indicate that it continued for some time.

32. FMDB, file 02B, Morry and Carter Families; and HE, notes provided during interview by author, Ferryland, 20 July 1999.

33. PANL, MG 31, Carter Family Papers, file 45(b), Will of Sarah Carter, 7 September 1866.

34. FMDB, file 02B, Morry and Carter Families; and HE, notes provided during interview by author, Ferryland, 20 July 1999. Harriet's maternal first cousin Ann Williams Hutchings married Arthur's brother, Lieutenant Robert Carter, further demonstrating the interconnectedness of these families.

35. PANL, MG 31, Carter Family Papers, George Williams to "My dear Niece" [Harriet Carter], 6 August 1826.

36. See PANL, MG 31, Carter Family Papers, files 4 and 10.

37. PANL, MG 31, Carter Family Papers, file 10, George Williams to Harriet Carter, 5 March 1833.

38. PANL, MG 31, Carter Family Papers, file 10, draft of letter from Arthur Carter to Tom Skinner, 1847.

39. PANL, Church of England Parish Records, Petty Harbour Parish, Ferryland District, box 2. Arthur was the only "gentleman" listed in the records; all his contemporaries' occupations were recorded more specifically—e.g., "merchant," "merchant/planter," "master of merchant vessel," etc. (see Chapter 3, n. 54). It is likely, then, that he had no source of income other than family money, although his adult male relatives were all engaged in mercantile operations, the navy, or the professions.

40. PANL, MG 31, Carter Family Papers, file 36. Arthur's request for a government position, however, was refused. See PANL, GN 2/1/A, vol. 38, 400, James Crowdy, Colonial Secretary, to Arthur H. Carter, Ferryland, 15 October 1832.

41. PANL, MG 31, Carter Family Papers, file 26, Harriet Carter to "My dear uncle" [George Williams], ca. late 1820s or early 1830s.

42. PANL, MG 31, Carter Family Papers, files 5, 19, and 26.

43. PANL, MG 31, Carter Family Papers, file 19, Excerpt of letter to "My dear Sir" without signature but, from the context, obviously George Williams to Arthur Carter, 13 March 1827.

44. PANL, MG 31, Carter Family Papers, file 19, George Williams to [Arthur Carter], 13 May 1827.

45. PANL. MG 31, Carter Family Papers, file 26, Harriet Carter to [George Williams], ca. late 1820s or early 1830s. All the following quotations from Harriet are excerpts from this letter.

46. In an 1826 letter, for example, George indicated to Arthur that when he went to Liverpool to find a vessel to carry his mail to Newfoundland, he would send out some "trifle" and a brief note to Harriet. See PANL, MG 31, Carter Family Papers, file19, excerpt of an undated and unsigned letter, but obviously George Williams to Arthur Carter, likely accompanying a short note to Harriet Carter dated 6 August 1826. And on 13 March 1827, George again wrote to Arthur: "I was desirous of sending Harriet some little article of dress by this vessel, but my daughters who are the more competent judges in such important matters say that we had better wait till the 'Spring fashions' come out when we shall be enabled to supply the demands of Ferryland with the newest specimen of taste." See PANL, MG 31, Carter Family Papers, file 19, George Williams to [Arthur Carter], 13 March 1827.

47. PANL, Church of England Parish Records, Petty Harbour Parish, Ferryland District, box 2. Harriet's death was also briefly noted in PANL, MG 920, Robert Carter Diary, 20 July 1835.

48. Maternal mortality rates were high in the late eighteenth and the nineteenth centuries. Ulrich estimates that the maternal mortality rate experienced by Martha Ballard's patients was 5 per 1,000 births, compared with the late-twentieth-century rate in the United States of 1 per 10,000 births. Still, her record was impressive compared with rates in seventeenth- and eighteenth-century English villages (ranging from 10 to 29 per 1,000) or late eighteenth-century London and Dublin hospitals (generally ranging from 8 to 39 per 1,000, with some exceptionally high rates in epidemic years). See Laurel Thatcher Ulrich, *A Midwife's Tale: The Life of Martha Ballard, Based on Her Diary, 1785–1812* (New York: Knopf, 1990), 170–73 and Table V. British sources also report high maternal mortality rates during the period. The British Lying-In Hospital rates for 1749–88 ranged from 16 to 60.8 per 1,000, and the Queen Charlotte's Hospital mean rate for 1860–64 was 42.4 per 1,000. In England and Wales overall, however, rates had dropped to 5 to 6 per 1,000 by 1850–60. Still, they were high compared with late twentieth-century rates of 0.15 per 1,000 in England and 0.17 per 1,000 in Scotland. See: Irvine Loudon, "Deaths in Childbed from the Eighteenth Century to 1935," in *Childbirth: Changing Ideas and Practices in Britain and America, 1600 to the Present*, ed. Philip K. Wilson, vol. 5 (New York: Garland, 1996), 196–97 and 214, and Tables 1 and 4; and Margaret F. Myles, *Textbook for Midwives*, 8th ed. (Edinburgh: Churchill Livingstone, 1975), 635. Statistics on maternal mortality are not available for Newfoundland for the study period. However, Mcnaughton provides some early twentieth-century data, indicating that rates were still in the range of 6 to 9 per 1,000 well into the 1920s. Indeed, in 1923, Newfoundland's rate of 6.2 per 1,000 was in the high range for Western countries (which had average rates from 2 to 6.6 per 1,000). See Janet Mcnaughton, "The Role of the Newfoundland Midwife in Traditional Health Care, 1900 to 1970" (Ph.D. diss., Memorial University of Newfoundland, 1989), 66–73 and Tables 1, 3, and 4. All the above sources agree that only in the 1930s did maternal mortality rates begin to decline significantly, and quite precipitously, as standards of obstetric care improved dramatically.

49. See PANL: Church of England Parish Records, Petty Harbour Parish, Ferryland District, box 2; and MG 708, Mary Ann Simms Scrapbook, 1839–44, particularly the typed family tree charts inserted at the front of the collection.

50. PANL, MG 708, Mary Ann Simms Scrapbook.

51. I refer here to the handwritten poems (as opposed to the typeset poems by published poets that appear occasionally throughout). Some appear in Mary Ann's hand; many more were obviously written in the book by friends, as they were addressed to her, written in different hands, and/or signed or initialed by other parties.

52. A marriage settlement is mentioned in PANL, MG 247, Carter–Benger–Nason Papers, file 18, but no details are given. Richard's will of 8 April 1818 also refers to the marriage settlement (apparently, it was dated 8 January 1754), but the only provision mentioned was that a trust of £500 was to be created to provide for any children who had not reached the age of majority and inherited property in Ireland or been properly accommodated by way of marriage settlements by the time of Richard's death. See PANL, MG 247, Carter–Benger–Nason Papers, file 7, Will of Richard Nason, 8 April 1818.

53. Dorcas had died sometime before her sister Rachel left Ferryland in 1782. Speculating that she was in her twenties when she married, it is reasonable to assume that she was between forty-five and fifty-five years of age at her death. See PANL, MG 247, Carter–Benger–Nason Papers, files 3 and 37.

54. See: FMDB, Benger Family; PANL, MG 247, Carter–Benger–Nason Papers, especially files 3, 18, and 37; and Mannion Name Files, Ferryland, "Benger" and "Nason."

55. PANL, MG 247, Carter–Benger–Nason Papers, files 3 and 37, letter from Elizabeth and Emmeline Bennett to Robert and Peter Weston Carter, 26 June 1847, and notes from a Dobel family Bible. See also Mannion Name Files, Ferryland, "Benger" and "Dobel."

56. Various court cases involving Mary Ludwigg's estate have been cited in Chapter 6. See also Mannion Name File, Ferryland, "Ludwigg."

57. In PANL, MG 31, Carter Family Papers, file 29, there is a certified true copy of a will executed by Peter Weston, dated 14 June 1775, which leaves his entire estate to his wife, Catherine, and two daughters, Catherine and Sarah, in equal shares to be held severally. His wife's share was to be a life interest and, at her death, was to devolve to the two daughters or the survivor of them. Daughter Catherine was to receive her share on her wedding day. Daughter Sarah was to receive her third upon attaining the age of eighteen years. Weston's wife and Edmund Gormond were named executors of the estate and guardians of his daughters. (Note that their daughter Ann received nothing by the will; likely, she had already received her portion in a marriage settlement when she married William Carter.) On 26 September 1776, Governor John Montagu issued a grant of the estate to mother and daughters as co-heiresses and co-executors. See PANL, GN 2/1/A, vol. 6, 149–53.

58. Cyril J. Byrne, ed., *Gentlemen-Bishops and Faction Fighters: The Letters of Bishops O Donel, Lambert, Scallan, and Other Irish Missionaries* (St. John's: Jesperson Press, 1984), 105–6, particularly 106, Father Phelan to Archbishop Troy, 4 February 1788. Phelan was likely correct in his assumption about Lanagan, because the English Protestant, middle-class community, including Catharine and her son-in-law William Carter, continued to shelter Power for some time thereafter.

59. Only two middle-class marriages in the nineteenth century involved Irish Protestant spouses—both wives, both from outside the area (see Table 3.3). Still, it is dif-

ficult to speculate whether or not ethnicity trumped class in marriages among the local elite because the Irish Protestant presence in the area had been too small and too fleeting.

60. The Rules of the Supreme Court established in 1826 stipulated that grand jurors be drawn from "the principal Merchants and Gentlemen" of the community (Rule 20). Petty jurors were to be drawn from those male inhabitants between twenty-one and sixty years of age who owned real property of any amount or rented property at an annual rental of at least £12 per annum; also included on the lists were the sons of the aforesaid while they lived with their fathers (Rule 24). See PANL, GN 5/2/C/1, box 1, Royal Charter instituting the Supreme and Circuit Courts, January 1826, with attached General Rules and Orders of the Supreme Court of Newfoundland.

61. PANL, 5/4/C/1, Ferryland, box 2, *Regina v. Catherine Payne and Sarah Payne,* 22 June 1842.

62. PANL, GN 5/4/C/1, Ferryland, box 2, *Regina v. Catharine Payne, Sarah Payne, Elizabeth Frost, and Barbara Sisk,* 12 August 1851.

63. Sarah herself had other life-experiences that were not atypical for plebeian women on the southern Avalon. She had a child with George Jones in August of 1842; the Anglican minister initially recorded the birth as illegitimate, then crossed out the notation; but Sarah's surname was listed separately, which the minister only did in cases of illegitimacy. The couple had another child in 1845, and this time, the parents were listed as George and Sarah Jones. However, there was no record of the couple having married within the church, either between the two births, or indeed any time from 1829 onwards, when the marriage records began. It seems likely, then, that Sarah and George may have entered into an informal family arrangement (hence, the minister's uncertainty in recording Sarah's surname and her first child's status). The court references to her as Sarah "Payne" in 1842, 1851, and 1854 reinforce this interpretation. (There is no other Sarah Payne in the Anglican records for this period; Sarah's daughter, born in 1842, was also named Sarah, but likely used the surname of her acknowledged father, Jones. Regardless, she would have been too young to have been involved in any of these incidents that found their way to the courtroom.) Several other plebeian couples within the English Protestant community appeared as parents in the baptismal records, but no corresponding marriages were entered in the marriage records. Given that Anglican ministers were not consistently available in the area, these couples, too, may have entered into informal marriages.

64. PANL, GN 5/4/C/1, Ferryland, box 2, *Mary Ann Perryman v. Marmaduke Clow,* 13 July 1854.

65. PANL, GN 5/4/C/1, Ferryland, box 2, *Regina v. Peter Payne and Sarah Payne,* 14 July 1854.

66. Marmaduke's marriage to Mary Johnson the following year records his place of residence as Port-aux-Basques. See PANL, Church of England Parish Records, Petty Harbour Parish, Ferryland District, box 2, 2 September 1855.

10. THE SLENDER THREAD CAST ON

By the second half of the eighteenth century, the slender thread had begun to stretch across the North Atlantic, as Irish women came to the southern Avalon from the southern counties of Ireland: Wexford, Waterford, Kilkenny, Tipperary, and Cork. Like the broader waves of Irish migrants to the island of Newfoundland, they weighed their choices—balancing land shortage, economic recession, and the contraction of domestic textile work in the homeland against opportunity in the Newfoundland fishery, a potential that was always tempered with risk in this persistently uncertain industry. Leaving behind the comfort and security of familiar landscapes and broader kinship groups, they set out as single women or within nuclear family groups to negotiate their way through new territory—not just in terms of geographical place but also in terms of shifting social and economic terrains.

Given that the Newfoundland passenger trade was largely unregulated, the passage for most Irish migrants to the southern Avalon was difficult, the provisions ranging from very basic to dangerously inadequate; the accommodations, from rudimentary to appalling. Still, the majority survived the Atlantic crossing and either landed on the southern Avalon or disembarked at St. John's and wended their way southward. Some women crossed the Atlantic "on order" from local employers; others shipped themselves when they arrived. Some ventured to the New World alone, while others arrived in family groups, accompanying husbands or fathers who had already had some experience as servants in the fishery and were hoping to strike out on their own. As increasing numbers of women arrived, they had a stabilizing effect on community populations, for they tended to be permanent immigrants, and they provided marriage or cohabitation partners for the still largely transient male fishing population. Along the southern Avalon, large numbers of male fishing servants increasingly found wives among incoming Irish women and, more significantly in the nineteenth century, among first- and second-generation Irish Newfoundland women in the area. Matrilocal and uxorilocal residence patterns often featured in community formation, as male immigrants settled in the home communities of their wives. Irish women played another vital role in the establishment of the Irish population in the area as numerous English Protestant patrilines were brought into the Irish Catholic ethnoreligious group through intermarriage with Irish Newfoundland women. By the early decades of the nineteenth century, a thriving Irish planter society had established itself along the southern Avalon.

The reception that the Irish received from British authorities on the island, however, was grudging at best. Irish servants became the backbone of the fishing labor force from the mid-1700s onwards, yet authorities greeted their ever-expanding presence with increasing alarm. In particular, official discourse focused on those who remained behind in St. John's in the off-season, equating Irishness with idleness, drunkenness, and disorder. Treachery, too, was set forth as an essential characteristic of the Irish, particularly among those to the south of St. John's, who were seen as constantly poised to take advantage of any weakness in the British defenses on the island and ever ready to join forces with the French and Americans. Part of this official discourse shaped an image of Irish women as immoral and unproductive.

Yet this was not the construction of Irish womanhood that evolved on the southern Avalon. As Irish women accommodated themselves to the new rhythms of a fishing/subsistence agriculture economy, their ability to contribute to the productive and reproductive power of their households became an intrinsic part of how they were perceived by the plebeian community and how they defined themselves. Almost all adult women worked in subsistence agriculture, performing physically challenging tasks such as clearing, digging, planting, weeding, manuring, harvesting, gleaning, and animal husbandry. Women were also responsible for processing their families' raw production for household use. Increasingly from the late 1700s onwards, women performed shore work for household production units in the fishery, gradually replacing transient male shore crews and ultimately filling the void left on shore by the collapse of the traditional planter fishery based on hired labor. Women's vital role in household production was reflected in a household division of labor that delegated work routines in terms of pragmatism and availability, not on gendered equations of men's work with outdoor, productive, or skilled labor and women's work with domestic, reproductive, or unskilled tasks.

Neither did the concept of woman primarily as *helpmate* to her husband evolve within the plebeian community of the area. In the essential work of fishery and subsistence production, women worked along with the men; and while some specific tasks were differentiated roughly by sex, there was also much overlapping of routines, with members of each sex occasionally *helping* the other as necessity demanded. Indeed, women in the plebeian community felt they had equal stakes and equal responsibilities in family enterprises. Certainly, they did not aspire to be freed from outdoor work through the hiring of servants; rather, servants were hired for domestic work to enable their mistresses to participate in more important productive work. Women also worked in various economic capacities outside household production: as domestic and fishing servants, as laundresses and seamstresses, in the hospitality trade and health care. Some combined household production with paid work and/or the sale of agricultural surplus in a package of economic coping strategies that helped their families survive or even enjoy some small luxuries. The working woman, then, was not problematic within the plebeian community in the study area. The "good, hard-working stump of a girl"—a construction that was transported from the home country—rooted well in southern Avalon soil.

The status and authority that Irish plebeian women enjoyed in family economies spilled over into other aspects of family and community life. These women were usually the primary household managers; indeed, a woman's ability to juggle household demands and resources could make the difference between comfort and poverty, even survival for those families living close to the margin. The names of women—single, widowed, and married—appeared in various capacities in merchant ledgers, indicating that they were a significant part of the exchange economy that supported the local fishery. In general, their visible presence in the broader economic sphere—in their work routines and economic agency—was a source of power for these women well beyond the study period. Religion was another source of female power within the largely Irish plebeian community. Not only did women play a custodial role in formal religion—performing baptisms and marriages in the absence of priests, teaching children their prayers—but they also had a powerful place as mediators in the alternative pre-Christian religious system that operated in combination with formal Catholicism. And women's information networks—whether functioning as sites of networking, group preservation, female resistance, or competition—were inextricably bound up in the power relations of early communities in the area.

Irish plebeian women also wielded authority as they maneuvered within and between two systems of justice and conflict resolution. Within the plebeian population, women frequently took matters into their own hands, using verbal and physical aggression in a show of informal power that was consistent with their status and authority in family and community. As an alternative to, or sometimes in conjunction with, the politics of informal confrontation, women brought their quarrels and their abusers into the courthouse. The formal legal system, at least at the local level, was not hostile terrain, but rather a milieu that offered a viable option for these women in obtaining the justice that they perceived to be their due. Indeed, as the court system became more formalized, Irish women seemed to embrace this system based on individual right rather than discretionary justice. Granted, women were excluded from the formal system in terms of legislative or official functions; but they were a vital part of local court life: as civil litigants, as complainants and defendants in criminal matters, as witnesses and petitioners. As a result, the courtroom was more often a venue for their empowerment than a site of their oppression. Furthermore, within both systems, formal and informal, women participated not purely in an extension of their roles as wives and mothers—an interpretation that limits our understanding of their actions to the bounds of pre-conceived gender roles—but also as self-interested parties in pursuit of individual rights. Moreover, both systems of justice were receptive to their participation on these terms.

Because Irish women on the southern Avalon were successful in carving out territory for themselves in the social, economic, and political life of their communities in the period of early settlement, there was little concerted effort within plebeian culture to circumscribe their lives. A semblance of patriarchal authority was maintained outside the home; in most families, however, this veneer masked a more equitable sharing of decision-making and production responsibilities between spouses. Indeed, a significant number of plebeian women were not bound by the legal restrictions of formal marriages and coverture, particularly up to the early 1800s, as a relatively benign regime on female sexuality permitted various informal family arrangements and the options of informal separation and divorce. But even the majority of women who did enter into formal marriages were not easily constrained in terms of informal status and authority because of their vital role as producers in family economies.

But what of outside influences—middle-class ideology and Catholic Church discourse—that were constructing femininity in terms of domesticity, fragility, sexual passivity, and economic dependence? Such rhetoric made few incursions in plebeian culture because it clashed with the reality of women's lives. Indeed, local middle-class families also showed little interest in encouraging such standards of behavior for plebeian women, because these families constituted a local mercantile network that was reliant on plebeian women's presence in public spaces: in shore work, in support services for the local fishing population, and in the exchange economy that underpinned the resident fishery.

These families would have therefore been poorly served by encouraging plebeian women to move into the "respectability" of the private sphere.

But the Catholic Church found no such clash between ideology and economic reality as it pursued its civilizing mission on the southern Avalon from the late 1700s onwards. With the priests came an increasing restriction of female sexuality, a denigration of women's outdoor productive work, and an idealization of Irish motherhood based on self-denial, virtue, and domesticity. While church rhetoric often conflicted with the lived experience of Irish Newfoundland women, some impact was being felt by the latter decades of the period, as pronouncements from the pulpit and disciplinary mechanisms—such as shaming and denial of the sacraments—whittled away at plebeian women's sense of selfhood.

Still, Irish plebeian women in the study area maintained their status more effectively than did middle-class women in the area. Women of the eighteenth-century elite had been involved in the economic activity of their families. Although they would not have been present on flakes or in fields like plebeian women, they supervised household affairs and led relatively public and active lives in their communities. By the turn of next century, however, the lives of these women were becoming increasingly circumscribed by middle-class ideology. Indeed, the economic idleness and increasing gentility and domesticity of these women helped to maintain class boundaries in small fishing communities where middle-class and plebeian men frequently interacted, thus blurring the edges of class perimeters. Although middle-class women enjoyed greater wealth, education, and physical comfort than plebeian women, they were, in many ways, less powerful than women from the plebeian community.

Irish women on the southern Avalon also maintained greater status and autonomy into the nineteenth century than those who had remained in the home country. In Ireland, the massive economic and demographic changes that occurred throughout the 1800s provoked a severe decline in the status of rural women. The transition from tillage to pasturage, the mechanization and masculinization of agricultural work and dairying, and the contraction of the domestic textile industry led to a devaluation of women's productive work. Meanwhile, the collapse of the potato culture at mid-century suspended the practices of subdivision and partible inheritance that had permitted universal and early marriage. The farming class that predominated in post-famine Ireland turned increasingly to the restrictive practices of impartible inheritance, primogeniture, and the arranged match, with family hopes and resources pinned on the inheriting son and the first-married daughter. Many rural Irish women thus found themselves as "surplus" daughters, with limited opportunities for paid work. Many responded by emigrating.

But on the southern Avalon, the continuing value of women's productive work remained unchallenged in the study period, and Irish women's status as essential contributors to family productive units endured. Furthermore, the relative availability of land for fishing premises and subsistence agriculture, disproportionate sex ratios in early communities, equitable testation practices, and the desirability of large families to share in family production enhanced women's opportunities to become mistresses of their own households. Thus, while social and economic flux eroded the status of rural women in Ireland, along the southern Avalon, Irish plebeian women's status as essential producers and reproducers within family economies remained intact and provided them with considerable influence, both within their households and throughout the broader network of community power relations. The slender thread thus proved to be quite resilient within the context of New World experiences along the southern Avalon.

BIBLIOGRAPHY

1. PRIMARY SOURCES AND UNPUBLISHED MANUSCRIPTS

A. *Manuscripts*

CNS and CNS Archives

C.O. 194 Series. Correspondence between authorities at Newfoundland and the Colonial Office in Britain.

MF 236. Will of John Bole, Ferryland, 10 October 1759.

Whelan, Sister. Elizabeth. "History of the Community of St. Mary's." Unpublished research paper dated 4 April 1972.

FMDB

Files on the following families: Benger, Carter, Coady, Costelloe, Culleton, Curran, Goff, Healey, Hynes, Johnston, Keough, Morry, Mountain, Ryan, Sullivan, Swain, Williams.

Robert Carter Diary, 1832–52.

MHA

Alan Goodridge and Sons Limited fonds, 1840–1909.

Corrigan, Francis. "The Ryans of Biscay Bay (1850–1970): A Study of Settlement," MHA, 43-A-1-42, Geography 2000 Collection, [early 1970s].

Hawco, Lorraine. "Ledwell, Calvert, Caplin Bay." MHA, 43-B-1-47. Geography 2000 Collection, [early 1970s].

Keith Matthews Collection. Early census material of British naval authorities at Newfoundland and correspondence to the Board of Trade, Britain.

MF-053. Robert Carter Diary, partial typescript, 1832–37. MF-105. Letterbook of Capt. Michael Richards, Commander at Fort William, 1700–3.

MF-191. Letterbook of Edward Kough, 1818–34.

R 95/20. "List of Inhabitants' Names, the No. of Their Families, 1708." Transcribed from C.O. 194, vol. 4, fols. 253–56, by W. Gordon Handcock.

Undergraduate Research Papers. Anthropology 2230 Collection.

Undergraduate Research Papers. Geography 2000 Collection.

Undergraduate Research Papers. History Collection.

MUNFLA

Johnson, Zita. "Calendar Customs and Rites of Passage at Renews." MUNFLA ms. 68-011D. Unpublished research paper, Memorial University of Newfoundland, 1967–68.

O'Brien, Andrew. "Wake, Funeral and Burial Customs in Cape Broyle." MUNFLA ms. 68-016C. Unpublished research paper, Memorial University of Newfoundland, 1967–68.

——. "Songs from Cape Broyle." MUNFLA Tape 68-16/490. Memorial University of Newfoundland, 1967–68.

NLGS

Various genealogical records for communities in the study area, including birth, marriage, and death records and gravestone listings.

PANL

GN 2/1/A. Outgoing correspondence from the Newfoundland governor's office as recorded by the local colonial secretary, 1749–1834.

GN 2/2. Incoming correspondence to the Newfoundland governor's office as recorded by the local colonial secretary, 1825–91.

GN 2/39/A. Early census material for the study area, 1675, 1677, and 1681, as well as submissions to the Board of Trade respecting the advantages and disadvantages of the planter fishery, 1675, 1677, and 1691.

GN 5/1. Registry of Wills, vols. 1 and 2.

GN 5/1/C/1, 5/1/C/6, 5/1/C/9, 5/2/C/1, 5/2/C/3, 5/2/C/4, 5/2/C/8, and 5/4/C/1. Court and probate records (various), Ferryland and Trepassey–St. Mary's Districts.

GN 5/2/A/1. Court records, Central district.

GN 21/1/A. Department of Education, Minute Book of the Protestant Board of Education for the District of Ferryland, 1836–37 and 1843–78.

GN 21/6/2. Department of Education, Minute Books of the Roman Catholic Board of Education for the District of Conception Bay, 1836–57.

MG 31. Carter Family Papers.

MG 49. Sweetman Collection, various loose materials, including business correspondence and accounts.

MG 204. Papers of Governor Thomas Duckworth.

MG 205. Papers of Governor Charles Morice Pole, including copy of a nominal census of Ferryland district comprising: register of families, 1 January 1800; list of masters, servants, and dieters, winter 1799 and spring 1800; and list of masters, servants, and dieters, 13 August 1800. Original held at the National Maritime Museum, Greenwich, WYN/109/9. Copy also held at the National Archives of Canada, MG 24 A 46, Sir Charles M. Pole fonds, reel A-134.

MG 206. Papers of Governor Thomas Cochrane.

MG 237. Matthew Morry Papers.

MG 247. Carter-Benger-Nason Papers.

MG 473. Alan Goodridge and Son Collection, particularly the business ledgers for 1839 and 1841.

MG 598,. Society for the Propagation of the Gospel in Foreign Parts Collection, particularly Series C, D, E, and G.

MG 708. Mary Ann Simms Scrapbook.

MG 920. Robert Carter Diary, 1832–52.

Mildred Howard Collection. Vital statistics from Newfoundland newspapers.

Parish Records

Church of England

Petty Harbour Parish, Ferryland District:
baptisms—1823 onward
marriages—1829 onward
deaths—1827 onward.
(Other records for the study area are available but fall outside the time frame.)

Roman Catholic

Bay Bulls Parish:
baptisms—1830 onward.

Witless Bay Parish:
baptisms—1831 onward;
marriages—1830 onward;
deaths—1901 onward.

Brigus South Parish:
headstone data, 1879–1900.

Renews Parish:
baptisms—1857 onward;
marriages—1838 onward.

Trepassey Parish:
baptisms—1843 onward;
deaths—1856 onward.

St. Mary's Parish:
baptisms—1843 onward;
marriages—1844 onward;
deaths—1891 onward.
(Other records for the study area are available but fall outside the time frame.)

PCA

Condon, Raymond J. "A Brief History of the Early Catholic Missionaries on the Southern Shore." Unpublished research paper, Labrador City, 23 April 1983.

"The Four Foundresses First Letters Home to Ireland." File containing letters of Mother Mary Bernard Kirwan and Sisters Magdalene O'Shaughnessey, Mary Xavier Lynch, and Mary Xavier Molony, 1833–34.

PRL

340.9 N45. Surrogate Court Records, Ferryland and Trepassey–St. Mary's districts, 1773–1804.

971.8/SA8/NR. Sweetman Letterbook, 1788–1804, and miscellaneous items.

RCAASJ

100 Series. Bishop James O Donel Papers, 1784–1806.
101 Series. Bishop Patrick Lambert Papers, 1807–16.
102 Series. Bishop Thomas Scallan Papers, 1817–29.
103 Series. Bishop Michael A. Fleming Papers, 1829–50. Includes Dean Patrick Cleary, "A note on church history" [1784–1850].

Private Collections

Mannion, John. Name File Collection. Database on Irish immigrants to Newfoundland from the eighteenth century onward. Private Collection, St. John's, Newfoundland.

Unidentified mercantile journal, 1881–92, found in the White–Maher house at Ferryland prior to its demolition circa 1960s and currently in the possession of HE of Ferryland.

B. Newspapers

Newfoundland

Newfoundlander
Public Ledger
Royal Gazette and Newfoundland Advertiser

Ireland

Clonmel Gazette
Cork Evening Post
Waterford Chronicle
Waterford Herald
Wexford Herald

C. *Unpublished Manuscripts from the Study Area*

Barnable, Gerald. "The Ferryland Magistracy." Unpublished manuscript, Ferryland, n.d.

———. "An Outline of Renews History." Unpublished manuscript, Ferryland, December 1992.

Calvert Come Home Year Committee. "From Caplin Bay, 1920 to Calvert, 1995." Calvert: Calvert Come Home Year Committee, 1995.

Croft, Agnes, Janet Curran, Sheila Hynes, Catherine Fennelly, Dot Fennelly, Rick Kenny, and Randy Crane. "A Glimpse into the Past." Unpublished manuscript, Ferryland, n.d. Sketches by Jack Barnable.

Ferryland Historical Society. "Ferryland Bibliography." Unpublished listing of newspaper items relating to Ferryland, n.d.

Hurd, Lisa, Donald Hurd, Guy Barnable, Jennifer Power, and Jim Walsh. "Research Report on Living History Potential at Ferryland." Unpublished manuscript, Ferryland, April 1995.

O'Brien, James Joseph (Jim Joe). "Cape Broyle, 1959–60." Unpublished community history, [1960]. Copy in possession of author.

———. "Cape Broyle." Unpublished chronicle of the old families of Cape Broyle, 1971. Copy in possession of author.

———. "Leahy Family." Unpublished and untitled notes on the Leahy family at Cape Broyle, [1971?]. Copy in possession of author.

———. "The Oldridge Family." Unpublished notes on the Oldridge family at Cape Broyle, [1971?]. Copy in possession of author.

Power, Jennifer. "Research Reports." Unpublished manuscripts, Ferryland, February 1995 (background notes for the report, cited above, by Hurd et al.; review of secondary literature and numerous oral interviews on a range of topics relating to historical Ferryland, including general history, religion, medicine, the role of women, social customs, superstitions, shipwrecks, education, and the economy).

Untitled and undated directory of inhabitants of Ferryland from the seventeenth century to the nineteenth century. Prepared for the Colony of Avalon site, Ferryland, n.d.

D. *Published Manuscripts and Documents*

Anspach, Rev. Lewis A. A *History of the Island of Newfoundland*. London: Anspach, 1819.

Chappell, Lieut. Edward, R.N. *Voyage of the Rosamond to Newfoundland and the Southern Coast of Labrador*. London: n.p., 1818.

Fleming, Mons. Michael Anthony. "The State of the Catholic Religion in Newfoundland Reviewed in Two Letters by Monsignor Fleming to Rev. P. John Spratt." Rome, 1836.

——. *Report of the Catholic Mission in Newfoundland in North America.* Submitted to the Cardinal Prefect of Propaganda. Rome: Printing Press of the Sacred Congregation, 1837.

——. "Letter on the State of Religion in Newfoundland." Addressed to the Very Rev. Dr. A. O'Connell, Dublin, 11 January 1844. Dublin: James Duffy, 1844.

Howley, Rev. Michael F. *Ecclesiastical History of Newfoundland.* Boston: Doyle and Whittle, 1888; reprint, Belleville, ON: Mika, 1971.

Pedley, Rev. Charles. *The History of Newfoundland.* London: Longman, Green, Longman, Roberts, and Green, 1863.

Reeves, John. *History of the Government of the Island of Newfoundland.* London: n.p., 1793; reprint, Yorkshire: S. R. Publishers, 1967.

Thomas, Aaron. *The Newfoundland Journal of Aaron Thomas*, edited by Jean M. Murray. London: Longmans, Green, 1968.

Journal of the Legislative Council. St. John's: Queen's Printer, 1836–78.

Newfoundland Population Returns, 1836. St. John's: Queen's Printer, 1836.

Newfoundland Population Returns, 1845. St. John's: Ryan and Withers, 1845.

Newfoundland Population Returns, 1857. St. John's: Queen's Printer, 1858. Extract from the Journal of the House of Assembly, 1858 (Sessional Papers).

Statutes of Newfoundland, 1834–60.

E. Oral Interviews and Personal Correspondence from Informants

AG. Ferryland. Interview, 21 July 1999.

EO. Calvert/Caplin Bay. Interview, 26 August 1999.

ESF. Cape Broyle. Interview, 25 August 1999.

ESX. Calvert/Caplin Bay. Interview, 19 July 1999.

EW. Calvert/Caplin Bay (formerly of Trepassey). Interviews, 21 July and 30 August 1999.

EC. St. Mary's (formerly of Gaskiers). Interview, 10 September 1999.

HE. Ferryland. Interview, July 20, 1999. Also, handwritten notes, July 1999, and letters to author dated 8 March 1999 and 31 January, 13 March, and Christmas 2000.

ISF. St. John's (formerly of Cape Broyle). Interview, 4 May 2001.

IT. Calvert/Caplin Bay. Interview, 19 July 1999.

IV. Calvert/Caplin Bay. Interview, 23 August 1999.

JSF. St. John's (formerly of Cape Broyle). Interviews, 1972 and 1974.

JA. Cape Broyle. Interview, 1974.

KO. St. John's (formerly of Cape Broyle). Interviews, 1972, 1974, 15 May 1998, and 26 March and 4 May 2001.
NNSF. Cape Broyle. Interviews, 1972 and 1974.
NO. Ferryland . Interview, 24 August 1999.
NSF. Cape Broyle (formerly of Calvert / Caplin Bay) . Interviews, 1972 and 1974.
NXSF. Cape Broyle. Interviews, 1972 and 1974.
NA. Ferryland . Interview, 9 May 2000.
QH. Ferryland. Interviews, 27 July and 24 August 1999.
QO. Renews. Interview, 31 August 1999.
QSF. Cape Broyle. Interview, 22 July 1999, and handwritten notes, July 1999.
QC. St. Mary's. Interview, 11 September 1999.
VF. St. John's (formerly of Calvert/Caplin Bay). Interview, 26 March 2001.
VN. Ferryland. Interview, 9 May 2000.
XF. Brigus South. Interview, 22 June 1999.
XT. Calvert / Caplin Bay. Interview, 19 July 1999.
Byrne, Cyril (coordinator of Irish Studies at Saint Mary's University, Halifax). E-mail to author, 8 September 2000.

F. Other

Displays at the Capt. William Jackman Museum, Renews.

2. SECONDARY SOURCES

Adams, William Forbes. *Ireland and Irish Emigration to the New World from 1815 to the Famine.* 1932. Reprint, New York: Russell and Russell, 1967.
Akenson, Donald H. *Being Had: Historians, Evidence, and the Irish in North America.* Don Mills, ON: P. D. Meany, 1985.
——. *Small Differences: Irish Catholics and Irish Protestants,* 1815–1922: *An International Perspective.* Kingston: McGill-Queen's University Press, 1988.
——. "The Historiography of the Irish in the United States of America." In *The Irish in the New Communities,* edited by Patrick O'Sullivan. Irish World Wide Series. Vol. 2. Leicester: Leicester University Press, 1992, 99–127
——. *The Irish Diaspora: A Primer.* Toronto: P. D. Meaney, 1993.
——. *The Irish in Ontario: A Study in Rural History.* 2nd ed. Montreal: McGill-Queen's University Press, 1999.

——. "Irish Migration to North America, 1800–1920." In *The Irish Diaspora*, edited by Andy Bielenberg. Harlow: Longman, 2000, 111–38.

Antler, Ellen. "Women's Work in Newfoundland Fishing Families." *Atlantis* 2, no. 2 (1977): 106–13.

Backhouse, Constance. *Petticoats and Prejudice: Women and Law in Nineteenth-Century Canada*. Toronto: Osgoode Society, 1991.

Baines, Dudley. *Emigration from Europe, 1815–1930*. Economic History Society Studies in Economic History. Houndmills, Hampshire: Macmillan Education, 1991.

Bannister, Jerry. *The Rule of the Admirals: Law, Custom, and Naval Government in Newfoundland, 1699–1832*. Toronto: University of Toronto Press with the Osgoode Society for Canadian Legal History, 2003.

Barnable, Gerald J. "The Ferryland Riots of 1788." *An Nasc* 7 (summer 1994): 4–9.

Berg, Maxine. "Women, Property and the Industrial Revolution." *Journal of Interdisciplinary History* 24, no. 2 (autumn 1993): 233–50.

Bergman, Jérg R. *Discreet Indiscretions: The Social Organization of Gossip*. Translated by John Bednarz Jr. New York: Aldine de Gruyter, 1993.

Berkin, Carol. *First Generations: Women in Colonial America*. New York: Hill and Wang, 1996.

Berkin, Carol, and Leslie Horowitz, eds. *Women's Voices, Women's Lives: Documents in Early American History*. Boston: Northeastern University Press, 1998.

Bielenberg, Andy, ed. *The Irish Diaspora*. Harlow: Longman, 2000.

——. "Irish Emigration to The British Empire, 1700–1914." In *The Irish Diaspora*, edited by Andy Bielenberg. Harlow: Longman, 2000, 215–34.

Biemer, Linda Briggs. *Women and Property in Colonial New York: The Transition from Dutch to English Law, 1643–1727*. Ann Arbor: UMI Research Press, 1983.

Bittermann, Rusty. "Women and the Escheat Movement: The Politics of Everyday Life on Prince Edward Island." In *Separate Spheres: Women's Worlds in the Nineteenth-Century Maritimes*, edited by Janet Guildford and Suzanne Morton. Fredericton: Acadiensis Press, 1994, 23–38.

Black's Law Dictionary. 7th ed. 1999.

Blessing, Patrick. "Irish Emigration to the United States, 1800–1920: An Overview." In *The Irish in America: Emigration, Assimilation and Impact*, edited by P. J. Drudy. Irish Studies, no. 4. Cambridge: Cambridge University Press, 1985, 11–37.

Boase, Leonard, ed. *Catholic Book of Knowledge*. Vol. 3. London: Virtue and Company, 1961; reprint, Chicago: Catholic Home Press, 1962.

Bourke, Angela. "The Irish Traditional Lament and the Grieving Process." *Women's Studies International Forum* 11, no. 4 (1988): 287–91.

Bourke, Joanna. *Husbandry to Housewifery: Women, Economic Change, and Housework in Ireland, 1890–1914*. Oxford: Clarendon, 1993.

Bradbury, Bettina. *Working Families: Age, Gender, and Daily Survival in Industrializing Montreal*. Toronto: McClelland and Stuart, 1993.

Brown, Kathleen M. *Good Wives, Nasty Wenches, and Anxious Patriarchs: Gender, Race, and Power in Colonial Virginia*. Chapel Hill: University of North Carolina Press, 1994.

Burke, Johnny. "Betsy Brennan's Blue Hen." In *Doryloads*, edited by Kevin Major. St. John's: Breakwater Books, 1974, 79–81.

Bury, John B. *The Life of St. Patrick*. 1905; reprint, Freeport, NY: Books for Libraries Press, 1971.

Byrne, Cyril J., ed. *Gentlemen-Bishops and Faction Fighters: The Letters of Bishops O Donel, Lambert, Scallan, and Other Irish Missionaries*. St. John's: Jesperson Press, 1984.

——. "The Case of the Schooner Fanny from Waterford to St. John's, 1811." *An Nasc* 3, no. 1 (spring/summer 1990): 19–22.

——. "The Brig *Thomas Farrell*," *An Nasc* 4, no. 1 (winter 1991): 6–7.

Cadigan, Sean. *Hope and Deception in Conception Bay: Merchant-Settler Relations in Newfoundland, 1785–1855*. Toronto: University of Toronto Press, 1995.

——. "Whipping Them into Shape: State Refinement of Patriarchy among Conception Bay Fishing Families, 1787–1825." In *Their Lives and Times: Women in Newfoundland and Labrador: A Collage*, edited by Carmelita McGrath, Barbara Neis, and Marilyn Porter. St. John's: Killick Press, 1995, 48–59.

Callista, Agnes. "Canada's Immigration Policy and Domestics from the Caribbean: The Second Domestic Scheme." In *Race, Class, Gender: Bonds and Barriers*, edited by Jesse Vorst et al. Toronto: Between the Lines in cooperation with the Society for Socialist Studies, 1989, 133–65.

——. "Race, Gender, and Canadian Immigration Policy: Blacks from the Caribbean, 1900–1932." In *Gender and History in Canada*, edited by Joy Parr and Mark Rosenfeld. Toronto: Copp Clark, 1996, 70–87.

Cameron, Deborah, ed. *The Feminist Critique of Language: A Reader*. London: Routledge, 1990. Revised Edition, 1998.

Campbell, Gail G. "Disenfranchised but not Quiescent: Women Petitioners in New Brunswick in the Mid-Nineteenth Century." In *Separate Spheres: Women's Worlds in the Nineteenth-Century Maritimes*, edited by Janet Guildford and Suzanne Morton. Fredericton: Acadiensis Press, 1994, 39–66.

Campbell, Malcolm. *The Kingdom of the Ryans: The Irish in Southwest New South Wales, 1816–1890*. Sydney: University of New South Wales Press, 1997.

Carlson, Terry. "Dealing with Offenders: An Historical Perspective on Corrections in Newfoundland." In *Ties That Bind: An Anthology of Social Work and Social Welfare*, edited by Gale Burford. St. John's: Jesperson, 1997, 91–125.

Casey, George. "Irish Culture in Newfoundland." In *Talamh An Eisc: Canadian and Irish Essays*, edited by Cyril Byrne and Margaret Harry. Halifax: Nimbus, 1986, 203–27.

Casway, Jerrold. "Irish Women Overseas, 1500–1800." In *Women in Early Modern Ireland*, edited by Margaret MacCurtain and Mary O'Dowd. Edinburgh: Edinburgh University Press, 1991, 112–32.

Cell, Gillian. *English Enterprise in Newfoundland, 1577–1699*. Toronto: University of Toronto Press, 1969.

Clark, Anna. "Humanity or Justice? Wifebeating and the Law in the Eighteenth and Nineteenth Centuries." In *Regulating Womanhood: Historical Essays on Mar-*

riage, *Motherhood, and Sexuality*, edited by Carol Smart. London: Routledge, 1992, 187–206.

———-. *The Struggle for the Breeches: Gender and the Making of the British Working Class*. Berkeley: University of California Press, 1995.

Clarke, Brian. *Piety and Nationalism: Lay Voluntary Associations and the Creation of an Irish-Catholic Community in Toronto, 1850–1895*. Montreal: McGill-Queen's University Press, 1993.

Clarkson, L. A. "Love, Labour, and Life: Women in Carrick-on-Suir in the Late Eighteenth Century." *Irish Economic and Social History* 20 (1993): 18–34.

———. "Ireland 1841: Pre-industrial or Proto-industrial; Industrializing or De-industrializing?" In *European Proto-industrialization: An Introductory Handbook*, edited.by Sheilagh C. Ogilvie and Markus Cerman. Cambridge: Cambridge University Press, 1996, 67–84.

Clear, Caitriona. "The Limits of Female Autonomy: Nuns in Nineteenth-Century Ireland." In *Women Surviving: Studies in Irish Women's History in the Nineteenth and Twentieth Centuries*, edited by Maria Luddy and Cliona Murphy. Dublin: Poolbeg Press, 1989, 15–50.

Coates, Jennifer. "Gossip Revisited: Language in All-Female Groups." In *Women in Their Speech Communities: New Perspectives in Language and Sex*, edited by Jennifer Coates and Deborah Cameron. London: Longman, 1988, 94–122.

Coates, Jennifer, and Deborah Cameron, eds. *Women in Their Speech Communities: New Perspectives in Language and Sex*. London: Longman, 1988.

Cole, Sally. *Women of the Praia: Work and Lives in a Portuguese Coastal Community*. Princeton: Princeton University Press, 1991.

Collins, B. "Irish Emigration to Dundee and Paisley During the First Half of the Nineteenth Century." In *Irish Population, Economy, and Society: Essays in Honour of the Late K. H. Connell*, edited by J. M. Goldstrum and L. A. Clarkson. Oxford: Oxford University Press, 1981, 195–212

———. "The Irish in Britain, 1780–1921." In *An Historical Geography of Ireland*, edited by B. J. Graham and L. J. Proudfoot. London: Academic Press Limited, 1993, 366–98.

Connell, Kenneth H. *The Population of Ireland, 1750–1845*. Oxford: Clarendon Press, 1950.

———. *Irish Peasant Society: Four Historical Essays*. Oxford: Clarendon Press, 1968.

Connolly, Sean J. *Priests and People in Pre-famine Ireland, 1780–1845*. Dublin: Gill and Macmillan, 1982.

———. "Popular Culture in Pre-Famine Ireland." In *Talamh An Eisc: Canadian and Irish Essays*, edited by Cyril Byrne and Margaret Harry. Halifax: Nimbus, 1986, 12–28.

Conrad, Margaret. "Recording Angels: The Private Chronicles of Women from the Maritime Provinces of Canada, 1750–1950." In *The Neglected Majority: Essays in Canadian Women's History*, edited by Susan Mann Trofimenkoff and Alison Prentice. Toronto: McClelland and Stewart, 1977, 41–60.

———. *Recording Angels: The Private Chronicles of Women from the Maritime Provinces of Canada, 1750–1950*. Ottawa: Canadian Research Institute for the Advancement of Women, 1982.

——. "'Sundays Always Make Me Think of Home': Time and Place in Canadian Women's History." In *Rethinking Canada: The Promise of Women's History*, edited by Veronica Strong-Boag and Anita Clair Fellman. Toronto: Copp Clark Pitman, 1986, 67–95.

——, ed. *Intimate Relations: Family and Community in Planter Nova Scotia, 1759–1800*. Planter Studies Series, no. 3. Fredericton: *Acadiensis*, 1995.

Conrad, Margaret, Toni Laidlow, and Donna Smyth. *No Place Like Home: Diaries and Letters of Nova Scotia Women, 1771–1938*. Halifax: Formac, 1988.

Conway, Sheelagh. *The Faraway Hills are Green: Voices of Irish Women in Canada*. Toronto: Women's Press, 1992.

Costa, Derek Mendes da, Richard J. Balfour, and Eileen E. Gillese. *Property Law*. 2nd ed. Toronto: Edmond Montgomery, 1990.

Crvecoeur, Hector St. John de. *Letters from an American Farmer*. London: J. M. Dent, 1912.

Cullen, Louis M. *The Emergence of Modern Ireland, 1600–1900*. New York: Holmes and Meier, 1981.

——. "Irish History Without the Potato." In *Nationalism and Popular Protest in Ireland*, edited by C. H. E. Philpin. Cambridge: Cambridge University Press, 1987, 126–38.

Cullen, Mary. "Breadwinners and Providers: Women in the Household Economy of Labouring Families, 1835–6." In *Women Surviving: Studies in Irish Women's History in the Nineteenth and Twentieth Centuries*, edited by Maria Luddy and Cliona Murphy. Dublin: Poolbeg Press, 1989, 85–116.

Cullum, Linda, and Maeve Baird. "'A Woman's Lot': Women and Law in Newfoundland from Early Settlement to the Twentieth Century." In *Pursuing Equality: Historical Perspectives on Women in Newfoundland and Labrador*, edited by Linda Kealey. Social and Economic Papers, no. 20. St. John's: Institute of Social and Economic Research, Memorial University of Newfoundland, 1993, 66–162.

Daly, Mary. "Women in the Irish Workforce from Pre-industrial to Modern Times." *Saothar* 7 (1981): 74–82.

Damousi, Joy. *Depraved and Disorderly: Female Convicts, Sexuality, and Gender in Colonial Australia*. Cambridge: Cambridge University Press, 1997.

Danaher, Kevin. *Irish Country People*. Cork: Mercier Press, 1966.

Davidoff, Leonore. *Worlds Between: Historical Perspectives on Gender and Class*. Cambridge: Polity Press, 1995.

Davidoff, Leonore, and Catherine Hall. *Family Fortunes: Men and Women of the English Middle Class, 1780–1850*. Chicago: University of Chicago Press, 1987.

Davis, Graham. *The Irish in Britain, 1815–1914*. Dublin: Gill and Macmillan, 1991.

——. "The Irish in Britain, 1815–1939." In *The Irish Diaspora*, edited by Andy Bielenberg. Harlow: Longman, 2000, 19–36.

David, Nanciellen. "Patriarchy from the Grave: Family Relations in Nineteenth-Century New Brunswick Wills." *Acadiensis* 13, no. 2 (spring 1984): 91–100.

Delaney, Enda. "Gender and Twentieth-Century Irish Migration, 1921–1971." In *Women, Gender, and Labour Migration: Historical and Global Perspectives*, edited by Pamela Sharpe. London: Routledge, 2001, 209–23.

Dictionary of Newfoundland English. 2nd ed. with suppl., edited by G. M. Story, W. J. Kirwin, and J. D. A. Widdowson. Toronto: University of Toronto Press, 1998.

Diner, Hasia R. Erin's *Daughters in America: Irish Immigrant Women in the Nineteenth Century*. Baltimore: Johns Hopkins University Press, 1983.

Dinn, Eileen M., and Carla S. Krachun. "Kirke, David." In *Encyclopedia of Newfoundland and Labrador*, edited by Joseph R. Smallwood. Vol. 3. St. John's: Harry Cuff, 1991.

Doyle, David. "The Irish in Australia and the United States: Some Comparisons, 1800–1939." *Irish Economic and Social History* 16 (1989): 73–94.

——. "The Irish in North America, 1776–1845." In *A New History of Ireland*, edited by W. E. Vaughan. Vol. 5. Oxford: Clarendon Press, 1989.

Doyle, Gerald S., ed. *The Old Time Songs and Poetry of Newfoundland*. St. John's: Gerald S. Doyle, 1927.

Dubinsky, Karen. "'Maidenly Girls or Designing Women?': The Crime of Seduction in Turn-of-the Century Ontario." In *Gender Conflicts: New Essays in Women's History*, edited by Franca Iacovetta and Mariana Valverde. Toronto: University of Toronto Press, 1992, 27–66.

——. *Improper Advances: Rape and Heterosexual Conflict in Ontario*, 1880–1929. Chicago: University of Chicago Press, 1993.

Dunbar, Robin. *Grooming, Gossip and the Evolution of Language*. London: Faber and Faber, 1996.

Edwards, Susan M. *Female Sexuality and the Law: A Study of Constructs of Female Sexuality as They Inform Statute and Legal Procedure*, edited by C. M. Campbell and Paul Wiles. Oxford: Martin Robertson, 1981.

Elliott, Bruce S. *Irish Migrants in the Canadas: A New Approach*. Kingston: McGill-Queen's University Press, 1988.

Ellis, Peter Berresford. *Celtic Women: Women in Celtic Society and Literature*. London: Constable, 1995.

English, Christopher. "The Development of the Newfoundland Legal System to 1815." *Acadiensis* 20, no. 1 (autumn 1990): 89–119.

——. "From Fishing Schooner to Colony: The Legal Development of Newfoundland, 1791–1832." In *Law, Society, and the State: Essays in Modern Legal History*, edited by Louis A Knafla and Susan W. S. Bunnie. Toronto: University of Toronto Press, 1995, 73–98.

——. "The Reception of Law in Ferryland District, Newfoundland, 1786–1812." Paper presented to a joint session of the Canadian Law and Society Association and the Canadian Historical Association, Brock University, 2 June 1996.

——. "Collective Violence in Ferryland District, Newfoundland, in 1786." *Dalhousie Law Journal* 21, no. 2 (fall 1998): 475–89.

English, Christopher, and Christopher P. Curran, "A Cautious Beginning: The Court of Civil Jurisdiction, 1791," *Silk Robes and Sou'westers: The Supreme Court, 1791–1991*. St. John's: Jesperson Press, 1991.

English, Tracy M. "Big Wages, Glorious Climate, and Situations Guaranteed: A Study of the Migration of Irish Women to Great Britain for the Period 1861 to 1911." Master's thesis, Memorial University of Newfoundland, 1999.

Erickson, Amy Louise. *Women and Property in Early Modern England*. London: Routledge, 1993.

Errington, Elizabeth Jane. *Wives and Mothers, Schoolmistresses and Scullery Maids: Working Women in Upper Canada, 1790–1840*. Montreal: McGill-Queen's University Press, 1995.

Fallows, Marjorie. *Irish Americans: Identity and Assimilation*. Englewood Cliffs: Prentice-Hall, 1979.

Faris, James C. *Cat Harbour: A Newfoundland Fishing Settlement*. St. John's: Institute of Social and Economic Research, Memorial University of Newfoundland, 1972.

Field, Agnes. "The Development of Government in Newfoundland, 1638–1713." Master's thesis, University of London, 1924.

Fingard, Judith. *The Dark Side of Life in Victorian Halifax*. Porter's Lake, NS: Pottersfield Press, 1989.

Fitzgerald, John E. "Conflict and Culture in Irish-Newfoundland Roman Catholicism, 1829–1850." Ph.D. diss., University of Ottawa, 1997.

Fitzpatrick, David. "The Modernisation of the Irish Female." In *Rural Ireland: Modernisation v. Change, 1600–1900*, edited by Patrick O'Flanagan, Paul Ferguson, and Kevin Whelan. Cork: Cork University Press, 1987, 162–80.

——. "Emigration, 1801–70." In *A New History of Ireland*, edited by W. E. Vaughan. Vol. 5. Oxford: Clarendon Press, 1989, 562–622.

Frager, Ruth A. *Sweatshop Strife: Class, Ethnicity, and Gender in the Jewish Labour Movement in Toronto, 1900–1939*. Toronto: University of Toronto Press, 1992.

Fyson, Donald. "Criminal Justice, Civil Society, and the Local State: The Justices of the Peace in the District of Montreal, 1764–1830." Ph.D. diss., Université de Montréal, 1995.

——. "The Biases of *Ancien* Régime Justice: The People and the Justices of the Peace in the District of Montreal, 1785–1839." In *Power, Place, and Identity: Studies of Social and Legal Regulation in Quebec*, edited by Tamara Myers, Kate Boyer, Mary Anne Poutanen, and Steven Watt. Montreal: Montreal History Group, 1998.

Galgay, Frank, and Michael McCarthy. *Shipwrecks of Newfoundland and Labrador*. 4 Vols. St. John's: Harry Cuff, 1987; and Creative Publishers, 1990, 1995, and 1997.

Galgay, Frank, Michael McCarthy, Sister Teresina Bruce, and Sister Magdalen O'Brien. *A Pilgrimage of Faith: A History of the Southern Shore from Bay Bulls to St. Shott's*. St. John's: Harry Cuff, 1983.

Gray, Breda. "'The Home of Our Mothers and Our Birthright for Ages'? Nation,

Diaspora, and Irish Women." In *New Frontiers in Women's Studies: Knowledge, Identity, and Nationalism*, edited by Mary Maynard and June Purvis. London: Taylor and Francis, 1996, 164–86.

Green, Anna, and Kathleen Troup, eds. *The Houses of History: A Critical Reader in Twentieth-Century History and Theory*. New York: New York University Press, 1999.

Gushue, Raymond. "The Law of Real Property in Newfoundland." *Canadian Bar Review* 4 (May 1926): 310–4.

Handcock, W. Gordon. *Soe longe as there comes noe women: Origins of English Settlement in Newfoundland*. St. John's: Breakwater Books, 1989.

Handlin, Oscar. *Boston's Immigrants*. Cambridge, Mass.: Harvard University Press, 1941.

Harris, Ruth-Ann. *The Nearest Place That Wasn't Ireland: Early Nineteenth-Century Irish Labor Migration*. Ames: Iowa State University Press, 1994.

———. "Searching for Missing Friends in the Boston *Pilot* Newspaper, 1831–1863." In *The Irish Diaspora*, edited by Andy Bielenberg. Harlow: Longman, 2000, 158–75.

Harvey, Kathryn. "Amazons and Victims: Resisting Wife-Abuse in Working-Class Montreal, 1869–1879." *Journal of the Canadian Historical Association* 2 (1991): 131–48.

Head, C. Grant. *Eighteenth Century Newfoundland: A Geographer's Perspective*. Toronto: McClelland and Stewart in association with the Institute of Canadian Studies, Carleton University, 1976.

Hearn, Mona. *Below Stairs: Domestic Service Remembered in Dublin and Beyond, 1880–1922*. Dublin: Lilliput Press, 1993.

Hedrick, Joan D. *The Oxford Harriet Beecher Stowe Reader*. New York: Oxford University Press, 1999.

Henderson, Jennifer. *Settler Feminism and Race Making in Canada*. Toronto: University of Toronto Press, 2003.

Higgs, Edward. "Domestic Service and Household Production." In *Unequal Opportunities: Women's Employment in England, 1800–1918*, edited by Angela John. Oxford: Basil Blackwell, 1986, 125–50.

Hill, Bridget. *Women, Work, and Sexual Politics in Eighteenth-Century England*. Oxford: Basil Blackwell, 1989.

———. *Servants: English Domestics in the Eighteenth Century*. Oxford: Clarendon Press, 1996.

———. "Women's History: A Study in Change, Continuity, or Standing Still?" In *Women's Work: The English Experience, 1650–1914*, edited by Pamela Sharpe. London: Arnold, 1998, 42–58.

Hoffman, Ronald. *Princes of Ireland, Planters of Maryland: A Carroll Saga, 1500–1782*. Collaborated with Sally D. Mason. Chapel Hill: University of North Carolina Press, 2000.

Hogan, Sister M. Williamina. *Pathways of Mercy in Newfoundland, 1842–1984*. St. John's: Harry Cuff, 1986.

Houston, Cecil J., and William J. Smyth. *Irish Emigration and Canadian Settlement: Patterns, Links, and Settlers.* Toronto: University of Toronto Press, 1990.

———. "The Irish Diaspora: Emigration to the New World, 1720–1920." In *An Historical Geography of Ireland,* edited by B. J. Graham and L. J. Proudfoot. London: Academic Press, 1993, 338–65.

Hoy, Suellen. "The Journey Out: The Recruitment and Emigration of Irish Religious Women to the United States, 1812–1914." *Journal of Women's History* 6–7, no. 1 (1994–95): 64–98.

Humfrey, Paula M. "'I saw, through a large chink in the partition . . .': What the Servants Knew." In *Women and History: Voices of Early Modern England,* edited by Valerie Frith. Toronto: Coach House Press, 1995, 51–80.

Hunt, Margaret R. "'The great danger she had reason to believe she was in': Wife-Beating in the Eighteenth Century." In *Women and History: Voices of Early Modern England,* edited by Valerie Frith. Toronto: Coach House Press, 1995, 81–102.

Iacovetta, Franca. "Making New Canadians: Social Workers, Women, and the Reshaping of Immigrant Families." In *Gender Conflicts: New Essays in Women's History,* edited by Franca Iacovetta and Mariana Valverde. Toronto: University of Toronto Press, 1992, 261–303.

Innis, Harold A. *The Cod Fisheries: The Study of an International Economy.* Rev. ed. Toronto: University of Toronto Press, 1954.

Jackson, James H., Jr., and Leslie Page Moch, "Migration and Social History of Modern Europe." In *Time, Family and Community: Perspectives on Family and Community History,* edited by Michael Drake. Oxford: Open University in association with Blackwell, 1994, 181–98.

Jensen, Katherine. "Oral Histories of Rural Western American Women: Can They Contribute to Quantitative Studies?" *International Journal of Oral History* 5, no. 3 (November 1984): 159–67.

John, Angela, ed. *Unequal Opportunities: Women's Employment in England, 1800–1918.* Oxford: Basil Blackwell, 1986.

Johnson, Trudi D. "Matrimonial Property Law in Newfoundland to the End of the Nineteenth Century." Ph.D. diss., Memorial University of Newfoundland, 1998.

Jones, Deborah. "Gossip: Notes on Women's Oral Culture." In The *Feminist Critique of Language: A Reader,* edited by Deborah Cameron. London: Routledge, 1990, 242–50.

Jones, Dot. "Counting the Cost of Coal: Women's Lives in the Rhondda, 1881–1911." In *Our Mothers' Land: Chapters in Welsh Women's History, 1830–1939,* edited by Angela V. John. Cardiff: University of Wales Press, 1991, 109–33.

Jones, Rosemary. "Women, Community, and Collective Action: The 'Ceffyl Pren' Tradition." In *Our Mothers' Land: Chapters in Welsh Women's History, 1830–1939,* edited by Angela V. John. Cardiff: University of Wales Press, 1991, 17–41.

Kaplan, Temma. "Women and Communal Strikes in the Crisis of 1917–1922." In *Becoming Visible: Women in European History,* edited by Renate Bridenthal, Claudia Koonz, and Susan Stuard. Boston: Houghton Mifflin, 1987, 429–49.

Karlsen, Carol F. "The Devil in the Shape of a Woman: The Economic Basis of Witchcraft." In *Women's America: Refocusing the Past*, edited by Linda Kerber and Jane Sherron de Hart. 3rd ed. New York: Oxford University Press, 1991, 57–72.

Kennedy, Liam, and Leslie A. Clarkson, "Birth, Death, and Exile: Irish Population History, 1700–1921." In *An Historical Geography of Ireland*, edited by B. J. Graham and L. J. Proudfoot. London: Academic Press, 1993, 158–84.

Kennedy, Robert E, Jr. *The Irish: Emigration, Marriage, and Fertility*. Berkeley: University of California Press, 1973.

Kent, Susan Kingsley. *Sex and Suffrage in Britain, 1860–1914*. Princeton: Princeton University Press, 1987.

Keough, Willeen. "The 'Old Hag' Meets St. Brigid: Irish Women and the Intersection of Belief Systems on the Southern Avalon." *An Nasc* 15 (spring 2001): 12–25.

——. "The Riddle of Peggy Mountain: The Regulation of Irish Women's Sexuality on the Southern Avalon, 1750–1860." *Acadiensis* 31, no. 2 (spring 2002): 36–70.

Kirkham, Graeme. "The Origins of Mass Emigration from Ireland." In Migrations: *The Irish at Home and Abroad*, edited by Richard Kearney. Dublin: Wolfhound Press, 1990, 81–90.

Koditschek, Theodore. "Gendering of the British Working Class." *Gender and History* 9, no. 2 (August 1997): 333–63.

Kross, Jessica. "Mansions, Men, Women, and the Creation of Multiple Publics in Eighteenth-Century British North America." *Journal of Social History* 33, no. 2 (1999): 385–408.

Lachance, André. "Women and Crime in Canada in the Early Eighteenth Century, 1712–1758." In *Crime and Criminal Justice in Europe and Canada*, edited by Louis A. Knafla. Waterloo: Wilfrid Laurier University Press, 1985.

Lahey, Raymond J. *James Louis O'Donel in Newfoundland, 1784–1807: The Establishment of the Roman Catholic Church*, edited by Shannon Ryan and G. M. Story. St. John's: Newfoundland Historical Society, pamphlet 8, 1984.

Larkin, Emmet. "The Devotional Revolution in Ireland, 1850–75." Chap. 2 in *The Historical Dimensions of Irish Catholicism*, edited by Emmet Larkin. New York: Arno Press, 1976.

Lewis, Johanna Miller. "Women and Economic Freedom in the North Carolina Backcountry." In *Women and Freedom in Early America*, edited by Larry D. Eldridge. New York: New York University Press, 1997, 191–208.

Leydesdorff, Selma, Luisa Passerini, and Paul Tompson, eds. *Gender and Memory. International Yearbook of Oral History and Life Stories*. Vol. 4. Oxford: Oxford University Press, 1996.

Light, Beth, and Alison Prentice, eds. *Pioneer and Gentlewomen of British North America, 1713–1867. Documents in Canadian Women's History*. Vol. 1. Toronto: New Hogtown Press, 1980.

Lindstrom, Varpu. *Defiant Sisters: A Social History of Finnish Immigrant Women in Canada*. 2nd ed. Toronto: Multicultural History Society of Ontario, 1992.

Little, Linda. "Plebeian Collective Action in Harbour Grace and Carbonear, 1830–40." Master's thesis, Memorial University of Newfoundland, 1984.

Lockhart, Audrey. *Some Aspects of Emigration from Ireland to the North American Colonies Between 1660 and 1775*. The Irish-Americans Series. New York: Arno Press, 1976.

Lochrie, Karma. *Covert Operations: The Medieval Uses of Secrecy*. Philadelphia: University of Pennsylvania Press, 1999.

Loudon, Irvine. "Deaths in Childbed from the Eighteenth Century to 1935." In *Childbirth: Changing Ideas and Practices in Britain and America, 1600 to the Present*, edited by Philip K. Wilson. Vol. 5. New York: Garland, 1996, 195–235.

Luddy, Maria. *Women in Ireland, 1800–1918: A Documentary History*. Cork: Cork University Press, 1995.

Lysaght, Patricia. "Women and the Great Famine." In *The Great Famine and the Irish Diaspora in America*, edited Arthur Gribben. Amherst: University of Massachusetts Press, 1999, 21–47.

MacKay, Margaret. "Nineteenth Century Tiree Emigrant Communities in Ontario." *Oral History* 9, no. 2 (autumn 1981): 49–60.

Mac Laughlin, Jim. *Historical and Recent Irish Emigration: A Critique of Core-Periphery and Behavioural Models*. London: University of North London Press, 1994.

——. "Emigration and the Construction of Nationalist Hegemony in Ireland: The Historical Background to 'New Wave' Irish Emigration." In *Location and Dislocation in Contemporary Irish Society: Emigration and Irish Identities*, edited by Jim Mac Laughlin. Cork: Cork University Press, 1997, 5–35.

MacRaild, Donald M. "Crossing Migrant Frontiers: Comparative Reflections on Irish Migrants in Britain and the United States during the Nineteenth Century." *Immigrants and Minorities* 18, nos. 2 and 3 (July/November 1999): 40–70.

——. *Irish Migrants in Modern Britain, 1750–1922*. New York: St. Martin's Press, 1999.

Mageean, Dierdre. "To Be Matched or to Move: Irish Women's Prospects in Munster." In *Peasant Maids—City Women: From the European Countryside to Urban America*, edited by Christiane Harzig. Ithaca: Cornell University Press, 1997, 57–97.

Mancke, Elizabeth. "At the Counter of the General Store: Women and the Economy in Eighteenth-Century Horton, Nova Scotia." In *Intimate Relations: Family and Community in Planter Nova Scotia, 1759–1800*, edited by Margaret Conrad. Planter Studies Series, no. 3. Fredericton: *Acadiensis*, 1995, 167–81.

Mannion, John J. "Irish Imprints on the Landscape of Eastern Canada in the Nineteenth Century: A Study in Cultural Transfer and Adaptation." Ph.D. diss., University of Toronto, 1971.

——. "The Irish Migrations to Newfoundland." Unpublished summary of a public lecture delivered to the Newfoundland Historical Society, St. John's, 23 October 1973.

——. *Irish Settlements in Eastern Canada: A Study of Cultural Transfer and Adaptation*. Toronto: University of Toronto Press, 1974.

——. "The Impact of Newfoundland on Waterford and Its Hinterland in the Eighteenth Century." Paper delivered at the Annual Conference of Irish Geographers, University College, Galway, 22 April 1977.

——. "Migration and Upward Mobility: The Meagher Family in Ireland and Newfoundland, 1780–1830." *Irish Economic and Social History* 15 (1988): 54–70.

——. "Tracing the Irish: A Geographical Guide," *The Newfoundland Ancestor* 9, no. 1 (spring 1993): 4–18.

——, ed. *The Peopling of Newfoundland: Essays in Historical Geography.* Social and Economic Papers, no. 8. St. John's: Institute of Social and Economic Research, Memorial University of Newfoundland, 1977.

Mannion, John J., and Gordon Handcock. "The Southeast Ireland Homeland," "The Southwest England Homeland," and "Origins of the Newfoundland Population, 1836." In *Historical Atlas of Canada,* edited by R. Louis Gentilcore. Vol. 2. Toronto: University of Toronto Press, 1983, plate 8.

Mannion, John J., and Fidelma Maddock. "Old World Antecedents, New World Applications: Inistioge Immigrants in Newfoundland." In *Kilkenny: History and Society–Interdisciplinary Essays on the History of an Irish County,* edited by William Nolan and Kevin Whelan. Dublin: Geography Publications, 1990, 345–404.

Marks, Lynne. "No Double Standard?: Leisure, Sex, and Sin in Upper Canadian Church Discipline Records, 1800–1860." In *Gendered Pasts: Historical Essays in Femininity and Masculinity in Canada,* edited by Kathryn McPherson, Cecilia Morgan, and Nancy M. Forestell. Oxford: Oxford University Press, 1999, 48–64.

Martin, Ronald, ed. and comp. *Poems of Action, Sentiment and Reflection.* St. John's: n.p., 1945.

Matthews, Keith. "A History of the West of England-Newfoundland Fishery." D.Phil. diss., Oxford University, 1968.

——. *Lectures on the History of Newfoundland, 1500–1830.* St. John's: Breakwater Books, 1988.

May, Allyson N. "'She at first denied it': Infanticide Trials at the Old Bailey." In *Women and history: Voices of Early Modern England,* edited by Valerie Frith. Toronto: Coach House Press, 1995, 19–49.

McCaffrey, Lawrence J. *The Irish Diaspora in America.* Bloomington: Indiana University Press, 1976.

McCarthy, Michael. *The Irish in Newfoundland, 1600–1900: Their Trials, Tribulations, and Triumphs.* St. John's: Creative Publishers, 1999.

McCormack, Bridget. *Perceptions of St. Patrick in Eighteenth-Century Ireland.* Dublin: Four Courts Press, 2000.

McGrath, Carmelita, Barbara Neis, and Marily Porter, eds. *Their Lives and Times: Women in Newfoundland and Labrador: A Collage.* St. John's: Killick Press, 1995.

McLintock, A. H. *The Establishment of Constitutional Government in Newfoundland, 1783–1832.* London: Longmans, Green, 1941.

Mcnaughton, Janet. "The Role of the Newfoundland Midwife in Traditional Health Care, 1900 to 1970." Ph.D. diss., Memorial University of Newfoundland, 1989.

McPherson, Kathryn, Cecilia Morgan, and Nancy M. Forestell, "Introduction: Conceptualizing Canada's Gendered Pasts." *Gendered Pasts: Historical Essays in Femininity and Masculinity in Canada,* edited by McPherson, Morgan, and Forestell. Oxford: Oxford University Press, 1999, 1–11.

Merritt, Susan E. *Her Story II: Women from Canada's Past*. St. Catharines, ON: Vanwell, 1995.

Miller, Kerby A. "Emigrants and Exiles: Irish Cultures and Irish Emigration to North America, 1790–1922." *Irish Historical Studies* 22, no. 86 (September 1980): 97–125.

——. *Emigrants and Exiles: Ireland and the Irish Exodus to North America*. New York: Oxford University Press, 1985.

——. "Emigration, Capitalism, and Ideology in Post-famine Ireland." In *Migrations: The Irish at Home and Abroad*, edited by Richard Kearney. Dublin: Wolfhound Press, 1990, 91–108.

——. "'Scotch-Irish,' 'Black Irish,' and 'Real Irish': Emigrants and Identities in the Old South." In *The Irish Diaspora*, edited by Andy Bielenberg. Harlow: Longman, 2000, 139–57.

——. "'Scotch-Irish' Myths and 'Irish' Identities in Eighteenth-and Nineteenth-Century America." In *New Perspectives on the Irish Diaspora*, edited by Charles Fanning. Carbondale and Edwardsville: Southern Illinois University Press, 2000, 75–92.

Miller, Kerby A., David Doyle, and Patricia Kelleher. "'For love and liberty': Irish Women, Migration, and Domesticity in Ireland and America, 1815–1920." In *Irish Women and Irish Migration*, edited by Patrick O'Sullivan. *Irish World Wide Series*. Vol. 4. London: Leicester University Press, 1995, 41–65.

Miller, Kerby A., Arnold Schrier, Bruce D. Boling, and David Doyle. *Irish Immigrants in the Land of Canaan: Letters and Memoirs from Colonial and Revolutionary America, 1675–1815*. Oxford: Oxford University Press, 2003.

Mokyr, Joel. *Why Ireland Starved: A Quantitative and Analytical History of the Irish Economy, 1800–1850*. London: George Allen and Unwin, 1983.

Mokyr, Joel, and Cormac O Grada, "Emigration and Poverty in Prefamine Ireland." *Explorations in Economic History* 19, no. 4 (October 1982): 360–84.

Monahan, Arthur P. "Canada." In *A History of Irish Catholicism*, edited by Patrick J. Corish. Dublin: Gill, 1971, 1–34.

Morgan, Cecilia. *Public Men and Virtuous Women: The Gendered Languages of Religion and Politics in Upper Canada, 1791–1850*. Toronto: University of Toronto Press, 1996.

——. "'When Bad Men Conspire, Good Men Must Unite!': Gender and Political Discourses in Upper Canada, 1820s–1830s." In *Gendered Pasts: Historical Essays in Femininity and Masculinity in Canada*, edited by Kathryn McPherson, Cecilia Morgan, and Nancy M. Forestell. Oxford: Oxford University Press, 1999, 12–28.

Murphy, James, comp. *Songs and Ballads of Newfoundland, Ancient and Modern*. St. John's: n.p., 1902.

Murphy, Maureen. "Charlotte Grace O'Brien and the Mission of Our Lady of the Rosary for the Protection of Irish Immigrant Girls." *Mid-America: An Historical Review* 74, no. 3 (1992): 253–70.

Murray, Hilda Chaulk. *More Than Fifty Percent: Women's Life in a Newfoundland Outport, 1900–1950*. St. John's: Breakwater Books, 1979.

Myles, Margaret F. *Textbook for Midwives*. 8th ed. Edinburgh: Churchill Livingstone, 1975.

Nead, Lynda. *Myths of Sexuality: Representations of Women in Victorian Britain*. Oxford: Basil Blackwell, 1988.

Nemec, Thomas F. "The Irish Emigration to Newfoundland," *Newfoundland Quarterly* 69, no. 1 (1972b): 15–24.

——. "Trepassey, 1505–1840 A.D.: The Emergence of an Anglo-Irish Newfoundland Outport," *Newfoundland Quarterly* 69, no. 4 (1973): 17–28.

——. "An Ethnohistorical and Ethnographic Study of the Cod Fishery at St. Shott's, Newfoundland." Ph.D. diss., University of Michigan, 1980.

——. "Irish Settlement in Newfoundland." In *Encyclopedia of Newfoundland and Labrador*, edited by Joseph R. Smallwood. Vol. 3. St. John's: Harry Cuff, 1991.

——. "Trepassey, 1840–1900: An Ethnohistorical Reconstruction of an Anglo-Irish Outport Society." In *Through a Mirror Dimly: Essays on Newfoundland Society and Culture*, edited by Maura Hanrahan. St. John's: Breakwater, 1993, 145–62.

Neville, Grace. " 'She Never Then After That Forgot Him': Irish Women and Emigration to the United States in Irish Folklore." *Mid-America: An Historical Review* 74, no. 3 (1992): 271–89.

Newson, Harry. *The Law of Salvage, Towage, and Pilotage*. London: William Clowes, 1886.

Nolan, Janet A. *Ourselves Alone: Women's Emigration from Ireland, 1885–1920*. Lexington: University Press of Kentucky, 1989.

——. "The Great Famine and Women's Emigration from Ireland." In *The Hungry Stream: Essays on Emigration and Famine*, edited by E. Margaret Crawford. Belfast: Centre for Emigration Studies, Ulster-American Folk Park, and Institute of Irish Studies, Queen's University, 1997, 61–70.

Nordvik, Helge W., and Lewis R. Fischer. "Peter M. Stuwitz and the Newfoundland Inshore Fishery in 1840." *Newfoundland Studies* 1, no. 2 (fall 1985): 129–40.

Norton, Judith. "The Dark Side of Planter Life: Reported Cases of Domestic Violence." In *Intimate Relations: Family and Community in Planter Nova Scotia, 1759–1800*, edited by Margaret Conrad. Planter Studies Series, no. 3. Fredericton: *Acadiensis*, 1995, 182–89.

O'Carroll, Ida. *Models for Movers: Irish Women's Emigration to America*. Dublin: Attic Press, 1990.

O'Connor, Thomas. *The Boston Irish: A Political History*. Boston: Northeastern University Press, 1995.

O'Day, Edward. "The 'Second Colonization of New England' Revisited: Irish Immigration Before the Famine." In *New Perspectives on the Irish Diaspora*, edited by Charles Fanning. Carbondale and Edwardsville: Southern Illinois University Press, 2000, 93–114.

O'Dea, Shane. "Simplicity and Survival: Vernacular Response in Newfoundland Architecture." *Society for the Study of Architecture in Canada Bulletin* 8, no. 2 (June 1983): 4–11.

O'Dowd, Anne. *Spalpeens and Tattie Hokers: History and Folklore of the Irish Migratory Agricultural Worker in Ireland and Britain*. Blackrock: Irish Academic Press, 1991.

——. "Women in Rural Ireland in the Nineteenth and Early Twentieth Centuries: How the Daughters, Wives, and Sisters of Small Farmers and Landless Labourers Fared." *Rural History* 5, no. 2 (1994): 171–83.

O'Farrell, Padraic. *Superstitions of the Irish Country People*. Dublin: Mercier Press, 1978.

O Grada, Cormac. *Ireland: A New Economic History, 1780–1939*. Oxford: Clarendon Press, 1994.

O'Neill, Kevin. *Family and Farm in Pre-famine Ireland: The Parish of Killashandra*. Madison: The University of Wisconsin Press, 1984.

O'Neill, Paul. *Upon This Rock: The Story of the Roman Catholic Church in Newfoundland and Labrador*. St. John's: Breakwater Books, 1984.

Oosterhoff, A. H. Text, *Commentary, and Cases on Wills and Succession*. 3rd ed. Toronto: Carswell, 1990.

O'Sullivan, Patrick, ed. *Patterns of Migration*. Irish World Wide Series. Vol. 1. Leicester: Leicester University Press, 1992.

——, ed. *The Irish in the New Communities*. Irish World Wide Series. Vol. 2. Leicester: Leicester University Press, 1992.

——, ed. *The Creative Migrant*. Irish World Wide Series. Vol. 3. Leicester: Leicester University Press, 1994.

——, ed. *Irish Women and Irish Migration*. Irish World Wide Series. Vol. 4. London: Leicester University Press, 1995.

——, ed. *Religion and Identity*. Irish World Wide Series. Vol. 5. London: Leicester University Press, 1996.

——, ed. *The Meaning of the Famine*. Irish World Wide Series. Vol. 6. London: Leicester University Press, 1997.

O'Toole, A. L. *Challenged: The Story of Edmund Rice and the Christian Brothers in North America Since 1825*. Bristol: Burleigh Press, 1975.

Parker, Stephen. *Informal Marriage, Cohabitation, and the Law, 1750–1989*. New York: St. Martin's Press, 1990.

Paulson, Kenneth. "Land, Family, and Inheritance in Lunenburg Township, Nova Scotia, 1760–1800." In *Intimate Relations: Family and Community in Planter Nova Scotia, 1759–1800*, edited by Margaret Conrad. Planter Studies Series, no. 3. Fredericton: *Acadiensis*, 1995, 110–21.

Perkin, Joan. *Women and Marriage in Nineteenth-Century England*. Chicago: Lyceum Books, 1989.

Perry, Adele. "'Oh I'm Just Sick of the Faces of Men': Gender Imbalance, Race, Sexuality, and Sociability in Nineteenth-Century British Columbia," *BC Studies* 105 and 106 (spring/summer 1995): 27–43.

———. *On the Edge of Empire: Gender, Race, and the Making of British Columbia, 1849–1871*. Toronto: University of Toronto Press, 2001.

Pocius, Gerald L. "English Styles and Irish Adaptations: The Emergence of Newfoundland House Forms on the Southern Shore." Paper presented to a joint meeting of the Irish Newfoundland Society and the Newfoundland Historical Society, 29 January 1981.

——. "Architecture on Newfoundland's Southern Shore: Diversity and the Emergence of New World Forms." *Society for the Study of Architecture in Canada Bulletin* 8, no. 2 (June 1983): 12–19.

——. *A Place to Belong: Community Order and Everyday Space in Calvert, Newfoundland.* Athens: University of Georgia Press, 1991.

Pope, Peter. "The South Avalon Planters, 1630–1700." Ph.D. diss., Memorial University of Newfoundland, 1992.

Porter, Marilyn. "She Was Skipper of the Shore Crew: Notes on the History of the Sexual Division of Labour in Newfoundland," *Labour/Le Travail* 15 (spring 1985): 104–25.

Porter, Roy. "Mixed Feelings: The Enlightenment and Sexuality in Eighteenth-Century Britain." In *Sexuality in Eighteenth-Century Britain,* edited by Paul-Gabriel Boucé. Manchester: Manchester University Press, 1982, 1–27.

Poutanen, Mary Anne. "Reflections of Montreal Prostitution in the Records of the Lower Courts, 1810–1842." In *Class, Gender and the Law in Eighteenth- and Nineteenth-Century Quebec: Sources and Perspectives,* edited by Donald Fyson, Colin Coates, and Kathryn Harvey. Montreal: Montreal History Group, 1993, 99–125.

——."The Homeless, the Whore, the Drunkard, and the Disorderly: Contours of Female Vagrancy in the Montreal Courts, 1810–1842." In *Gendered Pasts: Historical Essays in Femininity and Masculinity in Canada,* edited by Kathryn McPherson, Cecilia Morgan, and Nancy M. Forestell. Oxford: Oxford University Press, 1999, 29–47.

Prowse, Daniel W. *A History of Newfoundland from the English, Colonial, and Foreign Records.* London: MacMillan, 1895, reprint Belleville: Mika Studio, 1972.

Reece, Bob. "'Such a Banditti': Irish Convicts in Newfoundland, 1789–Part 1." *Newfoundland Studies* 13, no. 1 (spring 1997): 1–29.

Rendall, Jane. *Women in an Industrializing Society: England, 1750–1880.* Historical Association Studies. Oxford: Basil Blackwell, 1990.

Rhodes, Rita. *Women and the Family in Post-famine Ireland: Status and Opportunity in a Patriarchal Society.* New York: Garland, 1992.

Richter, Julie. "The Free Women of Charles Parish, York County, Virginia, 1630–1740." In *Women and Freedom in Early America,* edited by Larry D. Eldridge. New York: New York University Press, 1997, 290–312.

Ridner, Judith. "'To Have a Sufficient Maintenance': Women and the Economics of Freedom in Frontier Pennsylvania, 1750–1800." In *Women and Freedom in Early America,* edited by Larry D. Eldridge. New York: New York University Press, 1997.

Riley, Denise. *"Am I That Name?": Feminism and the Category of Women in History.* Minneapolis: University of Minnesota Press, 1988.

Roberts, Elizabeth. *A Woman's Place: An Oral History of Working-Class Women, 1890–1940*. Oxford: Basil Blackwell, 1984.

Rollmann, Hans. "Religious Enfranchisement and Roman Catholics in Eighteenth-Century Newfoundland." In *Religion and Identity: The Experience of Irish and Scottish Catholics in Atlantic Canada*, edited by Terrence Murphy and Cyril J. Byrne. St. John's: Jesperson Press, 1987, 34–52.

Rose, Sonya O. *Limited Livelihoods: Gender and Class in Nineteenth-Century England*. Berkeley: University of California Press, 1992.

Rosen, Deborah A. "Mitigating Inequality: Women and Justice in Colonial New York." In *Women and Freedom in Early America*, edited by Larry D. Eldridge. New York: New York University Press, 1997, 313–29.

Ross, Ellen. *Love and Toil: Motherhood in Outcast London, 1870–1918*. New York: Oxford University Press, 1993.

Rossiter, Ann. "In Search of Mary's Past: Placing Nineteenth Century Irish Immigrant Women in British Feminist History." In *Women, Migration, and Empire*, edited by Joan Grant. Stoke-on-Trent: Trentham Books, 1996, 1–29.

Rousseau, G. S., and Roy Porter, eds. *Sexual underworlds of the Enlightenment*. Chapel Hill: University of North Carolina Press, 1988.

Ryan, Mary P. *Womanhood in America: From Colonial Times to the Present*. New York: New Viewpoints, 1975.

Ryan, Shannon. "Fishery to Colony: A Newfoundland Watershed, 1793–1815." *Acadiensis* 12, no. 2 (spring 1983): 34–52.

——. *The Ice Hunters: A History of Newfoundland Sealing to 1914*. St. John's: Breakwater, 1994.

Sangster, Joan. "Telling Our Stories: Feminist Debates and the Use of Oral History." *Women's History Review* 3, no. 1 (1994): 5–28.

Scally, Robert James. *The End of Hidden Ireland: Rebellion, Famine, and Emigration*. New York: Oxford University Press, 1995.

Schrager, Samuel. "What is Social in Oral History?" *International Journal of Oral History* 4, no. 2 (June 1983): 76–98.

Scholten, Catherine M. "'On the Importance of the Obstetrick Art': Changing Customs of Childbirth in America 1760–1825." In *Women's America: Refocusing the Past*, edited by Linda Kerber and Jane Sherron de Hart. 1st ed. New York: Oxford University Press, 1982, 51–65.

Scott, Joan Wallach. *Gender and the Politics of History*. New York: Columbia University Press, 1988.

Seary, E. R., with Sheila Lynch. *Family Names of the Island of Newfoundland*. Rev. ed. St. John's: Memorial University of Newfoundland, 1984.

Shanley, Mary Lyndon. *Feminism, Marriage, and the Law in Victorian England, 1850–1895*. Princeton: Princeton University Press, 1989.

Shapiro, Ann-Louise. "History and Feminist Theory; or, Talking Back to the Beadle." In *Feminists Revision History*, edited by Ann-Louise Shapiro. New Brunswick: Rutgers University Press, 1994, 1–23.

Shannon, William V. *The American Irish*. New York: Macmillan, 1963.

Sharpless, Rebecca. "The Numbers Game: Oral History Compared with Quantitative Methodology." *International Journal of Oral History* 7, no. 2 (June 1886): 93–108.

Simon, Krista. "A Case Study in the Reception of Law in Newfoundland: Assessing Women's Participation in the Courts of Placentia District, 1757–1823." Honors diss., Memorial University of Newfoundland, 1999.

Sinclair, Alan M., and Margaret E. McCallum. *Introduction to Real Property Law*. Fourth ed. Toronto: Butterworths, 1997.

Smart, Carol. "Disruptive Bodies and Unruly Sex: The Regulation of Reproduction and Sexuality in the Nineteenth Century." In *Regulating Womanhood: Historical Essays on Marriage, Motherhood, and Sexuality*, edited by Carol Smart. London: Routledge, 1992, 7–32.

Smith, Babette. *A Cargo of Women: Susannah Watson and the Convicts of the "Princess Royal."* Kensington: New South Wales University Press, 1988.

Smith, Merril D. "'Whers Gone to She Knows Not': Desertion and Widowhood in Early Pennsylvania." In *Women and Freedom in Early America*, edited by Larry D. Eldridge. New York: New York University Press, 1997, 211–28.

Snell, James G. *In the Shadows of Law: Divorce in Canada, 1900–1939*. Toronto: University of Toronto Press, 1991.

Snell, K. D. M. "Agricultural Seasonal Unemployment, the Standard of Living, and Women's Work, 1690–1860." In *Women's Work: The English Experience 1650–1914*, edited by Pamela Sharpe. London: Arnold, 1998, 73–120.

Sundberg, Sarah. "Farm Women on the Canadian Prairie Frontier: The Helpmate Image." In *Rethinking Canada: The Promise of Women's History*, edited by Veronica Strong-Boag and Anita Clair Fellman. Toronto: Copp Clark Pitman, 1986, 95–106.

Swift, Roger, and Sheridan Gilley, eds. *The Irish in the Victorian City*. London: Croom Helm, 1985.

——. *The Irish in Britain, 1815–1939*. London: Pinter, 1989.

——. *The Irish in Victorian Britain: The Local Dimension*. Dublin: Four Courts Press, 1999.

Swyripa, Francis. *Wedded to the Cause: Ukrainian-Canadian Women and Ethnic Identity, 1891–1991*. Toronto: University of Toronto Press, 1993.

Taylor, David. *Crime, Policing and Punishment in England, 1750–1914*. New York: St. Martin's Press, 1998.

Tebbutt, Melanie. *Women's Talk? A Social History of "Gossip" in Working-Class Neighbourhoods, 1880–1960*. Aldershot: Scolar Press, 1995.

Thompson, E. P. *Customs in Common*. London: Merlin Press, 1991.

Thomson, Alistair. "Moving Stories: Oral History and Migration Studies." *Oral History* 27, no. 1 (spring 1999): 24–37.

——. "Tales of the Century: Biennial National Conference of the Oral History Association of Australia, 2–5 September 1999, State Library of Victoria, Melbourne." *Oral History* 28, no. 1 (spring 2000): 25–7.

Thomson, Alistair, Michael Frisch, and Paula Hamilton. "The Memory and History Debates: Some International Perspectives." *Oral History* 22, no. 2 (autumn 1994): 33–43.

Toulson, Shirley. *The Celtic Year: A Month-by-Month Celebration of Celtic Christian Festivals and Sites*. Shaftesbury: Element, 1996.

Trumbach, Randolph. "Modern Prostitution and Gender in *Fanny Hill*: Libertine and Domesticated Fantasy." In *Sexual underworlds of the Enlightenment*, edited by G. S. Rousseau and Roy Porter. Chapel Hill: University of North Carolina Press, 1988, 69–85.

Tucker, Ephraim W. *Five Months in Labrador and Newfoundland During the Summer of 1838*. Concord, 1839.

Ulrich, Laurel Thatcher. *Good Wives: Image and Reality in the Lives of Women in Northern New England, 1650–1750*. New York: Knopf, 1982.

——. *A Midwife's Tale: The Life of Martha Ballard, Based on Her Diary, 1785–1812*. New York: Knopf, 1990.

Valenze, Deborah. *The First Industrial Woman*. New York: Oxford University Press, 1995.

Van Kirk, Sylvia. "The Impact of White Women on Fur Trade Society." In *The Neglected Majority: Essays in Canadian Women's History*, edited by Alison Prentice and Susan Mann Trofimenkoff. Vol. 2. Toronto: McClelland and Stewart, 1985, 27–48. Originally published as "Women and the Fur Trade," The Beaver (winter 1972): 4–21.

Walker, David M. *The Oxford Companion to Law*. Oxford: Clarendon Press, 1980.

Walkowitz, Judith. *City of Dreadful Delight: Narratives of Sexual Danger in Late-Victorian London*. Chicago: University of Chicago Press, 1992.

Walter, Bronwen. *Outsiders Inside: Whiteness, Place, and Irish Women*. London: Routledge, 2001.

Williams, Alan F. *Father Baudoin's War: D'Iberville's Campaigns in Acadia and Newfoundland, 1696, 1697*, edited by Alan G. Macpherson. St. John's: Memorial University of Newfoundland, 1987.

Williamson, Jeffrey G. "The Impact of the Irish on British Labor Markets During the Industrial Revolution." *Journal of Economic History* 46, no. 3 (September 1986): 693–720.

Wokeck, Marianne S. *Trade in Strangers: The Beginnings of Mass Migration to North America*. University Park: Pennsylvania State University Press, 1999.

Wood-Martin, G. *Traces of the Elder Faiths of Ireland*. Vol. 2. London: 1902; reprint, Port Washington, NY: Kennikat Press, 1970.

Wright, Miriam. "Women, Men and the Modern Fishery: Images of Gender in Government Plans for the Canadian Atlantic Fisheries." In *Their Lives and Times: Women in Newfoundland and Labrador: A Collage*, edited by Carmelita McGrath, Barbara Neis, and Marilyn Porter. St. John's: Killick Press, 1995, 129–43.

Yogis, John A. *Canadian Law Dictionary*. 3rd ed. Hauppauge, NY: Barron's Educational Series, 1995.

3. INTERNET SOURCES

Dictionary of Newfoundland English Online. 2nd ed. with suppl., edited by G. M. Story, W. J. Kirwin, and J. D. A. Widdowson. Toronto: University of Toronto Press, 1998. Newfoundland and Labrador Heritage Web Site, Memorial University of Newfoundland, Web Link

Newfoundland and Labrador Heritage Web Site. Memorial University of Newfoundland. Web Link

Newfoundland Salt Fisheries: A Digital Exhibit. Canada's Digital Collections Program, Industry Canada. Web Link

GLOSSARY

This glossary contains words and terms related to the Newfoundland fishery or from the Newfoundland vernacular in the nineteenth century that appear in the text. The definitions reflect usage on the southern Avalon; some variations in meaning exist elsewhere on the island. Interested readers should also consult the *Dictionary of Newfoundland English*, edited by G. M. Story, W. J. Kirwin, and J. D. A. Widdowson, 2d ed., with supplement (Toronto: University of Toronto Press, 1998). An online version of the dictionary is available at the Dictionary of Newfoundland English Online.

BARM A mixture for leavening bread, made from hops, potato scrapings, and molasses or sugar.

BARRA (OR BARROW) A flat, wooden frame with handles at each end, like a stretcher, for carrying fish.

BIBE A banshee; a supernatural creature, gendered female, whose plaintive wail—usually a low-pitched moaning or sobbing, sometimes in combination with a whistling sound—was an omen of death. The spirit was usually heard at night and manifested herself to the person about to die (or to a close relative or friend) usually in or around that person's house, in graveyards, or on lonely stretches of road.

BLASTY BOUGH A windfall branch from a coniferous tree, dried but with reddish-brown needles still attached; used to make short, hot fires for cooking and baking.

BOATKEEPER (ALSO **BY-BOATKEEPER**) A fisher who fitted out a small inshore fishing craft or crafts that were operated by hired crews. Traditionally, boatkeepers were migratory fishermen who kept a small boat or boats at Newfoundland, buying passage for themselves and their hired crew each fishing season on board the larger fishing ships coming out from the West of England.

BOATMASTER The skipper of a small, undecked vessel used in the inshore boat fishery; the person in charge of a boat crew.

BOTTOMER A plain, flat cake made with buttermilk, eggs, and flour.

BRESNEY (OR **BRESHNEY**) A dried branch or twig collected in the woods and used for firewood; or a bundle of these windfall branches and twigs tied together and transported on the back.

BROKEN FISH Codfish that had been damaged in the body during processing. When salted and dried, such fish would not keep in the warmer climates of Newfoundland's fish markets and would attract a very low price. It was designated the lowest grade (*West India*) and was sometimes simply kept for local consumption. See also **cull**.

BUNKHOUSE A building where hired fishing servants and sharemen (see share) working for a family production unit were accommodated.

BUSKINS Knitted leggings worn as outer clothing in winter to keep snow out of boots.

CABOUSE (OR **CABOOSE**) An iron hearth and copper for cooking on board a passenger vessel.

CAPTAIN A member of a small boat crew, responsible for keeping the boat clean and cooking for the crew.

CHIPS Small, thin pieces of wood, usually remnants from chopping **junks** in the woodyard, although sometimes purposely cut, used to start fires or as fuel for quick cooking or baking jobs.

COASTING SCHOONER A decked vessel, rigged fore and aft, employed in the coastal trade, trading between settlements along a coastal area.

COOK ON THE DOG IRONS To prepare meals in iron kettles and pots hung over *dog irons*, metal supports set in hearths to hold firewood in place.

COOKROOM A structure on fishing premises for cooking food and accommodating fishing servants.

CRACKIE A small, yappy dog of questionable pedigree.

CRUBEEN (OR CRUBBEEN) A pig's foot, particularly the hock, pickled in brine for eating.

CULL The grade of **saltfish**; or to engage in the process of grading saltfish. Newfoundland saltfish was sorted by buyers into categories according to its overall appearance and quality. The superior grade of fish (thick, with a smooth surface, not showing blood stains or excessive salt, not sunburned) was called *merchantable*. The next grade, slightly inferior but still of good quality, was called *Madeira*, after one of its original markets. The lowest grade of fish (sunburnt, over-salted, **broken**, sour, etc.) was called West *India* and was designated for the Caribbean trade. see Audio Sample No. 24

DOCTORING FEES A local term for Greenwich hospital for the seamen's hospital in southeast London, England); an early form of medical insurance for seamen and fishermen whereby an amount was held back by vessel owners and fishing employers from seamen's and fishing servants' wages to cover the costs of care they might require from attending medical practitioners.

DIET Provisions for a fishing season, or for the off-season (*winter's diet*); in a broader sense, room and board. Fishing employers would usually provide *diet* to servants as part of their contracted terms of employment.

DIETER A servant in a fishing household who remained in Newfoundland beyond the fishing season, without contracted employment, and worked through the winter for room and board, or **diet**.

ENGLISH SHORE Part of the east and southeast coast of Newfoundland, between Cape Bonavista and Cape Race, where English fishermen traditionally cured their fish. (The fishery at Newfoundland had initially been an international fishery, involving English, French, Spanish, and Portuguese vessels. While the fishermen of other countries salted their catch and brought it home in a **green** state, the English developed a lightly salted cure that required shore space for drying.) The *English Shore* would eventually become the site of initial settlement by people from the British Isles.

FAGGOT A small pile of split and salted codfish, generally stacked in the evening and respread on the **flake** in the morning for further drying. As the fish dried, it was stacked in increasingly larger heaps until it was put into **pile**.

FAIRY BUN A piece of bread, blessed by lightly touching down on the dough to mark the sign of the cross, and carried out of doors to prevent the bearer from being **fairy-led**; frequently carried by children moving beyond the environs of the immediate household, but also carried by adults in back-meadows and woods.

FAIRY CAP A toadstool or mushroom; *fairy caps* in the woods were evidence that fairies were nearby, and children who picked them were in danger of being led astray by the *little people.*

FAIRY-LED Led astray by the fairies, often in out-of-the way, yet still familiar, surroundings such as back-meadows or frequented woods.

FAIRY PATH A small path in the woods not used by humans, yet remaining mysteriously clear; said to be used by the fairies.

FAIRY PIPE A pipe-like frond of a fern.

FAIRY-STRUCK Beset by a mental or physical paralysis and, hence, rendered senseless by the fairies.

FATPORK (ALSO **FATBACK PORK**) Salt-cured fat from a pig, used for a variety of purposes, from making soap to curing warts, but featuring most prominently in the local diet as a lard for cooking and baking.

FISH Codfish.

FISHING ADMIRALS In the heyday of the migratory fishery at Newfoundland, the masters of the first ships to reach a particular cove or harbor in any given fishing season. The first master to arrive was the admiral; the second, the vice admiral; the third, the rear admiral. The admirals had first choice of the fishing **rooms** in the harbor for the season and were responsible for maintaining some degree of law and order, exercising jurisdiction in property and employment disputes and in the enforcement of fishery regulations—with varying degrees of ability and diligence. (Web Link)

FISHOGUE (ALSO PISHOGUE) A tall tale; foolish yarn; complaint; story about the supernatural.

FLAKE wooden poles, or **longers**, covered with boughs and built on upright poles to allow air to pass beneath.

FLY-SPIT A deposit of eggs left on codfish by a fly; when the eggs hatched, the larvae made the fish maggoty and ruined the quality.

FOLLOW THE FISH (ALSO FOLLOW THE FISH AND OIL) Refers to a custom whereby a fishing servant had first claim to the produce of a fishing season to ensure payment of his or her wages. Even if the employer's fish and oil had already been collected by the supplying merchant, the servant could *follow the fish* to the merchant to demand full satisfaction of wage claims before any other creditor of the employer was paid.

FORESHIPMAN A fisherman stationed forward in a small craft used in the inshore boat fishery.

FROZY A flat cake containing **fatpork** (instead of butter) mixed with eggs, flour, spices, and molasses.

GAFF A long wooden pole with a hook on one end, used to draw water in buckets from wells and for various purposes in the cod and seal fisheries.

"GOD BE MERCIFUL" PIPE A communal pipe, shared by those at a house where a body was waking, with tobacco usually provided by the family of the deceased. The smoke was drawn into the mouth and then exhaled with the invocation "God be merciful." Men and women alike partook of the ritual.

GREEN Of codfish, split and salted but not dried. Of a fishing servant, inexperienced; see also **youngster**.

GROWING SEEDS Sowing and nurturing seedling fruits and vegetables.

GRUB BOX A container, like a small wooden bucket with a cover, for carrying food when fishing or going into the woods.

HABIT In the Irish Catholic community, letters *IHS* and a small white cross above and a small white heart below the insignia. (The letters *IHS* are a Latin approximation of the Greek letters *ΙΗΣ*, a contraction of the Greek word for Jesus, *ΙΗΣΟΤΣ*.)

HAG (ALSO **OLD HAG**) A supernatural creature who came in the night and sat on the chest of her prey in an effort to impede or stop the victim's breathing. The visitation produced a choking sensation or semiconscious state from which the sufferer could only be wakened by calling his or her name backward. Not all variations of the *hag* actually involved a female apparition; sometimes she manifested herself more diffusely in the form of a bad nightmare from which the sufferer could not wake or as a feeling of paralysis that kept the sufferer pinned to the bed. Still, such victims were said to be *hag-rode* or *hag-ridden*—bewitched into temporary but terrifying paralysis by the powers of this nocturnal female phantasm.

JUNK A billet, or short log of wood, for burning in a stove or fireplace. Also, more generally, a substantial piece—e.g., a *junk* of salt beef, a *junk* of ice.

LINHAY (ALSO **LINNEY** AND **BACK KITCHEN**) A small kitchen or storeroom with a lean-to roof and attached to the back of a house.

LIST A section of drying space on a **flake**, usually set off by **longers**.

LIVYER (ALSO **LIVIER**) A permanent resident or inhabitant of Newfoundland, as compared with a visiting, migratory fisherman. Given the reluctance of English/British authorities to encourage settlement in Newfoundland, the term *settler* is rarely seen in early records. Even more rare is the term *colonist*, outside the context of the proprietary colonies of the early seventeenth century. Usage of *livyer, resident*, and *inhabitant* was much more common.

LONGER A long wooden pole, made from a small tree approximately three to four inches in diameter, used as a fence rail or to build the surfaces of **stages** and **flakes**; also used to mark the divisions between **lists**.

MAKE (FISH) To cure or preserve codfish by washing, salting, and drying it on shore.

MASTER OF THE VOYAGE The supervisor of the **shore crew**, responsible for overseeing the processing of fish on land.

MIDSHIPMAN A fisherman stationed in the mid-section of a small craft used in the inshore boat fishery.

MUG-UP A drink of tea and a snack between meals, usually taken as a respite from work (the equivalent of the modern-day coffee-break) or before retiring for the night.

NATIVE A person of European (especially British or Irish) extraction living in Newfoundland, as distinguished from migratory fishermen from the British Isles. See also **livyer**.

NEWFOUNDLAND SUMMER In the Newfoundland fishery, a term of employment that encompassed two summer fishing seasons, with the intervening winter spent cutting wood, repairing premises and gear, or other fishery-related work. Often delineated in **shipping papers** as "two summers and a winter."

OIL PETTICOAT An apron waterproofed by treating it with oil and worn while processing fish.

OUTHARBOR A harbor other than the chief port (and, eventually, capital), St. John's. Also, the inhabited portion of such a harbor. See also **outport**.

OUTPORT The inhabited portion of an **outharbor**. A coastal settlement outside St. John's, the chief port (and, eventually, capital).

PALM A knitted mitten without fingers, worn to protect the palm of the hand when splitting fish or hauling ropes.

PASSENGER Traditionally, a migrant fishing servant brought to Newfoundland for employment in any of the branches of the fishery. By the latter half of the eighteenth century, the term also referred more generally to those coming to the Newfoundland fishery with the hope of settling. See also **servant**.

PEW A fish prong, comprised of a long handle with a single tine attached to the end for transferring fish from boat to stagehead. Also, to land fish by using a *pew.* see Audio Sample No. 27

PILE A large heap of salted and split cod, usually circular, with tails pointing inward, and either stacked on a **flake** during the drying process (covered with bark for protection from moisture), or placed in a fish **store** when fully cured. See also **faggot**.

PIPE A cask holding two hogsheads, or 126 gallons.

PLANTER A resident (as opposed to migratory) proprietor of fishing premises. Planters in the early centuries of the Newfoundland fishery relied almost exclusively on hired fishing and household servants for labor; by the late eighteenth and early nineteenth centuries, the term also referred to heads of household production units using family labor supplemented by some hired labor.

PLANTATION A large fishing room or fishing premises.

PRATE-BOX A person given to idle chatter or gossip.

PRONG A tined instrument or pitchfork. Also, to stab something with a prong or to transfer something (e.g., fish or hay) from one place to another using a prong.

PUPS Pustules around the wrists, commonly caused by chafing at the sleeve edge from jigging and hand-lining in oilskins.

QUINTAL (PRONOUNCED *KEN'T'L*) In the Newfoundland fishery, the basic unit of measurement used in reference to codfish, wet or dried. Equivalent to a hundredweight (112 lbs. avoirdupois, or 50.8 kgs.).

RAL A rowdy, vagrant, or lawless person.

RAMSHORN A wooden washing trough submerged in saltwater, latticed or perforated with holes to allow seawater to run through; used to wash codfish during processing.

ROOM Fishing premises, including stages, flakes, sheds, wharves, and fish stores for the landing, processing, and storing of fish, as well as cookrooms for the accommodation of the crew. See also **stage**, **flake**, and **cookroom**.

SALTBULK A pile of codfish that had been split, washed, and salted but not yet dried.

SALTFISH Codfish that had been split, salted, and dried on **flakes**.

SCALD CREAM Cream skimmed off the top of milk after it had been heated on the stove almost to boiling point; a small amount was set aside for eating, but most scald cream was churned into butter for the family's consumption or for sale or exchange.

SCULPS Cod cheeks, a local delicacy.

SERVANT An employee in the Newfoundland fishery; part of a fishing crew or shore crew or in household service. Fishing servants were usually hired for the fishing season from May to October, although "two summers and a winter" (a **Newfoundland summer**) was also a common term of employment. Servants generally worked for wages, shares, or some combination of the two.

SHARE A portion of the value of the catch of a fishing or sealing voyage assigned to the owner or a crew member after the expenses of the vessel (the *boat's share*) had been deducted.

SHAREMAN A crew member in the fishery who worked for a **share** of the **voyage**, rather than for wages.

SHEBEEN A place where illicit liquor was sold; an unlicensed tavern; hence, **shebeen-keeper**, a person who ran such a premises.

SHEELAGH'S BRUSH (ALSO SHEILA'S BRUSH OR JUST SHEELAGH/ SHEILA). A winter storm around 18 March, usually with freezing rain that left a heavy coating of ice on the landscape; attributed to *Sheelagh/Sheila*, the wife or companion of St. Patrick, whose feast day falls on 18 March. Traditionally, the March storms leading up to and including St. Patrick's Day, 17 March, were attributed to Patrick, while those immediately following were attributed to Sheelagh—a weather pattern known as *Patrick and Sheelagh*.

SHIPPED Hired for service in the Newfoundland fishery, either through a written employment contract or through verbal agreement. In a more general sense, hired for any type of work. See also **shipping paper**.

SHIPPING PAPER A formal written employment contract for service in the Newfoundland fishery, stipulating the terms of employment such as type of work, length of employment (usually a fishing season, but also commonly "two summers and a winter"), and compensation.

SHORE CREW The members of a fishing crew who were responsible for processing fish on shore.

SHOREMAN A member of a **shore crew**.

SOUND The air bladder that ran along the inside of the backbone of a codfish and controlled its buoyancy. *Sounds* were removed during the splitting process, salted, and cooked and eaten as a local delicacy.

SOUTHERN SHORE The portion of the **English Shore** that extended south of St. John's from Bay Bulls to Cape Race.

STAGE An elevated wooden platform on shore, with cutting table and sheds, where fish were landed, split, headed, gutted, washed, and laid in **saltbulk**; also, where cod-liver oil was processed and fishing gear and supplies were stored.

STAGEHEAD The end of a fishing stage, extending over the water, where fish were landed by *pewing* them from boats with a fish prong. See also **stage**.

STORE A building on a planter's or fisherman's fishing premises where gear and supplies were stored and **saltfish** and cod oil received from fishermen and was awaiting shipment.

TILT A temporary lean-to or shelter; a primitive, single-roomed hut, without windows, built of vertical studs or logs, chinked with moss and covered with canvas, bark, sods, or boughs; traditionally employed by the migratory fishermen at Newfoundland but also a temporary form of shelter for some new residents on the island.

VAMP A short, knitted sock covering only the foot and ankle.

VOYAGE A period of fishing, or the fish and oil produced during that period, as in the phrase *attach one's voyage* or *lose one's voyage*.

WATERHORSE Codfish that has been split, salted, washed in brine, and then stacked for draining before being brought to a flake or beach for drying.

WESTERN BOAT A schooner-rigged fishing boat used in fishing the banks off the south and southwest coast of the island; much smaller than the banking schooners that carried large complements of crew and dories for several weeks' fishing on the banks.

WHARF OF WOOD A large stockpile of tree poles to be cut into firewood, so named because its size and shape mimicked a harbor wharf.

YAFFLE An armful of dried, salted codfish; or the process of gathering an armful of saltfish. More generally, any small bundle or bunch.

YELLOW BELLY Various Irish factions of the southeast counties reestablished themselves in Newfoundland. *Yellow Belly* was an epithet for a person hailing from county Wexford. The name referred to the yellow sash often worn as an identifying mark. Other faction names included the Waterford *Whey Bellies*, the Kilkenny *Doonees* or *Doonaneens*, the Tipperary *Clear Airs*, and the Cork *Dadyeens*.

YOUNGSTER (ALSO GREEN MAN) A novice servant in the Newfoundland fishery. The term connoted inexperience, not necessarily age, although most youngsters were, indeed, young.

CASE FILE ARCHIVE

Note: These files contain typescripts of court records and governors' correspondence relating to selected criminal, civil, and estate matters discussed in the text. Other than headings, which have been inserted throughout for organizational purposes, the wording is as it appears in the original documents. The typography reflects my effort to render as faithfully as possible the idiosyncrasies of the original texts.

CASE FILE NO. 1

Elizabeth Cullen v. James Shortall
[26 September] 1787
Before Capt. Edward Pellew, Surrogate, with Robert Carter, JP

Elizth Cullen Complains that she was shipped in Ireland by a Mr. Pat^{k} Goff's wife to serve Mr. James Shortall on order in the Harbour of Ferryland but the vessel haveing along passage, the said Shortall shipped another person in the room of the s^{d} Cullen when the s^{d} Cullen arrived to Ferryland the said Shortall did not want [her] in his own House but reshipped her to a Mary Sanders in Ferryland the said Cullen served the s^{d} Sanders sometime but adisagreement happened They parted. The said Cullen went to the said Shortall but he would not let her in whereupon she got lodgings to a Hannah Gaffney.

1787	Elizth Cullen to Hannah Gaffney	D^{o} ~
	To 6 weeks & 5 days lodging @ 7/ p week~	£1.18.6

M^{r}. Shortall
You are to pay the amount of this demand for your Servants Lodging & diet & take her into your care~

(signed) Ed^{d}. Pellew Surrogate

Sources: PANL, GN 5/4/C/1, Ferryland, box 1, 43, *Elizabeth Cullen v. James Shortall,* [26 September] 1787.

CASE FILE NO. 2

James Rouse [also Rows] *v. Catharine Clements*
1784–1806

To John Campbell Esqr. Governor
and Commander in Chief in and over the Island
of Newfoundland

The Humble Petition of James Rows of Renews in the District of Ferryland.

That his Father William Rows an Inhabitant of Renews having a spot of Ground Granted hum by Captain Thomas Smith of His Majestys Ship Durrely Galley in the year Seventeen hundred and thirty two which my Father built thereon, Stages, Houses and Fish Flakes and carried on the Fishing Business for many years unmolested; he dying left a Wife with seven children, the said Fishing Premises went to Decay; My Mother Died in the Month of March last left the said fishing Premises to me; I had cut some Timber and put it on the said Fishing Premises; to build a Stage &c. Mrs Clemins a Widow living in the Harbour of Renews, whose fishing Premises Joined the spot of Ground granted my Father by the said Captain Smith, as the Grant will make appear, the said Mrs Clemins servants, Arthur Jackman and Stephen Power have molested and hindred me from Building my Stage and Trespassed upon the Flake foresaid [and] threatened and abused me.

Soon after the Fishing Admirals Arrival in Renews I presented a Petition setting forth the Trespasses &c. and prayed for Redress (got none) I then applied to Justice Carter of Ferryland who advised me to remain silent and lay the state before your Excellency in which I might rely upon your Excellency would do me Justice.

Whereas your humble Petitioner have received much hurt and Abuse ~ and sustained a considerable loss, being hinder'd Building my stage by Stephen Poor Master of Voyage for Mrs Clemins and by Arthur Jackman her Son in Law the 22nd and 31st July.

I pray that your Excellency will be so well pleased to Order him a Quiet and Peaceable Possession of the said Premises as a Restitution of the Damages I have sustained and your Petitioner as in Duty bound will Ever pray.

To which was Annexed the following Certificate

These are to certify that I know the said fishing premises, as the said William Rows in the Harbour of Renews situated on the North side of the said Harbour whereon the said William Rows carried on the Boat Fishery for Ten or Twelve Years and that I carried on a Boat Fishery next Room to him for Twelve years during which time there was no molestation or Disturbance by the said Rows a perfect harmony subsisted and that to the best of my knowledge no person or persons have any Claim or Demand upon the said Premises and that the said James Rows is the real Proprietor of the said Premises and his fair and honest in his Dealings and behaves very Orderly. In Testimony whereof I have hereunto set my Hand in Ferryland 14th August 1774

Robert Carter, Justice of the
Peace in Feryland
St Johns, Newfoundland 27th. August 1774

Sir,

You will please to enquire particularly into this matter and if it appears that Mrs Clemins does not Occupy the premises as Fishing Rooms according to the Act of Parliament [*Newfoundland Act*, 1699] I desire you will put the Petitioner into possession of the whole provided he means to build Stages and Flakes thereon or of such part thereof as he Actually intends Occupying for the use of the Fishery agreeable to the said Act

To
Captain Edgar
of His Majestys Ship
Leoradia

I am

Sir

Your most Obedient
humble servant
Jno. Campbell

Renewse
31 August 1785

Before Alexander Edgar, President, and Robert Carter and Henry Sweetland, JPs

[Unidentified deponent] Says he is a very old inhabitant at Renewse and that he knew very well the ground where James Rouse built on and says it was not occupied in the Fishery when said Rouse built thereon says that about Twenty years ago there was two Stages on it that he remembers those Stages being taken down but never remembers it being occupied since says he does not know who the owners were of these stages

Asked if he knew whose ground the Stages stood on says he cannot say whose ground it was but that they were not on Pottersby said Plantation (now Mrs Clements but separate from it) says that he believes the ground in dispute does not belong to either Clements or Rouse but he has been formerly been [sic] acquainted it belongs to a person in Bristol and that he himself once intended to have applied to the Person in Bristol for the said Ground to build on it himself having been told he might get it for about five Pounds says he does not know the persons name in Bristol -

Chris Pulman ~ (Sworn) Says he has seen and knows the Ground in dispute where Rouse built on and that it has been occupied as a beach for that last summer Mrs Clements dried fish on it ~ Asked if he thought the Beach was formed by Nature or if Mr Clements had made it ~ Says that he believes it was formed by Nature but that the sea breaks some times over it and that Mr Clements he believes kept it in repair he further sayeth that said James Rouse did build a flake on said Ground in dispute and that said Mrs Clements did pull it down by order of the Fishing Admiral at Renewse

Michl Carol ~ (Sworn) Asked by the Court if he ever saw the Flake Rouse built and how far it was from Mrs Clements Stage says he has seen it and that it is 30 or 40 feet from Mrs Clements premises says that he carried fish to wash last summer and that there was room enough for the *ramshorn* with-out molesting either party there being a vacant place for the purpose of washing Fish in the Landwash exclusive of the spot Rouse claims ~ Asked if ever Rouse hindered him from washing fish in that vacant spot between M[rs] Clements and the Ground alloted to Rouse says no he never asked him any liberty ~ Asked if Rouse ever hindered him from washing fish in the ramshorn says not but that he hindered him from washing under his Rouses flake ~ Asked if he had ever been ordered by M[rs] Clements to pull down Rouses Flake says not but that he was told by one of his fellow servants that it was ordered to be pulled down by Mr R[d]. Bulley the Fishing Admiral and that he did assist in pulling it down ~ ~ ~ ~ ~

William Tubrett (Sworn)	Asked if he assisted in pulling down said Rouses Flake says he did by order of Mr Rich[d]. Bully the Fishing admiral says that M[rs] Clements did not order him ~ Asked who was present when said Flake was pulled down says Mr Chris Pulman Mrs Catherine Clements Mr Richd Bully and Michl Byrne ~
Michl Byrne (Sworn)	Says he did not help or assist in pulling down said Flake he says he saw it pulled down and that he helped to carry it away says he does not know who gave orders to pull it down ~
James Rouse	Asked if he can bring any person to prove the spot of ground in dispute was ever in possession of his Father ~
Justice Carter	Says he knew the spot of Ground in dispute Twenty or Thirty years in his fathers possession says he once sold Potsburys Plantation now M[rs] Clements to John and David Miland and they sold it to Long & C[o] London who afterwards became insolvent and their assignees sold it to Henry Wall by Publick Auction and Wall since sold it to M[r] Clements says it is about ten years since he sold it says he well knows the spot and that he never remembers and can safely [attest] there was never any buildings on it ~ before Rouse built thereon
Catherine Clements	Asked if she ever spread any fish on the spot of Ground in dis pute where Rouse built his Flake ~ says Mr. Pullman knows ~. Asked how many boats she keeps answers Two and a skiff.
Mr. Justice Carter	Asked how many boats room M[r] Clements premises was for merly ~ Answer four Boats Asked if the four Boats rooms is exclusive of the Beach in dispute answers Yes ~

Mr. Justice Sweetland	Confirmed Mr. Justice Carters answers as above he once re sided at Renewse and knows the situation of Mrs Clements premises ~
Catherine Clements	Says said Rouse hindered her from Washing her Fish in the Land Wash ~ ~ ~ ~ ~
James Rouse called	Asked if Mrs Clements charge was true answers no he never refused her and that he left a space of 21 feet for the ramshorn agreeable to Justice Carters order ~ asked if he ever made known to Mrs Clements the Justices order says he believes it was made known to her ~ ~ ~
Note	The decree of the Fishing admiral at Renewse who last fall enquired into this affair by order of Mr. Justice Carter and by whose order they were to have put Rouse in possession say it is their opinion the said Beech is neither of said Clements right but as that said Clements had dried her fish there before they had given it her she being last in possession.
Mrs Clements	Says she did not claim said Beach but from ye above Decree

Copy

This is to certify whom it may concern That I John Drew an employer twenty years in this Harbor of Renewse do testify that the part of the beach whereon James Rouse has this season began to build a Flake has been occupied in carrying and making of fish by the former proprietors of Pottburys Plantation twenty three years past now in possession of Widow Clements ~

Renewse 31st August 1785 ~ as witness my hand

Signed

John Drew ~

Given by Mr Christ Pullman (on Oath that the above is John Drews hand writing and that he believes him a man of veracity ~

Note the above Certificate was delivered in Court by Mrs. Catherine Clements ~

Graham Little v. James Bryan
11 April 1791
[Before Robert Carter, Henry Sweetland, and Nicholas Brand?]

James Bryan appeard, to the suit of Graham Little, who complained [that] the s^{d} Bryan woud not pay him his Balance the Acc^{t}. was attested by the Court & Bryan orderd, to pay Little the Balance which was £2.16s.3½d, and an Order on M[rs] Catherine Clements was taken for the amount. ~

Fort Townshend 1st. Oct[r]. 1806

Sir,

James Rowse having presented to me certain Documents in support of his claim to a Fishing Room in Renewse, which he complains has been unjustly witheld from him by a person named Clements, I transmit you herewith the papers relating to this affair, and desire you will please to investigate it fully, and give the said Prowse such redress as you may judge him entitled to, but if any doubt should remain on your mind respecting his title to the said room, you will refer the whole of the evidence on both sides to the Governor for the time being, stating whether Rowse ever deserted or neglected the Room previous to its being occupied by another person.

I am,

William Carter Esq[r].
Surrogate
Ferryland

Sir,

Your most Obedient humble servant
E. Gower

Sources: PANL, GN 2/1/A, vol. 10, 49–51, Petition of James Rows, ca. 14 August 1784, together with Affidavit of Robert Carter, JP, Ferryland, 14 August 1784, and Order, Governor Campbell, 27 August 1784; PRL 340.9 N45, Ferryland, *James Rouse v. Catherine Clements*, 31 August 1785; PANL, GN 2/1/A, vol. 19, 75, Governor Erasmus Gower to William Carter, Surrogate, Ferryland, 1 October 1806; and PANL, GN 5/4/C/1, Ferryland, box 1, *Graham Little v. James Bryan*, 11 April 1791.

CASE FILE NO. 3

Regina v. Thomas Leary
2 and 4 January 1855
Before Matthew Morry, JP

Charles M[c]Carthy of Renews in his Examination this day Said that he bought Spirits from Thomas Leary of Renews and payed him for it, the Said M[c]Carthy son then Sworn, and proves that he did buy Spirits from Thomas Leary and pay him for it.

Whereupon a Summons was issued against the said thomas Leary to Show cause (if any) why he should not be Fined for selling Spirits without License.

Thursday January 4th.
Before Matthew Morry

Thomas Leary against whom a Summons was issued on the 2nd. Inst. was brought to the court by the officer Evans, and on bring asked why he should not be Fined for Selling Spirits without a License Said that his Wife applied for a License last fall whilst he was at Sea and that She was told by the officer Sullivan that a License would not be granted to her. that her husband was the proper person to make application, that he (Leary) was Sick ever Since he came from Sea, and not able to come to Ferryland to apply for a License.

Monday, 1 January 1855
Liquor license issued to Thomas Leary of Renews for a 12-month period. Bond—£40.

[In the court minutes, this entry appears after the court hearing on the matter, amidst February hearings, and doubtless was issued after the fact. In the clerk's drafts on file, the draft license, although also dated January 1, was written on a separate piece of paper, blue in color, and was pasted into the main text between entries for 28 December 1854, and 2 January 1855, without any mention of the court hearing, again creating the impression that the license was back-dated.]

Sources: PANL, GN 5/4/C/1, Ferryland, box 2, *Regina v. Thomas Leary*, 2 and 4 January 1855.

CASE FILE NO. 4

Elizabeth Sutton

License granted 30 September 1794

By Sir James Wallace Knt. Rear Admiral of
the White Governor and Commander in
Chief in and over the Island of
Newfoundland.

I James Wallace Knt. Governor of the Island of Newfoundland do allow and Licence Elizabeth Sutton of Trepassey Widow to keep a Common Ale House or Victualling

House and to utter and sell Victuals, Beer, Ale, Cyder and other exciseable Liquors to be drunk in any part of Trepassey where she may chuse to reside for One whole year from the Twenty Ninth day of this present Month of September and no longer so as the true assize in bread, Beer Ale, and other Liquors hereby allowed to be sold be duly kept, and no unlawfull Game or Games, Drunkness, or any other disorder be suffered in her House, Yard Garden or Backside, but that good Order and rule be maintained and kept therein according to the Laws of the Realm of England in that behalf made, and that she does not Harbour or entertain at improper times or Seasons, Seamen, Marines, or Soldiers belonging to His Majesty's Ships of War and that she do not secret, Harbour nor entertain with undue quantities of Liquors, Seamen and employed in the Merchants Service or Servants employed in the Fishery during the Fishing Season under such Penalties as the Court of Sessions can legally inflict exclusive of being deprived of her Licence.

Given under my hand and Seal at Fort
Townshend S^{t}. Johns 30th September 1794

License Renewal—12 October 1800

Whereas Elizabeth Sutton a Widow with a small helpless Family, having Petitioned Captain Larkan of His Majestys Ship Camilla my Surrogate the 22nd Ulto, to renew a License granted her by His Excellency Sir James Wallace, the 30th September 1794, for keeping a Public House in the District of Trepassey.

I do thereby grant the request of the Petitioner, and she is hereby authorized to keep a Public House in the District aforesaid, upon the conditions and on observing the wholesome Regulations contained in the License abovementioned: -

(signed) Charles Morice Pole, Governor

Re: Elizabeth Sutton
28 September 1802

Before Micajah Malbon, Surrogate

Copy of Notice to Elizabeth Sutton, to desist from keeping a public house at Trepassey, she having applied for a Licence and afterwards refused to pay the fees.

Court House Trepassey
Septem^{r}. 28th. 1802

It is my direction that you go to the house of Elizabeth Sutton of Trepassey aforesaid who lately kept a public house known by the sign of the Ship, and give her Notice to immediately take down the said sign and to desist from selling Ale Beer Spiritous liquors or other strong waters, as on the contrary her house will be pulled down and the penalty of £10 will be enforced against her

To Richard Lloyd	Mic. Malbon
Constable for the	
District of	Surrogate
Trepassey	

Note in Colonial Secretary's Letterbook
30 October 1802

Governor J. Gambier to Lt. McKellop (of the Trepassey Cutter), 30 October 1802.

Enclosing a complaint/petition of Michael Delahunty for his decision on arrival at Trepassey—& desiring that Eliz. Sutton may not be permitted to keep a Public House at that place unless she takes out a proper License for that purpose [details of Delahunty petition not given].

Re: Elizabeth Sutton
18 November 1802
Before Lieut. McKillop, Surrogate

Nov. 18th, 1802
Trepassey, Surrogate Lieut. McKillop
The following person Received a License to Keep Public House at Trepassey

Viz.	Elizabeth Sutton	£ s
	fee thereon	3..10..0

Sources: PANL, GN 2/1/A: vol. 12, 268, liquor license granted by Governor James Wallace to Elizabeth Sutton of Trepassey, 30 September 1794; vol. 16, 7–8, liquor license granted by Governor Pole to Elizabeth Sutton, 12 October 1800; and vol. 17, 35, Governor Gambier to McKillop, 30 October 1802; and PRL, 340.9 N45, Trepassey–St. Mary's, *Re: Elizabeth Sutton*, 28 September and 18 November 1802.

CASE FILE NO. 5

Dennis Stokes v. — Butler
[3 July] 1787
Before Robert Carter, JP

Comp^{lt}. That the said Stokes being violently taken ill ~ of a Rheumatic Fever ~ occasioned by a great Cold ~ by which his hands were benumbed & all his body was Affected with it the said Butler being Master of the Voyage to Edmond Colbert of Cape Broil Boatkeeper—also the said Stokes was Shipped to the said Colbert to serve him as a Cooper (as in his shipping ^{paper} underwritten will mention, the said Edmond Colbert was at the Westward when the said Stokes was taken ill ~ the said Butler being left as manager ~ turned the said Stokes off the room ~ & would not provide any Subsistance for the said Stokes for the recovery of his Health ~ whereupon the s^{d} Stoke[s] came before Justice Carter & Complain'd of the ill treatment of the s^{d} Butler ~ Justice Carter provided lodgings & a Nurse to take care of the said Stokes ~ after the said Stokes was recovered from his Illness ~ Justice Carter gave him an Order to be reinstated in the said Service ~ the said Order was rejected & not complyed with ~

(Coppy) Stoke's Shipping paper

St. Johns Newf^{d}Land 7th May 1787 ~

This day I have agreed & Shiped myself to Edmond Colbert & Co to serve him from the day hereof untill the Twentieth day of Octo^{r} next as a Cooper or anything else for the benefit of my Interest & in Consideration of my due performance ~ I am to give him for Wages fifteen Pounds & his passage from Waterford ~ & after my Country Charges being deducted ~ I am to have the balance of my Acct in good Bills of Ex^{e} ~ as Witness by hand

signed Edmond Colbert
his
Dennis X Stokes
mark

Order
Geo. 3^{d} &^{c}. &^{c}. &^{c}.

You are hereby required to receive into your Services again ~ Dennis Stokes ~ which was turned off the room Sick ~ at your perill find not ~ on pain of ten pounds ~

Given under my hand in Ferryland
June 18th 1787 ~

To
Edm^{d} Colbert
Capebroil

signed Robert Carter J.P.

Certificate
These Certify that the bearer Dennis Stokes has leave & permission to Ship himself to whom he please ~

Given under my hand in Ferryland
July 3[d]. 1787 ~
[Robert Carter]

To
all whom it may
Concern

Sources: PANL, GN 5/4/C/1, Ferryland, box 1, 38–39, *Dennis Stokes v. — Butler*, [3 July] 1787.

CASE FILE NO. 6

Mary Sweeny v. Patrick Fowler
7 October 1818
[Before Robert Carter, JP]

To Recover £6 .... for attendance Board & Lodging of James Aylward during his Illness ~

James Aylward was Servant to defendant who for the Convenience of Medical attendance was left in care of the pltiff for Board Lodging and Attendance in his illness and agreed topay her Twenty Shillings weekly for the same—at the end of Seven Weeks Aylward removed to his Service and the pltiff made a Charge against him of Six pounds only requesting it from Fowler who objected to the payment ~

An order of Court was sent to def[t]. requesting him to pay plaintiff Six pounds or appear to Shew reason to the Contrary ~

Sources: PANL, GN 5/1/C/1, Ferryland, 50, *Mary Sweeny v. Patrick Fowler*, 7 October 1818.

CASE FILE NO. 7

Re: Margaret Curry
and
M. D. Dutton v. Clapp & Co.

27 September 1802
Before Micajah Malbon, Surrogate

Copy of Notice to Margaret Curry ordering her to desist from practicing as a Doctress at Trepassey

Margaret Curry

I hereby give you Notice that you immediately desist from following your practice as a Doctress at Trepassey or any other place on the Island of Newfoundland, as if I find upon my return you continue to follow the practice, I will cause your house to be pulled down, and have you conveyed out of the Island.

Court House Trepassey
Septem^{r}. 27th. 1802

Micajah Malbon

Supreme Surrogate

M[ichael] D[avenport] Dutton v. Clapp & Co.
Undated
Before Lieut. McKillop, Surrogate

	£ s d
Action to recover	14 .. 9 .. 6

On account of Doctoring. it appears that Defendant Last spring. Warn'd the Plaintiff not to attend his People. that If he did he might Look to the People for payment as he wou'd not pay him. Plaintiff having attended several of said People in the fall applied to them for payment. they refus'd to pay saing that M^{r}. Clapp had stopt their Doctoring. on Plaintiffs applying to M^{r}. Clapp. he told him that the money was not stopt for him But for M^{rs}. Curry. M^{r}. Clapp contends that the custom of this country is for Masters to appoint A Doctor for his servants. It appears that M^{r}. Clapp Did not appoint a proper Person. As on the arrival of Cap^{n}. Malbon, Surrogate. It appears that she was desir'd to Desist from such Practice. and as Both Parties agree'd that this case shou'd be referr'd to the

Supreme Court. It is so
Order'd.

Together with the Depositions of the Under Mentioned Person's ~~~

Mich^{l}. Moore (Sworn) Declares that he was Shipp't to M^{r}. Clapp for the Last season that he was attended by D^{r}. Dutton that he never was Desir'd by M^{r}. Clapp to apply to M^{rs}. Curry. that he was always satisfied with D^{r}. Dutton's attendance and that he once visited him on M^{r}. Clapps Premises ~

W^{m}. Power (Sworn) gave the same Evidence except that D^{r}. Dutton never visited him on M^{r}. Clapps Premises

Jno. Welch (sworn) Declar'd that among others he applied to M^{r}. Clapp to be allowed to employ M^{rs}. Curry & that his reason for so Doing was on account of D^{r}. Dutton misbehaving to one of his fellow servants by making him an Improper Charge.

Jno. Mealey (sworn) Declares that he Did apply to M^{r}. Clapp to be allowed to Employ M^{rs}. Curry. his reason for so Doing was D^{r}. Duttons having refus'd to attend him or his family.

Jno. Beer (sworn) Declares that he is a Clerk to Mr. Clapp & has been for two years. that During that time he never Knew Mr. Clapp to refuse his servants their Accounts and that It was not a constant custom to charge the Doctoring. some were, some were not, that in the Spring he her'd Mr. Clapp tell Dr. Dutton that he shou'd not attend his people or if he Did that he wou'd not be answerable for the payment. Dr. Dutton reply'd that if the men sent for him he shou'd attend them & he had no Doubt but they wou'd satisfy him themselves.~

Thos. [-ean?] (sworn) Declares he is a Clerk to Mr. Clapp & gave some Evidence as above except that he knew nothing of the conversation Between Mr. Clapp and Dr. Dutton

Graham Little (sworn) Declares that in the spring some youngsters belonging to Mr. Clapp came to him for Credit. some he gave Credit. and Dr. Dutton finding this came to him and requested him to stop from those youngsters his Doctoring as he did not expect to get it thro Mr. Clapp. he spoke to the men and they were agreeable that he shou'd stop the money. But on receiving their accounts they found that the Doctoring was stopt for Mrs. Curry and they refus'd to pay Dr. Dutton saying they wou'd not pay two Doctors. But that Dr. Dutton was the Person that they meant to Pay

Jno. McKillop. Surrogate

Michael Dutton v. William Clapp & Co.
27 September 1803
Before Thomas Tremlett, Esquire, Chief Justice

It appeared that the Plaintiff did not apply to the Defendants for the sundry sums due from their Servants to Plaintiff for Medical Attendance, until after they had been paid by said William Clapp & Co. the balance of their wages, The High Sheriff is hereby ordered to receive from the present masters of the sundry persons indebted to Plaintiff, the respective sums due from them to the said Michl. D. Dutton for medical attendance for the year 1802—to be charged against the persons so indebted in proportion to their respective debts.

Thos. Tremlett,
Ch. Justice

Sources: PRL, 340.9 N45, Trepassey—St. Mary's: Notice re: Margaret Curry, 27 September 1802; and *M. D. Dutton v. Clapp & Co.*, undated hearing and Order, 27 September 1803.

CASE FILE NO. 8

Ellen [also Ellon] Veal v. Mary Bowen
22 July 1822
Before William Phipard, Justice of the Peace

Plaintiff complains of an assault—and states that she went to Defendants House to ask of her for what reason she shoud have caused such a report about her that Catharine St Croix had heard Ellon Tobin say she shoud have caried Lyes and storys up the harb in relation to M^{rs}. Bishop and her deceased Husband. which she denied to be true—a few words ensued when Defendant ran to me—and struck me several times, and drew blood ~~

Ellon Tobin Sworn}	And deposed—she was at Defendants house on Saturday the 20th. Ins^{t}. July ~ when Plaintiff came and stood at the door ~ bid her the time of the day which was returned by Defendant—She was then in the act of nursing a Child ~ which she put from her arms and went to the Plaintiff ~ saw both Plaintiff and Defendant very shortly after entangled with each other—and both in the act of striking and blood running from the Plaintiff—Defendant asked if she had enough of it—she replyed she had ~ when they parted ~ cant say which of the Parties struck first -
Mary Molly Sworn}	she was present when Plaintiff called at Defendants House on the 20 July—Asked Defendant what Lyes and Storys She had been saying about her up the Harbour—that Nell Tobin had told her so—Defendant requested her to go from the House not to stay there to make an oration of it—that if she did not She woud turn her off—Plaintiff swore God if She did, she woud break the Bucket over her head. Defendant then went to the Plaintiff, saw them directly after entangled with each other And in the act of stricking heard Plaintiff say she shoud not have but the half of it ~ cannot say which struck first ~

Defendant appearing in Court states that Plaintiff called at her House on the 20th. July ~ Asked her the reason why She shoud report such Lyes and storys about her ~ and that her Daughter shoud have received a pair of Shoes from James Barry—that Nell Tobin had told her so—I then ordered her imediately from my House and uphand [?] it ~ when She swore She woud not—puting away the Child that I had in my arms at the time—endeavoured to turn away—at which she resisted—and broke the Pipe that I was smoaking off in my mouth, and I struck Her -

This case to stand over for the decision of the first surrogate—visiting this Port.

Court of Sessions
1 August 1822
Before R. C. Curry, Surrogate and JP, and William Phipard, JP

The Court decreed that the parties should find Bail £5 each to keep the peace for One Twelve month-

Pat[k.] Fitzgerald [bondsman] for Deft
Jn[o]. Davis [bondsman] for Pltf -

1 August 1822
Before R.C. Curry, Surrogate and JP, and William Phipard, JP

Be it remembered that on the 1st day of August 1822 in the 2nd Year of the Reign of our Sovereign Lord the King-Ellen Veal & Mary Bowin—Pat[k]. Fitzgerald and John Davis all of the District of S[t]. Marys personally came before us R. C. Curry Esq[r]. Surrogate and William Phipard Esq[r]. Justice of the Peace in the said District and acknowledged to owe our Sovereign Lord the King that is to say Pat[k]. Fitzgerald and John Davis the Sum of £5 each of good and lawful Money of Great Britain to be made and levied of their Good & Chattels respectively to the use of our Lord the King his Heirs and Successors if the said Ellen Veal and Mary Bowin shall make default in the conditions hereunder written

The conditions are that the said Ellen Veal and Mary Bowin shall keep the Peace with all His Majestys Subjects particularly with themselves for One whole Year from the date hereof

Signed {

Jn[o]. Davis
Pat[k]. Fitzgerald

Acknowledged before us
R. C. Curry { Surrogate
& Justice Peace
William Phipard Justice Peace

Sources: PANL, GN 5/4/C/1, St. Mary's, 116–17 and 119–20, *Ellen Veal v. Mary Bowen*, 22 July and 1 August 1822.

CASE FILE NO. 9

The Berrigan women

John William Saunders & Co. v.Thomas Berrigan
17 September 1832
Before Justice Edward B. Preston with William Carter and Robert Carter, JPs

This is an action brought to recover £2.6.6 Stg. being the balance due Pltffs. for the Rent of a Room in Renews whereon the Def[d]. has a Fishery

Def[t]. having been called did not appear. Michael Jackman, serving officer, sworn proves the service of the Writ on Def[d].

J. W. Sanders, sworn, states the Defendant is justly and truly indebted to Pltffs the sum of £2.6.6. Stg

Judgment £2.6.6 Stg by Default

J. W. Saunders Esq[r]. v. Thomas Berrigan
Writ no. 8 issued 25 September for return 1 November 1836
Action in Ejectment
Remarks: 2/6 [costs] due Verdict for Defendant

John W. Saunders v. Thomas Berrigan
3 and 5 November 1836
Circuit Court
Before Chief Justice Augustus DesBarres with Robert Carter, JP

In Ejectment. The Parties appear in person and agree to be ready for Trial on Saturday the 5th Instant.

Saturday, November 5, 1836

In Ejectment. To recover possession of a Fishing Room and premises with the appurtenances sitiuated at Renews bounded on the North West by the Harbour on the South East by Crows nest Room and on the South West by Shuddy's Room and on the North East by Thomas's Room

Demurer laid 1st May 1835 Ejectment 2nd May 1835
Plaintiff [appears] in Person
Defendant [appears] in Person

The Defendant pleads the Gen[l]. Issue
[A Petty Jury is empanelled]

The Plaintiff states his case and calls the following Evidence

Thomas Mahoney Storekeeper to the Plaintiff sworn

Thomas Congdon Esqr sworn

The Defendant states his case and calls the following Evidence

Mary Gearing sworn

His Lordship charged the Jury who retired and on their return delivered into Court the following Verdict

Not Guilty
John Rossitter
Foreman

Regina v. Anastatia Berrigan et al.
3 September 1838
Before Robert Carter, Justice JP

Philip Wright Esqre. late Deputy Sheriff, complains of having been violently assaulted at Renews on the 16th day of August last whilst in the lawful execution of his duty by the following persons viz. Anastatia Berrigan, Edward Berrigan, Alice Berrigan Bridget Berrigan & Walter Barron, and prays that they may be bound to keep the peace towards him, and also to appear in the Supreme Court on the first day of next Term to stand their Trial for said offence ~ Warrants were accordingly issued to bring the parties before the Court

Wright also complains that one John Fitzgerald, a Labourer at Renewse, failed to offer him assistance in carrying the Queen's Writ into effect and asks that he be tried for the matter.

Regina v. Edward Berrigan, Alice Berrigan, Bridget Berrigan et al.
20 September 1838
Before Robert Carter, JP

Edward Berrigan, Alice Berrigan, and Bridget Berrigan against whom a Complaint was made on 3rd Inst. together with some others for having assaulted the Deputy Sheriff at Renewse on the 16th day of August, where this day brought up under Warrants, and entered into Sureties to appear in the Supreme Court on the first day of next Term to take theire Trial, and also to keep the peace for the next twelve months, the other parties against whom Warrants were issued gave the required Surety before Allan Goodridge Esqre. at Renewse, except Walter Barron, who did so at St. John's.

Regina v. William Berrigan, Anastatia Berrigan, Bridget Berrigan, and Alice Berrigan
31 December 1842
Before Robert Carter, JP

This day appeared John Stephenson Esquire, Deputy Sheriff of the Southern District and deposed on Oath,

That he was violently assaulted at Renews this day by William Berrigan, Anastatia, Bridget & Alice Berrigan while in the Execution of his Duty upon a Writ of Possession issuing out of the Supreme Court of this Island, against the property of Thomas Berrigan the Elder.

Whereupon, Warrants were issued against the said William, Anastatia, Bridget & Alice Berrigan, and delivered to Sullivan the Officer of the Court to execute.

Regina v. William Berrigan, Alice Berrigan, Bridget Berrigan, and Anastatia Berrigan
31 January 1843
Before Robert Carter, JP

This day, William, Bridget & Alice Berrigan of Renews was brought before the Sitting Magistrate by Sullivan the Officer, against whom Warrants were issued on the 3rd. Instant, for a violent assault on, and obstructing John Stephenson Esquire Deputy Sheriff, at Renews in the Execution of his Duty. The aforesaid parties having entered into their several Bonds to keep the peace for 12 Months and appear at the next General Quarter Sessions of the peace to answer the Complaint made against them by John Stephenson Esquire Deputy Sheriff, the said parties were discharged

Anastatia Berrigan being unable to attend from Sickness, her bond was forwarded to Alan Goodridge Esquire J.P. at Renews to be there perfected.

Regina v. William Berrigan, Alice Berrigan, Bridget Berrigan, and Anastatia Berrigan
23 February 1843
Before Robert Carter and Mathew Morry, JPs

Grand Jurors sworn.

Bills of Indictment were sent to the Grand Jury against the following persons for Riot and assault on John Stephenson Esquire, Deputy Sheriff in the Execution of his Office Grand Jury finds a True Bill. Petty Jurors sworn.

Crown Witnesses Sworn ~ ~ ~
John Stephenson Esquire (Dpty. Shff)
Francis Geary
Richard Sullivan

Witness for Prisoner's
Benjamin Willcox
Thomas Dinn Junr.
Christopher Horden
Thomas Berrigan Junr.

The Petty Jury return a Verdict
Not Guilty

Regina v. James Gearing Sr., Benjamin Wilcox [also Willcox], Edward Berrigan, Anastatia Berrigan, Thomas Berrigan Sr., and Thomas Berrigan Jr.
13 June 1843
Before Robert Carter, JP

Appeared this day John William Saunders Esquire of Renews and complained on Oath that he was assaulted on the 9th. Instant at Renews by James Gearing Senior and by him, prevented from exercising a right of a certain fishing Room, situate at Renews, aforesaid ~ ~ ~

The Complainant also deposeth on Oath, that he was assaulted, and put in bodily fear by Benjn. Wilcox also of Renews, (fisherman). and the said Complainant also deposeth on Oath that he/he was assaulted and threatened at Renews on the 12th. Instant by Edward, Anastatia and Thomas Berrigan Junior, as also by Thomas Berrigan Senior, and that the said John William Saunders considers that his Life is in Danger from the frequent assaults and threatenings of the said parties, Complainant therefore prays the intervention of the Law ~ ~ ~

Upon the said Complaint, warrants were issued against the said parties, namely, James Gearing Senior, Benjamin Willcox, Edward Berrigan, Anastatia Berrigan, Thomas Berrigan Senior, Thomas Berrigan Junior. ~ ~ ~

Regina v. Thomas Berrigan Sr., and Anastatia Berrigan
14 June 1843
Before Robert Carter, JP

Thomas Berrigan Senior and Anastatia, his Wife was brought to the Court this day by the Officer (Sullivan) against whom a Warrant was issued Yesterday the 13th. Instant for an assault upon John William Saunders Esquire of Renews, who having entered into the required securities to keep the peace for 12 Months from this date, was discharged.

Regina v. James Gearing Senior
20 June 1843
Before Robert Carter, JP

This day appeared James Gearing Senior Renews agt.. whom a Warrant was issued on the 13th. Instant upon examination of James Dutton on Oath there did not appear sufficient cause to enforce a peace bond against the said James Gearing Senr. who was discharged accordingly.

Regina v. Edward Berrigan
27 June 1843
Before Robert Carter, JP

This day appeared Edward Berrigan of Renews, (fisherman) against whom a Warrant was issued on the 13th. Instant upon the Complaint of John William Saunders Esquire of Renews, and the said Edward Berrigan having entered into security to keep the peace and appear when called on to appear and answer to any Indictment that may be exhibited against him was discharged.

Regina v. Thomas Berrigan Jr.
5 February 1844.
Before Robert Carter and Mathew Morry, JPs

Thomas Berrigan Junr. against whom a Warrant was issued on the 13th. day of June last, for an assault on John Wm. Saunders Esqr. of Renews was brought to the Court by Sullivan the Officer, and having entered into the required security to keep the peace for 12 Months was discharged.

Sources: PANL: GN 5/2/C/1, Box 2, 12, *John William Sanders & Co. v. Thomas Berrigan*, 17 September 1832; GN 5/2/C/4, Writ no. 8, *J. W. Saunders Esqr. v. Thomas Berrigan*, issued 25 September for return 1 November 1836, Action in Ejectment; GN 5/2/C/3, 1835-47 journal, 62 and 64–65, *John W. Saunders v. Thomas Berrigan*, 3 and 5 November 1836; GN 5/2/C/8, 74 and 76–77, *John W. Saunders v. Thomas Berrigan*, 3 and 5 November 1836; GN 5/4/C/1, Ferryland, box 1, *Regina v. Anastatia Berrigan et al.*, 3 and 20 September 1838; PANL, GN 5/4/C/1, Ferryland, box 2, *Regina v. William Berrigan, Anastatia Berrigan, Bridget Berrigan, and Alice Berrigan*, 31 December 1842 and 31 January and 23 February 1843; GN 5/4/C/1, Ferryland, box 2, *Regina v. James Gearing Sr., Benjamin Wilcox, Edward Berrigan, Anastatia Berrigan, Thomas Berrigan Sr., and Thomas Berrigan Jr.*, 13, 14, 20, and 27 June 1843; and GN 5/4/C/1, Ferryland, box 2, *Regina v. Thomas Berrigan Jr.*, 5 February 1844.

CASE FILE NO. 10

Elenor Evoy Welsh

Elenor Evoy v. Moses Rowe
29 December 1794
Before Robert Carter Sr. and Robert Carter Jr., JPs

The Plaintiff complained that the Defendant assaulted her at the House of Thomas Welsh on Friday the 26 Instant, and has Torn her Cloak, & handkerchief, the Defendant acknowledged the fact.

Ordered that Defendant do pay to the Plaintiff the sum of Two Pounds, Two Shillings for Damages & be fined one pound One Shilling for Breech of the peace, and bound to his Good Behaviour. ~

Michael Ryan v. Mary Whealon, Mary Neal, Elizabeth Morricy, and Elinor Evoy
21 July 1795
[Before Robert Carter Sr. and Nicholas Brand, JPs]

Michael Ryan stated in Petition No. 2 that he was assault[ed] and Batterd with Stones by Mary Whealon, Mary Neal, Elizabeth Morricy, and Elenor Evoy, Defendants in Justification said that the plaintiff had several times behav'd Rude to them, and as a Punishment they were Determin'd to Hustle him as they Term'd it,

The Defendants being young and no Malice, or Evil designs appearing fin'd the Parties Four Shillings & six pence each, and Reprimanded them.~

Elenor Evoy v. Michael Ryan
28 July 1795
[Before Robert Carter Sr. and Nicholas Brand, JPs]

Elenor Evoy stated in Petition No. 3 that she was assault[ed] by Michael Ryan, abused and her carector defamed, John Houlihan being Sworn deposed that he was on his Masters gallery he saw some Stones Thrown as he supposed to Michael Ryan, by some girls assembled, and heard Elenor Evoy advise said Ryan to go away and the girls would have no more to say to him, Ryan abused said Evoy and said she kept a Bawdy House.

John Sullivan deposed that he was standing by Mr. Carters garden Door and Michael Ryan afew paces from him, he heard said Evoy desire said Ryan to go inform the girls who were pelting him with stones, and that they would leave it off, Ryan abus'd Evoy, said he would Beat her, and Call'd her a Bawdy House Keeper.

Defendant in reply admitted that he had spoken the words but said it arose from Passion being then so Ill Treated by the Girls. Judgment to pay five Pounds to the King, to be Bound to keep the peace, himself & one surity, in the sum of Five pounds each, and pay Court Charges Twenty-seven shillings.

Michael Ryan v. Elenor Evoy
28 July 1795
[Before Robert Carter Sr. and Nicholas Brand, JPs]

Michael Ryan stated in Petition No. 4 that Elenor Evoy had abus'd him since the last Court day, defendant denied the Charge, Margret Aylward being call'd to support the charge, declar'd that she did not [see] Mrs. Evoy abuse Mr. Ryan, nor did she hear any words pass, She heard Evoy cough but knew not the Intention,

Plaintiff non suited to pay Court Charges-

Elenor Evoy v. Michael Ryan
3 August 1795
[Before Robert Carter Sr. and Nicholas Brand, JPs]

Michael Ryan appeared in Court and Entered into a Recognizance to keep the peace according to his Sentence last Court Day, and stated in a Petition No. 6 that oweing to the Ill Treatment he Receiv'd from Certain persons that assaulted him he was actuated by passion for his Offence, and Craves the Mercy of the Court to lessen the fine levied on him,

The Court took Michael Ryan's Petition into Consideration and Reduced the fine to five shillings.

Rex v. James Welsh
Court of Sessions
1 April 1803
[Before William Carter, Robert Carter, and Rev. Henry Wood, JPs]
An information brought by Adam M^c^Larthy for an assault

It appeared and was proved that James Welsh had entered the pltffs house, and had struck and illused M^c^Larthy who was a Constable~

Ordered that James Welsh pay a fine to the King of five pounds with Cost of Court and find security for his good behaviour, and a suspension of acting as Constable, untill his Excellency the Governors pleasure was known.

Rex. v. Sylvester Welsh
1 April 1803
[Before William Carter, Robert Carter, and Rev. Henry Wood?]

This information was brought by Ann M^c^Larthy for assaulting her in the passage leading to her house~

the assault was proved on oath, and that he came to the assistance of James Welsh who had assaulted her husband Adam M^c^Larthy.~

Ordered that he pay a fine to the King of five pounds, with Costs-and find security for his good behaviour and to keep the peace..~

Ann M^c^Larthy v. Patrick Evoy
1 April 1803
[Before William Carter, Robert Carter, and Rev. Henry Wood, JPs]

It appeared the defendant had abused the plaintiff and was with James & Sylvester Welsh at the time of the assault of M^c^Larthy's in their house~

Ordered that the defendant pay a fine of Twenty shillings, with Court charges, and find security for his Good behaviour~

Rex v. Elenor Welsh
1 April 1803
[Before William Carter, Robert Carter, and Rev. Henry Wood, JPs]

For assaulting Adam M^c^Larthy on the night of the 11th of february last~

The fact being proved the defendant was fined 50/- with Court charges, and to find security for her good behaviour and to keep the peace..~

Sources: PRL, 340.9 N45, Ferryland: *Elenor Evoy v. Moses Rowe*, 29 December 1794; *Michael Ryan v. Mary Whealon, Mary Neal, Elizabeth Morricy, and Elinor Evoy*, 21 July 1795; *Elenor Evoy v. Michael Ryan*, 28 July and 3 August 1795; and *Michael Ryan v. Elenor Evoy*, 28 July 1795; and PANL, GN 5/4/C/1, Ferryland, box 1, *Rex v. James Welsh, Rex v. Sylvester Welsh, Ann McLarthy v. Patrick Evoy*, and *Rex v. Elenor Welsh*, 1 April 1803.

CASE FILE NO. 11

Tobin and St. Croix families

Catharine St. Croix v. Martin Tobin
22 January 1820
Before William Phipard, JP

The complaint of Catharine S^t^. Croix—that on the 20th January~ She put a quantity of Clothes on her Garden fence to dry—That early on the same day she missed two Cotton Shirts ~ The snow then being on the ground she traced the foot^step^ of a man from said fence to the Dwelling of Martin Tobin ~ and for many other reasons—do firmly believe—and do more solemnly swear on Oath—that she do suspect the said Martin Tobin to be the agressor—and that the said Cotton Shirt [sic] has been deposited, or secreted in the said Tobins Dwelling—and prays that a Warrant be grant^d^ her ~ A search Warrant was accordingly granted—addressed to the D^y^ Sherriff—Sheriffs report that no property of the said Catharine S^t^. Croix was visible ~ in, or above the Dwelling of said Martin Tobin—

Ellen Tobin v. Ann S^t^. Croix
27 June 1823
Before William Phipard, JP

Plaintiff states that she called on M^rs^. Linnahan on the 27th Ins^t^. June—that the Defendant was then siting down—I asked her the reason why she so abused my Sister—and often in the habit of th[r]owing rocks at me and my Brother—She then took a stick from out of the fire and struck me several times on the face—The principal Evidence being on the point of confinement—this case stand over untill the first Court of Sessions or Surrogate Court held at St Marys.

Bridget S Croix v. Thom[s]*. Tobin*
30 June 1823
Before William Phipard, JP

Plaintiff complains—and states as she was coming from M[r]. Quiltys last evening—met with Thomas Tobin—when he accosted me and said now you vagabond hore I have you—I told him I woud not be wishing for him for a pair of Shoes to touch me—He then took a Broom stick —which I had in my hand—and struck me several times—and said that he would watch us day and night—to be revenged —

The Defendant being absent on the fishing account—This case remains over for the decision of a Surrogate.

Sources: PANL, GN 5/4/C/1, St. Mary's: 84, *Catharine St. Croix v. Martin Tobin,* 22 January 1820; 134, *Ellen Tobin v. Ann St. Croix,* 27 June 1823; and 135, *Bridget St. Croix v. Thomas Tobin,* 30 June 1823.

CASE FILE NO. 12

John Dollard v. John Neile (also Neale)
16 October 1818
Before Robert Carter, JP

To recover £2..10. for Washing for Commerford & others who had their fish cured on defe[ts]. Room ~

Plaintiff stated that sufficient fish was left with def[t]. by the persons for whom the Washing was done—to pay his demand—which the deft denying—Patrick Aylward was Sworn, who deposed—that he was present when M[rs] dollard demanded payment from Commerford for washing—That Commerford and dollard went together to John Neile, and Commerford asked Neile if he would pay for his Washing if he would leave fish for that purpose ~ and deponent said that Commerford did leave Seventeen quintals of fish with Neile on his leaving Fermuse, but cannot say for what purpose ~ Neale said he stopt fish belonging to Commerford to pay himself for curing his fish, but received no fish for the purpose of paying plaintiff~ No sufficient evidence appearing to prove that fish was left by Commerford to pay the Washing

Judgment Non Suit ~

Second Hearing
30 October 1818
Before Robert Carter, (local) Surrogate and JP

The was an Action, demanding fish from the defendant which plaintiff Stated was left on defendants fishing Room to be delivered to the plaintiff for washing done by his Wife for Commerford and others ~ which the deft. denying ~

Thomas Keith Master of the Voy^{e}. for def^{t}. house-deposed that Commerford carried all his fish to S^{t}. Johns except about 15 qtls which he left on the Room to pay for fish making and other debts which he owed to the def^{t}. and that he left no uncured fish on the Room ~ It appeared that the evidence of Aylward taken at D^{o}. was incorrect, which stated 4 quin^{s}. of part cured fish being left on the Room by Commerford ~ Judgm^{t} Non Suit ~ Confirmed

---

Sources: PANL, GN 5/1/C/1, Ferryland, 59 and 61, *John Dollard v. John Neile (also Neale)*, 16 and 30 October 1818.

CASE FILE NO. 13

Samuel G. Carter & Co v. William Coleman
19 January 1818
Before Robert Carter, JP

To Recover £3..15 for Blankets delivered to the order of the def^{t}. which he denied to have received and said he was not in the habit of sending orders for any Articles ~

Arthur Carter said he delivered a Blanket on account of the plaintiff to the order in writing of the deft which the def^{t}. acknowledges, but denied to have received the Blankets in question —

John W. Sanders who was Store Keeper with the plaintiffs employ and who had made the entry of the delivery of the Blankets was Summons'd and Sworn, and was questioned by the Court —

1st.	Question	— was you in the employ of Saml. G. Carter & Co—Ans^{r} I was —
2nd.	Question	— in what capacity was you in their employ—As Storekeeper—
3rd.	"	— did you make entry in the day Book of Saml. G. Carter & Co of apair Blankets delivered to the order of William Coleman on the 1st. december. Answer—Yes —
4th.	"	— was Coleman adealer in the House of Saml. G. Carter & Co—Answer—he was a partial dealer in that House —
5th.	"	— was you in the Habit of entering Articles ordered at the time of delivery—Answer—Yes —
6th.	"	— do you recollect who the Blankets were delivered to—Answer—to Margret Moody to the best of my knowledge

The defendant acknowledges that Margret Moody lived with him as Servant at that time, and that she was in the Habit of bringing Goods for him—and that his wife drew most of the orders in his name—

Question for deponant—prior to the entry on the 1st. of december, did you see any other orders, and by whom was the Goods delivered ~

Answer—I did see orders, and I believe the Goods ordered were Generally delivered to Margret Moody—I see orders from William Coleman for Goods subsequent to the order of the 1st. of december ~ I do not recollect to have seen any order for Blankets except the One which I entered myself ~ I was not in the habit of making entrys except for Goods delivered by myself

Question ~ did you deliver the Blankets charge[d] to Wm. Coleman on the 1st. of december 1813.

Answer ~ at this elapsed time I cannot recollect so as to be positive—to have delivered them, but I believe I delivered them otherwise I would not have charged them ~ Questions ~ in the Course of the Winter in which you was Acting as Store and Shop Keeper, did you know of any Goods delivered by yourself or Arthur Carter disputed ~ Ansr. I did not ~ Question ~ in consiquence of William Coleman sending an order for Blankets—and as he says, there being only one Blanket in the Shop and that damaged by Kats, do you recollect Blank[et]s were sent to the shop ~ Answer ~ I believe there were Blankets brought to the shop subsequent to Colemans 1st. order for Blankets ~ Question ~ was there any conversation between you and Mrs. Coleman respecting Blankets, and at what period ~ Answer ~ there was a Conversation between us prior to 1815 the subject was concerning the Blankets in question ~ and I think I desired Mrs. Coleman call at the Counting House of the plaintiffs. to refer to the day Book entry—I do no recollect that Mrs. Coleman came to the Counting House to make the enquiry ~ Since that time Mrs. Coleman did not speak to me concerning Blankets untill about aforthnight ago.

The evidence of Margret Moody, who was now at St. Johns, appearing to be necessary, ordered to lay over, untill her evidence was obtained—the deft. prayed the case as it no[w] stood may be submitted to the decision of a Jury. the parties Consenting ~

A Jury was impannelled and the whole case a set forth being laid before them—they withdrew, and after some deliberation they returned the following verdict in Writing ~

It is the opinion of the Jury, the evidence of John W. Sanders is perfectly correct, and verdict whereby given in favour of the plaintiff with Costs of Suit ~

William Teage foreman ~

Sources: PANL, GN 5/1/C/1, Ferryland, 24–26, *Samuel G. Carter & Co v. William Coleman*, 19 January 1818.

CASE FILE NO. 14

Samuel G. Carter v. John Power
19 January 1818
Before Robert Carter, JP

To Recover £3.5.3 for Goods Sold and delivered to Margret Neile previous to her marriage with the defendant ~

The debt was proved, and it was Also proved that the said Margret Neile was possessed of property previous to and at the time of the Marriage. Ordered that the defendant pay the ptffs £3.5.3 and Costs of Suit—the def[r]. not offering Satisfactory Security for payment of the Said Debt a feather bed belonging to the defts wife previous to her marriage was ordered to be attached as security.

Sources: PANL, GN 5/1/C/1, Ferryland, 26, *Samuel G. Carter v. John Power*, 19 January 1818.

CASE FILE NO. 15

Elizabeth Beaves

Hunt, Stabb, Preston & Co. v. the Estate of Thomas Beaves
6 November 1820
[Before Robert Carter, JP]

To recover £70. Balance of an Acc[t]. —the pltiffs stated that the deceased died in the year 1810. that at the time of his death he owed pltiffs £65- that the other part of the sum sued was supplied to his widdow up to the year 1818 Elizabeth Beaves, Widdow of the deceased, objected. that the debt was of a long standing and incorrect- [that] the property she possessed in Fishing Room, House and Gardens was left her by her Mother- that since the death of her Husband, no claim was made on her for her Husband's debt- and that no Account to that effect was rendered her since her Husbands death- altho she had dealings in pltiffs House every year since, and had balances in her favour until 1817, when she fell in debt and last year her fishing Room and all her premises were Sold by order of Ewen Stabb, agent for pltiffs, at public Auction, and purchased by themselves for £28. that the Sale was made without her Consent and without any lawful Authority—the Widdow pleaded the Act of Limitation so far as respects the debt of her deceased Husband and that the premises So Sold be restored into her possession. Proceedings in this Case was had in the Supreme Court previous to this hearing. Judgement was now Staid until them proceedings was known ~

Hunt, Stabb, Preston & Co. v. the Estate of Thomas Beaves
11 December 1820
[Before Robert Carter, JP]

This case was before the Court on aformer day to recover a debt of £78.9 contracted by the deceased Thomas Beaves with the pltiffs—on property in the possession of his Widdow Elizabeth Beaves ~ The point contended for is that the property was left to the Wife after her Marriage with Beaves—The property was left by Will to Elizabeth Thomas—it is admitted they were lawfully married—Beaves died intestate and in debt to Hunt Stabb Preston & C[o].—and the Supplies continued to be given and the Account Since has been carried on under the head of Elizabeth Beaves & Son—pleads the Statute of Limitation—under the present view of the Case as Stated on the 6th. of November last—and the pltiffs admitting there had been no right exercised on the property in question by def[t]. deceased nor have they looked thereto but Consider notwithstanding the property of the Wife is that of the Husband and liable for his debts—the Court observed that various Accounts in this Case have been Submitted to the Court and it has been attempted to continue the Accounts so as to prevent the Statute of limitation being abar to the debt of the deceased—With whatever ingenuity these attempts maybe made this Court is ever awake to prevent their effect being extended beyond legal bounds ~ the Statute of Limitation is a bar to the debt, but independent of the Statute it has been held to be law that property acquired of the Wife either before of after Marriage over which the Husband has exercised no manner of right or control is not liable to the debt of the Husband ~ Judgement-the Action against the property of the Widdow cannot prevail ~ pltiff nonsuited ~

Sources: PANL, GN 5/1/C/1, Ferryland, 124–25 and 162, *Hunt, Stabb, Preston and Co. v. the Estate of Thomas Beaves*, 6 November and 11 December 1820.

CASE FILE NO. 16

Frida Tobin v. Mary Bony
29 September 1818
Before John Gordon, Surrogate

Pltf complains of an assault and states that she was struck several times by the Deft her Mistress without any provocation, and that the Deft refuses to pay the wages due agreeably to the Shipping paper produced in Court by the Pltf being from 7th. April to 31st. Octr. 1818. The deft appearing in Court admits that she did assault the Pltf but does not refuse to pay the Wages

Decreed that deft do pay the Pltf the balance of Wages and a fine of two Shillings to our Sovereign Lord the King with Costs.

Sources: PANL, GN 5/4/C/1, *St. Mary's, 47–48, Frida Tobin v. Mary Bony,* 28 September 1818.

CASE FILE NO. 17

Catherine Lancrop v. John Doody, Jr.
29 September 1818
Before John Gordon, Surrogate

Pltf complains of an assault States that she served the Dft nearly one year and that he did not pay her passage out, she further states that Dft did strike her, drew blood from her and that she lay some time for dead

The Dft appearing in Court admits striking the Pltf and giving no reason why he should not pay the Plaintiffs passage Money

Decreed the Dft do pay afine of Forty Shillings to our Sovereign Lord the King for assaulting the Pltf also to pay the balance of her Wages together with the passage Money with Court Fees 2nd Class.

Sources: PANL, GN 5/4/C/1, St. Mary's, 52, *Catherine Lancrop v. John Doody,* Jr., 29 September 1818.

CASE FILE NO. 18

Jane Costeloe v. Bridget Whealon
3 August 1795
[Before Robert Carter, Sr., and Nicholas Brand, JPs]

Jane Costeloe stated in Petition No. 5 that she hired Bridget Whealon for one year, and that the said Whealon had Eloped from her service, Whealon, the Defendant acknowledged that she hired herself to the said Mrs. Costeloe, for three pounds for the year Virbally, but her reason for quiting her service are [sic] that she frequently Beat and Scolded her.

Order'd her to return to her Service & Reprimanded her. (no charges)

Sources: PRL, 340.9 N45, *Ferryland, Jane Costeloe v. Bridget Whealon,* 3 August 1795.

CASE FILE NO. 19

Barbara (also Barbary) Murphy

Order of Governor John Byron
29 October 1770

By His Excell. the Hon. Jno. Byron
Govr. &c. ~

Whereas it has been represented unto me by Willm. Coombs that he is in Possession of a Fishing Roome known by the Name of Langworthys Room on the South side of Petty Harbour containing in length along shore 20 feet; also in length East and West on the back thereof 220 feet, and in breadth North and South 205 feet; that he is Tenant to the Widow Barbara Murphy of Ferryland who has Let it to the said Coombs on a Building Lease; and that part of the said Premisses has laid waste & unoccupied for the Fishery for upwards of 20 years past, as appears by a Certificate under the hands of five of the most ancient Inhabitants of Petty Harbour. And Whereas the said William Coombs to comply with the Terms of the said Lease by erecting Fishing Works thereon and prayed me to secure the Proprietor & himself in the Peaceable and quiet Possession thereof; I do therefore hereby Order and direct that all the Houses, Stages Cookrooms, Trainfats Flakes and other Fishing Conveniences now standing on the said Premisses, & wch. shall and may hereafter be Built, Cut out and made thereof (if the same or any part thereof since the 25th. of March 1685 did not belong to Fishing Ships) the said Barbara Murphy shall and may peaceably and quietly enjoy to her own Use with^{t}. any Disturbance of or from any Person or Persons whatsoever agreeable to the Act of the 10th. and 11th. of William the 3^{d}. for encouraging the Trade to Newfoundland, she or the Tenant or Tenants in Possession thereof complying with the 9th. and 10th. Sections thereof; by employing the Fresh Men required by the said Act and producing Certificates thereof when lawfully Demanded. But it is to be observed that in case the Fishing Works so to be Erected as aforesaid, are not completed within two Years from the Date hereof; or if at any time hereafter the said Fishing Works shall be Neglected and fall to Decay, and not be employed for the purposes of taking Bait and Fishing; or for drying, curing or husbanding of Fish, it will revert to the Public and Fishing Conveniences may be Built Cut out and made thereon by any Person or Persons (except the said William Coombs) for his, her or their own Use, by Permission in Writing from the Gov[r]. and Commodore for the time being; with[t]. being Accountable to the said Barbara Murphy, her Executors, Admi[rs]. or Assigns or her or their Tenant or Tenants for the same. Given under my Hand at S[t]. Johns, this 29th. Oct[r]. 1770.

J. Byron

By Command of His Excell[y].
the Gov[r]. and Commodore
Hen Stacy

Deposition of Maurice Kane
Before Jonathon Pitts, Admiral, and Nicholas Mudge, Rear Admiral, Petty Harbour
12 September 1772

In the matter of a complaint by William Keen, merchant of St. John's, in relation to an alleged encroachment on his Fishing Room in Petty Harbour, known as "Paradice"

Maurice Kane being first duly Sworn Deposeth That about forty one or Forty two years ago, this Deponent bound himself an Apprentice to Hon. T. Efford of Brixham in the County of Devon Boatkeeper, who at time lived on a Fishing Room in Petty Harbour in Newfoundland known by the name of Paradice, which Room the said Hon. T. Efford Rented from Will[m]. Keen Esqr. of S[t]. John's, on which this Deponent lived two years and a half, at which time George Efford Occupied the other part of the said Room; the whole being four Boats Room, that some time after this Deponent became a Boatkeeper and rented a Fishing Room of Barbary Murphy next adjoining, and behind the Room belonging to said William Keen consisting of three Boats Room which he held fifteen years, and which he held as the whole of her Room at that time, and that about four years ago the said Barbary Murphy lett her Room to Will[m] Coombs and Partner at which time this Deponent was called upon by Barbary Murphy to point out and shew the Bounds of her Rooms, which he had Occupied as aforesaid, which this Deponent accordingly did and shew'd to her how far her Room extended, and where it [obliteration] Paradice Room [obliteration] to Will[m]. Keen [obliteration] present, the said Keens Room extending from a small run of Water which bound the Western part as Sam[l] Chafes Room does the Eastward part of the said Paradice Room belonging to Will[m]. Keen as aforesaid and the Back part towards the Woods being bounded by the said Barbary Murphy's Room; this Deponent further Sayeth that being now called by Will[m]. Keen of S[t]. John's Merchant to examine whether any Person or Persons have made any Encroachments on his said Room called Paradice; and after carefully examining the same finds that Will[m]. Coombs and Partner Tenants to Barbary Murphy have made great Encroachments on the said Room of the said Will[m] Keen, by Building a Fish Flake on the Westward part adjoining the run of Water mentioned by [previous deponent] W^{m}. Bailey with a small Studded House or Platform and a small Garden adjoining the Stage Occupied by Willm. Coombs at this time which Platform and Garden are Built on the said Keen's Room and obstruct the path from his Stage to the Flakes which path went from the Stage by a Well of water which was on the left hand of the said path, and he further Sayeth that the upper Flake built by said Coombs extends down the Hill even below their Right, and are entered on the Room of the said Keen some small matter, and further Sayeth that the Bound Stone placed at the Eastern bounds of the said Keen's has been moved some distance in on his Room and should be Close to Saml Chafes Flake. ~

Sworn before us in Petty Harb^{r}.
this 12 September 1772. ~
(Signed) Jno. Pitts ~ Admiral
Nich^{s}. Mudge. R. Adm^{l}.

(Signed) M^{ce}. Kane

Sources: PANL, GN2/1/A: vol. 4, 283–84, Order, Governor John Byron, 29 October 1770; and vol. 5, 134–36, Deposition of Maurice Kane before Jonathan Pitt, Admiral, and Nicholas Mudge, Rear Admiral, at Petty Harbour, 12 September 1772.

CASE FILE NO. 20

Mary Bryan
10 October 1780

Gov. R. Edwards to Justice Isaac Follet, Trepassey, October 10, 1780, to enquire into Mary Bryan's petition complaining of Mr. Townshend being about to turn her out of a Plantation

Having received a Petition from Mary Bryan of St. Maries setting forth that her Husband (who is insane) holds a Plantation by Lease, John Richards of the same place, who let it to Mr. Townshend last February, the term of the Lease, but as she says there is a Clause in it specifying 12 Months warning is to be given.

I desire you will inquire particularly into the matter, as the Poor woman and her family must naturally be distressed if turned out of their House at this time of . . . Year, settle it for her, as amicably as you can—tho I think Mr. Townshend has a right to possess it in time to carry on his fishery next year.

Sources: PANL, GN 2/1/A, vol. 9 (reverse end), 26, Governor Edwards to Justice Isaac Follet, 10 October 1780.

CASE FILE NO. 21

Mary McMahon v. John Quilty
8 October 1833
Before Justice A. Desbarres with J. H. Martin, JP

Action brought to recover £20.0.0 for a Trespass on Pltffs property

The Parties appeared in Court & agreed to leave all matters on things in dispute between them to Benjamin Sweetland Esqr. whose determination and award, after hearing the Parties, set down in writing and returned into this Court shall be final, and Judgment entered thereon, as on the verdict of a Jury

The following award was accordingly given in to Court
In the Case McMahon vs. Quilty

The Def^{d} is satisfied to give the Pltff, in addition to the spot on which her House is built, a spot adjoining thereto, bounded by a Slide Path running by Thomas Tobins fence, commencing at the corner nearest the Road, leading between William Burks Plantation and Thomas Tobins Garden and bearing about N.W by W. fifty seven yards, from thence N by E. fifty five yards and SE. by S. thirty five yards, from thence back to the stake from whence we started South forty seven Yards, and also to give her a Path through his Garden to the Well. That the Pltff is to remove her fence and longers now putting up, and to pay her own Costs, the Def^{d}. having made her the same liberal offer before this action was brought

St. Marys
8th Oct. 1833

B Sweetland
Arbitrator

Judgment pursuant to award

Sources: PANL, GN 5/2/C/1, box 1, 317–18, *Mary McMahon v. John Quilty*, 8 October 1833.

CASE FILE NO. 22

The King on the complaint of Catharine Payne v. Peter Winsor
16 May 1819
[Before Robert Carter, JP]

For a Violent Assault and Breach of the peace ~
Catharine Payne, Sworn, deposed and on her Oath Saith-

That on the 12th day of May instant about the Hour of Eleven OClock in the forenoon—the defendant came into her dwelling House, and ordered her to quit the same that Instant—on her refusing to Comply, deft struck her ablow with his fist on the face and Seizing her by the arms, used all his strength to drag her out—and failing therein, he Seized her by the neck, and held and draged her with such violence as nearly suffocated her, and that in this inhumane Struggle he marked her face and Bruised her very much in different parts of her Body, which at present is apparent—Evidence was Sworn, which proved the assault and the defendant Acknowledging the Same ~

Ordered that Defendant pay a fine of £5.. to the King and Court Charges £2.7.8—and that he find security to keep the peace for three months in the sum of £30 . . . which was done. ~

Sources: PANL, GN 5/1/C/1, Ferryland, 81, *Rex. v. Peter Winsor*, 16 May 1819.

CASE FILE NO. 23

Charlotte Flood

Regina v. William Mitchell
2 August 1841
[Before Robert Carter and Mathew Morry, JPs]

This day Charlotte, Wife of James Flood of Ferryland (fisherman) also appeared and complained on oath that the aforesaid William Mitchell several times in the absence of her Husband assaulted and beat her and repeatedly threatened to take her Life and that of Her Husband and Child. The said Mitchell being already in custody on the Complaint of Lewis M. Lynch [charged 31 July 1841, and found guilty 9 August 1841], remains for trial for this complaint also. [Mitchell was also found guilty of assault and battery against one Patrick Costello, 10 November 1840, and guilty of threatening John White (his master) with burning his house down and other injuries, 24 and 27 August 1840.]

Regina v. William Mitchell
9 August 1841
Before Robert Carter and Mathew Morry, JPs

The said William Mitchell was also called on to answer the Complaint of Charlotte, Wife of James Flood of Ferryland for an Assault and Battery and repeatedly threatening to take away her own as well as her Husbands and Childs lifes. The Court adjudged the said Mitchell to stand further committed for Trial, James Flood and Charlotte his Wife having entered into the required security to appear and prosecute the said Mitchell when called on so to do.

Regina v. William Mitchell
28 October 1841
Before Hugh A. Emerson, Acting Supreme Court Justice, with Robert Carter and Matthew Morry, JPs

The Queen against William Mitchell, for assault on one Charlotte Flood at Ferryland on the twenty second day of July last

A True Bill returned by Grand Jury-J. H. Carter, foreman
The Prisoner is arraigned and upon his arraignment pleads Not Guilty and ready for Trial
Petty Jury Sworn

Evidence for the Crown
Charlotte Flood
sworn

Prisoner addresses the Petty Jury
His Lordship charged the Petty Jury who retired and return into Court with the following Verdict
"Guilty"

The Court sentenced the Prisoner to twenty four hours imprisonment.

Sources: PANL, GN 5/4/C/1, Ferryland, box 2, *Regina v. William Mitchell,* 2 and 9 August 1841; GN 5/2/C/3, 1835-47 journal, *Regina v. William Mitchell,* 28 October 1841; and GN 5/2/C/8, 1835-42 journal, *Regina v. William Mitchell,* 28 October 1841.

CASE FILE NO. 24

Margret Kenney

Arthur Hunt [agent for Leigh & Co.] *and John Baker* [Agent for Holdsworth's] *v. John Kenny, Margret Kenny, William Power, William Broadfoot, Timothey Fowler, Patrick Burne, and Richard Dunphy*
6 [8?] October 1795
Before Robert Carter, (local) Surrogate

For Theft..~
The deposition of Margret Riely taken before Robert Carter Esqr. Surrogate..~ That in the spring of the year 1795, this depon^{t}. heared a conversation between John Kenny and his Wife late at night, as she believed respecting Hay, that immediately after such conversation they called up Timothy Fowler their servt. Who was there in Bed, and the said Fowler and John Kenny then went out of the House about 12 oClock at night with a Bag made of two sheets sewed together and in less than an Hour they returned to the said Kenny's House with the said Bag full of Hay ~ that the next morning the said Timothy Fowler told this deponant that when Kenny was taking the Hay out of M^{r}. Holdsworths Cow House, he was afraid of his life, this deponent further says that William Power a servant with M^{r}. Robert Holdsworth was frequently at Kenny's House dureing the Winter and that the deponant being present she heard the said Margret Kenny request some coals of the said William Power, and that he the said Power told her to send at night when she thought M^{r}. Angel was abed and that he would give her some, and she saw coals brought into the said Kennys House six or seven times by John Kenny in a Bag late at night ~..~

This deponant further sayeth that sometime last Winter Richard dunphy aservant with Mr. John Baker Ferryland had some conversation with Margret Kenny late at night that in consequence of such conversation ~ the said Margret Kenny called up her Winter servant who was then in bed and that she the said Margret Kenny gave the said servant a Bag~ that he went out of the House with the said dunphy, and in about an hour they returned to the said House with aBag filled with dryed fish Cutt into pieces..~..~..~

This deponant further sayeth that sometime last winter she hear'd Margret Kenny request of William Broadfoot to give her afire poker or fire shovell, that in sometime after in the night about Six oClock the said William Broadfoot brought a poker and fireshovell under his Packet and as he passed by this deponant he called the said Margret Kenny into the inner Room and there delivered the said poker and fireshovell to her. and that in a few days after the said William Broadfoot, at the request of the said Margret Kenny, delivered her two decanters.~ her
Elizabeth x Riely
mark

Arthur Hunt in behalf of Robert Holdsworth and John Baker in behalf of John Hill & Co. haveing appeared in Court, they respectively prayed that a prosecution may be had against the defendants, on the foregoing deposition,

A Jury being impannelled and the said deposition submitted to them after examination of the parties they withdrew and returned the following Verdict in Writing ~

It is the opinion of the undernamed Jurymen, that John Kenny is Guilty of Stealing the Hay.~

That John Kenny and William Power are Guilty of stealing the Coals, but would recommend the latter to the mercy of the Judge..~

That Margret Kenny's Winter servant (Patt Burn) brought the Bag full of fish to said Kenny's House, and from Circumstances in aclandestine manner~..~..~..~..~

James Shortall foreman	Thomas Norris	Michael Moran
John Power	Samuel Taylor	Michael Kelly
Lawrence Huolahan	John Badcock	Mathew Ronan
John Aylward	John Brown	Maurice Fitzgerald

It was Ordered that John Kenny and Margret Kenny be fined £3..~ each for stealing the Hay, that John Kenny be imprisoned and whiped for stealing the Coals, that Wm. Power pay afine of £2..10..~ that Patt Burn be imprisoned and whiped for stealing the fish, and that Richard dunphy pay afine of £1..1..~ John Kenny and Patt Burn haveing inlisted into his Majestys Newfoundland Regiment when in prison, their punishment was remitted~ Patt Burn fined £2..2..~ and each of the said offenders Bound to the Good behaviour~ which was accordingly done..~

Sources: PANL, GN 5/4/C/1, Ferryland, box 1, *Arthur Hunt* [agent for Leigh & Co.] *and John Baker* [Agent for Holdsworth's] *v. John Kenny, Margret Kenny, William Power, William Broadfoot, Timothey Fowler, Patrick Burne, and Richard Dunphy*, 6 [8?] October 1795.

CASE FILE NO. 25

Bridget Hegarthy and Mary Reed

Regina v. Bridget Murphy
3 April 1833
Before Robert Carter, JP

Bridget Murphy of Ferryland, married woman, was brought before Robert Carter Esq[r]. J.P. charged on the oath of Mary Read her daughter, with having received from her the said Mary Read a quantity of Provisions at different times well knowing the same were the property of Patrick Connors and stolen from the House of the s[d]. Patrick Connors by directions of her said Mother, Bridget Murphy

She was bound over to appear before the Honble the Southern Circuit Court on the first day of next term in Ferryland to stand her trial for the said offence.

Regina v. Bridget Hegarthy and Mary Reed
16 February 1842
Before Robert Carter, JP

Information was laid at about 11 O'Clock of the Night of this day by Benjamin Sweetland Morry of Ferryland Clerk and Storekeeper to James H. Carter Esquire, Merchant, (at present in England) that the Store of the said James H. Carter had been feloniously entered by some person or persons unknown to this Informant and a quantity of salted Beef and pork stolen therefrom and a strong suspicion having attached to Bridget Hegarthy (Wife of Charles Hegarthy) and Mary Reed, her Daughter. Informant prayed that a search Warrant may be granted to search the premises of Charles Hegarthy which was granted accordingly and given to the Officer Sullivan to execute.

Regina v. Bridget Hegarthy and Mary Reed
17 February 1842
Before Robert Carter, JP

The Officer (Sullivan) to whom a search Warrant was directed to search the premises of Charles Hegarthy at Ferryland, for the discovery of a quantity of salted Beef and pork feloniously stolen from the Store of James H. Carter on the evening or night of the 16th. instant, came into Court and informed the same that he had made diligent search on the premises of Charles Hegarthy for the said Beef and pork but could not discover the same, but on entering the cellar of said Charles Hegarthy in company with Benjamin S. Morry they discovered a quantity of Shop Goods, enclosed in a Cotton Shirt and a Bread Bag which was identified by said Morry as the property of said James H. Carter which Goods the Officer brought to the police office, as well [as] Bridget Hegarthy and Mary Reed.

the said Bridget Hegarthy and Mary Reed having undergone an examination and the depositions of Benjamin S. Morry, William Keefe, Richard Sullivan and John White taken, the said Bridget Hegarthy and Mary Reed were committed until tomorrow for the attendance of a second Magistrate.

Regina v. Bridget Hegarthy and Mary Reed
18 February 1842
Before Robert Carter and Mathew Morry, JPs

The above Magistrates having consulted on the case of Bridget Hegarthy and Mary Reed, the said Bridget Hegarthy and Mary Reed were fully committed to take their Trial at the approaching General Quarter Sessions of the peace on the 21st. Instant at Ferryland.

Contents of Bread Bag

2 pair Mens Boots	Valued at	£1.. 10..
3 pair Mens Shoes	"	.. 15..
3 pair Womens Shoes	"	.. 12..
4 Cotton Shirts	"	.. 10..
3 White serge d^o^	"	.. 15..
2 Blue d^o^ d^o^	"	.. 10..
3 pair Womens Black Hose	"	.. 3..
4¾ Yards flat Canvas	"	.. 2..4
16 Yards Calico	"	.. 8..
2 pair Mens Braces	"	.. 1..
2 pieces Black Tape	"	2
1 Ball Black Worsted	"	.. .. ..
13/8 Yards Flushing	"	.. 5..
4½ Yards Check	"	.. 2..3
3 lbs Bohea Tea	"	.. 7..6
3 Worsted Comforters	"	.. 1..6
1 pair Yarn Hose (Rat eaten)	"	3
1 tw [twist] Black Thread	"	.. 2..6
2¾ Yards Blue Flushing	"	..11..
		6..16..6

Contents of Cotton Shirt

12 Yards Calico 6/ 4¾ Yds Serge 4/9 1 Blue Shirt 5/	..15..9
2 lb Bohea Tea 5/ 1 Yard Calico 6d	.. 5..6
1 Cotton Shirt	.. 2..6
	£8..0..3

Regina v. Charles Hegarthy, Bridget Hegarthy, and Mary Reed
21 February 1842
Before Robert Carter, Peter Winser, John William Saunders, and Mathew Morry, JPs

A Bench Warrant was issued to apprehend Charles Hegarthy of Ferryland, fisherman, for having goods in his possession knowing the same to be stolen, and directed to the Deputy Sheriff, who returned wit the said Hegarthy in Custody to stand his trial for the Offence. [Grand Jurors were sworn.]

The following Indictments were sent to the Grand Jury

The Queen against Bridget Hegarthy & Mary Reed	}	Larceny
"Queen against Bridget Hegarthy Mary Reed & Charles Hegarthy	}	Having Goods in possession knowg them to be stolen

The foreman returned into Court with True Bills against the above prisoners, when Bridget Hegarthy and Mary Reed were placed at the Bar and Arraigned and pleaded Not Guilty . . .

[Petty Jurors were sworn.]
Witnesses on the part of the Crown, Benjn . S. Morry, Richard Sullivan, William Keeffe, John White. [No transcript of evidence.]
The Prisoners call no Witnesses.
Jury return into Court with their Verdict. Guilty
The Prisoners, Charles Hegarthy, Bridget Hegarthy and Mary Reed against whom a True Bill of Indictment was found for having Goods in their possession, knowing the same to have been stolen was placed at the Bar and arraigned, who pleaded, Not Guilty.

[Petty Jurors were sworn.]
Witnesses on the part of the Crown as before,
Prisoners call no Witnesses.
Jury return into Court with their Verdict Not Guilty
The Court then proceeded to pass Sentence on Bridget Hegarthy and Mary Reed. That the said Bridget Hegarthy and Mary Reed be imprisoned in the Gaol of Ferryland for the space of Twelve Calendar Months from this date.

Estate of William Carter v. Patrick Costelloe and Bridget Hegarthy
25 November 1844
Before Robert Carter, JP

This day appeared William Carter on behalf of his Father Arthur H. O. B. Carter (Agent and Attorney to the Estate of the Late William Carter Esquire deceased) and complained that some person or persons unknown to complainant, on or about Saturday last the 23rd. instant had stolen and taken away from a House belonging to the said Estate and formerly occupied by William Costelloe, 2 Studds, 7 or 8 Boards of a Loft, the whole of a back linhay and a Window Sash. Complainant under the above circumstances prays the interference of the Court for the detection of the/the Offenders. ~ ~ ~

Whereupon Patrick Costelloe and Bridget Hegarthy was summoned before the Court and underwent a strict examination when nothing being elicited by said examinations for the further interference of the Court upon the said complaint, the parties were dismissed.

Sources: PANL, GN 5/4/C/1, Ferryland: box 1, 48, *Regina v. Bridget Murphy*, 3 April 1833; and box 2: *Regina v. Bridget Hegarthy, and Mary Reed*, 16, 17, 18, and 21 February 1842; *Regina v. Charles Hegarthy, Bridget Hegarthy, and Mary Reed*, 21 February 1842; and *Estate of William Carter v. Patrick Costelloe and Bridget Hegarthy*, 25 November 1844.

CASE FILE NO. 26

Honour Tobin

——*Hogan v. Patrick Shea*
26–28 March 1787
Before Robert Carter and Henry Sweetland, JPs

Compl^{t} that his Uncle Redmond Ellward was beat & ill treated by Patrick Shea (a partner in the boat fishery with the said Ellward) so that his Death was occasioned by it~

[sample depositions]

The deposition of Richard Reddy taken before Robert Carter and Henry Sweetland Es^{rs} Justices of the peace for the district of Ferryland March 26th. 1787 ~

This deponent saith that on Friday the 16th Inst about 8 at Night Patrick Shea sent this Deponent to one William Burn at his House in Cape Broil to ask him or any of the rest of the Lads to come to the s^{d} Shea's House in the s^{d} Harbour of Cape Broil to drink some Grog (this deponent being a winter Servant to the s^{d} Shea) this Deponent went & saw Burn—invited him but he would not come but one Walter Fenor who is a dieter with the s^{d} Burn came with him close to the House of the s^{d} Shea but on his hearing a Noise in the House he returned back & did not go in on account of the noise in the House as this deponent believes ~ this deponent went into the House of the s^{d}. Shea & Saw Redmond Ellward bleeding from his forehead this deponent enquired how it came ~ one Patrick Bryan told him that the s^{d} Ellward stumbled as he was getting up & fell on an Iron pot ~ which this deponent saw ~ which stood just by the door of the s^{d} House ~ there this deponent got some kind of a Handkerchief to stop the Blood ~ which they did as well as they could ~ the said Ellward being in Liquor strove to keep off the Handkerchief from being put to ^{the} wound which he had received in his Head (the said Shea being in Liquor also) the said Shea got up follow^{d} Ellward & gave the said Ellward ablow with his fist in his Side the the s^{d} Ellward cryed Murder Murder ~ then this deponent & William Fenor put the s^{d} Ellward to bed ~ then Fenor went home ~ & left this deponent Pat[k] Bryan & said Shea in the s[d] Shea's House after about 6 or 7 Minutes the s[d] Ellward began to complain ~ then the said Shea got up from where he was sitting in the said House took a Clift of whitling & struck the s[d] Ellward as he lay in bed but says the blow did not hurt him ~ in less that a Quarter of an Hour after this he took another Clift & struck him again as he lay in bed Several times but the blows being given on the bed Cloaths it did not seem to hurt him ~ after this all the people at the House went to bed ~ but this deponent saith that he frequently complain[ed of a pain] in his side before he died ~ this deponent believed in his right side ~ & further this deponent says not.

The Deposition of Patrick Bryan taken before Robert Carter & Henry Sweetland Esq[rs] Justices of the peace Marcy 27th. 1787 ~

This deponent saith that he was going from Ferryland to Brigus in his way he call'd into Patrick Shea's House at Cape Broil on Friday the 16th Inst continued there in the s[d] Sheas House all that night saw Redmond Ellward to bleed from his forehead which was cut by a fall as this deponent believes against an Iron pot—which was in the s[d] Sheas House but this deponent saith that he saw Shea to strike Ellward wth his fist some way about his body when his wound was dressing to make him stand still as he believes ~ this deponent further saith that after the cut in his Head was dressed the s[d] Ellward was put to bed being very drunk ~ after the s[d] Ellward was in bed the s[d] Shea took a split of wood & went to strike the said Ellward as he was in bed but does not know whether he did or not but heard arattle with the s[d] Split about the Cabbin & bid him go to sleep but believes he was not hurted by it This deponent further saith that he did no see any more offers given the s[d] Shea to strike the s[d] Ellward after this ~ and further this deponent says not. ~

The Deposition of Honour Tobin taken before Robert Carter & Henry Sweetland Esq[rs]. Justices of the peace March 28th.1787 ~

This Deponent saith that on Sunday Evening the 18th Inst Patrick Shea came to this deponent & ask'd her to go & make a drink of Tea for Redmond Ellward as he was sick ~ which she did & saw the said Ellward bleeded by Michl Bryans Cooper ~ then she went home again ~ this deponent went to see the said Ellward on Monday Morning found the s[d] Ellward very Sick ~ this deponent stay'd with the s[d] Ellward all that day this deponent went home at the end of this day ~ the next day this deponent went to see the said Ellward again found him still very Sick ~ She continued there untill the s[d] Ellward died ~ which was about ten at night ~ She laid him out could not see any Marks of Violence on his Body in any part only a Cut in his forehead~ She further saith that the said Ellward never repeated any thing against the said Shea ~ nor does not know nor never heard any person to say how he came by the Cut in his forehead ~ & further this deponent says not.

Sources: PANL, GN 5/4/C/1, box 1, 28–33,—*Hogan v. Patrick Shea*, 26–28 March 1787.

CASE FILE NO. 27

Mrs. Warne

Thomas Murphy v. James Warne
20 November 1793
Before Isaac Follett, (local) Surrogate

Thomas Murphy complaining and produced a Note of hand of James Warne, which the sd Murphy still asserted to have been unpaid, and also that in a former acct. Mrs. Warne had overcharged him Six Pounds, and never settled with him for a three Pounds Bill which he delivered to the said Warnes wife ~

AffirmationsJames Warne and his wife have produced their Books and solemnly affirmed to the legality and Justness of their accts. and evidently made appear that Murphys charge was Malicious and illfounded.

The Court therefore decrees that Murphy in consequence of not being able to prove his charge, be confined on Bread and Water for three days, & fined Forty Shillings for the use of the King ~

Sources: PRL, 340.9 N45, Trepassey—St. Mary's, 15, *Thomas Murphy v. James Warne*, 20 November 1793.

CASE FILE NO. 28

Jane Holehan [also Hollehan] v. Catherine Walsh

8 October 1819
Before William Nugent Glascock, Surrogate

Ptf stated Def[t] had falsely accused her of Witchcraft and praying a Summons for Def[t] to appear before the Court.

A Summons was granted accordingly for Deft to appear on the 15 October 1819 before W[m] Phipard Esq[r] Magistrate who is requested to enter into the merity of the case.-

26 November 1819
Before William Phipard, JP

This case before William N. Glaskcock Esqr. Surrogate—folio 72—and defer'd untill the 15 October—by summons granted to Plaintiff.—The Parties appeared on the 26

November.— Plaintiff states that Def[t] has accused Plaintiff of Witchcraft . . . and when Plaintiff went to see Def[t]—said to James McGrath (now dead)—that the Plaintiff went over to Peters River—decidedly to take away the milk of a Cow by force of witchcraft ~ Plaintiff produced two Witnesses to prove.~

Hugh Kelly
Sworn } — and states that he heard Def[t]. say—that she suspected no other person else but the Plaintiff for the loss of her Cows milk ~.

Ellen Peddle
Sworn } — That she heard Def[t]. say—that she suspected no other Person—but the Plaintiff—for the taking away the Milk—from Def[ts] Cow—but still she coud not say that she did ~.

The case labouring under such inconsistencys—and Defendant not attending the summons in due course—Decree'd—the Defendant do pay the cost of summons—to the Constable serving—ten pence p[er] mile for thirty miles -
William Phipard J.P.

Sources: PANL, GN 5/4/C/1, St. Mary's, 72 and 83, *Jane Holehan [also Hollehan] v. Catherine Walsh*, 8 October and 26 November 1819.

CASE FILE NO. 29

Hannah McDaniel

Petition of Hannah McDaniel and Order of Governor John Campbell, received from the governor's office and entered in the Ferryland records 13 September 1784

His Excellency John Campbell Esq[r] ~
Adm[l] of the White Squadron Governor and Commander in Chief in and over the Island of Newfoundland &c. &c. &c.

The Humble Petition of Hannah M[c]Daniel Sheweth

That your Excellency's Petition[r] being anative of Ferryland who was left by last will and Testament to produce some plots of ground warranted by the Surrogate James Howell Jones Esq[r] & fully granted by warrant under his hand & seal untill your Excellencys will & pleasure to revoke Now may it please your Excellency Peter Weston Esq[r] of Ferryland deceased had some old arrears due him by Petitioners father by Law after making seizeor of all his Effects for said Debt before, since his decease Petitioners

Mother was furnished with Acct^{s} of them old arrears hemmed in by the said Westons Son in Law Mr Wm Carter by order of his Mother in Law the Widow Weston after dealing in the said House for seven years could never so much as to obtain an Account from them altho every fall demanded Now may it please your Excellency since the death of Petitioners Mother ~ and the said Peter Weston Esqr wants to come down on the premises before mentioned altho when Admiral Montague ordered petitn^{rs} Mother to come round & he would decide the same on wch Acct gave her afew lines underhand to indemnify her from them which was mislaid ~ Your Excellency will take petitn^{rs} Case into Consideration being apoor woman with avery great Charge seven helpless Children to support maintain & nourish ~ that never knew anything about these Accounts before ~ and petitioner as in duty bound will forever pray ~

St. John's 10th Sept 1784

As this matter ought to have been settled long ago and as no application has been made to the Surrogates who have at different times been at Ferryland by any of the Westons family ~ I desire you will secure Hannah McDonell and her Husband in the quiet and peaceable possession of the premises now Occupied by them so long as they shall Continue to employ it for the use of the fishery ~

Signed John Campbell

Catherine Weston v. Hannah and William McDaniel
8 March 1787
Writ issued by Robert Carter, JP, to William & Hannah McDaniel

You are required to appear before me tomorrow by Eleven in the forenoon ~ to answer for yourselves at your peril fail not~

9 March 1787

Appear'd Hannah McDaniel by Eleven in the forenoon & made known to the said Justice Carter that W^{m} McDaniel was gone in the woods ~ the said W^{m} McDaniel Appear'd before Robt Carter and Henry Sweetland Esq^{rs} Justices of the Peace by two in the afternoon ~ but was to appear by Eleven in the forenoon as ye Order sent him yesterday p [per] Wm Cox Constable ~ which was in order for him to give an obligation for a Debt due to late Peter Weston Esqr of £145.12.6/2 - deducting 25 p c^{t} [per cent] amounts to £109.4.5 the neat debt ~

the s^{d} W^{m} McDaniel was Ask'd by the Mes Justies whether he would comply with the Terms Offerr'd him ~ which was to pay — — ~ out of a fishing premises lett by the s^{d} McDaniel to Matthew Ronane & John Grace yearly untill the said Debt was fully paid ~ The Answer made by the said W^{m} McDaniel that he would not give a pair of shoes for the premises ~ when at the same time the yearly rent of the s^{d} premises is ^{lett} ^{att} £22 p ann^{m} paid by the s^{d} Ronane & Grace the Occupiers ~

The said McDaniel was further Ask'd by Justice Carter whether he was married to a Hannah McDaniel says he was not ~ at the same time the s^{d} W^{m} McDaniel & Hannah Carney (this being her maiden name) has lived together as man & wife (& has ^{had} several children) for anumber of years ~ & the said W^{m} McDaniel gave the lease of the fishing presmises to the s^{d} Ronane & Grace in his own name ~ which if he is not (as her says) married to the s^{d} Hannah Carney ^{he} had no right to lett the premises ~ all this seems to be only to stave off from paying the said Debt ~ the said premises was given by Will to the s^{d} Hannah Carney by her Mother Mary Shea the said Debt was contracted by the s^{d} Shea ~ the s^{d} W^{m} McDaniel nor Hannah Carney otherwise McDaniel would not comply to the Terms offerr'd them as aforesaid

before
Robt Carter
Henry Sweetland Esqr } Justices of the Peace

Order, 9 March 1787

"Matt^{w} Ronane George the 3^{d} by the grace of god &c &c &c
&
John Grace

You are hereby required & commanded to stop & retain in your hands all the whole rent of the fishing premises for the year Seventeen hundred eighty seven by virtue of alease bearing date the 20th Oct. 1785 at the yearly rent of Twenty two pounds under the hand of William M^{C}Daniel of Ferryland ~

You are further required not to advance a shilling of this years rent to the s^{d} W^{m} McDaniel or to his Assigns to hold the whole entire rent in your hands untill further orders from us this shall be your justification ~

Given under our hands in
Ferryland March 9th 1787
R.C. [Robert Carter] JP
H.S. [Henry Sweetland] JP

Order, Governor John Elliot, 5 October 1787

It evidently appears from the foregoing Order of Governor Campbells that he was satisfied of the illegality of Westons Claim ~ and as it would be the means of creating endless confusion throughout the Island ~ if the Governor for the time being was to enter into the merits ~ upon which his predecessors had founded all their decisions ~ I do hereby strictly enjoin the Magistrates of the district of Ferryland to see Governor Campbells said order punctually obeyed ~ This order with areference to Governor Campbells order) to be entered in the Records of the district and the paper (with a

Certificate of its Registry signed by the Keeper of the Rolls) to be delivered to the petitioner ~

St. John's Newfoundland 5th Oct 1787~
signed {J. Elliot

By Command of
the Governor
sign'd A. Graham

Catherine Weston v. William McDaniel
17 August 1790
Before Jacob Waller, Surrogate, and Henry Sweetland and Peter Romney, JPs

Catherine Weston of Ferryland made Complaint upon Oath that William McDaniel of Ferryland planter is justly Indebted to her in the Sum of one hundred and nine pounds four shillings and five pence sterling which he has refused to pay; . . . praying that justice may be done her. [William McDaniel summoned to appear in court on Friday, 27 August or the next court day thereafter to answer the complaint.]

Catherine Weston v. William McDaniel
15 September 1790
Before Jacob Waller, Surrogate, and Henry Sweetland and Peter Romney, JPs

Mrs. Catherine Weston of Ferryland Plaintiff on the 17th August last made Complaint upon Oath before Our Justices of our Court of Common pleas that William McDaniel of Ferryland planter is justly Indebted to her in the sum of One hundred and nine pounds four shillings and fivepence sterling being for the Amount of a Book-debt, and that he refuses payment thereof although thereunto frequently required.

In consequence of which Complaint a Writ was Issued and the defendant Summoned to appear on this day when the sheriff returned the Writ Endorsed as follows viz. 23rd. August demanded payment which was refused, demanded security which was likewise refused, served the defendant with notice of Trial and a Copy of the Petition Attached affishing Room, Dwelling houses, Stage and Flake, the property of the defendant. John Brenan Dy Sheriff.

Henry Sweetland Esqr. appeared for the Plaintiff and Hannah McDaniel appeared for the defendant her husband, and produced apetition Endorsed by Governors Campbell & Elliot.

The Court having fully heard and examined the Complaint before them and also what said Hannah McDaniel had to produce or alledge in defence thereof do consider that William McDaniel is justly Indebted to Catherine Weston the Plaintiff in the sum of One hundred and nine pounds four shillings and five pence, and that Judgment dopass against the defendant with all Costs of Suit.

Catherine Weston v. William McDaniel
15 October 1790
Before Jacob Waller, Surrogate, and Henry Sweetland and Nicholas Brand, JPs

The proceedings in the Court of Common pleas on Wednesday the 15th. September One thousand seven hundred and ninety in the cause of Catherine Weston versus William McDaniel are Rescinded by Consent of the parties, and the Writs of Attachment and Execution destroyed

Witness — for Cath Weston
G Hill — Hy Sweetland
Jno Baker — {Sealed}

Petition of Hanna McDaniel and Decision of Chief Justice John Reeves, received and entered in the Ferryland records 12 October 1791

The Honourable Lord Chief Justice Reeves High Judge of the
Island of Newfoundland &ca &ca &ca ~

The Humbel Petition of Hanna McDaniel otherwise Carney most humbly sheweth- That petitioner begs leave to inform your honor that one Mr. Baker in Ferryland has a bond of Petitioners husbd of One Hundred pounds Sterling these six years in his hands, & was to pay but Twenty pounds a year in part payment of said sum - by Agreement and in stead of that sum there was Twenty seven pounds ten shillings payd aforesaid Baker these two years past that is seven pounds ten shillings more then she Contracted Compound was because the aforesd Mr. Baker wanted to distress petitioner & her poor helpless charge of six Children. Petitioner set [let] a fishing Roome to maintain herself & familey- The aforesaid Baker took all this rent to himself tho his Compound agreement was to Receive but Twenty pounds a year and not allow Petitioner a hundred [weight of] Bread out of his store towards mantaining her heavey charge - The aforesaid Baker several Different times wanted petitioner to sell her Room to pay himself & likewise wanted her to sign him a Bond for the Intrest of the aforesaid sum after paying more than Compound agreed upon yearly the tinnant that ouccupies petitioners room pays the aforesaid Baker the rent of said Roome without the Petitioners order or Consent- Your Petitioner cannot get no Good of ye said Mr. Baker There fore Petitioner hopes your honor will Take it into consideration & vindicate the Cause then your Petitioner in Duty bound [obliterated] will be for Ever bound to pray -

Decision of John Reeves, Chief Justice

If it is Specified in the Bond that the amount is to be paid by instalments of Twenty Pounds p annum, Mr. Baker has no right to stop the whole Rent of the room amounting to Twenty seven pounds nor had he any right to dispose of either of the skiffs which appear to have been put into his possession only as asecurity for the payment of the Twenty Pounds p ann^{m}. Interest cannot be charged upon the Bond as upon the face of it (– if ye facts are as stated in the Memorial) It is to secure the payment of Twenty pounds a year &not for the payment of a Specific Sum of money with Intrest it is to be presumed that M^{r}. Baker writes off upon the Bond the several sums which he receives on acc^{t} of McDaniel & that when the whole amount has been received by him he will deliver up the Bond. and to prevent the Court being troubled unnecessarily with M^{c}-Daniel Complaints, M^{r}. Baker is desierd to Furnish her with a Stated account to this day and to transmit a Copy there of to the Sheriff at Saint Johns.

John Reeves Chief Judge

Michael Malone v. Hannah and John McDaniel
9 June 1797

The plaintiff haveing petitioned that John Mcdaniel by the Counsel of his mother had absented himself from his service and refused to serve out his time according to agreement..~

The pltff and defds. being in Court, on hearing it appeared that John Mcdaniel was hired to the pltff to go fishing with the pltff in his Boat this present season for Fifteen pounds wages. but the pltff haveing hired his said Boat to Martin Molloy & Thomas Clements, and had also transfered or hired out the said John Mcdaniel, without his Consent, to serve them, the said Mcdaniel refused to become their servant, alledging that he shipped himself to serve in the pltff's employ and that therefore he would not become the servant of any other person under such transfer..~..~

The Court being of opinion that the pltff could not dispose of his servant, as he had done with his private property, without the servants consent, and more especially as the servant shipped to fish out of the Harbour of Ferryland, he could not be compelled to serve out of any other Harbour~ the said Molloy & Clements on hearing the opinion of the Court, resolved to fish out of Ferryland, upon which the said ~ Mcdaniel agreed to serve them..~ the pltff paid the Costs of Suit 16/~. ~

Sources: PANL: GN 5/4/C/1, Ferryland, box 1, 50–52, copy of Order, Campbell, 10 September 1784, with attached Petition from Hannah McDaniel, [September 1784?], entered in the Ferryland court records October, 1787; GN 2/1/A, vol. 11, 245–57, copy of Order, Campbell, 10 September 1784, attached to Order, Governor Elliot, 5 October 1787; GN 5/4/C/1, Ferryland, box 1, 25–26, *Catherine Weston v. Hannah and William McDaniel*, 8 and 9 March 1787; GN 5/4/C/1, Ferryland, box 1, 3, 4–5, and 8, *Catherine Weston v. William McDaniel*, 17 August, 15 September, and 15 October 1790; GN 5/4/C/1, Ferryland, box 1, Petition of Hannah McDaniel, alias Carney, [September 1791?], together with Decision of Chief Justice John Reeves, received 12 October 1791; and GN 5/4/C/1, Ferryland, box 1, *Michael Malone v. Hannah and John McDaniel*, 9 June 1797.

CASE FILE NO. 30

Mary Kennedy v. William Tucker
13 October 1792
Before John Reeves, Chief Justice

This was to recover £4.

It appeared that the Plt. and Def^{t}. were brother & sister, and the only children of their father, who died without leaving a will properly executed. He left a plantation, which let for £11 a year, till the last year, when it produced only £8. The brother had taken possession, and had paid his sister £4. a year, as a bequest, or intended bequest of the father; But last year, he declared his father died intestate, and the plantation belonged to him as heir, and that he would no longer pay the plaintiff any thing.

Whereupon It was adjudged, & ordered, that the def^{t}. pay £4. the half of the last year's rent, and £7.10. the sum which make the £4 paid in former years to be half the Eleven pounds the former rent; And further It was Ordered that the plt be at liberty to take half the plantation to herself whenever she pleases, The Court being of opinion, that Lands & Plantations, in Newfoundland, are nothing more than Chattel Interests, and should, in case of Intestacy, be distributed as such.

It was ordered, that £4. be paid this year & £7.10 the next year.

Mr Morey
deft's master
was ordered
to pay £4
out of his
wages.

Sources: PANL, GN 5/4/C/1, Ferryland, box 1, 25–26, *Mary Kennedy v. William Tucker*, 13 October 1792.

CASE FILE NO. 31

Catharine Jackman

Renewse, March 27, 1813
Mortgage Catherine Jackman to
Hunt S.[tabb] P.[reston] & Co.
Consideration: £143 15s 8d

a Dwelling House, out Houses & 2 Head of Cattle, for the payment of Twenty pounds a Year on the 20th day of November & in default of payment to take possession, ~

Hunt, Stabb, Preston & Co. v. Estate of Catharine Jackman, Renews
6 June 1818
Court of Sessions
[Before Robert Carter, JP]

To Recover £160 on the estate of Catharine Jackman, deceased

It appeared a transfer of the deceaseds property as Security of the annual payment of £20 untill the debt was paid, had been Recorded in this Court and that on investigating the Account produced in the Court by the Administrators of the deceased, it appeared the Bond debt was Liquidated by payments made in the year 1813, between March, the time of executors said Bond in the same Year, and the Month of November next following to the Amount of £49 . . . and that a further payment of £43 was made by George Jackman

Jugt can not be had till the 20 day of November—the day on which the installment becomes due

A rehearing of this case was had on the 20th. of October 1818- and it appearing by authentic documents which was then produced in Court, that in the year 1817, the sum of £15 of the annual instalment was unpaid in that period ~

Judgment that the said Sum of £15. be paid on the 20th. of November next—and on the 20th. of November in each year thence following, the annual sum agreed to be paid according to the Tenor of the Mortgage, untill the whole debt for which the same was given be fully paid ~

Hunt, Stabb, Preston & Co. v. Estate of Catharine Jackman, Renews
25 April 1820
[Before Robert Carter, JP]

To recover £160. Balance of an account

Ordered to Stand over for ahearing at a future day on the Grounds that the children of Arthur and Catharine Jackman claiming interest in the said estate—the same could not be legally disposed of for payment of Catharine Jackman's debts, if such Interest was proved ~

Hunt, Stabb, Preston & Co. v. Estate of Catharine Jackman, Renews
7 November 1820
[Before Robert Carter, JP]

To Recover £160 due on a Bond debt

this Case was before the Court on the 25th. of April last and ordered to stand over in consequence of a claim by the children of the deceased on their Fathers property who died intestate—pltiffs endeavoured to justify their claim to the said property on the following circumstances—the deceased, Catharine Jackman, had been Supplied at various times by pltiffs up to March 1813, at which time she stood indebted the sum sued, and to secure the payment thereof Transferred all her right, title and Interest in a dwelling house and all the Appurtenances, and two head of Cattle—the debt to be paid by Annual instalments and in default of the payment at the time the same became due in any succeeding year, pltiffs to be at liberty to enter & possess the premises and effects so transferred—George Jackman pres[t]. Stated that his Father died intestate in the year 1807—at which time he was aminor and was totally ignorant of the Transfer now before the Court— in the year 1815 he paid £42 towards payment ofhis Mothers debt, to prevent the property being sold being then ignorant of any will made by his father leaving the whole property to his Mother—in 1816 his Mother died, and he Administered to the estate—Contends that as the debt was Contracted by his Mother, that it could not bind the property beyond the proportion she was by law entitled to his Father having died intestate—pltiffs Reply stated, Arthur Jackman to have died insolvent, and largely indebted to them at his decease ~

Ordered to stand over for producing pltiffs Accounts -

Hunt, Stabb, Preston & Co. v. Estate of Catharine Jackman, Renews
5 December 1820
[Before Robert Carter, JP]

This case was before the Court on aformer day and now application by pltiffs. for the foreclosure of the Mortgage of Catharine Jackman for the Sum of £160, upon which debt the sum of £40 remained unpaid—George Jackman appears, and resists the Claim of pltiffs the property being liable to him for a share, contending that his Mother had no authority to alienate or transfer the same ~ the Widdow Jackman died 1815 at which time said George Jackman administered to the said estate and together with his Brother paid all up to the Sum of £40—On the part of pltiffs it is contended that paying these sums after being of Age that he cannot plead ignorance ~ Judgmt. the Widdows one third to be disposed of for the benefit of her Creditors ~ the Garden which is in dispute if it can be shewn the party is entitled to a preference—to be further Considered by the Court—the Accounts to be adjusted by arbitration.

Sources: PANL, GN 5/1/C/1, Ferryland: 113, Mortgage, Catharine Jackman to Hunt, Stabb, Preston and Co., 27 March 1813; and 47, 110, 126, and 161, *Hunt, Stabb, Preston and Co. v. the Estate of Catharine Jackman*, 6 June 1818 and 25 April, 7 November, and 5 December 1820.

CASE FILE NO. 32

The Widow Brandy

Hunt, Stabb, Preston & Co. v. the Estate of William Brandy, Renews
25 April 1820
[Before Robert Carter, JP]

To recover £50. Balance of an Account

Thomas Codner Agent for pltiffs. pray Judgment and execution on def[ts]. effects, stating that def[t]. was possessed of a House and Gardens at Renewse, and that the same be sold for payment of the said debt ~ denis McCarthy of Renewse having claim to the said premises—proceedings was defered untill dennis McCarthy shoud appear to prove his claim ~

Hunt, Stabb, Preston & Co. v. the Estate of William Brandy, Renews
6 November 1820
[Before Robert Carter, JP]

To recover £50.. Balance of an Acct. ~

The deceased was drowned in June 1818, was adealer of ptiffs and died possessed of a House and Garden which he possessed of by marriage, with the Widdow of John doyle-

The deceased's Widdow objected that the said premises were the property of her former Husband who died intestate, leaving a child—which child she contended had a right to enjoy all her deceased fathers property ~

Judgm[t]. that the property in question, being considered from the circumstances of doyle's dying intestate, to belong, one third to the Widdow and two thirds to the children—That the Widdow's one third, as becoming the property of her second Husband thro marriage, is subject and liable to pay his debts—the other two thirds to remain for the Children.

Sources: PANL, GN 5/1/C/1, Ferryland, 109 and 123–24, *Hunt Stabb Preston Co. v. the Estate of William Brandy*, 25 April and 6 November 1820.

CASE FILE NO. 33

Catharine Delahunty v. James H. Carter

Writ No. 179
Initiated 3 October 1827—returnable 4 October 1827

4 October 1827
Before Chief Justice Richard A. Tucker with W. Carter, A. Morrison, and J. Preston, JPs

This action is to recover compensation for the loss of Services of Plaintiffs Daughter, inconsequence of her seduction by Defendant

Damages laid at £100.0.0

The Defendant having prayed a Special Jury the Court ordered one to be summoned, when the following Gentlemen appeared in Court and were sworn in as Special Jurors

Benjamin Sweetland foreman,

Gregory Brown, William Richards, Nicholas Stabb, Maurice Brazil, Thomas Norris, Matthew Morry, Peter Winser, Ewen Stabb, Noah Clift, William Goff, and John Killegrew.

Ellen Delahunty, Sworn, Is Daughter of the Pltff—Has no Father living. He has been dead sixteen years, lived with Plaintiff for the last Ten or Twelve years, and has worked for her. Pltff keeps no Servant but witness has performed the duties of one towards her. In 1826 witness first became acquainted with the Def[d]., the acquaintance commenced by witness going to Def[d]. for the price of a pair of Cuffs, which Plaintiff had made for one of the persons in Def[ds]. employment, thinks that she went soon after to Def[d]. with another message from Pltff and Def[d]. asked witness when she would come again. Witness said she had no business to come again, after this Kitty Kelly desired Witness to make some Socks for the Def[d]., which Wit. accordingly did and carried them to Def^{d}. who gave her Three shillings and Six pence for a pair of the socks and told her, she might get whatever she wanted, for the money in the shop, Def^{d}. also asked Wit. if Kitty Kelly had delivered her any messuage. Wit. said she had desired her to make the socks for him. Wit. afterwards occasionally met Def^{d}. in the Street and asked by him more than once when she would come to the shop—at one time Def^{d}. asked Wit. if she wou'd cut some Sounds on the Stage and she consented to do so, she cut four Firkins of sounds, and took up some articles of dress in the Shop on Credit, Def^{d}. sometimes asked Wit. if she had much washing and where she got firewood, He also ask'd her when she wou'd go into the woods for it, Wit. told Def^{d}. she was in the habit of going into the woods for it and Def^{d}. said he wou'd go too. Whenever Wit. went out she generally saw Def^{d}. who repeated his questions about going into the woods. Wit sometimes told Def^{d}. she would go into the woods tomorrow, and he said he wou'd be there too. This sort of acquaintance between Def^{d}. and Wit. continued up to July 1826 when Wit. one day met Def^{d}. in the woods, but no freedom was allowed. Wit. afterwards met Def^{d}. in the Street, and was again ask'd by him when she was going into the woods—Wit. said not until that day week and on that day she again met Def^{d}. in the woods, who ask'd her to speak a word to him. Wit. promised to do so provided he wou'd do nothing to her, when he said he wou'd not. Wit then went to him saying she wou'd take him at his word—Def^{d}. took Wit by the hand and seated himself by her Def^{d}. used some liberties and Wit desired him to desist. He said it was all Nonsense. Deft. then had connexion with Wit. on the ground and afterwards cut some wood for her, after this Wit had frequent connexion with Def^{d}. and produced a Child on the 29th. April last—The Def^{d}. is the Father of that Child—it was about a week after the first connexion that Wit had another in the woods and it was always in the woods that the connexion took place between them. Def^{d}. is certainly the Father of Wits. Child, during her pregnancy Wit. concealed her situation but it was discovered by D^{r}. Morrison about six or eight weeks before the birth of the Child, Wit. was living with Pltff at this time, before D^{r}. Morrison attended Wit. she was attended by D^{r}. Bryand but he did not find out her situation, When Wit. lay in her Mother attended her, for a long time before the birth of the Child, Wit. suffered from a stich in her side and a pain in her breast which prevented her from doing her usual work, and after this she was obliged to work when really not able to do so, From July to October, Def^{d}. had occasional carnal connection with her, but it did not take place very often.

Cross examined

Never told Def^{d}. she was with Child by him, but went several times with an intention of doing so, but could not find an opportunity

Plaintiffs case closed

Defendant calls
Andrew Morrison, Sworn, knows last Wit. and was call'd on sometime last Winter to attend her professionally, discovered that she was pregnant but found her most reluctant

to confess that she was so. Wit. thought then that she was about seven and a half months advanced in her pregnancy, and told Pltff he supposed she wou'd be deliver'd about the end of April or beginning of May.

Catharine Kelly, sworn, About one and a half months ago, Wit. who is Sister to Ellen Delahunty, cautioned her against walking with Robert Brine. Wit. did this because he was a married man does not know that her sister ever saw him after that

William Harris, sworn,
Martin Conway sworn has never seen Ellen Delahunty conduct herself differently from what well behaved Girls in her situation in life do,

His Lordship charges the Jury, who retire and on their return deliver into Court the following verdict.

For Plaintiff £30.0.0 Cur^{cy}.
Signed Benjamin Sweetland
foreman

Sources: PANL, GN 5/2/C/1, Ferryland, box 1, 142–45, *Catharine Delahunty v. James H. Carter*, 4 October 1827.

CASE FILE NO. 34

Catherine Oudle [also] Audle v. John Murry, Sr.
4 April 1791
Before Robert Carter and Nicholas Brand, JPs

The voluntary examination of Catherine Oudle of Ferryland in the s^{d}. District, single woman taken on Oath before Robt Carter and Nich^{l} Brand Esqr—two of his Majesty's Justices of the Peace in & for the s^{d}. District, this 3d Day of April 1791 ~

Who saith, that she is now with Child and that the said Child is likely to be born a Bastard & to be chargeable to the District of Ferryland and John Murray Senior of Ferryland, in the District, Fisherman, is the Father of the said Child

Taken & signed the
Day & Year above
written before us ~
Robt Carter J.P.
Nich^{l} Brand J.P.

the mark of
x
Catherine Oudle

The Court Ordered John Murry to appear & give bond for the maintenance of the Child ~

25 April 1791

Catherine Audle being delivered of a male Bastard Child, the following order of filiation & maintenance was issued ~

District of } Ferryland	The Order of Rob[t] Carter and Nich[l] Brand Esq[rs]~ two of His Majesty's Justices of the Peace for thes[d] District, made 25th. of April 1791 -

Concerning a male Bastard Child lately Born in the Harbor of Ferryland, of the Body of Catherine Audle single woman ~

Whereas it appears unto us ye s[d] Justices that the s[d]. Catherine Audle on ye 22d. Inst. was delivered of a male Bastard [Child] & that the s[d] Bastard is now chargeable on this Harbor & that Jn[o] Murry of this Harbour did beget the s[d] Bastard.

And whereas the s[d] Murry hath appeard before us & hath not shewd sufficient Cause why he should not be the reputed Father of the Child—we therefore upon the examination of the Circumstances, as well as upon the Oath of the s[d] Catherine Audle dohereby ajudge him ye s[d] Jn[o] Murry to be the reputed Father of the s[d]. Bastard Child—And thereupon we do Order, for the sustenance of the s[d] Child, that Jn[o] Murry dopay upon Notice of this our Order the sum of ten shillings, into the hands of Rob[t] Carter Esq[r]. toward the Laying in of the s[d] Catherine Audle & ye maintenance of ye s[d] Child, to the time of making this Order -

And we do further order ye s[d] Jn[o] Murry topay or Cause to be paid, into the hands of Rob[t] Carter Esqr.- the sum of two shillings weekly & ever[y] week from this present time for the maintenance of the s[d]. Child-so long as the Child shall be chargeable to the s[d]. Harbour ~

And we do further orderd s[d] Jn[o] Murry topay to Rob[t] Carter Esq[r].~ weekly & ever[y] week ye sum of two shillings & sixpence, in Case the s[d] Catherine Audle shall not Nurse or take Care of the Child herself~

Given &c ~

Sources: PANL, GN 5/4/C/1, Ferryland, box 1, *Catherine Audle [also Oudle] v. John Murray*, Sr., 3/4 (both dates appear in the record) and 25 April 1791.

CASE FILE NO. 35

Elizabeth Carney v. Manus Butler
16 May 1791
[Before Robert Carter and Nicholas Brand, JPs]

Elizabeth Carney complained of having a Child by Manus Butler & prayed assistance to compel ye s[d] Butler to maintain the Child—Butler present—admitted the complaint, & allow'd the Charges, viz.

	£ s d
To a midwife	1..1. 0
Expences during the illness Nursing &	2..2. 0
Nursing & Cloathing of Child fm	
10 Augst. to 16 May 1791—at 3/6 per week	6..16 .6
	9..19 .6

~ May 23.
gave an Order to
Eliz Kerny for 3/6
p week for
maintenance of
the child.

Sources: PANL, GN 5/4/C/1, Ferryland, box 1, *Elizabeth Carney v. Manus Butler*, 16 and 23 May 1791.

CASE FILE NO. 36

Catharine Power at the Suit of the Crown v. William Deringwater, alias Drinkwater
20 September 1806
Before William Carter and James Lowe, JPs

This was an action by information against the Defendant at the suit of the Crown, charging him with opening the door of the House in which the plaintiff dwelt at Renewse (in the district aforesaid [Ferryland]) and after so entering the dwelling house aforesaid between the hours of ten and twelve oClock at night, did assault and ill treat the Plaintiff against the Laws and statutes of the realm and against the peace of our said Lord the King. This charge resting on the unsoported solitary deposition of a woman of infamous character who by the deposition of John Hawsey was by him put into her bed intoxicated at Eight oClock the same night and it appearing by the testimony of three creditable witnesses that the Defendant was not from his house during the night the complaint was submitted to a Jury who immediately returned the following verdict. "from the Evidence before the Jury on the part of the defendant William deringwater we the undersigned are of opinion that the said William deringwater is not guilty of the charge alledged against him by Catharine Power"

Francis Tree Foreman	Thomas Head	John Sanders
John Pike	William Rion	Richard Gorman
John Steer	Thomas Colleton	
Thomas Norris	Matthew Ronan	
Richard Holman	Thomas Meagher	

The defendant was accordingly acquitted and the plaintiff Catharine Power ordered to be sent from here by the first opportunity to Ireland.

Sources: PANL, GN 5/4/C/1, Ferryland, box 1, *Catharine Power at the Suit of the Crown v. William Deringwater, alias Drinkwater*, 20 September 1806.

CASE FILE NO. 37

Mary Jenkins v. John Power, James Callinan, and Patrick Cahill
24 February 1794 [although possibly 1795, as the record falls between hearings dated 17 November 1794 and 20 May 1795]
Before Robert Carter, (local) Surrogate

For attempting a Rape ~
The Plaintiff exhibited the following complaint
To Robert Carter Esqr. Surrogate..~..~

The Humble petition of Mary Jenkins sheweth ~

that John Power, aman who lives in a House at the River head of Fermuse did last tuesday evening, the 10th day of february Instant about four oClock, come into the House where your petitioner and her Mother live in at Fermuse and laid hold on your petitioner and endeavoured by force to have carnal communication with her, he first draged her to atable and endeavoured to accomplish his designs on her there, then he draged her into a Room and tore her cloths, and would have obtained his ends (as your petitioners strength was exausted) had not her continual screeching detered him—the said Power called your petitioner whore several times—and he had two Accomplices with him namely James Callanan and Patt Cahill, who were present at his Brutal behaviour towards your petitioner, and did not afford her the least assistance—Your petitioner's mother was not at home when this happened—there was a shoemaker in the House all the time who was afraid to interfere in assisting your petitioner ..~..~..~

Petitioner humbly prays that you will Order the said John Power James Callinan and Patt Cahill to be brought to Justice and to redress her- Pet[r]. as in duty bound will ever pray ~

her
Mary x Jenkins
mark

At a Court held this day Present Rob[t]. Carter Esq[r]. Surrogate and a Jury impannelled, they brought in the following Verdict ~

We, the undersigned the Jury on a cause this 24th February 1794 between Mary Jenkins James Callanan and others, from the evidence we have heared, do give it as our Opinion, that James Callanan Patrick Cahill, are accessarys with Power, who hath absconded—more particularly, as they did not hinder the said Power from useing the said Mary Jenkins so ill, and we likewise give it as our Opinion ~ that Callanan and Cahill should pay Mary Jenkins two pounds each be fined one pound each, and Walter Toubret [the shoemaker] one pound ten shillings as a fine for not assisting the said Mary Jenkins, each to be bound over to keep the peace..~..~..~

John Baker foreman
Arthur Hunt
William Jennings
John Aylward
John Young
Francis Tree Junr.
James Connelly

his
Matthew x Ronan
mark

Richd. Eales
Matthew Costelly
John Saunders
James Shortall

Sources: PANL, GN 5/4/C/1, Ferryland, box 1, *Re: Mary Jenkins*, 24 February 1794 (or possibly 1795).

CASE FILE NO. 38

Magarett Hanahan v. Thomas Hanahan
31 January 1791
Before Robert Carter, Henry Sweetland, and Nicholas Brand, JPs

Deposed on Oath that on Sunday Ev^{g} 30th Jany. as she came home from her mother's house she heard, as she approach'd ye Door of her husband's House, her Youngest Child crying & on going in found it was in bed—asked her Husband what ye matter was with it, as it seem'd to Cry as tho it was stifling, he reply'd that he had coverd it over & it wou'd soon begone—she then exclaimd against him—& s^{d} wou'd you murder the Child—& going into the room to its relief found it almost suffocated -

She further deposes that he then took the Eldest Child & swore it shou'd have no supper & otherwise ill used it—some hours after ongoing to bed—he took a Bough & Flogged the Child, to oblidge it to make water—& on her Interfereing he told her that if she contradicted him ~ he woud take a Hatchet or anything he coud find & ill use her—nothing more pass'd that night & on this Day complained to us & Craved the Peace of him her s^{d} Husband ~
sworn before us ~

Robt Carter
H^{y} Sweetland
Nich^{l} Brand

In consequence of the above deposition a summons was issued—Court adjourned. -

Magarett Hanahan v. Thomas Hanahan
1 February 1791
Before Robert Carter, Henry Sweetland, and Nicholas Brand, JPs

Court assembled -

Thomas Hanahan was bro^{t}. in, was ordered to make his defence—which he not doing to the satisfaction of the Court—& there appearing Marks of Violence on the Children & wife.—the Court <u>Ordered him thirty Nine lashes on the bare back—</u> and $^{\text{tobe imprisoned}}$ $_{\text{while he}}$ find Security for the peace against his s^{d} wife—& she praying tobe separated from him was granted.

Magarett Hanahan v. Thomas Hanahan
11 April 1791
[Before Robert Carter, Henry Sweetland, and Nicholas Brand, JPs]

Thoms Handerhan, who was committed to Jail for want of Surety of the Peace, demanded by his wife was Liberated, on his proving John Pritchett, Planter, to be bound for him—who there upon was Orderd by the Court to quit the District & nevermore to come here except by the Approbation of the Magistrates.

Sources: PANL, GN 5/4/C/1, Ferryland, box 1, *Margarett Hanahan v. Thomas Hanahan*, 31 January, 1 February, and 11 April 1791.

CASE FILE NO. 39

Ann St. Croix v. Benjamin St. Croix
16 October 1821
Before Charles A. Baker, Surrogate and JP, and William Phipard, JP

Ptff a woman of 33 charged her husband the Defandant aged 77 with neglect and ill treatment for the last two years and prayed that he might be compelled to provide for her support and that of their seven Children—The parties not agreeing to live together;

Under an Order of Court the Defendant made an agreement to give up the use of his house and garden to the Ptff; to pay £6 at the end of the present season, and £5 per annum in future for the support of the children, who were to be left in her charge.

Ann St. Croix v. Edward Power
16 October 1822
Before William Phipard, JP

Plaintiff states her Husband did not cohabit with her since the Summer of 1819 and that a settlem[ent] took place in the Court of Sessions at S^{t}. Marys on the 16 day of October 1821—for the support of her Children through the medium of her Husband as in the records will now fully appear—That on the 17 of July 1822 she was delivered of a Male Child begotten by the reputed father Edwd. Power.

The Examination of Ann S^{t}. Croix of Saint Mary's in said Port married Woman, taken upon Oath before me William Phipard Esqr—One of His Majestys Justices of the Peace in, and for the said Port—this 16th day of October, who saith that on the 17th day of July now last past in the Port of St Marys aforesaid—She the said Ann S^{t}. Croix was delivered of a (Male) bastard Child and that the said bastard Child is likely to become chargeable to the said Port of S^{t}. Marys—and that Edward Power of the said Port S^{t}. Marys Fisherman, did get her with Child of the said bastard Child.

Taken and signed the day and year
above written before me
William Phipard J.P.

her
Ann x S^{t}. Croix
mark

The reputed father having eloped from the Port to evade Justice—an order was issued by the Court to detain in the hands of Mr Wm Rideout a ballance of £4..15..4 due to the said Edwd. Power untill further orders, in restitution made for the support etc of said bastard Child and sufficient recognisance entered into—Ordered that forty Forty shillings be paid for the necessary expences of laying in—and that three shillings p^r Week for the support of the said bastard Child—as far as the given sum of £4..15..4—laying in the hands of the aforesaid William Ridout.

William Phipard J.P.

Sources: PANL, GN 5/4/C/1, St. Mary's: 111, *Ann St. Croix v. Benjamin St. Croix*, 16 October 1821; and 130–31, *Ann St. Croix v. Edward Power*, 17 July 1822.

CASE FILE NO. 40

Mary Kearney v. Andrew Kearney
13 August 1804
Before Micaiah Malbon, Surrogate and JP

> Petitioned that her Husband might be obligated to allow her a maintenance, he having about 15 Months since turned her to Door, since which time she has been supported by her Brother Thos. Kennedy.

Andrew Kearney, Sworn, says he was married to Mary Kennedy now Mary Kearney, but cannot exactly recollect the time, that soon after the Marriage, his Wife behaved very Ill frequently getting drunk and totally neglecting her household affairs, it afterwards appeared that she was with child at the time of her Marriage and at the end of six months was delivered of a Male Child, that he did turn her to door and refused to support her./.

Mary Kearney (Sworn) says she was married to Andrew Kearney by the Romish priest at Trepassey on the 2^d. day of November 1802. had been absent from her Husband about 15 Months, since which time she had been supported by her Brother.

Thomas Kennedy, Sworn, says that he his [is] the Brother of Mary Kearney, and has paid or is accountable to pay for her Maintenance since the time she has been absent from her husband about the sum of twelve pounds Sterling.

In Consideration of the fair Character of the Husband, the Court decreed that he should allow her 3/ p. week for her separate Maintenance, and the following Agreement was entered into.

We Michael Kearney and Andrew Kearney of Biscay Bay in the Island of Newfoundland Husbandmen Do hereby agree to pay and allow from the day of the date hereof unto Mary Kearney the lawful Wife of the beforenamed Andrew Kearney the sum of three shillings p week for the Maintenance and support of her the said Mary Kearney And we do further promise and agree that the said sum of three shillings p. week shall be paid weekly and every week during the joint lives of us the said Michael Kearney and Andrew Kearney provided the said Mary Kearney shall so long happen to live, but if and in case it shall be proved to the satisfaction of any Court of Justice that the same [parties] may come before ~ that after the commencement of the said weekly payment that the said Mary Kearney shall have a Child or Children by any other Man, then that the said week[ly] payment shall cease and be void to all intents and purposes whatsoever ~ Witness our hands at the Court house in Trepassey this 13th. day of Augt. 1804.

Signed in the presence
of Mic. Malbon
Joseph Pearce./.

Michael Kearney
The X Mark
of
Andrew Kearney

Sources: PRL, 340.9 N45, *Mary Kearney v. Andrew Kearney*, 13 August 1804.

APPENDIX A

Plebeian and Elite Communities on the Southern Avalon

The term *plebeian* is used in this study in the sense that it was defined by E. P. Thompson in his discussion of eighteenth-century English society. As in England, the plebeian community on the southern Avalon was not working-class because it lacked a class consciousness—"a consistency of self-definition . . . ; clarity of objectives; the structuring of class organization." But there was a distinct and vigorous plebeian culture, with its own rituals, its own patterns of work and leisure, its own world view. Furthermore, the plebeian community did share a common consciousness and exert political pressure on specific occasions in relation to specific issues—either in the form of the "mob" in direct collective actions, or as the menacing presence behind anonymous actions and threats. As Thompson argues, plebeian culture was not revolutionary, but neither was it deferential: "It bred riots but not rebellions: direct actions but not democratic organizations."[1] On the southern Avalon, the plebeian community was composed primarily of fishing servants, washerwomen, seamstresses, midwives, artisans, small-scale boatkeepers, planters and, by the nineteenth century, numerous "independent" fishing families (in as much as they could be independent from their merchant suppliers).

The polar opposites to the plebs in Thompson's "societal field-of-force" were the English gentry (the patricians), who exercised cultural hegemony through their control over office and preferment, law, credit, the distribution and sale of goods or raw materials, the deployment of favors and charity, and the symbolism of hegemony. Their smaller-scale equivalent on the southern Avalon were local merchant-planters, merchants, merchants' agents, vessel owners and masters, Anglican clergy, and more substantial boatkeepers and planters, who functioned as a gentry in the study area with their control of employment opportunities, relief, supply and credit, and administrative and magisterial functions. By the late eighteenth and early nineteenth centuries, this group was adopting the lifestyles and ideologies that signaled an emerging middle class in Newfoundland (see Chapter 9).

I use the term *gentry* here in its broadest sense, to mean a group with high social ranking. A *landed gentry* did not develop in Newfoundland. This was a reflection of a prolonged perception of Newfoundland as a fishing station rather than a colony,[2] as well as the poor prospects for commercial agriculture along most of the English Shore. It was also a reflection of the tenuous nature of private property in Newfoundland—the result of a fishing regime that had traditionally privileged the migratory ship fishery in its use of prime waterfront property. After a century marked intermittently by disputes between migratory fishermen and resident fishers, the *Newfoundland Act* of 1699 (*10 & 11 Wm. III, Cap.* 25) permitted inhabitants of the island to occupy areas that had not traditionally been used by the migratory ship fishery. And throughout the following century, as the nature of fishing operations increasingly shifted from migratory to sedentary, British authorities permitted uninterrupted possession of additional shoreline properties, provided they were used for the purposes of the resident fishery. But even land designated for private use could not be held by freehold title, and the right of occupation could be withdrawn by the governor (although this was not common, unless fishing premises were not maintained).[3]

Official recognition of private property did not really begin to evolve until the early nineteenth century (1810s to 1830s), as the growing resident population demanded greater certainty in land titles. However, while the legal definition of property remained uncertain until that point, local communities had long recognized title by quiet possession, and residents disposed of property (by sale, mortgage, deed of gift, or testamentary bequest) as if no such ambiguity existed. On the southern Avalon, the merchant-planter gentry of the eighteenth century accumulated extensive properties (in several communities) on or near waterfronts, and either used the properties themselves or rented them to local fishing families, thus becoming substantial landlords in the area. In the nineteenth century, the mercantile elite still had significant holdings, although there was an increasing trend to sell these rental properties to community residents as the stability of settlement, the demand for property, and the certainty in land titles converged.

The local elite maintained social distance from the plebeian community through religious affiliation (most were English Protestant, as opposed to the largely Irish Catholic plebeian community) and exclusive patterns of socializing and marriage. Still, there was a reciprocity between plebeians and the gentry on the southern Avalon, for they were tied to each other through interdependence in the fishery. The relationship was far from equal, but, as Thompson notes, the concept of *paternalism and deference* that is frequently invoked to describe preindustrial societies would not do justice to the complexity and underlying tension of the relationship. The elite saw themselves as benevolent patrons, and plebeians accepted the gentry's paternalism, but on their own terms: deference was accorded only on a conditional basis, to the degree that it enabled them to extract what they needed for their own advantage and self-preservation. In the process, plebeians recognized the gentry's political and economic power, but they were also resistant to it, sometimes openly.

Linda Little has written about plebeian collective actions in Conception Bay in the 1830s that demonstrated a vibrant plebeian culture in that area.[4] Such episodes on the southern Avalon were not as frequent or of the same magnitude, perhaps because the area participated only marginally in the sealing industry—a site of nascent working-class consciousness in St. John's and Conception Bay in the first half of the nineteenth century—and also because ethnoreligious tensions were muted in the more homogeneous population of my study area. Still, resistance was articulated in forms of protest typically deployed by plebeian communities, such as anonymous notes, assaults, cattle maiming, vandalism, and theft directed against the gentry as well as parades and the use of symbols as mechanisms of group identity and unity.

Some of these episodes involved women and are discussed in Chapter 5. Several other examples will serve to demonstrate. Among the family papers of the Carters, merchants and magistrates on the southern Avalon, there are several anonymous notes and songs written about the local elite, including the following offering about the Morrys, a merchant family in Caplin Bay:

A set of rogues are in this town
Who truth and justice both disown
They are a petty pygmy clan
And named the motley maggot gang

Chorus
Sing loud the motley maggot gang
sing ho the motley maggot gang
come join my chorus every one
and echo loud the maggot gan[g]

The poor they oft oppress and wrong
and cloak it 'mong their g[u]iling throng
they are a bandit wicked clan
and named the motley maggot gang
Sing loud the motley &c &c[5]

The song continues in a similar vein for several more stanzas, concluding that "the cozening rob[bers] ought to hang." One verse refers to an animal-maiming incident—a form of popular protest that was a common manifestation of Whiteboyism in eighteenth-century Ireland and that was probably transferred to the southern Avalon, as there were several other incidents reported during the study period that had ethnic and class undertones.[6] And court records provide evidence of theft from and malicious damage to mercantile premises during the eighteenth and early nineteenth centuries.

The menacing presence of plebeians in the anonymity of the night also caused concerns among the local elite. In an 1835 presentment, for example, the grand jury for Ferryland district (assembled from the "principal inhabitants and merchants" of the area) expressed fear of the "great risk and danger to which we are nightly exposed of having our Houses and Stores and other Property destroyed by Fire from the Inhabitants in the different Towns carrying pieces of Wood on Fire in their hand thro' the Streets and Lanes in the said Towns."[7] Although this could be construed as merely a commentary on unsafe lighting practices, the issue certainly seemed to have a more sinister aspect in 1839, when the grand jury voiced the same concern about the carrying of firebrands in combination with the following complaint:

> That they view with indignation the anonimous papers now handed them (together with the certainty of a Cow and two horses having been shot) and deplore most fervently, that Individuals should be found capable of such atrocious conduct, and trust that means may be adopted to detect the perpetrators thereof and prevent a recurrence of the same.[8]

Clearly, the threat of plebeian reprisal underscored the gentry's worries about the nocturnal wanderings of local inhabitants.

Deputy sheriffs, bailiffs, and constables were frequently harried and assaulted in the performance of their duties, most notably in attaching property to satisfy court judgments for debt. Such was the case in 1817, for example, when local constable Edward Power, in the company of Ferryland magistrate Andrew Morrison, attempted to attach (or confiscate) the voyage of Patrick Kent and Patrick Crane of Cape Broyle for payment of a debt owing to W. and B. Sweetland and Co. Kent and his boat crew spirited the fish away to Kent's stage in

Island Cove, where Power caught up with them and attempted to seize the fish and boat. Bystander John Howlett provoked the crew, saying, "You are very quiet men or you would pew that fellows guts out." Defendant Kent declared that the constable "might as well attach his prick as that fish." Various spectators refused to render assistance, and the two court officials feared for their lives.[9]

Here, a discrepancy had arisen between the perceptions of the formal legal system and those of local fishermen in relation to the entitlement of a supplying merchant. Typically, such noncompliant behavior garnered the support of the plebeian community—either in direct action or through noncooperation with authorities. A number of these incidents involved women and are discussed in Chapter 5. A similar sense of plebeian justice motivated the overzealous salving of wrecked vessels in the area—again, episodes in which plebeian women participated (see Chapter 4). Pre-emptive removal of salvage and interference with magistrates, deputy sheriffs, and wreck commissioners were regular occurrences at wreck sites and demonstrated an alternative, plebeian interpretation of the equitable distribution of salvaged goods.

A different sense of fairness also underpinned the occasional plundering of merchants' and ships' stores, usually in periods of distress or emergency. The inhabitants of Bay Bulls and Renews, for example, removed supplies from fishing ships in their harbors and distributed them among their communities during the terrible *winter of the* rals (1817–18)—a period of high distress throughout the English Shore resulting from the recession following the Napoleonic Wars and from disastrous fishing seasons in 1816 and 1817. Similarly, when American privateers were harrying the southern Avalon during the Revolutionary War, the merchants and principal inhabitants of Renews complained that the local Irish population was plundering dry fish and stores,[10] an episode that was repeated in 1796, when the French were wreaking havoc in the area.[11] While these actions were interpreted by English Protestant merchants and government officials as evidence of the treasonous nature of the Irish population, it is more likely that the largely Irish plebeian community were simply taking advantage of the moment to enforce an alternate distribution of the fish and stores, with a pragmatic view that they were certainly more entitled to them than were the enemy.

Of course, real life is always messy, and this black-and-white division of plebeian and elite cultures masks various shades of grey. There were socioeconomic gradations within both groups: a small-scale planter, for example, was in a more privileged social and economic position than a fishing servant; a merchant with extensive fishing premises and several vessels was more comfortably situated than a clergyman. Furthermore, there was a middling group of modest-sized planters or boatkeepers and lesser court officials (sheriffs, constables, gaolers, etc.) who shared in the rituals and routines of the plebeian community but sometimes found their allegiance turning to the gentry either because of shared ethnoreligious background, dependence on the gentry for their commissions, or simple social ambition.

Furthermore, neither plebeians nor the local elite always acted in unanimity. Numerous court cases involving assault and civil litigation attest to small fissures between individual members of the plebeian community. And there were occasional cracks in gentry solidarity—especially when opportunity for preferment presented itself. Most disagreements were minor squabbles over government office and took place within the confines of the group. More public was the alliance of English Protestant merchant and magistrate Peter Winsor (also Winser) of Aquaforte with Catholic priest Father Duffy of St. Mary's in the 1836 election campaign. The two joined forces against a local candidate from a powerful English Protestant mercantile family, Lieutenant Robert Carter, to support a drop-in candidate from St. John's, Irish Catholic merchant Patrick Morris.[12] When the polls opened, Winsor spoke against Carter, using "very tantalizing language towards him to create popularity among the crowd."[13] He did his part in delivering at least some of the Protestant vote, for (according to Carter's diarist cousin) "Mr. Winsor, his son and brother with all the protestants in Aquaforte [a predominantly Protestant community] joined Rev. J. Duffy's party and voted for Patrick Morris to their shame."[14] By 24 November, Carter had withdrawn his candidacy, and Morris was declared elected on 28 November. (The election for the entire island, however, was declared null and void by the governor because proper seals had not been affixed to the election writs. Ultimately, this was a very satisfactory result for Peter Winsor, for he himself was elected in the newly called election in 1837.)

But while individual quarrels occurred within the plebeian community and among the gentry, the two groups appear distinctly in the historical record, each sharing a group consciousness that was separate from the other's, even as their mutual economic interdependence brought their worlds in proximity. The local elite wielded considerable local economic and administrative power and maintained their separateness through carefully arranged marriages, exclusive socializing, and different forms of consumption, housing, and conduct. The plebeian community acknowledged the gentry's power, but a mask of public deference hid a more subtle culture of resistance and reprisal.

NOTES

1. This discussion borrows from E. P. Thompson, *Customs in Common* (London: Merlin Press, 1991), chap. 2; quotations are from 57, 64, and 73.

2. Newfoundland was not granted the status of a crown colony until 1825.

3. For a discussion of understandings of the nature of property in Newfoundland up to the early nineteenth century, see Trudi D. Johnson, "Matrimonial Property Law in Newfoundland to the End of the Nineteenth Century" (Ph.D. diss., Memorial University of Newfoundland, 1998).

4. Linda Little, "Plebeian Collective Action in Harbour Grace and Carbonear, 1830–40" (master's thesis, Memorial University of Newfoundland, 1984).

5. PANL, MG 31, Carter Family Papers, file 64, "A Song." A similar offering, entitled "The Grinder", appears in file 65 of the series.

6. See, for example, PANL: GN 5/4/C/1, Ferryland, box 1, 73, *James Walsh v. John Rossiter*, 7 September 1835; GN 5/4/C/1, St. Mary's, 137, *Christopher and Burk v. Kielly*, 6 October 1823; and MG 920, Robert Carter Diary, Friday, 30 August 1839, "Robert Pitts Cow found so injured near Val Keefes Garden as to render it necessary to kill her. Person unknown."

7. PANL, GN 5/2/C/3, 11–14, Grand Jury Presentment, Ferryland, 3 November 1835.

8. PANL, GN 5/2/C/3, Grand Jury Presentment, Ferryland, 6 November 1839.

9. The court ordered Kent to pay a £20 fine and sentenced him to fourteen days in jail. The sentence was remitted in supreme court. Mannion Name Files, Cape Broyle, "Patrick Crane," and "Patrick Kent," citing PANL, GN 5/2/A/1, 14, 27, and 28 November and 10 and 17 December 1817.

10. PANL, GN 2/1/A, vol. 7 (reverse end), 96–98, Petition from the merchants and principal inhabitants of Renews to Governor Montagu, 29 July 1778.

11. Mannion Name File Collection, Renews.

12. The alliance was unusual, not only because of Winsor's class and ethnicity, but also because of the very recent acrimony between him and Father Duffy. According to Robert Carter's diary, Duffy had spent the winter of 1834 at Winsor's house, but he had abused the hospitality shown him by baptizing two of Winsor's daughters into the Catholic faith the following summer. Hard feelings carried through the next spring, for, when Winsor's vessel, the *Pelter*, was leaving for the seal hunt, Duffy cursed the boat and all who would dare to sail on it—a powerful deterrent within a largely Irish Catholic district. Nonetheless, by the fall of 1836, fences had been mended and the two joined forces to elect Morris. See PANL, MG 920, Robert Carter Diary, 10 August 1834 and 24 February 1835. Winsor also identified himself with the plebeian community on at least one other occasion. In June 1836, Robert Carter noted in his diary that a public notice had been attached to Mr. Wright's (likely Thomas Wright's) fence, warning people not to sign a paper in circulation in support of Mr. Wright as stipendiary magistrate because no one in the district had sufficient abilities for the position

but merchants or those connected with them, and, as a group, they were "unfitted thereby to hear a case." The notice was dated 4 June and signed "the friend of the people. P. Winsor." PANL, MG 920, Robert Carter Diary, 5 June 1836.

13. PANL, MG 920, Robert Carter Diary, 14 November 1836.

14. PANL, MG 920, Robert Carter Diary, 1 January 1837.

APPENDIX B

Historiography, Sources, Study Area, and Naming Patterns

HISTORIOGRAPHY

This study will attempt to add some understanding of women's experiences to two broad areas of historiography: the literature on early European settlement in Newfoundland and Canada, and the history of the Irish diaspora.

EARLY EUROPEAN SETTLEMENT IN NEWFOUNDLAND AND CANADA

> Almost every family history here begins with "Two brothers came out from Ireland or England . . ."
>
> —HE, resident of Ferryland, 20 July 1999[1]

This insight came from one of my oral informants as she tried to warn of the difficulties in mining the oral tradition for information about women's contribution to early community formation on the southern Avalon. She had certainly arrived at the crux of a methodological problem, for she was not only articulating the conventional opening for, but also identifying the main protagonists in most family histories in the Irish or English Newfoundland tradition. There are, of course, some departures from the formula: in one variation, an older brother remains in the home country while the younger leaves for Newfoundland; in another, a father and his sons cross the Atlantic to seek their fortune in the fishery. But in plot and focus, the stories are similar. The family narratives tell how those men carved a living out of relentless sea and barren soil, and how they bred large families in a mysterious process that, with its seeming absence of women, must surely have equaled the miracle of the Virgin Birth.[2] The sagas continue to follow the male line: sons and grandsons are named, their lives chronicled, while daughters remain peripheral—sometimes numbered, rarely named, often ignored altogether.

While my informant was discussing the oral tradition, her comments could also have applied well to the traditional historiography on Newfoundland settlement, in which this male-centered focus resounds. Granted, this preoccupation was rooted in the nature of the main industry of Newfoundland—the cod fishery—which, until the second half of the eighteenth century, was largely migratory in aspect and carried out primarily by men, with a smattering of planters' wives and female servants. Logically linking the course of settlement with the pursuit of the fishery and the vicissitudes of its migratory and sedentary branches, earlier writings either overlooked or vastly underplayed the one ingredient essential for the stabilization of the local population: the presence of women.

Traditional historiographical offerings explained settlement as a process that occurred within the context of conflict between inhabitant fishermen and avaricious merchants from the West of England, who controlled the migratory trade and effectively pressured successive governments to prohibit settlement, or at least to discourage it actively, in order to block the development of a competitive resident fishery. Hence, these historians argued, settlement in Newfoundland followed an erratic course, with resident fishermen relegated to marginal areas, their premises hidden in tiny coves or hanging precipitously off cliff faces—out of the way of the privileged migratory fishermen and out of the sight of visiting fishing admirals and naval authorities.[3]

This theory of "retarded settlement" was roundly challenged by later writers, who argued that, although the Western Adventurers had briefly opposed settlement, many of them soon came to realize that the migratory and sedentary branches of the fishery could be complementary, and evolved into suppliers and marketers for the inhabitant fishery while maintaining their migratory interests into the eighteenth century. The home government, spurred by its desire to preserve a "nursery for seamen" through the traditional migratory ship fishery, did attempt to restrict settlement by delaying the development of governance and property ownership in Newfoundland. Ironically, however, they were forced to establish increasingly sophisticated agencies to enforce the restrictive laws they were passing and to maintain law and order between residents and visiting fishermen (Web Link). The scattered nature of fishing communities therefore reflected not a fear of discovery by officials or harassment by migratory fishermen, but rather the suitability of the sites for exploiting the inshore cod resource: proximity to fishing grounds, for example, access to water and wood, and availability of other resources, such as seals and salmon. And large-scale, year-round settlement was made possible by the development of a spring seal fishery—a complementary industry to the cod fishery in that it employed fishermen, boats, and artisans in the off-season.[4]

Scholars also began to uncover information on the substantial numbers of Irish servants who came out to the Newfoundland fishery, particularly from the mid-eighteenth century onwards, and their imprint on the demographic and cultural patterns of early Newfoundland communities.[5] John Mannion, in particular, stressed the agency of Irish immigrants to Newfoundland, many of them from artisan or farming backgrounds who exercised choice in pursuing opportunity in the Newfoundland fishery in the face of declining (but not dire) prospects in the home country.

Yet as the historiographical debates on settlement in Newfoundland evolved, the movements of men were carefully traced and analyzed while the activities of women remained out of focus. Even though the Newfoundland fishery had been primarily (although not exclusively) a male enterprise up to the middle of the eighteenth century, in Newfoundland, as elsewhere, populations and communities did not stabilize until women were present in increasing numbers. But while the historical literature spoke of the rising supremacy of the resident fishery and the increasing stability of the population in the latter eighteenth century, women's experiences were absent, their voices muted. Occasional references appeared to fishermen's marrying "local women" (a term that generally referred to women of English or Irish, not aboriginal, descent)–as if their presence needed no further explanation, as if these women had somehow sprung from the ground. Like Topsy, a character of nineteenth-century American fiction, they had apparently just "grow'd."[6] Treating them as merely a factor in a demographic equation, the literature said little or nothing of their motives for emigrating, their lived experiences, or their role in early community formation.

Outside the disciplines of history and historical geography, feminist scholars began to question women's absence from accounts of early fishing communities.[7] Their writings offered insights on women's contributions to family fisheries of the latter nineteenth and early twentieth centuries, but they were observing phenomena that were rooted in an earlier period and begged several questions: How did the sexual division of labor evolve in early Newfoundland fishing villages? What were the value of women's work and the extent of women's influence in family and community in the period of initial settlement? Did gender relations transfer relatively intact from the Old World to the New, or did immigration and settlement experiences create a new playing field for the negotiation of gender?

By the late 1980s, some necessary (if somewhat conservative) adjustments were being made to the historiography of Newfoundland in terms of women's participation in the settlement process. Historical geographer W. Gordon Handcock introduced a gender component to his extensive study of English migration and settlement patterns in northeast Newfoundland, articulating the link between the presence of women and population growth by using the numbers of female winter inhabitants in Newfoundland as an index of permanence.[8] He also noted that matrilineal bridges played a role in family perpetuation before the 1800s, but underplayed their importance in terms of settlement continuity. Working from the assumption that "a consolidated, stable population tends to have a strong patrilineal-patrilocal character,"[9] he fell back on a male-centered demographic technique of surname sieving to measure the stability of settlement, noting some matrilineal extensions, but more as interesting diversions than as evidence of earlier, women-centered continuities.

Other scholars began to add sections on women's work and status to their examinations of early Newfoundland communities. In his interdisciplinary study of the English colonization effort at Ferryland in the seventeenth century, Peter Pope found that women were important contributors to planter households in terms of housewifery, animal husbandry, and their involvement in the fishery, noting that some widows became household heads or even prominent planters in their own right—a phenomenon that he found to be more anomalous than was actually the case. In general, he concluded that these women "were powerful relative to their sisters elsewhere, in a century in which women were powerful, relative to their great-granddaughters"—apparently assuming that patriarchy would re-root itself as a matter of course on the island and a slide in women's status would ensue as permanent settlement increased in the eighteenth and early nineteenth centuries.[10]

In his examination of merchant-settler relations in Conception Bay, Sean Cadigan also provided valuable insight into women's vital role in fishing households as the fishery moved from waged labor to family production in the early nineteenth century.[11] However, he assumed an unproblematic transplanting of patriarchy from the Old World to the New, untempered by immigration and early settlement experiences.[12] Women's work rhythms bent to the dictates of male-centered agendas and male decision-making, he argued, and women's status was secondary within a patriarchal family structure that was reinforced by the formal legal system and male "discipline . . . by the fist."[13] In these three writings, there was an assumption of an inexorable "evolution" towards a patrilineal, patriarchal society in which women's status and contributions were seen as secondary, diversionary, or anomalous.

In the 1990s, important contributions in the field of legal history delved into the impact of both formal and customary legal practices on women's lives in Newfoundland.[14] Still, there are significant gaps in our understanding of how women's experiences, especially in early fishing communities, played out on the ground. And there is still a reluctance in the literature on early settlement to perceive gender in terms of a dynamic, ongoing process that did not follow a straight and uncontested "evolutionary" course towards patriarchy.[15] But was the "march of patriarchy" as unproblematic in the Newfoundland context as much of the historiography has presupposed?

The paucity of scholarship on women in early Newfoundland communities corresponds with a traditional obscuring of the female experience in the Anglophone literature[16] on early European immigration to the rest of the territory that today forms Canada.[17] Since the late 1980s, women's historians have been working towards a more balanced interpretation of immigration history that incorporates more gender-inclusive categories of analysis. Writers such as Franca Iacovetta, Varpu Lindstrom, Ruth Frager, Agnes Calliste, and Francis Swyripa have examined ethnic women and cultural maintenance and/or adaptation, domestic service, the industrial workforce, labor politics, and radical activism—studies that have added significantly to our understanding of the interrelated processes of gender, race, and class.[18] But there is a late-nineteenth- and/or twentieth-century concentration in this literature and a focus on ethnic minorities and urban experiences. The history of women in earlier migrations from the British Isles to what is today Canada has, until recently, remained largely unexplored terrain; in much of the literature, these women have remained part of an amorphous entity, *white settler society*, with little recognition of the gendered dynamics of their experiences or the ways in which dimensions of race, ethnicity, and class also affected their lives.[19]

The Anglophone literature on colonial women in Canada has lagged behind its American counterpart.[20] Still, some promising contributions have been made to our understanding of women's lives in the pre-confederation period: for example, Beth Light and Alison Prentice's thematic collection of primary documents on women in British North America up to 1867;[21] Constance Backhouse's examination of women's encounters with the justice system in the nineteenth century;[22] Cecilia Morgan's discussion of the complex interplay between understandings of gender and public discourses in Upper Canada;[23] Elizabeth Errington's study of the essential nature of women's work in preserving Upper Canadian households;[24] Jennifer Henderson's examination of the writings of nineteenth-century Anglo-Protestant women within the context of moral regulation and the racial discourse of white settler culture;[25] and Margaret Conrad's mining of the diaries of Maritime women, who made life choices on the basis of gendered expectations as daughters, wives, and mothers.[26]

Many of these writings, however, demonstrate a pervasive difficulty in women's history—the problem of uncovering the lives of women from marginalized groups. Evidence from the white colonial elite—statutes, newspapers, diaries, correspondence, prescriptive writings—dominates the historical record for the period of early settlement. We can see how hegemonic feminine ideals were constructed and have some insight into their impact on elite women, but we have much more limited access to the meanings they created for women of aboriginal societies, ethnic minorities, and working-class or plebeian cultures. We can read interpretations of the lives of women on the periphery, but they have been mediated by middle-class editors, clergymen, and officials, and, occasionally, gentry women.

But although the presence of plebeian women in white settler society is quite muted in the written records, some recent historians have managed to find traces of their lives. The third volume of the Planter Studies Series published by Acadiensis contains some insightful contributions on women in Nova Scotian communities settled by New England planters in the latter part of the eighteenth century, most particularly in the areas of testamentary practices, exchange economies, and domestic violence.[27] Another Maritime collection, *Separate Spheres*, provides a discussion of women's participation in the Escheat Movement in Prince Edward Island in the 1830s and in petitioning in New Brunswick in the 1840s and 1850s.[28] A promising body of work on encounters between popular-class women and the formal legal system in eighteenth- and nineteenth-century Montreal has been developing since the 1990s.[29] Women's experiences during the push west in the late nineteenth century have also received some attention from recent writers such as Adele Perry and Sarah Brooks Sundberg.[30] However, there is still no comprehensive body of Anglophone literature on colonial women in Canada, and plebeian women in particular are barely visible. This study is merely one small drop in a slowly filling well.

THE IRISH DIASPORA IN NORTH AMERICA

The literature on Irish migrations to North America has traditionally been preoccupied with famine and post-famine migrations, resonating with motifs of disruption and alienation.[31] This concentration has had a profound impact on popular understandings of the diaspora on both sides of the Atlantic. There is a timeless sorrow, a lingering sense of mourning and loss, that clings to our perceptions of Irish movements to the New World. The very phrase *Irish emigration* evokes images of poverty and desperation—of suffering masses huddled in the dank holds of coffin ships, fleeing hunger, disease, and economic devastation in the home country. Such impressions emanate from one relatively brief but intensely poignant moment in the history of Irish emigration: the Great Famine and its immediate aftermath. But because of the magnitude of this mid-nineteenth-century trauma, such images linger in the popular consciousness as the essence of the Irish diaspora through time.

These shades and specters haunted the traditional historiography on Irish emigrations. Up to the mid-1980s, the *Great Hunger* often cast its pall over discussions of other movements of Irish people: vestiges lingered in explanations of later relocations; its shadow also stretched back in time as historians used earlier migrations to set the stage for the famine exodus without considering that previous movements may have had dynamics of their own. When movements in the late eighteenth and early nineteenth centuries were mentioned at all, they were usually presented as a prologue to the great Irish emigration drama of the mid-nineteenth century, and images of exile and exclusion pervaded the texts.

This is particularly true of the works of historians of the American Irish, from William Forbes Adams to Kerby Miller, whose writings, until the past decade or so, have tended to dominate the literature on Irish immigration to North America.[32] The perspectives they provide of the ghettoization of impoverished and unskilled Irish immigrants in urban landscapes do not supply useful models for understanding the experiences of Irish immigrants on the southern Avalon or in rural areas in general. Indeed, this portrayal of the Irish as predominantly disadvantaged urban dwellers has been roundly challenged by writers such as Donald Akenson, David Doyle, and Cecil Houston and William Smyth, who have effectively demonstrated that most of the Irish in North America ultimately fanned out into rural areas and were employed in primary industries—particularly farming, and, to a lesser extent, fishing or lumbering—with a smaller but still significant number entering skilled trades and professions. Those who lived in cities were not more numerous, they have argued, but merely more noticeable as minorities; and for many who first entered larger ports, life in the city was a temporary existence, the first stage of a series of moves that brought them eventually to the rural sector. This was especially true of pre-famine immigrants: the processes of urbanization, ghettoization, and proletarianization were a later phenomenon in the United States, and that model does not apply at all to Canadian experiences.[33]

In addition to his urban bias, Miller has also come under fire for his representation of Irish Catholics as a group handicapped by religious and cultural traditions in adapting to their new environments—casualties of modernization who clung to traditional goals and lifestyles and sought self-sufficiency rather than upward mobility. The Irish Protestant immigrant, by contrast, he presents as rational and responsive to changing conditions—a voluntary immigrant, able to embrace ambition and the individualistic and acquisitive values of entrepreneurship. Miller explains the phenomenon in terms of "a distinctive Irish Catholic world view," emanating from Gaelic culture and the Catholic religion, which devalued individual ambition and action, making Catholics less adaptable than Protestants as a group to increasing modernization and commercialization in Ireland and, ultimately, to immigrant experiences in the New World.[34] His treatment of the Irish Protestant as a superior immigrant type to the Irish Catholic has been challenged by several scholars who have found the contrast between the two groups largely overdrawn, especially if one moves beyond initial urban experiences and looks at adaptation over time.[35] This examination of the southern Avalon Irish will reinforce these findings, portraying a largely Catholic migrant group as responsive to opportunity and often upwardly mobile in their new environment.

Here, it will follow a major paradigm shift in the historiography since the late 1980s—a movement away from discourses of exile and alienation toward a view of Irish emigration as a rational, adaptive strategy employed in response to changing social and economic conditions. Increasingly, writers have presented Irish emigrants as informed individuals who evaluated information and made conscious choices to emigrate from a range of available alternatives—weighing deteriorating conditions in the old country against opportunity in the new and responding to the rises and downturns in employment opportunities in destination areas, based on large-scale, sensitive feedback networks between host economy and home country.[36] From this perspective, most pre-famine Irish migration experiences meshed with those of other European nations, where migration became a common adaptive strategy in the modern era as Europeans moved in significant numbers, over short, middle, and long distances, on both temporary and permanent bases, in response to socio-economic factors in their home communities as well as to the demands of an increasingly international economy.[37] Irish society was not exceptional, then, in adopting internal and external migration as a "habit of life" by the eighteenth century.[38]

A warning bell must be sounded, however, about the economic reductionism that often underscores these more recent interpretations of Irish emigration. As Jim Mac Laughlin observes, they tend to portray emigration purely as a "transfer mechanism," whereby emigrants responded to the logic of labor surplus at home and labor demand in overseas markets while muting the negative aspects of the experience—the fragmentation of families and home communities, the re-mapping of social and political terrains. This type of interpretation is an over-correction of the traditional literature, he argues, and overly sanitizes the phenomenon of emigration.[39]

Furthermore, there has been a continuing reluctance among historians of Irish emigration—particularly quantitative historians, who rose to prominence in the latter part of the twentieth century—to delve too deeply into pre-famine experiences because of the lack of "hard" evidence on population sizes and emigration figures for the period. Even writings that draw more heavily from qualitative sources, or use a combined methodology, rarely reach back further than the 1840s, particularly works dealing with movements beyond the British Isles.[40] One important exception is a recent annotated collection of emigrant letters by Miller, Schrier, Boling, and Doyle, which covers the period up to 1815; due to the nature and availability of sources, however, the collection focuses predominantly on Scots-Irish emigrants and overwhelmingly on American experiences.[41] Other recent efforts continue to tend towards later movements. For example, one of the most ambitious studies of Irish migration to date—an interdisciplinary compilation of six volumes edited by Patrick O'Sullivan—still focuses primarily on the period from the mid-nineteenth century onwards.[42] A more recent collection edited by Andy Bielenberg covers a broader time frame, but the leaning towards later migrations and later source materials is still apparent, while discussions of earlier emigrant groups are often preliminary and tentative.[43] There is thus still a need for Irish migration studies that emphasize earlier movements and emigrant agency without underplaying the human costs or reducing the phenomenon to a purely economic response mechanism.

John Mannion's work on the Irish in Newfoundland follows more recent trends in the literature, emphasizing the influx of Irish servants into the Newfoundland fishery as an adaptive response to declining opportunities in the homeland. His writings, however, illustrate a further limitation of the historiography until recent years: a tendency to homogenize Irish emigration in terms of male experiences. As late as 1993, Akenson aptly noted that women in the Irish diaspora were still "the Great Unknown."[44]

The low visibility of Irish women in emigration studies reflected a deficiency in the broader corpus of Irish historical writings until the past ten to fifteen years. Irish women's history in general had lagged behind its British and North American counterparts, although it has certainly come out of its pioneering stages with a growing body of research of increasing analytical rigor from the 1990s to present day. Still, a search for the female emigrant in much of the secondary literature becomes a frustrating hunt for random pieces of a puzzle that is missing essential interlocking parts. Two decades ago, L. A. Clarkson claimed that Kenneth Connell's mid-century work on rising fertility rates had finally brought Irish women into focus in the emigration saga.[45] However, Clarkson's optimism was premature. Once the Irish woman's role as a prodigious breeder of children had been established, she was left to linger on the periphery of migration experiences until recent years.

The search for Irish women emigrants is doubly confounded by a lack of attention to the pre-famine period.[46] This trend has already been observed in the general historiography, but it is also true of the writings that deal specifically with Irish female emigration. There are several community or regional histories and family chronicles that span several centuries, but women's lives are generally subsumed in the discussions under the experiences of men or the larger family unit.[47] Some other writings on women emigrants deal briefly with the pre-famine period, but they are heavily weighted towards the 1840s and later, and often deal with dysfunctional experiences in urban settings that were not shared by the Irish women who emigrated to rural areas such as the southern Avalon.[48] Indeed, while the literature about Irish women emigrants has grown in the 1990s, most offerings have examined movements from the mid-nineteenth century and beyond, when the Great Famine had established a new set of parameters for Irish emigration. This concentration is understandable, for the demographic and economic changes of the famine years and their aftermath had a particular impact on women and wrought a profound change in their status in Ireland.[49] But few of these writings provide insight into the motivations and experiences of earlier women emigrants.

In looking for the Irish woman emigrant of the late eighteenth and early nineteenth century, we find ourselves staring down a historiographical funnel. As we shift our perspective from overseas Irish emigration in general to focus on Irish female emigration experiences in particular, and finally hone in on earlier movements, our viewing screen becomes increasingly constricted. The story of the Irish women who emigrated to North America before the 1840s can only be patched together from pieces and fragments of evidence of an emigration phenomenon that is, in itself, fragmentary in the literature.

Much of the information on women emigrants in this earlier period is statistical: a relentless array of sex ratios, average ages, marital categories, fertility rates, and occupational profiles, drawn from aggregate data for a broad range of destination areas and extended time periods. These have revealed the trend that Irish women, particularly single Irish women, became increasingly prominent in overseas movements through the first half of the nineteenth century, much more so than women of other migrant groups from Western countries.[50] Fitzpatrick and Miller explain the predominance of single Irish women in the stream to North America as a rational response to the high demand for domestic servants in destination areas (an observation that is, itself, skewed towards the urban American experience by the aggregate data).[51] After parading out some statistical data on women, however, many of these writers allow the female emigrant of the pre-famine period to be eclipsed once again by male experiences.

Perhaps one of the most well-known proponents of quantitative over qualitative approaches in studying Irish migration is Donald Akenson, who has used aggregate data to provide a "yardstick"—based on average sex ratios and age, religious, and occupational profiles—against which Irish migrations to various parts of the English-speaking world can be measured. For the late nineteenth and early twentieth centuries, he also provides a breakdown of women emigrant "types" based on marital status and number of children. Again, however, his indices are based on data from the post-famine period to Partition. The pre-famine period remains veiled in mystery, he claims, although he does venture some aggregate findings and a periodization of women's migration from 1815 onwards.[52]

Akenson is trying to provide a tool to gauge the typicality of specific movements against a broad geographical and temporal canvas. Yet the problem in presenting the average as typical is that it overlooks the possibility that this statistical measurement may not reflect the actual experience of many, or even most, of the emigrants involved. In his effort to provide a template for the Irish diaspora worldwide, Akenson tends to blur the nuanced edges of specific migrations, seeming to imply that those experiences that do not fit the mold are irrelevant, or so anomalous as to be unworthy of historical examination other than as a curiosity. More troubling, his analysis leaves us with a series of unrelated, unexplained, and non-contextualized statements that provide little insight into migration experiences as they were actually lived by the people involved.[53]

Akenson's writings are representative of an increasing focus in the Irish historiography on quantitative analysis in the latter decades of the twentieth century, a shift which has led some critics to bemoan the predominance of cliometricians in the field. Nonetheless, these approaches have been quite useful in banishing stereotypes and blanket assumptions, and other historians have often been pleased to cite their findings (as I have done above), secretly relieved that someone else has performed the task of crunching the numbers. But without context and anecdotal vitality, such analyses remain clinical and bleak; without interpretation, they are unsatisfying. They demonstrate little understanding of emigration as a movement of people, not just economic or demographic variables. And they provide little insight into the multi-layered dynamics of emigration: how gender, ethnicity, and class affected emigration experiences, or how emigration, in turn, affected the negotiation of gender, ethnicity, and class in the New World.

In this study, I use a blending of qualitative and quantitative evidence, which I hope will provide a more comprehensive understanding of women's experiences as they left their Irish homeland and settled on the southern Avalon.

SOURCES

Several sources have enabled me to create a database from which I have extrapolated some basic quantitative information about Irish Newfoundland women: source areas in Ireland, intermarriage and assimilation, the growth of permanent population, the transition to the family production unit in the fishery, and the frequency of women's involvement in court proceedings, petitioning, and inheritance practices. Most helpful in this regard have been the following:

- a privately held, extensive collection of name files on Irish immigrants to Newfoundland, compiled by geographer John Mannion and his wife Maura from numerous primary sources in various repositories throughout the city of St. John's
- governors' annual returns on the fisheries and inhabitants of Newfoundland, in the Colonial Office [CO] 194 Series, of which microfilm copies are available at the Provincial Archives of Newfoundland and Labrador (PANL), St. John's, and the Centre for Newfoundland Studies (CNS) at Memorial University
- a nominal census for Ferryland district for 1799–1800 commissioned by Governor Charles M. Pole (the Pole Papers), housed at the PANL
- the court records of the southern districts of Ferryland and Trepassey–St. Mary's held at the PANL and the Provincial Reference Library (PRL), St. John's
- the Registry of Wills held at the PANL, which covers the period from 1824 onward
- the Mildred Howard Collection, an assemblage of vital statistics from early Newfoundland newspapers
- Newfoundland parish registers held at the PANL and the offices of the Newfoundland and Labrador Genealogical Society (NLGS)
- the Ferryland Museum Database (FMDB), a fledgling genealogical database (in progress) at the community museum in Ferryland

However, the collection and presentation of quantitative information has presented some difficulties, and several limitations must be noted. The problems with migration data in Ireland, for example, are echoed and magnified in the Newfoundland context (see Chapter 3). In addition, parish registers for the study area and period (see the bibliography for a complete listing) are not at all comprehensive. They were introduced in particular parishes at different times, with the earliest Catholic records appearing in the 1830s and the earliest Anglican records in the 1820s. Even after introduction, they were piecemeal—with births, marriages, and deaths covering different time spans even within specific parishes. And not all have survived. Nonetheless, a comforting number of earlier vital statistics for the southern Avalon appear in the Mannion Name File Collection—some from various sources in the late eighteenth century and a substantial number from the records for what is now the Basilica parish (Catholic), St. John's, from 1793 onward—and this material has helped to plug holes in my database.

The court records for the southern Avalon also require qualification. First, records for the area are available only from 1773 onward; any references to earlier cases appear only sporadically in governors' correspondence. Second, the court records are themselves incomplete. There are various temporal gaps, and while a system evolved whereby matters were entered under several heads—such as causes, writs, minutes, and judgments—rarely are the full set of records for any given case available (either they have not survived or they were never fully recorded in the first place); thus, one might find the writ and minutes of an action, for example, but not the final judgment, or the judgment may be given without particulars of the case. The minutes themselves are not verbatim court transcripts but summary descriptions (with occasional quotations from the parties involved), and the degree of their thoroughness depended on the ability, energy, and interest of the court clerk on any given day (surprisingly, some of the most detailed minutes were provided for hearings in the eighteenth century). Third, as noted below in the description of the study area, the cases examined here relate almost exclusively to the districts of Ferryland and Trepassey–St. Mary's, with only sporadic items from the area between Bay Bulls and Toad's Cove (now Tors Cove).

Still, the court records provide a broad range of cases to work with, and my database includes more than 500 entries on civil and criminal cases and estate matters involving women in the area. In gauging the significance of the number of cases found, the reader should bear in mind not only the limitations already described but also the fact that the number of adult women in the population of the area for which records have been examined thoroughly was quite small until the last couple of decades of the study period. Only by the 1830s did it exceed 400, as the following table indicates:

Furthermore, the 1857 figure is inflated by a change in the census age categories from 14^+ to 10^+; thus, the above table includes as "adults" for that year an additional segment of the population (children from the ages of eleven to thirteen), and one that was not usually before the courts.

Anecdotal evidence in general is more readily available—although sometimes the absence of women in the sources is as eloquent as their presence. I have tapped the oral tradition along the southern Avalon for collective historical memories of women's migration and settlement experiences. This use of

Year	Adult Women
1775	63
1785	150
1795	310
1805	287
1815	363
1825	307
1836	847
1845	994
1857	1,562

oral history is described in greater detail at the end of Chapter 1. Again, the court records for the area provide a rich lode of qualitative evidence on Irish Newfoundland women. Less inclusive but still useful in terms of discerning official attitudes toward the study group is government correspondence for the period. The CO 194 Series encompasses the correspondence of various governors stationed at Newfoundland with the Colonial Office. The PANL also contains the papers of specific governors of the period—John Duckworth and Thomas Cochrane—as well as copies of local incoming and outgoing correspondence of the governor's office as recorded by the local colonial secretary. Catholic clergy in Newfoundland frequently commented on the state of religion and social conditions they found on the island, with occasional references to women included. In this regard, the collection of letters of early bishops and missionaries compiled and edited by Cyril Byrne has been very useful,[54] as have the papers of Bishops O Donel, Lambert, Scallon, and Fleming and a notebook penned by Dean Cleary, parish priest of Witless Bay, all housed at the Roman Catholic Archdiocese Archives, St. John's [RCAASJ]. The collection of papers of the Society for the Propagation of the Gospel in Foreign Parts [SPG], available on microfilm at the PANL, helped in tracing the assimilation of the English Protestant population in the study area into the Irish Catholic ethnoreligious group. In addition, the published writings of several nineteenth-century clergymen on the island—such as Michael Howley, Lewis Anspach, and Charles Pedley—lent some insights to the perception of the Irish at Newfoundland.[55] Early Newfoundland newspapers housed at the CNS and PANL provided information about the horrors of the passenger trade from Ireland to Newfoundland, a perspective that was balanced by the more mundane descriptions of New Ross merchant Edward Kough in his letterbook, housed at the Maritime History Archives (MHA), Memorial University, and by letters written to the mother convent in Ireland by the first Presentation sisters to come out to Newfoundland, available at the Presentation Convent Archives (PCA) at the Mother House, Cathedral Square, St. John's. A number of other manuscript collections were mined for information on women: the papers of merchant firms Alan Goodridge and Sons (operating out of Renews; surviving ledgers for 1839–41 housed at the PANL and MHA) and Saunders and Sweetman (operating out of Placentia, with dealers in St. Mary's Bay and Trepassey; papers available at the PANL) were helpful in examining women's participation in the exchange economy of the area; and the Carter Family Papers, the Carter-Benger-Nason Papers (including letters written by Harriet Carter at Ferryland to her relatives in England), and the Mary Ann Simms Scrapbook (all available at the PANL) as well as the diary of nineteenth-century magistrate Robert Carter (housed at the PANL and the Ferryland Museum, with a partial typescript version at the MHA) revealed the gradual incursion of middle-class feminine ideals on elite women living in the study area and the sharpening contrast between the lives of these women and those of the Irish plebeian community.

In quoting various primary documents, I have tried to preserve their period ambience without imposing modern-day standards of spelling or grammar. In quotations, original (and sometimes conflicting) spellings, abbreviations, punctuation, and capitalization are maintained as much as possible and without the heavy-handed use of "[*sic*]." Very occasionally, I have filled in missing letters in square brackets or provided minimal punctuation for the sake of clarity. But for the most part, I have tried not to intrude in the style and cadence of the original.

One final note on sources from the PANL must be made. The PANL has recently transferred its records to a new location and, in the process, has reorganized some of its holdings. As a result, box and file numbers cited in this study, which were those that existed at the time of my research, may vary from new finding aids. The actual names and numbers of the main collections, however, remain the same.

STUDY AREA

The parameters of the study area require some qualification. Although I have defined the *southern Avalon* as extending along the coastline from Bay Bulls on the Southern Shore to Dog Point in St. Mary's Bay, the reader should be advised that the boundaries of the study area sometimes contract with the accessibility or organizational peculiarities of the sources.

All anecdotal information for the entire area was considered for inclusion in this discussion. Much of the quantitative data—including material on source areas, population growth, intermarriage and assimilation, and the transition to the family production unit—also relate to the entire study area. However, it became necessary to rein in the scope of research in relation to two major sources for my investigation: the court records and the oral tradition. By an organizational quirk of the court system, the portion of the study area from Bay Bulls to Toad's Cove was included within the jurisdiction of the central district of St. John's (although it was, more logically, included in Ferryland district in the electoral divisions that accompanied self-government in the 1830s). The collection of records for the central district court is massive, including as it does the numerous cases and estate matters emanating from the colony's capital. Most of the material is not indexed, and thus wading through it to find sporadic cases from Bay Bulls to Toad's Cove would have been far too time-consuming for the anticipated return and a task not manageable within the scope of the current research. Therefore, only those cases mentioned in governors' correspondence or in the Mannion Name File Collection for that section of the shore have been included in the database for this study (when Mannion provided specific references, the original court records were also checked). The exigencies of time and accessibility also dictated that the oral history component of this project be restricted. I therefore chose to carry out interviews in the same area as that covered by the court records—opting for depth of research rather than breadth (a decision that was reinforced by my stronger contacts on that part of the shore). This makes the coverage of the area from Brigus South to St. Mary's more comprehensive than that of the segment closer to St. John's. I am confident, however, that extended research on the Bay Bulls–Toad's Cove section would reveal more similarities than differences in the experiences of Irish Newfoundland women within the overall study area.

NAMING PATTERNS

Throughout this study, I have followed a pattern of using the first names of southern Avalon women whenever possible. I did this for the pragmatic reason of making women's identities stand out from the jumble of surnames so common in discussions of events and developments involving multiple parties. But I also wanted to respect and celebrate traditional practices of naming women on the southern Avalon—patterns that maintained a strong sense of women's pre-marital identity and individuality (see Chapter 5).

NOTES

1. HE, interview by author, Ferryland, 20 July 1999.

2. The Christian belief that Jesus Christ was miraculously conceived in the womb of his mother, Mary, through the power of the Holy Spirit, without sexual intercourse with a man.

3. See: John Reeves, in *History of the Government of the Island of Newfoundland* (London: 1793; reprint, Yorkshire: S. R. Publishers, 1967); Daniel W. Prowse, *A History of Newfoundland from the English, Colonial and Foreign Records* (London: Macmillan, 1895; reprint, Belleville, ON: Mika Studio, 1972); A. H. McLintock, *The Establishment of Constitutional Government in Newfoundland, 1783–1832* (London: Longmans, Green, 1941); and Harold A. Innis, *The Cod Fisheries: The Study of an International Economy*, rev. ed. (Toronto: University of Toronto Press, 1954).

4. See: Keith Matthews, "A History of the West of England–Newfoundland Fishery" (D.Phil. diss., Oxford University, 1968); C. Grant Head, *Eighteenth Century Newfoundland* (Toronto: McClelland and Stewart, in association with the Institute of Canadian Studies, Carleton University, 1976); Shannon Ryan, "Fishery to Colony: A Newfoundland Watershed, 1793–1815," *Acadiensis* 12:2 (Spring 1983): 34–52.

5. See: Matthews, "West of England–Newfoundland Fishery" and *Lectures on the History of Newfoundland, 1500–1830* (St. John's: Breakwater Books, 1988); Thomas F. Nemec, "The Irish Emigration to Newfoundland," *Newfoundland Quarterly* 69:1 (1972): 15–24; Nemec, "Trepassey, 1505–1840 A.D.: The Emergence of an Anglo-Irish Newfoundland Outport," *Newfoundland Quarterly* 69:4 (1973): 17–28; Nemec, "Irish Settlement in Newfoundland," in *Encyclopedia of Newfoundland and Labrador*, ed. Joseph R. Smallwood, vol. 3 (St. John's: Harry Cuff Publishers, 1991), 71-7; Nemec, "Trepassey, 1840–1900: An Ethnohistorical Reconstruction of an Anglo-Irish Outport Society," in *Through a Mirror Dimly: Essays on Newfoundland Society and Culture*, ed. Maura Hanrahan (St. John's: Breakwater, 1993), 145–62; John Mannion, "Irish Imprints on the Landscape of Eastern Canada in the Nineteenth Century: A Study in Cultural Transfer and Adaptation" (Ph.D. diss., University of Toronto, 1971); Mannion, *Irish Settlements in Eastern Canada: A Study of Cultural Transfer and Adaptation* (Toronto: University of Toronto Press, 1974); Mannion, "The Impact of Newfoundland on Waterford and its Hinterland in the Eighteenth Century" (paper presented at the Annual Conference of Irish Geographers, University College, Galway, 22 April 1977); Mannion, "Introduction," in *The Peopling of Newfoundland: Essays in Historical Geography*, ed. John J. Mannion, Social and Economic Papers, no. 8 (St. John's: Institute of Social and Economic Research [ISER], Memorial University of Newfoundland, 1977), 1–13; Mannion, "Patrick Morris and Newfoundland Irish Immigration," in *Talamh An Eisc: Canadian and Irish Essays*, ed. Cyril J. Byrne and Margaret Harry (Halifax: Nimbus Publishing, 1986), 180–202; Mannion, "Migration and Upward Mobility: The Meagher Family in Ireland and Newfoundland, 1780–1830," *Irish Economic and Social History* 15 (1988): 54–70; Mannion, "Tracing the

Irish: A Geographical Guide," *The Newfoundland Ancestor* 9:1 (Spring 1993): 4–18; and John Mannion and Fidelma Maddock, "Old World Antecedents, New World Applications: Inistioge Immigrants in Newfoundland," in *Kilkenny: History and Society–Interdisciplinary Essays on the History of an Irish County*, ed. William Nolan and Kevin Whelan (Dublin: Geography Publications, 1990), 345–404.

6. Topsy is a young female slave in Harriet Beecher Stowe's novel *Uncle Tom's Cabin*. When quizzed about her parentage and where she has come from, Topsy has no knowledge of her background, but ventures an opinion nonetheless: "I spect I grow'd. Don't think nobody never made me." See Joan D. Hedrick, *The Oxford Harriet Beecher Stowe Reader* (New York: Oxford University Press, 1999), 256.

7. Ellen Antler, "Women's Work in Newfoundland Fishing Families," *Atlantis* 2:2 (1977): 106–13; Hilda Chaulk Murray, *More Than Fifty Percent: Women's Life in a Newfoundland Outport, 1900–1950* (St. John's: Breakwater Books, 1979); and Marilyn Porter, "She was Skipper of the Shore Crew: Notes on the History of the Sexual Division of Labour in Newfoundland," *Labour/Le Travail* 15 (Spring 1985): 104–25.

8. Using the formula 2F+C (where F=the number of adult women in the over-wintering population, multiplied by 2 to allow for a male partner, and C=the number of children), Handcock found significant population growth through the late eighteenth and early nineteenth centuries as the numbers of women in the population increased, although the significance of this phenomenon was muted in the remainder of his discussion. See W. Gordon Handcock, *Soe longe as there comes noe women: Origins of English Settlement in Newfoundland* (St. John's: Breakwater Books, 1989).

9. Handcock, *Soe longe*, 140–41.

10. Peter Pope combined traditional historical sources with archeological evidence in his innovative study "The South Avalon Planters, 1630–1700" (Ph.D. diss., Memorial University of Newfoundland, 1992); quotation from 307. His observation applies more to elite women than plebeian women, although he does not differentiate between them here; even so, the process was not "inevitable" for either group of women.

11. Sean Cadigan, *Hope and Deception in Conception Bay: Merchant-Settler Relations in Newfoundland, 1785–1855* (Toronto: University of Toronto Press, 1995).

12. Summarizing Handcock's findings in relation to English settlement at Newfoundland, Cadigan concluded: "A process of transatlantic family migration in fact established the patriarchal family structure of West Country English society in Newfoundland in the early modern period." See Cadigan, *Hope and Deception*, 65.

13. Cadigan, *Hope and Deception*, 64–82; quotation from 82. Such conclusions regarding family power relations do not emerge from the southern Avalon data. However, Cadigan's study area contained a different ethnic mix of English and Irish from mine, and there was greater economic diversification in Conception Bay, with the development of the North Shore, Labrador, and seal fisheries, and various related trades. It is possible that these contrasting circumstances resulted in different gender relations within fishing households in the two areas—a possibility that I am exploring in my current research.

14. See: Linda Cullum and Maeve Baird, "'A Woman's Lot': Women and Law in Newfoundland from Early Settlement to the Twentieth Century," in *Pursuing Equal-*

ity: Historical Perspectives on Women in Newfoundland and Labrador, ed. Linda Kealey, Social and Economic Papers no. 20 (St. John's: ISER, 1993), 66–162; and Trudi D. Johnson, "Matrimonial Property Law in Newfoundland to the End of the Nineteenth Century" (Ph.D. diss., Memorial University of Newfoundland, 1998).

15. This lack is discussed in "Editors' Note: Women, the Migratory Fishery and Settlement," in *Their Lives and Times: Women in Newfoundland and Labrador: A Collage*, ed. Carmelita McGrath, Barbara Neis, and Marilyn Porter (St. John's: Killick Press, 1995), 22–26.

16. I confess my unfamiliarity with the Francophone literature on this period.

17. The confederation of Canada took place in 1867, when Canada West (Ontario), Canada East (Quebec), Nova Scotia, and New Brunswick tentatively joined forces (with little in common, some have argued, but debt and the fear of American expansionism). By 1905, all remaining provinces and territories had been brought into the union with the exception of Newfoundland, which entered the confederation in 1949.

18. See, for example, Franca Iacovetta, "Making New Canadians: Social Workers, Women and the Reshaping of Immigrant Families," in *Gender Conflicts: New Essays in Women's History*, ed. Franca Iacovetta and Mariana Valverde (Toronto: University of Toronto Press, 1992), 261–303; Varpu Lindstrom, *Defiant Sisters: A Social History of Finnish Immigrant Women in Canada*, 2nd ed. (Toronto: Multicultural History Society of Ontario, 1992); Ruth A. Frager, *Sweatshop Strife: Class, Ethnicity, and Gender in the Jewish Labour Movement in Toronto, 1900–1939* (Toronto: University of Toronto Press, 1992); Agnes Callista, "Canada's Immigration Policy and Domestics from the Caribbean: The Second Domestic Scheme," in *Race, Class, Gender: Bonds and Barriers*, ed. Jesse Vorst, et al. (Toronto: Between the Lines, in cooperation with the Society for Socialist Studies, 1989), 133–65; Calliste, "Race, Gender and Canadian Immigration Policy: Blacks from the Caribbean, 1900–1932," in *Gender and History in Canada*, ed. Joy Parr and Mark Rosenfeld (Toronto: Copp Clark, 1996), 70–87; and Francis Swyripa, *Wedded to the Cause: Ukrainian-Canadian Women and Ethnic Identity, 1891–1991* (Toronto: University of Toronto Press, 1993).

19. One early exception was Sylvia Van Kirk's examination of the impact of the arrival of white women on fur trade society: the increasing denigration of marriages *a la façon du pays* and social stratification of the community, as trading company, church, and white women asserted the cultural "superiority" of wives of European descent over aboriginal wives who had contributed so effectively—through their experience, their work, and their contacts—to the fur trade. See Van Kirk, "The Impact of White Women on Fur Trade Society," in *The Neglected Majority: Essays in Canadian Women's History, Volume 2*, ed. Alison Prentice and Susan Mann Trofimenkoff (Toronto: McClelland and Stewart, 1985), 27–48; first published as "Women and the Fur Trade," *The Beaver* (Winter 1972): 4–21.

20. The American literature is discussed extensively in my doctoral thesis, "The Slender Thread: Irish Women on the Southern Avalon" (Ph.D. diss., Memorial University of Newfoundland, 2001).

21. Beth Light and Alison Prentice, eds., *Pioneer and Gentlewomen of British North America 1713–1867*, Documents in Canadian Women's History, vol. 1 (Toronto: New Hogtown Press, 1980).

22. Constance Backhouse, *Petticoats and Prejudice: Women and Law in Nineteenth-Century Canada* (Toronto: Osgoode Society, 1991).

23. Cecilia Morgan: *Public Men and Virtuous Women: The Gendered Languages of Religion and Politics in Upper Canada, 1791–1850* (Toronto: University of Toronto Press, 1996); and "'When Bad Men Conspire, Good Men Must Unite!': Gender and Political Discourses in Upper Canada, 1820s-1830s," in *Gendered Pasts: Historical Essays in Femininity and Masculinity in Canada*, ed. Kathryn McPherson, Cecilia Morgan, and Nancy M. Forestell (Oxford: Oxford University Press, 1999), 12–28.

24. Elizabeth Jane Errington, *Wives and Mothers, Schoolmistresses and Scullery Maids: Working Women in Upper Canada, 1790–1840* (Montreal: McGill-Queen's University Press, 1995).

25. Jennifer Henderson, *Settler Feminism and Race Making in Canada* (Toronto: University of Toronto Press, 2003).

26. See Margaret Conrad: "Recording Angels: The Private Chronicles of Women from the Maritime Provinces of Canada, 1750–1950," in *The Neglected Majority: Essays in Canadian Women's History*, ed. Susan Mann Trofimenkoff and Alison Prentice (Toronto: McClelland and Stewart, 1977), 41–60; *Recording Angels: The Private Chronicles of Women from the Maritime Provinces of Canada, 1750–1950* (Ottawa: Canadian Research Institute for the Advancement of Women, 1982); and "'Sundays Always Make Me Think of Home': Time and Place in Canadian Women's History," in *Rethinking Canada: The Promise of Women's History*, ed. Veronica Strong-Boag and Anita Clair Fellman (Toronto: Copp Clark Pitman, 1986), 67–95. See also Conrad's collaborative effort with Toni Laidlow and Donna Smyth, *No Place Like Home: Diaries and Letters of Nova Scotia Women, 1771–1938* (Halifax: Formac Publishing, 1988).

27. See the following offerings in Margaret Conrad, ed., *Intimate Relations: Family and Community in Planter Nova Scotia, 1759–1800*, Planter Studies Series, no. 3 (Fredericton: Acadiensis, 1995): Kenneth Paulson, "Land, Family, and Inheritance in Lunenburg Township, Nova Scotia: 1760–1800," 110–21; Elizabeth Mancke, "At the Counter of the General Store: Women and the Economy in Eighteenth-Century Horton, Nova Scotia," 167–81; and Judith A. Norton, "The Dark Side of Planter Life: Reported Cases of Domestic Violence," 182–89.

28. Rusty Bittermann, "Women and the Escheat Movement: The Politics of Everyday Life on Prince Edward Island," and Gail G. Campbell, "Disenfranchised but not Quiescent: Women Petitioners in New Brunswick in the Mid-19th Century," in *Separate Spheres: Women's Worlds in the 19th-Century Maritimes*, ed. Janet Guildford and Suzanne Morton (Fredericton: Acadiensis Press, 1994), 23–38 and 39–66, respectively.

29. See, for example: Donald Fyson, "Criminal Justice, Civil Society, and the Local State: The Justices of the Peace in the District of Montreal, 1764–1830" (Ph.D. diss., Université de Montréal, 1995); Kathryn Harvey, "Amazons and Victims: Resist-

ing Wife-Abuse in Working-class Montreal, 1869–1879," *Journal of the Canadian Historical Association* 2 (1991): 131–48; Mary Ann Poutanen, "Reflections of Montreal Prostitution in the Records of the Lower Courts, 1810–1842," in *Class, Gender and the Law in Eighteenth- and Nineteenth-Century Quebec: Sources and Perspectives*, ed. Donald Fyson, Colin Coates, and Kathryn Harvey (Montreal: Montreal History Group, 1993), 99–125; and Poutanen, "The Homeless, the Whore, the Drunkard, and the Disorderly: Contours of Female Vagrancy in the Montreal Courts, 1810–1842," in *Gendered Pasts*, ed. McPherson et al., 29–47.

30. Adele Perry has studied assisted immigration of white women to British Columbia as an effort to "civilize" the white male homosocial culture of the region and discourage mixed-race marriages; the combined impact of a skewed gender ratio and colonial race politics resulted in enhanced heterosocial contact but restricted socio-economic opportunity for these women. See Perry, "'Oh I'm Just Sick of the Faces of Men': Gender Imbalance, Race, Sexuality, and Sociability in Nineteenth-Century British Columbia," *BC Studies* 105 and 106 (Spring/Summer 1995): 27–43; and Perry, *On the Edge of Empire: Gender, Race, and the Making of British Columbia, 1849–1871* (Toronto: University of Toronto Press, 2001). Sarah Brooks Sundberg has argued that the substantial contributions of prairie farm women as homemakers, home manufacturers, field hands, wage earners, and teachers was understated by the persistent image of "helpmates" in emigrant promotional literature in the late nineteenth century. See Sundberg, "Farm Women on the Canadian Prairie Frontier: The Helpmate Image," in *Rethinking Canada*, ed. Strong-Boag and Fellman, 95–106.

31. Although Ireland experienced a number of local crop failures and some widespread famines in the eighteenth and nineteenth centuries, the famine that is the focus of much of the historical literature on Irish emigration in that period is the Great Famine, which occurred in the late 1840s through the early 1850s. The term *famine* in this discussion refers to that mid-century disaster, unless the context specifically indicates otherwise.

32. See, for example, William Forbes Adams, *Ireland and Irish Emigration to the New World from 1815 to the Famine* (1932; reprint, New York: Russell and Russell, 1967); Oscar Handlin, *Boston's Immigrants* (Cambridge, MA: Harvard University Press, 1941); William V. Shannon, *The American Irish* (New York: Macmillan, 1963); Lawrence J. McCaffrey, *The Irish Diaspora in America* (Bloomington: Indiana University Press, 1976); Kerby A. Miller, "Emigrants and Exiles: Irish Cultures and Irish Emigration to North America, 1790–1922," *Irish Historical Studies* 22:86 (September 1980): 97–125; Miller, *Emigrants and Exiles: Ireland and the Irish Exodus to North America* (New York: Oxford University Press, 1985); and Miller, "Emigration, Capitalism, and Ideology in Post-Famine Ireland," in *Migrations: The Irish at Home and Abroad*, ed. Richard Kearney (Dublin: Wolfhound Press, 1990), 91–108.

33. See Donald H. Akenson: *Being Had: Historians, Evidence, and the Irish in North America* (Don Mills, ON: P. D. Meany Publishers, 1985), 40–42, 69–72, and 84–85; and *Small Differences: Irish Catholics and Irish Protestants, 1815–1922: An International Perspective* (Kingston: McGill-Queen's University Press, 1988), 102–3. See

also Cecil J. Houston and William J. Smyth: *Irish Emigration and Canadian Settlement: Patterns, Links, and Settlers* (Toronto: University of Toronto Press, 1990), 21; and "The Irish Diaspora: Emigration to the New World, 1720–1920," in *An Historical Geography of Ireland*, ed. B. J. Graham and L. J. Proudfoot (London: Academic Press Limited, 1993), 338–65, particularly 353. See also David Doyle, "The Irish in North America, 1776–1845," in *A New History of Ireland*, ed. W. E. Vaughan, vol. 5 (Oxford: Clarendon Press, 1989), 706.

34. Miller, "Emigrants and Exiles: Irish Emigration," and *Emigrants and Exiles: Irish Exodus*. Other historians of the American Irish have also sharply differentiated between Irish Protestant and Irish Catholic adaptation in America. See: Shannon, *American Irish*; Marjorie Fallows, *Irish Americans: Identity and Assimilation* (Englewood Cliffs, NJ: Prentice-Hall, 1979), 144–3; and Thomas O'Connor, *The Boston Irish: A Political History* (Boston: Northeastern University Press, 1995), 19–22.

35. See Donald Akenson: *Being Had*; *Small Differences*; "The Historiography of the Irish in the United States of America," in *The Irish in New Communities*, ed. Patrick O'Sullivan, Irish World Wide Series, vol. 2 (Leicester: Leicester University Press, 1992), 99–127; and *The Irish Diaspora: A Primer* (Toronto: P. D. Meaney, 1993). Akenson by-passed U.S. data in this analysis, as the religion of immigrants was not systematically recorded in America. See also: Bruce S. Elliott, *Irish Migrants in the Canadas: A New Approach* (Kingston: McGill-Queen's University Press, 1988); and David Doyle, "The Irish in Australia and the United States: Some Comparisons, 1800–1939," *Irish Economic and Social History* 16 (1989): 73–94, particularly 92–3.

36. See: Akenson, *Being Had*, *Small Differences*, and "Historiography of the Irish"; Doyle, "Irish in North America"; David Fitzpatrick, "Emigration, 1801–70," in *New History*, ed. Vaughan, 562–622; Patrick Blessing, "Irish Emigration to the United States, 1800–1920: An Overview," in *The Irish in America: Emigration, Assimilation and Impact*, ed. P. J. Drudy, Irish Studies 4 (Cambridge: Cambridge University Press, 1985), 11–37; Liam Kennedy and Leslie A. Clarkson, "Birth, Death and Exile: Irish Population History, 1700–1921," in *Historical Geography*, ed. Graham and Proudfoot, 158–84; and Houston and Smyth, "Irish Diaspora" and *Irish Emigration and Canadian Settlement*.

37. See: Dudley Baines, *Emigration from Europe, 1815–1930*, Economic History Society Studies in Economic History (Basingstoke: Macmillan Education, 1991); and James H. Jackson, Jr. and Leslie Page Moch, "Migration and Social History of Modern Europe," in *Time, Family and Community: Perspectives on Family and Community History*, ed. Michael Drake (Oxford: Open University, in association with Blackwell Publishers, 1994), 181–98.

38. Fitzpatrick, "Emigration, 1801–70," 564. See also David Fitzpatrick, "The Modernisation of the Irish Female," in *Rural Ireland: Modernisation v. Change, 1600–1900*, ed. Patrick O'Flanagan, Paul Ferguson, and Kevin Whelan (Cork: Cork University Press, 1987), 162–80, particularly 175.

39. Jim Mac Laughlin: *Historical and Recent Irish Emigration: A Critique of Core-Periphery and Behavioural Models* (London: University of North London Press, 1994), 9–11 and 45–46; and "Emigration and the Construction of Nationalist Hege-

mony in Ireland: The Historical Background to 'New Wave' Irish Emigration," in *Location and Dislocation in Contemporary Irish Society: Emigration and Irish Identities*, ed. Jim Mac Laughlin (Cork: Cork University Press, 1997), 5–35.

40. Still, some studies of migrations to North America have attempted to deal with earlier periods. Doyle, Fitzpatrick, and Miller have included brief discussions of earlier migrations in works already cited; Audrey Lockhart looks at earlier migrations to America and Newfoundland (although she tends to treat Newfoundland primarily as a stepping-stone to America, and uncritically accepts contemporary reports that Irish migrants to the island were vagrants and the refuse from Irish jails who had been pressed into service in Irish ports). See Lockhart, *Some Aspects of Emigration from Ireland to the North American Colonies Between 1660 and 1775*, The Irish-Americans Series (New York: Arno Press, 1976). Graeme Kirkham provides a brief overview of emigration from Ulster in the first half of the eighteenth century in "The Origins of Mass Emigration from Ireland," in *Migrations*, ed. Kearney, 81–90; Marianne S. Wokeck includes a chapter on eighteenth-century Irish immigration to the Delaware Valley in *Trade in Strangers: The Beginnings of Mass Migration to North America* (University Park, PA: Pennsylvania State University Press, 1999), 167–219. Miller has looked at the evolution of Scotch-Irish ethnicity in America in "'Scotch-Irish' Myths and 'Irish' Identities in Eighteenth-and Nineteenth-Century America," in *New Perspectives on the Irish Diaspora*, ed. Charles Fanning (Carbondale: Southern Illinois University Press, 2000), 75–92; and Edward O'Day provides an analysis of naturalization records in the northeastern states in the pre-famine period in "The 'Second Colonization of New England' Revisited: Irish Immigration Before the Famine," in *New Perspectives*, ed. Fanning, 93–114.

There is certainly a growing body of literature on Irish migrants to Britain in the pre-famine period, particularly seasonal laborers in agriculture and semi-skilled, unskilled, and casual workers in the textile, construction, and transportation industries. Again, there is a concentration on processes of urban ghettoization and proletarianization as seasonal movements gave way to permanent immigration—dynamics that contrast with the experiences of the Irish on the southern Avalon in the same period. See, for example: B. Collins, "Irish Emigration to Dundee and Paisley During the First Half of the Nineteenth Century," in *Irish Population, Economy and Society: Essays in Honour of the late K. H. Connell*, ed. J. M. Goldstrum and L. A. Clarkson (Oxford: Oxford University Press, 1981), 195–212; Collins, "The Irish in Britain, 1780–1921," in *Historical Geography*, ed. Graham and Proudfoot, 366–98; Roger Swift and Sheridan Gilley, eds., *The Irish in the Victorian City* (London: Croom Helm, 1985); Swift and Gilley, eds., *The Irish in Britain, 1815–1939* (London: Pinter Publishers, 1989); Swift and Gilley, eds., *The Irish in Victorian Britain: The Local Dimension* (Dublin: Four Courts Press, 1999); Ruth-Ann Harris, *The Nearest Place That Wasn't Ireland: Early Nineteenth-Century Irish Labor Migration* (Ames: Iowa State University Press, 1994); Jeffrey G. Williamson, "The Impact of the Irish on British Labor Markets During the Industrial Revolution," *Journal of Economic History* 46, no. 3 (September 1986): 693–720; Graham Davis, *The Irish in Britain, 1815–1914* (Dublin: Gill and Macmillan, 1991); Anne O'Dowd, *Spalpeens and Tattie Hokers: History and Folklore of the Irish*

Migratory Agricultural Worker in Ireland and Britain (Blackrock: Irish Academic Press, 1991); Donald M. MacRaild, *Irish Migrants in Modern Britain, 1750–1922* (New York: St. Martin's Press, 1999); and various contributions in *Irish Women and Irish Migration*, ed. Patrick O'Sullivan, vol. 4, Irish World Wide Series (London: Leicester University Press, 1995). A recent offering by Donald M. MacRaild examines the similar types of "frontiers"—economic, social, political, psychological—that had to be negotiated by Irish immigrants to Britain and America in the nineteenth century, but again, the concentration is on urban experiences from the 1840s and beyond. See MacRaild, "Crossing Migrant Frontiers: Comparative Reflections on Irish Migrants in Britain and the United States during the Nineteenth Century," *Immigrants and Minorities* 18:2 and 3 (July/November 1999): 40–70.

41. Kerby A. Miller, Arnold Schrier, Bruce D. Boling, and David Doyle, *Irish Immigrants in the Land of Canaan: Letters and Memoirs from Colonial and Revolutionary America, 1675–1815* (Oxford: Oxford University Press, 2003).

42. This series explores a variety of themes, as encapsulated in the titles of the various volumes. See Patrick O'Sullivan, ed., *Patterns of Migration*, vol. 1 (1992), *The Irish in the New Communities*, vol. 2 (1992), *The Creative Migrant*, vol. 3 (1994), *Irish Women and Irish Migration*, vol. 4 (1995), *Religion and Identity*, vol. 5 (1996), *The Meaning of the Famine*, vol. 6 (1997), Irish World Wide Series (Leicester and London: Leicester University Press, 1992–97). There are several studies in the collection that extend back into earlier time periods, but they deal with specialized groups such as indentured servants, religious personnel, and soldiers abroad.

43. See Andy Bielenberg, ed., *The Irish Diaspora* (Harlow: Pearson Education, 2000). Some contributions that do discuss earlier movements to varying degrees include: Graham Davis, "The Irish in Britain, 1815–1939," 19–36; Donald Akenson, "Irish Migration to North America, 1800–1920," 111–38; Kerby Miller, "'Scotch-Irish', 'Black Irish' and 'Real Irish': Emigrants and Identities in the Old South," 139–57; Ruth-Ann M. Harris, "Searching for Missing Friends in the Boston Pilot Newspaper, 1831–1863," 158–75; and Bielenberg, "Irish Emigration to The British Empire, 1700–1914," 215–34.

44. Akenson, *Primer*. The quotation comes from the title of chap.7: "Women and the Irish Diaspora: The Great Unknown."

45. L. A. Clarkson, "Love, Labour and Life: Women in Carrick-on-Suir in the Late Eighteenth Century," *Irish Economic and Social History* 20 (1993): 18–34, particularly 19. The reference to Connell's work relates to Kenneth H. Connell, *The Population of Ireland, 1750–1845* (Oxford: Clarendon Press, 1950).

46. There are exceptions, such as Jerrold Casway's "Irish Women Overseas, 1500–1800," in *Women in Early Modern Ireland*, ed. Margaret MacCurtain and Mary O'Dowd (Edinburgh: Edinburgh University Press, 1991), 112–32. His work concentrates on female indentured servants in America and the Caribbean, and harks back to the earlier "emigrant-as-exile" genre.

47. The most gender-inclusive of these is Malcolm Campbell's *The Kingdom of the Ryans: The Irish in Southwest New South Wales, 1816–1890* (Sydney: University of New South Wales Press, 1997). This study is still male-centered, focusing as it does "on two generations of the Ryan family, father, and son, whose leadership of the Irish

community played a vital role in shaping its composition, identity, and relationship with Australian society" (11). But Campbell does provide a discussion of the centrality of the Irish family in terms of economic production and cultural continuity, the importance of women in establishing and maintaining stable family life, and the impact of middle-class constructions of femininity and masculinity on rural Irish communities in Australia (chap. 5). Other, less inclusive sagas include: Elliott, *Irish in the Canadas*; Wokeck, *Trade in Strangers*; Akenson, *The Irish in Ontario: A Study in Rural History*, 2nd ed. (Montreal: McGill-Queen's University Press, 1999); and Ronald Hoffman, *Princes of Ireland, Planters of Maryland: A Carroll Saga*, 1500–1782, collaborated with Sally D. Mason (Chapel Hill: University of North Carolina Press, 2000).

48. For an overview, see Ann Rossiter, "In Search of Mary's Past: Placing Nineteenth Century Irish Immigrant Women in British Feminist History," in *Women, Migration and Empire*, ed. Joan Grant (Stoke-on-Trent: Trentham Books, 1996), 1–29.

49. Dierdre Mageean, for example, examines women's emigration from Munster in the nineteenth and early twentieth centuries, and provides a very enlightening discussion of the changes in women's lives before and after the mid-nineteenth century; but it is aimed at understanding the motivations of women who left home during the Great Famine and thereafter. See Mageean, "To Be Matched or to Move: Irish Women's Prospects in Munster," in *Peasant Maids—City Women: From the European Countryside to Urban America*, ed. Christiane Harzig (Ithaca, NY: Cornell University Press, 1997), 57–97. Other writings that deal with women's declining status and emigration from the famine onwards include: Robert E. Kennedy, Jr., *The Irish: Emigration, Marriage and Fertility* (Berkeley: University of California Press, 1973); Hasia R. Diner, *Erin's Daughters in America: Irish Immigrant Women in the Nineteenth Century* (Baltimore: Johns Hopkins University Press, 1983); Fitzpatrick, "Modernisation"; Janet Nolan, "The Great Famine and Women's Emigration from Ireland," in *The Hungry Stream: Essays on Emigration and Famine*, ed. E. Margaret Crawford (Belfast: Centre for Emigration Studies, Ulster-American Folk Park, and Institute of Irish Studies, Queen's University, 1997), 61–70; and Janet A. Nolan, *Ourselves Alone: Women's Emigration from Ireland, 1885–1920* (Lexington: University Press of Kentucky, 1989). Miller, Doyle, and Patricia Kelleher cover the nineteenth century in "'For love and liberty': Irish Women, Migration and Domesticity in Ireland and America, 1815–1920," in *Irish Women and Migration*, ed. O'Sullivan, 41–65. Their discussion is still focused on the famine and beyond, but they briefly touch upon some push factors of female emigration in the pre-famine period, primarily revolving around illiteracy and social and economic subordination. However, their conclusions on Irish women's lowly status before the famine appear to stem from middle-class understandings of femininity and are, therefore, unconvincing; they also run contrary to the other literature noted above. There are various other writings that deal primarily with Irish women emigrants from the mid-nineteenth century and beyond, including: Ida O'Carroll, *Models for Movers: Irish Women's Emigration to America* (Dublin: Attic Press, 1990); Sheelagh Conway, *The Faraway Hills are Green: Voices of Irish Women in Canada* (Toronto: Women's Press, 1992); Grace Neville, "'She Never Then After That Forgot Him': Irish Women and Emigration to the United States in Irish Folklore," *Mid-America: An Historical Review* 74:3 (1992):

271–89; Maureen Murphy, "Charlotte Grace O'Brien and the Mission of Our Lady of the Rosary for the Protection of Irish Immigrant Girls," *Mid-America: An Historical Review* 74:3 (1992): 253–70; Breda Gray, "'The Home of Our Mothers and Our Birthright for Ages'? Nation, Diaspora and Irish Women," in *New Frontiers in Women's Studies: Knowledge, Identity and Nationalism*, ed. Mary Maynard and June Purvis (London: Taylor and Francis, 1996), 164–86; Tracy M. English, "Big Wages, Glorious Climate and Situations Guaranteed: A Study of the Migration of Irish Women to Great Britain for the Period 1861 to 1911" (master's thesis, Memorial University of Newfoundland, 1999); Enda Delaney, "Gender and 20th-Century Irish migration, 1921–1971," in *Women, Gender and Labour Migration: Historical and Global Perspectives*, ed. Pamela Sharpe (London: Routledge, 2001), 209–23; and Bronwen Walter, *Outsiders Inside: Whiteness, Place, and Irish Women* (London: Routledge, 2001). Suellen Hoy's study period straddles the nineteenth and early twentieth centuries, but she is looking at a very specific occupational group, in "The Journey Out: The Recruitment and Emigration of Irish Religious Women to the United States, 1812–1914," *The Journal of Women's History* 6/7, no. 1 (1994–95): 64–98.

50. See: Adams, *Irish Emigration*, 223; Akenson, *Primer*, 166; Fitzpatrick, "Emigration, 1801–70," 573–4; Joel Mokyr, *Why Ireland Starved: A Quantitative and Analytical History of the Irish Economy, 1800–1850* (London: George Allen and Unwin, 1983), 247; and Mokyr and Cormac O Grada, "Emigration and Poverty in Prefamine Ireland," *Explorations in Economic History* 19, no. 4 (October 1982): 360–84, particularly 367.

51. See: Fitzpatrick, "Emigration, 1801–70," 574; and Miller, *Emigration and Exile: Irish Exodus*, 200.

52. Akenson, *Primer*, particularly chap. 7.

53. Akenson's study of the Irish in Ontario is an exception, although it focuses primarily on men's experiences. See Akenson, *The Irish in Ontario: A Study in Rural History*, 2nd ed. (Montreal: McGill-Queen's University Press, 1999).

54. Cyril J. Byrne, ed., *Gentlemen-Bishops and Faction Fighters: The Letters of Bishops O Donel, Lambert, Scallan and Other Irish Missionaries* (St. John's: Jesperson Press, 1984).

55. See: Rev. Lewis A. Anspach, *A History of the Island of Newfoundland* (London: Anspach, 1819); Rev. Charles Pedley, *The History of Newfoundland* (London: Longman, Green, Longman, Roberts and Green, 1863); and Rev. Michael F. Howley, *Ecclesiastical History of Newfoundland* (Boston: Doyle and Whittle, 1888; reprint, Belleville, ON: Mika, 1971).

APPENDIX C

Women's Presence in the Mercantile Accounts of the Southern Avalon

The following examples of women's particip ation in the exchange economy of the Southern Avalon are drawn from the Sweetman Coll ection (PANL, MG 49), Goodridge Collection (PANL, MG 473, 1839 and 1841) , and Alan Goodridge and Sons Limited fonds (MHA, 1840). Speci fic entries have been selected to illustrate the discussion in Chapter 5 (section 5.2). They are by no means exhaustive.

Note: The typography of this table reflects my effort to render as faithfully as possible the idiosyncracies of the original document.

1. Autonomous household heads

Account of Rachel Welsh and Son (Goodridge's, 1840 ledger, fol. 381)

D^r.			£ s d	C^r.			£ s d
Date	Folio			Date	Folio		
Augt 27	374	To 1/2 Cwt Bread	15	Sep^t 17	413	By McBride & Kerr	1. 2. 6
Augt 27	374	" 6 lb Butter	7. 6				
		£	1. 2. 6				

Account of Catherine Kenny and Sons (Goodridge's, 1840 ledger, fol. 363)

D^{r}.			£ s d	C^{r}.			£ s d
Date	Folio			Date	Folio		
June 1	190	To 2 Pair Deck Boots	2.16. -	Octr 15	468	By Fermews Estabm^{t}	
June 1	190	" 2 lb 2 ozs Leather	7. 6			[fish and oil]	6. 5. 8
June 1	190	" 1 lb Sparrowbills	1				
June 8	210	" 9 yards No. 5 Canvas	1. 2. 6	Augt 27	372	To Amount from opposite	6. 3. 5
June 8	210	" 1 yard Calico	10	Augt 27	372	" 1/2 lb Sparrowbills	6
June 19	241	" 1 Roughstone	1	Octr 14	466	" 1 lb N. H. Tobacco	1. 9
June 29	261	" Thread	4				
July 15	285	" 1 Pair Womens Shoes	7. 6				
July 15	285	" 5 3/8 yds Blue Serge	14.10				
Augt 10	341	" 1 lb Tea	4				
Augt 27	372	" 2 1/4 lb Leather	7.11				
		Amount opposite	£ 6. 3. 5				£ 6. 5. 8

Account of Catherine Kenny and Sons (Goodridge's, 1841 ledger, fol. 266)

D^{r}.

Date	Folio		£ s d
Jany 29	48	To 1 pair Mens Shoes	9
Feby 8	52	" 1/2 Brl oatmeal	15
Feby 8	52	"1 lb Leaf Tobacco	1. 2
Feby 17	56	" 2 lbs Coffee	3. 4
Feby 22	58	" 1 pair Womans Shoes	7. 6
Feby 22	58	" 5 yds Calico	4. 2
Feby 22	58	" 1 lb Leaf Tobacco	1. 2
March 8	64	1 pair mens Shoes	9
March 8	64	" 2 3/4 lbs Leather	11
March 12	65	" 4 lbs Sugar	2. 4
March 12	65	" 1/2 yard Cotton	10
March 19	68	" 1/2 yard Gown Cotton	6
March 24	70	" 1 pair Boys Lge Shoes	6. 6
March 24	70	" 10 ozs Leather	2. 6
March 24	70	" Thread	6
March 31	73	" 2 yds Calico	1. 8
March 31	73	" 1 lb 2 ozs Soap	8
April 2	75	3 yds Blay Calico	2. 6
April 22	84	5 lbs asst Nails	2.11
		Amount opposite	£ 4. 2. 3

C^{r}.

Date	Folio		£ s d
Septr 15	373	By House Expense— Wages p. Girl last winter & a Pr Shoes	1. 7. 6
Novr 19	481	By John Goodridge & Co.	3. 4. 9
			£ 4.12. 3
April		To amount from opposite	4. 2. 3
April 23	85	" 2 1/4 lbs Leather	9
Septr 24	382	" Thread	1. -
			£ 4.12. 3

Account of Jane Careen, 1820 (Sweetman's, box 3, file 4)

		Bread cwt	Butter lbs	Beef Bar^{ls}	Pork Bar^{ls}	Flour Bar^{ls}	Oatmeal Bar^{ls}
1820	Jane Careen	2	16	1/2	—	1/4	—

Fish on board Brig Concord, 1822 (Sweetman's, box 3, Accounts 1822–26, 11–13)

		Merchantable	Madeira	West Indies
		[amounts represent quintals of fish]		
p. 11	1822 Debit			
	Sept. 13—Widow Blanch & Son	9	34	
	Sept. 24—Widow Blanch & Son	9	67	
pp. 12–13	1822, Jersey Store Contra			
	Aug[t] 10—M[rs]. Blanch & Son	9	57	30
	Aug[t] 19—M[rs]. Blanch & Son	9	33 1/2	20
	Supra Dr.			
	Sept. 14—Widow Blanch & Son	9	—	26
	Sept. 24—Widow Blanch & Son	9	—	20
	Jersey Store Contra			
	Oct. 2—Widow Blanch & Son	9	—	12
	Nov[r] 14—M[rs]. Blanch & Son	9	6 3/4	—

Collection and disposal of fish oil, 1828 (Sweetman's, box 3, file 36)

Mary Morris	On Nov. 17, 1828, oil valued at £99/ . . / . . shipped

Fish Book Journal, 23 July–11 November 1838 (Sweetman's, box 2, file 4)

Date		Merchantable	Madeira [quintals of fish]	West Indies	Total
Aug. 3	Sarah McCarthy	64	12		76
Nov[r]. 10	Sarah McCarthy	23	11		34
Nov[r]. 10	Barter for Mrs. Murphy, Rams [place name]	2			2

Dry Fish Book, 7 January–31 December 1846 (Sweetman's, box 2, file 42)

Date		Merchantable	Madeira [quintals of fish]	West Indies	Amount £ s d
Aug. 17	Mary Murphy, Upper Rams	26	9		20. 2. 0
Aug. 24	Mary Murphy, Upper Rams	21	4		14.12.0
Oct. 14	Dorothy Cantwell	10			6. 0. 0
Oct. 20	Sarah McCarthy	9 7/8	5 1/4		8.11.0

2. Washerwomen and seamstresses

Note that the names of women's customers were entered in the credit side of the women's accounts, along with the amounts the customers owed the washerwoman or seamstress. A corresponding debit entry was made in each customer's account. This form of *contra* entry in merchant account books was usually how these women were paid in the period.

Nancy Kean, Renews Seamstress (Goodridge's, 1839 ledger, fol. 380)

D^{r}.			£ s d	C^{r}.			£ s d
Date	Folio			Date	Folio		
Jany 3	55	To 3 yards Calico	2. 3	1838			
Jany 3	55	" 1 lb Black Paint	1	Dec^{r}	18	By Balance	3. 4
Jany 3	55	" 1 Run Herring Twine	2. 2	1839			
Jany 16	68	" 3 yards Shirting	3	Sep^{t} 28	541	" Patrick Kennedy	5
June 12	268	" 1/2 Pint L'seed Oil	9	Sep^{t} 28	541	" Michael Mansfield	5
June 12	268	" 1 lb Black Paint	1	Octr 25	614	" Mathew Joyce	5
June 12	268	" 1 yard Calico	10	Decr 6	715	" Bad Debts	1. 2
July 1	325	" 3 1/4 yards Calico	3. 2				£ 1. 0. 6
July 24	391	" 2 1/2 yards Calico	2. 1				
July 30	401	" 1 1/2 yards Calico	1. 3	Octr 8	566	To Amount from opposite	19. 9
July 30	401	" 4 Knots Sw^{g} Twine	8	Octr 8	566	" 1/2 Pint L'seed Oil	9
July 30	401	" 1 lb Soap	7				
Oct. 3	555	" 1 lb Black Paint	1. -				
		Amount opposite	£ - 19. 9				£ 1. 0. 6

Mary Neill, Renews washerwoman (Good ridge's, 1840 ledger, fol. 337)

D^{r}.			£ s d	C^{r}.			£ s d
Date	Folio			Date	Folio		
1839							
Dec^{r}	14	To Bad Debts	9.11				
1840							
June 24	252	" 1 Pair Boys large shoes	7	June 24	251	By William Meagher	10
July 9	275	" 3 lb 6 ozs Soap	2	Augt 17	351	" Edward Fling	8
Augt 17	351	" 2 lb 7 ozs Soap	1. 5	Octr 10	457	" John Foley 10/	
Augt 17	351	" Thread	7			Edward Fling 2/	12
Augt 17	352	" 2 Gallons Molasses	7.	Novr 20	548	" Abatement	5
		Amount opposite	£ 1. 7.11				£ 1.10. 5
				Sep^{t} 11	405	To Amount from opposite	1. 7.11
				Sep^{t} 11	405	" 1 Pair Black Hose	2. 6
							£ 1.10. 5

Ann Kean, Renews washerwomen (Goodridge's, 1841 ledger, fol. 246)

D^{r}.			£ s d	C^{r}.			£ s d
Date	Folio			Date	Folio		
May 15	126	To 1 Pair Womans Shoes	7. 6	Sep^{t} 30	391	By Richard Tobin	12
May 24	157	" 2 1/2 yards No. 6 Canvas	6. 3	Sep^{t} 30	391	By John Ryan	12. -
June 14	187	" 1/4 lb Thread	1. 6				
July 20	276	" 1 yard blue Serge	2. 9			Washes 2 Men B^{t} [Boat] *Rose*	
July 20	276	" 2 ozs. Thread	1				
Oct. 14	412	" 1/2 lb Sen. Tea	3				
Oct. 14	412	" 3/4 yard Merino	2. -				
			£ 1. 4. 0				£ 1. 4. 0

Combined washing and sewing, St. Mary's–Placentia, 1823 (Sweetman's, box 3, file 17, fols. 20-1)

			£	s	d
Bess St. Croix					
—	2/140	Capt. J. Dunn @ 14/–			
		mother @ 10/–	1	4	"
—	2/142	Jno Clooney	"	8	"
—	2/41	Jno Gready	1	8	"
—	2/97	Wm Doyle	"	10	"
—	2/107	Ths Grant	"	3	6
—	2/145	Ml Mullowney	"	15	"
		Ent in Ledger No. 2 fo 47	4	8	6
Mrs. Jas Mulally					
—	2/161	Jno Moran	1	10	"
—	2/118	A. Tobin	"	18	"
—	2/25	R. Fitzpatrick	"	15	"
		to Cr Ledger No 2 fo 159	3	3	"
Mrs. Ths. McCarthy					
—	2/150	Michl Power	"	15	"
—	2/110	William Power	1	10	"
—	2/135	Jas Hartby	"	15	"
—	2/10	Rd Forrestal Junr.	"	15	"
—	2/178	Jerry McKew	1	10	"
		Cr in Ledger No 2 fo 43	5	5	"

Combined washing and sewing, St. Mary's–Placentia, 1823 (Sweetman's, box 3, file 18a, fol. 21)

			£	s	d
M[rs]. Ja[s] Barron					
—	2/156	Wm Wall	"	15	"
—	2/114	Jas Maher	1	10	"
—	2/151	Matw Lonergan	"	10	"
—	2/98	Dens Downey	1	10	"
—	2/152	Patk Neil	"	10	"
—	2/34	Jno Holden	1	10	"
—	2/106	Ths Grant	1	10	"
—	2/154	Jno Mackay	"	10	"
—	2/22	L. Keef	"	19	"
—	2/144	Ths McKay	"	10	"
—	2/112	Patk Fowler	"	10	"
—	2/42	Ml. Costelloe	"	15	"
—	2/14	Ml. Brennan	1	10	"
—	2/137	Wm. Aylward	1	10	"
—	2/17	Ct. Hawkins	1	"	"
		to Cr Ledger No 2 f. 69	14	19	"
Honor Sinnot					
—	2/102	Mau[ce] Morrissey	1	7	"
—	2/149	Jno Green Yr [Younger?]	"	10	"
—	2/106	Ths Gran a/c Wm Walsh	1	6	"
—	2/108	Ed Dunn	1	10	"
—	2/109	Lce Delahunty	1	10	"
—	2/117	Ml Walsh	1	10	"
—	2/141	Pk Lynch	"	10	"
—	2/165	Micl Shea	1	10	"
		to Cr. Ledger No 2 fo 65	9	13	"

3. Women fishing servants

Betsy Byrne, shore crew, Renews (Goodridge's, 1839 ledger, fol. 383)

D^{r}.			£ s d	C^{r}.			£ s d
Date	Folio			Date	Folio		
Augt 10	406	To 1 Pair Womans Shores	7. 6	Sep^{t} 19	514	By Fishing 2 Days Work	4
				Decr 6	715	" Bad Debts	3. 6
			£ 7. 6				£ 7. 6

Bridget Meagher, shore crew, Renews (Goodridge's, 1840 ledger, fol. 341)

D^{r}.			£ s d	C^{r}.			£ s d
Date	Folio			Date	Folio		
Augt 21	359	To 3 yds Blue Serge	8. 3	Sep^{t} 30	444	By Fishery 15 days' work	1.10
Augt 21	359	" 1 lb Soap	7				
Augt 21	359	" Thread	6	Sep^{t} 26	435	To amount from opposite	1. 8. 6
Augt 31	383	" 1 lb 1 oz Soap	8	Sep^{t} 26	435	" 5 ozs Congo Tead	1. 6
Sep^{t} 2	389	" 4 yards Brown Merino	11				£ 1.10. 0
Sep^{t} 2	389	" 1 Pair Black Hose	2				
Sep^{t} 7	398	" 6 ozs Tea	1. 6				
Sep^{t} 19	418	" 1/2 lb Congo Tea	2. 6				
Sep^{t} 19	418	" 1 1/2 yard Shirting	1. 6				
		Amount opposite	£ 1. 8. 6				

Nancy Gerian, shore crew, Renews (Goodridge's, 1841 ledger, fol. 306)

Dr.			£ s d	Cr.			£ s d
Date	Folio			Date	Folio		
Augt 24	335	To 1 Pair Womans Shoes	7	Oct 15	418	By 22 1/4 days [shore] work	2. 4. 6
Augt 27	340	" 3 yards Calico	2. 6				
Septt 4	357	" 1 Pair Chil[d]s Boots 6 1/2 Inches	3.10				
Octt 6	401	" 1 yard Shirting	1				
Octt 20	424	" 2 1/4 yards Black Merino	6. 2				
Octt 20	424	" 2 1/4 yards Calico	3. 2				
Octt 20	424	" 3 lbs Sugar	1. 8				
Octt 20	425	" Thomas Gerrian	14. 2				
Octt 20	425	" Cash	5. -				
			£ 2. 4. 6				

Female shore crew in Goodridge's fishery account, 1841 (1841 ledger, fols. 45–48)

	No. of days worked	Wages[a] £ s d
Julia McCarthy	13 1/2	1. 7. 0
Esther Cahill	45 1/2	4.11.0
Mary Power	4	8. 0
Mary Conway	47 1/4	4.14.6
Mary Ann Fowler	45 1/4	4.10.6
Fanny Devine	6	12.0
Fanny Rose	12 1/2	1. 5. 0
Catherine Cahill	22 1/4	2. 4. 6
Phoebe Squires	3 3/4	7. 6
Margaret Dunphy	29 1/2	2. 1. 9
Nancy Gerian	22 1/4	2. 4. 6
Bridget Meagher	4 3/4	9. 6

[a] Wage amounts are debited to the fishery account and appear as credits in the women's respective accounts.

4. Multiple services

Fanny Byrne, washing, sewing, and shore work, Renews (Goodridge's, 1839 ledger, fol. 377)

Dr.			£ s d	Cr.			£ s d
Date	Folio			Date	Folio		
Aug. 28	203	To 4 yards Blue Serge	11	June 15	280	By 17 Days [shore] work	1.14. 0
June 7	244	" 16 yards Calico	8. 4	July 20	382	" David Lee	12
June 8	257	" 1 Pair Black Hose	2. 9	July 25	394	" William Karney	12
June 15	280	" 10 lb soap	5.10	Augt 9	436	" Laurency Hunt	12. 6
June 15	280	" 4 yards Gingham	5	Octr 7	562	By William Meagher	12. 6
June 15	280	" 1 Cotton Handkf	1. 6				
July 8	361	" 1/2 lb thread	3				
July 20	382	" 1 1/4 lb Soap	6. 7				
July 20	382	" 2 1/2 yards Gingham	3. 1				
July 25	394	" 3 yards White Serge	7. 6				
Augt 7	428	" 8 1/2 yards double M . . . ing	1. 5. 6				
Septr 17	514	" 2 lbs 15 ozs soap	1. 9				
Octr 11	572	"1 1/4 lbs soap	8				
Octr 12	576	" 1 lb soap	6				
			£ 4. 3. 0				£ 4. 3. 0

Mary Ann Fowler, shore work and sale of oakum, Renews (Goodridge's, 1839 ledger, fol. 379)

D^{r}.			£ s d	C^{r}.			£ s d
Date	Folio			Date	Folio		
1838				1839			
Dec^{r}	16	To Balance	1. 0. 0	June 15	280	By 14 1/2 Days [shore] Work	1. 9. 0
1839				Octr 24	612	" 11 lbs Oakum	3. 8
May 27	201	" 7 lbs 6 ozs soap	4. 3	Decr 6	715	" Bad Debts	1.15.8
May 27	201	" 6 yards Blue Serge	16. 6				
June 1	222	" 1 Pair Womans Shoes	7. 6				
June 1	222	" 10 yards Cotton	8. 4				
June 14	276	" 1 Pair Black Hose	2. 9				
Sep^{t} 17	512	" 1 Pair Womans Shoes	7. 6				
Sep^{t} 20	525	" 1/4 lb Thread	1. 6				
			£ 3. 8. 4				£ 3. 8. 4

Ann Jackman, shore work and sale of hay, Re news (Goodridge's, 1840 ledger, fols. 336, 341)

D^r^.			£ s d	C^r^.			£ s d
Date	Folio			Date	Folio		
fol. 336							
1839							
Dec^r^	14	To Bad Debts	1.10. 0				
1840							
Augt 3	319	" 5 1/2 yards Shirting	5. 6	Sep^t^ 24	420	By 6 Ducks	7. 6
Augt 14	347	" 2 yards Shirting	2			Amount to Folio 341	
Augt 22	362	" 1/2 yards Gown Cotton	. 6	Sep^t^ 3	391	To Amount from opposite	1.18. 0
		Amount opposite	£ 1.18. 0	Sep^t^ 3	391	" 4 lb 7 ozs Soap	2. 8
						Amount to Folio 341	£ 2. 0. 8
fol. 341							
Sep^t^		To Amount from Folio 336	2. 0. 8			By am^t^ from Folio 336	7. 6
Sep^t^ 24	401	" 1 lb Leather 3/6		Sep^t^ 30	441	" Fishery 17 days work	
		1 lb offal 2.	5. 6			per B. M^c^Carthy	1.14. 0
Octr 14	464	" Thread & Sparrowbills	4	Octr 31	502	" 1 3/8 Cwt Hay	6.11
Octr 14	466	" Cash paid B. M^c^Carthy	1. 3. 0	Decr 11	576	" Bad Debts	1. 1. 1
			£ 3. 9. 6				£ 3. 9. 6

Mary Foley, washing, sewing, and sale of produce, Renews (Goodridge's, 1840 ledger, fols. 337, 342)

D^{r}.			£ s d	C^{r}.			£ s d
Date	Folio			Date	Folio		
fol. 337							
1839							
Dec^{r}	14	To Bad Debts	1. 2				
Decr 28	20	" 8 yards Calico	6. 8				
1840							
July 28	308	" 1 yard Black Merino	3	April 21	99	By 1 Doz^{n} Eggs	1
Augt 3	318	" 3 1/2 yards red Merino	9. 8	Augt 22	362	" 12 Ducks	15
Augt 3	318	" 5 1/4 yards slate color D^{o}	14. 6			Amount to Folio 342	£ - 16 -
Augt 3	319	" 1 Pair Small Boys Shoes	6	Aug^{t}		To amount from opposite	2. 1. 0
		Amount opposite	£ 2. 1. 0	Augt 8	339	" 3 lb Sugar	1. 9
				Septr 9	412	" 6 1/2 yds Shirting 6/6	
						5 yds Merino @ 2/9–13/9	1. 0. 3
						Amount to Folio 342	£ 3. 3. 0
fol. 342							
Dec^{r}		To Amount from Folio 337	3. 3. 0	Octr 20	486	By amount from Folio 337	16
Dec^{r}	607	" Balance due her	1. 0. 9	Octr 20	486	" Philip Power	6
			£ 4. 3. 9	Novr 5	519	" John Sheen	7
				Decr 8	568	" House Expense	
						Cream	19
				Decr 8	568	" 11 Ducks	13. 9
				Decr 8	568	" William Rowe	12
				Decr 8	568	" John Beer	10 -
							£ 4. 3. 9

Margaret Leary, washing and cooking, Renews (Goodridge's, 1840 ledger, fol. 339)

Dr.			£ s d	Cr.			£ s d
Date	Folio			Date	Folio		
June 17	234	To 6 yards Bleu Calico	5	Novr 18	542	By House Expense	
June 27	258	" 1Pair Childrens Shoes				1/2 year's washing	4. 0. 0
		4 3/4 Inches	2.10	Novr 18	542	" Cooking 2 Months each for	
June 29	260	" 2 lb Sugar	1. 2			Foley & McGrath	1. 0. 0
July 11	279	" 2 lb 6 ozs Soap	1. 5	Decr 14	580	" Ann Huffman Balance Acc^{t}	1. 0. 0
Augt 4	324	" 6 lb 13 ozs D^{o}	4	Decr 17	584	" 3/4 Months Cooking	
Augt 25	370	" Cash	5			p. P. Finn	3. 9
Sep^{t} 25	432	" Cash	2. 0. 0	Decr 17	584	" 1 3/30 Months Cooking	
Novr 6	520	" Thread	6			p. Capt	5. 6
Decr 14	580	" Mr Reid & Kerr order	2. 0. 0	Dec^{r}	606	" Balance due	8
Decr 17	584	" Ann Huffman reversed entry	1. 0. 0				£ 6. 9.11
Decr 17	589	" Cash p. Tho. at St. Johns	10. -				
			£ 6. 9.11				

Esther Cahill, washing and shore work, Rene ws (Goodridge's, 1841 ledger, fol. 245)

D^{r}.			£ s d	C^{r}.			£ s d
Date	Folio			Date	Folio		
May 24	157	To 2 lbs 2 ozs Soap	1. 3	1840			
May 24	157	" 1 yard Calico	9	Dec^{r}	14	By Balance	2
June 30	242	" 2 3/4 lbs soap and		1841			
		1/2 lb Sen. Tea	4. 5	Oc^{t} 9	405	" Patrick Kennedy	12
July 3	245	" 2 lbs Sugar and		Oc^{t} 9	405	" James Ryan Sr	12
		1/2 yard Gown Cotton	2. 2	Oc^{t} 15	417	" 45 1/2 days [shore] work	4.11. 0
July 5	250	" 1 1/8 yards black Merino	3. 1				
		Amount to Folio 305	£ - 11. 8			Amount to Folio 305	£ 5.17. 0

Margaret Dunphy, shore work and sale of poultry, [b] Renews (Goodridge's, 1841 ledger, fol. 306)

D[r].			£ s d	C[r].			£ s d
Date	Folio			Date	Folio		
Aug[t] 14	317	To 3 1/2 yards blue Serge	6.11	Aug[t] 23	328	By 9 Ducks	9
Aug[t] 14	317	" 1 Pair Black Hose	2. 9	Oc[t] 15	417	" 29 1/2 days [shore] work	2.19. 0
Aug[t] 23	328	" 1 yard blue Serge	2. 9				
Aug[t] 23	328	" 2 Pair Womans Shoes	14			£	3. 8. 0
Aug[t] 23	328	" 6 yards blay Calico	5				
Aug[t] 27	340	" 8 yards Gown Cotton	8	Oc[t] 1	392	To Amount from opposite	3. 6. 0
Sep[t] 7	352	" 4 1/2 yards Black Merino	12. 5	Oc[t] 1	392	" 2 5/8 yds blay Calico	2
Sep[t] 10	366	" 3 yards Black Merino	8. 3				
Sep[t] 13	370	" 1 yard black Merino	2. 9			£	3. 8. 0
Sep[t] 13	370	" 4 1/4 yards Calico	3. 2				
		Amount opposite £	3. 6. 0				

[b]Margaret's supplies suggest that she also did a considerable amount of sewing; however, there is nothing in the credit column of this particular account to indicate that she had customers in that regard.

5. Women servants or servants of women

1799 accounts, St. Mary's–Placentia (Sweetman's, box 3, 1799 ledger, fol. 44)

Catherine Hayse

D^{r}.		£ s d	Contra		£ s d
n.d.	To a/c Widow Hayse Servts Wages No. 1	1. 0. 0	n.d.	By money collected	1. 0. 0

Mrs. Botley (or Bolley)

D^{r}.					
May 9	To Cash in Poole	4. 0. 0	May 9	By wages @ £4.0.0 p month from this date to . . .	
May 9	John Sinnott	10			
Oct. 17	2 Qtls Fish			not given	
		to be Settled at Home			

Ann Huffman, household service, Renews (Goodridge's, 1840 ledger, fol. 340)

D^{r}.			£ s d	C^{r}.			£ s d
Date	Folio			Date	Folio		
June 18	236	To Cash	15	Novr 18	541	By House Expense Wages the summer	2. 2. 0
July 8	275	" 1 Pair Boys Shoes	7	Decr 17	584	" Margaret Leary reversed entry	1. 0. 0
Decr 14	580	" Margaret Leary Balance Acc^{t}	1. 0. 0				£ 3. 2. 0
Decr 17	584	" Cash	1. 0. 0				
			£ 3. 2. 0				

6. Rent transactions involving women

Mary Row account, Renews (Goodridge's, 1839 ledger, fol. 431)

D^r.			£ s d	C^r.			£ s d
Date	Folio			Date	Folio		
Feby 2	347	To Sterling rent Room	10. 0. 0	Novr 22	693	By John Power Senr Rent of Room this year	
April 25	356	" Exchange Acc^t [exchange rate, Nfld. Currency]	1.10.9	Decr 6	719	£10 Stg. @ 20d is by	12. 0. 0
Decr 31	747	" Balance	12. 0. 0	Decr 6	719	By W. B. Row for Rent Room credited him last year	11.10.9
			£ 23.10.9				£ 23.10.9

Mary Row account, Renews (Goodridge's, 1840 ledger, fol. 388)

D^r.			£ s d	C^r.			£ s d
Date	Folio			Date	Folio		
				1839			
				Dec^r	12	By Balance	12. 0. 0
1840							
March 1	330	To Sterling	10. 0. 0	Decr 8	569	" John Power Senr Rent of Room	
April	334	" Exchange Acc^t 20 pC^t on £10	2. 0. 0			£10 Stg in Cy	11.10.10
Dec^r	607	" Balance due her	11.10.10				£ 23.10.10
			£ 23.10.10				

Margaret Furlong, St. Mary's–Placentia (Sweetman's, box 3, file 92—1843 balances)

1843—Credit Balance—Margaret Furlong 1s. 4d.—rent

7. Women with credit and debit balances after settling up with merchant

Goodridge's, 1839 balances (fols. 454–55)

fo.	D[r]	£ s d	fo.	+C[r]	£ s d
			454	Mary Fowler Sen[r].	1. 2
			454	Susanna Goodridge	10. 7. 8
			454	Mary Row	12. 0. 1
455	Jane Power	3			

Goodridge's, 1840 balances (fols. 293–94)

fo.	D[r]	£ s d	fo.	+C[r]	£ s d
			393	Ann Brandy	1. 4
			393	Esther Cahill	2
			393	Mary Golway	2.11
			393	Mary Foley	1. 0. 9
			393	Susanna Goodridge	10. 7. 5
			393	Mary Row	11.10.10
			394	Ellen Fowler	8. 1
				Mary Pleace	1. 6. 7
				Margaret Leary	8

Goodridge's, 1841 balances (fols. 310–1)

fo.	D^{r}	£ s d	fo.	$^{+}$C^{r}	£ s d
			310	Ann Brandy	1. 4
			310	Mary Ann Fowler	6
			310	Mary Conway	12.11
			310	Esther Cahill	8. 4
			310	Nancy Shannahan	1
			310	Susanna Goodridge	27.11. 7
311	Margaret Leary	2. 6. 5			
311	Elizabeth Brown	1. 0. 0			

Sweetman's, 20 November 1802 (box 3, file 7)

Credit balances:		£ s d
—	Widow Lamb & Son	143. 0. 1
—	Anne St. Croix	3. 9. 7
—	Mary St. Croix	61. 1. 4
—	M^{rs}. John Sutton	26. 0. 0
—	M^{rs}. Simms	6. 0. 6
—	M^{rs}. Newman	13. 1.11
—	Jane Careen	3. 2. 4
—	Bridget Quan	4. 9. 0
Debit balances:		
—	Widow Conway	2. 6. 1
—	Mary Morris	62.12.8

Sweetman's, 1843 balances (box 3, file 92)

fo.	D^r	£ s d	fo.	^+C^r	£ s d
16	Bridgit Blanch	142. 1.11			
"	Cath Crotty, servant	18. 2	125	Sarah Delany	14. 8
200	Johanna Green	3. 8. 1	346	Mary Morris, paybl in goods	8.12. 9
"	Mrs. Juke, Rams	2. 2. 0	313	Mary McGrath	58. 3. 7
			314	Hannah Mullet	1.12. 4
			316	Mary Murphy, Rams	10. 0. 0
327	Sarah McCarty	191.18. 8			
328	Eleanor Mooney	29.13. 6	450	Mary Wallace	23.12. 3
352	Mary Mullins	1. 6.10			
409	Johanna Patterson	2.10. 5	158	Margaret Furlong, rent	1. 4
427	Bridgit Sinnot	29. 0.10	365	M^rs. Murphy, Lower Rams	12. 5. 3

8. Possible woman shopkeeper or tavernkeeper

Mary Morris account (Sweetman's, box 3, file 17, 1823 ledger, fols. 20–21)

(The nature of Mary's business is not explained but, given the large numbers of men and the range of amounts listed here for credit to Mary's account, it is possible that she was running a public house or a shop.)

f. 21				£	s	d
—	2/148	James Pendergast			1	6
—	2/21	Michl Grace		1	9	3
—	2/29	Wm Roche			2	6
—	2/115	Wm Walsh			1	"
—	2/8	B Murphy			13	6
—	2/106	Ths Grant		2	1	11
—	2/6	P. Shaw			7	
—	2/10	Rd Forrestal Junr			7	6
—	2/23	Jno Cain			9	6
—	2/12	Wm Gill			18	9
—	2/120	Lce Wickham	8.10.3	1	17	10
—	2/109	Lce Delahunty		2	6	8
—	2/112	Patk Fowler			18	
—	2/124	D. Sinnot		1	"	9
—	2/159	Jas. Mullally			10	
—	2/117	Ml. Walsh			7	6
—	2/161	Jno Moran		2	14	4
—	2/42	Ml Costelloe		3	5	"
—	2/14	Ml Brennan		4	6	2
—	2/147	Patk Walsh			12	6
—	2/54	Ths Duran	16.1.11	"	1	"

—	Carried forward		16.1.11			
—	2/88	Ml Whelan		1	15	8
—	2/137	Wm Aylward			9	3
—	2/22	Lce Keef		3	2	"
—	2/170	Jno Walsh		1	"	"
—	2/27	Pk? Walsh (Gar)		4	14	10
—	2/173	Jno Walsh (Cook)			12	6
—	2/165	Micl Shea		1	6	"
—	2/67	Ml. Foley	14.4. 6	1	"	9
—	2/199	Lce Walsh			3	6[c]
		to Cr. Ledger No. 1 fo 146		38	16	8

[c]This final entry, of 3s. 6d., was not included in the account's total.

APPENDIX D

Marital and Other Family Arrangements in Ferryland District, ca. 1800

Under instructions of Governor Pole, a nominal census of Ferryland district (extending from Lamanche southward to Renews) was compiled by local magistrate Robert Carter in 1799–1800. The census provides a listing of all fishing employers and servants in the area during the winter of 1799–1800 and another for the fishing season of 1800. The census also includes a "Register of Families" residing in the district in August 1800; this register identifies family groupings in each harbor and lists the names of fathers, mothers, and children, together with the sex and age of each child. Of the total 166 families identified, the following patterns emerge.

Note: The typography of this table reflects my effort to render as faithfully as possible the idiosyncracies of the original document.

A. Nuclear family or couple with shared surname Total 122

E.g., **Cape Broyle**			
Richard Welsh	Elenor Welsh	Mich[l]. Welsh	(15)
		Thomas	(11)
		John	(9)
		James	(7)
		Mary	(3)
Renewse			
James doyle	Ann doyle	[no children]	

A. Nuclear family or couple with shared surname   Total 122

These appear in the census as recognized formal marriages with legitimate children (if any). A cautionary note must be sounded, however. Given the lack of recording of vital statistics and the scarcity of clergy on the southern Avalon until the 1790s, some of these couples may not have been formally married, even though they presented themselves as such to Carter at the time. Unless he was personally aware of their circumstances, he would have had little cause to question their claims.

B. Widows with legitimate children   Total 7

E.g., **Ferryland**		
Margret Whelan	John Whelan	(27)
Widdow	James	(25)
	Michael	(17)
	Thomas	(14)
	Alice	(20)

In all seven cases, Carter specifically noted that these women were widows.

C. Widows who had remarried and were living with children by former and/or current husbands   Total 3

E.g., **Fermuse**				
James Ready	Mary Ready	{	Thomas Clancy	(23)
by her first husband		{	James Clancy	(22)
		{	Edmund Clancy	(12)
			Martin Ready	(9)
			James Ready	(3½)
			Mary Ready	(7)
			Margret Ready	(5)

In all three cases, Carter specifically noted that the children with surnames different from that of the current husband/partner were by a former husband of the mother.

D. Women living with children with different surname than current partner Total 7

E.g., **Ferryland**			
James Neill	Margret Neill	Ann Murphy	(18)
		Mary Furlong	(10½)
		Joan Furlong	(8)
		Bridget Neill	(4½)
		Catharine Neill	(1½)

The women in this category were living with children, some or all of whom had different surnames from that of the woman's current husband/partner. These cases differed from those discussed in section C in that Carter had not noted that such children were "by her first husband." Was this lack of such qualification merely an oversight on Carter's part, or did it indicate some ambiguity in relation to the legitimacy of the children or to the formality of the mother's previous relationship(s)?

E. Women without partners living with children with mixed surnames Total 1

E.g., **Renewse**		
Bridget doyle	William drinkwater	(35)
	Bridget doyle	(11)

Again, this suggests the possibility of illegitimate births or informal marriages and common-law relationships.

F. Women without partners living with children with same surname Total 13

E.g., **Cape Broyle**		
Sarah drohan	Catharine drohan	(19)
	Elenor drohan	(16)

By contrast to those women discussed in section A, Carter had not made any notation that these women were widows. Again, this may have been an oversight on his part. But again, the possibility exists that the children were illegitimate, or that the mother had been in some informal marriage or common-law relationship that no longer existed due to breakdown of the relationship or death. This category may also have included women who had been in a formal marriage but who had been separated or informally divorced from their husbands.

G. Men with no partners living with children with same surnames Total 5

E.g., **Ferryland**		
William Mcdaniel	James Mcdaniel	(23)
	Matthew	(20)
	John	(19)
	William	(16)
	Catharine	(14)

In none of these cases had Carter noted that the father was a widower, and so again the possibility exists that we are looking at the remnants of informal marriages or common-law relationships. We know this was actually true in the case of the Mcdaniels, as some of their family history appears in the court records. William Mcdaniel and his partner, Hannah, were involved in a lengthy legal battle with the Westons and Carters in Ferryland in the 1780s and 1790s. In the course of the proceedings, they revealed to the court that they had never been properly married but had been living common-law (see PANL, GN 5/4/C/1, Ferryland, box 1, 25-26, *Catharine Weston v. William and Hannah Mcdaniel*, 8 March 1787). Hannah's actual surname was Carney, and she was the daughter of Mary Shea (which raises interesting questions about her mother's marital arrangements as well). At any rate, William and Hannah's relationship was obviously quite stable, as it spanned at least two decades and resulted in the birth of seven children, five of whom were still living with their father by 1800. Hannah, however, was no longer in the picture at that point; but whether this was due to her death or the breakdown of the relationship is undetermined.

H. Definite illegitimacies, informal marriages, common-law relationships Total 7

E.g., **Ferryland**			
William Hennecy	Mary McCue	Martin Dunn	(13)
		John Hennecy	(11)
		Thomas Hennecy	(8)
		Margret Hennecy	(9½)
		Sarah Hennecy	(5½)

We know from a 1791 court case that Mary had been married to Timothy Dunn and successfully sued him for support of their child (Martin, born 1786/87). The court acknowledged the separation, although it had no jurisdiction to grant a divorce (see PANL, GN 5/4/C/1, Ferryland, box 1, *Mary Dunn v. Timothy Dunn*, 14 March 1791). From Carter's listing, we can see that she had since either gone back to her maiden name or had had another partner between Dunn and Hennecy. Regardless, her 1800 relationship with Hennecy was one at common law.

E.g., **Ferryland**		
Mary Blake	John Whelan	(17)

The different surnames of mother and son suggest either illegitimacy or a former informal marriage/common-law relationship.

E.g., **Ferryland**			
John Ellis	Margret Ellis	Mich[l]. Hanrahan	(13)
		Mary Hanrahan	(11)

In 1791, "Margarett Hanahan" had taken her former husband, Thomas, to court on charges of violent domestic abuse. She had two young children at the time. The court acknowledged their separation and awarded her support and the family home; ultimately, the magistrates ordered Thomas out of the district (see PANL, GN 5/4/C/1, Ferryland, box 1, *Margarett Hanahan v. Thomas Hanahan*, 31 January, 1 February, and 11 April, 1791). While this was effectively a divorce for the Hanahans, Newfoundland courts did not have jurisdiction to grant divorces at that time. So Margret's new relationship with John Ellis was an informal marital arrangement or common-law relationship.

unmarried	Edmund Power	(3)
	Catharine Sullivan	(11)
Cath[ne] Fling	John dwyer	(14)
unmarried	Matthew dwyer	(11)
	William doyle	(4)
	Mary Orchard	(1)
Ann dobbin	William Carroll	(10)
unmarried	John Mullins	(6)

Carter was not ambiguous about his opinion on the marital status of these women, although their children may still have been the result of informal marriages or (more likely) common-law relationships.

E.g., **Ferryland**		
John Sullivan	Eliz[a]. McCarthy	[no children]
	unmarried	
<u>Brigus</u>		
John Sloan	Anstice dwyer	[no children]
	unmarried	

Carter was equally unambiguous about these couples, although they may possibly have been in stable common-law relationships.

GPSR Authorized Representative: Easy Access System Europe, Mustamäe tee 50, 10621 Tallinn, Estonia, gpsr.requests@easproject.com

www.ingramcontent.com/pod-product-compliance
Lightning Source LLC
LaVergne TN
LVHW091515200926
848483LV00005B/420/J